The Former Yugoslavia at the Turn of the Twenty-first Century

Of the few authors sufficiently knowledgeable to write on all the thirty-plus countries moving from central planning to the market, Ian Jeffries is outstanding. This sequence of books, ranging from front-rank EU candidates to barely changed Cuba and North Korea, promises to be a 'must buy' for any university library.

Professor Michael Kaser (Universities of Birmingham and Oxford)

Following the highly successful *Economies in Transition: A guide to China, Cuba, Mongolia, North Korea and Vietnam at the turn of the twenty-first century* (published in the Routledge Studies in Development Economics series), and *Eastern Europe at the Turn of the Twenty-first Century: A guide to the economies in transition*, this book focuses on economic and political events in the former Yugoslavia.

The author presents a clear, detailed and accessible breakdown of the developments in the following countries: Bosnia-Hercegovina, Croatia, the Former Yugoslav Republic of Macedonia, Slovenia and the Federal Republic of Yugoslavia (Serbia and Montenegro).

International military and civilian involvement in the more unstable parts of the former Yugoslavia (dealt with in detail in this book) is seen as essential in maintaining peace and rebuilding economic and political structures. Such experience is invaluable in deciding what to do with 'failed states' such as Afghanistan. The 11 September 2001 terrorist attacks on the United States led to the rapid fall of the Taleban regime in Afghanistan, which had shielded international terrorists. The international community is looking closely at events in the former Yugoslavia for guidance regarding countries like the new Afghanistan.

This book provides a unique level of coverage of economic and political developments in the countries of the former Yugoslavia. It will provide an invaluable source of reference for all those interested in transitional and developing countries.

The fourth volume in this sequence, *The Former Soviet Union at the Turn of the Twenty-first Century: A guide to economies in transition*, will be published by Routledge in 2002.

Ian Jeffries is Member of the Centre of Russian and East European Studies at the University of Wales.

Routledge Studies of Societies in Transition

The Former Yugoslavia at the Turn of the Twenty-first Century

A guide to the economies in transition

Ian Jeffries

London and New York

First published 2002 by Routledge
11 New Fetter Lane, London EC4P 4EE

Simultaneously published in the USA and Canada
by Routledge
29 West 35th Street, New York, NY 10001

Routledge is an imprint of the Taylor & Francis Group

© 2002 Ian Jeffries

Typeset in Baskerville by Taylor & Francis Books Ltd

Printed and bound in Great Britain by Antony Rowe Ltd, Chippenham,
Wiltshire

British Library Cataloguing in Publication Data
A catalogue record for this book is available from the British Library

Library of Congress Cataloging in Publication Data
A catalog record has been requested for this title

ISBN 0–415–28190–3

Contents

Tables

Acknowledgements

The mammoth task of keeping up to date with rapidly changing economic and political events in thirty-five countries would not have been possible without the help of a magnificent library staff, certain other individuals and the portering/cleaning staff in general. Individuals deserving of particular mention are the following (in alphabetical order): Gwen Bailey (Library); Pam Beardsmore (Library); Michele Davies (Library); Dianne Evans (Library); Ray Jones (Library); Nigel O'Leary (Economics); Lis Parcell (Library); Ann Preece (Library); Paul Reynolds (Library); Kathy Sivertsen (Library); Clive Towse (Library); Ray Watts (Library); Chris West (Library).

The earliest possible access to quality newspapers and magazines has, as always, been ensured by the excellent Kays Newsagency, owned and managed by Russell Davies.

Professor Michael Kaser and Professor Paul Hare have continually provided external support and encouragement.

Armenia Economic Trends, Azerbaijan Economic Trends, Belarus Economic Trends, Georgia Economic Trends, Kazakhstan Economic Trends, Moldovan Economic Trends, Ukrainian Economic Trends and *Uzbekistan Economic Trends* are invaluable sources of information which have been provided free of charge. My thanks to all those involved in producing and sending them.

The staff at Routledge have, as always, provided support of the highest degree and professionalism of the highest standard. My thanks in particular (in alphabetical order) go to Yeliz Ali, Oliver Escritt, Tessa Herbert, Alan Jarvis, Liz Jones, Peggy Starling, Alfred Symons, Annabel Watson and James Whiting.

Ian Jeffries
Centre of Russian and East European Studies
University of Wales

Introduction and overview

A Guide to the Socialist Economies was published in 1990. Covering fourteen communist countries (accounting, in mid-1988, for 1.6 billion out of a world population of 5.1 billion), the final amendments to the book had been made in early October 1989. Shortly afterwards communism collapsed in Eastern Europe, followed in late 1991 by the disintegration of the Soviet Union (the largest country in the world by area, covering a sixth of the world's land area excluding Antarctica, and then a 'superpower' able to challenge the USA in terms of military capacity). Yugoslavia also disintegrated, and in a generally very bloody fashion. Academics like myself who had invested a lifetime in studying the communist countries saw their intellectual capital mostly vanish overnight. The effort of trying to comprehend profound changes, in many ways unique events and the multiplication of countries (as well as the disappearance of the GDR into a reunified Germany!) has been staggering.

My first stab at covering what became known as the transitional economies came in 1993 with the publication of *Socialist Economies and the Transition to the Market: A Guide*, which includes analyses of the basic features of command economies and the general issues involved in the transition to a market economy plus chapters on the original fourteen communist countries before 1989 and their individual experiences after 1989 (including the disintegration of the Soviet Union and Yugoslavia). While most countries opted for the market economy and political democracy, Cuba (initially) and North Korea retained the essential features of the traditional communist economic and political system. China, in contrast, adopted gradual and partial economic reform. Vietnam took note of the Chinese model, although there were speedier elements. Both China and Vietnam, however, remained firmly in the grip of the Communist Party.

A Guide to the Economies in Transition was published in 1996. Basically a companion volume to (as opposed to a revised edition of) *Socialist Economies and the Transition to the Market: A Guide*, it covers the period up to the mid-1990s. I am not an economic theorist but the volume includes an overview of the main issues in the transition from command planning to the market (including 'big bang'/'shock therapy' versus gradualism, China as an economic model and privatization). Although I am mostly interested in how economic and political systems actually change, I discuss the basic economic performance of individual countries. Since I am not an econometrician I simply provide readers with an idea both of broad economic magnitudes and of the difficulties of obtaining meaningful data during the transition. The other chapters are devoted to the major political and economic events in thirty-five countries (including the reunification of East and West Germany): the now fifteen independent countries of the former Soviet Union, the countries of Eastern Europe (broadly defined) and the non-European countries (China, Cuba, Mongolia, North Korea and Vietnam).

I am increasingly convinced of the artificiality of separating economics and politics. For example, the privatization programmes chosen may be profoundly affected by political factors such as the strength of the central government and whether or not to seek foreign debt forgiveness. I am not a political scientist and I am unable to interrelate the two disciplines to a desirable degree. Instead, I do attempt to do two things: (1) provide a basic guide to understanding how all the 'bits' fit together, and (2) present a richly endowed 'quarry' of up-to-date economic and political information (often presented chronologically where appropriate) to allow the reader to dig out any desired facts and figures.

This is not (and is not meant to be) original research but a broad-brush painting of the overall economic and political picture. I make use of a range of secondary sources in English (necessary given the large number of languages involved). Apart from journals and books, the sources include the following:

1   Reports such as the European Bank for Reconstruction and Development's (EBRD's) *Transition Report*, the United Nations' *World Economic and Social Survey*, the United Nations Economic Commission for Europe's *Economic Survey of Europe*, the United Nations Economic and Social Commission for Asia and the Pacific's *Economic and Social Survey of Asia and the Pacific*, the World Bank's *Transition*, the IMF's *World Economic Survey* and the OECD's *Economic Outlook*.
2   Quality newspapers such as the *International Herald Tribune* (*IHT*), *Financial Times* (*FT*), *The Times*, the *Guardian*, the *Independent*, the *Telegraph* and the *Baltic Times*.
3   Weeklies such as *The Economist* and the *Far Eastern Economic Review* (*FEER*).
4   Quarterlies/monthlies/fortnightlies such as *Business Central Europe*, *Eastern Europe* (*EEN*, formerly *Eastern Europe Newsletter*), *The World Today*, *Asian Survey*, *Current Digest of the Post-Soviet Press* (*CDSP*, before 5 February 1992 known as *Current Digest of the Soviet Press*), *Transition*, *Finance and Development*, *Armenia Economic Trends* (*ARET*), *Azerbaijan Economic Trends* (*AET*), *Belarus Economic Trends* (*BET*), *Georgia Economic Trends* (*GET*), *Kazakhstan Economic Trends* (*KET*), *Moldovan Economic Trends* (*MET*), *Russian Economic Trends* (*RET*), *Ukrainian Economic Trends* (*UET*) and *Uzbekistan Economic Trends* (*UZET*).

A review in the *Times Higher Education Supplement* (29 October 1993) kindly referred to my 'meticulous referencing', even though detailed referencing has the potential to be tiresome to readers. But since this is not original research and I am deeply indebted to many sources, I feel it necessary to make every effort to acknowledge the material used. It is not always feasible to name the correspondents or contributors, but I try, as far as possible, to ensure that credit goes where it is due. Partly for this reason and partly for accuracy I make extensive use of quotations, although where these include commonly quoted sayings or speeches I leave out specific sources.

My task in these four companion volumes is to cover mainly the period from the mid-1990s up to the turn of the century. I once naively thought that things would 'settle down' and that the follow-up volume (in the singular!) would be smaller than the 1996 one. Far from 'settling down', the amount of economic and political material to be processed has expanded almost exponentially! Routledge has kindly supported me in the gargantuan task of writing four separate volumes:

1   *Economies in Transition: A guide to China, Cuba, Mongolia, North Korea and Vietnam at the turn of the twenty-first century*

This was published in June 2001. The rationale for a separate volume was significantly enhanced by China, North Korea and Cuba on occasion being at the centre of world attention. China's rapid economic progress has aroused considerable interest worldwide in China as an economic model of gradualism. China is increasingly participating in globalization (witness events such as its prospective entry into the WTO). Its economic progress has enormous implications in terms of international affairs. Hong Kong and Macao have been reclaimed but relations with Taiwan remain edgy. China's human rights record is often the cause of friction, especially with the USA. The June 2000 summit between the leaders of North and South Korea turned out to be a dramatic event after decades of bitter division. The Elian Gonzalez case and the actions of his Miami relatives had important implications for US policy towards Cuba. Mongolia continues to provide a fascinating case study of continued commitment to market-orientated economic reform despite political squabbling and changes of government. Vietnam's attitude to economic reform has fluctuated. The Asian financial crisis, for instance, dampened enthusiasm. But in July 2000 the trade agreement with the USA was signed after a year's delay and greater encouragement has been given to the private sector and foreign direct investment.

2   *Eastern Europe at the Turn of the Twenty-first Century: A guide to the economies in transition*

This was published in February 2002. Part I covers Albania, Bulgaria, the Czech Republic, Hungary, Poland, Romania and Slovakia. Part II deals with general issues, relating to topics such as 'big bang'/'shock therapy' and privatization. It was felt that these issues were best analysed in this volume, e.g. Poland in 1990 was the first country to adopt 'big bang'/'shock therapy'. The major issues relating to German reunification had already been dealt with in the 1993 and

1996 volumes. The only thing I thought worth including in this volume was privatization in the eastern part of Germany as a revealing case study.

3   *The Former Yugoslavia at the Turn of the Twenty-first Century: A guide to the economies in transition*

The countries covered in this volume are Bosnia-Hercegovina, Croatia, the Former Yugoslav Republic of Macedonia, Slovenia and the Federal Republic of Yugoslavia (Serbia and Montenegro). Although Montenegro and Serbia still formally constitute one country, the Federal Republic of Yugoslavia, they are now essentially separate countries. It is deemed appropriate, therefore, to devote separate chapters to them.

The West intervened militarily to protect Moslems in Bosnia and in Kosovo, and international military and civilian involvement for the foreseeable future is proving critical in maintaining the peace and rebuilding economies and political structures. The terrible events of 11 September 2001, when terrorists attacked targets in New York and Washington, showed the dangers of allowing states like Afghanistan to fail. International terrorists were given sanctuary by the Moslem fundamentalist Taleban regime. There has been a profound change in the attitude of the administration of President George W. Bush towards US involvement in those countries of the former Yugoslavia affected by ethnic strife. The new president, inaugurated in January 2001, was initially very cool about the involvement of US troops. The Bush administration now sees the vital importance of the United States maintaining its presence in the more unstable parts of the former Yugoslavia.

4   *The Former Soviet Union at the Turn of the Twenty-first Century: A guide to the economies in transition*

The countries covered are Armenia, Azerbaijan, Belarus, Estonia, Georgia, Kazakhstan, Kyrgyzstan, Latvia, Lithuania, Moldova, Russia, Tajikistan, Turkmenistan, Ukraine, Uzbekistan.

The 11 September 2001 terrorist attacks on the United States had a profoundly positive effect on relations between the United States and Russia. Thus, for example, Russia gave its blessing to the use by the United States of air bases in Uzbekistan for launching attacks on the Taleban regime in Afghanistan. This and other extraordinary events will be dealt with in Volume IV.

The road to disintegration of the former Yugoslavia

Clashes occurred between Serbs and Croats in Croatia from March 1991 onwards, but the first action of the Yugoslav army (JNA) was in Slovenia after the declarations of independence by Croatia and Slovenia on 25 June 1991. However, the JNA was humiliated in a series of brief clashes, withdrew and then turned its attention to Croatia. The Yugoslav army backed the Serbs in a vicious war against the Croats.

Vukovar first came under JNA shelling in August 1991, and in October 1991 the Yugoslav army also started shelling Dubrovnik from the hills and the sea. The Yugoslav army then supported the Serbs in Bosnia-Hercegovina against the Moslems and Croats.

Federal Yugoslav authority gradually collapsed. On 12 March 1991 the collective presidency declared itself 'paralysed'. Serbia at first refused to allow the Croat Stipe Mesic to become president when his turn came under the revolving system on 15 May 1991. Serbia, in league with Montenegro, assumed control of the federal presidency and government on 3 October 1991. Mesic formally resigned on 5 December, declaring that 'Yugoslavia does not exist any more'. The federal prime minister, Ante Markovic, resigned on 20 December 1991. On 27 April 1992 Serbia and Montenegro declared a new Federal Republic of Yugoslavia.

The EU imposed an arms embargo on the whole of the former Yugoslavia in July 1991 and the UN Security Council did so on 25 September 1991. On 22 September 1992 the UN General Assembly refused to recognize the new Yugoslavia as the legal successor to the old one. On 16 June 1993 the new Yugoslavia was expelled from the seat held by the former Yugoslavia. On 30 May 1992 the UN Security Council imposed a trade ban on the new Federal Republic of Yugoslavia.

The process of disintegration was a bloody and complicated one. The collapse of the communist system in the Soviet Union and Eastern Europe removed the last vestiges of any external threat to the country and the struggle for land within the former Yugoslavia often took the most ugly of ethnic forms. Crude nationalism was exploited by ex-communists like Slobodan Milosevic and Franjo Tudjman for their own ends. Milosevic himself played a key role in the disintegration of Yugoslavia by rejecting early attempts to create a loose confederation. When the fighting started he strove to create a 'Greater Serbia' by backing ethnic Serbs in the other republics, and only distanced himself from the Bosnian and Croatian Serbs when their conflicts threatened his hold on power.

The late Franjo Tudjman desired a 'Greater Croatia', but international pressure helped thwart its attainment. As early as 25 March 1991 he and Milosevic agreed to share out Bosnia-Hercegovina between them, leaving only a rump Moslem state. In the end Tudjman went along with the idea of a (March 1994, US-brokered) Bosnian government–Bosnian Croat federation linked economically with Croatia in a loose confederation. Tudjman dealt with the ethnic Serbs in Croatia by effectively expelling most of them. A significant part of Croatia was under the control of the Croatian Serbs until the devastating Croatian successes in the military campaigns of 1–2 May and 4–7 August 1995.

Until mid-September 1995 some 70 per cent of Bosnia lay in the hands of the Bosnian Serbs, who had 'ethnically cleansed' whole areas and committed even worse crimes in the name of Serb nationalism. The Croats and Bosnian Croats have a lot to answer for, and it is not difficult to draw up a long list of atrocities committed by supporters of the Bosnian government. But the burden of guilt rests massively on the shoulders of the Serbs.

This is not to underestimate the complexities of the situation. Even though the Croats in Bosnia started off fighting alongside the Moslems against the Serbs, by the early summer of 1993 Bosnian Croats and Serbs had drawn up the essentials of a plan to divide an allegedly confederal Bosnia into three ethic states and their military forces were actively collaborating in the field against the Bosnian government. Even the seemingly eternal animosity between Croats and Serbs has thus occasionally been put aside when they have colluded at the expense of the Moslems. In fact there was cold and calculated switching of partners on occasion as the nightmare developed, with even the Serbs being involved. Bitter fighting between Bosnian government and Croat forces in central Bosnia started in the spring of 1993, with Serbs helping the latter. But in the late summer of 1993 there was some evidence of Serb–Moslem collaboration. On 25 February 1994 the Bosnian government and Bosnian Croat forces began a ceasefire, and on 3 November 1994 a combined force of Bosnian government and Bosnian Croat forces took the town of Kupres in central Bosnia.

Until Nato's resolute (and justifiable) action in the second half of 1995 (especially the start of massive air strikes against the Bosnian Serbs on 30 August 1995, which followed Croatia's routing of the ethnic Serbs in the Krajina), the West's prevarication not only allowed evils (almost unimaginable in present-day Europe) to take place but also almost irreparably damaged the credibility of the UN, Nato and the EU. The attempt to solve the problem of Bosnia through EU diplomacy was a massive failure. The USA took over the reins of negotiations in August 1995. It took a (belated) US intervention to bring about a military and political solution, the latter via the Dayton accords of late 1995 (inspired by the dynamic Richard Holbrooke).

The West's very first reaction was to try to preserve the former Yugoslavia, albeit in a looser form and with minority rights fully protected, but this soon proved to be unrealistic. Continued Bosnian Serb aggression resulted in attempts to increase international economic sanctions on the new Federal Republic of Yugoslavia (and by implication the Bosnian and Croatian Serbs) and the imposition of a 'no fly' zone over Bosnia. But leaky economic sanctions both by the international community and later by the Federal Republic of Yugoslavia were ineffective in controlling the Bosnian Serbs. Right at the start the West carelessly broadcast its unwillingness to intervene militarily or even to lift the arms embargo on the poorly equipped Bosnian government. US president Bill Clinton did argue for a 'lift and strike' strategy (though not unilaterally). But he did not apply sufficient pressure on other Western countries, especially strong opponents of military action like the French and British governments. Britain and France had the largest contingents of Unprofor (UN Protection Force) troops on the ground in Bosnia.

With the international community imposing an arms embargo on all the warring factions (including the Bosnian government) and initially ruling out the use of military force, a massive humanitarian aid programme was undertaken. But the West's decision to use Unprofor troops to escort aid convoys to besieged Moslem towns, despite the positive achievements, led to the charge of 'fed but dead'.

The international community relied heavily on the arch-villain Slobodan Milosevic to bring the Bosnian and Croatian Serbs to heel. The overriding goal of communist-turned-nationalist Milosevic was always to retain personal power (as opposed to creating a 'Greater Serbia') and he dumped the ethnic Serbs in Bosnia and Croatia. The 1995 agreement on Bosnia was negotiated by Serbia's foreign minister on behalf of the Bosnian Serbs. Kosovo was a victim of Dayton. The war there finally brought home to the West the folly of relying for solutions on the man most responsible in the first place for the troubles in the former Yugoslavia.

Thanks in part to lessons learned in Bosnia, the war in Kosovo brought forth a much speedier Western response. Nato's generally successful (and generally justifiable) bombing campaign, undertaken on humanitarian grounds (without a mandate from the UN Security Council because of opposition from Russia and China), was unimpeded by UN constraints. Kosovo has hardly been encouraging in ethnic tolerance terms, with many ethnic Serbs being driven out by vengeful ethnic Albanians (despite a substantial international presence) and the remainder generally sheltering in protected enclaves.

President George W. Bush of the United States (inaugurated in January 2001) was initially very cool about US military commitments in the Balkans. But this attitude soon began to be modified and it was changed fundamentally by the 11 September 2001 terrorist attacks on the World Trade Center in New York and on the Pentagon in Washington (although the intention remains to gradually reduce troop commitments in the Balkans). Nicholas Burns, the US ambassador to Nato:

> Nato must finish the job of bringing stability to the Balkans. In Bosnia, Kosovo and Macedonia the United States will remain with Nato, fully engaged militarily and politically, to staunch the kind of instability that let terrorists take root in Afghanistan.
>
> (*IHT*, 10 November 2001, p. 8)

Bosnia-Hercegovina

Political developments

In 1989 Bosnia-Hercegovina (henceforth Bosnia) accounted for 21 per cent of the area of the former Yugoslavia. Its 4.6 million comprised 19 per cent of the population and was split into 43 per cent Moslems, 32 per cent Serbs and 18 per cent Croats. Bosnia contributed 12 per cent of Yugoslav GNP and its index of *per capita* income was 66 (Yugoslav average = 100) (Deutsche Bank, *Focus Eastern Europe*, 1991, no. 25, pp. 15–16). The population in 1996 was an estimated 3.5

million, 2.5 million in the Moslem–Croat Federation and 1 million in the Republika Srpska (*IHT*, 14 September 1996, p. 7). It was one of the poorest parts of Yugoslavia, yet one of the most ethnically tolerant.

A free, multi-party election was held on 18 and 25 November 1990, with the parties splitting along mainly ethnic–religious lines. A collective presidency was established with the Moslem leader Alija Izetbegovic becoming president. (The presidency was meant to rotate, but a special clause in the constitution was invoked in December 1992 to enable Izetbegovic's term to be extended for the duration of the war.) On 15 October 1991, when Bosnia issued a 'memorandum on sovereignty', ethnic Serbian members of parliament walked out in protest. This memorandum implied that Bosnia would only be willing to accept a loose confederation (which included Croatia and Slovenia) as an alternative to inde-pendence. A referendum on independence was held 29 February–1 March 1992, attracting a turnout of only 63.4 per cent (there being a Serbian boycott). The 'yes' vote was 99.43 per cent.

Bitter fighting broke out in early April 1992, with the Bosnian Serbs, who started it, being aided by the Yugoslav army. (The killing on 5 April 1992, by a sniper, of a civilian while she was demonstrating in Sarajevo against the raising of barricades by Bosnian Serbs is taken as the start of the war.) The Bosnian Croats unilaterally declared an autonomous 'Croatian Community of Herceg-Bosna' on 5 July 1992. When the EU and the USA recognized Bosnia on 7 April 1992, the Serbs proclaimed an independent 'Serbian Republic of Bosnia' in order to remain within the truncated Yugoslavia. The fighting in Bosnia attracted world attention and UN mediation. Developments were particularly tragic in the light of Bosnia's history of ethnic tolerance and respect, arguably a vital factor in its survival in the past.

The UN Security Council declared an air exclusion ('no fly') zone on 9 October 1992 for military flights over Bosnia. But in the event of violations there was only to be urgent consideration given to 'further measures necessary to enforce the ban'. There were in fact mass violations of the ban, although the first (confirmed) bombing raid by Serbian planes did not take place until 13 March 1993. On 31 March 1993 the UN Security Council voted to enforce the ban, starting on 12 April. It is of some interest to note two things about the 'enforce-ment'. First, it represented the first ever combat role for Nato (albeit under the authority of the UN). Second, on 8 April 1993 the German constitutional court gave provisional permission for Germans to take part in the enforcement of the ban as radar operators in AWACS surveillance flights. This was the first combat role for German armed service personnel since the Second World War. The court was called in to determine whether the constitution allowed any combat role outside the Nato area. Third, the violations continued and no aircraft were shot down until 28 February 1994.

'Safe areas'

These came to include Sarajevo, Bihac, Gorazde, Srebrenica, Tuzla and Zepa.

The imminent fall of Srebrenica produced a very strong international reaction. On 16 April 1993 the UN Security Council declared the town and its environs a 'safe area', an area safe from 'armed attack or any other hostile act'. (The idea stemmed from the 'safe havens' for the Kurds in Iraq.)

On 11 May 1993 the USA failed to convince the Europeans to support its proposal to end the arms embargo on the Bosnian government. The Clinton plan involved a 'lift and strike' strategy, i.e. lift the embargo and bomb the Serbs until Bosnian government forces were sufficiently armed to prevent a predicted pre-emptive Serbian offensive.

Serious fighting had started in central Bosnia between Croats and Moslems in October 1992. The fighting intensified in April 1993. At first the Croats made most headway with 'ethnic cleansing', but a powerful Moslem offensive in the spring and summer of 1993, with many Moslem troops themselves victims of earlier cleansing, led to a turn of the tide. The Moslems felt that, since the international community had in effect accepted the Serbian and Croatian 'facts on the ground', survival meant having to indulge in retaliatory large-scale 'ethnic cleansing' of their own.

Mohammed Sacirbey, the Bosnian ambassador to the UN, described Srebrenica as an 'open concentration camp', where disease, hunger and despair 'have replaced shells and bullets as the tools of genocide'. President Clinton himself had shortly before raised the spectre of another Lebanon or Northern Ireland, while the US secretary of state, Warren Christopher, had only two weeks earlier described such areas as ethnic ghettos that would mean acceptance of 'ethnic cleansing'.

On 4 June 1993 the UN Security Council approved the sending of troops to the six 'safe areas' (the figure of 7,600 being approved on 18 June), with the ability to use force (including calling air strikes) to protect themselves. The troops were authorized 'to take the necessary measures, including the use of force' if the aid convoys were obstructed or there were 'bombardments against the safe areas by any of the parties or armed incursions into them'. (It was not clear whether the protection applied only to Unprofor troops. When, on 10 June 1993, Nato agreed to provide aircraft to defend Unprofor troops 'in performance of the overall mandate' there was disagreement as to whether the protection applied to the troops throughout Bosnia or just to those in the safe areas.)

The number of troops actually sent to protect the 'safe areas' was lower than hoped for and there were substantial delays. According to the *Guardian* (11 April 1994, p. 23), although the UN Security Council authorized the dispatch of 7,600 peacekeeping troops in June 1993, only 5,000 had arrived eight months later. Nato aircraft did not undertake a (totally ineffective, as it turned out) bombing raid (against Bosnian Serbs attacking Gorazde) until 10 April 1994. The Serbian assault on Gorazde, which started on 29 March 1994, turned into a near fiasco for the UN and Nato. The Bosnian Serbs brilliantly played on the divisions in the international community and the lack of UN troops on the ground to continue their attack while pretending to negotiate.

The threat of air strikes was further weakened by the other conditions laid down, apart from the fact that the Nato Council had to be unanimous. The UN secretary-general, Boutros Boutros Ghali, had a veto: 'The first use of our air power in the theatre shall be authorized by him.' Normally he would have to approve any requests from the commander of UN forces in the former Yugoslavia via the commander of UN forces in Bosnia. Thus the chances of actual air strikes seemed to be remote, given the resistance to air strikes by the UN commanders (and the co-chairmen of the Geneva talks) because of the fear of retaliatory attacks on Unprofor troops already in Bosnia, an allegedly certain adverse effect on the peace talks and a general disbelief in their effectiveness.

BIHAC

On 27 September 1993 the 'autonomous province of western Bosnia' was declared by the Bihac assembly. The next day President Izetbegovic ordered the military authorities to take control amid popular anti-central-government demonstrations. Their control turned out to be patchy and far from secure. On 29 September 1993 parliament voted sixty-one to one to remove Fikret Abdic from the collective leadership. (Abdic was the leader of the isolated and relatively unscathed north-western enclave of Bihac and a possible rival for the Bosnian presidency. He actually received more votes than Izetbegovic in the 1990 election. Abdic was a wealthy businessman who had gone on trading – via Agrokomerc – with the Croats and Serbs. In 1987 he was jailed for issuing unbacked promissory notes in the Agrokomerc scandal, an enterprise that he had built up.)

On 3 October 1993 government forces stormed a radio station and shot a policeman dead. The fighting then escalated. On 21 August 1994 Bihac effectively fell when Abdic's castle stronghold of Velika Kladusa was taken by Bosnian government forces.

On 8 September 1994 the Serbs launched a two-pronged attack on Bihac, won by Croatian Serbs from the Krajina. An anti-aircraft missile was fired at two UN (British) jets patrolling the area. But on 26 October 1994 Bosnian government forces began a highly successful offensive in the Bihac area. On 1 November there were reports that Bosnian Croats had begun to help Bosnian government forces in the Bihac area and around Kupres in central Bosnia. Kupres fell to Bosnian government and Bosnian Croat forces on 3 November 1994, the first relatively important town lost by the Bosnian Serbs. Fikret Abdic also sent people to fight on the side of the Bosnian Serbs.

On 27 November the UN and Nato did nothing while Serbs continued to take over the 'safe area' of Bihac and detain more Unprofor forces as hostages. Velika Kladusa fell on 17 December.

On 14 January 1995 Bosnian government forces retook some land around Bihac and there was some shelling of Bihac. Heavy fighting continued in the Bihac area, with Bosnian Serbs, Croatian Serbs and Abdic 'rebels' fighting Bosnian government forces. On 27 July 1995 Bosnian Croats, backed by units of the Croatian army, launched a major offensive to try to relieve the pressure of a three-pronged attack (beginning 19 July) on Bihac by Bosnian Serbs, Croatian Serbs and forces loyal to Fikret Abdic.

On 5 August 1995 Bosnian government forces broke out of Bihac and linked up with Croatian government forces after the latter's successful attack on the Krajina. On 7 August 1995 Bosnian government forces drove Abdic forces from Velika Kladusa.

GORAZDE

On 29 March 1994 the Bosnian Serbs began a large-scale assault on Gorazde. On 15 April, in defiance of the UN, the Bosnian Serbs launched an all-out assault on Gorazde and captured all the strategic points in the enclave. The UN was in disarray on 17 April 1994, as the Bosnian Serbs effectively took control of Gorazde while a ceasefire (plus a withdrawal of Serb heavy weapons three kilometres from the town) was being announced by Radovan Karadzic and Yasushi Akashi. The UN secretary-general called on Nato to sanction, if so requested, the use of air strikes to defend all six 'safe areas' themselves (as opposed to merely Unprofor personnel). On 22 April Nato gave the Bosnian Serbs an ultimatum. The UN secretary-general needed to approve only the first air strike. (Similar arrangements were made later for the other 'safe areas' of Bihac, Srebrenica, Tuzla and Zepa.) Yasushi Akashi announced an agreed ceasefire (as of noon local time, 23 April) after talks in Belgrade with the Bosnian Serb leaders (including General Ratko Mladic, who had personally led the assault on Gorazde). The assault continued on 23 April, but Yasushi Akashi refused to authorize air strikes before the midnight 23 April deadline. By 24 April the Bosnian Serbs had complied sufficiently with the ultimatum to avoid air strikes.

SREBRENICA AND ZEPA

On 6 July 1995 the Bosnian Serbs began an assault on Srebrenica. They blamed Bosnian government forces for launching raids out of the enclave. Two days later the Bosnian Serbs started overrunning UN observation posts in Srebrenica and took Dutch troops prisoners. They were later released. On 9 July the Bosnian Serbs were warned by the UN that Nato might be asked for 'close air support'. The following day the Bosnian Serbs issued an ultimatum to UN troops to leave Srebrenica. On 11 July the Bosnian Serbs captured Srebrenica despite two Nato air strikes on a tank column. (Srebrenica was the first 'safe area' to be declared and the first to fall.) On 12 July the Bosnian Serbs began transporting civilians out of Srebrenica and separating out males over the age of 16 for them to be 'screened for war crimes'. The UN Security Council unanimously passed a resolution demanding the immediate withdrawal of Bosnian forces from Srebrenica and full respect to be shown by both sides for Srebrenica's 'safe area' status.

More than 7,000 were murdered (Mark Danner, *New York Review of Books*, 24 September 1998, vol. XLV, no. 14). A UN report on the Srebrenica mass murder of July 1995 was published on 15 November 1999.

The report says that the UN's willingness to negotiate with the Bosnian Serb leaders, Radovan Karadzic and General Ratko Mladic, amounted to 'appeasement'. 'It was with the deepest regret and remorse that we have reviewed our own actions and decisions in the face of the assault on Srebrenica,' the report said. 'Through error, misjudgement and an inability to recognize the scope of evil confronting us, we failed to do our part to save the people of Srebrenica from the Serb campaign of mass murder ... The tragedy of Srebrenica will haunt us forever,' the report said. The report reserves its harshest criticism for the UN leadership, particularly former secretary-general Boutros Boutros Ghali, his senior commander, Lieutenant General Bernard Janvier of France, and his top envoy, Yasushi Akashi of Japan. While secretary-general Kofi Annan's personal role in the events in Srebrenica is not clearly addressed in the report, he says he has accepted general responsibility for the UN's failure in Bosnia. Mr Annan was head of the peacekeeping operation at the time ... The report also challenges a long list of UN decisions during the conflict. The UN now acknowledges that its arms embargo undermined the Bosnian Army's ability to defend itself. The report says the UN's persistent reluctance to use air power against the Bosnian Serbs was a mistake. And it repudiates a long-cherished assumption that the UN can be evenhanded in the face of an aggressor. The use of force, not diplomacy, is the only appropriate way to confront a determined aggressor, the report says ... 'In Bosnia as in Kosovo the international community tried to reach a negotiated settlement with an unscrupulous and murderous regime,' it says. 'In both instances it required the use of force to bring a halt to the planned and systematic killing and expulsion of civilians.'

(*IHT*, 16 November 1999, pp. 1, 10)

The lessons of the tragedy ... are drawn out in a 155-page report submitted to the Security Council. It has been written in the name of the UN secretary-general Kofi Annan. Mr Annan was in charge of peacekeeping at the time ... The misjudgements, Mr Annan writes, arose from an unwillingness to confront the Serbs with a sufficiently powerful military response. That itself resulted from 'an inability to recognize the scope of the evil confronting us' ... It is estimated that ... the Serb army rounded up and killed 7,600 men and boys over sixteen ... The Western powers negotiated with them [the Serbs] in a manner that 'amounted to appeasement' ... 'The cardinal lesson of Srebrenica is that a deliberate and systematic attempt to terrorize, expel or murder an entire people must be met decisively with all necessary means, and with the political will to carry the policy through to its logical conclusion,' the report says ... The report lingered on the refusal of the UN force in Bosnia, Unprofor, to agree to Bosnian requests for the return of weapons they had been forced to give up. 'This decision seems to have been particularly ill-advised given Unprofor's own unwillingness consistently to advocate force as a means of deterring attacks on the enclave,' it says.

(Independent, 17 November 1999, p. 19)

'War crimes investigators have found and exhumed more than 4,000 bodies from sites around the area [Srebrenica] but have been able to identify only eighty, according to ... the International Commission cn Missing Persons' (*IHT*, 13 July 2000, p. 5).

(It was announced on 1 November 1995 that Yasushi Akashi was to be replaced as UN special representative in the former Yugoslavia by Kofi Annan. On 1 January 1997 Kofi Annan replaced Boutros Boutros Ghali as UN secretary-general.)

MOSTAR

Mostar was not a 'safe area'. But it is appropriately dealt with here, as a signal failure to reintegrate ethnic Croats and Moslems.

In 1991 the population of Mostar was 35 per cent Moslem, 34 per cent Croat and 19 per cent Serb (*Independent*, 6 August 1996, p. 7).

A planned two-year EU administration, under Hans Koschnik (the former mayor of Bremen), began on 23 July 1994.

On 16 June 1996 Bosnian Croat hardliners announced, in Mostar, the formation of a new separate government for Herceg-Bosna.

On 31 July 1996 a US-mediated effort resulted in the Bosnian Croats agreeing to dismantle Herceg-Bosna and to set up power-sharing institutions by 8 August 1996. It was announced that the administrative arrangements of Herceg-Bosna 'cease to exist'.

On 19 December 1999 it was announced that Sfor (the Nato Stabilization Force for Bosnia) troops had raided buildings in Mostar on 14 October 1999.

> Nato troops ... say employees are actually intelligence agents of a clandestine, illicit network run by Croatia. Nato officials say they have clear evidence that the Croatian government of Franjo Tudjman, who died a week ago, has been secretly paying millions of dcllars a month to fund this network. Its aim, they say, was to support Bosnian Croat nationalists who oppose the return of Bosnian Moslems to Croat-dominated areas of the country, and thus keep alive the possibility that Croatia might ultimately be able to annex Bosnian territory. Some of the money was also used to promote criminal activity, including the apparent counterfeiting of credit cards and telephone debit cards, Nato officials say ... A senior Nato official said ... the raid had uncovered 'prima facie evidence of linkages' between the Croatian government and local intelligence cfficials that were designed to influence local politics and undermine the Dayton accords. 'This is illegal,' the official said. A small number of illegal weapons were also found.
>
> (IHT, 20 December 1999, p. 7)

Plans for Bosnia and events prior to Dayton

Before Dayton there had been a string of failed plans for Bosnia. An agreement was reached on 18 March 1992 which suggested that Bosnia should be 'cantonized' (the Carrington–Cutilheiro plan). The Vance–Owen plan for Bosnia of 28 October 1992 proposed that Bosnia be divided into ten largely autonomous provinces, with the three main ethnic groups (Moslem, Serb and Croat) to varying degrees in the majority in three provinces each (although all main groups had to be represented in provincial governments). The Serb–Croat plan for Bosnia of 16 June 1993 saw a territorial division between three constituent republics, a confederation of three constituent peoples. Union decisions would be taken by consensus, and there was intentionally nothing in reality in these proposals stopping the Serbs or Croats joining a 'Greater Serbia' or a 'Greater Croatia'. The Bosnian presidency's plan for Bosnia of 11 July 1993 put forward the following proposal: 'The constitutional make-up of Bosnia-Hercegovina should be along the lines of a federal state in which all citizens of three nationalities will have equal rights.' It was largely based on the Vance–Owen plan. But even the number of provinces was left vague (four to eighteen). There would be a pluralistic, democratic and secular federation, but with 'substantial provincial, cultural and social autonomy'. Each ethnic group would have parity at the federal level, but the provinces 'cannot be constituted solely on ethnic principles'. The Owen–Stoltenberg plan for Bosnia, the first draft of which was released for general publication on 6 August 1993 and the second draft on 20 August, was largely based on the Serb–Croat set of proposals. The republics were to be essentially ethnic-based. The 'Union of the Republics of Bosnia-Hercegovina' would be a confederation. The union government would have residual powers only, specifically confined to foreign policy and foreign trade.

Izetbegovic and Tudjman met in Geneva on 14 September 1993 and agreed a ceasefire between Bosnian government and Croat forces by 10 a.m. on 18 September at the latest. (Fighting actually continued even beyond the deadline.)

On 16 September 1993 a dramatic accord was signed by President Izetbegovic and Momcilo Krajisnik (chairman of the Bosnian Serb assembly). For example, after reaching an agreement on territorial division (this being deferred, with working groups considering the problem after the signing of a peace agreement) and

> during the initial two-year period of the union's existence, there would be provision for a referendum to be held on a mutually agreed date within the republics of the union on the question of whether citizens of any particular republic agree to remain in the union or to leave the union.

But this failed to gain acceptance.

By November 1993 the most commonly cited figures for the occupation of Bosnia as of that time were 15 per cent Moslem, 15 per cent Croat and 70 per cent Serb.

The British lieutenant-general Sir Michael Rose replaced Lieutenant-General Francis Briquemont of Belgium as commander of UN forces in Bosnia on 24 January 1994.

A Nato communiqué issued on 11 January 1994 stated that:

> We reaffirm our readiness, under the authority of the United Nations Security Council and in accordance with the Alliance decisions of 2 and 9 August 1993, to carry out air strikes in order to prevent the strangulation of Sarajevo, the safe areas and other threatened areas in Bosnia-Hercegovina.

On 28 January 1994 the UN secretary-general, Boutros Boutros Ghali, first delegated the authority to approve air strikes to his special representative in the former Yugoslavia, Yasushi Akashi.

On 5 February 1994 world attention once again switched to Sarajevo when a mortar bomb killed sixty-eight people in a Sarajevo market and injured more than two hundred others. A Nato communiqué followed on 10 February 1994 and read as follows:

> Ten days from 2400 GMT 10 February 1994, heavy weapons of any of the parties found within the Sarajevo exclusion zone, unless controlled by Unprofor, will, along with their direct and essential military support facilities, be subject to Nato air strikes which will be conducted in close co-ordination with the UN secretary-general.

The greatest pressure had come from France and the USA. The UK had been lukewarm. Canada had been one of the most reluctant and Greece actually dissociated itself from the statement. Prior to the meeting Manfred Wörner, Nato secretary-general, who was chairman despite being very ill, said: 'It is time to act. We have had enough words.' (He died of cancer on 13 August 1994.)

Disagreements emerged between Nato and the UN on 14 February 1994 about what precisely was meant by 'control' of heavy weapons and the deadline for compliance. The precise chain of authority for issuing air strike orders was also not crystal clear. (The Bosnian Serbs took advantage of the confusion to prevaricate and try to deepen the differences between Nato and the UN. But differences also emerged among Bosnian Serb political and military leaders.)

On 23 February 1994, military leaders of the Bosnian government and the Bosnian Croats, meeting in Zagreb, announced agreement on a ceasefire starting at noon on 25 February. Heavy weapons would be withdrawn by 7 March between six and twelve miles from the front lines or surrendered to UN control. UN troops would be positioned at key locations. The ceasefire began on 25 February 1994.

On 28 February 1994 Nato (US) fighters shot down four (out of six) Bosnian Serb jet aircraft that had been bombing targets in central Bosnia. (This was not only the first enforcement of the 'no fly' resolution, but also the first ever combat role for Nato. More than 1,600 violations of the flight ban had been recorded,

1,397 between 9 October 1992 and 1 January 1994: *FT*, 1 March 1994, pp. 2, 22.)

The Bosnian government–Croat plan for Bosnia emerged in March 1994. Tudjman went along with the idea of a US-brokered Bosnian government–Bosnian Croat federation linked economically with Croatia in a loose confederation. There would be a federation split up into cantons based not only on ethnic make-up. The central government was to be responsible for defence (there would be one army), foreign affairs and economic policy (including foreign trade), while the cantons would have authority over the police, education, housing and public services. The Bosnian Serbs were not interested in joining.

On 25 April 1994 it was announced in London that a 'contact group' of leading officials from the USA, Russia, the EU (the UK, France and Germany) and the UN had been established (the first meeting being held the following day). The 'contact group's' plan for Bosnia-Hercegovina proposed a federation split up into cantons based not solely on ethnic make-up.

On 23 January 1995, at the end of his controversial official term as Unprofor commander in Bosnia, Lieutenant-General Sir Michael Rose (seen by many as viewing all sides as equally bad and by the Bosnian government as actually pro-Serb) was replaced by Lieutenant-General Rupert Smith (also from the UK), a quiet and decisive man who made a dramatic difference to the course of the war in Bosnia.

On 6 March 1995, Croatia, the Bosnian government and the Bosnian Croat militia agreed to form a military alliance. On 20 March 1995 Bosnian government forces launched a major offensive to capture Bosnian Serb positions on peaks around Tuzla and Travnik (the targets including communications towers). There was also an offensive around Gradacac. On 25 March the Bosnian Serbs shelled Mostar and Gorazde.

On 27 March 1995 Lieutenant-General Smith's spokesman stated that attacks which came from outside a 'safe area' and which deliberately targeted civilians would meet a resolute response, including the use of air strikes. Bosnian government forces would not be protected if an attack came from within a 'safe area'.

On 7 May 1995 eleven people were killed when Sarajevo was shelled (near the entrance to the tunnel which forms the city's link with the outside world). The following day it was revealed that Yasushi Akashi (and General Bernard Janvier) had turned down a request from Lieutenant-General Rupert Smith for air strikes on the Bosnian Serbs. On 24 May Lieutenant-General Smith threatened air strikes against any transgressor if the following deadlines were not met: (1) all heavy weapons to cease firing in the Sarajevo exclusion zone by noon local time on 25 May; and (2) all such weapons to be either outside the exclusion zone or in UN-controlled collection sites by noon on 26 May.

On 25 May 1995, Nato jets attacked a Bosnian Serb ammunition dump near Pale when four guns taken from a UN collection site were not returned. The Bosnian Serbs responded by shelling Sarajevo and four other 'safe areas'. Seventy-one civilians were killed in Tuzla. The following day Nato jets launched another attack on the ammunition dump. The Bosnian Serbs retaliated by holding UN peacekeepers as hostages and using (unarmed) UN military observers as 'human shields' at likely targets of air strikes. On 27 May two (French) UN soldiers and four Bosnian Serbs were killed in a heavy exchange of fire over control of an observation post on a bridge in Sarajevo.

On 31 May 1995 President Clinton unexpectedly announced:

> I will carefully review any request for an operation involving the temporary use of our ground forces. If necessary, and after consultation with Congress, I believe we should be prepared to assist Nato if it decides to meet a request from the United Nations troops for help in withdrawal or in a reconfiguration and a strengthening of its forces.

(But on 3 June Clinton specified that the only other contingency that he had in mind was 'the remote, indeed highly unlikely event that Britain, France and other countries ... become stranded and cannot get out of a particular place in Bosnia'. On 7 June US defence secretary William Perry stated that 'We should be prepared to assist Nato in an emergency extraction of units, whose positions had become untenable, to points of safety in Bosnia.' Previously the USA had offered ground troops only for a withdrawal or to help police a final peace settlement. Also, on 31 May 1995, Lord Owen announced that he was to resign as EU mediator, i.e. as EU representative at the International Conference on the Former Yugoslavia. On 9 June 1995 he was replaced by Carl Bildt, the former prime minister of Sweden.)

An appeal from Milosevic made on 2 June 1995 resulted in the release of 121 UN hostages (about a third of the total). But the Bosnian Serbs took a further sixteen UN personnel hostage and shot down a Nato (US) jet on routine patrol. On 18 June the last twenty-six hostages were released.

On 3 June 1995 fifteen Western countries decided to set up a 'rapid reaction force' comprising up to 10,000 British, French and (to a much smaller extent) Dutch troops. On 18 June Unprofor forces abandoned the weapons collection points around Sarajevo, thus effectively ending the heavy weapon exclusion zone.

On 30 June 1995 the German Bundestag approved the use of German transport and fighter planes and the sending of a field hospital to support the 'rapid reaction force' and any future Nato withdrawal.

The Bosnian Serbs shelled UN headquarters in Sarajevo on 2 July, seemingly deliberately.

On 28 August 1995 thirty-seven civilians were killed in a mortar attack on Sarajevo.

Operation Deliberate Force began on 30 August 1995. Nato planes launched a series of massive air strikes against Bosnian Serb targets around Sarajevo in particular but also Tuzla, Gorazde, Zepa and Mostar. The 'rapid reaction force' also shelled targets around Sarajevo, with the announced aim of clearing the exclusion zone of heavy weapons.

Air strikes continued on 31 August, albeit on a reduced scale.

On 8 September 1995, while air strikes continued, the foreign ministers of Bosnia, Croatia and Serbia agreed on the 'basic principles' of a political settlement in Bosnia. US special envoy Richard Holbrooke described the agreement as 'an important milestone in the search for peace'.

An estimate made on 18 September was that the area held by the Bosnian Serbs was around 50 per cent. Control of the other 50 per cent was split more or less equally between the Bosnian government and the Bosnian Croats (*The Economist*, 4 November 1995, p. 55; *IHT*, 29 December 1995, p. 6).

The offensive in western Bosnia virtually ceased by 21 September.

On 5 October 1995 negotiations led by the USA resulted in a ceasefire agreement signed by Izetbegovic, Karadzic and Mladic.

On 8 October 1995 it was reported that heavy fighting continued in northern Bosnia. Troops from Croatia supported Bosnian government forces.

The ceasefire was delayed on 9 October 1995 because most preconditions had not been met, e.g. the restoration of utility services to Sarajevo.

It was announced that on 1 November Yasushi Akashi was to be replaced as UN special representative in the former Yugoslavia by Kofi Annan. (Yasushi Akashi had come in for bitter criticism from the Bosnian and US governments in particular for his resistance to air strikes against the Bosnian Serbs.)

The ceasefire began at 12.01 a.m. on 11 October 1995. It generally held, but fighting continued in places (e.g. around Sanski Most and Prijedor). On 18 October a UN aid convoy reached Gorazde from Sarajevo for the first time in two years.

On 8 November 1995 the USA and Russia announced that a Russian combat brigade (about 1,500 troops) would participate in the implementation force as part of a US division. The Russian commander would take orders from the US division commander, who, in turn, would take orders from General George Joulwan in his capacity as supreme commander of US forces in Europe rather than as supreme Nato (allied) military commander in Europe.

Dayton

A joint statement, issued by the international organizations supervising Bosnia on 21 November 1999 to mark the anniversary of the signing of the Dayton accords, included the following statement:

> We welcome the absence of war and the deepening of peace ... [But] we see what we lack for a truly durable peace: a functioning sovereign state that unites all peoples of Bosnia and Hercegovina; an economy free from political influence and corruption that can provide jobs and stability; and the ability for all refugees and displaced persons to return to their homes.
>
> (*FT*, Survey, 14 December 1999, p. 35)

The peace settlement talks began on 1 November 1995 at the Wright–Patterson Air Base near Dayton, Ohio, USA.

The peace agreement was initialled by Presidents Izetbegovic, Tudjman and Milosevic on 21 November 1995. (The formal signing ceremony was to be held in early December.) The main points were as follows:

1 Bosnia was to be preserved as a single state within its present borders and with international recognition. (The name of the country was to be changed from the 'Republic of Bosnia-Hercegovina' to 'Bosnia and Hercegovina'.)

2 Bosnia was to comprise the Bosnian–Croat Federation and the Republika Srpska, with a 'fair distribution of land between the two' (51 per cent and 49 per cent respectively).

3 The capital city of Sarajevo was to be reunited under federal authority, though with ten districts. There was to be an 'effective' central government, including a national parliament, presidency, constitutional court and central bank. The presidency and parliament would be chosen through free and democratic elections held under international supervision. The three-member presidency (one to be a Bosnian Serb) would rotate, but the Bosnian–Croat Federation would provide the first president. The central authorities would be responsible for foreign policy, foreign trade, common and international communications, inter-entity transport, air traffic control, monetary policy, citizenship and immigration. ('To counter the threat of financial instability, the authorities have decided that the new central bank will operate as a currency board for several years, issuing domestic currency only against full foreign exchange backing, and that there will be no domestic bank financing of public expenditure': United Nations Economic Commission for Europe 1996: 170.)

4 Refugees would be allowed to return to their homes.

5 Individuals charged with war crimes would be excluded from political and military life. Bosnia, Croatia and Serbia would co-operate fully in the investigation and prosecution of war crimes.

6 A land corridor would link Sarajevo and Gorazde.

7 The problem of Brcko and the Posavina corridor would be submitted to international arbitration. (The Bosnian Serbs were awarded the area in western Bosnia around Sipovo and Mrkonjic Grad which they lost in the summer of 1995.)

8 A 'strong international force' (a Nato implementation force) would supervise the separation of forces. (The Nato force was to number around 60,000, including some 20,000 US troops. In a 27 November 1995 speech advocating the sending of US troops, President Clinton said that 'this mission should and will take about one year'.)

9 On 22 November the UN Security Council announced that the arms embargo on the countries of the former Yugoslavia would be lifted over a six-month period and that economic sanctions on the Federal Republic of Yugoslavia would be suspended (for six months in the first instance). (The

agreement provided for a build-down of weapons by those who had a great
many and a build-up of the undersupplied Bosnian army: *The Economist*, 30
March 1996, p. 20.)

10 An international programme would provide humanitarian relief, assist
rebuilding and help refugees.

(Officials of the Bosnian–Croat Federation included the following: president,
Kresimir Zubak; vice-president, Ejup Ganic; prime minister, Izudin
Kapetanovic; defence minister, Vladimir Soljic: *Business Europa*, June–July 1996,
p. 28.)

On 5 December 1995 the foreign and defence ministers of Nato gave provisional approval to send some 60,000 troops to Bosnia (Ifor: Implementation
Force for Bosnia; Operation Joint Endeavour). The USA was to send roughly
20,000 troops, the UK 13,000, France 10,000 and Russia some 2,000. On 6
December 1995 the German Bundestag approved the sending of 4,000
personnel. They were mostly transport, medical and logistics specialists. Four
hundred German paratroopers and infantry were to provide protection, but
were not to take part in enforcing the separation lines.

The 'peace implementation conference' was held in London on 8–9
December 1995, dealing with civilian aspects. Carl Bildt was appointed 'high
representative', whose functions were (1) to co-ordinate civilian aid and the
reconstruction programme and (2) to act as liaison between the civilian and mili-
tary operations. A Peace Implementation Council (a replacement for the
International Conference on the Former Yugoslavia) was to have a Steering
Board comprising the G7 countries, Russia, the EU's presidency, the European
Commission and the Organization of the Islamic Conference. An OSCE
(Organization for Security and Co-operation in Europe) mission was to prepare
and conduct elections, while the United Nations High Commissioner for
Refugees was to be involved in that capacity. (The choice of Carl Bildt was criticized, especially in the USA. For example, a leader in the *New York Times*
commented as follows: 'Mr Bildt starts his new job burdened with a reputation
for accepting Bosnian Serb claims at face value and overlooking evidence of
atrocities against civilians. He mainly acquired that reputation when Bosnian
Serb forces overran Srebrenica in July … Mr Bildt has surprisingly suggested
that he divides his calendar between Sweden and the Balkans. Bosnia is not a
part-time job. If he cannot understand that, someone else should be found who
can': *IHT*, 18 December 1995, p. 8. The *New York Times* wrote in its leader
column that 'Mr Bildt has been shockingly slow in taking up his duties': *IHT*, 8
January 1996, p. 8.)

The formal signing of the peace agreement took place on 14 December 1995
at the Elysée Palace in Paris. Bosnia-Hercegovina and the Federal Republic of
Yugoslavia formally granted each other diplomatic recognition. The UN
Security Council approved the deployment of Ifor the following day. On 20
December 1995, Nato formally took over from the UN.

Invited by the USA, the presidents of Bosnia, Croatia and Serbia met 'contact group' members in Italy on 17–18 February 1996. Richard Holbrooke, who was to leave his post as assistant secretary of state for European affairs on 21 February, announced that the crisis threatening the Dayton peace agreement had been averted.

> Recent moves by the [Bosnian] government have called into question its commitment to an ethnically mixed city and country ... The moves began, Western officials say, with the failure of Bosnia's Moslem leadership to adequately assure Serbs in five Serbian-held suburbs surrounding Sarajevo that they would be welcome to stay in those areas once they transferred back to government control. They continued with the unwillingness of Moslem police to stop intimidation of Serbs around Sarajevo once those suburbs changed hands. They climaxed last week when Moslem authorities shut out Serbs and Croats in the formation of the capital's new government ... forty-five out of forty-seven seats were given to Moslems. Serbs and Croats were allotted one seat each. That move prompted Sarajevo's well-respected mayor, Tarik Kupusovic, to resign in protest.
>
> (John Pomfret, *IHT*, 18 March 1996, p. 6)

There were varying estimates of how many Serbs in total remained in the five suburbs. The UN believed that only 8,000–10,000 Serbs (10 per cent to 12 per cent of the pre-war population) remained (*Independent*, 19 March 1996, p. 11). Of the roughly 60,000 Serbs who lived in these suburbs during the 1992–5 war, only about 10,000 remained (*Independent*, 21 March 1996, p. 17). Only 11,000 Serbs remained in the five suburbs, less than a tenth of the pre-war figure (*Guardian*, 20 March 1996, p. 10). Some 60,000 left the five suburbs (*IHT*, 20 March 1996, p. 1; *The Times*, 20 March 1996, p. 15).

On 5 April 1996 it was alleged that in 1994 President Clinton had secretly given his approval for covert arms shipments from Iran to Bosnia via Croatia (which had taken its share) (*IHT*, 6 April 1996, p. 2). US officials learned in the autumn of 1992 that Iran had opened an arms smuggling route with the assistance of Turkey. The US administration turned a blind eye soon after coming to office in January 1993 (*IHT*, 13 May 1996, pp. 1, 6).

> [On 8 November 1996] the US Senate intelligence committee concluded that President Clinton did approve the secret decision to do nothing to stop the shipment of Iranian arms, which violated a UN embargo. Senior Clinton administration officials may have misled one another, Congress, America's allies and the American people. But they broke no laws, the arms helped the Bosnian government to survive and it was hard to prove that Iran's influence in the region increased.
>
> (Tim Weiner, *IHT*, 9 November 1996, p. 2)

On 13 April 1996 Haris Silajdzic announced the formation of the New Party for Bosnia-Hercegovina, committed to a genuinely multi-ethnic Bosnia. He was injured on 15 June 1996 when, campaigning for his New Party for Bosnia-Hercegovina, he was hit over the head with an iron bar by a supporter of the Moslem Union for Democratic Action. (On 21 January 1996 he announced he would resign as prime minister, effective 30 January, because the Bosnian parliament had passed a law that reduced the number of ministries in the federal government, thus weakening his authority. He became co-chairman of the cabinet after the September 1996 elections.)

On 15 May 1996 Radovan Karadzic dismissed the prime minister of the Republika Srpska, Rajko Kasagic. Kasagic, from Banja Luka, was considered to be a moderate willing to negotiate. Kasagic:

> Karadzic is an illegitimate president because he was not elected by the people as called for in the constitution, but only by a self-proclaimed parliament. I guarantee the salvation of the Serbian people, while he is leading the people to ruin. The Dayton agreement is the only future the Republika Srpska has.
>
> (*IHT*, 17 May 1996, p. 1)

Karadzic said that he would relinquish his role in international relations to his deputy Biljana Plavsic (known as the Iron Lady because of her extreme views) and concentrate on the economy, helping Bosnian Serb refugees and providing jobs for demobilized Bosnian Serb soldiers. There was considerable doubt as to whether these moves diminished Karadzic's influence. Kasagic described the moves as a 'farce': 'Through Biljana Plavsic, Karadzic can have full influence and implement the policy he has started' (*IHT*, 21 May 1996, p. 5).

On 18 June 1996 the UN Security Council lifted the arms embargo on the countries of the former Yugoslavia.

Karadzic was re-elected leader of the Serbian Democratic Party on 29 June 1996. On the following day it was revealed that in a letter dated 26 June Karadzic had said that he would step down as president, citing 'temporary inability' to perform his functions. (International sanctions had been threatened.) He was to hand over to Biljana Plavsic, but she said that Karadzic remained president until the 14 September elections and that she was vice-president. On 3 July 1996 Karadzic declared he would not be a candidate in the September elections. On 9 July he was appointed chairman of a new body, the Senate.

On 19 July Richard Holbrooke and Slobodan Milosevic reached agreement on Radovan Karadzic. Karadzic signed the following statement along with Momcilo Krajisnik (speaker of the Bosnian Serb assembly), Biljana Plavsic and Aleksa Buha (the Bosnian Serb foreign minister), while it was witnessed by Milosevic and Milan Milutinovic:

> The undersigned reaffirm their commitment to fulfil the General Framework Agreement for Peace and Annexes negotiated in Dayton and signed in Paris 14 December 1995, and state the following:

1 As of 19 July 1996 Dr Biljana Plavsic has assumed the office of Temporary Acting President of Republika Srpska until completion of the elections of 14 September 1996.
2 Dr Radovan Karadzic states that he shall withdraw immediately and permanently from all political activities.
3 As of 19 July 1996 Dr Radovan Karadzic relinquishes the office of President of the SDS [Serbian Democratic Party] and all the functions, powers and responsibilities of the President of the SDS shall be frozen until the SDS chooses a new President. These powers and responsibilities shall be taken over by Professor Buha.

On 14 August 1996, the US secretary of state Warren Christopher convened a meeting with Presidents Izetbegovic, Tudjman and Milosevic and gained their agreement to implement the Dayton accords. Presidents Izetbegovic and Tudjman reaffirmed their commitment to 'strengthening the Federation as the cornerstone of the peace process'. It was agreed that by 31 August 1996 Herceg-Bosna would 'cease to exist' and the Bosnian state would turn over its government institutions to the federation.

On 27 August 1996, OSCE postponed the municipal elections due to have been held on 14 September owing to 'widespread abuse of rules and regulations'. Criticism was especially levelled at the Serbs (the Bosnian Serbs and the authorities in Serbia) for the ways in which large numbers of Bosnian Serb refugees had been registered to vote in towns like Brcko and Srebrenica which formerly had Moslem majorities. Election rules, approved by OSCE, gave the three nationalist parties (the Croatian Democratic Union, the Moslem Party of Democratic Action and the Serbian Democratic Party) a monopoly on registering voters.

On 12 September 1996, Biljana Plavsic called for Serb secession. Such sentiments were, of course, contrary to the Dayton accords. The following day she was forced by OSCE to apologize publicly for campaigning for union with Serbia.

The Bosnian elections of 14 September 1996 and events thereafter

Those not living in their former areas had a choice as to where to vote – where they used to live, where they currently lived or where they would like to live. The elections went ahead despite the many arguments put forward for postponing them, e.g. the likely retrenchment of ethnic divisions, the lack of progress made with regard to refugees wishing to return to their homes, the lack of independent media, widespread intimidation of opposition parties, and the accusation that the timetable was set to suit the November 1996 US presidential election. The turnout seemed suspiciously high given the voter register. On 23 September OSCE took the controversial decision to increase the total number of registered voters. As predicted, the vote split mainly on ethnic lines. The final election results were announced by OSCE on 24 September 1996:

1   The three-member Bosnian presidency, a 'Bosniac' (an OSCE term indicating that 'Bosniacs' are not exclusively Moslems), a Bosnian Croat and a Bosnian Serb. There is a rotating presidency but the first president's term of office lasts for two years. Decisions by the three-man presidency need unanimity. Alija Izetbegovic became the Moslem representative, Momcilo Krajisnik the Bosnian Serb representative, and Kresimir Zubak the Bosnian Croat representative.

2   The Republika Srpska has a separate presidency, comprising two people and elected on the basis of one round of voting. The Moslem–Croat (Bosniac–Croat) Federation also has a presidency, but the federation is divided into ten cantons (districts), each with its own assembly (444 seats in total).

3   The House of Representatives of Bosnia and Hercegovina (the lower house of the federal legislature) comprises twenty-eight seats for the Bosniac–Croat Federation and fourteen for the Bosnian Serbs.

4   The House of Peoples (the upper house) of Bosnia and Hercegovina comprises fifteen delegates, split equally between Bosniacs, Croats and Serbs, and is elected indirectly. Fifteen delegates are from the House of Representatives of the Bosniac–Croat Federation and five from the National Assembly of the Republika Srpska.

5   There are separate assemblies for the Bosniac–Croat Federation and the Republika Srpska.

6   There are local councils in both entities.

Elections are by proportional representation except for the three-member Bosnian presidency and the presidency of the Republika Srpska.

> Multi-party elections for parliamentary and executive offices above the local level were held in Bosnia in September 1996, and, as earlier, the outcome, while seeming pluralist, did not represent the best result for a democratic Bosnia ... The flawed character of the 1990 elections – in particular the fact that the nature of the republic-level elections precluded holding federal elections – was relevant for post-Dayton elections.
>
> (Friedman 2000: 24–5)

> Ante Markovic, federal prime minister [January 1989 to 20 December 1991], attempted to establish a federation-wide party that would support his market economic policies and that would undercut the plethora of narrow interest parties that were arising throughout the country. However, [in 1990] there was no countrywide contest in which to introduce his new party ... Despite the fact that this party was one of the few that was devoted to maintaining the unity of Yugoslavia under a liberal democracy, the narrow, ethnically-oriented parties garnered the majority of votes ... The fact that Markovic's party was forced to compete in regional elections against region-

ally strong parties obviated what might have been a better showing at the federal level, should such a contest have been possible.

(pp. 23–4)

On 22 October 1996, OSCE postponed the local elections for the second time.

On 8 November 1996 Bosnian Serb president Biljana Plavsic announced that General Ratko Mladic and the rest of the general staff had been dismissed. (This was an early sign that Plavsic had turned against Karadzic and had become much more accommodating to the West.)

On 18 November 1996 Nato agreed to set up Sfor (Stabilization Force for Bosnia), comprising 31,000 troops. This was confirmed on 10 December at a meeting of Nato foreign ministers. On 17 December 1996 Nato defence ministers approved the 'activation order' for Sfor for a period of eighteen months. The UN approved a mandate for Sfor on 13 December. On the same day the German parliament approved the use of (2,000) German combat troops as part of Sfor, to operate in south-eastern Bosnia. This was the first time since the Second World War that German combat forces had been allowed to take full part in a ground mission with Western allies, albeit jointly with French forces. The total number of German military personnel involved was about 3,000. On 20 December 1996 Sfor took over from Ifor.

Roberts Owen (from the USA), who chaired the arbitration tribunal on Brcko, reported on 14 February 1997: 'We will make a final choice no later than 15 March 1998.' Until a final decision was made Brcko would be under international supervision, led by an 'international supervisor'. Although Brcko would remain in the hands of the Bosnian Serbs, provision would be made for the return of refugees and roads would be opened to Moslem and Croat travellers. (But on 15 March 1998 it was announced that a decision on Brcko would again be delayed, until at least early 1999: *IHT*, 16 March 1998, p. 1.)

On 30 May 1997 the Bosnian Peace Implementation Council threatened sanctions unless the Dayton accords were carried out in full. It was announced that Carl Bildt would be replaced as High Representative for Bosnia by Carlos Westendorp on 20 June 1997. (Westendorp, a former Spanish foreign minister, was then Spain's representative at the United Nations.)

On 27 June 1997 Bosnian Serb president Biljana Plavsic dismissed interior minister Dragan Kijac (who was loyal to Karadzic) for refusing to deal with the corruption that permeated the economy and enriched people like Karadzic. But prime minister Momcilo Krajisnik rescinded the dismissal the following day. On 29 June 1997 Plavsic was briefly detained at Belgrade airport by the Serbian police. The following day she was briefly detained by the Bosnian Serb police. She accused Karadzic of still running the Republika Srpska and of attempting a coup. On 3 July she attempted to dissolve the Bosnian Serb parliament and arrange fresh elections for 1 September 1997. 'The functioning of legal order ... is in a serious crisis in almost all fields,' she said. Parliament was 'carrying out orders from the informal centres of power', while the police were 'organizing criminal activities'. In February 1997 Plavsic placed an advertisement in Serbian papers calling for an investigation into the export–import companies controlled by Karadzic and Momcilo Krajisnik (who was also the Serb representative of the three-member Bosnian presidency).

> The Karadzic–Krajisnik companies are called Centrex and Select-Impex [Selkt-Impex] and bring in massive revenues from contraband … Dr Karadzic controls a nationwide secret police network … 'The consequence of this is an enormous accumulation of wealth by a relatively small number of our population,' Mrs Plavsic said in an extraordinary address from the Banja Luka studio of state television. 'Do they think that the rest of the population will be their slaves?' Yesterday government officials closed the studio.
>
> (Tom Walker, *The Times*, 5 July 1997, p. 17)

In an earlier article Chris Hedges (*IHT*, 7 April 1997, pp. 1, 7) reported that Karadzic oversaw a monopoly on the sale of gasoline, cigarettes and other goods in the Republika Srpska. He controlled the monopoly through two companies he ran with Momcilo Krajisnik. Plavsic stated that:

> The state has no control over the economy. Some private persons are making a lot of money behind the scenes and should be obliged to pay the state. I have given the order to investigate this, but unfortunately certain institutions, including the police, are involved. This monopoly does not just include gasoline, but extends to things such as building materials and cattle.

Karadzic started Centrex in 1993, which, with the protection of the police and the Serbian Democratic Party, secured exclusive rights to import and sell a variety of goods. In 1996 he formed Selkt-Impex along with the interior ministry of the Republika Srpska. It handled some imports but also supplemented the salaries of the Bosnian Serb police, whose basic wages were paid by the Serbian-dominated government of the Federal Republic of Yugoslavia.

On 19 July 1997 Plavsic was expelled from the Serbian Democratic Party. The following day, in Doboj, she addressed a rally of supporters: 'Now is the moment to establish a democratic Serb state based on legality, because we belonged – and will again belong – to Europe' (*IHT*, 22 July 1997, p. 9).

On 15 August 1997 the constitutional court ruled against Plavsic's attempt to dissolve parliament and call early elections.

On 16 August 1997 special police units loyal to Plavsic took over the Banja Luka Public Security Centre. Sfor troops then took over.

On 17 August 1997 Sfor troops left the centre and civilian police took over.

On 20 August 1997 Sfor troops (with Plavsic's 'mutual agreement') took over police stations in Banja Luka and seized unauthorized arms.

On 23 August 1997 the government of Republika Srpska announced that it would regard all Plavsic's decisions as 'irregular, illegitimate and non-binding'.

On 24 August 1997 the Banja Luka state television station (which covers the western part of Republika Srpska) made its first broadcast free of control of Pale (Karadzic's headquarters).

On 28 August 1997 clashes occurred between Sfor (US) troops and pro-Karadzic civilians in Brcko and Bijeljina when pro-Plavsic police tried to take control of police stations. Plavsic established a new party, the Serbian People's Union.

On 3 September 1997 army chief of staff Pero Colic met Plavsic in Banja Luka and afterwards referred to her as 'supreme commander'.

On 8 September 1997 Sfor troops and police loyal to Plavsic prevented most pro-Karadzic supporters from attending a rally in Banja Luka. Plavsic met Krajisnik.

On 9 September 1997 pro-Karadzic supporters (including Momcilo Krajisnik, interior minister Dragan Kijac and prime minister Gojko Klickovic) besieged in a Banja Luka hotel by pro-Plavsic supporters were rescued by Sfor troops.

Local elections were held in Bosnia on 13–14 September 1997. Voters were unable to nominate any place of residence (as they were previously). Voters had to choose either the area where they lived in 1991 (voting there or by absentee ballot) or the area where they had been resident since June 1996. ('The rules allowed them to register where they lived before the war or where they live now. Eighty-nine per cent chose their former abode': *Guardian*, 11 November 1997, p. 17.) The Croatian Democratic Union and the Serbian Democratic Party did not carry out their threats to boycott the elections. Plavsic's new party (the Serbian People's Union) was too late to take part.

There were a dozen towns in which exiles won majorities or a big share of the seats, e.g. Brcko, Dvar, Mostar and Srebrenica. In nine towns where inhabitants blocked exiles from taking office OSCE had to choose mayors itself and compelled councils to meet (*The Economist*, 11 April 1998, p. 34). In Srebrenica Moslem parties gained control with twenty-five seats (*FT*, 10 October 1997, p. 3). In January 1998 Serbs blocked the arrival of the twenty-five Moslem councillors and stoned the car of an OSCE official. On 6 April 1998 OSCE suspended the assembly and said it would appoint an administrator with wide powers (*The Economist*, 11 April 1998, p. 34). Following local authority polls in 1997 OSCE managed to install elected assemblies in all but two of Bosnia's 136 municipalities. One of the exceptions was Srebrenica, whose displaced Moslem population (still living as refugees) elected a Moslem-majority local assembly through the absentee voting system (Gabriel Partos, *The World Today*, vol. 54, nos 8–9, p. 210).

Municipal elections in Bosnia were organized by OSCE in September 1997. While the elections of the previous year were heavily weighted with nationalist candidates, the 1997 elections saw more than seventy parties represented and the use of absentee ballots for the Bosnian diaspora. However, only in Tuzla did non-ethnic parties dominate. In the rest of Bosnia, not surprisingly, the ruling nationalist parties captured most of the council seats ... There were some positive sides ... even though nationalism still ruled the area. The pro-Karadzic SDS [Serbian Democratic Party] in Republika Srpska did not capture as many votes as it was feared they would, although many disaffected voters cast their ballots for the more extreme nationalist Serbian Radical Party (SRS), the Bosnian branch of Vojislav Seselj's party in Serbia. Furthermore, candidates representing platforms for refugee return were elected in a number of seats in the federation and one in Republika Srpska.

(Friedman 2000: 26)

On 21 November 1997 OSCE reported that the various parties in Bosnia had completed the arms reductions agreed to in June 1996 (*IHT*, 22 November 1997, p. 2).

Elections were held in the Republika Srpska on 22–3 November 1997. The turnout was 77 per cent. The Serbian Democratic Party lost its majority, winning twenty-four of the eighty-three seats in the National Assembly. Plavsic's Serbian People's Union won fifteen seats, as did the Serbian Radical Party (an off-shoot of Seselj's Radical Party in Serbia). The Moslem-dominated Coalition for Bosnia and Hercegovina won sixteen seats, benefiting mainly from the absentee vote of refugees.

The Peace Implementation Conference held another session on 9–10 December 1997. Deadlines were set for various measures (e.g. the end of January 1998 for common car licence plates throughout Bosnia) and Carlos Westendorp was empowered to impose 'interim solutions ... when parties are unable to reach agreement'. 'At Bonn in December 1997 the Peace Implementation Council beefed up the High Commissioner's powers ... giving him authority to remove obstructive officials and to impose solutions where after lengthy delays the local leadership could not do so': Jacques Klein, *The World Today*, 1999, vol. 55, no. 6, p. 8.)

On 18 January 1998 Milorad Dodik, nominated by Biljana Plavsic, became prime minister of the Republika Srpska. (He was leader of the Independent Social Democrats, which had two seats in the National Assembly.) Pro-Karadzic supporters denounced Dodik as a tool of the West who had betrayed the Serbs and said that they would not recognize the new government. The coalition government had the support of Moslem and Croat deputies who would travel to sessions under UN protection.

Dodik blamed economic problems on 'needless spite, nonsense and egoism' by the previous rulers. He pledged strict implementation of the Dayton accords, the establishment of a free press and an end to censorship, an end to state corruption, an acceleration of privatization, and a separation of government from the Serbian Orthodox Church. Dodik wished to transfer the capital of Republika Srpska from Pale to Banja Luka (*IHT*, 21 January 1998, p. 5, and 22 January 1998, p. 8).

On 21 January 1998 Carlos Westendorp, the High Representative in Bosnia, imposed a solution for the design of a common currency (*IHT*, 22 January 1998, p. 5; *FT*, 22 January 1998, p. 2).

On 31 January 1998 the Bosnian Serb parliament voted in favour of transferring the capital from Pale to Banja Luka.

The Sarajevo Returns Conference was held on 3 February 1998. Sarajevo's population is now 87 per cent Moslem, whereas it was previously split much more evenly between Moslems (50 per cent), Serbs (27 per cent) and Croats (7 per cent). '[The] one-day conference will ... spotlight the failure of the government to allow – much less promote – minority resettlement' (R. Jeffrey Smith, *IHT*, 3 February 1998, p. 4).

On 4 February 1998 Carlos Westendorp unveiled the imposed national flag.

On 18 February 1998 the sixteen Nato ambassadors formally approved a third phase of peacekeeping in Bosnia. ('Sfor's mandate runs out at the end of June 1998. The number of troops – 35,000 – will remain the same at first but will be reduced to 20,000–25,000 after the Bosnian presidential and parliamentary elections are held in September 1998': *The Times*, 19 February 1998, p. 15.)

On 15 March 1998 a decision on Brcko was delayed until at least early 1999 (*IHT*, 16 March 1998, p. 1).

On 20 May 1998 Carlos Westendorp imposed a new flag after consensus was not reached.

In July 1998 new passports became available, containing only minor variations reflecting linguistic differences between the two entities (Gabriel Partos, *The World Today*, vol. 54, nos 8–9, pp. 210–11).

There was considerable delay before the results of the OSCE-organized elections (for all offices above the municipal level) were announced (12–13 September 1998).

Ultranationalist Nikola Poplasen was elected president of the Republika Srpska, beating Biljana Plavsic.

> Mr Poplasen's party is an offshoot of the Radical Party of Serbia's deputy prime minister Vojislav Seselj ... During the election campaign Mr Poplasen said that he would use all constitutional means to unite the Serb republic with Serbia ... Mr Poplasen boasts of having been a commander during the war ... A majority of voters chose Mr Poplasen on the grounds that other candidates would permit the return of Moslems and Croats who were ethnically cleansed in the war ... [Poplasen said that] 'I have not given up the Serbs' political and historical goals. They do not have to be achieved during my mandate, but in some five to ten years.'
>
> (Jonathan Steele, *Guardian*, 26 September 1998, p. 19)

The more moderate Zivko Radisic (Socialist Party) became the Serb member of the Bosnian three-person collective presidency, beating the hardline incumbent Momcilo Krajisnik.

'Last month's elections showed ethnic or confessional-based political parties losing ground. Non-confessional parties, such as the Social Democrats, gained ground' (*FT*, Survey, 21 October 1998, p. iii).

> The West would like Mr Dodik, whose party went up from two to six in September, to stay in the prime-ministership. It has made clear that, if he does, the Serb republic will continue to get the economic help that has brought in some $240 million worth of aid since July 1997.
>
> (*The Economist*, 21 November 1998, p. 46)

On 15–16 December 1998 a two-day conference of the Bosnian Peace Implementation Council was held in Madrid (the third such meeting). Extra powers were given to Carlos Westendorp (the High Representative), entitling him to block aid allocations or bar parties or political leaders from running for election if they failed to co-operate (*FT*, 17 December 1998, p. 3).

On 27 January 1999 it was announced that the size of the US military contingent in Bosnia would shrink from 6,900 to 6,200 over the two months as part of a Nato decision to trim its 32,000-strong peacekeeping force by 10 per cent (*IHT*, 28 January 1999, p. 6).

On 5 March 1999 a decision on Brcko was announced by Carlos Westendorp. The decision, however, was actually made by Roberts Owen, the US official who had supervised the Serb-run town of Brcko. The outlying area had been run by the federation. The ruling said that the two entities would be merged into a 'self-governing neutral district'. 'Both portions will now be held by both entities. The new government will be democratic and multi-ethnic.' The new entity would report to the federal government and would be administered under international supervision. On 8 March 2000 there was a formal announcement making Brcko a multi-ethnic district. The city has a multi-ethnic government approved by international officials and its residents are exempt from the draft.

Nikola Poplasen had earlier said that he was ready to 'take major decisions' in the event of an 'unjust solution'. He was later dismissed as president of the Republika Srpska by Carlos Westendorp (*IHT*, 6 March 1999, p. 2).

> On 5 March Roberts Owen, an American lawyer appointed by the International Court of Justice in The Hague, ruled that the entire pre-war municipality of Brcko should be a 'condominium' shared by Bosnia's two halves, with its own local administration … Only a few hours earlier Carlos Westendorp … had dismissed Nikola Poplasen … Mr Owen ruled that the Serb authorities – above all, Mr Poplasen – had blocked both the return of displaced Serbs living there and the return of displaced Serbs living there to the Moslem–Croat Federation.
>
> (*The Economist*, 13 March 1999, p. 55)

Carlos Westendorp (*IHT*, 15 March 1999, p. 10):

On 5 March I fired a president, the leader of the Bosnian Serbs ... The destiny of the Bosnian Serbs is no longer controlled by Belgrade. Nor would the great majority of the Serbs who live in Republika Srpska wish it to be ... President Poplasen had been warned ... But from the moment of his election last September [1998] he persistently abused his position to obstruct implementation of the Dayton peace agreement. Most serious was his refusal to nominate a viable candidate for prime minister ... It has been evident for many months that only one member of the National Assembly can command a workable majority, and that is Milorad Dodik, the prime minister of the last administration, who has been acting as caretaker. His government has shown a willingness to comply with the demands of the peace process. Mr Poplasen, a hardliner of the old school, responded by refusing to sign legislation legally passed by a majority vote of the National Assembly. The final straw came when he sought to remove Mr Dodik ... The decision [to remove him] has been further justified by his subsequent call for violent civil disobedience. The National Assembly initially responded with a vote of confidence in President Poplasen. That response, I believe, was in part based on the widely misunderstood (and wholly unrelated) decision on Brcko.

'Milorad Dodik ... has in fact continued to perform his duties much as normal' (*The Economist*, 13 March 1999, p. 55).

On 26 March 1999 the Russian contingent in Sfor opted out of US command in favour of its own command headquarters (*EEN*, 1999, vol. 12, no. 16, p. 9). (This was in protest at the Nato bombing of Yugoslavia which started on 24 March 1999.)

On 2 November 1999 it was announced that Sfor would be reduced by one-third to 20,000 by April 2000. ('Currently there are 30,000 troops, from about forty countries, down from about 60,000 just after the war': *FT*, 3 November 1999, p. 10.)

On 29 November 1999 Wolfgang Petritsch, the new high representative, dismissed twenty-two local politicians (nine Serbs, seven Bosniacs and six Croats), mainly for obstructing the return of minority group refugees (*FT*, Survey, 24 December 1999, p. 35). The mayor of Banja Luka was one of the nine Serbs (p. 37).

'Moslem co-chairman of the Council of Ministers Haris Silajdzic calls in an interview published in an Austrian newspaper [on 23 January 2000] for the Dayton agreement to be revised on the grounds that it is not being implemented.' He resigned on 11 February (*EEN*, 2000, vol. 12, no. 22, p. 4).

Local elections were held in Bosnia on 8 April 2000.

In most Moslem-dominated major cities the opposition Social Democratic Party defeated the governing Moslem Party for Democratic Action, according to preliminary results ... But the results also showed the nationalist Serb Democratic Party was winning the most votes in the

Serbian half of Bosnia ... The nationalist Croatian Democratic Union claimed victory.

(*IHT*, 11 April 2000, p. 4)

Municipal elections in April 2000 went furthest towards confirming the trend towards political moderation, with the stranglehold of the Social Democratic Party of Alia [Alija] Izetbegovic being surprised by defeats by the Social Democratic Party ... Nonetheless, the SDS [Serbian Democratic Party] still emerged as the majority party in the Republika Srpska, although its position had been eroded and it was clear that political sniping would continue, despite the trend towards moderate parties and towards more moderate candidates within all parties.

(Friedman 2000: 28)

On 6 June 2000 Alija Izetbegovic announced that he was to step down from the presidency when his term of office expired on 14 October 2000. (He remained chairman of the Party of Democratic Action.)

In an exodus that was partly orchestrated by the Serbian leadership and partly driven by panic, 100,000 Serbs abandoned their homes in the suburbs of Sarajevo ... All but a few thousand Serbs moved out. Now they are filtering back ... About 15,000 Serbs have returned to the Sarajevo area in the last eighteen months, nudging displaced people to return to other regions around the country. In the first five months of this year [2000] 15,665 people have registered after returning home throughout Bosnia. This change is largely due to property laws introduced in 1998, which international officials at the Office of the High Representative ... are using to eliminate local obstructions ... The authorities are evicting people from homes so owners can reclaim their property ... Alia Izetbegovic originally opposed the idea and his adviser, Mirza Hajric, blames the evictions for the recent fall in the popularity of Mr Izetbegovic's ... Party of Democratic Action. The few instances of Moslems returning to Serbian areas, while Sarajevo has welcomed so many Serbs, is one reason that Mr Izetbegovic, seventy-five, says he will resign his office [chairman of the multi-ethnic presidency of Bosnia] in October, Mr Hajric said.

(Carlotta Gall, *IHT*, 3 August 2000, p. 5)

Elections were held on 11 November 2000: for the Bosnian parliament; for the regional legislature and officials of ten regional cantons in the federation; and for president and vice-president in the Republika Srpska. Generally, voting went along ethnic lines, although the non-nationalist and multi-ethnic Social Democratic Party did well in Moslem areas.

'The landmark election last November ... brought to power the country's first non-nationalist government' (Wolfgang Petritsch, *IHT*, 26 March 2001, p. 10).

'The Croat member of Bosnia's tripartite presidency ... Ante Jelavic ... said

Wednesday [28 February 2001] that Croats could no longer take part in the joint federation with Moslems' (*IHT*, 1 March 2001, p. 11).

> The decision to withdraw recognition is set to be endorsed on Saturday [3 March] by the Croat National Congress, formed last year [2000] and dominated by Mr Jelavic's Croat Democratic Union ... Croats, the smallest of Bosnia's three main ethnic groups, have become increasingly unhappy since last October [2000], when OSCE changed rules on the election of Croat representatives shortly before November's general elections.
>
> (*FT*, 2 March 2001, p. 8)

> A meeting of the Croat National Congress on Saturday [3 March] in Mostar ... agreed to set up what it called an inter-cantonal council for Croats. The Congress, which has no formal legal standing, is dominated by the Croat Democratic Union (HDZ) ... Ante Jelavic ... [said] the new structure could be dismantled if, within fifteen days, international administrators revoked changes made to election rules just before November's general election.
>
> (*FT*, 6 March 2001, p. 10)

'The Croatian Democratic Union ... voted to establish its own mini-state in Bosnia if rules that favour multi-ethnic parties are not withdrawn in a fortnight' (*Telegraph*, 5 March 2001, p. 11). 'Wolfgang Petritsch ... dismissed ... Ante Jelavic ... and other senior Bosnian Croat officials on Wednesday [7 March]' (*IHT*, 8 March 2001, p. 4).

> Hard-line Croat separatists in Bosnia yesterday [28 March] set up their own defence headquarters as a mutiny spread among Croat soldiers serving in the Moslem–Croat federation army ... Reports ... suggested that the majority of the 7,500 Croat soldiers in the 22,500-strong common army were joining the mutiny ... The mutiny follows the establishment of a Croat national congress three weeks ago, which has called on all Croats to leave their jobs in the federation army, police and other public offices.
>
> (*Guardian*, 29 March 2001, p. 17)

'[On 5 March 2001] a full bilateral political and economic co-operation agreement is signed with Yugoslavia/Serbia during Yugoslav president Kostunica's visit to Banja Luka' (*EEN*, 2001, vol. 13, no. 4, p. 6).

> Bosnian Croats stoned Nato peacekeepers ... and attacked employees of international organizations Friday [6 April 2001] after the police and troops seized a major bank used by Bosnian Croat hard-liners bent on setting up their own state ... The trouble started when armed and masked UN and Bosnian police backed by Nato troops seized the Mostar headquarters of the Hercegovacka Banka and ten branches throughout Bosnia-Hercegovina

... The bank was believed to be used by the hard-line Croat Democratic Union to promote its campaign to establish a separate, Croat-run state in south-western Bosnia ... The raid triggered daylong rioting in Mostar.

(*IHT*, 7 April 2001, p. 2)

[On 9 April 2001] up to 150 Croatian war veterans protested in Split yesterday [9 April] against international attempts to prevent self-rule by the Croatian community in Bosnia. Police prevented the protest at a Nato supply base from turning into a repeat of the riots on Friday [6 April] in southern Bosnia.

(*Independent*, 10 April 2001, p. 14)

'[On 5 May 2001 there was a] serious outbreak of Serb violence against Moslems in the southern town of Trebinje during an attempted ceremony prior to the building of a new mosque' (*EEN*, 2001, vol. 13, no. 5, p. 5).

Angered by plans to rebuild a mosque in ... Banja Luka ... Bosnian Serbs beat dozens of Moslems on Monday [7 May]] and forced Western officials to take refuge in the Islamic centre ... Among the hundreds of people trapped for hours in the compound of the Islamic centre was the head of the UN mission in Bosnia, Jacques Klein, an American. With him were the British, Swedish and Pakistani ambassadors to Bosnia, who had come to attend the groundbreaking ceremony.

(*IHT*, 8 May 2001, p. 5)

[On 18 June 2001] the Bosnian Serb police clashed with nationalist rioters on Monday [18 June], using tear gas and water cannon to beat back mobs trying to disrupt a ceremony to mark the rebuilding of a medieval mosque. Hundreds of Bosnia Serbs in the city of Banja Luka attacked the police with stones and bottles ... but failed to stop the ceremony.

(*IHT*, 19 June 2001, p. 5)

On 11 September 2001 there were terrorist attacks on New York and Washington.

In Bosnia-Hercegovina, where I work as the leading representative of the international community – I am responsible for implementing the civilian provisions of the 1995 Dayton Peace Agreement – roughly half of the country's population of 4 million are Moslems. Much has been made of the residual influence of the mujahidin fighters who stayed after the 1992–5 war. But no evidence has been produced that the country has served as a base for Qaida [al-Qaeda, or 'the Base' is the terrorist network led by Osama bin Laden]. Allegations made by some Serbian extremists that the wars in the former Yugoslavia were fought to fend off Moslem fundamentalism are ridiculous. What is truly worthy of note is that the influence of fundamentalist Islam in the Balkans has been so weak ... The government is demonstrating its commitment to fighting global terrorism.

(Wolfgang Petritsch, *IHT*. 29 November 2001, p. 7)

War crimes

War criminals need to be punished if whole peoples are not to be blamed for the formers' deeds.

Atrocities were committed by all sides, but the Serbs were by far the worst offenders (Bosnian Moslems being the principal victims). The Moslems were not blameless by any means (e.g. there was a massacre in a Bosnian Croat village on 15 September 1993), but offended much less than the Croats, who came under increasing criticism.

On 14 August 1992 the UN Human Rights Commission appointed the former Polish prime minister Tadeusz Mazowiecki as special rapporteur. In his first report, published at the end of August 1992, he attached most blame for human rights violations to the Serbs. On 1 December 1992 the commission decided that the Bosnian Serbs were primarily responsible for the atrocities and posed the question whether 'ethnic cleansing' was a form of genocide.

On 9 March 1994 the UN Human Rights Commission in Geneva said that both the Serbs and the Croats had practised 'ethnic cleansing' in Bosnia, but the primary responsibility lay with the Serbian forces.

The International Criminal Tribunal for the former Yugoslavia

On 22 February 1993 the UN Security Council unanimously approved the setting up of an international court (International Criminal Tribunal for the former Yugoslavia) for war crimes at The Hague: 'An international tribunal shall be established for the prosecution of persons responsible for serious violations of international law committed in the territory of the former Yugoslavia since 1991.' This was the first war crimes tribunal since Nuremberg and Tokyo at the end of the Second World War, although the death penalty was not to be allowed on this occasion. Although the accused could not be tried *in absentia*, evidence could be presented and a record of the crimes established. The South African judge Richard Goldstone was named as the first chief prosecutor on 8 July 1994.

After he had stepped down on 1 October 1996 Richard Goldstone said: 'Ifor ... had both the legal, political and military power of arrest. Yet its masters at Nato refused to adopt a robust policy and ordered that indicted people were only to be arrested when stumbled upon during the ordinary course of duty' (*The World Today*, 1997, vol. 53, no. 2, pp. 106–7). (Sfor's arrest rate has improved over time; see below.)

Louise Arbour (Canada) replaced Richard Goldstone as chief prosecutor on 1 October 1996. She finished her term on 1 September 1999 and was replaced by Carla del Ponte of Switzerland.

The first person to be charged with war crimes was the Bosnian Serb Dusan Tadic on 14 October 1994.

On 24 April 1995 the tribunal named Radovan Karadzic and General Ratko Mladic (the Bosnian Serb army commander) as suspected war criminals. On 25 July 1995 the international tribunal issued arrest warrants. On 16 November 1995 fresh indictments were issued against Karadzic and Mladic for their part in the Srebrenica atrocities. (The tribunal charged that they planned, instigated and ordered the 'systematic mass killings' of as many as 8,000 Moslem refugees missing since Srebrenica fell in July 1995: *IHT*, 17 November 1995, p. 1.) On 11 July 1996 the war crimes tribunal issued international warrants for the arrest of Karadzic and Mladic on charges of genocide and war crimes. This meant that they could be arrested in any member country of the UN.

On 29 November 1996 the war crimes tribunal delivered its first verdict when Drazen Erdemovic was sentenced to ten years in jail for his part in the massacre of over 1,200 Moslems in Srebrenica. (On 5 March 1998 this was reduced to five years on the grounds of his remorse, youth and co-operation.)

On 7 May 1997 former chief prosecutor Richard Goldstone commented: 'There is a feeling it is a historic day: the first time in fifty years an international court has found someone guilty of crimes against humanity.' He was referring to the fact that Dusan Tadic (whose trial had started on 7 May 1996) had been found guilty on eleven counts of persecution and beatings, including two killings which had not been charged as murder but had been brought under the persecution charge. Tadic was found not guilty on nine counts of murder (because of insufficient evidence) and a further eleven charges ('grave breaches of the 1949 Geneva Conventions') were deemed inapplicable. On 14 July 1997 Tadic was sentenced to twenty years in prison. The judges said that he should serve a minimum of ten years. (See below.)

On 27 June 1997 agents of the international war crimes tribunal (assisted by international peacekeepers) arrested the Croatian Serb (and former mayor of Vukovar) Slavko Dokmanovic in Eastern Slavonia. (There was a 'sealed' or 'non-public' indictment in March 1996 in connection with the November massacre of about 260 people taken from Vukovar hospital in Croatia. The idea of 'sealed indictments' is to make it easier for Sfor to capture 'unsuspecting' suspects.)

On 10 July 1997 Sfor (British) troops were involved in an operation to arrest Bosnian Serbs who were not on the published list of indicted war criminals (thus Sfor received so-called 'sealed indictments'.)

On 10 July General Wesley Clark was sworn in as overall Nato commander. His predecessor, General George Joulwan, was less inclined to use Nato troops to arrest indicted war criminals.

In the first United Nations case to focus exclusively on rape as a war crime, a Bosnian Croat paramilitary commander, Anto Furundzija, was found guilty on war crimes on 10 December 1998 and sentenced to ten years in prison.

Slobodan Milosevic was indicted on 27 May 1999, the first time that this has happened to a sitting head of state. The charge: 'The accused planned, instigated, ordered, committed or otherwise aided and abetted in a campaign of terror and violence directed at Kosovo Albanian citizens.' On 28 June 2001 the Serbian government handed over Slobodan Milosevic to the war crimes tribunal in The Hague.

> Bosnia's Serb republic came under heavy pressure yesterday [4 July 2001] to surrender the indicted war criminals Radovan Karadzic and Ratko Mladic after Slobodan Milosevic's historic first appearance at the Hague tribunal [on 3 July 2001]. UN prosecutors … told its prime minister, Mladen Ivanic, that the time had come to start co-operating with the tribunal … 'After Serbia started co-operating with the transfer of Milosevic, Republika Srpska is the last region in former Yugoslavia that is not co-operating,' a tribunal spokesman said.
>
> (*Guardian*, Thursday 5 July 2001, p. 12)

On 9 October 2001 the tribunal formally indicted Slobodan Milosevic with war crimes and crimes against humanity during the war in Croatia. On 23 November 2001 the tribunal formally indicted him on charges relating to the war in Bosnia, including genocide.

On 2 August 2001 General Radislav Krstic, a Bosnian Serb, was sentenced to forty-six years in prison for his role in organizing the Srebrenica massacre of July 1995. Among other things he was found guilty of genocide. This was shorter than the maximum sentence of life imprisonment sought by the prosecution. But the sentence was the longest to date, one year greater than that given to Tihomir Blaskic. General Krstic was the first convicted in Europe by an international court under the international 1948 law on genocide.

> [On] Tuesday [2 October 2001] the parliament of the Bosnian Serb Republic adopted a long-awaited law on co-operation with the UN war crimes tribunal in The Hague … The government of the Bosnian Serb Republic has been the last regional authority in the former Yugoslavia refusing to hand over war crimes suspects to the Hague tribunal. From a legal point of view the measure was not required, since the obligation to co-operate with the tribunal derives from Bosnia's constitution and the Dayton peace accords that ended the war. But since the end of the conflict in 1995 Bosnian Serbs have ignored the requirement, contending that the tribunal had an anti-Serb bias.
>
> (*IHT*, 3 October 2001, p. 5)

On 14 January 2000 five Bosnian Croats were sentenced for their part in the Ahmici massacre on 16 April 1993, involving 116 Moslems including thirty-three women and children. Some villagers were burned alive. The court said the aim was to expel Moslems from the village (i.e. it was the first case focusing solely on 'ethnic cleansing'), but fell short of genocide.

On 3 March 2000 the Bosnian Croat commander General Tihomir Blaskic was sentenced to forty-five years in prison (the harshest sentence to date).

Although he was not charged with murder himself, he was found guilty of bearing 'superior criminal responsibility'. The crimes committed by forces under his command included the 16 April 1993 massacre at Ahmici. General Blaskic is the highest-ranking military commander brought to trial to date for war crimes during the Balkan conflict. The court also commented on the role of Croatia itself: 'The Republic of Croatia did not content itself with merely remaining a spectator on the sidelines or even seek simply to protect its borders. It intervened in the conflict, pitting Moslems and Croats of central Bosnia against each other.'

On 13 March 2000 the trial began of a Bosnian Serb general, Radislav Krstic, the charges including genocide. Tribunal prosecutor Mark Harmon (commenting on Srebrenica): 'At least 7,574 people are missing and presumed dead.' The missing males include boys as young as 14.

On 3 April 2000 French-led Sfor troops arrested the Bosnian Serb Momcilo Krajisnik (under a sealed indictment) and sent him to The Hague. George Robertson (Nato secretary-general): 'This arrest ... represents the capture by Sfor of the highest-ranking person indicted for war crimes in the former Yugoslavia thus far.'

Deaths, casualties and refugees

> Seventy per cent of our country is occupied. More than 200,000 civilians have been killed, including 17,000 children. More than 400,000 people have been wounded. More than 2 million have been expelled from their homes. All this, and our pre-war population was only 4.3 million.
> (Haris Silajdzic, the prime minister of the Republic of Bosnia-Hercegovina, *IHT*, 23 February 1995, p. 8)

More than 250,000 people were killed in the Bosnian war, over 200,000 were wounded and 13,000 were permanently disabled (*FT*, 21 December 1995, p. 2).

The World Bank estimated that about 250,000 people were killed, more than 200,000 wounded and 2.3 million displaced (*Transition*, November–December 1995, vol. 6, nos 11–12, p. 30).

By way of comparison, the war in Slovenia lasted a week and eight Slovenes were killed; the war in Croatia lasted six months and killed an estimated 20,000; the war in Bosnia has lasted two years and killed 200,000 (*FT*, 3 March 1994, p. 22). The ten-day war in Slovenia against the Yugoslav People's Army cost the lives of a handful of Slovenes, several Turkish truck drivers and some fifty young conscript soldiers (*FT*, Survey, 12 April 1994, p. 31). The casualty figure in the ten-day war in Slovenia was thirty-seven Yugoslav soldiers and twelve Slovenes killed (Zimmerman 1995: 13). The war in Croatia has to date resulted in at least 10,000 dead (*Independent*, 15 September 1993, p. 12). The war in Croatia left 10,000 dead or missing and created more than a million refugees (*Business Central Europe*, March 1995, p. 15).

It is estimated that around 2.5 million Bosnians have either fled or been forcibly expelled from their homes since the beginning of the war in April 1992. That is more than half of the 1991 population of 4,377,033. About 1.2 million are living as so-called internally displaced persons in other parts of Bosnia, mostly in areas controlled by the armed forces of their own nationality. Some 600,000 are in the other successor states of the former Yugoslavia. Of those probably 450,000 (mostly Serbian) refugees are in Serbia and Montenegro. There are about 700,000 Bosnian refugees in other European countries (330,000 in Germany). So far some 50,000 people, mostly internally displaced people, have returned to their homes. Of those 20,000 are Serbs who have gone back to villages in western Bosnia returned to the Bosnian Serbs under the Dayton agreement (Christopher Cviic, *The World Today*, June 1996, vol. 52, no. 6, pp. 144–5).

The return of displaced people was slow, especially to areas controlled by a different ethnic group. But the process has speeded up.

Economic developments

There was massive destruction in the war zones and massive dislocation in most places. By late 1995 Bosnia's economy had shrunk to 25 to 30 per cent of its pre-war size, while industrial output was at little more than one-tenth of Yugoslav-era capacity (Business Central Europe 1995: 42). Preliminary data collected by the World Bank painted a bleak picture of Bosnia. Annual *per capita* income had fallen from $1,900 in 1990 to about $500 (*Transition*, November–December 1995, vol. 6, nos 11–12, p. 30). Unemployment is very high.

The World Bank, in co-operation with the EBRD, the European Commission and UN agencies, proposed a $5.1 billion reconstruction programme over four years (United Nations Economic Commission for Europe 1996: 168).

After the war recovery was rapid (albeit from such a dismal condition), although the Republika Srpska has generally lagged behind the federation in terms of economic reform.

Assessments of economic performance has been summarized by EBRD in Table 1.1 (p. 182). The table shows hugely negative GDP growth figures for 1993 and 1994. Double-figure increases in GDP were typically recorded from 1995 onwards. As regards consumer price inflation, the figures are split between the federation and the Republika Srpska. The rates in 1994 were 780 per cent and 1,061 per cent, respectively. By 1999–2000 consumer price stability had been achieved in the former and inflation was only around 14 per cent in the latter.

Assessments of Bosnia's overall progress vary. But there is agreement about the major obstacles to economic progress, including crime and corruption, payments bureaux and labour market rigidities.

The system that governs the Bosnia and Hercegovina economy is to a large extent the same as it was in the days of communism. Many of the old command economy structures are still in place, notably the notoriously intransparent payment bureaux, through which all commercial and public bank transfers must pass. They levy a substantial sum for the service along the way. The banking system, in many cases on the verge of bankruptcy, is also in dire need of overhaul ... The first stage [of privatization], opening the books of the big state sector companies to independent audit, prior to devaluation, met fierce political resistance. Perhaps this was inevitable, since the state companies, like the payment bureaux, are a cash-cow for the major political parties ... We are moving ahead with privatization now; and the payment bureaux will be abolished this year [2000].

(Wolfgang Petritsch, High Representative for Civilian Implementation of the Dayton Peace Accords, *The World Today*, 2000, vol. 56, no. 4, p. 24)

On 9 November 1995 the Bosnian government pronounced the Deutschmark an official currency (exchangeable at 100 dinars each).

In June 1997 a so-called 'quick-start package' was introduced of laws governing state institutions, including a budget, a law on the central bank, on customs, and on the responsibility for foreign debt. The most significant advance so far at the state level has been the opening of a common central bank on 11 August 1997, which has begun to issue a common currency and to centralize foreign exchange reserves. The 'convertible marka' (KM: *konvertibilna marka*) is fully convertible and pegged at parity with the DM. The KM will have different designs (which have yet to be agreed on) but its use remains limited to non-cash transactions for the time being. In the interim, cash payments will be made in the currencies now in use in the two entities, and the DM will continue to be used as a medium of exchange. The entities are not legally obligated to take on the KM, but budgetary operations with the state government will have to be conducted in the new currency (EBRD 1997b: 157). Since mid-1998 all receipts and payments to the state budget have been settled in KM (EBRD 1998b: 156). The convertible marka is now used for official payments in both entities and the use of the DM and Croatian kuna for all non-cash payments is to be phased out by mid-1999 (EBRD 1999a: 34). Acceptance of the convertible marka (KM) is highest in the Bosniac-majority areas and lowest in the Bosnian–Croat areas. The currency board arrangement is functioning well (EBRD 1999b: 198–9).

'[Note] the Republika Srpska's decision this autumn [1999] to ban the use of the Yugoslav dinar as legal tender. Only the Konvertibilna Marka is used now in the Republika Srpska' (*FT*, Survey, 14 December 1999, p. 37).

'The payments system is undergoing much-needed reform. It is envisaged that by the end of 2000 all transactions will be transferred from the payments operations bureaux into commercial banks' (EBRD 2000a: 44).

The dismantling of the payments bureaux ... is now complete [January 2001]. The new clearing system, a real time gross settlements system and a wholesale clearing system, will increase transparency and confidence and remove one of the major obstacles for investment ... In late 2000 the Office of the High Representative imposed a number of amendments to labour

and pension laws in both Entities. These amendments are designed to eliminate features of the labour market, such as large unemployment benefit
entitlements and the inability to lay off excess labour, that were hindering
investment in state enterprises.

(EBRD 2001a: 52)

'Progress towards creating a single economic space has been slow. The
authorities have taken steps recently towards this goal' (EBRD 2001b: 122–3).

The first sales under the small privatization scheme began in 1999.
Completion of this programme for all state-owned small and medium-sized
enterprises is planned for mid-2000. The beginning of large privatization has
been delayed (EBRD 2000a: 44).

> Small-scale privatization in the Federation ... [began] in the second half of
> 1999. Enterprises are being sold either by auction or tender ... Large, state-
> owned enterprises continue to dominate the economy in both Entities and
> progress in their privatization has been slow. However, the pace has
> increased recently.
>
> (EBRD 2000b: 142)

'After a slow start privatization has gained momentum over the last six
months. Small-scale privatization has made progress in both Entities, particularly
in Republika Srpska (RS)' (EBRD 2001a: 52). 'Privatization [is] proceeding
slowly ... most economic activity remaining in the state sector ... Small-scale
privatization is under way ... Large-scale privatization has made some progress
but governance problems remain ... Numerous delays [have been encountered]
and several transactions were marred by a lack of transparency' (EBRD 2001b:
122).

In mid-1998, mid-1999 and mid-2000 the private sector accounted for
roughly 35 per cent of GDP. This figure had increased to 40 per cent by mid-
2001 (EBRD 2001b: 12, 124).

Foreign direct investment has been negligible. (See Table 1.1.)

> [On 18 September 2000 EU foreign] ministers approved an EU package
> granting duty-free access to 95 per cent of imports from Albania, Bosnia,
> Croatia, Macedonia and Montenegro ... The package includes abolition of
> tariffs on most industrial and farm products to the EU. However, some limits
> remain on exports of fish products and wine.
>
> (*FT*, 19 September 2000, p. 10)

Croatia

The situation in 1989 was as follows: area 21 per cent of the former Yugoslavia;
the population of 4.7 million (20 per cent of the Yugoslav total) comprised 75

per cent Croats and 12 per cent Serbs; Croatia contributed 26 per cent of Yugoslav GNP; index of *per capita* income 130 (Yugoslav average = 100).

President Franjo Tudjman (seriously at fault for his stridently nationalistic tone when independence was declared on 25 June 1991) would have been very happy to carve Bosnia up between Croatia and Serbia. A significant part of Croatia was under the control of the Bosnian Serbs until the devastating Croatian successes in the military campaigns of 1–2 May and 4–7 August 1995.

On 1 May 1995 Croat forces launched what was to be a successive three-pronged attack on the Serb-held (isolated and most vulnerable) area in Sector West Krajina (western Slavonia; one of the four sectors of Krajina). On 27 July 1995 the Bosnian Croats, backed by units of the Croatian army, launched a major offensive to try to relieve the pressure of a three-pronged attack (which had begun on 19 July) on Bihac (Bosnia) by Bosnian Serbs, Croatian Serbs and forces loyal to Fikret Abdic. (Presidents Tudjman and Izetbegovic had met on 22 July. Croatia agreed to provide emergency military aid to help defend Bihac and a defence pact was also agreed.) The combined Croat forces made early gains, capturing the strategic Serb-held Bosnian towns of Grahovo and Glamoc the very next day. On 3 August talks began between the Croatian government and the Croatian Serbs (preceded by skirmishes between their military forces; the Bosnian Serbs shelled the outskirts of Dubrovnik). But on 4 August 1995 Croatia launched a full-scale military assault on Sectors North and South Krajina (but not Sector East Krajina, known as Eastern Slavonia). The Croatian government forces made spectacular gains, e.g. they captured Knin on 5 August (considered by the Croatian Serbs to be their capital) and Petrinje and the Ubdina air base the following day (claiming that 80 per cent of their goals had been achieved by then). (Note that during the offensive Nato aircraft had knocked out Croatian Serb anti-aircraft positions.) Despite assurances given by the Croatian government there took place a massive exodus of Croatian Serb refugees; some later estimates put the figure at up to 200,000. The flood was encouraged by civilian attacks on fleeing refugees as well as looting and destruction of Serb property. Later on there were claims that mass graves had been found. On 2 October 1995 a report by EU monitors spoke of a systematic campaign of killings, arson and looting by the Croatian army. Croatian government forces were accused of deliberately targeting a UN observation post, killing three UN troops (others being allegedly used as human shields). On 9 January 1996 the United Nations Security Council condemned Croatia for human rights abuses against its Serb citizens, the victims of atrocities and murders. The council urged the abandonment, not just suspension, of laws making the return of Serb property conditional. There was an exodus of some 180,000 Serbs, whose 'rights to return in safety and dignity are being severely curtailed'. The UN also called for the handing over of six Croats to the war crimes tribunal (*FT*, 10 January 1996, p. 2). (On 6 October 1997 ten Bosnian Croats flew from Croatia and surrendered to the war crimes tribunal in The Hague.)

Croatia declared the military operation to be at an end on 7 August 1995, but some fighting continued. (A ceasefire was agreed, but collapsed; an official figure of 118 Croatian government troops killed in the operation was given.) On 8 August the UN negotiated a ceasefire, with the UN collecting heavy weapons from the Croatian Serb forces in return for the safe passage of some 40,000 refugees in the northern part of the war zone. On 9 August the UN reported that the last major pocket of Croatian Serb resistance ended when the town of Dvor fell. There were reports of a number of atrocities committed by Croatian and Bosnian government forces.

On 12 August 1995 Croatian government forces attacked Croatian Serb positions in the hills overlooking Dubrovnik, whose outskirts had come under renewed attack. Four days later it was reported that Croatian government forces were massing for an attack on Serb-held Trebinje in Bosnia in order to push Serb artillery out of range of Dubrovnik. On 25 August 1995 Serbia and Croatia signed a ceasefire over Eastern Slavonia, but skirmishes were reported. On 3 October 1995, in talks co-hosted by UN envoy Thorwald Stoltenberg and US ambassador to Croatia Peter Galbraith, Croatia and the Croatian Serbs agreed in principle on the future of Eastern Slavonia. It would remain part of Croatia and 'a transitional authority shall be established by the UN Security Council to administer the region during the transition period'.

On 12 November 1995 Croatia and the Croatian Serbs signed an agreement relating to Eastern Slavonia drafted by Tudjman and Milosevic during talks in the USA. Eastern Slavonia would return to Croatian control after a transitional term of no more than two years. (The minimum year could be lengthened by up to an additional one year if at least one side requested it.) During the transitional period there would be administration by the United Nations, whose Security Council would decide on the implementation force of peacekeepers and police. Demilitarization would be achieved within thirty days of their deployment. The area would have a multi-ethnic nature, with ethnic Croat refugees allowed to return and ethnic Serbs to remain.

On 9 September 1999 full diplomatic relations were established between Croatia and Yugoslavia. Refugees would be allowed to return.

The UN transitional administration in Eastern Slavonia came to an end on 15 January 1998:

1   The UN High Commissioner for Refugees reckons that 15,000 to 20,000 of Eastern Slavonia's 100,000 or so Serbs have left in the past two years. The UN transitional administration has concluded agreements with Croatia to encourage the 60,000 Serbs native to Eastern Slavonia to stay. OSCE is sending 250 monitors, 100 to Eastern Slavonia alone, to encourage Croatia to treat its minorities well. In addition, 180 UN police monitors will remain in Eastern Slavonia, at Croatia's request, to allay foreign suspicions that the local police will mistreat Serbs (*The Economist*, 10 January 1998, pp. 37–8).

2   Many of the 120,000 Serbs in the region still live in Eastern Slavonia (*IHT*, 12 January 1998, p. 5).

3   An OSCE spokesman says that Serbs in Eastern Slavonia 'are very much concerned about their future'. 'Recently there have been signs of economic

discrimination', e.g. layoffs of Serbs and problems with pensions and social benefits (*FT*, 20 February 1998, p. 2).

4   'Of the 120,000 ethnic Serbs who lived in the eastern Slavonian enclave two years ago, nearly half have fled, and the number of departures is rising daily, according to relief agencies' (Chris Hedges, *IHT*, 20 March 1998, p. 4).

5   An OSCE report estimates that as many as 200,000 Croatian Serbs fled the country between 1991 and 1995. During the 1995 military operations, around 190,000 people, mainly Croatian Serbs, fled Croatia chiefly to Serbia and the Republika Srpska (*FT*, Survey, 7 July 1998, p. i). Since the handover about 17,000 of the estimated 82,000 Croats displaced in 1991 have returned home. Returning Croats have resorted to violence and intimidation to evict Serbs, despite laws permitting them to remain until their homes can be occupied. Croatia has given citizenship (and in many cases abandoned Serb houses) to Bosnian Croat refugees. There are an estimated 400,000 refugees outside the country, including about 80,000 Serbs living in Bosnia (p. iii).

6   'Even today an estimated half of the ethnic Serbs who once lived in Croatia remain refugees beyond its borders' (*IHT*, 28 December 1999, p. 8).

7   'Though Yugoslavia and Croatia resumed diplomatic relations in 1996, only 20,000 of the estimated 300,000 refugees from Croatia have returned to their homes. Denied Yugoslav citizenship, the right to work, vote or own property, they survive on handouts and the charity of local relatives' (*FT*, 30 December 1999, p. 4).

8   'The [January 2000] election [in Croatia] was seen as a quiet but significant milestone for members of Croatia's slowly returning Serbian community. Before independence they represented 12 per cent of the population, but 100,000 still live in exile in Yugoslavia or in Bosnia' (*Guardian*, 4 January 2000, p. 10).

During 1991–2 around 30 per cent of fixed assets were damaged or destroyed (Radosevic 1994: 490). According to government estimates, there was $27.1 billion of direct damage during the war. Some 135,000 houses and apartments were destroyed along with more than 100 bridges and 200 churches (*FT*, Survey, 30 May 1996, p. iv). The Croatian government maintains that damage caused directly and indirectly by the war totals more than $50 billion. As much as 10 per cent of the housing stock (more than 170,000 homes and apartments) was destroyed or damaged. The damage to public utilities and social infrastructure is estimated at $4.2 billion, while the loss in economic output from 1991 to 1996 is put at $22.5 billion. At the height of the war there were over 1.2 million refugees and displaced persons (*FT*, Survey, 14 December 1998, p. 28). According to *Business Central Europe* (June 1996, p. 18), only about 10 per cent of fixed industrial capital was destroyed.

The general election of 29 October 1995 was for the 127 seats in the House of Representatives (three more than in the 2 August 1992 election). Twelve MPs were elected by the 'diaspora' (including the preponderant Bosnian Croats). As expected, the Croatian Democratic Union (CDU or HDZ) was victorious, stressing the recent military victories. The CDU won ten of the twelve 'diaspora' seats. But the party was disappointed not to win the two-thirds majority in parliament necessary to change the constitution in favour of a stronger presidency. The party did badly in Zagreb and other cities. Opposition parties, although complaining of lack of proper access to the media, successfully played on economic and social problems such as unemployment and on corruption in political life.

On 24 April 1996 the parliamentary assembly of the Council of Europe voted to admit Croatia. But on 14 May 1996 the Council of Europe's Committee of Ministers postponed Croatia's entry, the first time that the committee had voted against the parliamentary assembly (*Independent*, 15 May 1996, p. 81). On 5 June the Council of Europe set five conditions for admission, calling for concrete steps to be taken 'as rapidly as possible': the handing over of war crimes suspects; facilitating free elections in Bosnia; allowing the return of Serb refugees; dropping prosecutions against the independent media; allowing the opposition-controlled Zagreb council to elect a mayor (*Guardian*, 5 June 1996, p. 13). Croatia did not become the fortieth member of the Council of Europe until 6 November 1996.

Zagreb's city council, which appoints the mayor and is dominated by the opposition, was dissolved on 30 April 1996. President Tudjman subsequently appointed one of his own nominees as mayor. In April 1997 the CDU won twenty-four seats (two short of a majority) in the Zagreb city assembly. Two of the three elected members of the Croatian Peasants' Party subsequently defected to the CDU. The CDU did poorly in the municipal elections generally but benefited from a divided opposition in Zagreb.

On 26 September 1996 two journalists were cleared in court of the charge of defaming President Tudjman. (A new clause in the criminal code allowed a maximum sentence of three years for insulting high officials.)

On 20 November 1996 the government refused to renew the licence of Radio 101, the last independent radio station, allegedly because the station was 'not objective'. The licence was later extended to mid-January 1997. On 24 January 1997, Radio 101 was granted a five-year broadcasting licence.

On 15 June 1997, Tudjman won a second five-year term as president (despite reports that he had stomach cancer). The head of the OSCE observers concluded that the election 'did not meet the minimum standards for democracies'. 'Croatia has experienced a free but not fair election. While candidates were able to operate freely, the process leading up to the election was fundamentally flawed.' There was also a formal OSCE report: 'The electoral process afforded enormous advantages to the ruling party candidate and limited the ability of the opposition candidates to campaign freely.' The advantages included the degree of state control of the media (especially television) and the disparity in campaign resources. Ethnic Serbs who had fled the country were disenfranchised, while ethnic Croats in Bosnia were allowed to vote.

Croatia's isolation during the Tudjman era was such that it was not a member of Nato's Partnership for Peace and did not benefit from the EU's Phare programme (which provides financial and technical assistance to transitional economies).

In late January 1999 OSCE reported on human rights in Croatia. The report has not been made public, but it says: 'There has been no progress in improving respect for human rights, the rights of minorities and the rule of law.'

> The report ... is filled with damning details – about repression of the media by the Croatian government, about the lack of co-operation with the international war crimes tribunal in The Hague, and above all about its harsh treatment of ethnic Serbs. Only a small percentage of the approximately 300,000 ethnic Serbs forced to flee their homes here during the war have been allowed to return ... The [US] state department, in a human rights report made public last week, described Croatia as 'nominally democratic' but 'in reality authoritarian' ... The European group said that under pressure from the United States and the EU, the Croatian government had made commitments to freedom of the press. But Croatian television, the main source of news for as many as 90 per cent of Croatians, 'remains subject to political control by the ruling party', the report said. On the international war crimes tribunal, the report said the Croatian government had embarked on a campaign to 'encourage distrust and hostility' towards it among the Croatian populace.
>
> (Raymond Bonner, *IHT*, 4 March 1999, p. 9)

The CDU suffered internal splits even while Tudjman was alive, but quickly fell from power when he died. In 1996 President Tudjman was treated in a Washington clinic for what American sources said was cancer, a claim he denied. He underwent an emergency intestinal operation on 1 November 1999. On 26 November 1999 the constitutional court declared President Tudjman to be 'temporarily incapacitated'. Parliamentary speaker Vlatko Pavletic took over for an interim but renewable period of sixty days. Tudjman died of stomach cancer on 10 December 1999 (although this cause was not officially admitted). Tudjman's funeral took place on 13 December. The only foreign head of state present was the president of Turkey. The prime ministers of Hungary, Macedonia, Slovenia and Montenegro were present, along with the Croat member of the three-person Bosnian presidency.

One report talked of: 'The increasing unpopularity of Mr Tudjman's umbrella party, since the economy is stagnant, corruption is visible and unemployment is very high' (*IHT*, 26 November 1999, p. 7).

> Officials in Croatia's new government say [that there was] a sustained, successful campaign by President Franjo Tudjman and his allies to plunder billions of dollars from the treasury ... during almost ten years of absolute, nationalist rule that ended with Mr Tudjman's death in December [1999].

Over that decade top Croatian officials enriched friends, family members and political allies by manipulating the privatization of state-owned companies and handing out lucrative contracts and suspect loans, government officials now say ... It now appears that the officially sanctioned thievery in Croatia ... was greater on a *per capita* basis than any other East European nation undergoing transition, diplomats, officials and foreign experts say.

(Jeffrey Smith, *IHT*, 14 June 2000, p. 13)

When the Mesic team began opening up rooms in the presidential palace they found an archive of some 830 tapes and 17,000 transcripts of conversations between Tudjman and just about every single person who had visited him since 1991 ... Tudjman was obsessed with history. That is why he taped everything ... They have revealed that Tudjman's Croatia was rotten to the core; that with his blessing the HDZ elite pillaged every public institution in sight and virtually bankrupted the country ... [It is] widely believed that much of the most sensitive material was removed in the three weeks between Tudjman's death and the election of the new government ... If it is true that sensitive documents were removed, however, those who took them did not have time to smuggle out of the presidential palace the transcripts concerning the wholesale plunder of the economy by Tudjman's entourage.

(Tim Judah, *New York Review of Books*, 2000, vol. XLVII, no. 13, pp. 20–2)

Secret tape recordings made by the late President Franjo Tudjman of Croatia prove that he and his close circle were directly involved in perpetuating war crimes ... The tapes also reveal that Tudjman and his apparent enemy Milosevic ... ignored pledges to respect Bosnia's sovereignty. Even after the signing of the Dayton accord they were still plotting to carve up the region.

(*Independent*, 1 November 2000, p. 16)

The Croatian Democratic Union was swept from office in the general election of 3 January 2000 in a defeat even more decisive than generally anticipated. It soon started to splinter. The victor was the six-party opposition bloc led by Ivica Racan of the Social Democratic Party and Drazen Budisa of the Social Liberals. Although Stipe Mesic beat Drazen Budisa in the second round of the presidential election held on 7 February 2000, all three individuals share the common goal of moving away from the former policies which, under Tudjman, kept Croatia distant from Europe and the West in general. (Under Tudjman Croatia did not even participate in Nato's Partnership for Peace programme. Participation did not begin until 25 May 2000.) Thus all three new men have promised much greater co-operation with the international criminal tribunal in The Hague, to do much more to increase the return of ethnic Serb refugees to Croatia, to stop meddling in the affairs of Bosnia, to decrease the powers of the presidency, to make Croatia much more democratic and to tackle the country's massive economic problems.

> All three main candidates [in the presidential election], of the nine who ran, promised an open democratic Croatia, less authoritarian and nationalist, with closer ties to the EU and the USA. All of them also promised to dismantle part of the monarchic, all-powerful presidency that Mr Tudjman left behind him, along with many of its trappings ... Mr Tudjman's aggressive nationalism isolated Croatia from the European mainstream. He was reluctant to co-operate fully with the UN tribunal on war crimes, refusing to hand over some indicted Croats, often citing medical reasons. Also, Zagreb intervened in Bosnia, financing and promoting a separate Bosnian Croat identity despite formal support for the Moslem–Croat federation that Washington demanded. Mr Tudjman's government also put complicated legal and administrative obstacles in the way of Serbs who wanted to return to the homes they had fled in the face of a Croatian military offensive in 1995 that asserted Zagreb's authority. All of Mr Tudjman's likely successors promised to co-operate more fully with the tribunal, to allow Serbian refugees who fled their homes to return more easily and to stop meddling in Bosnia. These policies will be easier to accomplish in conjunction with a new government, to be led by Ivica Racan, the reformist communist leader who built the opposition coalition in conjunction with Mr Budisa ... In a sense, Croatia's 4 million voters, unlike the pattern in the rest of the Balkans, concentrated on voting for the future, not the past. Croatians voting for Mr Mesic were also seeking a balanced, unthreatening, humorous personality.
>
> (Steven Erlanger, *IHT*, 26 January 2000, p. 7)

An EU–Balkan summit meeting was held in Zagreb on 24 November 2000. Albania, Bosnia, Macedonia and Yugoslavia were formally invited. 'The summit also saw Macedonia's signing of the first so-called Stabilization and Association Agreement with the EU – a new kind of agreement intended for western Balkan countries. Croatia also formally started negotiations on such an agreement' (*FT*, 25 November 2000, p. 6). ('[In May 2001] Croatia signed a Stabilization and Association Agreement with the EU, which will liberalize trading terms and increase EU funding': *Business Central Europe*, June 2001, pp. 16, 43.)

'Many wonder whether the fractious coalition can survive until elections due in two-and-a-half years' time' (*FT*, Survey, 19 June 2001, p. 41).

One of the divisive issues was that of suspected war criminals. There have been a number of arrests of suspected war criminals from Croatia (for trial within Croatia) and ethnic Croat suspects from Bosnia have been handed over to the war crimes tribunal in The Hague. But the government split on 7 July 2001 when a majority of the cabinet voted to co-operate with the tribunal and hand over two indicted army generals. Veteran organizations reacted angrily. Prior to this, on 28 August 2000, a key witness in the war crimes investigations had been murdered. The government comfortably survived a no-confidence vote in parliament.

GDP growth turned positive in 1994, but the growth rate declined sharply in 1998 and was actually negative in 1999. 'The economy slipped into recession by the end of 1998' (EBRD 1999b: 206).

> Croatia's recession ended in the second quarter of 1999, but growth for the full year was −0.3 per cent. The performance of the economy had been negatively affected both by the Kosovo conflict, which lowered tourism revenues significantly, and by the political uncertainty (now resolved) over the succession to President Tudjman.
>
> (EBRD 2000a: 5)

Positive GDP growth was restored in 2000. In 2000 GDP was an estimated 80 per cent of the 1989 level (EBRD 2001b: 59). There was hyperinflation in 1993 (1,518 per cent), but the rise in the retail price level fell sharply the following year and was in single figures thereafter. (See Table 2.1, p. 227.)

A managed floating exchange rate regime was introduced at the end of 1993 (Deutsche Bank, *Focus: Eastern Europe*, 1994, no. 108, p. 3). There is now a high degree of current account convertibility, but some capital controls are still in force (EBRD 1994: 21). The kuna has been convertible for current payment transactions in accordance with Article 8 of the IMF statutes since the end of May 1995 (Deutsche Bank, *Focus: Eastern Europe*, 1996, no. 157, p. 16). In practice the floating exchange rate is pegged around the DM (*FT*, Survey, 7 July 1998, p. i). The foreign trade system is liberal (EBRD 1994: 21). 'In July 2000 the WTO general council approved the entry of Croatia, which has committed to reduce agricultural and industrial protection' (EBRD 2000b: 150).

> [On 18 September 2000 EU foreign] ministers approved an EU package granting duty-free access to 95 per cent of imports from Albania, Bosnia, Croatia, Macedonia and Montenegro ... The package includes abolition of tariffs on most industrial and farm products to the EU. However, some limits remain on exports of fish products and wine.
>
> (*FT*, 19 September 2000, p. 10)

Croatia has reached agreement with the Paris Club of official creditors on rescheduling its foreign debt. The $1 billion debt would be repaid over fourteen years, with repayments starting in 1996. Another $100 million, borrowed after 1992, was to be repaid immediately (*Business Central Europe*, April 1995, p. 51). On 26 April 1996 Croatia reached agreement in principle with the leaders of the London Club of commercial bank creditors, accepting a 29.5 per cent share of the debt of the former Yugoslavia. But creditor banks holding at least two-thirds of the debt had to agree to this arrangement and the Federal Republic of Yugoslavia has raised legal objections (*FT*, 29 April 1996, p. 2; 30 April 1996, p. 2).

The private sector accounted for roughly 15 per cent of GDP in mid-1990. In mid-2001 the figure was 60 per cent (EBRD 1999b: 24, 208; and 2001b: 12, 132).

The large majority of privatizations have been management or worker buy-outs. Shares not sold when enterprises were converted were taken up by the Privatization Fund (two-thirds) and the Pension Fund (one-third). Ten per cent of capital was set aside as a provision for restitution claims (United Nations Economic Commission for Europe 1993: 224).

In October 1996 parliament passed the law on compensation for property taken during Yugoslav communist rule, regulating the denationalization of property confiscated or nationalized since 1945. It gives preference to restitution of property where possible (agricultural land, forests, some housing) and provides for compensation in other cases (other housing, developed construction, land) (EBRD 1997a: 28).

Small privatization is now largely complete (EBRD 1994: 20). By the end of 1995 about 1,200 of the total 2,750 enterprises had been converted and wholly sold to their employees or management. In a further 900 enterprises the state retained only a minority stake. Ten of the largest enterprises, most utilities and the banks are to be privatized under separate legislation (EBRD 1995b: 38). By early 1997 over 1,000 out of a total of 2,550 commercialized enterprises had been fully privatized and in another 1,350 the state retained only a minority stake. Most of the fully privatized enterprises are relatively small and the state still accounts for about 40 per cent of the net asset value and of employment in the 2,550 enterprises. The new privatization law also provides guidelines for the sale of large public enterprises, including the oil and gas conglomerate, electricity generation and distribution, television and radio, and telecommunications. It is envisaged that foreign bidding will be permitted for some of these enterprises (EBRD 1997b: 161–2).

Croatia's privatization policy came in for much criticism from some quarters:

1   'Resources of privatized state firms have disappeared into the pockets of the chosen few, including members of Tudjman's family' (*EEN*, 31 December 1996, vol. 10, no. 25, p. 6).

2   'His [Tudjman's] privatization policy has succeeded in concentrating vast economic power in the hands of a small oligarchy' (Misha Glenny, *The Times*, 7 August 1996, p. 14).

3   'Privatization ... often favours leading members of President Franjo Tudjman's party, the Croatian Democratic Union, at the expense of outside bidders, Western economists say' (Jane Perlez, *IHT*, 21 August 1996, p. 2).

4   Much of the privatization completed by the end of 1995 did not greatly accelerate restructuring. 'In most privatized enterprises the absence of a strong majority owner has inhibited restructuring' (EBRD 1996b: 144–5).

> Enterprise restructuring is inhibited by poor corporate governance that typically results from the absence of a strong majority shareholder and

from large residual state holdings. As a result of a privatization process largely by management and employee buy-outs, small shareholders (mostly employees) own the great majority of shares in privatized companies. The state privatization fund and the state pension fund – the largest shareholders in many majority privatized companies – have not taken an active role in management and enterprise restructuring.

(EBRD 1998b: 160)

5 'Industrial restructuring has so far been limited in scope, given industry's incestuous relationship with banks and a privatization scheme biased towards management buy-outs. Those industries that have been restructured are doing well ... Croatian shipyards, for instance' (Business Central Europe 1997: 38).

There have been further developments in privatization. A new privatization law was approved in February 1996. This provides a framework for the privatization of large public enterprises. Vouchers were to be distributed to refugees, war invalids and other displaced persons (perhaps some 300,000 people in total), who could use them to bid for shares either directly or via investment funds. It was envisaged that foreign bidding would be permitted for at least some of the large public enterprises such as the oil and gas conglomerate, the electricity generator, telecoms and television and radio stations (EBRD 1996b: 144–5). The long-delayed voucher-based privatization programme is under way. Three bidding rounds were scheduled for mid-1998 (EBRD 1998a: 34). More than two years after a privatization law was passed to accelerate the process one of its integral parts, a mass privatization programme, is finally under way. Some 225,000 voucher holders are to acquire shares in 471 firms, either directly or through one of seven competing privatization funds. By mid-1998 the funds had collected about 90 per cent of all vouchers. During three bidding rounds in mid-1998 about 80 per cent of the assets were sold (EBRD 1998b: 160). The long-delayed voucher privatization scheme was implemented in 1998, selling stakes in 471 enterprises. The next step is the consolidation of shares among the seven funds involved in the programme and their listing on the stock exchange (EBRD 1999a: 35). There are a number of large state entities not covered by the 1991 privatization law, accounting for about a quarter of employment in originally state-owned companies. The method of privatization is decided on a case-by-case basis (EBRD 1999b: 206). 'The privatization process gained momentum in 1999' (EBRD 2000a: 48).

The Former Yugoslav Republic of Macedonia

The situation in 1989 was as follows: area 11 per cent of the former Yugoslavia; the population of 2.2 million (9 per cent of the Yugoslav total) comprised 67 per cent Macedonians, 20 per cent Albanians (see below) and 4 per cent Turks;

Macedonia contributed 6 per cent of Yugoslav GNP; index of *per capita* income 61 (Yugoslav average = 100).

Ethnic Albanians

Ethnic Albanians claim that they constitute up to 40 per cent of the population. But in the 1991 census, boycotted by most Albanians, the official figures showed that the population was split 65 per cent ethnic Macedonian and 21.7 per cent ethnic Albanian. Likewise, the 21 June–10 July 1994 census was boycotted by most Albanians and to some extent by the Turk and Serb minorities.

The final results of the 1994 census were not released until December of that year. The total population was given as 1,936,877, of which Macedonians accounted for 1,288,330 (66.5 per cent) and Albanians 442,914 (22.9 per cent) (in 1953 the respective proportions were 65.59 per cent and 12.45 per cent). But in fact the number of Albanians is closer to 800,000 (40 per cent plus of the population) (*EEN*, 1995, vol. 9, no. 10, p. 2).

> Macedonia has many minority groups, with none representing an over-whelming majority, yet Slavic Macedonians occupy more than 90 per cent of public sector jobs and make up more than 90 per cent of the police force and 90 per cent of the university student population.
>
> (William Walker, *IHT*, 8 June 2001, p. 8)

President Kiro Gligorov struggled hard to maintain ethnic harmony and the integrity of the country.

On 16 February 1995 ethnic Albanians opened a university (in Tetovo) in defiance of government orders. 'An Albanian protester has been shot dead, the founder of the university is in prison and Albanian MPs are boycotting parliament' (Iso Rusi, *IHT*, 7 March 1995, p. 8). 'He was released four months later on bail … both communities have been careful not to let the situation get out of hand' (Kerin Hope and Anthony Robinson, *FT*, Survey, 7 July 1995, p. 36).

> One of the three new deputy prime ministers is from an Albanian party. The unofficial university in Tetovo remains closed, but its lecturers are allowed to teach people in their homes. More Albanians are being accepted at Skopje university, while degrees from Tirana university are to be recognised.
>
> (*The Economist*, 6 April 1996, p. 45)

(On 1 February 1997 the rector of Tetovo University was released from jail: *EEN*, 1997, vol. 11, no. 3, p. 8.) 'The government refuses to recognize the self-proclaimed Albanian University of Tetovo set up almost four years ago by the local community, with the support of the Kosovo Albanians' (*FT*, Survey, 17 December 1997, p. ii).

In mid-February 1997 Slav students began protests against a government-sponsored law on the enhanced use of Albanian in the pedagogical faculty in Skopje. The protests 'turned into organized daily rallies of up to 10,000 people' (*EEN*, 30 March 1997, vol. 11, no. 6, p. 6). 'Hundreds of [Slav] students have been protesting against a law – passed after strong American and EU urging – that lets Albanian be the language of tuition in just one branch of Skopje's university' (*The Economist*, 29 March 1997, p. 54).

On 8 July 1997 parliament passed a law restricting the use of non-Macedonian flags. (In May 1997 the constitutional court had ruled that other countries' flags should not be flown in public. On 8 July parliament approved a new law permitting the flags of ethnic minorities to fly outside municipal buildings only on public holidays: *FT*, Survey, 17 December 1997, p. ii.) On 9 July violence occurred in the ethnic Albanian towns of Tetovo and Gostivar as police tried to prevent the flying of the Albanian national flag. Several people were killed (*EEN*, 1997, vol. 11, no. 14, p. 7). The radical mayor of Gostivar insisted on flying the Albanian flag alongside the Macedonian flag outside the town hall. The clashes left three dead and more than 200 injured. But Gostivar quickly returned to calm.

> Even after the riots the Social Democrats have managed to retain the support of the moderate Albanian Party for Democratic Prosperity. The two parties have co-operated in government since 1992, with the ethnic Albanians holding five cabinet posts. A parliamentary commission has been set up to investigate the Gostivar riots.
>
> (*FT*, Survey, 17 December 1997, p. ii)

(On 13 April 1998 Arben Xhaferi, chairman of the Democratic Party of Albanians, announced his withdrawal of the party from parliament: *EEN*, 1998, vol. 12, no. 5, p. 6.)

On 17 September 1997 the ethnic Albanian mayor of Gostivar was sentenced to thirteen years in jail for not carrying out orders to lower the Albanian flag from public buildings in Gostivar (*EEN*, 1997, vol. 11, no. 18, p. 7). This was later reduced to seven years (*The Economist*, 7 March 1998, p. 54). The mayor of Tetovo received a two-and-a-half-year prison term for a similar offence (*Guardian*, 23 July 1998, p. 12).

The general election of 18 October and 1 November 1998 resulted in a coalition government. VMRO–DPMNE formed an alliance with Democratic Alternative. They invited the Democratic Party of Albanians, led by Arben Xhaferi, to join them. (See below.)

> The influx of Kosovar Albanian refugees [during the war in Kosovo] created panic and fears among the Slav majority that the balance of power and population in Macedonia would be changed dramatically. But when the war ended in the summer of 1999 most of the refugees returned to rebuild their shattered homes and lives ... The local Albanian community helped by both absorbing some 360,000 Kosovan refugees .. and then by calming the

Slav majority's fears of being swamped by helping Kosovar families to return home once the bombing stopped.

(Anthony Robinson, *FT*, Survey, 19 February 2001, p. 14)

On 25 July 2000 parliament passed a law allowing for higher education in the Albanian language (*EEN*, 2000, vol. 12, no. 24, p. 5). 'The current government, bowing to pressure from OSCE and other international bodies in support of these demands, has agreed to allow the building of a $50 million private university in Tetovo ... It will provide higher education in Albanian for up to 2,500 students' (*FT*, Survey, 19 February 2001, p. 13). 'A new university, sponsored by the international community, is due to open in Tetovo in October [2001] ... Some courses will be taught in Albanian as well as English and Macedonian' (*FT*, 6 March 2001, p. 10).

(Ethnic Albanian militancy is dealt with below.)

The name of the country

Macedonia escaped the wars that ravaged many parts of the former Yugoslavia in the first half of the 1990s.

A 'yes' vote of 99 per cent led to the declaration of independence on 18 September 1991. Bulgaria and Turkey soon recognized Macedonia, but EU recognition was held up by Greece's objection to the name, especially since it allegedly implied territorial claims. It was not until 8 April 1993, after interminable wrangling, that Macedonia was admitted to the UN (member number 181) under the temporary name of 'The Former Yugoslav Republic of Macedonia'. The final name was supposed to be the subject of international arbitration. However, Greece withdrew from the formal negotiations in late October 1993 after the general election there. On 13 October 1993 China recognized the country as 'The Republic of Macedonia'. On 16 December 1993 Germany, France, the Netherlands, Denmark and Italy established formal diplomatic links with 'The Former Yugoslav Republic of Macedonia'. Finland followed the next day and Japan on 21 December. On 9 February 1994 the USA recognized 'The Former Yugoslav Republic of Macedonia'.

On 16 February 1994 Greek prime minister Andreas Papandreou said that 'the Greek government has decided to suspend the activities of its consulate in Skopje and on the suspension of goods to and from Skopje through the port of Salonika, except those that are absolutely necessary for humanitarian reasons, such as food and medicines'. (The finance ministry said later that the embargo would apply to all customs points in Greece. Salonika normally handles 70 per cent of Macedonia's imports and exports: *IHT*, 28 March 1994, p. 6. Another source puts the figure at around 80 per cent of foreign trade: *Independent*, 29 March 1994, p. 8.) This was a somewhat surprising move, since only in late January 1994 there had been hints of a more conciliatory approach by the Greek government. These concerned possible concessions by Macedonia over: (1) the constitution, which states that 'The Republic cares for the status and rights of those persons belonging to the Macedonian people in neighbouring countries'; and (2) the flag, specifically the use of the star of Vergina (a sunburst symbol found on a gold casket in the tomb, unearthed in 1977, of Philip II of Macedonia and also associated with his son Alexander the Great). On 31 March 1994 more than a million Greeks demonstrated in Salonika in support of government policy. Greece's actions caused considerable anger among its partners. On 6 April the EU gave Greece a week to lift its blockade or face a referral to the European Court of Justice for violation of EU trade laws. Greece did not respond. On 29 June 1994 the court refused the EU's request for an emergency interim injunction (which can be granted only on the grounds of 'grave and irreparable harm' to the EU).

On 6 December 1994 there were reports that Greece had relaxed its embargo, e.g. allowing through fuel for humanitarian purposes. On 4 September 1995 simultaneous announcements in Washington, Athens and Skopje revealed that the Greek and Macedonian foreign ministers were to meet to take the first steps towards 'the creation of a basis for friendly relations between the two countries'. Only the name of the former Yugoslav republic had yet to be agreed. But other disputes had been resolved. The star of Vergina was to be removed from the Macedonian flag, while sections of the Macedonian constitution considered by Greece to be threatening were to be amended. In return Greece would lift its economic embargo and diplomatic relations would be established. The USA would also establish diplomatic relations with the former Yugoslav republic. Greece lifted its economic embargo on 15 October 1995. The agreement was signed on 13 September 1995, taking effect after thirty days.

The Macedonian parliament approved the 4 September agreement on 9 October 1995.

On 25 September 1999 Greece's state-run Olympic Airways began regular flights between Athens and Skopje (*IHT*, 27 September 1999, p. 2).

A sign of improving relations is the growing importance of Greek investment in the Macedonian economy. (See below.)

The Macedonian presidential and parliamentary elections of 16 October 1994 and events thereafter

Alleging serious irregularities, the Democratic Party (which campaigned on a platform of nationalism, the free market and clean government) and VMRO (Internal Macedonian Revolutionary Organization, a hardline nationalist party) boycotted the second round (which took place on 30 October, when the turnout was only 35 per cent). International observers were far from being happy, but thought the election results should stand.

The presidential election was, as forecast, won by the incumbent, Kiro Gligorov. Pro-Gligorov forces won about 82 per cent of the seats in parliament, with the under-represented opposition threatening civil resistance campaigns. The Party of Democratic Prosperity (the ethnic Albanian party) joined the Social Democratic Party in government.

President Gligorov, although badly hurt, survived an assassination attempt when a car bomb exploded in Skopje on 3 October 1995. He made a good recovery.

The Federal Republic of Yugoslavia and the 'Republic of Macedonia' signed an accord on 8 April 1996 normalizing relations.

The foreign, economy and justice ministers were dismissed on 29 May 1997 after a series of scandals that included the collapse of some pyramid investment schemes (*The Economist*, 31 May 1997, p. 4). (In February 1997 the Tat savings house collapsed amid widespread accusations of corruption and involvement by government officials. In April two modernizers, the deputy prime minister and the foreign minister, were dismissed. The central bank governor was forced to resign and his deputy was placed under arrest on charges of abusing his authority: *FT*, Survey, 17 December 1997, pp. i–ii.)

The general election of 18 October and 1 November 1998

VMRO–DPMNE formed an alliance with Democratic Alternative. They invited the Democratic Party of Albanians, led by Arben Xhaferi, to join them in a coalition government.

VMRO–DPMNE (Internal Macedonian Revolutionary Organization–Democratic Party) was led by Ljubco Georgievski. 'Mr Georgievski … talked of bringing in $1 billion in foreign investment … [and] of compensating for losses in financial scams' (Business Central Europe 1998: 39).

Democratic Alternative was led by Vasil Tupurkovski.

> A new, pro-business party founded by Vasil Tupurkovski … a law professor who served as Macedonia's special envoy to the USA. [He has] pledged to bring in $1 billion in foreign investment to reduce unemployment and speed Macedonia's transition to a market economy.
>
> (*FT*, 2 November 1998, p. 4)

'VMRO, led by Ljubco Georgievski who served briefly as Macedonia's vice-president in the early 1990s, has renounced its nationalist platform since teaming up with Democratic Alternative early this year' (Kerin Hope, *FT*, 2 November 1998, p. 4).

> The Social Democrats have governed in partnership with the moderate Albanian Party for Democratic Prosperity during six years in power. But Branko Crvenkovski, prime minister, faces criticism over the slow pace of reforms aimed at giving Albanians equal status with Slavs. The more radical Democratic Party of Albanians is fighting the election in alliance with the PDP.
>
> (Kerin Hope, *FT*, 19 October 1998, p. 2)

VMRO's ... [was] one of the world's first modern-style terrorist organizations ... For people in the southern Balkans VMRO is an acronym redolent of violence. Between the two world wars VMRO's *komitas* [brigands] carried out political assassinations, terrorized villages and exacted tribute on the ground of fighting for an independent Macedonia ... Disbanded under communism, VMRO went underground. But when Macedonia declared independence ... in 1992 it reappeared as VMRO–DPMNE ... [which] revived the dream of uniting western Bulgaria and northern Greece in a Greater Macedonia ... Seven years later, however, VMRO has succeeded in persuading voters that it is a party of peace ... This transformation from nationalist pressure group to centre-right political party owes much to Vasil Tupurkovski, a US-educated international lawyer who founded the DA earlier this year ... [He has] political skills and popularity with young voters ... Mr Tupurkovski has worked especially hard to persuade VMRO to abandon its traditional hostility towards Macedonia's large Albanian minority ... The VMRO–DA coalition is negotiating with the Democratic Party of Albanians, a radical party which used to promote separatism ... Mr Tupurkovski also helped VMRO underline its break with the past by focusing its election campaign on Macedonia's economic prospects ... [Mr Georgievski stressed the need] to create jobs and opportunities to build small businesses ... [Mr Tupurkovski] has pledged to bring $1 billion in foreign investment, with assistance from ethnic Macedonians in the USA and Australia ... 'Macedonia should become a high-quality agricultural producer and food-processor supplying markets abroad. The way to beat unemployment is to encourage development of family-sized agri-business units' [he said].

(Kerin Hope, *FT*, 3 November 1998, p. 2)

VMRO [is] descended ... from nationalist brigands of the 1920s and 1930s ... But over the past six months it has shed its wild image. Its [32-year old] leader, Ljubco Georgievski, is eloquent about cracking down on corruption and making Macedonia less risky for investors. The DA is run by Vasil Tupurkovski, an American-educated international lawyer, who once headed Yugoslavia's communist youth movement, but now talks about raising money abroad to develop the economy. Mr Tupurkovski ... has helped bring about VMRO's transformation ... [It has made an offer] of a law banning discrimination against Albanians and Macedonia's smaller Turkish and Gypsy minorities.

(*The Economist*, 7 November 1998, p. 56)

Ljubco Georgievski [32, who will be the new prime minister] started negotiating with Arben Xhaferi – whose support he does not need to govern – to see how they could work together ... Last June [1998] ... Alajdin Demiri began a two-year prison sentence for raising an Albanian flag outside the city hall of Tetovo ... When ethnic Albanian politicians began to talk with

Mr Georgievski one of his first concessions was that Mr Demiri and another mayor convicted of the same offence be released. According to Mr Xhaferi, they also agreed on a plan to give much more power to local governments and to settle a sometimes violent rallying point for both sides: a university where instruction is in the Albanian language … Mr Georgievski, at considerable political risk, has agreed to use state funds to support the Albanian-language university, Mr Xhaferi said … Mr Xhaferi, who in the past has hinted that Albanians here may have to secede in order to secure political rights, now says they must learn to work with Macedonian politicians. Foreign diplomats and Macedonian politicians say even the most radical people here now see that the landlocked country, sandwiched between Serbia, Albania, Greece and Bulgaria, will remain poor and isolated unless its leaders learn to co-operate.

(Mike O'Connor, *IHT*, 1 December 1998, p. 5)

Political developments after the 1998 general election

On 22 February 1999 a declaration of co-operation is signed by prime minister Ljubco Georgievski of Macedonia and prime minister Ivan Kostov of Bulgaria. The declaration was signed in two copies in the official languages of both countries.

Thus Georgievski could claim … that the Bulgarian side for the first time had agreed to an explicit endorsement of the Macedonian language. Kostov meanwhile was able to tell the Bulgarian public that Macedonian is merely a technical variation of Bulgarian. The Bulgarian side also insisted that the declaration contained an undertaking by the Macedonian side that the Macedonian constitution would never be used as a pretext for interference in the internal affairs of Bulgaria 'to defend the status and rights of persons who are not citizens of the Republic of Macedonia'. This formula is an exact copy of the formula used in the interim agreement between Macedonia and Greece in 1995, and it has the same aim: to prevent Macedonia from using Article 49 of the constitution which obliges the Macedonian state to care for the status and rights of Macedonians in neighbouring states … In their 'declaration' Bulgaria and Macedonia also included a stipulation that they would prevent the activities of institutions and private citizens that fostered violence or hatism directed at the other side.

(*EEN*, 1999, vol. 12, no. 15, pp. 4–5)

Bulgaria is to donate military equipment. Other agreements included the promotion and protection of investments, trade co-operation, international road traffic and air services (*ibid.*).

Bulgaria and Macedonia ... have signed a declaration of principles, which allows them to sidestep the thorny issue of Bulgaria's unwillingness to hitherto recognize the Macedonian language and nationhood ... The formula ... will allow the countries to sign bilateral treaties in the languages recognized by the two countries' constitutions.

(*FT*, Survey, 8 March 1999, p. i)

Prime ministers Georgievski and Kostov renounced territorial claims upon one another, declared that neither would allow its territory to be used by groups hostile to the other, and noted that the common language of the document they signed was 'Bulgarian, in accordance with the constitution of Bulgaria, and Macedonian, in accordance with the constitution of the Republic of Macedonia'.

(William Pfaff, *IHT*, 9 March 1999, p. 6)

Georgievski formed a curious coalition between VMRO–DPMNE (with its strong pro-Bulgarian faction in its leadership), the Democratic Alternative of Vasil Tupurkovski (his party representing a bunch of former Yugoslav apparatchiks that had been left out by the Social Democratic Alliance in the 1990s) and the radical Democratic Party of Albanians ... The strongest criticism of the new Macedonian–Bulgarian relationship comes from the SDSM and [President] Gligorov ... He said that the amnesty for the Albanian mayors of Tetovo and Gostivar ... the recognition of Taiwan and the negotiations with Bulgaria had ignored the institution of the president and had led to the adoption of policies dangerous to Macedonian sovereignty.

(*EEN*, 1999, vol. 12, no. 15, pp. 4–6)

('Some [money] is coming from Taiwan, which Macedonia has recognized diplomatically. To show its thanks, Taipei is paying $20 million to build Macedonia's first free trade zone': Business Central Europe 1999: 36.)

'Mr Georgievski ... has fulfilled an election promise to free the radical mayors of Tetovo and Gostivar' (*FT*, 29 March 1999, p. 2).

On 12 March 1999 the defence ministers of Macedonia and Bulgaria signed a defence co-operation agreement (*EEN*, 1999, vol. 12, no. 16, p. 10).

On 13 October 1999 a free trade agreement is signed with Bulgaria (*EEN*, 1999, vol. 12, no. 20, p. 4).

Although Boris Trajkovski (VMRO) came second (to Tito Petrovski of the Social Democratic Alliance) in the first round of the presidential election held on 31 October 1999, he eventually won the race (albeit after second-round reruns were ordered, on account of irregularities, in western Macedonia, where most ethnic Albanians live).

'Local elections [held on 10 September 2000] are easily won by opposition parties led by the Social Democratic Party of Macedonia' (*EEN*, 2000, vol. 12, no. 25, p. 4).

> Flawed local government elections … were marred by violence and criti-
> cised by international observers for irregularities … VMRO did badly in
> bigger towns and cities where the effects of an unemployment rate of
> between 25 and 35 per cent are felt most keenly.
>
> (*FT*, Survey, 19 February 2001, p. 11)

An EU–Balkan summit meeting was held in Zagreb on 24 November 2000.
Albania, Bosnia, Macedonia and Yugoslavia were formally invited. 'The summit
also saw Macedonia's signing of the first so-called Stabilization and Association
Agreement with the EU – a new kind of agreement intended for western Balkan
countries. Croatia also formally started negotiations on such an agreement' (*FT*,
25 November 2000, p. 6).

On 23 November 2000 the Democratic Alternative, led by Vasil Tupurkovski,
left the ruling coalition. On 30 November prime minister Ljubco Georgievski
announced a new cabinet following a coalition agreement between the
VMRO–DPMNE, the Liberals and the Democratic Party of Albanians (*EEN*,
2001, vol. 13, no. 2, p. 5).

'The Democratic Party of Albanians … became the government's main coalition partner after a political shake-up last November [2000]' (*FT*, 2 March 2001,
p. 8). 'Last November [2000] the DPA acquired five cabinet portfolios –
including the post of deputy prime minister' (*FT*, 6 March 2001, p. 10).

> [There have been] no fewer than five acrimonious cabinet reshuffles. The
> most recent cabinet upheaval resulted in the departure from the coalition of
> the Democratic Alternative, led by Vasil Tupurkovski … The Democratic
> Alternative was replaced as a coalition partner by the Liberals, with Srgjan
> Kerim … taking over the post of foreign minister … A telephone-tapping
> scandal is the latest crisis to confront Mr Georgievski. The Social Democrats
> accuse the interior ministry of using sophisticated electronic equipment
> provided by the USA for counter-terrorism purposes to tap the mobile
> phones of senior Macedonian politicians, including Mr Trajkovski and Mr
> Crvenkovski. Purported transcripts of taped conversations, provided by the
> Social Democrats, have appeared in Macedonian newspapers.
>
> (Kerin Hope, *FT*, Survey, 19 February 2001, p. 11)

> EU foreign ministers yesterday [9 April 2001] signed a political and
> economic accord with Macedonia … The 'stabilization and association
> agreement' holds out the promise of eventual EU membership to
> Macedonia if it introduces a package of reforms. But ministers refused
> Macedonia's request to be immediately recognized as an EU candidate.
>
> (*FT*, 10 April 2001, p. 9)

'In April 2001 FYR Macedonia became the first country in south-eastern
Europe to sign a Stabilization and Association Agreement with the EU' (EBRD
2001b: 146).

Although there had been occasional incidents involving ethnic Albanian militants, the self-styled National Liberation Army (NLA) was proclaimed in January 2001. Fighting with government forces escalated to the point where civil war was a possibility. Ethnic Albanian militants in Macedonia have close links with kindred groups in Kosovo and Serbia proper. Indeed, some NLA members are from those places and from Albania itself (although official representatives in Kosovo and Albania have spoken out against the use of violence). Militants have taken advantage of the buffer zone between Kosovo and estranged Serbia despite efforts by Kfor to intercept them. EU diplomacy was particularly prominent at first, but it took a joint effort by the EU and the USA (the latter being especially trusted by ethnic Albanians) to produce an agreement on a ceasefire (starting on 5 July 2001) and a political settlement negotiated between the ethnic Slav and Albanian parties. The so-called ceasefire did not prevent escalating fighting, but a peace accord was signed by political leaders on 13 August 2001. Thereafter the ceasefire became far more effective, although incidents continued to cause concern, and in November 2001 a seemingly small number of extremist ethnic Albanian militants calling themselves the Albanian National Army started to cause trouble. Many 'ethnic Slav Macedonians' (who typically resent the label) felt that they were forced to give in under duress and that Nato had leaned too much in favour of the rebels. There were immense strains within the coalition government (both between the ethnic parties and between Slav elements), but it held together long enough to produce an EU–US-brokered settlement enhancing the rights of the ethnic Albanians. In a staged process, Nato's 'Operation Essential Harvest' successfully gathered the weapons declared by the NLA (undoubtedly other weapons remained undeclared) while parliament voted on legislation designed to improve the position of ethnic Albanians. On 27 September 2001 its leader stated that the NLA had been disbanded. A smaller, German-led follow-up Nato force (the mission being called 'Amber Fox') was set up to protect civilian observers monitoring the peace agreement. There were many parliamentary delays and there were incidents which nearly derailed the whole process. It was not until 16 November 2001 that parliament adopted the constitutional changes. President Boris Trajkovski declared an amnesty for the former guerrillas hours after parliament ratified the reforms. All former ethnic Albanian guerrillas, including about 120 detainees and convicts, were to be covered by the amnesty, except those indictable by the United Nations war crimes tribunal. The situation remained fragile, but a March 2002 aid package indicated international approval (see p. 358).

Economic developments

Economic performance was generally pretty grim in the first half of the 1990s. Though poorly enforced, Macedonia's participation in sanctions on the Federal Republic of Yugoslavia did not help. But GDP growth turned positive in 1996. 'FYR Macedonia's economy was affected more severely [than Bulgaria's] by the Kosovo crisis, both through trade effects and the influx of large numbers of refugees. Nevertheless, the economy made a strong recovery in the second half of the year [1999]' (EBRD 2000a: 5). In 2000 GDP was an estimated 77 per cent of the 1989 level (EBRD 2001b: 59). There was hyperinflation in 1992 (1,664 per cent). Consumer prices were more or less stable in 1997–9. The inflation rate rose to just under 10 per cent in 2000. (See Table 3.1, p. 357) Fighting in 2001 had an adverse effect on the economy.

Net financial transfers from the federal government of the former Yugoslavia had been of the order of 5 to 7 per cent of GDP (United Nations, *World Economic and Social Survey*, 1996, p. 33).

The denar has been floating since the beginning of 1994. There is near full current account convertibility except for citizens wishing to holiday abroad. Controls remain on the capital account. The liberalization of the foreign trade regime is well advanced (EBRD 1994: 25, 109). Officially the denar has been floating since the beginning of 1994, but in practice it has remained closely aligned to the DM (EBRD 1996b: 151). The denar was devalued by 14 per cent in July 1997 (EBRD 1997b: 169). There is a *de facto* peg of the exchange rate to the DM (EBRD 1999b: 218).

'The government continues to control the prices of most utilities and miscellaneous items such as oil, mail and motor insurance' (EBRD 2001b: 146).

Various incomes policies have been use as part of stabilization packages.

On 24 October 1996 the London Club of bank creditors reached agreement in principle with Macedonia on repaying its share of the former Yugoslavia's commercial bank debt of $5.6 billion. (The debt arose from the 1988 rescheduling agreement, called the New Financing Arrangement.) Macedonia would take on 5.4 per cent of the principal and 3.65 per cent of the interest, i.e. some $280 million in total (*FT*, 25 October 1996, p. 3). Agreement was reached on 26 March 1997, with Macedonia issuing new bonds totalling $228.7 million in exchange for its share of the total Yugoslav debt of around $5.6 billion in principal and interest (*FT*, 27 March 1997, p. 2).

> [On 18 September 2000 EU foreign] ministers approved an EU package granting duty-free access to 95 per cent of imports from Albania, Bosnia, Croatia, Macedonia and Montenegro ... The package includes abolition of tariffs on most industrial and farm products to the EU. However, some limits remain on exports of fish products and wine.
>
> (*FT*, 19 September 2000, p. 10)

'In April 2001 FYR Macedonia became the first country in south-eastern Europe to sign a Stabilization and Association Agreement with the EU' (EBRD 2001b: 146).

The private sector accounted for roughly 15 per cent of GDP in mid-1990. In mid-2001 the figure was 60 per cent (EBRD 1999b: 24, 220; and 2001b: 12, 148).

Over 90 per cent of small enterprises are already privately owned (EBRD 1994: 24). By mid-1995 about 120 enterprises had been privatized, primarily through management buy-outs (EBRD 1995b: 42). More than half of the enterprises (representing at least half of the former state assets in the enterprise sector) have been privatized through management and employee buy-outs (p. 23). By the end of 1997 almost all enterprises designated in 1993 for privatization had completed the process, representing more than three-quarters of all enterprises. Management and employee buy-out remains the most common method, however, and progress on improving corporate governance is slow (EBRD 1998a: 35). By mid-1998 roughly four-fifths of all 'socially owned' enterprises identified for privatization had been privatized, mostly through management and employee buy-outs. However, most of these are small and medium-sized enterprises. There are a number of large loss-making industrial enterprises with majority state ownership which are being restructured and are to be sold to strategic investors or otherwise liquidated. The government is also preparing international tenders for stakes in telecoms, energy and the oil refinery.

> Improvements in corporate governance have been slow. This is due in part to the prevalence of management and employee buy-outs in the privatization process, which can act as a hindrance to enterprise restructuring ... Foreign investors have been deterred by high political risk in the region. Their participation in the privatization process amounted to less than 2 per cent of equity privatized.
>
> (EBRD 1998b: 166–7)

The situation has greatly improved in 1998, facilitated by an improved economic climate and greater emphasis on sales to outsiders in privatization. It is planned to privatize infrastructure on a case-by-case basis. The intention is to sell at least one-third of Macedonian Telecommunications to an international strategic investor (EBRD 1998b: 166–7). The privatization of agriculture has lagged behind the rest of the economy. But the pace has increased in 1998. By May 1998, 70 per cent of all agricultural enterprises had been privatized (representing about 40 per cent of employment in the sector). The rest are scheduled for privatization by the end of 1998 (EBRD 1998b: 166). By the end of June 1999, small privatization was largely complete with 1,458 enterprises sold. Large privatization has been slow. Most privatizations in agriculture have been sales to existing managers and farmers (EBRD 1999b: 218–19).

> Extensive use of management–employee buy-outs has resulted in poor corporate governance and improvement is slow ... Large-scale privatization has been slow to take off ... Privatization of the agricultural sector has proceeded steadily and more than three-quarters of agricultural land is privately owned. The law on agricultural land passed in 1999 abolished restrictions on land ownership and gave impetus to the enlargement of existing farms. Full privatization of the sector is expected by the end of 2000.
>
> (EBRD 2000a: 54)

'The privatization of large-scale enterprises has accelerated' (EBRD 2000b: 162–3). 'Progress has been made on large-scale privatization, but several large loss-makers remain in state hands' (EBRD 2001b: 28).

> Privatization in the agricultural sector is nearly complete with 418 companies privatized. Attention is now focussed on forty large loss-making enterprises scheduled for privatization or closure by the end of 2002 ... Strategic investors [are being sought]. The internal ethnic conflict has led to a delay in the programme. However, in June 2001 the government announced the liquidation of five of these enterprises (with 7,000 employees).
>
> (*ibid.* p. 146)

Most processing of agricultural products is still carried out by some 200 agro-kombinats, state conglomerates which control some 30 per cent of farmland. Private farmers produce about 75 per cent of agricultural output on fragmented holdings with an average size of 2.8 ha (*FT*, Survey, 15 November 1996, p. ii).

On 21 April 1998 parliament passed a law which allowed restitution of land and assets expropriated since 1945 (*EEN*, 1998, vol. 12, no. 6, p. 7).

Macedonia has attracted little direct foreign investment. (See Table 3.1.) Greek capital is important.

Slovenia

The situation in 1989 was as follows: area 8 per cent of the former Yugoslavia; the population of 2 million comprised 91 per cent Slovenes; Slovenia contributed 19 per cent of Yugoslav GNP; index of *per capita* income 210 (Yugoslav average = 100).

Despite some difficulty in forming stable governments, economically Slovenia (albeit experiencing problems with its economic reform) has pushed miles ahead of its erstwhile partners in the former Yugoslavia. It is in the leading ranks of candidates for admission to the EU despite experiencing various problems.

Slovenia is populated mainly by Slovenians, comprising 91 per cent of the 2 million population in 1989. It was the wealthiest part of the former Yugoslavia and the gap between it and its erstwhile partners has widened.

As regards relations with Italy, Slovenia and the EU initialled a trade and political co-operation agreement on 15 June 1995. But Italy had not lifted its veto on Slovenia having an association agreement with the EU until 6 March 1995. The dispute between Slovenia and Italy was about the property rights of Italians who fled from the Istrian peninsula after the Second World War. Slovenia's promise to the EU did not mean that Italians would be allowed to claim back their property or to take part in auctions. On 4 February 1998 Italy accepted $62 million from Slovenia in compensation for property seized from ethnic Italians who fled after the Second World War. An association agreement was signed with the EU on 10 June 1996. An exchange of letters was annexed to the agreement: (1) Slovenia will allow all EU citizens to buy land and property, on a reciprocal basis, within four years of the agreement being ratified; and (2) any EU citizens who have previously 'permanently resided on the present territory of the Republic of Slovenia for a period of three years' will be allowed to buy property immediately the agreement is ratified (*FT*, 10 June 1996, p. 2). (On 14 July 1997 parliament endorsed the amendment to Article 68 of the constitution to allow foreigners to own land.)

On 17 April 1998, Slovenia, Hungary and Italy agreed to establish a new joint peacekeeping brigade under Italian command as from January 1999 (*EEN*, 1998, vol. 12, no. 6, p. 9).

Nato's secretary-general Javier Solana Madriaga said on 8 July 1997 that:

> Today the heads of state and government have agreed to invite the Czech Republic, Hungary and Poland to begin accession talks with Nato ... We affirm that Nato remains open to new members ... We will review the process at our next meeting in 1999. With regard to aspiring members, we recognize with great interest and take account of the positive developments toward democracy and the rule of law in a number of south-eastern European countries, especially Romania and Slovenia.

(A majority of the sixteen Nato countries, led by France, supported the inclusion of Romania and Slovenia in the first wave of invitations. But the USA was adamant that only three countries would be invited to become members of Nato in the first wave.)

On 16 July 1997 the European Commission recommended that Slovenia opens negotiations (along with Cyprus, the Czech Republic, Estonia, Hungary and Poland) in early 1998 for entry to the EU. (The invitation was formally approved at an EU summit on 13 December 1997, formal negotiations for membership beginning on 31 March 1998.)

> The EU's negative progress report of November 1998 shook Slovenia ... The EU's criticisms centred on the country's slow progress in adopting the *acquis communautaire*, or EU legislation. That failure stems from Slovenia's weak government: it is a divided three-party coalition, with a parliamentary majority of just one vote. Decision-making is therefore as slow as economic and legislative reform.
>
> (Business Central Europe 1998: 30)

On 13 October 1999, however, the European Commission recommended that EU leaders at the December 1999 meeting in Helsinki allow Bulgaria, Latvia, Lithuania, Malta, Romania and Slovakia to begin accession negotiations in 2000. Slovenia is considered to have a functioning market economy. Malta and Cyprus have already met the economic terms set by the EU, being able to cope with competitive pressures and market forces in the EU. Hungary and Poland come next in economic terms, followed by Slovenia, Estonia and then the

Czech Republic. Hungary, Poland, Estonia and Slovenia have improved their ability to cope with competitive pressures and market forces 'in the medium term' (meaning more than one year from 2000) (*FT*, 14 October 1999, pp. 1, 10; *IHT*, 14 October 1999, p. 5; *Guardian*, 14 October 1999, p. 14; *Independent*, 14 October 1999, p. 18; *The Times*, 14 October 1999, p. 21; *Telegraph*, 14 October 1999, p. 20).

Despite some familiar concerns expressed in the 8 November 2000 EU assessment, Slovenia remained a front runner for membership.

On 13 November 2001 the EU published its progress reports on the twelve EU applicants for EU membership with which negotiations have begun. There are thirteen applicants in all (including Cyprus, Malta and Turkey), but negotiations have not yet begun with Turkey. Slovenia received another generally very favourable report, but what was different this time was that the EU indicated that it might admit up to ten new members at once. Günter Verheugen (EU enlargement commissioner): 'The aim of achieving the first accessions before the European Parliament elections in 2004 remains a demanding one. But it is not a utopian dream; it is a realistic and feasible challenge' (*FT*, 14 November 2001, p. 12). Bulgaria and Romania were excluded from early entry.

On 11 January 2000 the party leaderships of the Social Democratic Party and the Slovenian Christian Democrats approved a draft agreement for an electoral agreement (*EEN*, 2000, vol. 12, n 22, p. 6).

On 15 March 2000 the Slovenian People's Party announced its intention to leave the ruling coalition government following its merger with the Slovenian Christian Democrats (*EEN*, 2000, vol. 12, no. 23, p. 11). 'The government collapsed [on 8 April 2000] when the National Assembly refused to approve a new cabinet sought by prime minister Janez Drnovsek, a Liberal Democrat' (*IHT*, 10 April 2000, p. 4).

> Slovenia's opposition has agreed on a candidate to replace Janez Drnovsek as prime minister … The newly formed conservative Slovenian People's Party and the centre-right Social Democrats agreed late on Saturday [15 April] to nominate Andrej Bajuk … But the two parties hold just forty-four seats out of ninety in parliament … Mr Drnovsek's centre-left coalition lost a no confidence vote last week after the conservative People's Party quit the government to merge with the opposition Christian Democrats, forming the Slovenian People's Party and leaving Mr Drnovsek without a majority.
>
> (*FT*, 17 April 2000, p. 6)

On 7 June 2000 parliament narrowly approved a new government under a new prime minister, Andrej Bajuk.

Bajuk is an Argentine-Slovak banker (*Business Central Europe*, June 2000, p. 15).

'Parliament … finally elected, by a margin of one vote, a right-wing government led by Andrej Bajuk, a recently returned émigré … The 7 June success was down only to two maverick independent MPs who switched sides.' Fifty-seven-year-old Andrej Bajuk is vice-president of the new party, which is called the

SKD (Christian Democrats) + SLS (People's Party) Slovene People's Party. His parents fled Slovenia in 1945.

> They went to South America to escape recriminations for their wartime support for Slovenia's Nazi German and Italian fascist occupiers against the communist-led partisans. Some fear that the aggressive political style of his government risks reopening the long-running left–right divisions symbolized by Mr Bajuk's own life story. Many fears concern Janez Jansa, the defence minister and leader of the junior coalition Social Democratic Party, seen as the government's most powerful figure. The worries prompted Milan Kucan, the president, to warn about the dangers to national unity – and the EU accession process – at a 22 June press conference to mark the ninth anniversary of Slovenia's referendum on independence from Yugoslavia.
>
> (*FT*, Survey, 11 July 2000, p. 35)

> From April to June [2000] the country endured a spell of political uncertainty … Many have seen the subsequent two months of wrangling as a waste of scarce parliamentary time. The EU has sounded concerned about the effects of the hiatus on passage of legislation for membership … The president … [has been concerned] by the new government's conduct. With only months to govern, and a business backlog to clear, it has concentrated on replacing heads of a wide variety of state-influenced organizations with its own appointees.
>
> (*FT*, Survey, 11 July 2000, p. 35)

In the general election of 15 October 2000, Janez Drnovsek's Liberal Democracy of Slovenia did well, emerging at the head of a coalition government.

Slovenia is a really bright spot in the former Yugoslavia, although problems remain. GDP growth turned positive in 1993. (See Table 4.2, p. 373.) In 1998 GDP was an estimated 4 per cent in excess of the 1989 level. The figure for 1999 was 9 per cent (EBRD 2000a: 4, and 2000b: 65). The figure for 2000 was 14 per cent in excess (EBRD 2001b: 59). The annual rate of inflation peaked in 1990 (549.7 per cent), but it did not reached single figures until 1996.

The private sector accounted for roughly 15 per cent of GDP in mid-1990 (EBRD 1999b: 24, 268). In mid-2001 the figure was 65 per cent (2001b: 12, 196).

There is a liberal foreign trade regime and the economy quickly began being integrated into the world economy. The EU is the dominant trade partner.

On 9 June 1995 a tentative debt agreement was reached with Western commercial banks, with the signing perhaps taking place in September. Slovenia was to be responsible for 18 per cent of the former Yugoslavia's total debt of $4.65 billion owed to the banks. Slovenia had already secured debt rescheduling with the Paris Club of creditor governments (*FT*, 12 June 1995, p. 2). On 28 February 1996 the Slovenian parliament approved the agreement with the

London Club, Slovenia taking over 18 per cent of the former Yugoslavia's total debt to the commercial banks. The total debt was valued at $5.58 billion (of which $4.4 billion represented principal), but certain secondary market transactions were to be deducted. Slovenia was the first of the former Yugoslav states to finalize an agreement and was released from the 'joint and several liability' clause in the 1988 agreement. But the Federal Republic of Yugoslavia threatened legal action to halt the deal, demanding a general agreement on the debt and on the estimated $2 billion of gold and hard currency assets frozen around the world (*FT*, 1 March 1996, p. 2; 13 March 1996, p. 2; 30 April 1996, p. 2; Deutsche Bank, *Focus Eastern Europe*, 1996, no. 153, p. 5).

A new (convertible) currency, the tolar, was introduced on 8 October 1991 and a floating exchange rate adopted. Convertibility is full for current account purposes and the remaining restrictions on the capital account are to be phased out (EBRD 1994: 37, 109). On 1 September 1995 the tolar became externally convertible in accordance with the provisions of Article 8 of the IMF. To counter exchange rate appreciation the central bank increased quantitative controls on the capital account (EBRD 1998a: 41). Capital account restrictions were introduced in early 1997. In October 1998 further restrictions were introduced on portfolio flows, forcing foreign investors to hold Slovenian shares for at least seven years (EBRD 1998b: 190–1). 'Recent actions taken by the central bank to curb foreign capital inflows … have been justified on the grounds that the rising wave of capital inflows, in particular of foreign portfolio investment, was undermining the conduct of monetary policy' (*FT*, Survey, 28 April 1997, p. i).

'With a view to harmonization with EU requirements the central bank has substantially reduced restrictions on capital inflows … On 1 February 1999 the central bank substantially reduced restrictions on capital account inflows that had been in place since 1995' (EBRD 1999a: 43–4). The foreign exchange operations law passed in March 1999 and the implementing regulations adopted in July and September 1999 are significant steps towards full liberalization of capital flows. The law and its implementation so far leave restrictions for the most part only on the inflow of short-term capital (EBRD 1999b: 266).

'[The abolition of] restrictions on foreign portfolio investments … became effective on 1 July [2001]' (*FT*, Survey, 9 July 2001, p. 12). 'Effective from July 2001 foreign portfolio investments for all long-term securities (shares and bonds) are no longer subject to these obstacles, although some restrictions remain for investments in short-term securities of less than six months' (EBRD 2001b: 194).

Monetary, fiscal and incomes policies have all been employed in the quest for macroeconomic stabilization.

Restitution laws have been passed.

Privatization of socially owned enterprises is governed by the December 1992 law. The government aimed to privatize a total of 1,549 enterprises concerned. The sale was to take place through mass privatization involving the issuing of 'ownership certificates' to all Slovene nationals. They are exchangeable for either enterprise or investment funds shares. Enterprises can distribute a maximum of 20 per cent of the shares to incumbent employees free of charge. A further 40 per cent is transferable to three state-run funds (20 per cent to the development fund, 10 per cent to the pension fund and 10 per cent to the restitution fund set up to compensate individuals for previous nationalizations). The remainder may be sold to management/employees or to outsiders (EBRD 1996b: 175). Employees own a majority stake in enterprises representing 44 per cent of the book value of privatized enterprises (EBRD 1997a: 33). Large capital-intensive enterprises have tended to choose other privatization options, such as public offerings on the stock market (EBRD 1997b: 201). The privatization of socially managed enterprises was completed by mid-1997. But large public enterprises are still majority state-owned, as are the two large banks and several large conglomerates (EBRD 1998a: 41).

Almost all small trade and service activity is operated by the private sector (EBRD 1994: 36, 65). Large privatization has been slow (EBRD 1994: 36, 65). 'While privatization of socially (i.e. employee) managed enterprises is nearly complete, progress has been very slow in privatizing large firms' (EBRD 1999a: 24). 'The state still owns more than 50 per cent of total assets in the economy, including two large banks, fixed-line telecoms, energy, ports, highways and large enterprises in the steel and aluminium sectors ... The pace of bank privatization remains slow' (EBRD 2000a: 78).

> While the majority of the 'socially owned' enterprises (mostly small and medium-sized enterprises) had been privatized by the end of 1998, the state still holds shares in around 180 mainly large companies (eighty with a majority interest and 100 with a minority interest).
>
> (EBRD 2000b: 210)

'At mid-2001 the state still held shares in around 200 mainly large companies' (EBRD 2001b: 194).

> Just as most other central European countries are reaching the final stages of their privatization programmes, Slovenia is starting to sell its largest companies ... According to a new privatization law passed in April [2001], the emphasis will be on securing good strategic investors ... The next twelve to eighteen months should see the privatization of the two biggest banks, the dominant insurance company, the telecoms utility and a string of industrial assets, including the national steelworks and the Adriatic port of Koper.
>
> (*FT*, Survey, 9 July 2001, pp. 11–12)

Slovenia's privatization policy has been heavily criticized in some quarters:

1 'Slovenia's privatization programme not only fails to improve corporate governance – control of companies remains with management, where it has always been – it also results in minority shareholders being treated with contempt. And foreign investors are avoiding the country until the mess is sorted out ... Most [enterprises], predictably, went for a predominantly

management–employee buy-out option, so that control of Slovene industry will be little changed … Some of Slovenia's biggest and capital-rich companies were too expensive for insiders to gain a majority. These companies, around 100 in total, have opted to privatize by offering their shares to the general public in return for ownership certificates … With big-company ownership so widely dispersed, management calls the shots' (*Business Central Europe*, September 1996, p. 31). 'The exception to MBO [management–employee buy-out] privatization is the 100-odd companies privatized through the stock exchange … Slovenia's fund managers are employed by state-owned banks, and so will be no more distant from politics than their notorious Czech cousins' (p. 7). 'There are still the utilities, a couple of big banks and several other sectors that remain firmly in state hands. But let that pass … [Investment funds] have not exercised much corporate governance' (*Business Central Europe*, September 1997, p. 34).

2 'Barely half of state industry has been privatized and its new owners are mainly managers and workers … Companies have been slow to revamp themselves' (*The Economist*, 2 November 1996, p. 58).

3 'In the best cases funds – which have begun to build up holdings in companies by trading stakes between themselves – are beginning to exercise some much needed corporate governance … But others are taking advantage of the lack of transparency and market information – the vast majority of the newly privatized companies are not listed – by buying shares from individuals at low prices and selling them on for large profits' (Virginia Marsh, *FT*, Survey, 18 May 1998, p. iii).

4 'Privatization through management and employee buy-outs has effectively perpetuated the Yugoslav system of "social management" of enterprises … Most enterprises have undergone little restructuring … Foreign direct investment has been discouraged by excluding foreigners from the privatization process' (EBRD 1998b: 190). 'However, existing ownership structures are changing slowly, with some consolidation of ownership through takeovers and mergers' (EBRD 1999b: 267).

5 'Priority was given to the management and employees, who selected the transformation method … Unlike some Central and Eastern European countries (e.g. Hungary), Slovenia has been much more reluctant to allow foreign ownership and since "real" ownership changes have not been substantial insider-owners are still in the majority … The privatization of the Slovene former "socially-owned" enterprises did not generally bring new and different managers … Managers in the former "socially-owned" enterprises … remain a dominant force' (Bojnec 1999: 90–1). 'The majority of employment is still in "socially-owned" enterprises, while the majority of gross profits and total revenues is generated by private enterprises and those with mixed ownership; this implies that private enterprises are more efficient than "socially-owned" enterprises' (p. 71).

6 '[A] challenge … will be to keep crony politics in check. In recent years a string of high-profile public officials have become directors of companies

they helped to privatize. Now there is a growing sense of the coalition parties focusing more on dividing the spoils than on governing' (Business Central Europe 1997: 30).

The volume of direct foreign investment has been relatively low. (See Table 4.2.) But obstacles are gradually being removed.

Foreigners cannot own land (EBRD 1996b: 176). The constitution did not allow the sale of land to foreigners (*FT*, 6 April 1995, p. 35). This was the case until 14 July 1997. 'A widespread fear of selling out to foreigners continues to deter foreign investment' (Kevin Done, *FT*, Survey, 18 May 1998, p. iii).

Under the February 1999 reciprocity law, EU nationals who have permanent residence in Slovenia for at least three years may now purchase Slovene property (EBRD 1999b: 267).

The Federal Republic of Yugoslavia: Montenegro

In 1989, poor and mountainous Montenegro (the name means 'black mountain') constituted 5 per cent of the area of the former Yugoslavia but contributed only 2 per cent of its GDP. Its index of *per capita* income was 73 (compared with a Yugoslav average of 100). Its 0.7 million accounted for 3 per cent of the Yugoslav total and comprised 69 per cent Montenegrins, 13 per cent Moslems and 6 per cent Albanians. (The 1991 census gave a population of 616,327, of which Montenegrins accounted for 61.8 per cent, Slav Moslems 14.6 per cent, Serbs 9.3 per cent and Albanians 6.6 per cent: *EEN*, 1995, vol. 9, no. 10, p. 4.)

What has distinguished Montenegrin politics is the growing estrangement between it and Serbia after agreeing to stay united as the former Yugoslavia disintegrated. A referendum held on 1 March 1992 attracted a turnout of 66 per cent, and 96 per cent voted to remain part of Yugoslavia. On 27 April 1992 Serbia and Montenegro declared a new Federal Republic of Yugoslavia, with 44 per cent of the area and 39 per cent of the population of the old one. (Montenegro accounts for only about 5 per cent of the population, GNP and assets of the Federal Republic of Yugoslavia: *The Economist*, 23 July 1994, p. 42.) The December 1990 election had produced a win for the Communist Party, which became known as the Democratic Party of Socialists in June 1991. The then president was Momir Bulatovic. Montenegro supported Serbia as the threat of disintegration grew.

Montenegrin president Milo Djukanovic is facing severe constraints on his room to manoeuvre as regards sovereignty:

1   The extent of pro-Serb feeling that still exists within Montenegro.

> A referendum held in the early 1990s, when other Yugoslav republics voted to secede from the federation, showed overwhelming support for continued union. But a poll taken several weeks ago found the population deeply divided, with about 30 per cent favouring each side and the

remainder undecided or uninterested. Mr Djukanovic said independence must be supported by two-thirds of the population to prevent
such a move from causing social unrest.

(*IHT*, 28 November 1998, p. 7)

'About one-third of Montenegro's 680,000 people favour retaining an
alliance with Serbia – that is they support Mr Milosevic and the Yugoslav
federation, opinion surveys show. Others want complete independence just
as firmly' (*IHT*, 25 May 2000, pp. 1, 5). 'Nearly a third of Montenegro's
population view themselves as Yugoslavs' (Irena Guzelova, *FT*, 19
September 2000, p. 10). 'Mr Djukanovic broke from Mr Milosevic in 1997
... About 35 per cent to 40 per cent of Montenegro's 650,000 people
support union with Serbia' (Steven Erlanger, *IHT*, 19 September 2000, p. 6).
'About a third of Montenegrins firmly support independence; a third want
no loosening of ties with Serbia; the remainder are in the middle' (*The
Economist*, 15 July 2000, p. 29).

On 11 June 2000 local elections were held in the capital Podgorica and
in the coastal town of Herceg Novi.

Mr Djukanovic is hoping his governing For a Better Life coalition, a
three-party alliance, will defeat the main anti-independence SNP
[Socialist People's Party] – and the pro-independence Liberal Party –
and so keep his options open on the highly contentious independence
issue.

(Irena Guzelova, *FT*, 10 June 2000, p. 6)

About one-third of the electorate live in Podgorica. The total population of Montenegro is a little over 600,000 (*FT*, 13 June 2000, p. 10). The
two local elections involve about a third of the electorate (*Independent*, 13
June 2000, p. 16).

The result reflected the political divisions in Montenegro as regards
relations with Serbia:

In Podgorica the fifty-four seats were split as follows: For a Better Life
coalition, twenty-eight (a gain of one); the pro-Milosevic Yugoslavia
Coalition, twenty-two seats (a loss of one); the Liberal Alliance, four.

In Herceg Novi the thirty-five seats were split as follows: Yugoslavia
Coalition, nineteen (a gain of six); For a Better Life coalition, fourteen;
the Liberal Alliance, two.

The result was generally greeted with relief within Montenegro and in the
West. It was felt that a more one-sided outcome would have been destabilizing.

2   The very real danger of Milosevic's Serbia using force to prevent Montenegrin independence, especially since part of the Yugoslav army remains within Montenegro (friction already being caused over, for example, border controls). 'Mr Djukanovic controls the police while Mr Milosevic controls the army. Local analysts say there may be 10,000 police and 20,000 army troops' (*FT*, 22 May 1999, p. 2). 'Mr Milosevic has as many as 20,000 soldiers posted inside Montenegro and on its borders, including paramilitary forces believed to be far better trained and equipped than Montenegro's growing police force of some 15,000' (*IHT*, 25 May 2000, p. 5).

   Vojislav Seselj (leader of the extreme right-wing Serbian Radical Party, July 1999): 'If anyone tries to secede we will use all measures to protect the integrity of the state.'

3   The West's desire to avoid boundary changes in order to avoid knock-on effects elsewhere in the Balkans. During the war in Kosovo, Nato vowed to take action against Serbia if Montenegro was threatened, but post-war Nato statements became much more cautious and vague. Djukanovic was against Serbia's use of force in Kosovo and advocated a substantial degree of autonomy for the province.

   The United States and its allies have pursued a strategy similar to the 'strategic ambiguity' that the United States employs toward China with regard to Taiwan. The West has offered Montenegro just enough support to give Milosevic pause about invading the republic, but has refrained from a blanket security guarantee that might embolden Milosevic to separate so definitely from Belgrade as to provoke a war.

   (Editorial, *Washington Post*, in *IHT*, 10 July 2000, p. 8)

For a while even President Bulatovic distanced himself from Milosevic and an attempt to declare Montenegrin independence was not out of the question. Even as late as December 1996 Bulatovic publicly criticized the rigging of local election results in Serbia.

But the battle of estrangement became increasingly taken on by the then prime minister (and future president) Milo Djukanovic: 'There is no question that Milosevic's policy is not the policy for the future of the people of Serbia and Yugoslavia ... [Milosevic is an] ... incompetent politician ... [and should be removed from] any office in Yugoslavia's political life' (February 1997).

   I believe that Yugoslavia ... should be a country of deep reforms, a developed democracy, and integrated in the world economy ... President Bulatovic feels that we do not have the right to show much initiative, and that we should have great respect for Slobodan Milosevic. However, a passive stance such as this will only lead to an unconditional acceptance of Yugoslavia the way Mr Milosevic and Serbia see it ... Not only can

Montenegro be an equal member of the federation, but thanks to its reformist ideas it can also become the leader of the federation.

(June 1997)

Bulatovic had left the Democratic Party of Socialists in spring 1997 and taken seventeen MPs, forming a separate parliamentary faction. Djukanovic narrowly won the rerun presidential election held on 19 October 1997. Bulatovic, whose term as president was to expire on 15 January 1998, disputed the result, accusing Djukanovic of changing electoral lists and being involved in cigarette smuggling. In return, Djukanovic accused Bulatovic of embezzlement. Demonstrations followed. On 21 April 1998 Bulatovic presided over the inauguration of the new Socialist People's Party of Montenegro formed out of the pro-Bulatovic wing of the Democratic Party of Socialists.

On 18 May 1998 Yugoslav prime minister Radoje Kontic (a Montenegrin) was dismissed after a vote of no confidence had been passed in both federal houses of parliament. 'Formally, Mr Kontic was accused of incompetence in running the country's economy. But Mr Djukanovic said Mr Kontic was punished for refusing to impose a state of emergency in Montenegro when Mr Bulatovic lost presidential elections there in October' (*IHT*, 19 May 1998, p. 6). The Montenegrin parliament deemed the removal of Kontic to be illegal. The following day Montenegro's parliament voted not to recognize the new Yugoslav government headed by prime minister Momir Bulatovic.

In the general election of 31 May 1998, Djukanovic's coalition To Live Better won a more convincing victory than generally expected. The coalition (comprising the Democratic Party of Socialists, the Social Democratic Party and the People's Party) could also rely on the support of the Liberal Alliance of Montenegro and the ethnic Albanian MPs.

Economic links have been continually weakened. In July 1998, for example, the Montenegrin government unilaterally issued its own export and import licences. Transfers of tax revenue to the federal government have been halted. (See the section on the economy, below.)

Talks began on 14 July 1999 between Montenegro and Serbia (at the former's request) on redefining their relationship. Djukanovic: 'I want first of all to see Montenegro as a democratic country, economically developed and integrated into Europe. If Montenegro can achieve this in its present status as a member of the Yugoslav federation then that is good. If that should prove impossible, however, then the issue of independence will be imposed as an inevitable alternative' (*IHT*, 15 July 1999, p. 6). The talks were not successful, Montenegro demanding a very loose confederation (with control exercised, for example, over its own army and foreign policy).

The Yugoslav government never answered a Montenegrin proposal last August [1999] to restructure the constitutional relationship between the two republics. Mr Djukanovic had promised to hold a referendum on independence if the proposal was not answered in six weeks, but now, nine months later, he says there is no hurry.

(*IHT*, 25 May 2000, pp. 1, 5)

Measures include a new pro-Belgrade media offensive in the republic and the setting up of a special forces unit ... A pro-Serbian television station loyal to the United Yugoslav Left, the party of Mr Milosevic's wife, Mirjana Markovic, has begun broadcasting Belgrade's propaganda using military transmitters. A paramilitary unit has also been set up within the Yugoslav army in Montenegro. The Seventh Military Police battalion is made up of pro-Milosevic Montenegrins, local sources say, and their numbers have been increased from 400 to 900 trained saboteurs and special forces.

(*Telegraph*, 7 March 2000, p. 23)

President Milo Djukanovic ... accused Mr Milosevic of recruiting a special army battalion to be used to overthrow the government of Montenegro ... Last weekend [25–6 March], under pressure from Belgrade, Mr Djukanovic said, his government agreed to allow Yugoslav army troops to join Montenegrin police at border posts facing Albania and ... Kosovo ... Montenegro has no security or economic guarantees from the West ... Mr Djukanovic said he opposed the creation of a special military police unit within the Yugoslav Second Army based in Podgorica and numbering about 1,000 men, Montenegrins led by Serbs who are loyal to Mr Milosevic. 'They are in fact a paramilitary unit and their party association is unanimous,' he said. 'They are devoted to Mr Milosevic. Over 50 per cent of them have criminal records. They are not being retained to protect the country but to overthrow the government.'

(*IHT*, 29 March 2000, p. 6)

The Montenegrin government, parliament and president rejected the federal constitutional changes of July 2000. President Milo Djukanovic said that Montenegro would not take part in the federal elections (later set for 24 September 2000). On 6 July 2000 both houses of the Yugoslav parliament approved two constitutional changes, requiring the direct election through a popular ballot of the Yugoslav president and the upper house of parliament. They also allow two four-year terms for the president and raise the threshold for impeachment.

The effect will be to give Mr Milosevic a very good chance of remaining in power past July of next year [2000], when his current one-year term expires. Until now the federal president was elected by both houses of the federal parliament and could only serve one four-year term, while the upper house of the federal parliament was itself elected by the republic parliaments. The changes also put the federal government in charge of organizing elections, instead of the two republics, Serbia and Montenegro.

(Steven Erlanger, *IHT*, 7 July 2000, pp. 1, 8)

'The upper chamber has, until now, given both republics in the federation equal weight ... The move to elect deputies directly annuls the balance stipulated in the 1992 constitution' (*Independent*, 7 July 2000, p. 13). 'Henceforth it [Montenegro] will have no more weight than its share of Yugoslavia's population – about 7 per cent' (*The Economist*, 15 July 2000, p. 45). 'The new election rules, intended to put into effect constitutional changes pushed through this month [July], were overwhelmingly adopted [on 24 July] by both houses of the Federal Assembly' (*IHT*, 25 July 2000, p. 2). 'On Monday [24 July] the Yugoslav parliament went ahead with the adoption of new electoral laws allowing candidates to be elected by a simple majority' (*Independent*, 28 July 2000, p. 13).

On 8 July 2000 the chairman of the supreme court declared that Yugoslavia no longer existed. On 10 August the government resolved unilaterally to take over federal insurance companies in Montenegro (*EEN*, 2000, vol. 12, no. 24, p. 5).

In the 22 April 2001 general election, pro-independence parties won a much slimmer majority of seats than expected.

There were heavy falls in GDP in the Federal Republic of Yugoslavia between 1990 and 1993. (See Table 5.2, p. 409) But the economy grew in 1994. The GDP growth rate fell sharply in 1998 and turned heavily negative in 1999. Positive growth returned in 2000. In 2000 the level of GDP in the Federal Republic of Yugoslavia was still only 47 per cent of the 1989 level (EBRD 2001b: 59). Table 5.2 shows the conquering of hyperinflation, although inflation began to rise again in 1998. (See Serbia for details.)

Montenegro has obviously been dragged down by its association with Serbia. 'Since the introduction of UN sanctions, local industry has either closed or cut production to 20 per cent or less of capacity ... Unemployment is high but hard to quantify (well over 15 per cent)' (*EEN*, 15 March 1995, vol. 9, no. 6, p. 3).

But its increasing political estrangement from Serbia and its anti-war stance over Kosovo brought rewards in the form of lighter Nato bombing and partial exclusion from international economic sanctions.

Montenegro zoomed ahead of Serbia in the Milosevic era as regards privatization. 'Montenegro has privatized 90 per cent of industry, whereas in Serbia industry remains 90 per cent state-owned' (*EEN*, 15 March 1996, vol. 10, no. 4, p. 4). The process of privatization is well under way (*FT*, Survey, 27 January 1998, p. 14). The first phase of privatization is now all but complete (*Business Central Europe*, February 1998, p. 25).

A new privatization plan in Montenegro was approved in 1998 and led to the establishment of a privatization council. The plan, which has yet to be implemented, targets about 300 enterprises, most of which will be privatized either by a mass voucher scheme or by international tender.

(EBRD 2000b: 9)

'Montenegro has had a privatization plan since 1998, but implementation is slow' (EBRD 2001a: 62). 'But the recent political changes ... are giving a new impetus to the process' (p. 28). 'Privatization in Montenegro has been more advanced than that in Serbia, although progress has slowed down in recent years. The government plans to accelerate the process' (EBRD 2001b: 143). In mid-2000 the private sector's share of (Yugoslav) GDP was roughly 40 per cent (p. 144).

> Aluminium and tourism are the mainstays of the ... economy ... High taxes on legal employment have distorted competition, pushing more than 40 per cent of the economy into the shadows, and encouraged illegal and criminal activities, such as smuggling cars and cigarettes in response to trade sanctions on Yugoslavia ... Thus far the only big privatization by a foreign strategic investor was the purchase of Niksic brewery by Interbrew of Belgium in 1997. The pace is about to quicken, however.
>
> (*FT*, Survey, 10 July 2001, pp. 14–15)

Privatization, however, has not been without criticism. There have, for example, been allegations of cronyism. (See, for instance, *FT*, 8 December 1998, p. 2.)

Estrangement has also come in other forms. On 2 November 1999 Montenegro decided to make the DM legal tender alongside the dinar. Prime minister Filip Vujanovic: 'I believe this mechanism will protect us from [Belgrade's] destructive monetary policy which is threatening to turn into chaos.' Montenegro then launched its new currency, the marka. It was to trade alongside the DM at par. A currency board (governed by one Montenegrin and four other nationals from the G7 countries) has been introduced.

'Montenegro abolished the Yugoslav dinar in November 2000, leaving the DM (Euro) as the sole legal tender in the republic' (EBRD 2001b: 20).

> The prices of staple consumer goods, i.e. bread and milk, were partially liberalized over the past year. Both bread and milk increased in price by nearly 60 per cent in January [2001] and a further 100 per cent in August. Post and telecommunications charges were raised by nearly 100 per cent in June 2001. Further liberalization is planned for 2001 on controlled prices of items such as transportation, telecommunications and municipal services.
>
> (p. 142)

'The Montenegrin government has prepared a tax action plan' (p. 142).

> The Yugoslav national bank in Belgrade has hit back by blocking all payments between the two republics. Some 18,000 pensioners living in Montenegro who get their pensions from Belgrade have had their payments blocked; 8,000 military employees and 2,000 civil servants are in the same boat. To make matters worse, Serb police this week stopped dozens of

trucks with fresh food from crossing into Montenegro ... Montenegrin businessmen owed money by firms on either side of the border have no way of getting it back.

(*The Economist*, 4 December 1999, pp. 48, 51)

Serbia has imposed a full economic blockade on Montenegro ... The embargo, which local newspapers said came into effect at the weekend [4–5 March], will further tighten the economic noose on Montenegro, which traditionally relies heavily on Serbian exports ... Since Serbia began blocking wheat exports last year [1999] the Montenegrin government has been forced to import from Slovenia and Croatia, which are considerably more expensive.

(*Telegraph*, 7 March 2000, p. 23)

'Serbia ... largely sealed the border between the republics this month [March], preventing any trade between Serbia and Montenegro' (*IHT*, 18 March 2000, p. 4).

'Yugoslavia's newly democratic government has already abolished Milosevic-era trade barriers against Montenegro' (*Business Central Europe*, June 2001, p. 42).

Chris Patten, the EU commissioner for external relations, became the first Western politician to visit ... [Montenegro] since the Kosovo conflict ... Mr Patten ... promised yesterday [10 March] to boost planned help of Euro 60 million by a further Euro 5 million to fund infrastructure projects ... As part of Yugoslavia, Montenegro cannot receive significant aid from most international institutions. Mr Patten's Euro 5 million package will avoid being channelled through the government by going to specific projects, including a bridge at Mora and a road linking the capital with its airport.

(*Independent*, 11 March 2000, p. 14)

On 8 May 2000 EU finance ministers decided to provide Euro 20 million of special assistance, the money being allocated before by-elections in two Montenegrin cities on 11 June (*FT*, 9 May 2000, p. 10).

European foreign ministers ... approved [on 18 September 2000] an EU package granting duty-free access to 95 per cent of imports from Albania, Bosnia, Croatia, Macedonia and Montenegro ... The package includes abolition of tariffs on most industrial and farm products to the EU. However, some limits remain on exports of fish products and wine.

(*FT*, 19 September 2000, p. 10)

'The EU agreed to ... allow Croatia, Bosnia and Albania to export 95 per cent of their industrial and agricultural products to EU countries duty free. Montenegro will be allowed to export aluminium' (*The Times*, 19 September 2000, p. 14).

'Over the last three years the EU and USA delivered DM 450 million in aid, with a further DM 280 million pledged for this year [2001]' (*FT*, Survey, 10 July 2001, p. 13).

The Federal Republic of Yugoslavia: Serbia

Background

The situation in 1989 was as follows: area 34.5 per cent of the former Yugoslavia; the population of 10 million (41 per cent of the Yugoslav total) comprised 67 per cent Serbs, 13 per cent Albanians and 4 per cent Hungarians; Serbia contributed 35 per cent of Yugoslav GNP; index of *per capita* income 85 (Yugoslav average = 100).

Political developments prior to Dayton

In July 1990 the Serbian League of Communists and the Socialist Alliance merged to form the Serbian Socialist Party (SSP), with Slobodan Milosevic appointed chairman. Milosevic was born in Serbia, but is of Montenegrin descent. (He was born in 1941 of mixed Montenegrin and Serbian parentage: *EEN*, 1997, vol. 11, no. 1, p. 3.) He convincingly won the December 1990 Serbian presidential election with 65 per cent of the vote. Vuk Draskovic of the Party for Serbian Renewal came an unexpectedly poor second, with only 16 per cent. The SSP convincingly won the December 1990 Serbian parliamentary election on a platform of Serbian nationalism, a strong federation and promises of economic security (the party being lukewarm on economic reform in general). On 27 April 1992 Serbia and Montenegro declared a new Federal Republic of Yugoslavia. The 31 May 1992 general election in the new Yugoslavia was formally boycotted by the Serbian opposition and by the ethnic Albanians of Kosovo. Most opposition politicians, perhaps not surprisingly, curried nationalist favour while ethnic Serbs were fighting in other parts of the former Yugoslavia.

Milosevic comfortably won the Serbian presidential election of 20 December 1992. But he could not be elected for a third term as Serbian president unless the constitution was changed. (In fact, he subsequently became Yugoslav president.) In the Serbian parliamentary election the SSP led by Milosevic remained the largest party in the 250-seat Serbian National Assembly with 101 seats. The extreme nationalist Serbian Radical Party led by Vojislav Seselj made great strides to come second with seventy-four seats. The DEPOS (Democratic Movement of Serbia) opposition alliance won a disappointing forty-nine seats, with other parties as follows: Democratic Union of Hungarians in Vojvodina, nine; Democratic Party, seven; Citizens of Kosov-Methija, five. The Albanians in Kosovo boycotted the election as did most Moslems in the Sanjak (which straddles Serbia and Montenegro). In the words of the CSCE observers in Serbia, 'the electoral process was seriously flawed'.

The general election did take place on schedule, on 19 December 1993, with some reruns on 26 December owing to irregularities. All parties played the nationalist tune and played on the collective paranoia of the whole world seeming to be against Serbia. Draskovic openly advocated a 'Greater Serbia' and even criticized Milosevic for supporting the Owen–Stoltenberg proposals. The Socialist Party won 123 seats, just three short of an absolute majority. DEPOS won forty-five seats and the Serbian Radical Party thirty-nine. The Serbian Unity Party (founded on 3 November 1993 by Zeljko Raznatovic, also known as 'Arkan') did surprisingly poorly, winning only one seat. (Six of the forty-five DEPOS MPs went over to Milosevic soon after the election: *The Economist*, 23 July 1994, p. 42.)

Post-Dayton Serbia

On 7 August 1996 Presidents Milosevic and Tudjman met in Greece and agreed to establish diplomatic relations by the end of the month. (This actually occurred on 9 September 1996.) The statement talked of them being 'ready to proceed to full normalization'.

On 1 October 1996 the UN Security Council voted fifteen to nil to lift trade, travel and transportation sanctions permanently. This was in line with the Dayton accords, which made the lifting automatic ten days after declaring 'free and fair' elections. But the so-called 'outer wall' of sanctions (admittance to international institutions such as the UN, the IMF and the World Bank) were to remain until other conditions were met, such as compliance with the war crimes tribunal, resolution of the Kosovo problem and resolution of the debt/assets problem with the other countries of the former Yugoslavia.

On 3 October 1996 Milosevic and President Izetbegovic of Bosnia-Hercegovina met in Paris and pledged to establish full diplomatic relations.

Yugoslav (federal) elections were held on 3 November 1996. The federal parliament (Chamber of Citizens) has 138 seats. Serbia is allocated 108 seats and Montenegro thirty seats. There were only a few foreign observers (*FT*, 5 November 1996, p. 2). 'Though monitoring of the elections was wholly inadequate, there was no major fraud, certainly not enough significantly to have changed the results' (*EEN*, 1996, vol. 10, no. 22, p. 3).

The SSP (whose president is Slobodan Milosevic), the Yugoslav United Left (jointly led by Mirjana Markovic, Milosevic's wife) and the New Democracy Party won a total of sixty-four seats.

Zajedno ('Together') was an alliance between the Serbian Renewal Movement (led by Vuk Draskovic), the Democratic Party of Serbia (led by Zoran Djindjic), the Democratic Party (led by Vojislav Kostunica) and the Civic Alliance of Serbia (led by Vesna Pesic). Despite the resignation (on health grounds) of Dragoslav Avramovic as coalition leader on 9 October 1996, the leaders 'say that they will stick to Avramovic's liberal economic programme entailing privatization, an open economy and the reestablishment of relations with the international financial community' (*EEN*, 1996, vol. 10, no. 21, p. 2). 'A disparate grouping of liberals and Serb nationalists who freely admit entering a

temporary marriage of convenience in an attempt to break the left-wing monolith' (Julian Borger, *Guardian*, 2 November 1996, p. 17). Zajedno won twenty-two
seats.

Zoran Djindjic has shifted position many times. He was a student anarchist in
the 1970s, an anti-nationalist in the 1980s and a Serb nationalist as recently as
September 1996. He supported Karadzic during the war (John Pomfret, *IHT*, 31
December 1996, p. 2).

Vesna Pesic always opposed the ethnic wars (*Independent*, 6 December 1996, p.
16). She said:

> Only complete freedom of expression and legal equality of all political
> factions can enable solutions to be established which will not be questioned
> afterwards, a crucial question for the Balkans. This is especially true for
> Kosovo, which is tearing Serbia apart from within. Traumas and new poten-
> tial conflicts can only be avoided by establishing a state of law and respect
> for basic human rights – in other words, democracy.
>
> (*Guardian*, 1 January 1997, p. 9)

The second round of the local elections was held on 17 November 1996, the
first having been held on 3 November. The Zajedno alliance claimed to have
won elections in fifteen of the eighteen largest cities or towns in Serbia, including
Belgrade (the result in the capital being initially accepted by the electoral
commission). But the electoral commission or local courts began to declare
results invalid. (Zajedno victories were reversed in all but one city: *IHT*, 6
December 1996, p. 9.) The annulments led to massive demonstrations by
supporters of opposition parties and by students (with their chants including 'red
bandits'). The largest number of demonstrators in Belgrade at one time may
have been as high as 250,000 and in Nis up to 40,000. (Note that daily separate
demonstrations were typically being held by students and Zajedno supporters,
the former being the first to take place.)

On 11 December 1996 an organized group of workers joined the demonstrations for the first time. Workers downed tools in six factories in Belgrade, one in
Nis and one in Mladenovac (*IHT*, 12 December 1996, p. 9).

On 2 January 1997 an emergency meeting of the council of the Serbian
Orthodox Church issued the following statement (signed by, among others,
Patriarch Pavle):

> He [Milosevic] has already set us against the whole world and now wants to
> pit us against each other and trigger bloodshed just to preserve power. The
> Serbian Orthodox Church strongly condemns the falsifying of people's
> votes, the stifling of political and religious freedoms, and especially the
> beating up and murder of people on the streets.

The statement calls on the government to 'respect the results' of the local
elections held on 17 November. 'This is the only way of restoring our people's

faith in a peaceful and better future.' The statement accuses the regime ('Communist, Godless and Satanic') of 'bringing the country and the nation to complete collapse and making people beggars', and of 'betraying' the Serbs of the Krajina and Bosnia.

> The stinging rebuke by the Orthodox bishops contrasted with a generally passive and even approving stance by the Church toward the Milosevic government in the past, and with the Church's failure to condemn the three-and-a-half-year war in Bosnia-Hercegovina … The Church … has given tacit support to the political aims of both the Krajina and the Bosnian Serbs.
>
> (Michael Dobbs, *IHT*, 3 January 1997, p. 1)

On 4 February 1997, Milosevic wrote to prime minister Mirko Marjanovic:

> In keeping with its constitutional competence, I propose that the Serbian government submit to parliament a draft emergency law which will proclaim as final, results of a part of local elections in Serbia in keeping with the findings of the OSCE mission. I wish to stress that the state interest of improving relations of our country with the OSCE and the international community far exceeds the importance of any number of council seats in a handful of towns. I believe that the election disputes … especially in Belgrade … have inflicted great damage on our country at the internal and international level and that this is the final moment for the problem to be resolved in the highest institutions of our republic, the government and the national assembly.

On 15 February 1997, Zajedno leaders called for a halt to demonstrations, but threatened to resume them if state controls on the media were not relaxed by 9 March 1997. Zoran Djindjic was elected mayor of Belgrade on 21 February. On 7 March the rector of Belgrade University offered his resignation to the university council. Students ended their demonstrations.

On 11 April 1997 a gunman killed Radovan Stojicic in a restaurant. (Stojicic was deputy interior minister and head of Milosevic's security apparatus.)

On 15 July 1997 Milosevic was elected president of the Federal Republic of Yugoslavia for (one only) four-year term. He ran unopposed, the lower house of the federal parliament voting eighty-eight for and ten against and the upper house voting twenty-nine for and two against. On 23 July he was sworn in as federal president and stepped down as Serbian president.

Parliamentary and presidential elections were held on 20–1 September 1997. The elections were boycotted by the Democratic Party of Serbia (led by Zoran Djindjic) and the Civic Alliance of Serbia (led by Vesna Pesic). The split with Draskovic widened since he contested the election. There are 250 seats in parliament. The three-party ruling coalition, including the Yugoslav United Left led by Mira Markovic (Milosevic's wife) won 110 seats, thus losing its majority in parliament. The neo-fascist Radical Party, led by Vojislav Seselj and advocating a 'Greater Serbia', saw a big increase in their seats to eighty-two. The Serbian Renewal Party, led by Vuk Draskovic, won forty-five seats. Five smaller parties won thirteen seats. OSCE observers talked of a 'climate of mistrust' and of their 'serious concerns'. The 'process leading to the election was flawed', although 'technical' polling on election day was lawful in most places. There were cases where ballot papers were not numbered and there was bias in the media. In its formal report OSCE concluded that the elections were 'fundamentally flawed', with widespread potential for vote-rigging and bias in the state media in favour of the governing Socialists (*IHT*, 10 December 1997, p 7).

On 30 September 1997, in a vote inspired by Vuk Draskovic's Serbian Renewal Movement, Zoran Djindjic was voted out of office as mayor of Belgrade by the city assembly. (A number of demonstrations followed but these were easily controlled by the riot police.)

On 24 October 1997 Zoran Todorovic was assassinated. '[He was] the third and highest-ranking member of Mr Milosevic's circle to be shot fatally this year … Opposition politicians were quick to seize on the killing as a sign of the links between political power and crime in Yugoslavia.' Todorovic was director of Beopetrol (which has a virtual monopoly on oil imports) and secretary-general of Mira Markovic's Yugoslav United Left (*IHT*, 25 October 1997, p. 2).

On 24 March 1998 the Radical Party joined the Socialist Party and the Yugoslav United Left in a coalition government. Vojislav Seselj became one of five deputy prime ministers. The coalition had 187 of the 250 deputies.

Kosovo: the road to war

It is unfortunate for the ethnic Albanian majority that Serbs claim Kosovo to be the 'cradle' and spiritual centre of Serbian Orthodox civilization before the Turkish conquest. The Ottomans defeated the Serbs at the Battle of Kosovo Polje in 1389.

Kosovo was the poorest area in the former Yugoslavia. Before the war Kosovo's population was around the 2 million mark and, owing to rapid population growth and a net outflow of Serbs, over 90 per cent Albanian. There was Albanian agitation for autonomy in the late 1960s and for republican status after the death of Tito in May 1980. In March 1989 Kosovo's autonomy was reduced, in March 1990 Serbia took control of the police and on 5 July 1990 Serbia dissolved Kosovo's government and parliament (in response to an earlier statement of Albanian deputies, which declared 'an independent and equal union within the Yugoslav federation with the same contractual status as the other republics'). On 28 September 1990 Serbia promulgated a new republican constitution, which annulled the status of both Kosovo and Vojvodina under the 1974 federal constitution (which was not itself altered).

Compared with the wars in Bosnia and Croatia, Kosovo escaped relatively unscathed for a long time. 'Some 150 have died in ethnic violence' (*FT*, 3 September 1996, p. 2). But the situation deteriorated over time. On 25

December 1992 former US president George Bush wrote to Milosevic and the chief of staff of the Yugoslav army in these terms: 'In the event of conflict in Kosovo caused by Serbian action, the United States will be prepared to employ military force against the Serbs in Kosovo and in Serbia proper.' On 24 November 1993 the International Helsinki Federation for Human Rights (IHF) published a worrying report entitled *From Autonomy to Colonization: Human Rights Violations in Kosovo 1989–1993*.

> The methods of harassment range from verbal insults and meaningless identity checks in the street to arbitrary detention and torture or ill-treat-ment – not infrequently with fatal consequences, including death – and summary shootings of demonstrators or killing of unarmed individuals ... The region has been placed under virtual colonial control which has resulted in a total marginalization of the Albanian majority in Kosovo. The entire province has been gradually Serbianized ... The IHF is deeply concerned that the Serbian oppressive policies carried out in Kosovo aim at a permanent change in the demographic structure of the region.

The Dayton accords of 1995 essentially ignored Kosovo.

> The minority Serbian population there [in Kosovo], radicalized by tense relations with the Albanian majority, invariably voted for supporters of Milosevic or other ultra-nationalist candidates. With little backing for more moderate Serbian opposition parties and the Albanians boycotting the polls, Kosovo regularly elected to parliament a solid bloc of pro-Milosevic candi-dates. Knowing that Kosovo provided an unfailing core of loyal parliamentary supporters, Milosevic felt little incentive to engage in serious dialogue with the Albanian political leadership on territorial compromise, short of independence.
>
> (Thomas 1998: 118)

Owing to discrimination and sackings the ethnic Albanians of Kosovo ran a 'second economy', i.e. they set up their own structures, such as education estab-lishments and a health service.

On 24 May 1992 the Albanians managed to run their own unofficial presi-dential and parliamentary elections, with Ibrahim Rugova becoming president and the Democratic League of Kosovo being the successful party. Rugova, the leader of the Democratic League of Kosovo, proposed a UN protectorate. (The then president of Albania, Sali Berisha, refrained from stirring the nationalist pot, but nevertheless expressed the opinion that Kosovo should be under UN control and declared a neutral zone.) Although a consistent believer in non-violence, Rugova's advocacy changed from greater autonomy to outright independence for Kosovo.

'He [Ibrahim Rugova] insists on Gandhiesque peaceful means ... But on the central goal he is quite unyielding: self-determination for his people, statehood for the republic [of Kosovo] which he claims already exists' (Timothy Garton Ash, *The Times*, 19 March 1997, p. 18).

Ibrahim Rugova (11 March 1998):

> I insist that the best, the optimal and most viable solution and the best for the region and the neighbouring countries – Albania, Serbia, Macedonia and the rest – would be an independent Kosovo with all guarantees for the local Serb population and Serb interests in Kosovo.
>
> (*Guardian*, 12 March 1998, p. 14)

Details were released on 20 September 1998 of an interim solution to the status of Kosovo proposed by Rugova's negotiating team. Kosovo was envisaged as 'temporarily part of Yugoslavia, as an independent entity equal to the other two republics [Serbia and Montenegro] in the federation'. Kosovo would have its own parliament, government and courts as well as its own police and an independent central bank, but would share the market and a common economy with the rest of Yugoslavia. Control of Kosovo's borders could remain in the hands of the Yugoslav army and federal customs authorities. If negotiations failed to come up with a lasting solution to Kosovo's status during a three-year interim period, Kosovo's residents would vote on the proposals in a referendum. The United States had recently released details of a proposal for a three-year interim solution restoring the autonomy enjoyed by Kosovo until 1989 (*IHT*, 21 September 1998, p. 6).

The Kosovo Liberation Army (KLA) argued that aeons of non-violence had not worked.

> The armed movement [Kosovo Liberation Army] was organized six years ago to fight for independence and closer affiliation with Albania, the guerrillas said ... The rebel group carried out its first attack in 1993, but it was not until the middle of last year [1997] that it began to mount regular and sustained assaults.
>
> (Chris Hedges, *IHT*, 3 March 1998, p. 5)

'The KLA has been active in the Kosovo region since April 1996' (Thomas 1998: 118.)

The ambushing of Serb police patrols in Kosovo on 27–8 February 1998 left four policemen dead. On 28 February 1999 up to 3,000 ethnic Albanians commemorated the anniversary of what they regard as the start of the war in Kosovo, when Serb forces attacked a car containing KLA members.

On 23 February 1998 the US special envoy to the Balkans, Robert Gelbard, described the Kosovo Liberation Army, as 'without question, a terrorist group' (*IHT*, 11 March 1998, p. 6).

'The ethnic Albanian Kosovo Liberation Army, which began as a ragtag, peasant resistance movement, has after eight months of fighting, become a high-tech, mobile guerrilla force, and come next spring [1999] it expects renewed fighting.' Adem Demaci is the KLA's general political representative (*IHT*, 2 January 1999, p. 2).

'Only a year ago the rebels [the KLA] numbered no more than 2,000, but they are now estimated to have as many as 17,000 fighters' (*IHT*, 7 June 1999, p. 7). 'The rebel group [is] said to include 10,000 hardened fighters and 30,000 irregulars who joined after being driven from their homes this spring' (*IHT*, 22 June 1999, p. 1). On 13 August 1998 the KLA named Adem Demaci as its first political representative. 'Hashim Thaci, the KLA's thirty-year-old political leader and prime minister of the provisional government, agreed at the Paris peace talks in March [1999] … said the KLA had around 20,000 armed soldiers inside Kosovo' (*FT*, 27 May 1999, p. 2). 'In Washington US officials said the KLA was growing … The KLA had grown from around 5,000 troops in March [1999] to nearly 17,000' (*FT*, 29 May 1999, p. 3). 'The rebel group [is] said to include 10,000 hardened fighters and 30,000 irregulars who joined after being driven from their homes this spring' (*IHT*, 22 June 1999, p. 1).

Refugees

Sadako Ogata, United Nations High Commissioner for Refugees:

> The refugee exodus from Kosovo constitutes one of the most deplorable episodes in modern European history. Driven from their homes, stripped of their possessions and deprived of their identity documents, the Kosovars are the victims of a shameful and systematic campaign of persecution and abuse. Using the most brutal methods imaginable to erase a population from the map, the Yugoslav authorities have acted in a way that is morally repugnant and in direct violation of international law.
>
> (*FT*, 20 April 1999, p. 18)

According to the 1991 census, the population of Kosovo was 1,956,196, of which more than 1.8 million were ethnic Albanians (*IHT*, 23 April 1999, p. 4; *FT*, 23 April 1999, p. 2).

Refugees before the Nato bombing campaign began on 24 March 1999

The following give some indication of the magnitude of refugees before the Nato bombing campaign began on 24 March 1999:

1   Since 1990 about 250,000 of Kosovo's ethnic Albanians have left. The great majority have ended up in the USA and Germany (*Independent*, 21 March 1996, p. 17). Nearly 350,000 ethnic Albanians have left (*IHT*, 24 December 1996, p. 8).
2   International observers estimate that some 150,000 people have been displaced by the fighting (*IHT*, 30 July 1998, p. 5).
3   Sadako Ogata (United Nations High Commissioner for Refugees):

My agency estimates that the conflict has driven up to a quarter of a million people out of their homes, with some 170,000 displaced within Kosovo alone. In addition to helping the displaced in Kosovo, my agency, the International Committee of the Red Cross and other aid agencies are dealing with 13,000 Kosovo refugees in Albania and another 30,000 in Montenegro. More than 10 per cent of Kosovo's population is now displaced.

(*IHT*, 17 August 1998, p. 8)

4   'The UNHCR estimates that around 80,000 people have been displaced in fighting since the first round of peace talks ended inconclusively a month ago. Over the past year about 400,000 people – more than a fifth of Kosovo's population – have fled their homes' (*FT*, 22 March 1999, p. 2).

5   'In the previous twelve months ... before 24 March 1999 ... Serb forces had driven more than 300,000 Albanians out of their homes – homes which, in many cases, they then looted and burnt. Roughly 2,000 people had been killed, some of them in massacres such as the one at Racak where forty-five civilians were murdered' (Noel Malcolm, *Telegraph*, 24 March 2000, p. 28).

Refugees after the start of the Nato bombing campaign on 24 March 1999

The start of the Nato bombing campaign on 24 March 1999 was accompanied by a sharp increase in 'ethnic cleansing' and in the number of ethnic Albanian refugees.

The number of displaced people is believed to exceed 1 million – nearly 60 per cent of the roughly 1.8 million ethnic Albanians in Kosovo (*IHT*, 7 April 1999, pp. 1, 4).

'A [British] ministry of defence official said that 1.1 million out of a total ethnic Albanian population of 1.8 million had now become refugees since the civil war began about a year ago' (*The Times*, 7 April 1999, p. 1).

The UNHCR estimates that more than 430,000 people have fled Kosovo since 24 March, with 262,000 refugees in Albania, 120,000 in Macedonia and the rest in Montenegro and elsewhere. There are 260,000 displaced people in Kosovo itself (*IHT*, 7 April 1999, p. 4).

According to the 1991 census, the population of Kosovo was 1,956,196, of which more than 1.8 million were ethnic Albanians. Since March 1998 more than 770,000 have fled or been expelled. Since 24 March 1999 the figure is 591,600. The refugees are distributed as follows: Albania, 359,000; Macedonia, 132,100; Montenegro, 68,200; Bosnia, 32,000; Croatia, 5,000; Turkey, 4,000; Bulgaria, 2,500 (*IHT*, 23 April 1999, p. 4; *FT*, 23 April 1999, p. 2.).

'The UNHCR estimates that ... the total number of refugees in Macedonia is 200,900 ... 93,370 are being put up by host families among Macedonia's 600,000 ethnic Albanians' (*FT*, 6 May 1999, p. 2).

'The UNHCR estimates that as of 5 May 1999 the number of refugees outside Kosovo stood at 700,000' (*IHT*, 7 May 1999, p. 5).

'A new US government report [made public on 10 May 1999 and entitled *Erasing History: Ethnic Cleansing in Kosovo*] ... [estimated that] ... 1.5 million [ethnic Albanians had been] displaced as of last week' (*IHT*, 12 May 1999, p. 7).

The UNHCR estimates the number of Kosovars 'internally displaced' within Yugoslavia at about 743,000, including 64,000 in Montenegro. There are also 226,300 in Macedonia and 433,400 in Albania (*Telegraph*, 25 May 1999, p. 17).

More than 981,000 ethnic Albanians have fled Kosovo since the start of the crisis some fifteen months ago, according to the UNHCR. About 782,100 left after the start of Nato air strikes on 24 March 1999 (*Telegraph*, 4 June 1999, p. 3).

The UNHCR estimates that nearly 860,000 have fled Kosovo since 24 March 1999 (*IHT*, 10 June 1999, p. 17).

'[There are] more than 780,000 [refugees] in the countries neighbouring Kosovo, with 445,000 in Albania, 250,000 in Macedonia and around 66,000 in Montenegro. A further 75,000 refugees have been evacuated from Macedonia to third countries' (*FT*, 7 June 1999, p. 2).

(One of the issues not covered by any agreement was that of ethnic Albanians from Kosovo held in Serbian jails. The lowest estimates put the number at around 1,400. Under Milosevic there were concerns that many of them were falsely accused of things as serious as terrorism and that a ransom racket may have been involved.)

Refugees after the entry of Nato troops on 12 June 1999

After the entry of Nato troops on 12 June 1999 there was a massive reverse flow of ethnic Albanians and a sharply accelerated outflow of ethnic Serbs and Gypsies.

An OSCE report details human rights abuses in Kosovo from mid-June 1999 to the end of October 1999. 'The evidence of recent violations indicates that the cycle of violence has not yet been broken'; 'The desire for revenge has created a climate in which the vast majority of human rights violations have taken place' and led to 'the assumption of collective guilt', so 'that the entire remaining Kosovo Serb population was seen as a target'. The violence is attributed to 'the intolerance that has emerged within the Kosovo Albanian community' (*IHT*, 6 November 1999, p. 4; *The Times*, 7 December 1999, p. 16; *Independent*, 7 December 1999, p. 13; *Telegraph*, 7 December 1999, p. 18; *Guardian*, 6 December 1999, p. 12).

'The UNHCR estimates that only about 100,000 Serbs remain of the province's pre-war population of 200,000' (*FT*, 28 June 1999, p. 23).

An estimated 90,000 Serbs remain in Kosovo from the pre-conflict population of about 180,000 (Bernard Kouchner, head of UNMIK, *IHT*, 27 October 1999, p. 8).

According to the UNHCR, an estimated 230,000 Serbs and other non-Albanians, including more than 40,000 Gypsies, have fled Kosovo since Nato troops entered Kosovo in June 1999. About 200,000 are now in Serbia and about 30,000 are in Montenegro. The Serbian population stood at 200,000 to

250,000 before the war. The Serbs from Kosovo have added to the sum of Serbs, now more than 700,000, forced out of their homes in the former Yugoslavia in the past decade (*IHT*, 18 February 2000, p. 7).

> Members of Mr Djindjic's Democratic Party yesterday [18 August 1999] held a protest in Belgrade recalling that 700,000 ethnic Serbs fled to Serbia from wars in Croatia and Bosnia and 140,000 from Kosovo. Half a million Serbs had left the country to live abroad in the past decade.
>
> (*FT*, 19 August 1999, p. 2)

'The United Nations refugees agency this week gave its most precise estimate this week of the number of non-Albanians who fled the province after Nato marched in last year [1999]: about 180,000 went to Serbia proper and 30,000 to Montenegro' (*The Economist*, 27 May 2000, p. 42).

'Some 100,000 of the 125,000 Roma have fled or been forced to flee by the victorious ethnic Albanians, who say the Roma collaborated with the Serbs' (*IHT*, 3 April 2000, p. 6). 'Gypsies [are] a group that was considered [by the KLA] to be in league with the Serbs during the war' (*IHT*, 19 June 1999, p. 5).

Robin Cook (British foreign secretary; 24 March 2000): 'A year ago there were 850,000 refugees driven out by Milosevic's ethnic cleansing; 800,000 of them are now back in Kosovo' (*Telegraph*, 25 March 2000, p. 17).

Ethnic Serb enclaves in Kosovo

'A pattern of protected enclaves [for Serbs], as in Orahovac, Kosovska Mitrovica and Gracanica' (*IHT*, 12 August 1999, p. 5).

> The northern Kosovo city of Mitrovica has become the most serious flash-point and Serb special agents from Belgrade have been suspected of trying to provoke clashes in a bid to permanently divide the city into Serb and Albanian enclaves and ultimately destabilize the peacekeeping effort.
>
> (*IHT*, 11 March 2000, p. 2)

> The Ibar river running through the grimy industrial city of about 100,000 separates 80,000 Albanians in the south from 10,000 Serbs in the north. Adding to the tensions is the presence of 2,000 Albanians in the north, living under great pressure from Serb extremists to leave, as 8,000 already have.
>
> (*FT*, 24 March 2000, p. 10)

> Until last year [1999] Albanians were a majority on both sides of the river [Ibar] which runs through the town [Mitrovica]. Now the north is mainly Serbian. The [recent] attacks caused around 1,500 Albanians to flee in panic ... Because the town is close to Kosovo's border with Serbia proper – with only Serbian villages in between – hard-liners ... have been hoping to

detach the northern part of the city and its hinterland from the rest of Kosovo. An alternative for them would be to create an enclave on the model of the Serb-run entity in northern Bosnia.

(*Guardian*, 21 February 2000, p. 11)

'Mitrovica is the largest Serbian enclave. Albanians ... fear that they will never control the area in and around the Trepca mine complex ... This is the richest part of Kosovo' (*IHT*, 21 February 2000, p. 8).

The Ibar river has become a virtual dividing line between Serbs in the northern fifth of Kosovo and ethnic Albanians to the south ... Mitrovica and points north are seen as a test-case because they are the only bits of Kosovo where ethnic Serbs (perhaps 50,000 of them) have stayed on in significant numbers since Nato troops took charge last June [1999], enabling the return of nearly 1 million ethnic Albanian refugees. ... At least 100,000 Serbs have been displaced since Nato's arrival ... In January [2000] some 2,500 ethnic Albanians were hanging on in the town's northern part.

(*The Economist*, 26 February 2000, p. 55)

There have been violent clashes between ethnic Albanians and Serbs and between Kfor troops and elements from both ethnic communities, with some loss of life. Mitrovica is in the French zone, but troops from other countries have helped out on occasion (although US troops have been forbidden to return to Mitrovica after clashes with Serb demonstrators in February 2000). Kfor has been largely unsuccessful to date in returning refugees to their homes in the part of the city held by the opposing ethnic group. So-called 'confidence zones' have been set up on both sides of the main bridge over the Ibar river (a bridge controlled by Kfor troops) to allow the free movement of ordinary citizens, but the city essentially remains divided.

Milosevic the survivor

The short-sighted policy of using the arch-villain Milosevic as a negotiator for other Balkan problems and of neglecting Kosovo in the 1995 Dayton accords came home with a vengeance.

On 27 May 1999 the UN's International Criminal Tribunal for the former Yugoslavia indicted Slobodan Milosevic, the first time that this has happened to a sitting head of state. The charge: 'The accused planned, instigated, ordered, committed or otherwise aided and abetted in a campaign of terror and violence directed at Kosovo Albanian citizens.' (The indictment was not without its critics, however, even among Milosevic's enemies. The argument was that it left Milosevic cornered, making him even more unwilling to give up power voluntarily. But on 28 June 2001 the new Serbian government handed over Milosevic to the tribunal in The Hague. On 9 October 2001 the tribunal formally indicted Milosevic with war crimes and crimes against humanity during the war in

Croatia. On 23 November 2001 the tribunal formally indicted him on charges relating to the war in Bosnia, including genocide.)

Milosevic survived for a long time despite opposition from many quarters.

1 There was a lack of unity among opposition parties

Zoran Djindjic and Vuk Draskovic detest one another. (On 18 January 1999 Serbian Renewal Movement chairman Vuk Draskovic was appointed Yugoslav deputy prime minister for international relations. He was dismissed on 28 April 1999 for saying that everything was negotiable except for Serbia's sovereignty over Kosovo.)

> The British foreign secretary [29 April] yesterday challenged Slobodan Milosevic to air a 'startlingly frank' interview given to the BBC by Vuk Obradovic, a former general and leader of the small opposition Social Democratic Party. The interview was censored by the Yugoslav military.
>
> (*FT*, 30 April 1999, p. 2)

> Mr Obradovic, a former general, is the president of the country's Social Democratic Party ... A BBC spokesman said that Mr Obradovic told Mr Simpson: 'President Milosevic is a problem of the democratic forces in Serbia who we are going to get rid of' ... Earlier this week Mr Obradovic gave his view of the president [Milosevic] to *The Guardian*: 'His political initiative is over ... He should leave on his own now. And if he does not, we will make him leave.'
>
> (*Guardian*, 30 April 1999, p. 3)

> Vuk Obradovic, president of the Social Democratic Party and once a rising star in the Yugoslav army ... was quoted in the Italian newspaper *La Repubblica* as saying: 'Milosevic should resign – especially because it is clear that he will fall anyway.'
>
> (*Independent*, 20 April 1999, p. 4)

On 29 June 1999 there took place the first of a series of anti-government demonstrations organized by the Alliance for Change, an umbrella group of around thirty opposition parties. Demands included the resignation of Milosevic and early elections. (On 12 June 1999 the main Serbian opposition parties, excluding Vuk Draskovic's Serbian Renewal Movement, had met in Herceg Novi in Montenegro with representatives of the ruling Montenegrin Democratic Party of Socialists to form the Alliance for Change, composed of around thirty parties and movements. The meeting was attended in part by some senior foreign emissaries, including US envoy Robert Gelbard: *EEN*, 1999, vol. 12, no. 18, p. 9.)

'The Alliance for Change ... attracted 10,000 people to a rally in the town [of Kragujevac] on Thursday [15 July]' (*Guardian*, 17 July 1999, p. 17).

On 17 July some 20,000 people in Kragujevac attended the first rally organized by Vuk Draskovic's Serbian Renewal Movement (*IHT*, 19 July 1999, p. 4).

On 24 July 1999 Vuk Draskovic spoke at a rally in Nis attended by around 25,000 people.

> This will be Mr Draskovic's last mass rally for some time, senior aides said Saturday [24 July] ... His aides say he will hold no more meetings for at least several weeks ... Mr Draskovic is concentrating instead on trying to choose a transitional government of experts agreed on by most or all opposition parties, and then trying to push Mr Milosevic to empower that government and finally to step aside after new elections ... The Alliance for Change demands Mr Milosevic's resignation first, before any transitional government.
>
> (*IHT*, 26 July 1999, p. 4)

> An independent group of experts Monday [2 August 1999] outlined a plan for the formation of a transitional government to lead Yugoslavia out of economic misery and prepare for new elections. The group called for a major rally to be held in the capital Belgrade on 19 August in support of the idea. An independent economist [Mladjan Dinkic] said the head of the Serbian Orthodox Church, Patriarch Pavle, and all opposition leaders and independent figures, including the former army chief General Momcilo Perisic, would be invited to attend ... The so-called Stability Pact for Serbia, which details a plan for an interim government, has been drafted by a still-anonymous group of prominent Serbs ... It says both the ruling parties and the opposition should agree to give up their aspirations to power for one year, when free and fair elections would be held.
>
> (*IHT*, 3 August 1999, p. 5)

> Mladjan Dinkic is the thirty-five-year-old leader of the Group 17 organization of independent Yugoslav economists and an up-and-coming politician ... The creation of a transitional government is at the heart of a new 'pact for the stability of Serbia', a document drawn up by a group of economists and academics in response to the regional stability pact unveiled by world leaders in Sarajevo ... According to the draft released yesterday [3 August], the transitional government would have a one-year mandate.
>
> (*Guardian*, 4 August 1999, p. 13)

> The head of Serbia's Orthodox Church and the country's main opposition leaders [including Zoran Djindjic and Vuk Draskovic] agreed on Monday [10 August 1999] to join a mass anti-government rally in Belgrade on 19 August ... Opposition leaders and a group of independent economists met the head of the Serbian Orthodox Church, Patriarch Pavle, and other Church dignitaries in its Belgrade seat.
>
> (*IHT*, 10 August 1999, p. 5)

'Patriarch Pavle, the church leader, met with opposition leaders Monday [9 August] and the two sides agreed to form a transitional government of experts that would prepare for elections within a year and democratic and economic reforms' (*IHT*, 11 August 1999, p. 4).

> The 19 August rally is being organized by independent economists, Mladjan Dinkic and Predag Markovic, the creators of the stability pact for Serbia ... The authors of the stability pact for Serbia and others [such as Zoran Djindjic] ... insist that Mr Milosevic must step down before any transition government can take over ... But Mr Draskovic ... is arguing for a transitional government that includes some sort of power-sharing deal with Mr Milosevic.
>
> (*IHT*, 12 August 1999, p. 5)

On 11 August 1999 the Serbian Orthodox Church, after a meeting of its highest body, the Holy Synod, called for the resignation of Yugoslav president Slobodan Milosevic and Serbian president Milan Milutinovic. There was also a call for a transitional 'government of [non-party] experts' to prepare fresh elections and democratic and economic reforms (*IHT*, 12 August 1999, p. 5).

> The leader of the largest opposition party and an influential former army general Tuesday [17 August 1999] pulled out of a major anti-Milosevic rally scheduled for Thursday [19 August]. Vuk Draskovic ... said he would not participate in the rally because of the actions and behaviour of the Alliance for Change ... Momcilo Perisic ... said he did not support a transitional government of experts, one of the aims of the rally, but early elections for a new government. That puts Mr Perisic closer to Mr Draskovic, who also favours early elections ... Mr Djindjic, the Alliance for Change generally and the Clinton administration want Mr Milosevic to resign as a first step and for him to be delivered, perhaps within six months, as a war criminal to The Hague. They want a transitional government of experts to serve for one year to prepare fresh elections. The Alliance does not call for early elections. Mr Draskovic ... has proposed either new, internationally supervised elections to replace Mr Milosevic, or a transitional government, to be negotiated with the regime, that would render Mr Milosevic a figurehead.
>
> (*IHT*, 18 August 1999, p. 2)

Vuk Draskovic unexpectedly addressed the crowd on 19 August 1999.

> Mr Draskovic ... called for elections under international supervision. Referring to Mr Milosevic's pariah status internationally, Mr Draskovic said 'Serbia is in jail.' 'We are in jail,' he said, because Serbia 'is led by those who are totally isolated by the world' ... But he also denounced other opposition parties for making 'unrealistic' plans for 'some transitional governments' that no one will recognize. Such criticism, however, was not well received.

As Mr Draskovic left the speaker's stand he was booed and jeered by many in the crowd.

(*IHT*, 20 August 1999, pp. 1, 4)

Only about 3,000 people attended a demonstration in Belgrade on 23 September 1999. Zoran Djindjic: 'If there is no support, no energy, we'll say people in Serbia do not want to go to the streets to demand their rights. We'll say we are not the people they want as leaders' (*FT*, 24 September 1999, p. 2).

On 30 September 1999 leaders of the Alliance for Change and the Serbian Renewal Movement met to try to resolve differences about early elections.

On 3 October Vuk Draskovic was involved in a car accident. A lorry swerved into three cars. He was only slightly injured, but three of his bodyguards and his brother-in-law were killed. Draskovic: 'It was an obvious assassination attempt.' (Another theory is gang warfare. Draskovic's brother-in-law was director of the board for municipal building sites in Belgrade, generally recognized as a corrupt source of rich pickings.)

Mr Draskovic was shocked by what he perceived as an assassination attempt on 3 October, when a truck swerved into his car, killing his brother-in-law, and then struck the car behind him, killing three of his bodyguards. The police have not found the truck's driver or its current owner, lending credibility to Mr Draskovic's immediate charges of an attempted political hit by the Milosevic regime.

(Steven Erlanger, *IHT*, 15 October 1999, p. 6)

(On 15 June 2000 Draskovic was shot at and slightly injured at his holiday house in Montenegro. He blamed agents sent by Milosevic.)

The opposition parties said Thursday [7 October 1999] they had agreed on the most important conditions for early elections. 'Following a constructive discussion, participants have agreed on all important issues concerning election conditions and election laws,' said a statement ... Another session would be held next week. The conditions agreed on Thursday include a proportional voting system, a revision of election lists, and the presence of domestic and foreign observers at all stages of the voting process. The statement also said the opposition would demand new electoral commission members, the replacement of a restrictive media law, and new laws governing political parties and international rules for the campaign.

(*IHT*, 8 October 1999, p. 2)

On 14 October 1999 opposition parties published a joint document specifying the conditions needed for early elections. These included a proportional voting system, revision of election lists, the presence of domestic and foreign observers, and a free media (*FT*, 15 October 1999, p. 10).

'Nightly street demonstrations ... have all but fizzled out' (*IHT*, 21 October 1999, p. 5).

Daily opposition rallies in Belgrade ended on 18 December 1999 after dwindling attendance (*EEN*, 2000, vol. 12, no. 21, p. 6). (The numbers were by then down to a few hundred.)

On 10 January 2000, after a meeting organized by the Serbian Renewal Movement, seventeen opposition parties agreed to join forces. They demanded early elections at all levels by the end of April 2000 or demonstrations would begin in March.

A peaceful anti-Milosevic demonstration actually took place in Belgrade on 14 April 2000 and attracted a larger crowd than expected (in excess of 100,000 by most estimates). The demonstration was a combined effort by opposition parties. Vuk Draskovic and Zoran Djindjic not only attended but also shook hands. The student-based organization Otpor ('Resistance'), which was formed in October 1998, also took part.

There were further demonstrations in May 2000 in protest at government seizure of opposition-controlled television and radio. Otpor was very active despite harsh measures taken against members. The movement is playing an increasingly important role given the divisions among opposition parties.

On 6 August 2000, Vuk Draskovic's Serbian Renewal Party announced that it would put forward its own presidential candidate, the mayor of Belgrade, Vojislav Mihajlovic.

> The announcement was made at the start of two days of meetings involving sixteen opposition parties to decide whether to present a united front against President Milosevic ... Other opposition parties back Vojislav Kostunica, leader of the centre-right Democratic Party of Serbia.
>
> (*IHT*, 7 August 2000, p. 6)

The following day the fifteen remaining opposition parties formally named Vojislav Kostunica, a moderate nationalist, as their presidential candidate. 'Opinion polls show that if Serbia's fractious opposition were to unite behind one candidate they could beat Milosevic' (*FT*, 7 August 2000, p. 7). 'In a recent opinion poll [Vojislav Kostunica] was backed as a united opposition candidate by 42 per cent, against 28 per cent for Mr Milosevic' (*The Times*, 7 August 2000, p. 13).

'Serbia's single largest opposition party decided Thursday [24 August 2000] to run candidates in next month's parliamentary elections in Yugoslavia, dropping a boycott threat. But the Serbian Renewal Party said it would contest the vote independently' (*IHT*, 25 August 2000, p. 7).

2 *The attitude of the Serbian Orthodox Church*

> [There was] a generally passive and even approving stance by the Church toward the Milosevic government in the past ... [There was] the Church's failure to condemn the three-and-a-half-year war in Bosnia-Hercegovina ... The Church ... has given tacit support to the political aims of both the Krajina and the Bosnian Serbs.
>
> (Michael Dobbs, *IHT*, 3 January 1997, p. 1)

But the attitude of the Church changed. On 15 June 1999 a statement was issued by the Holy Synod of the Serbian Orthodox Church:

> Every sensible person has to realise that numerous internal problems and the isolation of our country on the international scene cannot be solved or overcome with this kind of government and under the present circumstances. Faced with the tragic situation in our nation and our country we demand that the current President of the country and his government resign in the interest of the people and their salvation so that new officials acceptable at home and abroad can take responsibility for the people and their future as a national salvation government ... We also appeal to our brothers in Kosovo to stay in their homes and not to leave their relics ... [The Church is] convinced that the final justice is with our Lord and not in the hands of an instrumentalized court in The Hague.

> The church was generally associated with Serbia's expansionist wars in the nineties, but its bishops turned against the regime after the 1995 Bosnian peace deal which they saw as a sell-out ... The church is particularly associated with Kosovo; the seat of the Orthodox patriarch is in Pec and the present Patriarch, Pavle, is a former bishop of the diocese of Prizren.
>
> (Marcus Tanner, *Guardian*, 16 June 1999, p. 2)

> In the frankest admission by a senior cleric of Serb atrocities committed against Moslem Albanians, Bishop Artemije of Kosovo spoke of the 'evil' committed by Serbs. But he insisted that there was no collective guilt and reiterated the Church's demand that Yugoslav president Slobodan Milosevic resign. 'We Serbs have lived in great pain and compassion at what was happening to our Albanian neighbours. We were sorry for every innocent victim,' said Bishop Artemije in Gracanica monastery.
>
> (*FT*, 29 June 1999, p. 1)

On 11 August 1999 the Serbian Orthodox Church, after a meeting of its highest body, the Holy Synod, called for the resignation of Yugoslav president Slobodan Milosevic and Serbian president Milan Milutinovic. There was also a call for a transitional 'government of [non-party] experts' to prepare fresh elections and democratic and economic reforms (*IHT*, 12 August 1999, p. 5).

3 Milosevic clamped down on the independent media

Unexplained deaths were even more worrying.

> Unidentified gunmen on Sunday [11 April] shot and killed a well-known opposition publisher outside his apartment in Belgrade. The publisher, Slavko Curuvija, the owner of the *Dnevni Telegraf* and the news biweekly *Evropljanin*, was shot as he returned home ... In the widespread crackdown by President Slobodan Milosevic against the independent media, *Dnevni Telegraf* and *Evropljanin* were heavily fined last year [1998] for breaching Serbia's restrictive information law, passed in October [1998], and then banned. Mr Curuvija reregistered them in Montenegro ... They were printed in Croatia, but their distribution in Serbia was widely curtailed.
>
> (*IHT*, 12 April 1999, p. 8)

Milosevic used state-controlled media against opponents and clamped down on the independent media through such means as heavy fines, seizure of transmission equipment and even seizure of entire television and radio stations. Journalists were harassed, one even imprisoned on espionage grounds.

4 There were purges among the elite

> Serbia's chief of secret police [Jovica Stanisic] ... has been dismissed [28 October 1998] after losing a political struggle against hard-liners heading a campaign of internal repression ... Over the past two years [he] was widely credited with blocking hard-line factions led by Mira Markovic, wife of Mr Milosevic, and the ultra-nationalist Radical Party chief, Vojislav Seselj ... Also at risk is General Momcilo Perisic, chief of staff of the federal Yugoslav army, who last week expressed his opposition to the confrontation with Nato ... A tough new media law has led to the closure of four independent newspapers and one magazine.
>
> (*FT*, 29 October 1998, p. 2)

> The daily *Vijesti*, published in Montenegro ... linked the dismissal [of Jovica Stanisic, head of the public and state security department] and that of Milorad Vucelic, vice-president of Serbia's ruling Socialist Party, with the Kosovo issue ... Belgrade commentators saw the security chief as the leading pragmatist in Mr Milosevic's entourage and a man who in the past had shown resistance to President Milosevic's authoritarian excesses on the political front. There is speculation that he objected to the rise of extremist Serbian nationalist leaders now allied with Mr Milosevic. The Yugoslav president has been using the right this month to spearhead his drive against dissent in Serbia – and not only in the independent media but also at

Belgrade University … So far this month the government has shut down three newspapers.

(*Guardian*, 29 October 1998, p. 17)

On 24 November 1998 General Momcilo Perisic was dismissed as head of the armed forces. He was replaced by General Dragoljub Ojdanovic.

President Slobodan Milosevic has dismissed the chief of the army, General Momcilo Perisic, in what observers said was a continuing purge of the military … Senior army officers are reported to be unhappy with Milosevic's having agreed to Nato's surveillance of Kosovo. General Perisic's dismissal follows the dismissal of the Yugoslav air force commander, General Ljubisa Velickovic, on 30 October. Three days earlier the chief of Serbia's security service, Jovica Stanisic, had been dismissed.

(*IHT*, 26 November 1998, p. 5)

Slobodan Milosevic of Yugoslavia has conducted an extraordinary purge of his innermost circle, dismissing the leaders of the army, the air force and the intelligence service, as well as one of his most trusted political commissars … The purge, conducted in the wake of Mr Milosevic's agreement 13 October to pull troops out of Kosovo, culminated last week with the dismissal of Momcilo Perisic, the long-serving army chief of staff and an architect of the war in Bosnia … The purges began shortly after the departure from Belgrade of the US envoy, Richard Holbrooke, who persuaded Mr Milosevic to agree to international observers in Kosovo, and were preceded by the closing of independent newspapers and academic dismissals at Belgrade University. The removal of General Perisic on Tuesday [24 November] was perhaps the least surprising. He publicly criticized Mr Milosevic last month [October] for allowing what is left of Yugoslavia to become a pariah state … General Perisic, who led the Yugoslav National Army during the atrocities in Bosnia, was reported to have opposed the use of soldiers against ethnic Albanian citizens in Kosovo during the summer offensive there.

(Jane Perlez, *IHT*, 30 November 1998, p. 1)

The first senior officer to be removed was Jovica Stanisic, the head of state security services. Along with Mr Stanisic, a dozen top operational officers of the security service were forced into retirement or removed. Mr Milosevic next dismissed Milorad Vucelic, the deputy leader of Mr Milosevic's Socialist Party, who served as the president's political disciplinarian. The head of the air force, General Ljubisa Velickovic, who protested against Mr Milosevic's agreement to allow Nato surveillance flights over Kosovo, was also removed.

Milosevic has managed to manipulate the currency so that he can pay about three-quarters of the annual state pensions due and keep the police and army paid. With help from Russia, which provides natural gas even though Yugoslavia is late in its payments, and with deals like a recent oil purchase from Libya, Mr Milosevic is able to provide energy for the long-suffering people.

(Jane Perlez, *IHT*, 30 November 1998, p. 9)

'Milosevic yesterday [23 March] sacked the second most powerful figure in the Yugoslav army, General Alexander Dimitrijevic, the head of military security' (*FT*, 24 March 1999, p. 1).

On 15 January 2000 Zeljko Raznatovic (known as Arkan) was shot dead in Belgrade's Intercontinental Hotel. A friend and a bodyguard were also killed. Intense speculation surrounded the assassination, e.g. a gangland killing or one ordered by Milosevic to ensure that Arkan would never be able to reveal what he knew about Milosevic's role in the Balkan wars. On 7 February 2000 Yugoslav defence minister Pavle Bulatovic was shot dead in a Belgrade restaurant. He was a Montenegrin and represented the pro-Serbia Democratic Party of Socialists in Montenegro. There was intense speculation as to the likely motive.

5 There were popular demonstrations

In May 1999 there were reports of anti-Milosevic demonstrations in the Serbian towns of Krusevac and Aleksandrovac, mainly by women and children related to reservists. Those taking part numbered around 3,000 and 1,000 respectively. Further demonstrations took place in these towns and others (such as Pancevo, Cacak and Raska). Reservists themselves also took part in the demonstrations.

6 Milosevic contrived constitutional changes to prolong his hold on power

On 6 July 2000 both houses of the Yugoslav parliament approved two constitutional changes, requiring the direct election through a popular ballot of the Yugoslav president and the upper house of parliament. They also allowed two four-year terms for the president and raised the threshold for impeachment.

> The effect will be to give Mr Milosevic a very good chance of remaining in power past July of next year [2000], when his current one-year term expires. Until now the federal president was elected by both houses of the federal parliament and could only serve one four-year term, while the upper house of the federal parliament was itself elected by the republic parliaments. The changes also put the federal government in charge of organizing elections, instead of the two republics, Serbia and Montenegro.
>
> (*IHT*, 7 July 2000, pp. 1, 8)

'The upper chamber has, until now, given both republics in the federation equal weight ... The move to elect deputies directly annuls the balance stipulated in the 1992 constitution' (*Independent*, 7 July 2000, p. 13). 'Henceforth it

[Montenegro] will have no more weight than its share of Yugoslavia's population – about 7 per cent' (*The Economist*, 15 July 2000, p. 45). 'The changes reduced the role of Montenegro from that of an equal partner in the federation, with a 50 per cent say in the House of Republics, to a minor partner with a symbolic 6.5 per cent say corresponding to its share of the electorate' (*IHT*, 15 August 2000, p. 8). 'The new election rules, intended to put into effect constitutional changes pushed through this month [July], were overwhelmingly adopted [on 24 July] by both houses of the Federal Assembly' (*IHT*, 25 July 2000, p. 2). 'Under the new rules ... Mr Milosevic can win by gaining a simple majority of votes cast, no matter how low the turnout ... Appointees [of Mr Milosevic] will have complete control of the procedures for both presidential and municipal elections to be held the same day' (*IHT*, 31 July 2000, p. 9). 'On Monday [24 July] the Yugoslav parliament went ahead with the adoption of new electoral laws allowing candidates to be elected by a simple majority' (*Independent*, 28 July 2000, p. 13).

The Montenegrin government, parliament and president rejected the constitutional changes. President Milo Djukanovic said that Montenegro would not take part in the federal elections (later set for 24 September 2000).

> President Slobodan Milosevic is the head of the country's army under a new military doctrine adopted this month [August] ... The president of the republic commands the Yugoslav army in wartime and in peacetime as supreme commander. Until the change the president's command had been based on decisions by the supreme defence council, which he heads. The council has not met since the October 1997 election of Milo Djukanovic ... [as] president of Montenegro.
>
> (*IHT*, 23 August 2000, p. 6)

Rambouillet

The Rambouillet talks started on 6 February 1999. The extended talks lasted until 23 February. The sticking points were the Serbian objections to a Nato-led peacekeeping force and ethnic Albanian demands for a referendum on Kosovo's future status after three years. International mediators said that there was a 'consensus' on a political agreement on autonomy for Kosovo, but neither side signed any agreement. The ethnic Albanian delegation said that it needed to hold 'technical consultations' with its 'political and military' base in Kosovo. The document did not refer to a referendum after three years. Instead, there was reference to 'taking into account the political will of the local population' and the 1975 Helsinki Final Act. The Serbs said that they were ready to 'discuss the scope and character of an international presence'. The peace talks were suspended until 15 March 1999, when a 'peace implementation conference' would be convened.

The peace talks reconvened in France (this time in Paris) on 15 March 1999. The ethnic Albanian delegation said that it was willing to sign the agreement. Politically, the proposals involved a three-year period of autonomy. Self-government would centre on elected bodies. Kosovo would remain part of Serbia. The whole arrangement would be reviewed in three years. The draft peace plan said that 'an international meeting' would be held after three years 'to determine a mechanism for a final solution to Kosovo on the basis of the will of the people' and other factors (*FT*, 16 March 1999, p. 3). An international meeting would take account of the 'will of the people' and the 'opinions of relevant authorities' (*IHT*, 16 March 1999, p. 8). The political plan was to be enforced by a Nato-led force (Kosovo Peace Implementation Force or Kfor) comprising around 28,000 troops. Yugoslav armed forces would have to leave the province except for 1,500 border guards, who would have to stay in their frontier positions under rules enforced by Nato troops.

> Under an annex of the Rambouillet accords that were to govern the behaviour of the purely Nato forces, they were to be given full access to go anywhere they wanted in the Federal Republic of Yugoslavia and will be immune from any legal process.
>
> (*IHT*, 5 June 1999, p. 4)

The annex says: 'Nato personnel shall enjoy, together with their vehicles, vessels, aircraft and equipment, free and unrestricted passage and unimpeded access throughout the FRY, including associated airspace and territorial waters' (*IHT*, 11 June 1999, p. 7). ('In the crucial weeks before Nato bombing began, [Madeleine] Albright telephoned Milosevic to suggest a meeting in Geneva, at which time the [US] administration was prepared to discuss changes in the Rambouillet accords that the Serbs had rejected. These previously undisclosed contacts show clearly that the West offered Milosevic every reasonable opportunity to resolve the Kosovo crisis diplomatically': James Rubin, former US state department spokesman *FT*, Weekend, 30 September 2000, p. i. 'Albright, in fact, made two rare and unpublicized telephone calls to Milosevic, one before Rambouillet and one prior to the bombing. She offered, for the first time since the crackdown on Kosovo began, to meet him ... Albright called Milosevic a second time while the talks were in progress. During this conversation she offered to meet him face to face, saying they could discuss the critical question of Nato peacekeepers at such a meeting. She suggested they meet in Geneva, after the Rambouillet conference concluded ... Albright clearly signalled in that second phone call that the US was prepared to be flexible in reaching an agreement ... Some observers have pointed to inflexibility in the wording of the military annexe prepared for Rambouillet as the reason the Serbs balked. This is nonsense. The Serb delegation was told time and time again that the document was negotiable': James Rubin, *FT*, Weekend, 7 October 2000, pp. i, ix.)

On 18 March 1999 representatives of the ethnic Albanian delegation signed the agreement. Russia's mediator, Boris Mayorsky, refused to sign as a witness.

The talks in Paris were called off on 19 March 1999. The 1,380 OSCE verifiers prepared to leave the following day.

Yugoslavia's decision to reject an international plan ... led to the collapse of the peace talks in Paris last week. It also signalled the start of a major new offensive by nearly 40,000 Serbian soldiers and security forces based in and around Kosovo.

(*IHT*, 22 March 1999, p. 6)

President Clinton [22 March 1999]: 'More than 40,000 Serb security forces are poised in and around Kosovo, with additional units on the way.'

On 22 March Richard Holbrooke began fresh talks with Milosevic, but by the following day it was clear that the mission had failed.

On 23 March 1999 the Yugoslav government declared a state of 'immediate threat of war'. 'Milosevic yesterday [23 March] sacked the second most powerful figure in the Yugoslav army, General Alexander Dimitrijevic, the head of military security' (*FT*, 24 March 1999, p. 1). Russian prime minister Yevgeni Primakov, on his way to a visit to the USA, turned around in mid-flight over the Atlantic after a telephone discussion with US Vice-President Al Gore. A US official said: 'The Vice-President could not assure Primakov that bombing would not take place while he was here.'

Nato's seventy-eight-day bombing campaign

Nato began missile and air attacks on 24 March 1999. Among the first targets were Serbian air defences. (The bombing campaign was called Operation Allied Force. A formal suspension of Nato bombing was announced on 10 June 1999 after a start to the Yugoslav withdrawal had been verified. But Nato air strikes actually stopped when the military technical agreement was signed the day before. A decision to launch air strikes has to be made unanimously, but afterwards no single Nato member can call a halt although objectors can withhold use of their military forces: *FT*, 30 March 1999, p. 2. The most commonly quoted figure is that the USA provided about 80 per cent of the planes involved in the bombing campaign. The technological gap between the USA and Europe was exposed.)

'The decision by Nato to attack a sovereign nation for the first time in its fifty-year history represents a momentous transformation for a defensive alliance conceived to protect Western Europe from an invasion by the Soviet Union' (*IHT*, 24 March 1999, p. 1).

'The war with Serbia to stop tyranny and ethnic cleansing in Kosovo was a milestone ... It was the first war that was not for conquest, or defence or the imposition of political power, but to assert standards of behaviour' (Flora Lewis, *IHT*, 18 March 2000, p. 8).

German planes took part in combat for the first time since the end of the Second World War. (On 16 October 1998 the Bundestag voted in favour of committing German fighter planes to any Nato air strikes, the vote being 503 to sixty-three with eighteen abstentions. 'It was the first time Germany had approved the possible use of force outside Nato territory without a United Nations mandate': *IHT*, 17 October 1998, p. 2.)

Russia suspended co-operation with Nato and participation in the Partnership for Peace programme.

The government of Montenegro declared that it would not recognize the declaration of an 'imminent state of war' and other decisions made by the federal government. The declaration was a prelude to a state of war or emergency, which would give sweeping powers to the federal government (*FT*, 25 March 1999, p. 2).

> Nato gave unusual written assurances Wednesday [24 March] to five countries neighbouring Serbia that the alliance would consider any military strikes against them by Belgrade's forces to be 'unacceptable'. Allied officials said that they had given the assurances after Albania, Bulgaria, Macedonia, Slovenia and Romania had expressed concern about threats to their own safety … Officials said that Mr Solana's letters had gone out before Yugoslavia warned Romania, Albania, Hungary, Bulgaria and Macedonia not to support Nato bombing raids or the ethnic Albanian rebels in Kosovo.
> (*IHT*, 25 March 1999, p. 5)

Nato's bombing campaign was highly controversial, of course. For one thing, Nato did not seek a UN Security Council resolution to approve the bombing campaign because both Russia and China would have opposed it. Instead:

1   Nato argued that humanitarian considerations outweighed the usual considerations of state sovereignty. (Serbia's sovereignty over Kosovo in the context of the disintegration of the former Yugoslavia, however, has been challenged.)

It was discovered on 16 January 1999, for example, that forty-five ethnic Albanian citizens (including three women and a child) had been killed the day before, allegedly by Serbian forces, in the village of Racak. (On 17 March 1999 the team of Finnish forensic scientists declared Racak a 'crime against humanity' but the word 'massacre' was not used.)

2   Nato also argued that its actions were in the spirit of previous resolutions (on 31 March 1998 and 23 September 1998).

On 31 March 1998 the UN Security Council imposed an arms embargo on the Federal Republic of Yugoslavia. A resolution condemned the 'excessive force' used by Serbia and urged 'the authorities in Belgrade and the leadership of the Kosovar Albanian community to enter into a meaningful dialogue on political status issues'. The outcome of a dialogue should include 'an enhanced status for Kosovo which would include a substantially greater degree of autonomy and meaningful self-administration'.

On 23 September 1998 the UN Security Council approved (with China abstaining) a France–UK resolution demanding an immediate ceasefire, an end to 'all action by security forces affecting civilians', the immediate withdrawal of 'security units used for civilian repression' and 'rapid progress on a clear timetable' for peace talks. 'Further action and additional measures' would be taken in the event of non-compliance. The situation in Kosovo 'constitutes a threat to peace and security in the region'. The resolution referred to 'enforcement provisions' of Chapter 7 of the UN Charter. (Under the UN Charter a Chapter 7 resolution is militarily enforceable: *IHT*, 24 September 1998, p. 7. 'Chapter 7 of the UN Charter [is] that part of the treaty which envisages the use of force in order to stop a situation which may threaten international security': *Newsbrief*, 1998, vol. 18, no. 10, p. 74.)

(Note also that on 26 March 1999 the Security Council rejected by twelve votes to three – including Russia and China – a Russian resolution calling for an immediate cessation of bombing and a return to negotiations.)

With reservations about aspects such as the height at which Nato planes flew, the bombing campaign was both justified and successful. (Criticisms relating to civilian casualties are dealt with below, in the section on the toll.) It was clearly a mistake to openly declare at the start that a ground invasion was not going to happen, although it is not difficult to appreciate both the domestic political constraints operating and the differences of opinion among Nato members on the issue.

> If the threat of ground troops was a factor then we would have been better off had our public posture not appeared to rule out ground troops from the beginning. There was legitimate political reason not to speculate about ground troops when Nato's air campaign began. We needed congressional support for air strikes and if we had pointed to the strong possibility of ground troops, I believe we could have lost the modest majority we managed to muster in the Senate. For example, if we had said explicitly in March [1999] that air strikes could well be followed by ground troops, I doubt a third of the Senate would have supported us. But, in retrospect, I believe we leaned too far in the other direction. Instead of appearing to rule out ground troops, we should have said that we were determined to prevail, that we were confident the air strikes would succeed – and simply refused to speculate on what would happen if air strikes did not work. Some in Congress would have objected, but I think we could have promised to consult them again if our strategy changed. Indeed, that is precisely what we were about to do in June [1999] when planning for ground troops matured.
>
> (James Rubin, former US state department spokesman, *FT*, Weekend, 7 October 2000, pp. i, ix)

There is no doubt that the start of the bombing campaign was accompanied by a rapid acceleration of the 'ethnic cleansing' of ethnic Albanians. But what critics fail to appreciate is what would have happened if Nato had simply been bluffing. Milosevic would have had a clear run to carry out what he had always intended to do. Human rights violations would have run riot. It is worth remembering two points:

1   On 24 November 1993 the International Helsinki Federation for Human
    Rights (IHF) published a worrying report entitled *From Autonomy to
    Colonization: Human Rights Violations in Kosovo 1989–1993*. 'The IHF is deeply
    concerned that the Serbian oppressive policies carried out in Kosovo aim at
    a permanent change in the demographic structure of the region' (*FT*, 3
    September 1996, p. 2).

2   ' "Operation Horseshoe" … was known to have been conceived by Mr
    Milosevic and his advisers in October [1998]' (William Drozdiak, *IHT*, 21
    July 1999, p. 4).

According to German government sources, this programme for purging
Kosovo of its Albanian population was prepared at the end of last year
[1998] under the codename 'Horseshoe' … Horseshoe was designed to
produce a permanent solution, and was launched even before the
Rambouillet discussions in February [1999].

> (William Pfaff, *IHT*, 15 April 1999, p. 6)

The bombings were indeed the trigger for most of the ethnic cleansing. The
campaign had already begun, directed at Albanian villages thought friendly
to the KLA. A plan, 'Operation Horseshoe', had been prepared in Belgrade
for the full-scale expulsion and murder of Kosovo Albanians, and it was
ordered into action during the hours following the start of the bombings.
But ethnic cleansing was clearly a result, as well as the cause, of the Nato
bombing campaign.

> (William Pfaff, *IHT*, 8 July 1999, p. 8)

In early 1999 there were clear signs of preparation for an intensification of
this campaign: a build-up of Serb forces, the introduction of paramilitaries
to the region and a new integration of police and military units, designed
specifically for operations against the civilian population. The new wave of
expulsions which started after 24 March [1999] was well organized and
systematic. What happened after the bombing began, therefore, was probably a speeded-up version of what would have happened anyway. Of
course, the 'what if' questions of history can never be answered with
certainty; but one thing here is quite clear: if Nato had not intervened and if
hundreds of thousands of Albanians had been driven out of Kosovo in the
spring and summer of 1999, those refugees would still be in exile today.

> (Noel Malcolm, *Telegraph*, 24 March 2000, p. 28)

Nato's bombing strategy was and still is criticized for starting with the
campaign with just a few selected and publicized targets in the hope that
Milosevic would use this as a cover for capitulating. But he did not. Factors in his
decision included the hope that the stresses and strains among Nato members
would bring the campaign to a premature halt, and the openly declared unwillingness of Nato to commit ground troops for an invasion of Kosovo. On 27

March 1999 Nato announced that phase two of the bombing campaign was to begin, including attacks on Serbian ground forces in Kosovo (which were not at all decisive and led to far fewer losses in Serbian troops and armaments than initially thought by Nato). It was only when Nato attacked infrastructure and other economic and communications targets within Serbia itself that Milosevic started to buckle. Phase three started when the interior ministry building in Belgrade was attacked on 3 April 1999. The targets included power stations, oil refineries, bridges, party and government buildings, television stations and allegedly dual civilian/military factories (e.g. cars and armaments). They were considered to be legitimate military targets because they helped the war effort and because they struck at the economic power of Milosevic and his cronies. Other factors affecting Milosevic's capitulation included the build-up of Nato forces in countries such as neighbouring Albania and Macedonia (there to look after refugees) coupled with Nato announcing that no options were ruled out. (President Clinton, for example, in an article published in the *IHT* on 24 May 1999, stated that: 'While I do not rule out other military options, we are pursuing our present strategy.') Nato secretary-general Javier Solana played a crucial role in maintaining cohesion among Nato members. General Wesley Clark from the USA, Nato's supreme allied commander in Europe, proved to be a dogged and highly intelligent leader (although controversial in some ways, e.g. the row with Britain's first head of Kfor, General Mike Jackson, about the Russian takeover of Pristina airport before the entry of Kfor troops into Kosovo; Russia's move was generally seen as a response to not being allocated a separate sector and as an attempt to divide Kosovo into Serbian and ethnic Albanian parts). (Among the three new Nato members Poland was the most supportive, Hungary was next and the Czech Republic was by far the least enthusiastic. The governments of countries seeking future Nato membership, such as Albania, Bulgaria, Croatia, Romania, Slovenia and Slovakia, actively assisted Nato despite varying degrees of enthusiasm among their populations.)

(Javier Solana took charge of the EU's foreign and security policy on 18 October 1999, a newly created post of co-ordinator or high representative of the EU's common foreign and security policy. He has combined this role with that of secretary-general of the WEU (Western European Union). George Robertson, formerly Britain's foreign secretary and now Lord Robertson, replaced Solana as Nato secretary-general on 14 August 1999. On 8 October 1999 General Klaus Reinhardt of Germany replaced the UK's General Sir Michael Jackson as head of Kfor. On 3 May 2000 General Joseph Ralston became Supreme Allied Commander, Europe, replacing General Wesley Clark. Although officially denied, General Clark's early relinquishing of this role was commonly attributed to his criticisms of Western political leaders' wariness over issues such as bombing targets and a ground invasion of Kosovo.)

In November 2001 Ibrahim Rugova drew parallels between Nato's bombing campaign and the bombing of targets in Afghanistan by the United States (aided by the United Kingdom) after the 11 September 2001 terrorist attacks in New York and Washington:

To describe it as a war against Islam ... is as senseless as describing the Nato air campaign [against Milosevic] as a war against Orthodox Christianity ... Some people in Nato countries criticised their governments for intervening. Fortunately for us they were ignored ... We knew that if the bombing stopped Milosevic would win and we would all pay a dreadful price ... When Milosevic refused to capitulate after only a few days of bombings, the critics queued up to say the military campaign was flawed and failing ... [Then came] Slobodan Milosevic's sudden capitulation in 1999 ... The rapid collapse of the Taleban [in Afghanistan] after weeks of bombing reminds me of [that sudden capitulation] ... Another criticism of the Nato air campaign in Kosovo at the time was that it created rather than averted a humanitarian crisis there. People are today saying the same thing about the military campaign in Afghanistan. But in Kosovo, as in Afghanistan, what many people failed to realise is that the humanitarian crisis had begun much earlier ... [In both cases] military action was the only way to create the conditions for resolving the humanitarian crisis ... Without Nato's intervention and determination [in Kosovo] hundreds of thousands would still be living in tents all over Europe ... More than $1.5 billion has been invested in Kosovo's future by the international community over the past two years – more than $750 for each person here. The uncomfortable reality is that military force is sometimes necessary to protect human rights and enforce the rule of law ... Military force brought an end to four years of suffering in Bosnia. It reversed the ethnic cleansing that had begun in Kosovo on a massive scale in 1998. And Nato forces have delivered many of those indicted for war crimes in the former Yugoslavia tc The Hague.

(*Telegraph*, 20 November 2001, p. 24)

The toll

'German foreign minister Joschka Fischer has recounted that when he went to Belgrade shortly before Nato started bombing, Mr Milosevic told him: "I am ready to walk on corpses and the West is not. That is why I shall win"' (Flora Lewis, *IHT*, 4 June 1999, p. 8).

'[The bombing campaign ended with] the lack of a single allied casualty in combat' (*IHT*, 11 June 1999, p. 1).

Only two Nato planes were shot down, although one was a US stealth bomber. Both pilots were rescued. (Two US pilots were killed in a training accident involving Apache helicopters.) 'Nato officials acknowledged Tuesday [22 June] that the alliance knocked out a good deal less Serbian military equipment in Kosovo than had been thought' (*IHT*, 23 June 1999, p. 1).

Nato estimates that 5,000 Yugoslav servicemen have been killed in the air campaign. The Yugoslav military command has admitted to only 1,800 dead (*FT*, 4 June 1999, pp. 1–2). 'Some 5,000 Serbian troops were killed and 10,000 wounded, the alliance estimates ... The Serbs contend that 1,500 civilians were killed during the bombing' (*IHT*, 7 June 1999, p. 9). In Belgrade a war crimes tribunal included in its indictment the names of 503 civilians, 240 soldiers and 147 politicians killed during the Nato bombing campaign (*Independent*, 19 September 2000, p. 12; *Guardian*, 19 September 2000, p. 17).

> The Yugoslav army chief of staff, General Dragoljub Ojdanovic, said Wednesday [21 July 1999] that 524 Yugoslav soldiers were killed during and after the eleven-week-long Nato bombing campaign against Yugoslavia ... General Ojdanovic said that thirty-seven soldiers were still listed as missing ... On 10 June ... President Slobodan Milosevic said that the army had lost 462 soldiers and 114 Serbian policemen had been killed.
>
> (*IHT*, 22 July 1999, p. 5)

(Slobodan Milosevic, in a television address: 'From 24 March [1999] until today [10 June 1999] 462 Yugoslav army soldiers and 114 police were killed.')

> United Nations forensic investigators searching for the bodies of ethnic Albanians killed by Yugoslav army and paramilitary forces in Kosovo now expect the final toll of confirmed killings to be between 4,000 and 5,000. This is half the total estimated during Nato's seventy-eight-day bombing campaign ... Two figures were frequently quoted: 100,000 missing and 10,000 murdered by the Serbs.
>
> (*The Times*, 19 August 2000, p. 13)

On 6 February 2000 a report was issued by Human Rights Watch (based in New York). It estimated that at least 500 civilians had been killed by Nato during the seventy-eight-day bombing campaign. The report said that: 'Human Rights Watch has found no evidence of war crimes ... [But] the investigation did conclude that Nato violated international humanitarian law.' Nato may have breached the Geneva Convention in five areas. For example, attacks were made on targets of questionable military legitimacy. 'Nine incidents were a result of strikes on non-military targets that Human Rights believes were illegitimate', including Radio Television Serbia in Belgrade, the New Belgrade heating plant and seven bridges that were neither on major transportation routes nor had military functions. Bridges were bombed during daylight hours when civilians were most likely to be crossing them (*Independent*, 7 February 2000, pp. 1, 3; *IHT*, 8 February 2000, p. 7).

On 2 June 2000 chief war crimes prosecutor Carla del Ponte said:

> I am now able to announce my conclusion, following a full consideration of my team's assessment of all complaints and allegations, that there is no basis for opening an investigation into any of those allegations or into other incidents related to the Nato bombing ... Although some mistakes were made by Nato, I am very satisfied that there was no deliberate targeting of civilians or unlawful military targets by Nato during the bombing campaign.
>
> (*IHT*, 3 June 2000, p. 1; *Guardian*, 3 June 2000, p. 21)

Carla del Ponte (26 January 2001):

> I received new information from Serbia that Nato advised Mr Milosevic ahead of time that the television station would be bombed. He then only told some of the directors, but he did not inform the working technicians so they could leave. So Mr Milosevic himself obliged people to stay in the building knowing it would be bombed so he could manipulate the situation against Nato. Our preliminary review of the bombing incident [on 23 April 1999] has come to the conclusion that there is insufficient cause so far to open an inquiry. We have asked the Serbian authorities for more evidence and if there is cause to open an inquiry we will do it. I have to say that this issue of Nato bombing arises all the time. How can this be a priority when each time I visit Bosnia-Hercegovina or Kosovo and observe the exhumation of thousands of bodies from mass graves? Our priority is prosecuting genocide and crimes against humanity. That is our goal now. Of course, the sixteen dead [at the bombed television headquarters] are not unimportant, but they cannot be my priority.
>
> (*IHT*, 1 February 2001, p. 8)

On 7 June 2000 Amnesty International published a report highly critical of Nato.

> [The report accused Nato] of committing serious violations of the rules of war, unlawful killings and – in the case of the bombing of Serbia's television headquarters – a war crime … The Amnesty report … states that 'Civilian deaths could have been significantly reduced if Nato forces had fully adhered to the rules of war' … Amnesty records that Nato aircraft flew 10,484 strike missions over Serbia and that Serbian statistics of civilian deaths in Nato raids range from 400–600 up to 1,500. It specifically condemns Nato for an attack on a bridge at Varvarin on 30 May last year [1999], which killed at least eleven civilians. 'Nato forces failed to suspend their attack after it was evident that they had struck civilians,' Amnesty says. When it attacked convoys of Albanian refugees near Djakovica on 14 April and in Korisa on 13 May, 'Nato failed to take necessary precautions to minimise civilian casualties.' The report says Nato repeatedly gave priority to pilots' safety at the cost of civilian lives … Of the Nato destruction of the train at Gurdulica bridge on 12 April … Nato had not, Amnesty adds, 'taken sufficient precautionary measures to ensure there was no civilian traffic in the vicinity of the bridge before launching the first attack'.
>
> (*Independent*, 7 June 2000, p. 17)

On 7 May 1999 the Chinese embassy in Belgrade was bombed. Nato described the bombing as a 'terrible accident', an explanation which China did not accept. It was the result of 'faulty information' as regards targeting, mistaking the building for the federal directorate of supply and procurement (a military office). (It was later revealed that an outdated map had been used and that personnel formerly used to check targets were switched to finding new targets.) Three Chinese journalists were killed. Angry demonstrations followed in China, including three days of mob attacks on US and UK embassies.

Milosevic concedes

Kosovo has, in effect, become a UN protectorate. The UN's Security Council Resolution 1244 placed UNMIK (UN Mission in Kosovo: the interim administration in Kosovo) in overall charge of civilian affairs. A Nato-led force (Kfor) provides the main security. Criticisms include the slowness of the UN administration to get itself organized (a vacuum initially exploited by the KLA) and of the international community in providing enough policemen. The judicial system and implementation of the rule of law leave a lot to be desired. Non-Albanians have left in droves despite the international community's aim of a multi-ethnic community. Those non-Albanians remaining generally shelter in protected enclaves.

But the international community's civilian and military support, for the foreseeable future, in Kosovo (and, indeed, elsewhere in the former Yugoslavia) has been an indispensable precondition for stability in the whole region. The terrible events of 11 September 2001, when terrorists attacked targets in New York and Washington, showed the dangers of allowing states like Afghanistan to fail. There has been a profound change in the attitude of the administration of President George W. Bush towards the former Yugoslavia. The new president, inaugurated in January 2001, was initially very cool towards the stationing of US troops in the Balkans. The new Bush administration now sees the vital importance of the United States maintaining its presence in the more unstable parts of the former Yugoslavia.

Russia played a vital role in securing a diplomatic settlement of the Kosovo crisis. When Russia distanced itself from Milosevic he knew that the game was finally up. Russian envoy Viktor Chernomyrdin and Finnish president and EU envoy Martti Ahtisaari flew to Belgrade on 2 June 1999 after extensive talks in Bonn at an EU summit (with US deputy secretary of state Strobe Talbott in attendance) which resulted in an international peace plan to be presented to Slobodan Milosevic. Martti Ahtisaari: 'It is neither negotiations nor an ultimatum. It is making an offer for peace and spelling out in no uncertain terms what the conditions are.'

> Speaking Thursday evening [3 June] in Cologne, where he was briefing the fifteen EU leaders upon his return from Belgrade, Mr Ahtisaari agreed that it was necessary for everybody to communicate the same message to Belgrade. 'To me it was absolutely vital that there would be no doubt and no misunderstanding about what was being discussed,' he said. When he presented the peace package in Belgrade on Wednesday evening [2 June], Mr Ahtisaari made a point of reading the entire document aloud. The

Finnish president said there was never any question of negotiating with Mr Milosevic. 'My role was to answer questions about the document, and there were plenty of them,' he said, the most pointed being whether he could improve on the conditions that the paper laid out. 'I had to say that it was the best offer the international community was in a position to make,' Mr Ahtisaari said. Rather than say more, he urged Mr Milosevic to discuss the terms with members of his government and deliver his decision at a meeting the following day.

(*IHT*, 5 June 1999, p. 4)

The Yugoslav government and Serbian parliament accepted the international peace plan brought by Martti Ahtisaari and Viktor Chernomyrdin on 3 June 1999. (Note that the footnote mentioned in point 10 below was not voted upon: *IHT*, 8 June 1999, p. 8.)

The text of the document was as follows:

1   The immediate and verifiable end of violence and repression in Kosovo.
2   The verifiable withdrawal from Kosovo of all military, police and paramilitary forces according to a rapid time schedule. (Note the word 'all'.)
3   Deployment in Kosovo, under the aegis of the United Nations, of effective international civilian and security presences.
4   The international security presence with substantial Nato participation must be deployed under unified command and control and authorized to establish a safe environment for all people in Kosovo and to facilitate the safe return to their homes of all displaced persons and refugees.
5   The establishment of an interim administration for Kosovo as part of the international civilian presence under which the people of Kosovo can enjoy substantial autonomy within the FRY (Federal Republic of Yugoslavia) to be decided by the Security Council of the United Nations. The interim administration to provide transitional administration while establishing and overseeing the development of provisional democratic self-governing institutions to ensure conditions for a peaceful and normal life of all inhabitants in Kosovo.
      (On 2 June 1999 Bernard Kouchner, the French health minister, was named as the special representative of the UN secretary-general [SRSG] for Kosovo, the head of the UN civil administration in Kosovo [UNMIK]. Bernard Kouchner arrived in Kosovo on 15 July 1999.)
6   After withdrawal an agreed number of Yugoslav and Serbian personnel will be permitted to return to perform the following functions: liaison with international civil mission and international presence; marking/clearing minefields; maintaining a presence at Serb patrimonial sites; maintaining a presence at key border crossings.
7   Safe and free return of all refugees and displaced persons under the supervision of the UNHCR and unimpeded access to Kosovo by humanitarian aid organizations.

8   A political process towards the establishment of an interim political frame-work agreement providing for a substantial self-government for Kosovo, taking full account of the Rambouillet accords and the principles of sovereignty and territorial integrity of the FRY and the other countries of the region, and the demilitarization of the UCK (KLA). Negotiations between the parties for a settlement should not delay or disrupt the estab-lishment of democratic self-governing institutions.

9   Comprehensive approach to the economic development and stabilization of the crisis region. This will include the implementation of a Stability Pact for South-Eastern Europe with broad international participation in order to further promotion of democracy, economic prosperity, stability and regional co-operation.

10   Suspension of military activity will require acceptance of the principles set forth above in addition to agreement to other, previously identified, required elements, which are specified in the footnote. A military–technical agree-ment will then be rapidly concluded.

A second footnote refers to the composition of the international force. It is understood that Nato considers an international security force with 'substantial Nato participation' to mean unified command and control and having Nato at the core.

The Kosovo Liberation Army (KLA)

On 21 June 1999 Nato and the KLA announced a detailed demilitarization agreement drawn up by Nato officers and KLA commanders. The agreement allows for the 'formation of an army in Kosovo on the lines of the US National Guard in due course as part of a political process designed to determine Kosovo's future status'. It will have a core of 4,000 professionals plus reservists.

> Hashim Thaci, the KLA's political head, said yesterday [21 June 1999] that under the deal the movement would transform itself into a national guard. The agreement also offers 'special consideration' to KLA fighters in the formation of civilian administration and the police force 'in view of the expertise they have developed'.
>
> (*FT*, 22 June 1999, p. 3)

> The paragraph says the international community should take full account of the KLA's contribution during the Kosovo crisis. There should be recogni-tion that the KLA is 'committed to propose individual current members to participate in the administration and police force of Kosovo, enjoying special consideration in view of the expertise they have developed'.
>
> (*FT*, 23 June 1999, p. 3)

'The National Guard analogy removes the implication of Kosovo sovereignty, as American states have them' (*IHT*, 24 June 1999, p. 10). 'The US National Guard ... [is] a citizens' militia which can use heavy weapons' (*The Economist*, 26 June 1999, p. 49).

'The success of the KLA in assuming civil power in much of the province – with international community administrators yet to arrive – is a foretaste of troubles to come' (William Pfaff, *IHT*, 24 June 1999, p. 10).

> Nato and UN officials have agreed to the formation of a civilian emergency force from the remnants of the KLA ... tentatively called the Kosovo Corps ... Although Nato sees the Kosovo Corps as a civilian force, the rebel army's officers see it as a potential core of a future national army ... [There is a] 19 September deadline for complete demilitarization of the 9,000 KLA troops ... The new force is expressly civilian and is intended to cope with national emergencies such as forest fires, earthquakes, mountain rescue and reconstruction. Nevertheless, it will have 3,000 members, with a military structure formed from the core commanders and brigades of the present KLA.
>
> (*IHT*, 4 September 1999, p. 2)

'Composed of 3,000 regulars and 2,000 part-timers, this force [the Kosovo Corps] would be used for emergency relief, infrastructure rebuilding and ceremonial duties' (*FT*, 9 September 1999, p. 2).

> Leaders of the KLA accepted [on 21 September 1999] the plan to transform the ethnic Albanian rebel organization into a civil defence group after a personal appeal by General Wesley Clark ... and after winning a concession from Nato on the group's name. The agreement came Monday night [20 September] ... Negotiations between Nato and the KLA revealed fundamental differences between the two sides over the rebel group's future ... The accord was reached after top KLA officials, including all but one of the rebel army's regional commanders, won agreement from Nato to call the new ethnic Albanian group 'the Kosovo Protection Corps'. The group, which Nato had wanted to name 'the Kosovo Corps', will oversee humanitarian assistance and disaster assistance ... General Sir Michael Jackson gained a renewed promise from the KLA leadership that the rebel group would officially cease to exist at midnight Tuesday [21 September] ... The new head of the Kosovo Protection Corps ... will be Agim Ceku, the KLA chief of staff.
>
> (*IHT*, 22 September 1999, p. 5)

The deadline for decommissioning KLA weapons expired on 19 September 1999. Kfor was generally satisfied that this would be met. But the KLA and Kfor said that they were to delay signing a demobilization agreement from the morning to midnight on 19 September. Later on it was announced that the deadline for signing the demobilization agreement would be shifted by forty-eight hours from midnight on 19 September to midnight on 21 September.

> Serb leaders in Kosovo yesterday [22 September 1999] pulled out of the
> United Nations' civilian advisory body, protesting against the creation of ...
> the Kosovo Protection Corps ... The Yugoslav government and Russia have
> already criticized the ethnic Albanian dominance of the force. The Serb
> leaders say they will continue to stay in contact with the international
> administration, despite leaving the transitional council.
>
> (*FT*, 23 September 1999, p. 2)

'The political leadership that emerged from the KLA is suffering a collapse of
its support in the province, according to voter surveys, interviews with ordinary
ethnic Albanians and even senior figures in the former rebel movement' (Peter
Finn, *IHT*, 18 October 1999, p. 10).

The Liberation Army of Presevo, Medvedja and Bujanovic (UCPMB)

The UCPMB was formed in January 2000, composed largely of former KLA
members. The organization is named after towns inside Serbia that have
majority ethnic Albanian populations. The UCPMB operated in the area of
Serbia adjacent to eastern Kosovo where ethnic Albanians predominate. The
aim of UCPMB seemed to be to cause sufficient trouble with Serbia to involve
Nato and thus incorporate the area into Kosovo. Nato's displeasure took such
forms as Kfor (US) troops undertaking operations to find UCPMB weapons.
Nato thought it had come to an agreement with the organization to halt its activities. But elements continued their provocations until agreement was reached
with the post-Milosevic government in Serbia.

The end of the Milosevic era

The end of the Milosevic era came suddenly and relatively peacefully. Open
indictment by the war crimes tribunal in The Hague did not prove to be an insu-
perable obstacle to the removal of Milosevic as pessimists thought (the argument
being that indictment would leave Milosevic with no choice but to retain power
at all costs). Calling an early Yugoslav presidential election proved to be a fatal
political error for Milosevic. (It was not long after his fall that figures began to
emerge about the large sums of money that had been illegally transferred out of
Serbia by his family and cronies.) Milosevic attempted to cheat in the first round
of voting but to no avail.

The new leaders faced massive problems in their quest to establish a more
normal political and economic system. (On 20 September 2000 Vojislav
Kostunica said in a campaign speech: 'I am like you, an ordinary person ... You
want to live in an ordinary, average state, in which everything is more or less
average': *New York Review of Books*, 2001, vol. XLVIII, no. 2, p. 44.) The
economic problems were both short-term (such as a severe energy shortage) and
long-term. It had long been predicted that the disparate eighteen-party DOS
coalition was more than likely to fall apart after it came to power in Serbia. But

optimists saw that as a natural progression to 'normal' political life. The personal friction between the cautious, legalistic Kostunica and the impetuous Djindjic did not impede progress towards electoral success. (They agreed pre-election, for example, to share seats equally between their parties although the latter's was much larger.) The Serbian people will also have to come to terms with their tendency to see themselves as victims. The international community will be more inclined to support the people of Serbia if they recognize the evil deeds committed in their name during the 1990s than if they seem merely to have thrown out Milosevic because he failed to achieve the aim of a Greater Serbia.

The first round of the presidential election was held on 24 September 2000. Also held were elections for the Yugoslav parliament (in which the ruling coalition retained its majority). In local elections in Serbia opposition parties predominated.

The candidate of the eighteen-party Democratic Opposition of Serbia (DOS), Vojislav Kostunica, won in the first round of the presidential election. A constitutional lawyer and a moderate nationalist who is critical of the Nato bombing campaign and of the war crimes tribunal in The Hague (to which he said he would not send Milosevic), he was generally recognized as an honest democrat who wanted a 'normal' country and a return to Europe. He seeks a peaceful solution to relations with Montenegro and Kosovo and with all neighbouring countries. He had never even met Milosevic (before 6 October 2000), let alone been 'bought off' at any stage of his career. Milosevic miscalculated. Most of the opposition parties had finally united behind a credible candidate.

The EU and the USA announced before the election that sanctions would be lifted if Milosevic lost.

Organizations such as OSCE were not allowed to monitor the elections. The United Nations mission allowed voting in Kosovo but only appointed so-called 'witnesses' to monitor polling organized by ethnic Serbs. President Djukanovic of Montenegro boycotted the elections but did not prevent voting by those who wished to take part. The turnout in Montenegro was less than 30 per cent of the electorate, with most voting for Milosevic. (There was the argument that ethnic Albanians from Kosovo and President Djukanovic of Montenegro wanted Milosevic to win because support from the West for independence would be easier to gain.)

In the first round of the presidential election the official Federal Election Committee gave Kostunica 48.96 per cent of the vote and Milosevic 38.62 per cent. (The Yugoslav United Left initially gave Kostunica 31.4 and Milosevic 56.3 per cent!) The Democratic Opposition of Serbia claimed that Kostunica won in the first round by 52.54 per cent to 35.01 per cent. For example, the Federal Election Committee claimed that 140,000 votes in Kosovo were for Milosevic, while the UN mission there said that its 'witnesses' counted only around 45,000 voters in total.) Kostunica refused to compete in the second round. (Vojislav Seselj's Radical Party thought that Kostunica won in the first round.)

There was a debate about whether Milosevic could stay until his term of office finished in July 2001 even if he conceded that he had lost in the first round.

The opposition decided on a programme of civil disobedience, including rallies, strikes and road blocks.

Russia offered to mediate. But at first President Vladimir Putin was ambiguous as regards whether he thought Kostunica had won in the first round. Russia belatedly recognized Kostunica's victory on 6 October.

Measures taken by the regime included arrests of strike organizers.

On 4 October 2000 police failed to take over the Kolubara mines, foiled by the miners themselves and others who came in support. Also on 4 October the constitutional court, after a challenge by the opposition, announced that 'part' of the first round of the presidential election had been annulled.

What may be described as a popular revolution took place on 5 October 2000. Crucial was the participation of workers, who joined other groups such as students and intellectuals. Casualties were low. One demonstrator was reported dead, the result of an accident. One man died of a heart attack.

In the morning of 5 October the constitutional court declared that the first round of the presidential election had been annulled and that a fresh election was necessary.

What were generally described as 'hundreds of thousands' of demonstrators (perhaps half a million) from Belgrade and outside the capital (with those from Cacak playing a notable role) took over key buildings, such as the Yugoslav federal parliament, the state-controlled television (Radio Television Serbia) and other television stations. Fires were started in the parliament and Radio Television Serbia buildings. The state news media Tanjug referred to 'President Kostunica'. Kostunica declared himself president.

The police offered little resistance and the army did not intervene. Some police and soldiers fraternized and even collaborated with the demonstrators.

'The new authorities … may arrest him [Milosevic] on charges of corruption, attempted electoral fraud or even for ordering the police and army to fire on the demonstrators on 5 October – an order they ignored' (Tim Judah, *The World Today*, 2000, vol. 56, no. 11, p. 6).

Milosevic (in a recorded address broadcast on 6 October): 'I congratulate Mr Kostunica on his electoral victory.' (It was later revealed that army personnel, including chief of staff Nebojsa Pavkovic, had visited Milosevic and ordered him to meet Kostunica.)

Russian foreign minister Igor Ivanov (after meeting Milosevic in Belgrade on 6 October):

> During the talks Milosevic emphasized his intention to seek a solution in a peaceful and legal manner, to avoid the use of force. Being the leader of the largest political party in Serbia he intends to continue to play a political role in the country.

On 6 October the constitutional court announced that Kostunica had won in the first round of the presidential election, Belarus offered political asylum to Milosevic, and the two Britons and the younger Canadian who had been arrested in early August were released from prison. The army announced that it would not intervene unless its bases and personnel were threatened. (The four Dutchmen arrested at the end of July 2000 were released from prison on 9 October.)

Kostunica was sworn in as Yugoslav president on 7 October 2000. The EU and the USA were quick to lift some of the sanctions (remaining ones including those aimed at Milosevic and his cronies) and to provide economic aid. Prominent early resignations included federal prime minister Momir and Serbian interior minister Vlajko Stojiljkovic (both on 9 October). (Customs controls on the Serb–Montenegrin border were lifted on 7 October: *EEN*, 2000, vol. 13, no. 1, p. 4.)

There were tense negotiations with and resistance from pro-Milosevic elements as Kostunica tried to set up a government for Yugoslavia (initially called a 'crisis committee'). The Serbian Socialist Party eventually agreed (on 13 October) to early elections for the Serbian parliament (to be held in December 2000) and (on 16 October) to a transitional power-sharing arrangement for Serbia. The Serbian Renewal Party was also involved, but the Radical Party refused to take part in the arrangement. The increasingly split Serbian Socialist Party called for an exceptional congress on 25 November 2000, with some members openly calling for the removal of Milosevic as party leader.

President Kostunica quickly faced the prospect of losing control. There were cases where workers spontaneously forced out pro-Milosevic managers, while some members of the Democratic Opposition of Serbia (especially Zoran Djindjic) attempted to replace pro-Milosevic personnel in various state bodies (such as the customs office) with their own people. ('In ministries, newspapers and all manner of companies self-proclaimed crisis committees were taking over': Tim Judah, *The World Today*, 2000, vol. 56, no. 11, p. 5. 'As the political parties met for coalition talks about a new federal government, self-appointed "crisis committees" in factories and offices sacked their former bosses – in the name of the people': Timothy Garton Ash, *New York Review of Books*, 2000, vol. XLVII, no. 18, p. 8.)

On 14 October 2000 Kostunica attended an EU meeting in Biarritz (France). The EU promised emergency aid worth Euro 200 million ($170 million) for things like food, medicine and fuel.

Kostunica then turned his attention to the appointment of a new Yugoslav (federal) government and prime minister. Under the federal constitution the prime minister must be from Montenegro if the president is, like Kostunica, from Serbia. President Kostunica visited Montenegro on 17 October 2000 but he failed to persuade President Djukanovic to take part in a federal government.

Kostunica visited Bosnia on 22 October 2000, the first visit by a leader of Serbia since 1992. He declared support for the Dayton agreement.

A new Serbian government was agreed on 23 October. The Serbian parliament approved the transitional government the following day.

Kostunica (in an interview on Kosovo held on 24 October): 'I am ready, how to say, to accept the guilt for all those people who have been killed.'

On 25 October Kostunica attended a summit of Balkan leaders in Skopje (the capital of the FYR of Macedonia). The following day Yugoslavia was admitted into the Stability Pact for South-Eastern Europe.

Kostunica visited Russia on 27 October. President Putin: 'You have managed to escape the difficult situation without bloodshed and lead your country out of international isolation ... Very soon Russia will reestablish energy deliveries interrupted this year to Yugoslavia, including gas supplies.' (Russia's Gazprom cut off supplies earlier in 2000 because of unpaid bills.)

Kosovo's municipal elections, held on 28 October 2000, attracted a high turnout from Kosovo Albanians and a boycott by the vast majority of Serbs. The elections resulted in a resounding win for Ibrahim Rugova's Democratic League of Kosovo. The Democratic Party of Kosovo (PDK), led by Hashim Thaci, was a poor second. All the Albanian parties stood on an independence platform. ('[The PDK is a] party formed by the KLA guerrillas who had fought the Serbian overlords ... Since the United Nations took control of Kosovo the KLA has controlled twenty-seven out of the province's thirty municipalities ... When Mr Thaci's LKA arrived in Nato's wake it seized as much power as it could get, in any way it could get it, and often abused it. That eventually provoked its massive ... repudiation in Saturday's election outcome': William Pfaff, *IHT*, 2 November 2000, p. 11.)

As regards Kosovo Albanians held in Serbian jails, Flora Brovina was released on 1 November 2000 on the orders of President Kostunica. Others were then released.

On 4 November 2000 the Yugoslav parliament approved the new Yugoslav government. Of the sixteen cabinet posts, Democratic Opposition of Serbia (DOS) had nine, including economics, foreign affairs and the interior. The other seven portfolios were held by the Montenegrin Socialist People's Party (SPP), including the posts of prime minister, defence minister and finance. The prime minister was Zoran Zizic (SPP). The deputy prime minister was Miroljub Labus (DOS). ('He is chairman of a group of opposition economists and policy experts known as G17 Plus, which was instrumental in drawing up the government's programme': *IHT*, 6 November 2000, p. 5.) The foreign minister was Goran Svilanovic (DOS; leader of the Civic Alliance). ('Goran Svilanovic ... is a long-time human rights activist, a lawyer by education': *Independent*, 6 November 2000, p. 14.) The interior minister was Zoran Zivkovic (DOS), the mayor of Nis.

On 17 November 2000 diplomatic relations were restored with the USA, the UK, France and Germany.

On 22 November it was reported that ethnic Albanian guerrillas had killed four Serb policemen in the Presevo Valley in an attack that had begun the day before. This was the latest incident in the valley. Also on 22 November one person (the residence's driver) was killed in a bomb attack in Pristina at the home of Yugoslavia's chief representative in Kosovo. He is head of the Yugoslav government's liaison committee with the international administration in Kosovo.

An EU–Balkan summit meeting was held in Zagreb on 24 November 2000. Albania, Bosnia, Croatia, Macedonia and Yugoslavia were formally invited.

The EU, which has taken prime responsibility for reconstruction and stability in the Balkans, will hold its first summit meeting with regional leaders on Friday [24 November] ... The EU is offering the main countries of the western Balkans – Macedonia, Croatia, Bosnia, Yugoslavia and Albania – Euro 4.65 billion from 2000 to 2006 ... It does not include Euro 200 million in emergency aid for energy, food and medicine ... for Serbia to help it get through the winter ... The Europeans ... are negotiating agreements with these countries, called Stabilization and Association Agreements, that lay out reforms that could put these countries on the path toward joining the EU. In Zagreb Macedonia will sign such an agreement with the EU, while the host, Croatia, will formally begin its negotiations toward one ... The EU would not invite Milo Djukanovic as the head of a delegation, but only as part of the Yugoslav one. Mr Djukanovic got a special invitation from the French and 'special status', with a chance to speak, normally reserved for national leaders.

(*IHT*, 24 November 2000, p. 5)

(The Euro 4.65 billion aid package is worth around $4 billion: *IHT*, 25 November 2000, p. 2.)

'Ibrahim Rugova ... is staying at home ... Bernard Kouchner will, however, be attending' (*Independent*, 24 November 2000, p. 18). 'There were no Kosovo Albanian representatives' (*The Times*, 25 November 2000, p. 24).

On 25 November Milosevic was re-elected as leader of the Serbian Socialist Party. 'Mr Milosevic, the sole candidate for party leader, got 85 per cent of the votes of 2,300 delegates at the special congress in Belgrade' (*Independent*, 27 November 2000, p. 15). But the party had already begun to split.

The general election in Serbia was held on 23 December 2000. Despite the relatively low turnout, the eighteen-party DOS (Democratic Opposition of Serbia) coalition achieved its expected victory. In fact it won more than the two-thirds of seats necessary to change the constitution. Zoran Djindjic was to be prime minister. ('Serbia has wiped the names of 900,000 Kosovan Albanians from the voting register ... Spokesmen in Belgrade vehemently deny the move advances independence or partition, claiming they were forced to abandon organizing the election in the Albanian parts of Kosovo because ... Kfor would not guarantee security if polling occurred': *Guardian*, 23 December 2000, p. 13.)

Events in Serbia have moved at breathtaking speed. Under pressure from the West (including conditional aid) the Serbian government handed over Slobodan Milosevic to the war crimes tribunal at The Hague on 28 June 2001[2] (although the manner in which it was done caused further friction between Serbian prime minister Zoran Djindjic and Yugoslav President Vojislav Kostunica). Yugoslav forces began (with Kfor permission) to return to the buffer zone between Kosovo and Serbia proper and in May 2001 an agreement was reached with ethnic Albanian rebels regarding the Presevo Valley. Elections for a national assembly in Kosovo were held on 17 November 2001. Ibrahim Rugova was the clear winner.

Despite all the considerable economic and political problems that Serbia faces, it has turned its face decisively towards the West and towards Europe in particular. Its new leaders are united in striving to ensure that Serbia becomes a 'normal' country.

The economy of Kosovo was, of course, massively disrupted by the upheavals there and is plagued by problems such as crime and corruption. Kosovo became heavily dependent on international aid, but things are improving as the economy revives (helped by active home reconstruction and small-scale enterprise by the people of Kosovo themselves).

> In 2000 the Kosovo consolidated budget was financed significantly with external grants (almost 50 per cent) ... Some 70 per cent ... [of] the budget for 2001 is expected to be financed by domestic revenues (primarily import duties, excises and sales tax), with donor contributions making up the balance ... The main outstanding legal and political issue relates to owner-ship of the so-called socially-owned enterprises (SOEs), which constitute the bulk of Kosovo's industrial sector. In late 2000 and early 2001 a handful of SOEs were tendered for management contracts. Local managers and employees generally resisted this move and it did not raise much interest among investors. More recently UNMIK circulated a proposal for the priva-tization of SOEs.
>
> (EBRD 2001b: 21)

> The United Nations administration in Kosovo announced yesterday [3 September 1999] that it was dropping the Yugoslav dinar and that from today [4 September] all official dealings would be in German marks ... All currencies would be legal tender, but the province would use the German mark as its preferred currency ... The Yugoslav currency, until now the only currency officially accepted, was still valid but its use would be discouraged. All taxes would be collected in marks and not sent to Belgrade. The decree merely legalizes the existing situation. In Kosovo, as in much of the Balkans, the mark is the main currency in daily use.
>
> (*The Times*, 4 September 1999, p. 19)

In the Milosevic era economic conditions deteriorated drastically for most Serbian citizens. Only a privileged handful benefited from an economy riddled with crime, corruption and regulations. Important positions were often political appointments. Nato bombed much of Serbia's infrastructure in 1999.

In the Milosevic era Serbia's overall economic record was dismal, with falling living standards and rising levels of poverty and unemployment (aggravated by wage arrears). There has been a massive brain drain from Serbia, especially among the educated and/or young. Refugees from Bosnia, Croatia and Kosovo have substantially added to the economic burden. 'Serbia has the highest number of refugees in the Balkans with almost 900,000 people displaced by wars in Croatia, Bosnia and now Kosovo' (Fiona Fox, *The World Today*, 2000, vol. 56, no. 4. p. 21). 'About 900,000 refugees and internally displaced persons live in Yugoslavia' (*Transition*, 2000, vol. 11, no. 6, p. 39).

'In 2000 ... in the Federal Republic of Yugoslavia ... the ratio of external debt to GDP was about 140 per cent' (IMF, *World Economic Outlook*, May 2001, p. 45).

Economic reform in the Milosevic era was very limited.

> About 40 per cent of GDP is produced by the private sector but much of it is in the informal economy. There has been negligible progress on structural reforms. Nearly all large industrial enterprises continue to be in state hands, despite the 1997 privatization law in Serbia.
>
> (Willem Buiter, chief economist at the EBRD, *Guardian*, 12 October 2000, p. 29)

> While it is impossible to give a precise estimate of the size of the private sector, a rough estimate puts the private sector share of GDP at about 40 per cent, with most small-scale enterprises in private hands. The true size of the private sector may be significantly higher once the informal or illegal economy is taken into account.
>
> (EBRD 2000b: 9)

Serbia has had to grapple with massive economic problems in general. There were heavy falls in GDP in the Federal Republic of Yugoslavia between 1990 and 1993. (See Table 5.2) But the economy grew in 1994 and Serbia's ability to feed itself has always been a positive factor. The GDP growth rate fell sharply in 1998 and turned heavily negative in 1999. Positive growth resumed in 2000. In 2000 the level of GDP in the FRY was still only 47 per cent of the 1989 level (EBRD 2001b: 59). Shortages have been severe and some basic products have been rationed. The cost of supporting the wars in Bosnia and Croatia was enormous. Table 5.2 shows the conquering of hyperinflation, although inflation began to rise again in 1998.

Although there have been varying estimates, hyperinflation reached staggering proportions. 'By January 1994 the rump Yugoslavia was suffering from a monthly inflation rate of 313 million per cent, breaking the world records set by Weimar Germany and post-World War II Hungary' (Steve Hanke, *Transition*, 1997, vol. 8, no. 1, p. 9). 'At its peak, in January 1994, the monthly inflation rate reached 313 million per cent ... In addition, the Yugoslav hyperinflation lasted twenty-four months' (Petrovic *et al.* 1999: 336).

A massive increase in the money supply (caused by the printing of money to cover enormous budget deficits) in an economy with falling output was the root cause of hyperinflation. A new 'super-dinar' was introduced on 24 January 1994 as part of an anti-inflation package. The new dinar was to be backed by gold and hard currency reserves and convertible into Deutschmarks at par. The Deutschmark had come to dominate transactions during the hyperinflation. Together with an austerity programme the currency reform soon produced impressive results. There were subsequent official devaluations of the new dinar (coupled with wide disparities between official and black market rates) and inflation again became a problem (including 'hidden' inflation caused by price controls), albeit relatively mild compared with the recent past. (See Table 5.2.)

Post-Milosevic Serbia has set its sights firmly westwards politically and economically. Its quest for a more normal political and economic system is being encouraged by Western aid and advice. The EBRD describes economic reforms thus: 'The most dramatic progress in structural reform in the past year' (EBRD 2001b: 20).

Notes

1 'More than 200,000 ... Bosnian refugees ... in the past three years ... [have returned] to areas in which they are an ethnic minority ... 90,000 last year [2001] alone ... The number of [Nato-led soldiers] in Bosnia has dropped from nearly 60,000 when the war ended to around 17,000 today ... American troops in Bosnia have dropped from a third to a sixth of the peacekeeping force' (*The Economist*, 9 March 2002, p. 53).

2 'The trial of Slobodan Milosevic began on 12 February 2002. 'Slobodan Milosevic ... is the first head of state to be tried for genocide. He is not the first head of state to be tried for war crimes: that was Admiral Karl Dönitz, who led Germany for a week after Hitler died. Dönitz spent ten years in prison' (*IHT*, 18 February 2002, p. 5).

1 Bosnia-Hercegovina

POLITICS

Events prior to the Dayton peace accords are dealt with in the Introduction and Overview.

Dayton and its aftermath

1 November 1995: the peace settlement talks begin at the Wright–Patterson Air Base near Dayton, Ohio, USA.

8 November 1995: the USA and Russia announce that a Russian combat brigade (about 1,500 troops) will participate in the implementation force as part of a US division. The Russian commander will take orders from the US division commander, who will, in turn, take orders from General George Joulwan in his capacity as supreme commander of US forces in Europe rather than as supreme Nato (allied) military commander in Europe. The question of overall political control of the peacekeeping operation remains.

> The first step was taken on 15 October 1995, when a Russian General Staff delegation, led by Colonel General Leontiy Shevtsov, arrived at my head-quarters in Brussels ... We developed a special arrangement that placed the Russian contingent under my command, through General Shevtsov, who would serve as my deputy for Russian forces ... The Russian force operates within the boundaries of Multi-National Division (North). The commander, Major-General Bill Nash of the US army, does not have the authority to assign it missions or tasks. However, he can exercise tactical, or day-to-day, control of its duties.
>
> (General George Joulwan, *IHT*, 30 April 1996, p. 8)

9 November 1995: it is announced that the economic embargo on the Federal Republic of Yugoslavia is to be eased slightly to permit the delivery of natural gas from Russia for home heating purposes.

10 November 1995: an agreement is signed which strengthens the Federation of Bosnia and Hercegovina. Warren Christopher describes the accord as giving the federation 'the power to govern effectively' by creating common political and economic institutions. Mostar is to be reintegrated and more conducive conditions created for the return of refugees.

21 November 1995: the peace agreement is initialled by Presidents Izetbegovic, Tudjman and Milosevic. (The formal signing ceremony will be held in early December.) The main points are as follows:

1   Bosnia is to be preserved as a single state within its present borders and with international recognition. (The name of the country is to be changed from 'the Republic of Bosnia-Hercegovina' to 'Bosnia and Hercegovina'.)

2   Bosnia is to comprise the Bosnian–Croat Federation and the Republika Srpska, with a 'fair distribution of land between the two' (51 per cent and 49 per cent respectively). (Of the 51 per cent, Dayton gives 27 per cent to the Moslems and 24 per cent to the Croats: *The Economist*, 20 January 1996, p. 24. The Bosnian Serbs control 50 per cent of the area, the Bosnian Moslems 30 per cent and the Bosnian Croats 20 per cent: Chris Hedges, *IHT*, 28 June 1997, p. 4.).

3   The capital city of Sarajevo is to be reunited under federal authority, though with ten districts. There is to be an 'effective' central government, including a national parliament, presidency, constitutional court and central bank. The presidency and parliament will be chosen through free and democratic elections held under international supervision. The three-member presidency (one to be a Bosnian Serb) will rotate, but the Bosnian–Croat Federation will provide the first president. The central authorities will be responsible for foreign policy, foreign trade, common and international communications, inter-entity transport, air traffic control, monetary policy, citizenship and immigration. ('To counter the threat of financial instability, the authorities have decided that the new central bank will operate as a currency board for several years, issuing domestic currency only against full foreign exchange backing, and that there will be no domestic bank financing of public expenditure': United Nations Economic Commission for Europe 1996: 170.)

4   Refugees will be allowed to return to their homes. People will be able to move freely throughout Bosnia and the human rights 'of every Bosnian citizen' will be monitored by an independent commission and an internationally trained civilian police force.

5   Individuals charged with war crimes will be excluded from political and military life. Bosnia, Croatia and Serbia will co-operate fully in the investigation and prosecution of war crimes.

6   A land corridor will link Sarajevo and Gorazde.

7   The problem of Brcko and the Posavina corridor will be submitted to international arbitration. (The Bosnian Serbs were awarded the area in western Bosnia around Sipovo and Mrkonjic Grad which they lost in the summer of 1995.)

8   A 'strong international force' (a Nato implementation force) will supervise

the separation of forces. (The Nato force was to number around 60,000, including some 20,000 US troops. In a 27 November speech advocating the sending of US troops President Clinton said that 'this mission should and will take about one year'.)

9   On 22 November the UN Security Council announced that the arms embargo on the countries of the former Yugoslavia would be lifted over a six-month period and that economic sanctions on the Federal Republic of Yugoslavia would be suspended (for six months in the first instance). (The agreement provides for a build-down of weapons by those who have a great many and a build-up of the undersupplied Bosnian army. The baseline is the present 'determined holdings' of the remnant Yugoslavia, made up mostly of Serbia. This well-armed force will be cut to 75 per cent of its existing baseline. Croatia will be entitled to 30 per cent of the baseline, the Bosnian Federation 20 per cent and the Bosnian Serbs 10 per cent. These ratios will require substantial upgrading of the Bosnian army, especially in heavy weapons: Anthony Lewis, *IHT*, 2 December 1995, p. 10. If Serbia, Croatia and Bosnia could not strike a deal by June 1996, a ratio of 5:2:2 respectively would be applied to weapons stocks. The Bosnian Federation would have two-thirds of Bosnia's total and the Bosnian Serbs one-third: *The Economist*, 30 March 1996, p. 20.)

10   An international programme will provide humanitarian relief, assist rebuilding and help refugees.

(Officials of the Bosnian–Croat Federation include the following: president, Kresimir Zubak; vice-president, Ejup Ganic; prime minister, Izudin Kapetanovic; defence minister, Vladimir Soljic: *Business Europa*, June–July 1996, p. 28.)

30 November 1995: the UN Security Council votes to withdraw the last of the UN peacekeeping troops in Bosnia by 31 January 1996. (Those in Croatia are to be withdrawn by 15 January 1996, while the mandate for those in Macedonia is renewed for a further six months.)

Bosnia establishes diplomatic relations with Russia and Greece.

5 December 1995: the foreign and defence ministers of Nato give provisional approval to send some 60,000 troops to Bosnia (Ifor: Implementation Force for Bosnia; Operation Joint Endeavour). The only Nato country not to send troops is Iceland, which does not have an army.

The USA is to send roughly 20,000 troops, the UK 13,000 and France 10,000. Other countries participating are Austria, Estonia, Latvia, Lithuania, Finland, Sweden, the Czech Republic, Slovakia, Hungary, Poland, Romania, Russia (some 2,000 troops), Ukraine, Pakistan, Egypt and Malaysia (*IHT*, 6 December 1995, p. 8; 14 December 1995, p. 7).

6 December 1995: the German Bundestag approves the sending of 4,000 personnel. They are mostly transport, medical and logistics specialists (400 German paratroopers and infantry are to provide protection, but are not to take part in enforcing the separation lines).

8 December 1995: the Bosnian government pledges, in line with the Dayton accords, to remove all foreign Islamic fighters within thirty days of signing the peace agreement in Paris. (The USA and the UK in particular fear attacks on their troops.)

8–9 December 1995: the 'peace implementation conference' is held in London, dealing with civilian aspects. Carl Bildt is appointed 'high representative', whose functions are (1) to co-ordinate civilian aid and the reconstruction programme and (2) to act as liaison between the civilian and military operations. A Peace Implementation Council (a replacement for the International Conference on the Former Yugoslavia) is to have a Steering Board comprising the G7 countries, Russia, the EU's presidency, the European Commission and the Organization of Islamic Conference. An OSCE mission is to prepare and conduct elections, while the United Nations High Commissioner for Refugees is to be involved in that capacity. (The deputy 'high representative' of the Peace Implementation Council is Michael Steiner of Germany.)

The choice of Carl Bildt has been criticized. For example, a leader in the *New York Times* commented as follows:

> Mr Bildt starts his new job burdened with a reputation for accepting Bosnian Serb claims of good behaviour at face value and overlooking evidence of atrocities against civilians. He mainly acquired that reputation when Bosnian Serb forces overran Srebrenica in July. He announced a deal allowing Red Cross access to the male civilians the Serbs said they were holding prisoner. But the Serbs had deceived him. The Red Cross visits never took place and thousands of the prisoners were killed ... Mr Bildt ... has surprisingly suggested that he intends to divide his calendar between Sweden and the Balkans. Bosnia is not a part-time job. If he cannot understand that, someone else should be found who can.
>
> (*IHT*, 18 December 1995, p. 8)

12 December 1995: the two French pilots shot down on 30 August 1995 are released by the Bosnian Serbs.

The Bosnian Serbs hold a referendum in the Serb-held parts of Sarajevo asking whether they wish to come under federal control. There is a 99 per cent 'no' vote in a 91 per cent turnout, according to Bosnian Serb figures.

14 December 1995: the formal signing of the peace agreement takes place at the Elysée Palace in Paris. Bosnia-Hercegovina and the Federal Republic of Yugoslavia formally grant each other diplomatic recognition.

15 December 1995: the UN Security Council approves the deployment of Ifor.

18 December 1995: a meeting starts near Bonn to discuss guidelines for disarmament.

20 December 1995: Nato formally takes over from the UN.

At a donors' conference in Brussels (which finished the following day) a target of $518 million is set to cover urgent reconstruction in the first three months of 1996 (*FT*, 21 December 1995, p. 13).

Bosnia becomes a member of the IMF, which awards an emergency credit. (In line with the accords the IMF will have substantial powers over monetary policy, including the appointment of a central bank governor from outside the region: *FT*, 19 December 1995, p. 2.)

24 December 1995: the first batch of prisoners since the peace agreement was signed are exchanged between the Bosnian government and the Bosnian Serbs.

26 December 1995: the Bosnian Serbs ask Admiral Leighton Smith for an extension from 19 March 1996 to September 1996 of the deadline for transfer of control of their parts of Sarajevo to the federal government. (The request was formally turned down on 30 December. Admiral Smith from the USA is Nato's commander in Bosnia, while General Michael Walker from Britain is Nato's commander of ground forces in Bosnia.)

27 December 1995: Bosnian government and Bosnian Serb forces vacate designated front-line positions around Sarajevo before the midnight deadline.

2 January 1996: the Bosnian government complains to Ifor about the abduction by the Bosnian Serb police of Bosnian citizens travelling since Christmas through the Serb-held Sarajevo suburb of Ilidza. Ifor says it is a civilian matter. (There are also complaints about the slowness of Carl Bildt. He planned to be on holiday until 8 January but was 'persuaded' to arrive in Sarajevo on 3 January. He complained about the lack of funds to operate.)

The *New York Times* wrote in its leader column that:

> Mr Bildt has been shockingly slow in taking up his duties. Although he insists that his other job as leader of Sweden's parliamentary opposition will not distract him, he did not manage to arrive in Bosnia until late last week. Despite the evident danger to Bosnian civilians, Mr Bildt seems in no rush to assemble the international monitoring force that is supposed to oversee local law enforcement.
>
> (*IHT*, 8 January 1996, p. 8)

3 January 1996: US defence secretary William Perry visits Bosnia.

4 January 1996: arms reduction talks begin in Vienna under the auspices of OSCE.

After the USA contacts Milosevic, the Bosnian Serbs release sixteen Bosnian citizens. The Bosnian government says that the seventeenth remains a captive and that three more citizens have been abducted.

Two Moslem policemen are shot at and wounded by Bosnian Croats in Mostar. (A Moslem youth was shot at and killed by the Bosnian Croat police on New Year's day. A Bosnian Croat policeman was shot dead on 6 January. Nato troops from Spain began patrols.)

5 January 1996: the first Nato (Italian) soldier is deliberately shot at and wounded (by a sniper, thought to be Bosnian Serb, in Sarajevo).

6 January 1996: UN (British) troops return fire when a sniper targets them near Sanski Most.

8 January 1996: two Apache helicopters are deployed to patrol Sarajevo after small-arms attacks on aircraft using the airport.

9 January 1996: a rocket-propelled grenade fired from a Serb-held suburb of Sarajevo kills one person and injures others when a tram is hit. Nato troops return fire.

The official end of the Sarajevo aid airlift, which began on 3 July 1992.

13 January 1996: President Clinton visits Tuzla in Bosnia (where he meets US troops and Bosnian political and religious leaders) and Zagreb (the capital of Croatia).

19 January 1996: the deadline for withdrawal from the front lines is considered by Ifor to be generally met. There is also a deadline for the exchange of about 900 prisoners, but the exchange is far less satisfactory (about 220 of the prisoners are released). (The Bosnian government has been the most reluctant. On 15 January it postponed the first major exchange, demanding an explanation of what had happened to 24,742 people missing in Serb-held territory. About 4,000 are thought by the Bosnian government to be in detention, but the fate of the others is unknown, including some 5,000 men from Srebrenica: Chris Hedges, *IHT*, 16 January 1996, p. 6. The Red Cross estimated that there were 645 prisoners still being detained, 318 by the Bosnian government, 150 by the Bosnian Serbs and 177 by the Bosnian Croats: *IHT*, 25 January 1996, p. 6.)

21 January 1996: prime minister Haris Silajdzic announces that he is to resign (effective 30 January) because the Bosnian parliament has passed a law that reduces the number of ministers in the federal government from twelve to six (one of them without portfolio), thus weakening its authority. He is to be replaced by Hasan Muratovic, Bosnia's minister for relations with Ifor.

24 January 1996: three Ifor troops (two Portuguese and one Italian) are killed in an accidental explosion at their base.

27 January 1996: around 380 prisoners are released by the Bosnian government and Bosnian Croats.

28 January 1996: seventy-four prisoners are released by the Bosnian Serbs (out of a planned 150) and seventy-six prisoners are released by the Bosnian government. (The Red Cross estimated that at least 112 prisoners were still being held. Sixty-three were considered war criminals by their captors and forty-nine were considered by the Red Cross to be held in breach of the peace agreement: *IHT*, 30 January 1996, p. 6.)

Three Nato (British) troops are killed when their armoured vehicle hits a mine.

1 February 1996: the Bridge of Brotherhood and Unity, connecting the two parts of Sarajevo, is reopened.

A Bosnian Serb sniper is shot dead by Nato (French) troops and another sniper is captured.

3 February 1996 (midnight): Ifor reports the satisfactory withdrawal of rival armed forces from the 'areas of transition' to be yielded. Ifor will take over and forty-five days will elapse before the rival forces are able to reoccupy these areas. (The Serb-held areas of Sarajevo caused the biggest problem. It was agreed that for forty-five days Bosnian Serb police would be permitted to remain on condition that they would be joined by non-Serb police and that they would be supervised by the international police task force. It was hoped that this would help prevent a mass exodus by Bosnian Serb civilians. Note that there has been difficulty in finding policemen for the international task force, planned to total 1,721.)

The first US soldier dies, killed in an accidental explosion.

7 February 1996: there is a riot by Bosnian Croats when the EU administrator outlines the plan for Mostar. The plan involves a central administration, with Mostar to be divided into seven districts, three for each side and one neutral district for the city centre. (Croat Mostar seems to be the home of powerful criminal gangs which would lose out under the new arrangements.)

8 February 1996: the Bosnian Serb military say they will suspend contacts with Ifor until the detainees are released.

Richard Holbrooke is to return to Bosnia on 11 February to try to defuse the situation.

10 February 1996: four detainees are released and Bosnian Serb political leaders say that contacts with Ifor should be resumed. But meetings with international organizations about arms control and elections will be boycotted until all detainees have been released.

16 February 1996: Ifor announces the capture of an alleged 'terrorist training camp' in central Bosnia and eleven people are detained. Eight are members of the Bosnian interior ministry and three are Iranian citizens described as military advisers. The Bosnian government says that the camp, in the process of being closed down, is a training centre for 'anti-terrorist units' specializing in the arrest of war criminals. (The eight Bosnian detainees were released on condition that the Iranians were deported.)

18 February 1996: invited by the USA, the presidents of Bosnia, Croatia and Serbia meet 'contact group' members in Italy on 17–18 February.

Richard Holbrooke, who is to leave his post as assistant secretary of state for European affairs on 21 February, announces that the crisis threatening the Dayton peace agreement has been averted:

1   Richard Holbrooke says that 'The three sides have agreed that all military and civilian contacts which had broken down in recent days will resume on schedule.'
2   The Bosnian Serbs of Sarajevo are reassured that their freedom will be protected.
3   Moves are announced to suspend UN sanctions against the Bosnian Serbs once Ifor affirms that they are complying with the Dayton peace agreement.
4   Acceptance of the EU's 'comprehensive solution for the integration of Mostar as a unified city, including the delimitation of the central zone' (although the central zone is reduced in size). The deployment of a unified police force will start at noon on 20 February with joint patrols, while on the same day 'complete and unlimited freedom for all' will come into effect. Refugees and displaced persons will be allowed to return to all areas of the

city. The EU is requested to prolong for six months the mandate of the European Administration.

5   Richard Holbrooke comments on the new 'rules of the road' on the arrest of suspected war criminals: 'People are not supposed to be picked up at random, on the basis they may be of interest to somebody later.'

6   Presidents Milosevic and Izetbegovic are to meet within a month and they have decided to set up a telephone hotline.

7   The remaining prisoners of war are to be released.

(Despite the agreement, problems remained, e.g. there were clashes in Mostar on 20 February and the Bosnian Serb military resisted contacts.)

19 February 1996: the Bosnian Serb military representative (deputy commander) fails to attend a meeting with his counterparts and Ifor.

22 February 1996: President Izetbegovic is admitted to hospital with heart trouble.

23 February 1996: federal police (a mixed force of Moslem, Bosnian Croat and Bosnian Serb officers, monitored by an international police force unarmed and without powers of arrest) start to patrol Vogosca, the first of the five Serb-held suburbs of Sarajevo to be transferred. (But the majority of Bosnian Serbs have already left Vogosca, encouraged by propaganda emanating from the Bosnian Serb leadership in Pale and the cutting off of basic services. There was friction between UN officials and Ifor over the latter's agreement to allow Bosnian Serb army vehicles to help in the exodus.)

Russia unilaterally suspends its sanctions against the Bosnian Serbs.

26 February 1996: Hans Koschnick announces that he is to resign as EU administrator for Mostar once a successor is found. (On 25 March the Spaniard Ricardo Perez Casado was named.)

27 February 1996: the Federal Republic of Yugoslavia and the UN suspend sanctions against the Bosnian Serbs after Ifor affirms their compliance with the zones of separation agreement.

29 February 1996: the Sarajevo suburb of Ilijas is returned to federal control, the Bosnian government pronouncing the official end of the siege of Sarajevo. It is estimated that only around 2,000 of the 17,000 inhabitants of Ilijas remain.

6 March 1996: Hadzici, the third suburb of Sarajevo, comes under federal control.

11 March 1996: the USA announces that around $100 million will be made available for arming and training the Bosnian (federal) forces. (The donor conference held on 15 March in Ankara was not a success. The USA's $98.4 million was publicly pledged along with Turkey's $2 million for training, dependent on the merger of Bosnian government and Bosnian Croat forces and on the departure of all 'foreign forces'. The target was $800 million. Thirty-two countries were represented, with EU countries attending only as observers. Russia did not attend. Light arms were allowed ninety days after the signing of the Dayton agreement and heavy weapons after 190 days.)

12 March 1996: Ilidza, the fourth suburb of Sarajevo, comes under federal command. There has been widespread intimidation, looting and arson by gangs of Bosnian Serb extremists. (There was friction between Bosnian Moslem and Bosnian Croat policemen over the colour of uniforms. There were reports of intimidation of Bosnian Serbs and looting by Moslem gangs.)

Sarajevo's mayor resigns because of the exclusion of Bosnian Croats from the Sarajevo cantonal assembly (*The Times*, 13 March 1996, p. 11).

> Recent moves by the [Bosnian] government have called into question its commitment to an ethnically mixed city and country … The moves began, Western officials say, with the failure of Bosnia's Moslem leadership to adequately assure Serbs in five Serbian-held suburbs surrounding Sarajevo that they would be welcome to stay in those areas once they transferred back to government control. They continued with the unwillingness of Moslem police to stop intimidation of Serbs around Sarajevo once those suburbs changed hands. They climaxed late last week when Moslem authorities shut out Serbs and Croats in the formation of the capital's new government … forty-five out of forty-seven seats were given to Moslems. Serbs and Croats were allotted one seat each. That move prompted Sarajevo's well-respected mayor, Tarik Kupusovic, to resign in protest.
>
> (John Pomfret, *IHT*, 18 March 1996, p. 6)

18 March 1996: the USA invites leaders of Bosnia, Croatia and Serbia to Geneva to bolster the Dayton accords.

19 March 1996: Grbavica, the fifth and final suburb of Sarajevo, comes under federal control. (Only 1,500 Serbs, Moslems and Croats remained in Grbavica: *Guardian*, 19 March 1996, p. 12. About 2,000 people, mostly elderly, refused to leave their homes: *The Times*, 20 March 1996, p. 15. Around 3,000 residents did not join the Serb exodus: *Independent*, 20 March 1996, p. 10.)

There are varying estimates of how many Serbs remained in the five suburbs. The UN believes that only 8,000–10,000 Serbs (10 per cent to 12 per cent of the pre-war population) remained (*Independent*, 19 March 1996, p. 11). Of the roughly 60,000 Serbs who lived in these suburbs during the 1992–5 war, only about 10,000 remained (*Independent*, 21 March 1996, p. 17). Only 11,000 Serbs remained in the five suburbs, less than a tenth of the pre-war figure (*Guardian*, 20 March 1996, p. 10). Some 60,000 left the five suburbs (*IHT*, 20 March 1996, p. 1; *The Times*, 20 March 1996, p. 15).

23 March 1996: the 'contact group' declares that the April conference on reconstruction aid will be postponed unless all sides agree to release the remaining prisoners of war (excluding suspected war criminals) by 30 March. (Soon afterwards the Bosnian government releases 110 prisoners and the Bosnian Croats release ten Bosnian Serbs.)

30 March 1996: the Bosnian government and the Bosnian Croats agree on measures to strengthen the federation, e.g. the establishment of a customs union, a single state budget, a unitary banking system and a new federation flag.

3 April 1996: Ron Brown, the US commerce secretary, dies when his plane (which took off from Tuzla) crashes on the approach to Dubrovnik. He was on a trade mission to Bosnia and Croatia, accompanied by other US officials and US business executives. (Thirty-five died altogether in the accident, including six crew members. Thirty-three were American citizens.)

5 April 1996: it is alleged that in 1994 President Clinton secretly gave his approval for covert arms shipments from Iran to Bosnia via Croatia (which took its share) (*IHT*, 6 April 1996, p. 2). (US officials learned in the autumn of 1992 that Iran had opened an arms smuggling route to Bosnia with the assistance of Turkey. The US administration turned a blind eye soon after coming to office in January 1993: *IHT*, 13 May 1996, pp. 1, 6.) ('[On 8 November 1996] the US Senate intelligence committee concluded that President Clinton did approve the secret decision to do nothing to stop the shipment of Iranian arms, which violated a UN embargo. Senior Clinton administration officials may have misled one another, Congress, America's allies and the American people. But they broke no laws, the arms helped the Bosnian government to survive and it was hard to prove that Iran's influence in the region increased': Tim Weiner, *IHT*, 9 November 1996, p. 2.)

6 April 1996: the Bosnian Serbs are declared not to have met the midnight (5 April) deadline for the release of sixteen prisoners of war.

10 April 1996: the Bosnian Serbs refuse the invitation because they demand separate representation (as opposed to being part of the Bosnian delegation) and equal status with the Bosnian Federation.

11 April 1996: Bosnia becomes a member of the EBRD.

12–13 April 1996: representatives of fifty countries attend a conference on aid for the reconstruction of Bosnia hosted by the World Bank and the EU. They estimate that $5.1 billion will be needed over the next three to four years, $3.7 billion for the Bosnian Federation and $1.4 billion for the Bosnian Serbs.

At the conference an additional $1.23 billion is pledged, thus reaching the goal of $1.8 billion for 1996. The USA pledges an extra $219 million (i.e. on top of the earlier $62.7 million pledged at the first aid conference; these sums bring the total US contribution to civilian aid for Bosnia in 1996 to $550 million: *IHT*, 15 April 1996, p. 7). The EU pledges $260 million, the World Bank $160 million and Japan $130 million. Little aid will go to the Bosnian Serbs while Radovan Karadzic and Ratko Mladic remain in power. Each donor country will choose its own projects.

(Another source breaks the total pledge of $1.283 billion as follows: EU, $200 million; bilateral pledges from EU member states, $197.7 million; USA, $219 million; Japan, $130 million; Canada, $1.08 million; Moslem countries, $144 million; other donor countries, $79.1 million; EBRD, $70 million; Islamic Development Bank, $25 million; World Bank, $200 million: *Business Europa*, June–July 1996, p. 28.)

13 April 1996: Haris Silajdzic announces the formation of the New Party for Bosnia-Hercegovina, committed to a genuinely multi-ethnic Bosnia.

19 April 1996: Ifor says that although the opposing sides have not completed the tasks of withdrawing their troops to barracks and placing their heavy weapons in storage by the Dayton deadline, it was satisfied that technical factors were behind the delay.

25 April 1996: the Bosnian government and the Bosnian Croats agree to establish a joint police force and a network of human rights monitors.

26 April 1996: the US defence department says that some US and other Ifor troops will remain in Bosnia for at least a month after the original pullout deadline of 20 December 1996 (*IHT*, 27 April 1996, p. 5).

28–30 April 1996: the Moslem Feast of the Sacrifice is celebrated. There are reports of clashes and even loss of life as Moslems try to visit family members and/or family graves in areas in which they used to live. (Ifor troops stop some Moslems from visiting in order to prevent violence between antagonists.)

5 May 1996: President Izetbegovic visits Gorazde.

15 May 1996: Radovan Karadzic dismisses the prime minister of the Republika Srpska, Rajko Kasagic. (Kasagic, from Banja Luka, is considered a moderate willing to negotiate.)

16 May 1996: Kasagic considers Karadzic's move as 'illegal, null and void' and says that the Bosnian Serb parliament has yet to ratify the dismissal.

> Karadzic is an illegitimate president because he was not elected by the people as called for in the constitution, but only by a self-proclaimed parliament. I guarantee the salvation of the Serbian people, while he is leading the people to ruin. The Dayton Agreement is the only future the Republika Srpska has.

The Serbian government considers the dismissal as 'illegal, null and void', while the Yugoslav Tanjug news agency describes it as 'an illegal act, undemocratic and totally unacceptable' (*IHT*, 17 May 1996, p. 1).

18 May 1996: the Bosnian Serb parliament votes to ratify the dismissal of Kasagic (fifty-five of the eighty-three members). Karadzic says that he will relinquish his role in international relations to his deputy Biljana Plavsic (known as the Iron Lady because of her extreme views) and concentrate on the economy, helping Bosnian Serb refugees and providing jobs for demobilized Bosnian Serb soldiers. The new prime minister is another hardliner, Gojko Klickovic. (There is considerable doubt as to whether these moves diminish Karadzic's influence. Kasagic described the moves as a 'farce': 'Through Biljana Plavsic, Karadzic can have full influence and implement the policy he has started': *IHT*, 21 May 1996, p. 5.)

30 May 1996: President Clinton appoints Richard Sklar as his special representative in Bosnia to oversee the US civilian reconstruction effort there.

2 June 1996: the presidents of Bosnia, Croatia and Serbia meet representatives of the USA, Russia, France, Germany and the UK amid uncertainty about the power exercised by Karadzic.

13–14 June 1996: the Peace Implementation Council meets in Florence to review the Dayton peace accord. The controversial decision is made to confirm the 14 September 1996 election date. (The USA was particularly keen to go ahead.) The final statement says of Karadzic: 'He should remove himself from the political scene.'

14 June 1996: the parties to the conflict, including Serbia and Croatia, sign an arms control agreement. (The original deadline was 6 June.) The Bosnian Serbs are required to reduce the number of heavy weapons, but the Bosnian Federation is permitted to acquire some heavy weapons in order to attain a two to one ratio with the Bosnian Serbs (*IHT*, 17 June 1996, p. 7).

15 June 1996: Haris Silajdzic is injured when, campaigning for his New Party for Bosnia-Hercegovina, he is hit over the head with an iron bar by a supporter of the Moslem Union for Democratic Action.

16 June 1996: Bosnian Croat hardliners announce, in Mostar, the formation of a new separate government for Herceg-Bosna.

18 June 1996: the UN Security Council lifts the arms embargo on the countries of the former Yugoslavia.

19 June 1996: Nato and the WEU announce that 'enforcement operations have been suspended' in relation to the naval blockade in the Adriatic.

The Bosnian Serb assembly votes to establish its own court to try those accused of war crimes.

25 June 1996: the chairman of OSCE reluctantly gives the final approval for the 14 September elections. Despite the 'extremely high risks', he says, a delay 'could heighten political uncertainty and political division even more' (*IHT*, 26 June 1996, p. 6).

26 June 1996: the USA certifies that the Bosnian government has fulfilled its obligations to expel Iranian military units. (Outside Moslems have either left or have been removed from the Bosnian army and security services: *IHT*, 8 July 1996, p. 5.)

Bosnia-Hercegovina becomes the twenty-sixth member of the European Bank for Reconstruction and Development.

29 June 1996: Karadzic is re-elected leader of the Serbian Democratic Party.

30 June 1996: it is revealed that in a letter dated 26 June Karadzic said he will step down as president, citing 'temporary inability' to perform his functions. (International sanctions had been threatened.) He was to hand over to Biljana Plavsic, but she says that Karadzic remains president until the 14 September elections and that she is vice-president.

There is a turnout of 60 per cent in the election in Mostar (originally fixed for 31 May 1996), with people voting where they lived in 1991. The event was peaceful. The forty-eight seats in the city council were to be split as follows: sixteen seats apiece were to be reserved for the Moslems and Croats and five were to be reserved for small minorities such as the Serbs (there were four minority parties). The voting went along predictable lines, with the Moslem Party of Democratic Action winning 49 per cent of the vote and the Croatian Democratic Union winning 45 per cent of the vote.

'Although most seats were reserved for either Muslims or Croats, the Muslims fared best in the open seats prompting local Croat bigwigs brazenly to reject the results' (*The Economist*, 20 July 1996, p. 38).

When it became clear after elections in the southern city of Mostar last month that Muslims would have a narrow majority over Croats on the city's newly united council, the HDZ [Croatian Democratic Union] mayor of Croat-held west Mostar, Mijo Brajkovic, declared that his party would boycott the council.

(Tony Barber, *Independent*, 20 July 1996, p. 10)

The five minority representatives sided with the Moslem Party of Democratic Action, thus bringing their combined voting power to twenty-one. The Bosnian Croats boycotted the first meeting of the council on 23 July, claiming that there had been irregularities in a ballot in Bonn for refugee voters (dismissed by the EU as not important enough to affect the election result; the number of ballots exceeded the number of voters by twenty-six). The EU threatened to pull out of Mostar by midnight 4 August if an agreement could not be reached, but further talks ensued. Agreement was reached on 6 August. The council would meet once to elect the mayor (a Croat) and his deputy (a Moslem). (The council met on 14 August.) Regular meetings would take place only when a constitutional court is set up and ruled (within sixty days) on the validity of the election.

On 31 July a US-mediated effort resulted in the Bosnian Croats agreeing to dismantle Herceg-Bosna and to set up power-sharing institutions by 8 August 1996.

(In 1991 the population of Mostar was 35 per cent Moslem, 34 per cent Croat and 19 per cent Serb: *Independent*, 6 August 1996, p. 7.)

3 July 1996: Karadzic says he will not be a candidate in the September elections.

9 July 1996: Karadzic is appointed chairman of a new body, the Senate.

12 July 1996: the US administration asks Richard Holbrooke to undertake a special mission to persuade Milosevic to comply fully with the terms of the Dayton accords, especially the removal of Karadzic and Mladic from power.

15 July 1996: it is announced that OSCE has postponed the start of official campaigning for the elections (due to start on 14 July).

It is announced that Ricardo Perez Casado is to be replaced (on 22 July 1996) as EU administrator for Mostar by Britain's Sir Martin Garrod.

19 July 1996: Richard Holbrooke and Slobodan Milosevic reach agreement on Radovan Karadzic. Karadzic signs the following statement along with Momcilo Krajisnik (speaker of the Bosnian Serb assembly), Biljana Plavsic and Aleksa Buha (the Bosnian Serb foreign minister), while it is witnessed by Milosevic and Milan Milutinovic:

The undersigned reaffirm their commitment to fulfil the General Framework Agreement for Peace and Annexes negotiated in Dayton and signed in Paris 14 December 1995, and state the following:

1 As of 19 July 1996 Dr Biljana Plavsic has assumed the office of Temporary Acting President of Republika Srpska until completion of

the elections of 14 September 1996, scheduled in accordance with the Dayton Peace Agreement, when a new President will be elected. So that, therefore, on 19 July 1996 Dr Radovan Karadzic has relinquished the office of President of the Republika Srpska and has relinquished all powers associated therewith.

2   Dr Radovan Karadzic states that he shall withdraw immediately and permanently from all political activities. He will not appear in public or on radio or television or other media or means of communication, or participate in any way in the elections.

3   As of 19 July 1996 Dr Radovan Karadzic relinquishes the office of President of the SDS [Serbian Democratic Party] and all the functions, powers and responsibilities of the President of the SDS shall be frozen until the SDS chooses a new President. These powers and responsibilities shall be taken over by Professor Buha.

(Richard Holbrooke told Milosevic that failure to reach agreement would have resulted in 'the disenfranchisement of the SDS and the reimposition of sanctions in the next few days': *IHT*, 20 July 1996, p. 5. Robert Frowick, the US head of OSCE's electoral mission in Bosnia, had warned that unless Karadzic had stepped down as president of the SDS the party would have been banned from standing in the September elections. Admiral Leighton Smith, commander of Nato forces in Bosnia, was empowered to reimpose sanctions – as was Carl Bildt who thought that Dayton allowed Karadzic to be president of the SDS – and Smith had stated that he was prepared to seek out and arrest Karadzic if so ordered.)

23–4 July 1996: vice-president Ejup Ganic leads a trade delegation to Belgrade.

It was agreed to restore telephone, rail, bus and air links and that civilians crossing the Bosnia–Serbia border would no longer require visas.

26 July 1996: the last of the four Catholic churches in Bugojno (mainly Moslem) in west-central Bosnia is blown up after a mosque was set on fire the previous day in nearby Prozor (mainly Croat) (*EEN*, 1996, vol. 10, no. 16, p. 2).

30 July 1996: a train leaves Sarajevo station for Ploce in Croatia (on the Adriatic coast). This is the first train to depart since 2 May 1992.

31 July 1996: Admiral Leighton Smith's last day as commander of Nato forces in Bosnia. He is to be replaced by Admiral Joseph Lopez.

7 August 1996: the first organized tour party (from Spain) to visit Sarajevo since April 1992.

10 August 1996: the Bosnian Serbs, in contravention of the Dayton agreement, deny Ifor access to a heavy weapons site at Bosnian Serb army staff headquarters at Han Pijesak. (But on 12 August they said they would allow an inspection after Ifor took preparatory measures for possible military action. It subsequently came to light that the Bosnian Serbs had originally laid down the unacceptable condition that Ratko Mladic should escort the small inspection party. The inspection took place on 13 August.)

14 August 1996: US secretary of state Warren Christopher convenes a meeting with Presidents Izetbegovic, Tudjman and Milosevic and gains their agreement to implement the Dayton accords.

Presidents Izetbegovic and Tudjman reaffirm their commitment to 'strengthening the federation as the cornerstone of the peace process'. It is agreed that by 31 August 1996 Herceg-Bosna will 'cease to exist' and the Bosnian state will turn over its government institutions to the federation.

15 August 1996: Sarajevo airport reopens for commercial flights. (The UN took control of the airport in April 1992: *IHT*, 14 August 1996, p. 1.)

19 August 1996: Ifor starts to destroy 300 tonnes of ammunition discovered on Bosnian Serb territory in contradiction of the Dayton accords.

27 August 1996: OSCE postpones the municipal elections due to have been held on 14 September owing to 'widespread abuse of rules and regulations'. Criticism is especially levelled at the Serbs (the Bosnian Serbs and the authorities in Serbia) for the ways in which large numbers of Bosnian Serb refugees have been registered to vote in towns like Brcko and Srebrenica which formerly had Moslem majorities.

> Election rules, approved by the organization [OSCE], gave the three nationalist parties – the Croatian Democratic Union, the Muslims' Party of Democratic Action and the Serbian Democratic Party – a monopoly on registering voters. The Serbian Democratic Party responded by engaging in a fraud so massive that the European agency was forced to postpone municipal elections – the most difficult and perhaps the most important vote of all. The Organization for Security and Co-operation in Europe also allowed members of nationalist parties to run all of the local election commissions, the organizations that will be carrying out the vote. On election day Saturday [14 September 1996], its supervision will be minimal. International election supervisors will each be responsible for five polling stations. A senior organization official estimated that only 20 per cent of the voting will be watched by an independent monitor.
>
> (John Pomfret, *IHT*, 14 September 1996, p. 7)

29 August 1996: Ifor troops detain uniformed and armed Bosnian Serb policemen who beat up Moslems returning to the village of Mahala.

30 August 1996: Bob Dole, the Republican presidential nominee, calls the 14 September elections 'a sham in the making'. Under present conditions the elections would amount to 'fraud with an American stamp of approval' (*IHT*, 31 August 1996, p. 1).

31 August 1996: it is announced that the administrative arrangements of Herceg-Bosna 'cease to exist'.

12 September 1996: Biljana Plavsic calls for Serb secession. (Such sentiments are contrary to the Dayton accords.)

13 September 1996: Biljana Plavsic is forced by OSCE to apologize publicly for campaigning for union with Serbia. (OSCE threatened to disbar leading members of her party from standing in the election.)

The Bosnian elections of 14 September 1996

The current population is an estimated 3.5 million, 2.5 million in the Moslem–Croat Federation and 1 million in the Republika Srpska. The ethnic composition of the pre-war population was 43.7 per cent Moslem, 31.3 per cent Serb, 17.7 per cent Croat and 7.3 per cent other (*IHT*, 14 September 1996, p. 7.)

Persons who were at least 18 years of age and appeared on the 1991 census were eligible to vote. Those not living in their former areas had a choice as to where to vote: where they used to live, where they currently lived or where they would like to live. The elections were monitored by 2,000 OSCE observers. (The number of refugees eligible to vote abroad, in fifty-five countries, was 641,000: *IHT*, 14 September 1996, p. 7.)

The elections went ahead despite the many arguments put forward for postponing them, e.g. the likely retrenchment of ethnic divisions, the lack of progress made with regard to refugees wishing to return to their homes, the lack of independent media, widespread intimidation of opposition parties, and the accusation that the timetable was set to suit the November 1996 US presidential election.

During the campaign there were many reports of pressure being exercised, especially by the Bosnian Serbs and Bosnian Croats, to induce people to vote in the places where they currently lived or in other ethnically cleansed areas. But reports of Moslem intimidation also surfaced in, for example, Bihac.

On the day of the election the Party of Democratic Action threatened not to recognize the results in the Republika Srpska. The following day the Bosnian Serbs stopped counting for a while, claiming alleged irregularities in the refugee ballot.

Although the voting process was generally peaceful, there was considerable unease about the vote itself. The turnout (put at 82 per cent by OSCE) seemed suspiciously high given a voter register of 2.92 million. On 23 September OSCE took the controversial decision to change the total to 3.2 million. OSCE's provisional election committee overruled its electoral appeals sub-committee's recommendation of a recount. The sub-committee talked of 'a significant possibility of double voting, other forms of fraud, or counting irregularities. This recount is necessary to rebut the possible inference that the high turnout is due to miscalculations in the count or fraud'. OSCE formally certified the election results on 29 September 1996.

As predicted, the vote split mainly on ethnic lines. The final election results were announced by OSCE on 24 September 1996:

1   The three-member Bosnian presidency, a 'Bosniac' (an OSCE term indicating that 'Bosniacs' are not exclusively Moslems), a Bosnian Croat and a Bosnian Serb. There is a rotating presidency but the first president's term of office lasts for two years.

> Decisions by the three-man presidency need unanimity, but, in a complex system, two votes can suffice – unless the odd man out declares

that his group's 'national interests' are threatened. In that event, he must then also get two-thirds of his area's parliament to back him – and thus block the other two presidents' decision.

(*The Economist*, 21 September 1996, p. 50)

The results in terms of votes were as follows: Alija Izetbegovic, the Moslem representative, 729,034 (Haris Silajdzic, 123,784); Momcilo Krajisnik, the Bosnian Serb representative, 690,373 (Mladen Ivanic, 305,803; this was considered a surprisingly good showing, although his vote was swelled by Moslem and Croat voters choosing to vote in the Republika Srpska; Ivanic is 'a staunch autonomist who nevertheless advocated co-operation and compromise with Bosnia's Muslims and Croats': *IHT*, 19 September 1996, p. 10; Ivanic is 'a socialist with links to Serbia's president, Slobodan Milosevic ... Though no believer in an integrated Bosnia, he does want Serbs to co-operate with the other Bosnians': *The Economist*, 21 September 1996, p. 47); Kresimir Zubak, the Bosnian Croat representative, 342,007 (Ivo Komsic, 38,261).

2   The Republika Srpska has a separate presidency, comprising two people and elected on the basis of one round of voting. The Moslem–Croat (Bosniac–Croat) Federation also has a presidency, but the federation is divided into ten cantons (districts), each with its own assembly (444 seats in total). Under the Dayton accords the Bosnian Croats are not allowed to rule both the 'mixed' cantons, numbers six (Lasva–Vrbas) and seven (Neretva, including Mostar). The other cantons are Una Sana (one), Posavina (two), Tuzla–Podrinje (three), Zenica–Doboj (four), Gorazde (five), West Hercegovina (eight), Sarajevo (nine) and Tomislavgrad (ten).

3   The House of Representatives of Bosnia and Hercegovina. The lower house of the federal legislature comprises twenty-eight seats for the Bosniac–Croat Federation and fourteen for the Bosnian Serbs.

The number of seats gained by each party was as follows:

Party of Democratic Action: nineteen. (Led by Alija Izetbegovic.)

Serbian Democratic Party: nine. (Led by Biljana Plavsic.)

Croatian Democratic Union: eight. (Led by Kresimir Zubak.)

United List of Bosnia and Hercegovina: two. (This is a five-party coalition, including the Union of Bosnian Social Democrats. It is sometimes classified as 'centre-left' but two of the parties are leftist, one is centrist and two are rightist. The United List's members come from all ethnic groups and the platform is a non-sectarian one. The liberal mayor of Tuzla, Selim Beslagic, is a candidate for the United List.)

Alliance for Peace and Progress: two.

Party for Bosnia and Hercegovina: two.

4   The House of Peoples (the upper house) of Bosnia and Hercegovina comprises fifteen delegates, split equally between Bosniacs, Croats and Serbs, and is elected indirectly. Fifteen delegates are from the House of Representatives of the Bosniac–Croat Federation and five from the National Assembly of the Republika Srpska.

5   There are separate assemblies for the Bosniac–Croat Federation and the Republika Srpska. In the Bosniac–Croat Federation there is a House of Representatives (elected on a party list basis and comprising 140 seats) and a House of the Peoples (elected on a geographical basis; comprises thirty Bosniacs, thirty Croats and others). In the Republika Srpska there is simply an eighty-three-seat National Assembly.

The number of seats gained by each party in the House of Representatives was as follows:

Party of Democratic Action: seventy-eight.

Croatian Democratic Union: thirty-five.

Party for Bosnia and Hercegovina: eleven.

United List of Bosnia and Hercegovina: eleven.

Democratic People's Union: three.

Croatian Party of Rights: two.

The number of seats gained by each party in the National Assembly was as follows:

Serbian Democratic Party: forty-five.

Party of Democratic Action: fourteen.

Alliance for Peace and Progress: ten.

Serbian Radical Party: six. (Closely allied to the Serbian Democratic Party.)

Democratic Patriotic Bloc of the Republika Srpska: two. (Led by Predag Radic, the mayor of Banja Luka.)

Party for Bosnia and Hercegovina: two.

Serb Party of Krajina: two.

United List of Bosnia and Hercegovina: two.

Serb Patriotic Party: one.

6   There are local councils in both entities. There are 109 municipalities (*opstinas*) plus a number of extra constituencies created where opstinas lie astride the inter-entity boundary line. There are some 150 local elections in

all. (The local elections were postponed on 27 August 1996: see entry for that date.)

Elections are by proportional representation except for the three-member Bosnian presidency and the presidency of the Republika Srpska.

Socialist Party of the Republika Srpska: led by Zivko Radisic, this party is effectively the Bosnian branch of President Slobodan Milosevic's Socialist Party in Serbia itself.

Serbian Unity Party: led by Zeljko Raznatovic ('Arkan'), although he cannot run in the election because he is a citizen of Serbia.

Liberal Party: led by Miograd Zivanovic, who advocates a multi-ethnic Bosnia. (He joined the Union for Peace and Progress, a coalition led by Radisic's Socialist Party of the Republika Srpska, because of the lack of support.)

Multi-party elections for parliamentary and executive offices above the local level were held in Bosnia in September 1996, and, as earlier, the outcome, while seeming pluralist, did not represent the best result for a democratic Bosnia ... The flawed character of the 1990 elections – in particular the fact that the nature of the republic-level elections precluded holding federal elections – was relevant for post-Dayton elections.

(Friedman 2000: 24–5)

Ante Markovic, federal prime minister [January 1989 to 20 December 1991], attempted to establish a federation-wide party that would support his market economic policies and that would undercut the plethora of narrow interest parties that were arising throughout the country. However, [in 1990] there was no countrywide contest in which to introduce his new party, as the regional elites opposed the holding of federal elections. Markovic's entry of his party, the Alliance of Reform Forces, into regional elections in Bosnia, Macedonia, Montenegro, Serbia and Vojvodina was unsuccessful. Despite the fact that this party was one of the few that was devoted to maintaining the unity of Yugoslavia under a liberal democracy, the narrow, ethnically-oriented parties garnered the majority of votes ... The fact that Markovic's party was forced to compete in regional elections against regionally strong parties obviated what might have been a better showing at the federal level, should such a contest have been possible. Yugoslav citizens were thus denied the ability to place their allegiance in a specifically Yugoslav solution, but were instead forced to choose among the plethora of narrow, ethnic-based parties featured in the regional elections ... In the 1990 elections ... the lack of strong federal organizational processes precluded the Yugoslav people from making their election choices between narrow, region-based (and mostly ethnic-based) parties and Yugoslav-wide parties.

(pp. 23–4)

Events after the September elections

19 September 1996: interior ministers of Germany's Länder decide to start repatriating refugees as of 1 October 1996. (Bavaria was the first to start the process, on 9 October.)

30 September 1996: the three members of the presidency meet for the first time in a motel on the outskirts of Sarajevo. (There was a dispute about where to meet.)

1 October 1996: the USA announces that about 5,000 US troops will soon begin moving into Bosnia (staying until March 1997) to help cover the withdrawal of 52,000 Ifor troops, including 15,800 US troops. The Ifor mandate expires on 20 December 1996 (*IHT*, 3 October 1996, p. 6).

3 October 1996: Izetbegovic and Milosevic meet in Paris and pledge to establish full diplomatic relations. They also agree to freedom of trade and transport, to visa-free travel for their nationals and to refrain from 'political and legal acts which do not contribute to the improvement of friendly relations and co-operation'.

5 October 1996: the inauguration ceremony for the collective presidency and the House of Representatives of Bosnia and Hercegovina takes place in the national theatre in Sarajevo despite the absence of the Bosnian Serbs. 'Mr Krajisnik and the ten Serbian representatives refused to sign the oath because it requires a pledge of loyalty to a unitary state' (John Pomfret, *IHT*, 7 October 1996, p. 11).

22 October 1996: Krajisnik meets Izetbegovic and Zubak in Sarajevo for the first working session of the presidency and signs the oath of loyalty.

OSCE postpones the local elections for the second time. According to Robert Frowick, this was because of 'continuing political problems in municipalities across Bosnia'. The elections will be held 'as soon as possible'. (Most reports mentioned spring 1997 as the most likely date.) (Last week OSCE changed the rules for the local elections, so that people will only be able to cast their votes where they lived before 1992: *FT*, 22 October 1996, p. 2.)

25 October 1996: it is reported that the USA is not releasing arms held at the Croatian port of Ploce (under the 'equip and train' programme for the Bosniac–Croat Federation's army) because of the USA's displeasure at what it perceives as the Bosnian deputy defence minister's close links with Iran and at the slowness of integration of the armed forces. (On 15 November President Izetbegovic announced that the federal defence minister and his deputy were to be dismissed, the former, a Bosnian Croat, going on 18 November and the latter, a Moslem, going two days later. On 20 November the USA announced that the arms would be released.)

7 November 1996: General William Crouch takes over as commander of Ifor from Admiral Joseph Lopez.

8 November 1996: Bosnian Serb president Biljana Plavsic announces that General Ratko Mladic and the rest of the general staff have been dismissed. (Rumours were reported some two weeks earlier. Mladic's successor as commander of the Bosnian Serb army, Major-General Pero Colic, was sworn in on 10 November. Mladic did not resign until 27 November and a ceremony for Colic was not held until 28 November 1996.)

11 November 1996: a group of about a hundred high-ranking officers in the Bosnian Serb army issue a statement expressing

> full support for the main headquarters led by General Mladic, as they are the only ones to guarantee the survival of the Serb Republic ... [the main headquarters are] fully in control of the situation, and in command of all the units, in which the situation is completely normal.
>
> (*IHT*, 12 November 1996, p. 8)

12 November 1996: the Bosnian Serb military occupy a television transmitter. (Control was not relinquished until 18 November.)

12–14 November 1996: in north-eastern Bosnia two Moslems are reportedly killed in clashes between Bosnian Serbs and Moslem refugees trying to return home.

14 November 1996: there is a meeting of Western foreign ministers and the Bosnian collective presidency in Paris. In the 'guidelines' the Bosnian presidency pledge 'as a high priority to establish all the joint institutions provided for in the constitution and make them fully operational as soon as possible'. The guidelines also include reminders that aid can depend on implementation of the peace agreement. 'There is a link,' they say, 'between the availability of international assistance and the degree to which all the authorities of Bosnia and Hercegovina fully implement the peace agreement, including co-operation with the International Criminal Tribunal' (*Independent*, 15 November 1996, p. 13). Warren Christopher says that 'the UN Security Council will consider imposing measures if they fail to significantly meet their obligations under the peace agreement'.

15 November 1996: President Clinton announces that the USA will contribute about 8,500 troops to the follow-up force after Ifor's mandate runs out on 20 December 1996. 'We will propose to our Nato allies that by the June of 1998 the mission's work should be done and the forces should be able to withdraw.' The total number of US troops will be reviewed every six months and about half should be withdrawn by the end of 1997.

18 November 1996: Nato agrees to set up Sfor (Stabilization Force for Bosnia), comprising 31,000 troops. (This was confirmed on 10 December at the meeting of Nato foreign ministers. On 17 December 1996 Nato foreign ministers approved the 'activation order' for Sfor for a period of eighteen months.)

4–5 December 1996: the peace implementation conference in London stresses that international aid is dependent on fulfilling the conditions of the Dayton agreement. Somewhat greater assistance will be given to the war crimes tribunal and the investigation branch of the international police task force. Among other things, the final statement calls for an integrated telephone system and a single system of car number plates.

13 December 1996: the UN approves a mandate for Sfor.

The German parliament approves the use of (2,000) German combat troops as part of Sfor, to operate in south-eastern Bosnia. This is the first time since the Second World War that German combat forces have been allowed to take full part in a ground mission with Western allies, albeit jointly with French forces. (The total number of German military personnel involved is about 3,000).

20 December 1996: Sfor takes over from Ifor.

31 December 1996: Mostar comes under the general authority of Bildt (although Britain's Sir Martin Garrod remains in charge).

1 January 1997: Kofi Annan replaces Boutros Boutros Ghali as UN secretary-general.

3 January 1997: there takes place the first full session of the Bosnian House of Representatives (forty-two members, dealing mainly with foreign relations). (Serbian delegates boycotted the inaugural session in October 1996, objecting to an oath pledging loyalty to Bosnia as a single state. Since then all the Serbian deputies have signed the 'solemn declaration' to the Bosnian constitution but have avoided taking the oath in a public ceremony: *IHT*, 4 January 1997, p. 2.)

The House of Representatives approves the cabinet (Council of Ministers) proposed by the collective presidency, with just one abstention: co-chairmen, Haris Silajdzic (Moslem) and Boro Bosic (Serb); foreign minister, Jadranko Prlic (Croat); foreign trade, Hasan Muratovic (Moslem); minister of communications, Spasoje Albijanic (Serb). Each minister has two deputies and the posts are distributed equally among the three national communities.

16 January 1997: former Bosnian Serb deputy vice-president Nikola Koljevic attempts to commit suicide (his fifth attempt).

10 February 1997: Moslems are shot at when they attempt to visit a cemetery in the Croat part of Mostar. (One died and at least twenty were wounded. It was observed by members of the International Police Task Force, whose report put the blame on some ethnic Croat policemen: *IHT*, 28 February 1997, p. 6.)

14 February 1997: Roberts Owen (from the USA), who chairs the arbitration tribunal on Brcko, reports: 'We will make a final choice no later than 15 March 1998.' Until a final decision is made Brcko will be under international supervision, led by an 'international supervisor'. Although Brcko will remain in the hands of the Bosnian Serbs, provision will be made for the return of refugees and roads will be opened to Moslem and Croat travellers.

28 February 1997:

> The Bosnian Serb leadership in Pale ... signed an agreement with the government in Belgrade that included a promise of military co-operation. The agreement, which Muslim leaders and Western diplomats said violated the Dayton peace agreement, also spelled out co-operation in areas such as foreign trade, border traffic, citizenship and customs.
>
> (Chris Hedges, *IHT*, 12 March 1997, p. 8)

16 March 1997: the Bosnian Serb parliament endorses the agreement, although Biljana Plavsic urged rejection of the agreement on the grounds that it was against both the constitution and the Dayton accords (*Guardian*, 17 March 1997, p. 10).

28 March 1997: agreement is reached on a power-sharing arrangement for Sarajevo, paving the way for the election of a mayor.

4 April 1997: agreement is reached on the formation of a hundred-strong joint police force for central Mostar.

12–13 April 1997: the Pope visits Sarajevo. He meets all three members of the three-man presidency.

30 May 1997: it is announced that Carl Bildt will be replaced as high representative for Bosnia by Carlos Westendorp on 20 June 1997. (Westendorp, a former Spanish foreign minister, is currently Spain's representative at the United Nations.)

The Bosnian Peace Implementation Council threatens sanctions unless the Dayton accords are carried out in full.

31 May 1997: US secretary of state Madeleine Albright is highly critical of Tudjman and Milosevic in personal meetings with them. She is especially critical of Croatia's policy towards ethnic Serb refugees and indicted war criminals and of Serbia's shielding of indicted war criminals.

2 June 1997: the Croatian Democratic Union and the Party of Democratic Action in Mostar sign an agreement on the administration of six municipalities in Mostar as proposed by the EU representative (*EEN,* 1997, vol. 11, no. 11, p. 8).

27 June 1997: Bosnian Serb president Biljana Plavsic dismisses interior minister Dragan Kijac (who is loyal to Karadzic) for refusing to deal with the corruption that permeates the economy and enriches people like Karadzic.

28 June 1997: prime minister Momcilo Krajisnik rescinds the dismissal.

29 June 1997: Plavsic is briefly detained at Belgrade airport by the Serbian police.

30 June 1997: Plavsic is briefly detained by the Bosnian Serb police. She accuses Karadzic of still running the Republika Srpska and of attempting a coup.

3 July 1997: Plavsic attempts to dissolve the Bosnian Serb parliament and arrange fresh elections for 1 September 1997. 'The functioning of legal order … is in a serious crisis in almost all fields,' she says. Parliament is 'carrying out orders from the informal centres of power', while the police are 'organizing criminal activities'.

4 July 1997: the Bosnian Serb parliament meets after the constitutional court overrules both of Plavsic's orders. Opposition MPs, including the fourteen members of the Party of Democratic Action, do not attend (*IHT,* 5 July 1997, p. 2). Plavsic tells her supporters in Banja Luka that 'I am sorry this happened, but crime must be stopped. Victims [of war] did not fall for a state of thieves, but for a state of honest people' (*The Times,* 5 July 1997, p. 17). (Plavsic has threatened to arrest Karadzic for corruption: *IHT,* 21 July 1997, p. 5. Plavsic has said that 'According to our constitution, not only Karadzic but no one else can be extradited': *The Times,* 26 July 1997, p. 16.)

In February 1997 Plavsic placed an advertisement in Serbian papers calling for an investigation into the export–import companies controlled by Karadzic and Momcilo Krajisnik (who is also the Serb representative of the three-member Bosnian presidency).

> The Karadzic–Krajisnik companies are called Centrex and Select-Impex [Selkt-Impex] and bring in massive revenues from contraband … Dr Karadzic controls a nationwide secret police network … 'The consequence of this is an enormous accumulation of wealth by a relatively small number of our population,' Mrs Plavsic said in an extraordinary address from the Banja Luka studio of state television. 'Do they think that the rest of the population will be their slaves?' Yesterday government officials closed the studio.
>
> (Tom Walker, *The Times*, 5 July 1997, p. 17)

In an earlier article Chris Hedges (*IHT*, 7 April 1997, pp. 1, 7) reported that Karadzic oversees a monopoly on the sale of gasoline, cigarettes and other goods in the Republika Srpska. He controls the monopoly through two companies he runs with Momcilo Krajisnik. Plavsic stated that:

> The state has no control over the economy. Some private persons are making a lot of money behind the scenes and should be obliged to pay the state. I have given the order to investigate this, but unfortunately certain institutions, including the police, are involved. This monopoly does not just include gasoline, but extends to things such as building materials and cattle.

Karadzic started Centrex in 1993, which, with the protection of the police and the Serbian Democratic Party, secured exclusive rights to import and sell a variety of goods. In 1996 he formed Selkt-Impex along with the interior ministry of the Republika Srpska. It handles some imports but also supplements the salaries of the Bosnian Serb police, whose basic wages are paid by the Serbian-dominated government of the Federal Republic of Yugoslavia.

5 July 1997: the Bosnian Serb parliament passes a number of measures designed to weaken the powers of the president (e.g. easier impeachment rules) and to pave the way towards a referendum on whether to dismiss President Plavsic. (The constitution requires that parliament call a referendum to remove the president: *IHT*, 21 July 1997, p. 5.)

12 July 1997: President Clinton: 'I believe the present [Sfor] operation will have run its course by then [30 June 1998] and we'll have to discuss what, if any, involvement the United States should have there' (*IHT*, 14 July 1997, p. 10).

19 July 1997: Plavsic is expelled from the Serbian Democratic Party.

20 July 1997: in Doboj Plavsic addresses a rally of her supporters: 'Now is the moment to establish a democratic Serb state based on legality, because we belonged – and will again belong – to Europe' (*IHT*, 22 July 1997, p. 5).

21 July 1997: joint police patrols begin in Mostar (*Independent*, 22 July 1997, p. 9). (An agreement on a joint police force was signed on 10 July 1997: *EEN*, 1997, vol. 11, no. 14, p. 6.)

1 August 1997: the deadline for agreement on naming Bosnia's ambassadors passes.

2 August 1997: Moslems who have returned to Croat-controlled Jajce in Bosnia are forced out by mobs.

3 August 1997: Germany suspends contacts with Bosnia's existing ambassador in Bonn.

4 August 1997: the UK, Germany, Sweden, Austria and Italy suspend contacts with Bosnia's existing ambassadors in these countries.

5 August 1997: the USA and the Netherlands suspend contacts with the existing Bosnian ambassadors. The USA criticizes Carlos Westendorp for allegedly spending too little time in Bosnia and for extending various deadlines.

5 August 1997: Bosnian Croat authorities agree to allow Moslem refugees to return and agree to form a joint Moslem–Croat police force by the end of August.

6–9 August 1997: Richard Holbrooke is sent on a special mission to Bosnia, Croatia and Serbia after increasing concern about the lack of progress in implementing the Dayton accords. He is accompanied by Robert Gelbard (the US envoy to Bosnia). Holbrooke secures agreement on the allocation of Bosnian ambassadors, on the Bosnian telephone system and on the setting up of a Bosnian military commission. In addition, Bosnia and Croatia make a fresh commitment to the principle of the 'organized, voluntary and safe return of displaced persons to their homes'. (There have been incidents when Moslems have obstructed the return of ethnic Serb and Croat refugees.) Holbrooke also extracts a promise from Krajisnik to exclude Karadzic from political activities. There is no progress on the common currency and the question of citizenship.

On 8 August it was announced that special police (paramilitary) forces in the Republika Srpska were either to come under the control of Sfor (if considered soldiers) or to come under the control of the United Nations International Police Task Force (if considered police). On that day Sfor ordered special police units to return to barracks or face seizure of their weapons, while regular inspections followed. On 15 August Sfor signed an agreement that would remove special police protection from indicted war criminals (*IHT*, 16 August 1997, p. 2).

11 August 1997: it is announced (by its French head) that the Central Bank of Bosnia has started operations (*Transition*, 1997, vol. 8, no. 4, p. 29).

15 August 1997: the constitutional court of the Republika Srpska rules against Plavsic's attempt to dissolve the parliament and call an early election. (One of the seven judges on the constitutional court later revealed that he had been beaten and told to vote against Plavsic. There were also rumours of others being intimidated.)

The president of the Banja Luka branch of the Serbian Democratic Party resigns.

16 August 1997: special police units loyal to Plavsic take over the Banja Luka Public Security Centre. Sfor troops then take over and find evidence that the centre has been used for spying on Plavsic.

On Saturday [16 August 1997] the international agency responsible for overseeing civilian aspects of the peace agreement interceded forcefully for Mrs Plavsic by issuing what amounted to a decree that she had the right to dissolve the legislature and hold new elections … In July American soldiers began round-the-clock protection for several hundred Muslim and Croatian refugees returning to homes in a Bosnian Serb area.

(*IHT*, 20 August 1997, p. 5)

17 August 1997: two ministers from the government of Republika Srpska resign.

18 August 1997: Sfor troops leave the centre and civilian police take over.

The police chief of Banja Luka, appointed by Plavsic, is briefly detained by the Republika Srpska security service.

The finance minister of the government of Republika Srpska resigns.

20 August 1997: Sfor troops (with Plavsic's 'mutual agreement') take control of police stations in Banja Luka and seize unauthorized arms.

22 August 1997: Pero Colic (the Bosnian Serb army chief of staff) says that he will 'not sit back with arms folded' and watch the Republika Srpska split. A statement is released after a general staff meeting: 'If individual actors in the crisis should continue to destroy the state, the army of the Republika Srpska shall no longer tolerate and warn, but shall … undertake measures to defend integrity, sovereignty and constitutional order.'

23 August 1997: the government of Republika Srpska announces that it will regard all Plavsic's decisions as 'irregular, illegitimate and non-binding'.

24 August 1997: the Banja Luka state television station (which covers the western part of Republika Srpska) makes its first broadcast free of the control of Pale (Karadzic's headquarters).

25 August 1997: Dragoljub Mirjanic, the vice-president of Republika Srpska, resigns.

26 August 1997: four of the eight main army commanders meet with Plavsic in Banja Luka. (A majority of the eleven commanders in total attend, accounting for two-thirds of the army: *Independent*, 27 August 1997, p. 8.) Colic and the three other main commanders decline the invitation. (The president is supreme commander of the army.)

27 August 1997: Plavsic meets Patriarch Pavle, head of the Serbian Orthodox Church.

The Doboj television transmitter (north-east of Banja Luka) is taken by pro-Plavsic supporters and then retaken by pro-Karadzic supporters.

28 August 1997: clashes occur between Sfor (US) troops and pro-Karadzic civilians in Brcko and Bijeljina when pro-Plavsic police try to take control of police stations.

Plavsic establishes a new party, the Serbian People's Union.

29 August 1997: an explosion in Banja Luka, near the bus and railway stations, kills one person. There are two explosions in Doboj.

1 September 1997: pro-Karadzic supporters stone Sfor (US) troops guarding a television transmitter (near Bijeljina) which was taken over on 28 August.

2 September 1997: Sfor (US) troops return the transmitter to the control of

Karadzic supporters on condition that Pale does not incite violence against Sfor and the international community, allows opposition politicians and President Plavsic reasonable airtime, and gives Carlos Westerdorp a half-hour slot to explain Sfor's actions in Brcko.

3 September 1997: army chief of staff Pero Colic meets Plavsic in Banja Luka and afterwards refers to her as 'supreme commander'. He also says that Plavsic can name the interior minister attending the Republika Srpska's supreme defence council.

4 September 1997: Sfor (US) troops dismantle their checkpoint on the bridge over the Sava river connecting the Republika Srpska with Croatia.

7 September 1997: Banja Luka's police chief bans all public meetings until the 13–14 September 1997 local elections.

8 September 1997: Sfor troops and police loyal to Plavsic prevent most pro-Karadzic supporters from attending a rally in Banja Luka.

Plavsic meets Krajisnik.

9 September 1997: pro-Karadzic supporters (including Momcilo Krajisnik, interior minister Dragan Kijac and prime minister Gojko Klickovic), besieged in a Banja Luka hotel by pro-Plavsic supporters, are rescued by Sfor troops.

11 September 1997: the USA announces that three aircraft will fly over Bosnia on 13–14 September (when local elections are to be held) capable of broadcasting programmes furthering the Dayton accords and of jamming radio and television broadcasts incompatible with the Dayton accords.

12 September 1997: Krajisnik ends his boycott of Bosnian presidential meetings (*EEN*, 1997, vol. 11, no. 18, p. 6).

13–14 September 1997: local elections are held in Bosnia.

These were organized by OSCE. There were 2.5 million registered voters, including 400,000 outside Bosnia (*IHT*, 15 September 1997, p. 10). Eighty-three parties, nine coalitions and 159 independent candidates competed (*IHT*, 13 September 1997, p. 2). Voting took place in 136 municipalities plus six precincts in Mostar.

Voters were unable to nominate any place of residence (as they were previously). Voters had to choose either the area where they lived in 1991 (voting there or by absentee ballot) or the area where they had been resident since June 1996.

The Croatian Democratic Union and the Serbian Democratic Party did not carry out their threats to boycott the elections. Plavsic's new party (the Serbian People's Union) was too late to take part.

The results took a long time to appear and were released only gradually. Some of the results were as follows:

> *Brcko:* three Serb parties win fifty-six seats, while five parties from the Bosniac–Croat Federation win twenty-six seats (Independent, 11 October 1997, p. 12). On 30 December 1997 a multi-ethnic administration was appointed by the international supervisor Robert Farrand (EEN, 1998, vol. 11, no. 25, p. 7). On 30 December 1997 a multi-ethnic municipal assembly convened, with Moslems in important posts. A multi-ethnic police force was formed soon afterwards (The Economist, 14 March 1998, p. 47).

Dvar: Dvar is controlled by Croats. Although there is a Serb mayor, who returned from exile in the Republika Srpska, he needs a two-thirds majority to get anything through the council. A mere 600 of more than 15,000 refugees from the town have returned (*The Economist*, 11 April 1998, p. 34).

On 16 April 1998 an elderly Serb couple who had recently returned to Dvar were killed by Croats. Dvar was 98 per cent Serb before it was overrun by the Croats in 1995. Some 1,500 Serbs have returned but around fifty arson attacks on Serb homes have taken place since the start of 1998 (*Guardian*, 17 April 1998, p. 2). Around a thousand Serbs have returned (*FT*, 17 April 1998, p. 2). Over thirty Serb houses have been burned since the beginning of 1998 (*IHT*, 17 April 1998, p. 5). On 23 April 1998 a cardinal and hundreds of other Croat Catholics were attacked after they ignored warnings not to visit and hold a mass in Serb-controlled territory east of Dvar. The following day Croats burned buildings and stoned overturned UN vehicles in Dvar (*IHT*, 25 April 1998, p. 2).

> 'In several towns, such as Dvar, in the Moslem–Croat Federation, where many Serbs have returned, the ethnic balance has tipped against the Croats without, yet, provoking the ructions that many feared' (*The Economist*, 19 August 2000, p. 35).

Mostar: the Moslem Party of Democratic Action gain control with fourteen seats. The Croatian Democratic Union, with ten seats, appeal (EEN, 1997, vol. 11, no. 20, p. 5).

Srebrenica: Moslem parties gain control with twenty-five seats. The two main Serb parties win twenty seats (*FT*, 10 October 1997, p. 3). In January 1998, Serbs blocked the arrival of the twenty-five Moslem councillors and stoned the car of an OSCE official. In March 1998, Serb councillors played the Bosnian Serb anthem at the council's inaugural session and the Moslems walked out. On 6 April 1998, OSCE suspended the assembly and said it would appoint an administrator with wide powers. The administrator was to control most municipal assets and would head an 'interim executive board' consisting of four Serbs and four Moslems. If the board failed to agree, he could rule by decree (*The Economist*, 11 April 1998, p. 34).

Tuzla: advocates of multi-ethnic toleration gain control (*The Economist*, 11 October 1997, p. 58).

Velika Kladusa: on 22 December 1997 Fikret Abdic returned to power after his party's victory (*EEN*, 1998, vol. 11, no. 25, p. 7).

> The local elections in September showed that most displaced Bosnians want to roll back the ethnic cleansing and go home. The rules allowed them to register where they lived before the war or where they live now. Eighty-nine per cent chose their former abode.
>
> (Jonathan Steele, *Guardian*, 11 November 1997, p. 17)

OSCE has certified 125 of the 136 municipalities, which means that the council has met at least once and its deputies have been chosen. There are a dozen towns in which exiles won majorities or a big share of the seats, e.g. Brcko, Dvar, Mostar and Srebrenica. In nine towns where inhabitants have blocked exiles from taking office OSCE has had to choose mayors itself and compel councils to meet (*The Economist*, 11 April 1998, p. 34).

Following local authority polls in 1997 OSCE has managed to install elected assemblies in all but two of Bosnia's 136 municipalities. One of the exceptions is Srebrenica, whose displaced Moslem population (still living as refugees) elected a Moslem-majority local assembly through the absentee voting system (Gabriel Partos, *The World Today*, vol. 54, nos 8–9, p. 210).

> Municipal elections in Bosnia were organized by OSCE in September 1997. While the elections of the previous year were heavily weighted with nation-alist candidates, the 1997 elections saw more than seventy parties represented and the use of absentee ballots for the Bosnian diaspora. However, only in Tuzla did non-ethnic parties dominate. In the rest of Bosnia, not surprisingly, the ruling nationalist parties captured most of the council seats ... There were some positive sides ... even though nationalism still ruled the area. The pro-Karadzic SDS [Serbian Democratic Party] in Republika Srpska did not capture as many votes as it was feared they would, although many disaffected voters cast their ballots for the more extreme nationalist Serbian Radical Party (SRS), the Bosnian branch of Vojislav Seselj's party in Serbia. Furthermore, candidates representing platforms for refugee return were elected in a number of seats in the federation and one in Republika Srpska.
>
> (Friedman 2000: 26)

17 September 1997: a UN helicopter crashes with the loss of twelve lives. Among those killed is Gerd Wagner (from Germany), deputy to Carlos Westendorp.

19 September 1997: a car bomb explodes in the western (Croat-controlled) part of Mostar near the police station run by the joint Moslem–Croat police force (agreed in July 1997).

20 September 1997: pro-Plavsic police take control of the police station in Prnjavor.

23 September 1997: Serbs attack Sfor troops guarding a checkpoint outside Doboj.

24 September 1997: Plavsic and Krajisnik meet Milosevic in Belgrade. Agreement is reached to hold a parliamentary election in the Republika Srpska on 15 November 1997 and elections for the two presidencies (presently held by Plavsic and Krajisnik) on 7 December 1997. The official radio and television stations will broadcast on alternate days from Banja Luka and Pale and interna-tional authorities will be given one hour each evening.

28 September 1997: Plavsic claims that Karadzic has transferred DM 49 million into foreign bank accounts (*The Times*, 29 September 1997, p. 14).

29 September 1997: the first stone from the Mostar bridge is retrieved from the Neretva river at the start of the bridge's reconstruction. (Built by the Ottoman sultan Suleiman the Magnificent in 1566, it was finally destroyed by the Bosnian Croats in November 1993.)

30 September 1997: the Bosnian Serb Pale faction led by Momcilo Krajisnik refuses to endorse Plavsic's decision to hold parliamentary elections on 23 November rather than 15 November as provisionally agreed with Milosevic (*EEN*, 1997, vol. 11, no. 19, p. 7).

1 October 1997: Sfor troops seize control of four radio and television transmitters (controlled by pro-Karadzic supporters), namely those near Doboj and Bijeljina (in the north), Trebinje (in the south-east) and Sarajevo. Control is handed over to pro-Plavsic supporters.

13 October 1997: Plavsic and Krajisnik agree in a meeting in Belgrade to hold parliamentary elections on 23 November (*EEN*, 1997, vol. 11, no. 20, p. 5).

16 October 1997: Pale mysteriously manages to resume television broadcasting.

19 October 1997: the pirate relay station is taken over by Sfor troops.

3–4 November 1997: Bosnia attends a meeting of Balkan countries which is also attended by Greece (the host nation), Turkey, the Federal Republic of Yugoslavia, Macedonia, Albania, Bulgaria and Romania.

11 November 1997: Sfor troops seize a police station in Doboj controlled by pro-Karadzic special police.

21 November 1997: OSCE reports that the various parties in Bosnia have completed the arms reductions agreed to in June 1996 by destroying close to 6,600 pieces of weaponry, including more than 700 tanks and 80 armoured combat vehicles, close to 60 combat aircraft and more than 5,700 pieces of artillery (*IHT*, 22 November 1997, p. 2).

22–3 November 1997: elections are held in the Republika Srpska. The turnout is 77 per cent. The Serbian Democratic Party loses its majority, winning twenty-four of the eighty-three seats in the National Assembly. Plavsic's Serbian People's Union wins fifteen seats, as does the Serbian Radical Party (an off-shoot of Seselj's Radical Party in Serbia). The Moslem-dominated Coalition for Bosnia and Hercegovina wins sixteen seats, benefiting mainly from the absentee vote of refugees.

9–10 December 1997: the Peace Implementation Conference holds another session. The three members of Bosnia's collective presidency announced agreement on passports and citizenship. The measures still have to be agreed by the federal parliament in Sarajevo (*FT*, 10 December 1997, p. 2).

Deadlines were set for various measures (e.g. the end of January 1998 for common car licence plates throughout Bosnia) and Carlos Westendorp was empowered to impose 'interim solutions … when parties are unable to reach agreement'. (Westendorp vowed to sack Krajisnik if he continued his blocking tactics: *Guardian*, 11 December 1997, p. 13.)

Yugoslav and Bosnian Serb delegates walked out shortly before the end of the session in protest at a reference in the final communiqué to 'increasing ethnic tension' in Kosovo. 'Those concerned' were urged to 'refrain from activities that might exacerbate existing difficulties'.

'At Bonn in December 1997 the Peace Implementation Council beefed up the High Commissioner's powers ... giving him authority to remove obstructive officials and to impose solutions where after lengthy delays the local leadership could not do so' (Jacques Klein, *The World Today*, 1999, vol. 55, no. 6, p. 8).

13 December 1997: Momcilo Krajisnik signs a dual citizenship agreement with the Yugoslav foreign minister Milan Milutinovic (*EEN*, 1997, vol. 11, no. 24, p. 7).

18 December 1997: President Clinton says that US troops should stay in Bosnia beyond the June 1998 deadline, until peace is 'self-sustaining'. 'It is imperative that we not stop until the peace here has a life of its own, until it can endure without us.' What is now needed are 'achievable, concrete benchmarks, not a deadline'. 'The progress in Bosnia is unmistakable, but it is not yet irreversible ... If we pull out before the job is done, Bosnia will almost certainly fall back into violence, chaos and ultimately a war as bloody as the last one.'

21 December 1997: the Luciano Pavarotti Music Centre in Mostar is opened by the opera singer himself. He and his friends raised the funds for the centre.

22 December 1997: President Clinton visits Sarajevo and US troops in Tuzla.

23 December 1997: Chancellor Kohl of Germany visits German troops in Sarajevo.

27 December 1997: Republika Srpska's National Assembly meets but adjourns until 12 January 1998 after failing to agree on new assembly and government officials.

18 January 1998: Milorad Dodik, nominated by Biljana Plavsic, becomes prime minister of the Republika Srpska. (He is leader of the Independent Social Democrats, which has two seats in the National Assembly.) Pro-Karadzic supporters denounce Dodik as a tool of the West who has betrayed the Serbs and say that they will not recognize the new government. The coalition government has the support of Moslem and Croat deputies who will travel to sessions under UN protection.

Dodik blames economic problems on 'needless spite, nonsense and egoism' by the previous rulers. He pledges strict implementation of the Dayton accords, the establishment of a free press and an end to censorship, an end to state corruption, an acceleration of privatization, and a separation of government from the Serbian Orthodox Church. Dodik wishes to transfer the capital of Republika Srpska from Pale to Banja Luka (*IHT*, 21 January 1998, p. 5, and 22 January 1998, p. 8).

19 January 1998: the Yugoslav government recognizes the Dodik administration (*FT*, 21 January 1998, p. 2). Milosevic says that he believes the Dodik government will 'co-operate completely' in the peace process and that he supports this (*IHT*, 22 January 1998, p. 8).

21 January 1998: Carlos Westendorp, the high representative in Bosnia, imposes a solution for the design of a common currency. This will be binding on both entities until they can agree among themselves. The 'convertible marka' (convertible one for one into the DM) will in fact have two designs. Both series of notes will have Cyrillic and Latin lettering. But one will feature leading Moslem and Croat historical and cultural figures, while the other will feature only famous Serbs. UN officials consider it unlikely that the marka will dethrone the DM as the central feature of every major private business transaction. But the marka will eventually play a central role in all transactions conducted with the government and it will have legal standing in the two entities (*IHT*, 22 January 1998, p. 5; *FT*, 22 January 1998, p. 2).

22 January 1998: Dodik meets Milosevic in Belgrade (*FT*, 23 January 1998, p. 2).

26 January 1998:

> Mr Dodik has swiftly signed agreements to unify his police with the Moslem and ethnic Croatian forces, to issue common passports, to establish a common currency and licence plates and to draw up a proper budget. He has dismissed a host of corrupt officials, including customs officials, the head of the financial police, the entire board of directors at the Bosnian power company and at Energopetrol, the fuel enterprise. He has also fired the nationalist editor of the state-owned daily *Glas Srpski*, and the directors of the two oil refineries, the iron mines in Ljubija and the major brewery and cigarette factories in Banja Luka. He said he would also soon remove the hardline chief of the Bosnian Serb army ... Mr Dodik, unlike the Bosnian Serb president Biljana Plavsic ... appears to genuinely support the calls to rebuild a multiethnic Bosnia ... Mr Dodik, thirty-nine, is forming rival ministries in Banja Luka and has announced that the seat of government will move to the city from the Karadzic stronghold in Pale. Most important, he has endorsed an international plan to begin large transfers of refugees to their homes ... The European Union has given Mr Dodik's fledgling administration $6.7 million to pay back salaries and to operate. Once a budget ... is complete the government will be eligible for a large part of the $1.5 billion in aid pledged by the international community for Bosnia ... By Monday [2 February 1998], with the assistance of EU customs inspectors, all border and customs stations will be in the hands of Dodik loyalists who will divert the tens of millions of dollars in revenue from Pale to newly established government bank accounts in Banja Luka ... Mr Dodik has demanded that all records and state documents be transferred from Pale to Banja Luka. Mr Westendorp ... promised international intervention if it did not ... Mr Dodik, a local politician who was blacklisted by the nationalist government for his repeated condemnation of the war, is largely unknown in the Serbian entity.
>
> (Chris Hedges, *IHT*, 29 January 1998, pp. 1, 6)

30 January 1998: the Croatian defence minister agrees in Washington that the Adriatic port of Ploce can be leased to the Bosnian federation for thirty years (*EEN*, 1998, vol. 12, no. 2, p. 7).

31 January 1998: the Bosnian Serb parliament votes in favour of transferring the capital from Pale to Banja Luka.

2 February 1998: Carlos Westendorp unveils the imposed common car-registration plates. The neutral design reveals neither ethnicity nor place of origin.

3 February 1998: the Sarajevo Returns Conference insists that at least 20,000 Serbian and Croatian refugees be allowed to resettle in Sarajevo by the summer of 1998. Sarajevo must be 'truly multi-ethnic'. The Bosnian government is given two weeks to revoke the 1995 legislation governing the return of property to Serbs and Croats (see below). President Izetbegovic says that he will not accept the demand unless the Republika Srpska is made to reciprocate (*IHT*, 4 February 1998, p. 6, and 5 February 1998, p. 5; *Guardian*, 5 February 1998, p. 11).

Sarajevo's population is now 87 per cent Moslem, whereas it was previously split much more evenly between Moslems (50 per cent), Serbs (27 per cent) and Croats (7 per cent). In Bosnia as a whole less than 9 per cent of the 400,000 refugees who have returned to their homes since 1995 are minorities in their immediate communities. Foreign officials talk of 'the Bosnian government's failure to implement repeated pledges to foster the rebirth of a multi-ethnic society'.

> After the war ended in 1995 the two newly established entities in Bosnia, the Serb Republic and the Moslem–Croat Federation, each enacted laws and regulations meant to freeze communal concentrations and obstruct the return of minority refugees to their prewar homes … [The] one-day conference will … spotlight the failure of the government to allow – much less promote – minority resettlement. The conferees will set a series of short deadlines for the government to adopt new laws, resolve dozens of housing disputes and permit thousands of minority refugees to return to Sarajevo. To ensure that the message is heard US and European diplomats at the conference also plan to threaten a cutoff of tens of millions of dollars in aid to Sarajevo if the deadlines are not met … The principal obstacle to allowing minority refugees to return is a 1995 Bosnian law that gave former residents two weeks to reclaim their homes after the 22 December ceasefire that year … If they did not meet it their property was declared abandoned and given to someone else. Because the law was never publicized outside the country, hundreds of thousands of refugees are now without legal recourse … The Bosnian parliament has also voted to deny refugees the right to return to thousands of apartments owned by the Yugoslav army before the war by nullifying contracts for the sale of those apartments to their prewar inhabitants. The Bosnian army has declared many of the apartments abandoned and transferred them to favoured war veterans.
>
> (R. Jeffrey Smith, *IHT*, 3 February 1998, p. 4)

4 February 1998: Carlos Westendorp unveils the imposed national flag.

18 February 1998: the sixteen Nato ambassadors formally approve a third phase of peacekeeping in Bosnia. Sfor's mandate runs out at the end of June

1998. The number of troops (35,000) will remain the same at first but will be reduced to 20,000–25,000 after the Bosnian presidential and parliamentary elections are held in September 1998 (*The Times*, 19 February 1998, p. 15).

15 March 1998: a decision on Brcko is delayed until at least early 1999 (*IHT*, 16 March 1998, p. 1).

22 April 1998: agreement is reached by both sides to re-establish a Bosnia-wide postal service.

23 April 1998: according to senior US and diplomatic officials, American and allied military forces abruptly shelved plans for an operation in August 1997 to capture Radovan Karadzic after it was discovered that a French officer had held secret meetings with Karadzic. US officials believed that key details of the arrest plans may have been leaked at these meetings. The French officer was transferred to Paris in December 1997 (based on a report in the 23 April issue of the *Washington Post* in *IHT*, 24 April 1998, pp. 1, 5).

(Milos Stankovic, a British army major with Serbian parents, was arrested in 1997 and questioned by British police. US officials alleged that he handed Nato plans to Ratko Mladic. Major Stankovic has since been released from detention on bail: *FT*, 24 April 1998, p. 2.)

28 April 1998: a conference takes place in Banja Luka, with all sides represented, aimed at speeding up the return of refugees.

20 May 1998: Carlos Westendorp imposes a new flag when consensus is not reached.

21 May 1998: a scheduled flight between Sarajevo and Belgrade takes place for the first time since 1992 (*IHT*, 22 May 1998, p. 2).

June 1998:

> In June Kresimir Zubak, the Bosnian Croats' representative on Bosnia's three-member presidency, left the hardline nationalist Croatian Democratic Union to set up the New Croatian Initiative, a party that appears to favour a more positive approach towards Bosnia's integration.
>
> (Gabriel Partos, *The World Today*, vol. 54, nos 8–9, p. 210)

The Marka made its first appearance in June 1998 (p. 211).

July 1998: in July 1998 new passports became available, containing only minor variations reflecting linguistic differences between the two entities (Gabriel Partos, *The World Today*, vol. 54, nos 8–9, pp. 210–11).

30 July–1 August 1998: US secretary of state Madeleine Albright visits Croatia and Bosnia.

12–13 September 1998: there was considerable delay before the results of the OSCE-organized elections (for all offices above the municipal level) were announced.

> European observers criticised the management of Bosnia's general elections … Roughly 200,000 voters could not find their names on the register and had to be given special ballot forms. That was four times more than were

left unregistered in last year's local elections. Computer glitches and late deliveries of ballot forms also caused large queues at many polling stations … They also attacked the poor security provided for parties campaigning in areas controlled by ethnic rivals …[But] the current head of OSCE hailed the elections as 'the most successful' since 1995.

(Jonathan Steele, *Guardian*, 15 September 1998, p. 16)

Ultranationalist Nikola Poplasen is elected president of the Republika Srpska, beating Biljana Plavsic.

Mr Poplasen's party is an offshoot of the Radical Party of Serbia's deputy prime minister Vojislav Seselj … During the election campaign Mr Poplasen said that he would use all constitutional means to unite the Serb republic with Serbia … Mr Poplasen boasts of having been a commander during the war … A majority of voters chose Mr Poplasen on the grounds that other candidates would permit the return of Moslems and Croats who were ethnically cleansed in the war … [Poplasen said that 'I have not given up the Serb's political and historical goals. They do not have to be achieved during my mandate, but in some five to ten years.'

(Jonathan Steele, *Guardian*, 26 September 1998, p. 19)

The more moderate Zivko Radisic (Socialist Party) becomes the Serb member of the Bosnian three-person collective presidency, beating the hardline incumbent Momcilo Krajisnik. 'Zivko Radisic, a relative moderate, won enough votes from Moslem and Croat refugees to defeat Momcilo Krajisnik for the Serb seat on Bosnia's three-man collective presidency' (Jonathan Steele, *Guardian*, 26 September 1998, p. 19).

Ante Jelavic (HDZ Party) wins the Croatian seat on the three-person presidency and Alija Izetbegovic (SDA) wins the Bosniac seat.

Mr Poplasen's room for manoeuvre is indeed limited. The nationalist coalition of his Radical Party and the former-ruling Serb Democratic Party is well short of a majority in the Bosnian Serb assembly. The search for a new prime minister is likely to be a drawnout process that could well lead to new elections. In the meantime Milorad Dodik … remains in office with the silent support of Moslem deputies holding the balance of power.

(*FT*, Survey, 21 October 1998, p. ii)

Last month's elections showed ethnic or confessional-based political parties losing ground. The SDA-dominated coalition of the wartime leader, Alija Izetbegovic, lost its absolute majority in the federation assembly, dropping from eighty-eight to sixty-eight seats in the 140-seat body. The hardline Croat HDZ party also dropped back a little. Non-confessional parties, such as the Social Democrats, gained ground.

(*FT*, Survey, 21 October 1998, p. iii)

The SDA and its coalition partners captured 48 per cent of the vote in last year's general election in the Bosniac–Croat Federation. The two biggest Croat parties between them took 23 per cent. The SDA's vote fell, but the two Social Democratic parties, the biggest non-ethnic parties, took only 17.5 per cent between them.

(*FT*, Survey, 14 December 1999, p. 37)

Although he [Poplasen] won the presidency, his party took only eleven of the eighty-three seats in the Bosnian-Serb area's parliament. Even with the help of Mr Karadzic's former ruling party and other hardliners, it can collect only thirty-three, well under the majority needed to form a government ... Carlos Westendorp ... dismissed the vice-president of Mr Karadzic's party for saying bellicose things about the possible repercussions in Bosnia of Nato intervention against Serbia in Kosovo. Nato peacemakers expelled Mr Seselj, the deputy prime minister of Serbia, from the Serb republic while he was visiting Mr Poplasen ... On 14 November Mr Poplasen ... invited Dragan Kalinic, another hardliner close to Mr Karadzic, to lead the government ... [But] so far only one member of parliament has switched allegiance. The West would like Mr Dodik, whose party went up from two to six in September, to stay in the prime-minister-ship. It has made clear that, if he does, the Serb republic will continue to get the economic help that has brought in some $240 million worth of aid since July 1997. If the pressure works, and Mr Dodik stays in the job, the West will try to make sure he lives up to earlier promises. He had said that he would let 70,000 Croat and Moslem refugees back into the Serb republic this year. So far only 2,000 have made it.

(*The Economist*, 21 November 1998, p. 46)

23 November 1998: Bosnia and Croatia sign an accord under which Bosnia receives the right to use the Adriatic port of Ploce, while Croatia is given free transit through Neum, a short strip on the Adriatic coast. The parties are committed to draft detailed annexes to the accord by July 1999 (*FT*, 24 November 1998, p. 2).

12 December 1998: a new federal government under premier Edhem Bicakcic is approved by parliament (*EEN*, 1998, vol. 12, no. 13, p. 6).

15–16 December 1998: a two-day conference of the Bosnian Peace Implementation Council is held in Madrid (the third such meeting). There is a call for urgent action to achieve a lasting peace (*IHT*, 16 December 1998, p. 6, and 17 December 1998, p. 5).

A programme is approved for economic, legal and political reforms to reduce Bosnia's reliance on outside support. Extra powers are given to Carlos Westendorp (the high representative), entitling him to block aid allocations or bar parties or political leaders from running for election if they fail to co-operate (*FT*, 17 December 1998, p. 3).

31 December 1998:

In an attempt to end a political deadlock, President Poplasen of Republika Srpska ... named Brane Miljus, a moderate, as prime minister designate after a hardliner failed to win parliamentary approval. Mr Miljus is a member of the pro-Western Party of Independent Social Democrats run by Milorad Dodik, the current prime minister. The parliament must approve Mr Miljus.

(*The Times*, 1 January 1999. p. 13)

(Miljus was voted down by the Bosnian Serb parliament on 25 January 1999: *EEN*, 1999, vol. 12, no. 14, p. 6.)

27 January 1999: the size of the US military contingent in Bosnia will shrink from 6,900 to 6,200 over the two months as part of a Nato decision to trim its 32,000-strong peacekeeping force by 10 per cent (*IHT*, 28 January 1999, p. 6).

5 March 1999: a decision on Brcko is announced by Carlos Westendorp. The decision, however, was actually made by Roberts Owen, the US official who had supervised the Serb-run town of Brcko. The outlying area had been run by the federation. The ruling says that the two entities will be merged into a 'self-governing neutral district'. 'Both portions will now be held by both entities. The new government will be democratic and multi-ethnic.' The new entity will report to the federal government and will be administered under international supervision.

Nikola Poplasen had earlier said that he was ready to 'take major decisions' in the event of an 'unjust solution'. He was later dismissed as president of the Republika Srpska by Carlos Westendorp (*IHT*, 6 March 1999, p. 2).

> Carlos Westendorp ... sacked Mr Poplasen, saying he 'consistently acted to trigger instability in Republika Srpska' and had abused his office by trying to remove its pro-Western prime minister, Milorad Dodik. Mr Dodik, however, resigned in protest at the decision on Brcko ... Mr Poplasen ... has blocked refugee returns and has refused to hand over control of the RS army to Bosnia's collective presidency, as ordered by Westendorp ... Last month ... a large cache of sophisticated weapons smuggled into Bosnia was found by Nato troops in the hands of the RS army near Brcko.
>
> (*FT*, 6 March 1999, p. 2)

> On 5 March Roberts Owen, an American lawyer appointed by the International Court of Justice in The Hague, ruled that the entire prewar municipality of Brcko should be a 'condominium' shared by Bosnia's two halves, with its own local administration ... Only a few hours earlier Carlos Westendorp ... had dismissed Nikola Poplasen ... Mr Owen ruled that the Serb authorities – above all, Mr Poplasen – had blocked both the return of displaced Serbs living there and the return of displaced Serbs living there to the Moslem–Croat Federation.
>
> (*The Economist*, 13 March 1999, p. 55)

Carlos Westendorp (*IHT*, 15 March 1999, p. 10):

> On 5 March I fired a president, the leader of the Bosnian Serbs … The destiny of the Bosnian Serbs is no longer controlled by Belgrade. Nor would the great majority of the Serbs who live in Republika Srpska wish it to be … President Poplasen had been warned … But from the moment of his election last September [1998] he persistently abused his position to obstruct implementation of the Dayton peace agreement. Most serious was his refusal to nominate a viable candidate for prime minister … It has been evident for many months that only one member of the National Assembly can command a workable majority, and that is Milorad Dodik, the prime minister of the last administration, who has been acting as caretaker. His government has shown a willingness to comply with the demands of the peace process. Mr Poplasen, a hardliner of the old school, responded by refusing to sign legislation legally passed by a majority vote of the National Assembly. The final straw came when he sought to remove Mr Dodik … The decision [to remove him] has been further justified by his subsequent call for violent civil disobedience. The National Assembly initially responded with a vote of confidence in President Poplasen. That response, I believe, was in part based on the widely misunderstood (and wholly unrelated) decision on Brcko.

(The arbitration procedure allowing for multi-racial district of Brcko was completed on 18 August 1999: *EEN*, 1999, vol. 12, no. 19, p. 3.)

6 March 1999: an armed Serb civilian is shot dead by a US soldier, allegedly because Sfor troops were threatened by a Serb gang (*Guardian*, 8 March 1999, p. 13).

9 March 1999: Milorad Dodik says he is prepared to resume his duties as caretaker prime minister once Serb anger cools (*IHT*, 10 March 1999, p. 7).

'Milorad Dodik … has in fact continued to perform his duties much as normal; it is becoming increasingly clear that he intends to stay on … Mr Dodik has met Brcko's international supervisor to discuss implementation of the decision' (*The Economist*, 13 March 1999, p. 55).

15 March 1999: Dodik withdraws his resignation (*EEN*, 1999, vol. 12, no. 16, p. 9).

16 March 1999: Moslem–Croat Federation deputy interior minister Jozo Leutar (a Croat) is fatally injured in a car bombing incident in Sarajevo (*EEN*, 1999, vol. 12, no. 16, p. 9).

26 March 1999: the Russian contingent in Sfor opts out of US command in favour of its own command headquarters (*EEN*, 1999, vol. 12, no. 16, p. 9). (This was in protest at the Nato bombing of Yugoslavia which started on 24 March 1999.)

22 October 1999: Zeljko Kopanja is badly injured in a car bomb explosion in Banja Luka. He is a publisher and editor of the liberal newspaper *Nezavisne Novine*, which has recently published a series of articles about war crimes. 'It was the first time a Bosnian Serb media outlet gave such a detailed account of ethnic cleansing crimes committed by Serbs from Bosnia against their former Moslem neighbours' (Anna Husarska, *IHT*, 26 October 1999, p. 6).

2 November 1999: it is announced that Sfor will be reduced by one-third to 20,000 by April 2000. Currently there are 30,000 troops (from about forty countries), down from about 60,000 just after the war (*FT*, 3 November 1999, p. 10).

15 November 1999: a UN report on the Srebrenica mass murder of July 1995 is published.

> The report says that the UN's willingness to negotiate with the Bosnian Serb leaders, Radovan Karadzic and General Ratko Mladic, amounted to 'appeasement'. 'It was with the deepest regret and remorse that we have reviewed our own actions and decisions in the face of the assault on Srebrenica,' the report said. 'Through error, misjudgement and an inability to recognize the scope of evil confronting us, we failed to do our part to save the people of Srebrenica from the Serb campaign of mass murder ... The tragedy of Srebrenica will haunt us forever,' the report said. On 6 July 1995, as Bosnian Serb forces began a five-day assault on the town, senior UN commanders repeatedly rejected appeals from the Dutch peacekeeping force for Nato air support, while the UN's local officer refused to release weapons to the Bosnian Moslems to defend themselves. When assistance finally came, it was 'too little, too late', according to a UN cable. The blame for the fall of Srebrenica was not the UN's alone, according to the report. It says the fifteen-nation UN Security Council was the chief architect of a policy that was doomed from the start. The out-gunned, lightly armed Dutch peace-keepers also came under criticism for failing to fire on the forces besieging the town or to warn of the enormous danger facing the enclave. And the major powers, including the United States, refused to provide intelligence on Serbian troop movements, the report says. But the report reserves its harshest criticism for the UN leadership, particularly former secretary-general Boutros Boutros Ghali, his senior commander, Lieutenant General Bernard Janvier of France, and his top envoy, Yasushi Akashi of Japan. While secretary-general Kofi Annan's personal role in the events in Srebrenica is not clearly addressed in the report, he says he has accepted general responsibility for the UN's failure in Bosnia. Mr Annan was head of the peacekeeping operation at the time ... The report also challenges a long list of UN decisions during the conflict. The UN now acknowledges that its arms embargo undermined the Bosnian army's ability to defend itself. The report says the UN's persistent reluctance to use air power against the Bosnian Serbs was a mistake. And it repudiates a long-cherished assumption that the UN can be evenhanded in the face of an aggressor. The use of force, not diplomacy, is the only appropriate way to confront a determined aggressor, the report says ... 'In Bosnia as in Kosovo the international community tried to reach a negotiated settlement with an unscrupulous and

murderous regime,' it says. 'In both instances it required the use of force to bring a halt to the planned and systematic killing and expulsion of civilians.'

(*IHT*, 16 November 1999, pp. 1, 10)

The lessons of the tragedy ... are drawn out in a 155-page report submitted to the Security Council. It has been written in the name of the UN secretary-general Kofi Annan. Mr Annan was in charge of peacekeeping at the time ... The misjudgements, Mr Annan writes, arose from an unwillingness to confront the Serbs with a sufficiently powerful military response. That itself resulted from 'an inability to recognize the scope of the evil confronting us' ... It is estimated that ... the Serb army rounded up and killed 7,600 men and boys over sixteen ... The Western powers negotiated with them [the Serbs] in a manner that 'amounted to appeasement' ... 'The cardinal lesson of Srebrenica is that a deliberate and systematic attempt to terrorize, expel or murder an entire people must be met decisively with all necessary means, and with the political will to carry the policy through to its logical conclusion,' the report says ... The report lingered on the refusal of the UN force in Bosnia, Unprofor, to agree to Bosnian requests for the return of weapons they had been forced to give up. 'This decision seems to have been particularly ill-advised given Unprofor's own unwillingness consistently to advocate force as a means of deterring attacks on the enclave,' it says.

(*Independent*, 17 November 1999, p. 19)

21 November 1999: a joint statement, issued by the international organizations supervising Bosnia to mark the anniversary of the signing of the Dayton accords, includes the following statement:

We welcome the absence of war and the deepening of peace ... [But] we see what we lack for a truly durable peace: a functioning sovereign state that unites all peoples of Bosnia and Hercegovina; an economy free from political influence and corruption that can provide jobs and stability; and the ability for all refugees and displaced persons to return to their homes.

(*FT*, Survey, 14 December 1999, p. 35)

29 November 1999: Wolfgang Petritsch, the new high representative, dismisses twenty-two local politicians (nine Serbs, seven Bosniacs and six Croats), mainly for obstructing the return of minority group refugees (*FT*, Survey, 24 December 1999, p. 35). The mayor of Banja Luka was one of the nine Serbs (p. 37).

19 December 1999: it is announced that Sfor troops raided buildings in Mostar on 14 October 1999.

Nato troops ... say employees are actually intelligence agents of a clandestine, illicit network run by Croatia. Nato officials say they have clear evidence that the Croatian government of Franjo Tudjman, who died a week ago, has been secretly paying millions of dollars a month to fund this network. Its aim, they say, was to support Bosnian Croat nationalists who oppose the return of Bosnian Moslems to Croat-dominated areas of the country, and thus keep alive the possibility that Croatia might ultimately be able to annex Bosnian territory. Some of the money was also used to promote criminal activity, including the apparent counterfeiting of credit cards and telephone debit cards, Nato officials say ... A senior Nato official said ... the raid had uncovered 'prima facie evidence of linkages' between the Croatian government and local intelligence officials that were designed to influence local politics and undermine the Dayton accords. 'This is illegal,' the official said. A small number of illegal weapons were also found.

(*IHT*, 20 December 1999, p. 7)

23 January 2000: 'Moslem co-chairman of the Council of Ministers Haris Silajdzic calls in an interview published in an Austrian newspaper for the Dayton agreement to be revised on the grounds that it is not being implemented.' He resigned on 11 February (*EEN*, 2000, vol. 12, no. 22, p. 4).

8 March 2000: there is a formal announcement making Brcko a multi-ethnic district. As of 8 March 2000 the city has a multi-ethnic government approved by international officials and its residents are exempt from the draft (*IHT*, 9 March 2000, p. 5).

Brcko becomes a neutral territory under a district administration appointed by international supervisor Robert Farrand (*EEN*, 2000, vol. 12, no. 23, p. 8).

8 April 2000: local elections are held in Bosnia. The turnout was about 70 per cent.

Bosnia's opposition Social Democrats said Sunday [9 April] that early local election results pointed to a shift away from nationalists in Moslem areas ... But the hard-line parties that have dominated Bosnia since before the 1992–5 ethnic war [the Serb Democratic Party and the Croatian Democratic Union] said they continued to enjoy broad support in Serbian and Croatian regions in the voting on Saturday [8 April] ... The multi-ethnic Social Democrats, who controlled only the northern town of Tuzla prior to Bosnia's second postwar municipal elections, said they were on track to become the biggest national party, helped by victory in Sarajevo ... Election organizers have said that early results in Bosnian Serb areas should be treated with some caution since they did not include absentee ballots cast by Moslem refugees expelled from their homes.

(*IHT*, 10 April 2000, p. 4)

In most Moslem-dominated major cities the opposition Social Democratic Party defeated the governing Moslem Party for Democratic Action, according to preliminary results ... But the results also showed the nationalist Serb Democratic Party was winning the most votes in the Serbian half of Bosnia ... The nationalist Croatian Democratic Union claimed victory.

(*IHT*, 11 April 2000, p. 4)

'The Serbian Democratic Party ... claimed it had even won in the western city of Banja Luka, a haven for moderate Serbs' (*Telegraph*, 11 April 2000, p. 20).

> Municipal elections in April 2000 went furthest towards confirming the trend towards political moderation, with the stranglehold of the Social Democratic Party of Alia [Alija] Izetbegovic being surprised by defeats by the Social Democratic Party ... Nonetheless, the SDS [Serbian Democratic Party] still emerged as the majority party in the Republika Srpska, although its position had been eroded and it was clear that political sniping would continue, despite the trend towards moderate parties and towards more moderate candidates within all parties.
>
> (Friedman 2000: 28)

'In April the harsh nationalists who ruled their respective roosts during the civil war did worse than usual in local elections across Bosnia ... The arch-nationalists did fairly badly in April's local elections' (*The Economist*, 19 August 2000, p. 35).

6 June 2000: Alija Izetbegovic announces that he will step down from the presidency when his term of office expires in mid-October 2000.

> In an exodus that was partly orchestrated by the Serbian leadership and partly driven by panic, 100,000 Serbs abandoned their homes in the suburbs of Sarajevo ... All but a few thousand Serbs moved out. Now they are filtering back ... About 15,000 Serbs have returned to the Sarajevo area in the last eighteen months, nudging displaced people to return to other regions around the country. In the first five months of this year [2000] 15,665 people have registered after returning home throughout Bosnia. This change is largely due to property laws introduced in 1998, which international officials at the Office of the High Representative ... are using to eliminate local obstructions ... The authorities are evicting people from homes so owners can reclaim their property ... Alia Izetbegovic originally opposed the idea and his adviser, Mirza Hajric, blames the evictions for the recent fall in the popularity of Mr Izetbegovic's ... Party of Democratic Action. The few instances of Moslems returning to Serbian areas, while Sarajevo has welcomed so many Serbs, is one reason that Mr Izetbegovic, seventy-five, says he will resign his office [chairman of the multi-ethnic presidency of Bosnia] in October, Mr Hajric said.
>
> (Carlotta Gall, *IHT*, 3 August 2000, p. 5)

14 October 2000: Alija Izetbegovic retires. The new president is Zivko Radisic. Izetbegovic remains chairman of the Party of Democratic Action (*EEN*, 2000, vol. 13, no. 1, p. 6).

11 November 2000: elections are held: for the Bosnian parliament; for the regional legislature and officials of ten regional cantons in the federation; and for president and vice-president in the Republika Srpska. The elections were administered by OSCE.

Generally voting went along ethnic lines, although the non-nationalist and multi-ethnic Social Democratic Party (led by Zlatko Lagumdzija) did well in Moslem areas. Nationalist parties performed strongly in ethnic Croat and Serb areas.

> Nationalists retained a big lead in the Serb part of Bosnia and were running strongly in the Moslem–Croat Federation ... A multi-ethnic party had a narrow lead in the Moslem–Croat Federation, based on 70 per cent of the ballots cast ... OSCE said urban votes lay behind a swing toward the multi-ethnic Social Democratic Party in the Moslem–Croat Federation. The nationalist Serbian Democratic Party remained well ahead in the Serb republic.
>
> (*IHT*, 15 November 2000, p. 6)

> With most of the votes counted ... only the Bosniacs – Bosnia's Moslems – appear to have heeded his [Petritsch's] advice ... In the Republika Srpska ... the Serbian Democratic Party ... won 37.5 per cent of the vote for the Bosnian Serb assembly and 41 per cent of the votes for the Serb seats in the national parliament ... Mirko Sarovic ... defeated ... Milorad Dodik by 49 per cent to 30 per cent. In Croatian areas ... the Croatian Democratic Union ... organized their own referendum parallel to the official elections ... demanding a 'third entity' for the Croats in Bosnia. Despite declaring the referendum illegal the authorities allowed it to go ahead ... The good showing of the Serbian Democratic Party was helped by widespread allegations of corruption against the current Western-backed prime minister Milorad Dodik ... The Bosniacs ... split their vote almost equally between the nationalist Party of Democratic Action and the multi-ethnic Social Democratic Party.
>
> (*Guardian*, 16 November 2000, p. 19)

The nationalist Serbian Democratic Party (led by Dragan Kalinic) became the biggest party but did not win enough seats for a majority. Mirko Sarovic won the election for president of the Republika Srpska with 50.1 per cent of the vote, thus defeating Milorad Dodik. The Party of Democratic Progress is led by Mladen Ivanic, while the Independent Social Democrats is led by Milorad Dodik.

'The Serbian Democratic Party ... was the single largest party, winning 36 per cent of the vote' (*IHT*, 22 November 2000, p. 1).

'Mr Dodik ... has become unpopular in his own community – and is perceived to have used Western protection as a cover for incompetence and misrule' (*The Economist*, 18 November 2000, p. 68).

With 97 per cent of votes counted the Social Democratic Party (SDP) won 26.1 per cent of the votes for seats in the lower house of the federation's parliament, against 13.7 per cent in 1998. The Party of Democratic Action's share fell from 49.2 per cent to 26.8 per cent. 'The Party for Bosnia-Hercegovina of Haris Silajdzic, one of Bosnia's most moderate wartime politicians, may back the SDP to form a government' (*FT*, 21 November 2000, p. 12).

The nationalist Croatian Democratic Union Nationalist is led by Ante Jelavic (the Croatian representative on the three-member collective national presidency).

'The hard-line Croatian Democratic Union ... organized an unauthorized referendum asking Croats if they backed its campaign for an internationally recognised Croatian ministate, and claimed 70 per cent support among Croats' (*IHT*, 13 November 2000, p. 5).

'The landmark election last November ... brought to power the country's first non-nationalist government' (Wolfgang Petritsch,*IHT*, 26 March 2001, p. 10).

> In Sarajevo yesterday [12 November] Wolfgang Petritsch ... announced the imposition of six laws to strengthen the central state. The laws include the establishment of a state court with jurisdiction in both halves of the country and a law on pensions – both of which had been stalled by nationalists in the outgoing parliament.
>
> (*Guardian*, 13 November 2000, p. 16)

28 February 2001:

> The Croat member of Bosnia's tripartite presidency said Wednesday [28 February 2001] that Croats could no longer take part in the joint federation with Moslems ... Ante Jelavic said the way the Moslem–Croat federation and separate Serb republic had been implemented by international peace officials had cut the Croats out of the picture. 'It is high time to say clearly that we cannot participate in this process any more,' said Mr Jelavic, whose Croat nationalist HDZ party has been accused by Western officials of exploiting ethnic fears for its own political and financial gain. 'From today the federation is a Bosniac national entity,' he said, referring to Bosnian Moslems, 'but without Croats. These authorities in Bosnia are illegal, illegitimate.'
>
> (*IHT*, 1 March 2001, p. 11)

> Ante Jelavic, the Croat member of the Bosnian presidency described the authorities as 'illegal, illegitimate,' and insisted: 'We will neither participate in them nor shall we recognize their decisions.' Mr Jelavic's party, the HDZ, has moved increasingly towards breakaway in recent months ... A spokesman for the High Representative ... described Mr Jelavic's statement as 'extremist nonsense'.
>
> (*Independent*, 1 March 2001, p. 17)

Ante Jelavic, Croat member of Bosnia's collective presidency, said at a rally on Wednesday [28 February] ... that Croats no longer recognized the government of the Moslem–Croat Federation ... 'From today the Federation is a Bosniac [Bosnian Moslem] national entity, but without Croats,' Reuters quoted Mr Jelavic as saying, in support of Croats convicted of war crimes. 'These authorities in Bosnia are illegal, illegitimate.' The decision to withdraw recognition is set to be endorsed on Saturday [3 March] by the Croat National Congress, formed last year [2000] and dominated by Mr Jelavic's Croat Democratic Union ... Croats, the smallest of Bosnia's three main ethnic groups, have become increasingly unhappy since last October [2000], when OSCE changed rules on the election of Croat representatives shortly before November's general elections.

(*FT*, 2 March 2001, p. 8)

3 March 2001:

A meeting of the Croat National Congress on Saturday [3 March] in Mostar ... agreed to set up what it called an inter-cantonal council for Croats. The Congress, which has no formal legal standing, is dominated by the Croat Democratic Union (HDZ) ... Ante Jelavic ... [said] the new structure could be dismantled if, within fifteen days, international administrators revoked changes made to election rules just before November's general election. The new council would take on legislative, judicial and executive powers ... Joint institutions [have] failed to form in many mixed cantons.

(*FT*, 6 March 2001, p. 10)

'The Croatian Democratic Union ... voted to establish its own mini-state in Bosnia if rules that favour multi-ethnic parties are not withdrawn in a fortnight' (*Telegraph*, 5 March 2001, p. 11).

Wolfgang Petritsch ... dismissed ... Ante Jelavic ... and other senior Bosnian Croat officials on Wednesday [7 March] ... Ante Jelavic ... was also barred from holding any other elected post ... A statement from Mr Petritsch's office said: 'As a member of the presidency of Bosnia-Hercegovina and the party president of the HDZ, it was Mr Jelavic's duty to uphold the constitutional order of the country. Instead he forced his party to withdraw from political institutions and to violate the constitutional order' ... The Bosnian Croats base their decision on a change in election laws last year [2000] that they say makes it impossible to retain positions which they held since the 1995 agreement. The changes involved shifting seats held by Bosnian Croats in local governments from areas where the HDZ was strong to other districts where the party has less influence. The Bosnian Croats gave the international administrator [Wolfgang Petritsch] fifteen days to reverse the law ... Mr Petritsch also dismissed Ivo Andric-Luzanski, former president of the federation and a member of parliament, and Marko Tokic and Zdravko Batinic as vice presidents of the Jelavic party.

(IHT, 8 March 2001, p. 4)

Three deputy presidents of the party were also dismissed from their party posts and from various elected posts ... Mr Petritsch said ... '[Mr Jelavic's action] has led me to believe Mr Jelavic is not concerned about the well-being and position of the Croats he allegedly represents, but the well-being and position of extreme nationalists, and perhaps even criminal elements in his party.'

(FT, 8 March 2001, p. 36)

'Bosnian Croat nationalists vowed Thursday [8 March] to defy international peace officials and to continue seeking self-rule' *(IHT*, 9 March 2001, p. 4).

This month, with the full agreement of the international community, I removed Ante Jelavic as a member of Bosnia's joint presidency and as a leader of the nationalist Croat Democratic Union. He had openly supported two war criminals convicted by the Hague tribunal for crimes against humanity. His party had carried out banned campaigning on election day last November [2000]. The final straw was a declaration of 'Croat self-rule', which would effectively have torn up the Dayton peace accords and the country's delicate constitution ... The landmark election last November ... brought to power the country's first non-nationalist government ... The victory of Dayton and international engagement has been a lasting peace, a slow but perceptible lessening of fear in Bosnia and Hercegovina and an increasing focus among ordinary citizens on issues that really matter: jobs, a decent education for one's kids, a state that can do business with the outside world.

(Wolfgang Petritsch, head of the international administration of Bosnia-Hercegovina,*IHT*, 26 March 2001, p. 10)

Hardline Croat separatists in Bosnia yesterday [28 March] set up their own defence headquarters as a mutiny spread among Croat soldiers serving in the Moslem–Croat federation army ... Reports ... suggested that the majority of the 7,500 Croat soldiers in the 22,500 strong common army were joining the mutiny ... The mutiny follows the establishment of a Croat national congress three weeks ago, which has called on all Croats to leave their jobs in the federation army, police and other public offices. The aim of the congress is to establish a 'third entity' or Croat statelet in Bosnia ... Most Croat generals seem to have walked out with their men. In the police force officers in largely Croat areas have for years ignored a law requiring them to wear Bosnian insignia alongside the chequer-board Croat badge on their uniforms. But Western officials yesterday drew some comfort from the fact that an estimated 250 Croats working in the federation interior ministry in Sarajevo have not responded to the nationalist call to abandon their posts. Police and soldiers have been warned that anyone who joins the illegal Croat structures will lose their jobs, pay and pension rights in the federation.

(*Guardian*, 29 March 2001, p. 17)

'Several thousand appear to have ... [left] the federal army ... although they have not taken their weapons with them' (*The Economist*, 7 April 2001, p. 29). '[The] Croat National Assembly ... got some 8,000 Croat soldiers to desert the federal army, luring them with a promise of good pay' (*The Economist*, 14 April 2001, p. 40). 'Sfor says it retains control of the mutinous troops' arms dumps' (*Telegraph*, 7 April 2001, p. 16). 'Sfor said ... weapons storage sites ... are safe and secure' (*The Times*, 7 April 2001, p. 18).

5 March 2001: 'A full bilateral political and economic co-operation agreement is signed with Yugoslavia/Serbia during Yugoslav president Kostunica's visit to Banja Luka' (*EEN*, 2001, vol. 13, no. 4, p. 6).

12 March 2001: 'The federal parliament (Croat and Moslem) votes in a new government under premier Alija Behman' (*EEN*, vol. 13, no. 4, p. 6).

6 April 2001:

Bosnian Croats stoned Nato peacekeepers ... and attacked employees of international organizations Friday [6 April] after the police and troops seized a major bank used by Bosnian Croat hardliners bent on setting up their own state ... The trouble started when armed and masked UN and Bosnian police backed by Nato troops seized the Mostar headquarters of the Hercegovacka Banka and ten branches throughout Bosnia-Hercegovina ... The bank was believed to be used by the hardline Croat Democratic Union to promote its campaign to establish a separate, Croat-run state in south-western Bosnia ... The raid triggered daylong rioting in Mostar.

(*IHT*, 7 April 2001, p. 2)

UN police, backed by Sfor troops, moved to close down the Hercegovacka Banka chain, suspected of being used to launder funds for the Bosnian Croats extremists' independence campaign ... The police raids ... were ordered by the UN-appointed high representative in Bosnia, Wolfgang Petritsch ... The Croatian foreign minister, Tonino Picula, spoke yesterday [6 April) of Bosnian Croat politicians 'exercising harmful politics'.

(*Independent*, 7 April 2001, p. 1)

'In some branches ... of the bank ... the officials had met and were still meeting resistance ... At other branches inspections were carried out quite peacefully and without difficulty' (*The Times*, 7 April 2001, p. 18).

The worst clashes were in Grude, south-west of Mostar, where the rioters took hostages and threatened to kill them ... The separatists have appealed to Croat soldiers serving in the joint Moslem–Croat Federation army to desert ... Most soldiers and officers obeyed the call, prompting Nato peace-keepers on Saturday [7 April] to seize arms depots held by the Croats since the end of the 1992–5 Bosnian war. The Croats are pushing ahead with their plans, despite much condemnation – most notably from the Croatian government in Zagreb ... Zagreb ... [supplies funds] to the Croat compo-nent of the Bosnian armed forces. Intelligence sources in Zagreb estimate that half that money ended up in private hands and a part is now being used to bankroll the new Croat 'statelet'.

(Guardian, 9 April 2001, p. 12)

Once self-rule was declared ... the Hercegovacka Banka ... which collects taxes and customs duties in the federation ... began to withhold funds from the federation's government ... Sfor ... was supposed to guard international administrators seizing control in several towns of branches of a bank suspected of involvement in illegal activities run by Croat nationalists. But in hardline areas such as Mostar mobs stormed the banks in advance, looting funds, stealing documents and assaulting the foreigners ... At Grude, a town near the border with Croatia, eleven of the would-be administrators were carried off at gunpoint ... Croat hardliners, led by the Croatian Democratic Union (HDZ), lost financial support from Croatia after their sister party lost power there in January 2000 and their own vote dropped (as did those of Serb and Moslem extremists) in last November's general election in Bosnia ... The HDZ managed to keep moderate Croat parties from entering government for three months after the elections. But the UN's administrator, Wolfgang Petritsch, at last overrode their stalling.

(The Economist, 14 April 2001, p. 40)

Headquartered in Mostar the Hercegovacka Bank is controlled by a group of ethnic Croats known as the 'young generals', men who became rich during the 1992–5 Bosnian war selling arms and food and were rewarded with appointments to military rank, mostly without formal training. Some were also senior officials of the Bosnian branch of the hard-line nationalist Croatian Democratic Union ... The party says Croats must get their own republic. Western investigators and Bosnian Moslem police officers say that party officials, supporters and appointees are deeply involved in the region's lucrative illegal trade in oil, contraband cigarettes and liquor, and stolen cars. Western officials say that huge profits from the illegal trade, as well as taxes collected by Croat authorities and payments from the government of neighbouring Croats to Bosnian Croat war veterans, are churned through Hercegovacka Bank ... The most dangerous standoff occurred in Grude, where the auditors and their escorts were held for more than twelve hours ... The mob leaders in Grude refused to give up the hostages until all bank documents ... were returned ... The records were returned ... The 6 April confrontation underscored the new reality of peacekeeping in the Balkans: increasingly powerful alliances between ethnic nationalist politicians and

organized criminals now form the greatest impediment to long-term reconciliation ... Western officials say the riots here were organized by
politician-gangsters who want to set up a Croat-only state in Bosnia.
Officials say the aim is to preserve a stream of illicit income ... The 6 April
operation was met with organized assaults on Nato soldiers and Western
personnel at several sites in four Bosnian cities. Twenty-nine Western and
Bosnian participants were injured, several seriously.

(R. Jeffrey Smith, *IHT*, 28 June 2001, p. 2)

8 April 2001:

The head of Croatia's largest veterans' association said Sunday [8 April]
that members would block a base [Divulje] on Monday [9 April] near Split
used by Nato-led forces in Bosnia-Hercegovina to express solidarity with
Bosnian Croats' demands for a separate state there ... The Nato-led force
maintains bases in Croatia to support the peacekeeping operation in Croatia
... Croatian veterans would also hold rallies near other military bases,
including one at the port of Ploce, the Croatia–Bosnia border crossing point
at Kamensko, and all other areas used by allied forces to support the Bosnia
peacekeeping operation.

(*IHT*, 9 April 2001, p. 7)

9 April 2001:

Up to 150 Croatian war veterans protested in Split yesterday [9 April]
against international attempts to prevent self-rule by the Croatian community in Bosnia. Police prevented the protest at a Nato supply base from
turning into a repeat of the riots on Friday [6 April] in southern Bosnia.

(*Independent*, 10 April 2001, p. 14)

10 April 2001:

A moderate Bosnian Croat government minister blamed Croat nationalists
yesterday [10 April] for a car bomb attack that badly damaged his house ...
The car, owned by the company run by the minister, Mladen Ivankovic, and
his brother Jerko, a parliamentary deputy, was blown up yesterday morning
in front of their family house ... The brothers, whose meat-processing
company is the most successful in Bosnia and whose support for the new
government was a big blow to the nationalist Croatian Democratic Union,
alleged the party was behind the attack ... Earlier ... a UN spokesman said
... the United Nations mission ... would act against Croat police involved in
violence in Mostar.

(*Independent*, 11 April 2001, p. 12)

13 April 2001: Colin Powell, the US secretary of state, visits Sarajevo and condemns what he calls 'extremist elements'.

15 April 2001:

> The federation's defence minister, Mijo Anic, a moderate Croat, claimed some success last week in stemming the desertions, reporting that around three-quarters of the soldiers in central and north-eastern Bosnia had gone back to barracks. In the hardline nationalist region of Hercegovina it was less than half. But Nato-led peacekeepers in Bosnia said yesterday [15 April] that they had begun removing weapons from several Croat-controlled barracks ... In elections in December [2000] the SDS – the party of Radovan Karadzic ... emerged as the strongest part in the Serb areas of the republic. In Bosnia's Croatian areas the equally nationalist Croatian Democratic Union, HDZ, won close to 90 per cent of the vote ... [But] Bosnia's Moslems, for the first time since the war, gave half their vote to parties with a civic rather than a nationalist agenda ... Four years after Dayton more than 800,000 Bosnians were still internally displaced, with another 300,000 living as refugees abroad. Only 100,000 had gone back to homes in areas where their ethnic group was a minority. Now the pace of 'minority returns' is picking up ... Enforcement of the new property laws, which allow people to reclaim their flats, has helped, as have the officials' efforts to arrange swaps.
>
> (Jonathan Steele, *Guardian*, 16 April 2001, p. 13)

> The authorities have begun an investigation [into the disturbances connected with the bank branches] and have already brought charges against two Bosnian Croat police chiefs suspected of egging on the rioters ... Dragan Mandic, the police chief of Mostar ... is under investigation for possibly causing a public disturbance ... Peacekeepers were forced to move in to remove heavy weapons from several of the army's storage sites ... An army colonel who complained of threats from the Croatian Democratic Union has disappeared and a political opponent has blamed the party for a car bomb outside his house ... Short of money and losing support among a weary electorate ... the Croatian Democratic Union ... launched what many see as a bid for survival – a campaign for self-rule for Bosnia's Croats.
>
> (Carlotta Gall, *IHT*, 17 April 2001, pp. 1, 9)

5 May 2001: '[There is a] serious outbreak of Serb violence against Moslems in the southern town of Trebinje during an attempted ceremony prior to the building of a new mosque' (*EEN*, 2001, vol. 13, no. 5, p. 5).

7 May 2001:

> Angered by plans to rebuild a mosque in ... Banja Luka ... Bosnian Serbs beat dozens of Moslems on Monday [7 May] and forced Western officials to take refuge in the Islamic centre ... Among the hundreds of people trapped

for hours in the compound of the Islamic centre was the head of the UN mission in Bosnia, Jacques Klein, an American. With him were the British, Swedish and Pakistani ambassadors to Bosnia, who had come to attend the groundbreaking ceremony.

(*IHT*, 8 May 2001, p. 5)

Violence by Serb extremists in Banja Luka ... yesterday prevented a start on the rebuilding of a [sixteenth-century] mosque ... the finest of more than twenty mosques destroyed on 7 May 1993 in Banja Luka ... [This was] the second incident in three days ... On Saturday [5 May] a Serb mob in Trebinje ... prevented the start of rebuilding work on the town's Osman Pasa mosque.

(*FT*, 8 May 2001, p. 8)

'The building in central Banja Luka ... was surrounded by a mob of more than a thousand Serb protesters' (*Independent*, 8 May 2001, p. 11).

'[There were] thousands of Serb demonstrators' (*The Times*, 8 May 2001, p. 14).

'Thousands of Bosnian Serb nationalists attacked Moslems and international officials ... in Banja Luka' (*Telegraph*, 8 May 2001, p. 13).

29 May 2001:

Under a plan approved by Nato ambassadors last week and expected to be announced Tuesday [29 May], the alliance's peacekeeping force will be reduced to 18,000 from 21,000. The US contingent in Bosnia, which is already in the process of being cut to 3,600, would be reduced to 3,100.

(*IHT*, 28 May 2001, p. 5)

15 June 2001: President George W. Bush (speaking in Poland): 'America's role is important, and we will meet our obligations. We went into the Balkans together, and we will come out together. Our goal must be to hasten the arrival of that day' (*IHT*, 16 June 2001, p. 4).

18 June 2001:

The Bosnian Serb police clashed with nationalist rioters on Monday [18 June], using tear gas and water cannon to beat back mobs trying to disrupt a ceremony to mark the rebuilding of a medieval mosque. Hundreds of Bosnia Serbs in the city of Banja Luka attacked the police with stones and bottles ... but failed to stop the ceremony ... Riots a month ago killed a Moslem man and forced the postponement of the cornerstone ceremony for rebuilding the sixteen-century Ferhadja mosque, which was destroyed by Serb extremists in 1993.

(*IHT*, 19 June 2001, p. 5)

'Belgrade provides substantial funding for Republika Srpska's armed forces.

Almost 4,000 officers hold dual rank in the Yugoslav and Bosnian Serb armies. Belgrade trains them and pays their salaries and pensions' (Gareth Evans, *IHT*, 27 June 2001, p. 8).

22 June 2001:

> Bosnia's prime minister [Bozidar Matic] resigned Friday [22 June] in protest over the parliament's failure to adopt an election law ... An acceptable electoral law is a main condition put forward by the Council of Europe ... for the Balkan country to become a member. The law was needed to govern the election of members of the state presidency and parliament and would also stipulate the principles governing elections at all levels of authority in the country ... International officials had given Bosnia a deadline of Friday to adopt the law in an effort to push the nation to govern itself as a democracy ... The 1995 Dayton Peace Agreement ... had stipulated that Bosnia's elections would be supervised by international officials until the nation was ready to hold its own.
>
> (*IHT*, 23 June 2001, p. 4)

27 June 2001:

> Seven governments ... yesterday [27 June] signed an agreement aimed at liberalizing trade in at least 90 per cent of goods trade between them. The move by Albania, Bosnia-Hercegovina, Bulgaria, Croatia, Romania, Macedonia and Yugoslavia marks the latest stage in efforts, under the EU's Stability Pact for South-Eastern Europe, to enhance stability in the region through economic growth. Moldova is expected to join the arrangement shortly. Croatia, Bosnia and Yugoslavia also reached agreement on measures to resettle the remaining 1.2 million refugees and displaced persons in their countries. Initiatives include reconstruction programmes and housing loan schemes.
>
> (*FT*, 28 June 2001, p. 8)

July 2001:

> On 25 August 1999 Bosnia's *Nezavisne Novine* published the first in a series of articles about a 1992 massacre of more than 200 Bosnian Moslems ... The articles alleged that a group of Bosnian Serb policemen killed the Moslems and that Bosnian Serb authorities covered up the crime ... The newspaper is based in Banja Luka, capital of Republika Srpska ... Two months after the series began, someone blew up the car of *Nezavisne Novine*'s editor, Zeljko Kopanja ... He was nearly killed and lost both legs from above the knee ... Later he began work on plans to make *Nezavisne Novine*, which means Independent News, into Bosnia's first national newspaper, writing for Serbs, Croats and Moslems alike ... *Nezavisne* has bureaus in Mostar and Sarajevo ... and employs 136 people, drawn from all three ethnic groups ... *Nezavisne*

is not alone in carrying objective coverage of current events and investigating the wartime conduct of its own group's leaders. Journalists at the Sarajevo weeklies *Dani* and *Slobodna Bosna*, the Banja Luka weekly *Reporter* and Banja Luka's ATV station are doing the same. ATV, its signal retransmitted by the international community, can be heard in most of the nation. But of the print media only *Nezavisne* has gained national circulation.

(Tina Rosenberg, *IHT*, 10 July 2001, p. 8)

24 July 2001: 'President George W. Bush visits US troops in Kosovo. The USA contributes 5,400 of Kfor's 36,200 troops, i.e. 15 per cent' (*IHT*, 25 July 2001, p. 4).

President Bush:

[The United States] will not draw down our forces in Bosnia or Kosovo precipitously or unilaterally. American and allied forces came into Bosnia and Kosovo together and we will leave together. Our goal is to hasten the day when peace is self-sustaining, when local, democratically elected authorities can assume full responsibility and when Nato forces can go home. America has a vital interest in European stability and therefore peace in the region.

'Bosnian Serb police sent a 176,000 pounds sterling bill to the organizers of a [recent] commemoration for the Moslems massacred in Srebrenica, saying those who arranged the event must pay for security' (*Guardian*, 25 July 2001, p. 15).

11 September 2001: there are terrorist attacks in the United States. (War in Afghanistan followed.)

18 October 2001:

US and British officials shut down their embassies in ... Sarajevo ... after receiving threats. The US embassy and two other satellite offices in the cities of Mostar and Banja Luka will be closed until further notice. The British embassy and its cultural centre also closed.

(*IHT*, 18 October 2001, p. 7)

24 October 2001:

Nato said Wednesday [24 October] that it had spearheaded a crippling blow against a Bosnia-based network linked to Middle East extremists ... Nato had worked with the Bosnian authorities ... Among the dozens of suspects the Bosnian police have detained and questioned since the 11 September attacks on New York and Washington six [all of Algerian origin] are now under investigation by the supreme court ... The US and British embassies reopened Monday [22 October].

(*IHT*, 25 October 2001, p. 4)

'Nato-led peacekeepers said yesterday [25 October] they had discovered links to Osama bin Laden's al-Qaeda network ... [and that they] have been disrupted' (*Guardian*, 26 October 2001, p. 9).

28 November 2001:

> In Bosnia-Hercegovina, where I work as the leading representative of the international community – I am responsible for implementing the civilian provisions of the 1995 Dayton Peace Agreement – roughly half of the country's population of 4 million are Moslems. Much has been made of the residual influence of the mujahidin fighters who stayed after the 1992–5 war. But no evidence has been produced that the country has served as a base for Qaeda [al-Qaeda, or 'the Base' is the terrorist network led by Osama bin Laden]. Allegations made by some Serbian extremists that the wars in the former Yugoslavia were fought to fend off Moslem fundamentalism are ridiculous. What is truly worthy of note is that the influence of fundamentalist Islam in the Balkans has been so weak ... The government is demonstrating its commitment to fighting global terrorism.
>
> (Wolfgang Petritsch, *IHT*, 29 November 2001, p. 7)

> On 28 November ... the Croat party – known as the HDZ ... resumed their seats in the parliament of the Federation ... During their ten-month boycott [which started in January 2001 when it] refused to accept exclusion from the new government ... the HDZ ... had tried every imaginable option to demand greater rights for its people. Its leaders established an autonomous Croat government. There was also an abortive army mutiny. Yet, faced with apathy from ordinary Croats, its funding cut off and international organizations' determination to stop them ... they resumed their seats ... The stand-off created a tense, sometimes violent, environment for the early days in office of new Alliance for Change governments at Federation and state level ... Built around the ... Social Democratic Party and Haris Silajdzic's Party for Bosnia-Hercegovina, the alliance has excluded the main nationalist parties from government for the first time since the war ... A second raid ... [on 18 April 2001, on the] Hercegovacka Banka [was successful] ... The new administrators stopped the bank's funding of Croat self-rule institutions. Croat soldiers, who had walked out of Federation army barracks, were then presented with an ultimatum to sign new contracts and return. Knowing that the Croat self-government could not pay them, most signed ... Mladen Ivanic became prime minister of ... Republika Srpska ... eleven months [ago] ... [He] has embarked on a programme designed to reform the economy, attract investment and increase transparency ... [But] Mr Ivanic governs in coalition with the Serb Democratic Party (SDS) ... [which] after elections in November 2000 ... became the largest party in parliament, winning thirty-one of the eighty-three seats.
>
> (*FT*, Survey, 20 December 2001, p. 17)

18 December 2001:

Defence secretary Donald Rumsfeld on Tuesday [18 December] proposed reducing Nato peacekeeping forces in Bosnia by a third next year [2002], saying the mission is straining the United States and other Nato members 'when they face growing demands from critical missions in the war on terrorism' ... Senior US defence officials said that with 18,000 peacekeepers in Bosnia, including 3,100 US soldiers, Mr Rumsfeld's proposed reduction of about a third could reduce the force by about 6,000. If applied proportionately to all nations' forces, the officials estimated about 1,000 Americans could end up going home or departing for other, more pressing, overseas assignments. There are a total of 57,000 peacekeepers in Bosnia, Kosovo and Macedonia, 8,800 of whom are Americans. A separate British proposal under consideration to create a unified command in the Balkans could bring further reductions, US and Nato officials said. The Pentagon asked Nato for help in eight different areas immediately after the 11 September terrorist attacks, including the surveillance AWACS flights over the United States and replacements for specialized US units withdrawn from the Balkans and redeployed to fight the war in Afghanistan ... Nato's secretary-general, Lord Robertson ... said that Mr Rumsfeld, in proposing troop withdrawals in Bosnia, had endorsed the concept that Nato allies had gone into the Balkans together and would 'only leave together' ... [Lord Robertson also said that] Nato forces ... are 'smashing al-Qaeda cells in Bosnia and Kosovo'.

(*IHT*, 19 December 2001, pp. 1, 8)

1 January 2002:

The introduction of Euro notes and coins [on 1 January 2002] appears to be boosting previously weak banking sectors in parts of the former Yugoslavia as residents seek to convert cash DM savings ... Bank collapses and government seizures of hard currency savings drove many in former Yugoslavia away from the formal economy in the 1990s ... In Bosnia-Hercegovina the changeover is leading to the withdrawal of DMs which have circulated alongside the country's own currency, the Konvertibilna Marka, pegged at a one-for-one exchange rate with the DM. The change has accelerated a rise in bank deposits following the arrival of foreign banks in Bosnia's Moslem–Croat Federation area.

(*FT*, 10 January 2002, p. 7)

18 January 2002:

In an operation co-ordinated with the Bosnian government, US troops took custody Friday [18 January] of six Arab terror suspects after their court-ordered release from a Bosnian prison and prepared to fly them to the US military base at Guantanamo Bay, Cuba ... The six men ... were arrested by the Bosnian authorities in October [2001] … The operation was reportedly conducted by US troops acting independently of the Nato-led force … [The six] are accused of plotting to blow up the US embassy and planning other attacks on Americans in Bosnia … A Bosnian court ruled Thursday [17 January] that there was insufficient evidence to continue holding the men.

(*IHT*, 19 January 2002, p. 5)

22 January 2002: 'Bosnia … was given the green light Tuesday [22 January] by the Council of Europe's parliamentary assembly … to join the pan-European organization' (*IHT*, 23 January 2002, p. 4).

THE ECONOMY

Losses

There was massive destruction in the war zones and massive dislocation in most places. Some indication of the economic losses can be gleaned from the following:

1   In 1991 unemployment was 17 per cent and inflation was 117.4 per cent (*Business Europa*, April–May 1995, p. 60).
2   Industrial output fell by 16.2 per cent in 1991 and by 25 per cent in 1992 (United Nations Economic Commission for Europe 1994: 52, and 1995: 70).
3   Average *per capita* income has fallen to only $500 from $1,900 in 1990. Around 80 per cent of the Moslem–Croat Federation is at least partially dependent on humanitarian food aid. In 1994 industrial output was about 5 per cent of the level of 1990, while electricity consumption was below 10 per cent of the 1990 level (*FT*, 24 November 1995, p. 2). During the war Bosnia's economy shrank to less than a third of its former level (*FT*, 15 May 1999, p. 2, and 7 June 1999, p. 23).
4   By late 1995 Bosnia's economy had shrunk to 25 to 30 per cent of its pre-war size, while industrial output was at little more than one-tenth of Yugoslav-era capacity. GDP per head had fallen to $500, from $1,900 in 1990. But the Bosnian government has already laid the foundations for recovery by keeping inflation in check (the expected rate for 1995 being under 10 per cent) and pegging the Bosnian dinar to the Deutschmark (Business Central Europe 1995: 42).
5   As the World Bank has pointed out, 90 per cent of the population of Bosnia is now wholly or partly dependent on food aid. Waterborne diseases are increasingly common. More than a third of the health infrastructure has been damaged or destroyed. Two-thirds of the housing stock has been damaged and one-fifth destroyed. Industrial output fell by about 95 per cent between 1990 and 1994, coal production has declined to less than 10 per

cent of its pre-war level and 70 per cent of electricity generating capacity is damaged or out of action. Income per head has fallen by three-quarters, to $500. The telecommunications and transport infrastructure has been seriously damaged. Donors are being asked for some $5 billion over the next three to four years (*FT*, 21 December 1995, pp. 2, 13).

6   The World Bank estimates reconstruction costs for Bosnia at $4.9 billion, excluding rescheduling of the $3.2 billion debt (*FT*, 11 December 1995, p. 22). The World Bank estimates minimum reconstruction costs at $3 billion for areas under Bosnian government control, plus another $2 billion for the rest of the country (Business Central Europe 1995: 42). The World Bank, in co-operation with the EBRD, the European Commission and UN agencies, has proposed a $5.1 billion reconstruction programme over four years, with disbursements in 1996 (about $1 billion), in 1997 ($1.6 billion), in 1998 ($1.4 billion) and in 1999 ($1.09 billion) (United Nations Economic Commission for Europe 1996: 168). (In February 1996 Bosnian prime minister Hasan Muratovic estimated that Bosnia would need $3 billion a year for five years to rebuild its economy: *Guardian*, 5 February 1996, p. 8.)

7   Bosnia's economy is heavily dependent on agriculture, with a major emphasis on sheep and cattle. The government estimates that the livestock count has fallen by 70 per cent. The UN's International Fund for Agricultural Development is considering a plan to lend pregnant livestock to Bosnian farmers who will then repay their debt in live animals (*IHT*, 29 January 1996, p. 9). But when the scheme was implemented the overwhelming majority of farmers opted to repay loans in cash because it was cheaper (*IHT*, 10 October 1996, p. 19).

8   Preliminary data collected by the World Bank painted a bleak picture of Bosnia (*Transition*, November–December 1995, vol. 6, nos 11–12, p. 30):

> Annual *per capita* income has fallen from $1,900 in 1990 to about $500. (*Per capita* income was $1,872 in 1991 and $524 in 1995: *Business Central Europe*, September 1996, p. 80.)

> Around 45 per cent of all industrial plants, including perhaps 75 per cent of all oil refineries, have been destroyed. A much higher percentage has been robbed of machinery and equipment. The surviving industry operates at 5 to 6 per cent of pre-war capacity. Seventy-eight per cent of electrical generating capacity is out of commission and coal production is less than 10 per cent of pre-war levels.

> About 35 per cent of roads and 40 per cent of bridges have been damaged or destroyed.

> One-third of all health care facilities and half of Bosnia's school buildings have been damaged or destroyed.

> Seventy per cent of the housing stock has been destroyed or damaged.

Domestic food production satisfies only 35 per cent of the country's needs. About 80 per cent of Bosnia relies on outside food aid.

Total foreign debt amounts to $4.2 billion. IMF membership was approved on 21 December 1995 and a $45 million credit emerged. The IMF supported a plan whereby the new central bank was to operate for at least six years as a currency board, issuing currency only with full foreign exchange backing. Furthermore, the government and public sector entities were to refrain from financing expenditures through domestic bank loans. Longer-term projects, primarily rebuilding infrastructure, transport, water and sewerage, would require around $5 billion over the three-year period.

9   In 1990 Bosnia's GDP was $10 billion, while it is now only $2 billion (*IHT*, 20 February 1996, p. 6).

10 *Per capita* income has fallen to a quarter of pre-war levels, while industrial production is barely 10 per cent. One million refugees are scattered around Europe, while of those who stayed three-quarters are unemployed and require humanitarian aid (*IHT*, 15 April 1996, p. 7).

11 The World Bank figure for unemployment is 50 to 60 per cent. Industrial production is still only 10 to 15 per cent of the pre-war level (*IHT*, 7 January 1997, p. 5). Before the war 1.1 million were employed and 350,000 were unemployed. Today the figures are 210,000 and 650,000 respectively (*Transition*, January–February 1996, vol. 7, no. 1, p. 5). The unemployment rate in the second quarter of 1995 was nearly 40 per cent, but may well have been higher given the exclusion of the self-employed and the private sector in agriculture from the figures (United Nations Economic Commission for Europe 1996: 168).

12 Unemployment is stagnating at 30 per cent to 40 per cent after improvements in 1996–8 (EBRD 1999b: 199).

13 The official unemployment rate is 40 per cent (Business Central Europe 1999: 32).

14 'The end of the war saw some 150,000 dead, countless injured and 2 million people displaced. Sixty per cent of housing units, 50 per cent of schools, 30 per cent of hospitals and 60 per cent of livestock were destroyed. Roads, railways, bridges and water and energy supply were severely damaged. Perhaps 6 million unexploded mines were spread through villages and fields. A large part of the population was entirely dependent on humanitarian aid … More than 450,000 refugees have returned and an 80 per cent unemployment rate has been reduced to 50 per cent … But endemic corruption would have to be eliminated and new laws enforced to attract external investment, which is at present virtually non-existent … At present the international community seems set to remain for decades. The costs … amount to $9 billion annually' (Frederick Bonnart, *IHT*, 27 November 1998, p. 8).

Historical and religious treasures have also been vandalized or destroyed, e.g. the Serbs' early bombardment of Dubrovnik in Croatia, the loss of many priceless books when Sarajevo's National Library was destroyed, and continuing whole-sale destruction of mosques in Bosnia (the last two coming under the category of what may be called 'cultural cleansing'). The Serbs started the shelling, but on 9 November 1993 it was the Croats who finally destroyed the famous Mostar bridge (Stari Most, or 'Old Bridge'). It had been built over the River Neretva in 1557–66 on the orders of Suleiman the Magnificent.

Recovery

Assessments of economic performance have been summarized by EBRD in Table 1.1. The table shows hugely negative GDP growth figures for 1993 and 1994. Double-figure increases in GDP were typically recorded from 1995 onwards. As regards consumer price inflation, the figures are split between the federation and the Republika Srpska. The rates in 1994 were 780 per cent and 1,061 per cent, respectively. By 1999–2000 consumer price stability had been achieved in the former and inflation was only around 14 per cent in the latter.

In 1995 the rate of GDP growth for the country as a whole was 7 per cent. In 1996 the Moslem–Croat Federation's GDP grew by 35 per cent and enjoyed low inflation, whereas the Republika Srpska had virtually zero growth and suffered from high inflation (and received only 2 per cent of aid for Bosnia) (Deutsche Morgan Grenfell, *Focus: Eastern Europe*, 3 March 1997, p. 71).

> Last year [1996] Bosnia's economy grew by 40 per cent; industrial output recovered to some 10 per cent of its 1991 level; real wages grew about three-fold … and the unemployment rate fell to some 50 to 60 per cent of the labour force from its postwar high of 90 per cent … Prices have been stabilized … But the country's GDP (adding up the figures of the two entities …) is still only one-third of its prewar level. *Per capita* GDP is estimated at $500 compared with the $1,900 seen in 1991 … It is estimated that in Bosnia's Croat territory industrial output has recovered to 85 per cent of its prewar level … The Serb Republic has so far received only 2 per cent of donor support. Economic growth there has been close to zero, wages are one-third of the level in the Federation and inflation is high.
>
> (*Transition*, February 1997, vol. 8, no. 1, p. 11)

(The unemployment rate in the Republika Srpska is 90 per cent. Of the 800,000 Bosnian Serbs, 300,000 were displaced from their homes by the war: *IHT*, 12 March 1997, p. 8. Since the end of the war total output in the Moslem–Croat Federation has doubled and unemployment has fallen from 90 per cent to 50 per cent. By the end of 1997 output should reach something like half the pre-war level. In the Republika Srpska, however, unemployment remains at 90 per cent, with barely 3 per cent of the $1.36 billion in official reconstruction aid in 1996 going to that part of Bosnia: *IHT*, editorial, 1

Table 1.1 Bosnia-Hercegovina: selected economic indicators 1990–2000

Economic indicator	1990	1991	1992	1993	1994	1995	1996	1997	1998	1999	2000 (estimate)
Rate of growth of GDP (%)				-40.0	-40.0	20.8	86.0	37.0	10.0	10.0	5.0
Rate of growth of industrial output (%)						33.0	38.1	51.4	18.5	10.5	9.5
Rate of growth of agricultural output (%)						-9.7	28.4	22.8	8.6		
Inflation rate (consumer, %) Federation					780.0	-4.4	-24.5	14.0	5.1	-0.3	1.9
Republika Srpska					1,061.0	12.9	16.9	-7.3	2.0	14.0	14.7
Budget surplus or deficit (% of GDP)						-0.3	-4.4	-0.5	-6.9	-7.0	-5.5
Unemployment rate (end of year, %)								37.0	38.0	40.0	40.1
Balance of payments (current account, $billion)					-0.177	-0.193	-0.748	-1.060	-0.790	-0.971	-0.909
Foreign direct investment (net, $million)									100	90	150
Population (million)[a]			4.2	4.1	4.2	4.2	4.1	4.2	4.2	4.3	4.3

Source   Various issues of European Bank for Reconstruction and Development, Transition Report.

Note   [a] Includes refugees abroad

September 1997, p. 8.) Bosnia's economy grew by about 40 per cent in 1996, but GDP was still only one-third of its pre-war level. In the Bosniac–Croat Federation it is estimated that industrial output recovered to 85 per cent of its pre-war level. Foreign trade turnover increased briskly and prices were stabilized. Economic growth in the Republika Srpska was close to zero; wages were one-third of the level in the federation and inflation was high. The unemployment rate in Bosnia as a whole fell to some 50 to 60 per cent of the labour force from its worst point of 90 per cent (United Nations, *World Economic and Social Survey*, 1997, p. 24).

The federation's economy grew by 50 per cent in 1996 and the World Bank estimates that growth in 1997 will be about 35 per cent. Inflation is negligible. Unemployment is 50–60 per cent in the federation and higher in the Republika Srpska. Industrial production is still only 15 per cent of its pre-war level and many people still live from soup kitchens. Customs duties and value-added tax, not income tax, are the government's main revenue sources. In the Republika Srpska much of the farmland lies idle (*IHT*, 11 December 1997, pp. 13, 17).

GDP continued to recover in 1997, with the federation area reporting a 37 per cent increase. Growth continued to be driven by the power, food-processing and construction sectors (EBRD 1998a: 33).

Bosnia is rapidly recovering from the war which caused $20 billion worth of damage to its industry and infrastructure, cut its GDP to one quarter of its pre-war level of $2,000 a head and reduced industrial output to 10 to 15 per cent of its pre-war level. The economy grew by 50 per cent in 1996 and 36 per cent in 1997 and it is likely to grow by 25 per cent in 1998, according to the World Bank (*FT*, Survey 1998, p. i). Apart from the railways, which are nominally unified throughout the country, other utilities (electricity, post and telecommunications) are still run as three separate organizations, two of them within the federation, one for Croats, one for Moslems (p. iii). Unemployment is still running at around 40 per cent, according to the Bosnian government (p. iv). The unemployment rate is roughly 30 per cent (*FT*, Survey, 14 December 1999, p. 35). Some 90 per cent of foodstuffs are imported (p. 36).

The following economic statistics for Bosnia-Hercegovina as a whole are provided by the United Nations *Economic Survey of Europe* (2000, no. 1, pp. 42, 83, 230 and 23): industrial output: 1997, 35.7 per cent; 1998, 23.8 per cent; 1999, 10.6 per cent; agricultural output: 1997, 15.4 per cent; inflation rate (consumer): 1990, 594.0 per cent; 1991, 116.2 per cent; 1992, 64,825.1 per cent; 1993, 38,825.1 per cent; 1994, 553.5 per cent; 1995, −12.1 per cent; 1996, −21.2 per cent; 1997, 11.8 per cent; 1998, 4.9 per cent; 1999, −0.6 per cent; unemployment rate (end of year): 1997, 39.0 per cent; 1998, 38.5 per cent; 1999, 39.1 per cent.

Economic aid

With UN approval the USA (amid much spiteful derision) began (increasingly successful) aid airdrops (parachuted relief supplies) on 28 February 1993. France and Germany joined in later.

The UN High Commission for Refugees made many complaints about the amount of aid donated. In July 1993 it appealed for an additional $1 million to $1.5 billion. Between September 1991 and the end of June 1993 the total aid of $1.285 billion for the former Yugoslavia was donated as follows: the EU, $872 million (68 per cent of the total); the USA, $164 million (13 per cent); Japan, $32 million (2 per cent); and others, $217 million (17 per cent) (*FT*, 14 July 1993, p. 2).

A significant portion of aid did not reached its final destination (e.g. the Bosnian Serb forces at checkpoints demanded some). The EU estimated that 20 to 30 per cent of its aid had gone missing (*IHT*, 9 June 1995, p. 5).

At a donors' conference in Brussels on 20–1 December 1995 a target of $518 million was set to cover urgent reconstruction costs in the first three months of 1996 (*FT*, 21 December 1995, p. 13).

Bosnia became a member of the IMF on 20 December 1995 and was awarded an emergency credit. (In line with the accords the IMF was to have substantial powers over monetary policy, including the appointment of a central bank governor from outside the region: *FT*, 19 December 1995, p. 2.)

Representatives of fifty countries attended a conference held on 12–13 April 1996 on aid for the reconstruction of Bosnia hosted by the World Bank and the EU. They estimated that $5.1 billion would be needed, $3.7 billion for the Bosnian Federation and $1.4 billion for the Bosnian Serbs. At the conference an additional $1.23 billion was pledged, thus reaching the goal of $1.8 billion for 1996. The USA pledged an extra $219 million (i.e. on top of the earlier $62.7 million pledged at the first aid conference; these sums brought the total US contribution to civilian aid for Bosnia in 1996 to $550 million: *IHT*, 15 April 1996, p. 7). The EU pledged $260 million, the World Bank $160 million and Japan $130 million. Little aid was to go to the Bosnian Serbs while Radovan Karadzic and Ratko Mladic remained in power. Each donor country would choose its own projects. (Another source broke down the total pledged of $1.283 billion as follows: EU, $200 million; bilateral pledges from EU member states, $197.7 million; USA, $219 million; Japan, $130 million; Canada, $1.08 million; Moslem countries, $144 million; other donor countries, $79.1 million; EBRD, $70 million; Islamic Development Bank, $25 million; World Bank, $200 million: *Business Europa*, June–July 1996, p. 28.)

On 26 June 1996 Bosnia-Hercegovina became the twenty-sixth member of the European Bank for Reconstruction and Development.

The third international conference on aid for Bosnia, held on 23–4 July 1997, pledged $1.2 billion. The conferences in December 1995 and April 1996 had together secured $1.85 billion for the first year of the reconstruction programme. By mid-1997 projects worth some $926 million had reportedly been implemented under the priority reconstruction programme, with the Moslem–Croat Federation receiving some 98 per cent of the funds and just 2 per cent being channelled to the Republika Srpska (*Transition*, 1997, vol. 8, no. 4, p. 29).

On 26 January 1998 the EU announced an Ecu 6 million (£4 million) aid package for the Republika Srpska to be used to pay the salary arrears of police, teachers and other essential workers. The World Bank pledged a $17 million (£10.1 million) credit, representing the first element of a $65 million project to repair water and power networks, build houses and aid farmers (*FT*, 27 January 1998, p. 2).

The international reconstruction programme for 1996–2000 is worth $5.1 billion (*FT*, Survey, 21 October 1998, p. i). The World Bank is the largest institutional lender in Bosnia. From the start of 1996 to mid-1998 it has lent or given $533 million for twenty-four reconstruction projects, the largest being to restore transport and electric power. The EBRD has signed nine projects, totalling Ecu 73.6 million. In May 1998 the IMF approved a twelve-month $80 million stand-by credit. Bosnia is getting about $1 billion a year in bilateral aid, with nearly half coming from the USA and the EU in more or less equal amounts (p. iii). 'External financing needs for the reconstruction effort in Bosnia from 1996 to 1999 have totalled $5.1 billion, of which around $3.3 billion has been spent so far' (*FT*, 25 June 1999, p. 3). 'The list [of things needed for a durable peace] is daunting – and in some ways an indictment of an international aid effort costing $5.1 billion from 1996 to the end of this year [1999]' (*FT*, Survey, 24 November 1999, p. 35).

On 20 May 1999 an international donors' conference in Brussels pledged a further $1 billion for Bosnia (*EEN*, 1999, vol. 12, no. 13, p. 8).

'In Bosnia over $5 billion was pledged over four years, with Europe paying more than half. But actual payments proved slow, holding back reconstruction' (*IHT*, 21 June 1999, p. 5).

On 5 March 1998 five members of the anti-fraud committee of the Moslem–Croat Federation, in a meeting in London, accused the federation government of being 'completely unwilling to co-operate' with an enquiry into misuse of foreign reconstruction aid. Western figures showed that some $1.5 billion worth of aid had been spent on projects, but the anti-fraud committee claimed that the real disbursement was only about $1 billion (*FT*, 6 March 1998, p. 2). The committee, established in August 1997, claimed that almost $600 million in aid given by the USA, the EU and the UN had gone missing (*The Times*, 6 March 1998, p. 17).

As much as a billion dollars has disappeared from public funds or been stolen from international aid projects through fraud carried out by the Moslem, Croatian and Serbian nationalist leaders who keep Bosnia rigidly partitioned into three enclaves, according to an exhaustive investigation by a US-led anti-fraud unit ... set up by the Office of the High Representative ... The report names several officials linked to the governing nationalist parties as profiting from the fraud. Even though the Office of the High Representative has dismissed fifteen officials or prevented them from holding office, most retain their authority ... Bosnia has received $5.1 billion in international aid since the end of the war in 1995. The corruption has also played a pivotal role in driving away foreign investment ... The Office of the High Representative has been reduced to promising money and aid projects to towns and cities that say they will allow some refugees to return, promises that are usually never kept.

(IHT, 18 August 1999, pp. 1, 4)

The opening paragraph of [the article] ... referred incompletely to the losses estimated at $1 billion. According to the anti-fraud unit of the Office of the High Representative ... at least $20 million of that total was in foreign aid from a variety of countries. But the vast majority of the money was either stolen from Bosnian public funds or lost through the failure of officials in Bosnia to collect taxes, either through corruption or mismanagement.

(IHT, 21 August 1999, p. 2)

Assessments of Bosnia's progress

Assessments of Bosnia's progress vary. Included among the more pessimistic are the following:

1   'The leaders of Bosnia, Serbia and Croatia have refused to loosen their grip on the economies that gave each of them a power base during the war, say Western economists, business leaders and government officials. By perpetuating their fiefdoms built on spoils and patronage, the politicians are obstructing the economic changes – and development of entrepreneurs and regional markets – that could help dilute the virulent nationalism that propelled the conflict ... All over the region loans to start businesses remain almost unattainable from government-controlled banks. Still persisting are the import–export licences and tariff barriers from which politicians-cum-war-profiteers made fortunes. Air, rail and telephone links that would help citizens move about and foster businesses are slow in coming because there is fear of competition damaging to government monopolies ... In many instances the heads of Bosnia's important government agencies, like the major utility Electropiverta, are also senior members of the governing political party, the Party of Democratic Action' (Jane Perlez, *IHT*, 21 August 1996, p. 2).

2   'With the ravages of war still very obvious and an economy still run by communist-era rules, doing business in Bosnia remains so unattractive that there is very little foreign investment. The economy survives in large part on international aid and the money spent to support foreign organizations and tens of thousands of foreigners working here ... Only three big foreign companies have ventured into Bosnia and their commitments are tentative. Volkswagen, which had operated a large plant outside Sarajevo ... is opening a much-scaled-down operation. With about 400 workers it will assemble 10 per cent of the Skoda cars made at the company's plants in the Czech Republic. Coca-Cola has a bottling venture in Bosnia and DHL operates a courier service ... Bosnian politicians refuse to provide the kind of business environment that most large foreign investors

demand. Foreign economists say there is often favouritism in the way taxes are collected and laws are applied. They say the lack of a commercial banking system or privatization also keeps investors away ... Bosnian leaders allow, and often profit from, corruption, tax evasion and tax regulations so burdensome that companies often must bribe officials or break the law. Most workers still do not have jobs and only 30 per cent of the prewar industrial capacity has been revived. Some countries are starting programmes they hope will foster free enterprise' (Mike O'Connor, *IHT*, 23 November 1998, p. 4).

(Volkswagen formally resumed car production in Sarajevo on 31 August 1998: *IHT*, 1 September 1998, p. 5. The joint venture between Volkswagen and Unis (the Yugoslav industrial conglomerate which owned 51 per cent of the shares) died in April 1992. The new operation – Volkswagen Sarajevo – is 58 per cent owned by Volkswagen, effectively in exchange for pre-war debts. Unis has to contribute new capital to gain its 42 per cent stake: *FT*, Survey, 21 October 1998, p. iv.)

3   Robert Barry, head of OSCE's mission to Bosnia and Hercegovina (*FT*, 22 October 1999, p. 23):

> While slow and steady progress has been made on the political front – as the monopoly of the ruling nationalist parties slowly gives way to political pluralism – much less progress has been made towards creating a functioning market economy in Bosnia. Despite billions of dollars of reconstruction aid, the political and economic conditions that would allow investors and entrepreneurs to replace international peacekeepers do not yet exist. Consequently, economic insecurity today represents as grave a threat to stability as renewed military confrontation. With the benefit of hindsight, it is clear that the international community made a fundamental mistake at the beginning of the Dayton implementation process in 1996. Too much emphasis was placed on physical reconstruction and not enough on fundamental economic reform. The consequences are all too visible. Bosnia's rule of law, investment climate and economic strength is among the worst in Central and Eastern Europe. Unemployment remains chronically and unacceptably high, while the average wage across the country – at least officially – is less than DM 350 a month. Instead of preparing itself for free-market capitalism, Bosnia has become dangerously donor-dependent. A large part of the problem is that the Bosnian leadership has so far been unwilling to commit itself to the task of building a market economy. Instead, it seeks to consolidate its control over the economy, which provides it with funds and sources of patronage ... For Bosnia, taking advantage of the economic promise of the stability pact [for south-eastern Europe] will require radical reform on a number of fronts:

(a) The forest of regulations that choke economic life must be cleared away. Within Bosnia's Moslem–Croat Federation, for example, every enterprise is required to have a minimum number of employees. Similarly, a recently passed labour law contains a provision obliging companies to provide benefits to workers employed in 1991. Combined with extensive barriers to trade between Bosnia's two entities, such provisions not only strangle legitimate economic activity, but also foster corruption.

(b) Bosnia and Hercegovina's notorious payments bureau system must be dismantled. A legacy of socialist-era Yugoslavia, this system requires that almost all economic transactions be channelled through party-controlled payments bureaux. These institutions bankroll the leading nationalist parties, undermine the emergence of a viable banking system, breed corruption, drive much of the local economy underground, and generally act as a brake on economic growth and development.

(c) Corruption must be brought under control.

(d) Fundamental tax reform must be an urgent priority. The present complex web of taxation makes it all but impossible to make a profit.

(e) Privatization must proceed quickly. While legislation is now in place in both entities, bureaucratic and political foot-dragging has delayed implementation.

4   'Bosnia's leaders show little commitment to the type of reforms necessary to create a prosperous, or at least sustainable, economy … They have maintained control and tolerate, if not participate in, a system rife with corruption – all in the service of what they define to be their nationalist political interests. For example, no real banking system has been permitted to develop because, to date, the Bosnians have insisted on maintaining the Yugoslav payments system, which allows them to track every transaction in the country and to skim off the top to fund nationalist political activities. The same type of ethnic politics now threatens to distort the privatization process … Multiple approvals by a wide array of petty officials are required for almost any type of economic activity, opening the door to widespread graft. Taxes are unevenly collected. (It is believed that the non-payment of taxes accounts for much of the oft-cited $1 billion lost to corruption.) And according to one senior member of the judiciary, 90 per cent of the judges are viewed as compromised and needing to be replaced. The result is an economy that has grown almost completely dependent on foreign aid' (Daalder and Froman 1999: 109).

5   'Criminal gangs – using skills gained circumventing blockades and embargoes during the 1992–5 Bosnian war – are smuggling in thousands of cartons of untaxed cigarettes and unknown quantities of illegal drugs a week. They have also established well-protected corridors for trafficking in

stolen cars from Western Europe and prostitutes from Eastern Europe. Unofficial markets "have mushroomed throughout the country", said a recent European Commission report on organized crime in Bosnia. Western officials say that 40 per cent to 60 per cent of the Bosnian economy appears to be based on black-market commerce. This has fuelled the rise of a wealthy criminal class that wields enormous political influence and annually diverts hundreds of millions of dollars in potential tax revenue to itself. Although there is little evidence of direct diversion of foreign aid to private hands, the siphoning off of public revenue has helped ensure the country's continued dependence on outside assistance for many years to come, officials say ... Some officials say the Arizona market [opened in spring 1996 in the Brcko municipality] is an example of how the West's policies here – particularly its preoccupation with physical reconstruction instead of the more difficult task of orchestrating lasting economic and political reform – have fostered the enormous expansion of criminal activity' (R. Jeffrey Smith, *IHT*, 27 December 1999, p. 5).

Among the more optimistic is Rory O'Sullivan (the World Bank's special representative for south-east Europe and its former representative in Sarajevo):

It is imperative that we set the record straight on how the generosity of international donors offers real hope and opportunity to countries ravaged by conflict. One country which has benefited greatly from this generosity and made significant strides in rebuilding after years of trauma is Bosnia. It is now enjoying peace and growing prosperity, but it is unfairly portrayed as squandering its chances for economic recovery ... The task of rebuilding bridges, roads and other infrastructure damaged by bombing or shelling has been completed on schedule. Economic growth has been impressive, although reform along market lines is not over by any means ... Roads and bridges are now generally working again, and people and freight can move around the country without any special inconvenience ... The railway system is rolling again. Power stations are back in full production. More people have telephones and running water than before the war ... The law and rules needed to operate a modern economy are just about there ... Progress [as regards implementation] has been slower than many would like. If the slow but steady progress now being achieved in implementing these laws continues, the future of Bosnia's children will be assured. But if the delaying tactics often used by special interest groups succeed, the future will be one of decline and poverty ... The real achievements of the past four years seldom get the recognition they deserve. Allegations of corruption have recently seized headlines, while the tangible day-to-day achievements that are gradually transforming the economy are ignored. Corruption is a problem ... But the impression that some commentators give of international donors being systematically fleeced is simply wrong. Most donors use tough chasing and auditing measures that keep their money safe ... Another

common complaint from outside Bosnia is that international donors pay all
the bills and local people pay nothing. Not true. People do pay taxes, which
finance the bulk of the recurrent expenditures budgeted by the various levels
of government. In 1999 the tax intake across the country will have risen to
some DM 2 billion, the equivalent of 35 per cent of the country's GDP ...
It is true that much hatred persists ... But most local people can also cite
countless cases of solidarity across ethnic divides.

(Rory O'Sullivan, the World Bank's special representative for south-east Europe
and its former representative in Sarajevo, *IHT*, 22 December 1999, p. 6)

Economic policy

On 9 November 1995 the Bosnian government pronounced the Deutschmark an
official currency (exchangeable at 100 dinars each).

On 23–4 July 1996 vice-president Ejup Ganic led a trade delegation to
Belgrade. It was agreed to restore telephone, rail, bus and air links and that civilians crossing the Bosnia–Serbia border would no longer require visas.

On 20 June 1997 the Bosnian parliament passed its first laws, a 'quick-start
package' that should create a central bank, a common currency, a customs union
and common external tariffs (*The Economist*, 28 June 1997, p. 43). The broad
package of fiscal, trade policy and customs laws, called the 'quick-start package',
aimed at restoring Bosnia's financial institutions. 'The package came on the heels
of another accord by Bosnia's Serb, Croat and Moslem leaders to form a single
central bank and an interim currency, though with different designs for each
territory' (*Transition*, June 1997, vol. 8, no. 3, p. 30). The governor of the central
bank of Bosnia and Hercegovina wrote, in a letter to *The Economist*, that currency
issuance is the sole prerogative of the head office of the central bank, under the
authority of its governing board, which is bound by a strict currency-board rule
for money creation (*The Economist*, 12 July 1997, p. 10). It was announced on 11
August 1997 (by its French head) that the Central Bank of Bosnia had started
operations (*Transition*, 1997, vol. 11, no. 4, p. 29).

In June 1997 a so-called 'quick-start package' of laws was introduced
governing state institutions, including a budget, a law on the central bank, on
customs, and on the responsibility for foreign debt. Direct telecommunications
links and co-operation in air traffic between the two entities were only re-established in September 1997. The most significant advance so far at the state level
has been the opening of a common central bank on 11 August 1997, which has
begun to issue a common currency and to centralize foreign exchange reserves.
The 'convertible marka' (KM: *konvertibilna marka*) is fully convertible and pegged at
parity with the DM. The KM will have different designs (which have yet to be
agreed on) but its use remains limited to non-cash transactions for the time being.
In the interim, cash payments will be made in the currencies now in use in the
two entities, and the DM will continue to be used as a medium of exchange. The
entities are not legally obligated to take on the KM, but budgetary operations
with the state government will have to be conducted in the new currency (EBRD

1997b: 157). Since mid-1998 all receipts and payments to the state budget have been settled in KM (EBRD 1998b: 156). The convertible marka is now used for official payments in both entities and the use of the DM and Croatian kuna for all non-cash payments is to be phased out by mid-1999. A commons custom tariff has been established covering both entities, preferential entity trading regimes with Croatia and Yugoslavia are being eliminated and several steps have been taken to harmonize taxes (EBRD 1999a: 34). While a common customs tariff was agreed in March 1998, containing four rates and a low average, its effective implementation has been delayed by free-trade agreements between the federation and Croatia and between the Republika Srpska and the Federal Republic of Yugoslavia. Tax avoidance through the rerouting of trade has been further encouraged by sharp differences in excise and sales taxes across the entities. As a result, non-tariff impediments on the internal market have abounded. Recently the Republika Srpska has taken steps to reduce sales taxes and adjust excise taxes, bringing rates broadly into line with the federation. The free trade agreements with Croatia and the Federal Republic of Yugoslavia were ended in May 1999. At the same time temporary import surcharges imposed by the federation were replaced by a common list for Bosnia. There is current account convertibility. Acceptance of the convertible marka (KM) is highest in the Bosniac-majority areas and lowest in the Bosnian-Croat areas. In the Republika Srpska more than 50 per cent of commercial bank deposits are now in KM. The Kosovo conflict has increased demand for the KM at the expense of the Yugoslav dinar. There is agreement to ban the use of the DM and Croatian kuna (originally scheduled for June 1999) and mandate it as the unit of account for all financial transactions. But targets dates are slipping. The currency board arrangement, however, is functioning well. KM inflation is in low single figures. Currency board rules prevent Bosnia's different levels of government from contracting domestic debt. The Payments Bureaux (inherited from the former Yugoslavia) prevent banks from offering payments services and provide opportunities for bureaucratic interference and control. A recent agreement with the IMF envisages a phasing out of the system by the end of 2000 (EBRD 1999b: 198–9).

On 21 January 1998 Carlos Westendorp, the High Representative, imposed a solution for the design of a common currency. (See the entry for that date in the political section above.)

The European Commission's customs union has taken over the borders from the Bosnian Serb government (*IHT*, 1 June 1998, p. 10).

On 1 April 1998 the Bosnian Serb government declared the DM an official temporary currency as the Yugoslav dinar was devalued. All public salaries and pensions would be paid in DMs this month. The introduction of a 'double monetary system' would enable Bosnian Serbs to open DM bank accounts (*The Times*, 2 April 1998, p. 15).

The newly established Central Bank of Bosnia-Hercegovina introduced its new currency, the convertible mark (KM), on 22 June 1998. The aim is to replace the three existing currencies, the Croatian kuna, the Bosnian dinar and the Yugoslav dinar. The central bank will operate under a currency board regime, which pegs the KM to the DM at a rate of one to one. Currency in circulation plus commercial bank deposits with the central bank will be fully covered by foreign currency (Deutsche Bank Research, *Emerging Europe Weekly*, 26 June 1998, p. 2).

> In June last year [1998] came the birth of the marka … It ranks among the youngest currencies in the world, but also, Peter Nicholl [a New Zealander who is governor of the central bank of Bosnia] insists, among the most stable. A pure currency board system ensures that the marka lives up to its name, trading at a strict one-to-one against the DM (and so, since 1 January 1999, at one-to-0.51 against the Euro). The DM was chosen because it has traditionally been the most trusted currency in the Balkans … Within Sarajevo the marka is now trusted so much that it circulates interchangeably with the DM … Outside Sarajevo take-up of the Bosnian notes has been slowest in the Croat-dominated south and west. Croatia is the main trading partner there and the Croatian kuna – a stable enough currency in its own right – prevails. But in the Serb-dominated north and east of Bosnia, where Serbia is the main trading partner, the trend has been better. The traditional local currency, the Yugoslav dinar, printed with periodic abandon in Belgrade, fell sharply over the winter. Bosnian Serbs responded by deserting the dinar for the more reliable domestic product. At least half the monetary transactions in the Serb-dominated parts of Bosnia are now in markas.
>
> (*The Economist*, 1 May 1999, p. 102)

> Until this year payment bureaux, a state-owned bureaucracy for cash payments, enjoyed a monopoly on payments in Bosnia over DM 50 – and charged a 0.4 per cent fee on every transaction … The payment bureaux are only now approaching closure. After years of discussion a deadline of the end of next year [2000] has been set for abolition … Some of the most important steps towards abolishing the bureaux this year were late. But all have been taken or are under way, including the scrapping of the bureaux' monopoly on non-cash. The DM, the Croatian kuna and the Yugoslav dinar … have also been removed from the system.
>
> (*FT*, Survey, 14 December 1999, p. 38)

> Nato bombing caused considerable collateral damage to the Republika Srpska economy. Last year [1998] Yugoslavia took 70 per cent of Republika Srpska exports and accounted for nearly a quarter of its GDP. The annual value of this trade has now been halved … Some decline in Republika Srpska links with Yugoslavia was inevitable following the latter's decision to exclude the Republika Srpska from its payments system and the Republika Srpska's decision this autumn [1999] to ban the use of the Yugoslav dinar as legal tender. Only the Konvertibilna Marka is used now in the Republika Srpska.
>
> (*FT*, Survey, 14 December 1999, p. 37)

The system that governs the Bosnia and Hercegovina economy is to a large extent the same as it was in the days of communism. Many of the old command economy structures are still in place, notably the notoriously intransparent payment bureaux, through which all commercial and public bank transfers must pass. They levy a substantial sum for the service along the way. The banking system, in many cases on the verge of bankruptcy, is also in dire need of overhaul ... The first stage [of privatization], opening the books of the big state sector companies to independent audit, prior to devaluation, met fierce political resistance. Perhaps this was inevitable, since the state companies, like the payment bureaux, are a cash-cow for the major political parties ... We are moving ahead with privatization now; and the payment bureaux will be abolished this year [2000].

(Wolfgang Petritsch, High Representative for Civilian Implementation of the Dayton Peace Accords, *The World Today*, 2000, vol. 56, no. 4, p. 24)

'From January 2001 the country's non-cash payment system finally moves to the commercial banks and away from the payments bureaux' (Business Central Europe 2000: 36).

'The payments system is undergoing much-needed reform. It is envisaged that by the end of 2000 all transactions will be transferred from the payments operations bureaux into commercial banks' (EBRD 2000a: 44).

The governments of the two Entities agreed in June 1999 that they would harmonize excise taxes ... The final implementation of these measures, however, was delayed until March 2000 ... Since October 1999 all non-cash transactions between the two Entities and within the Federation have been in KM only ... In June 2000 the governments of both Entities announced their commitment to revising [labour] laws ... including the elimination of waiting lists and the reduction of severance costs for those already on them, more flexible provisions on fixed-term contracts and less restrictive provisions on cancelling employment contracts, were approved by the Federation parliament in August 2000 and are expected to be approved shortly in the RS [Republika Srpska].

(EBRD 2000b: 142)

The dismantling of the payments bureaux ... is now complete. The new clearing system, a real time gross settlements system and a wholesale clearing system, will increase transparency and confidence and remove one of the major obstacles for investment ... In late 2000 the Office of the High Representative imposed a number of amendments to labour and pension laws in both Entities. These amendments are designed to eliminate features of the labour market, such as large unemployment benefit entitlements and the inability to lay off excess labour, that were hindering investment in state enterprises.

(EBRD 2001a: 52)

The dismantling of the payments bureaux was successfully completed in January 2001 ... The Office of the High Representative (OHR) imposed amendments to the labour laws of both Entities in late 2000. In the Federation the new law ... reduces high unemployment benefit entitlements and enables employers to lay off excess labour. In RS in November 2000 the OHR amended the existing labour law, reducing compensation payments to employees on 'wait lists'. These measures ... will help to increase the attractiveness to investors of enterprises undergoing privatization. However, contractual obligations will remain on investors to maintain certain levels of employment ... Progress towards creating a single economic space has been slow. The authorities have taken steps recently towards this goal, including the decisions recently by both Entity parliaments in May 2001 to equalize the sales tax rate ... Direct taxes ... tend to be lower in RS ... valuation of goods for customs purposes [differ] and [there are] different foreign investment laws. Preparations are advanced for the introduction of a harmonized income law in January 2000 ... In June 2001 Bosnia and Hercegovina was one of seven signatories in the south-east European region to sign a memorandum of understanding on free trade, thereby committing to free trade within the region by 2006.

(EBRD 2001b: 122–3)

[On 18 September 2000 EU foreign] ministers approved an EU package granting duty-free access to 95 per cent of imports from Albania, Bosnia, Croatia, Macedonia and Montenegro ... The package includes abolition of tariffs on most industrial and farm products to the EU. However, some limits remain on exports of fish products and wine.

(*FT*, 19 September 2000, p. 10)

On 19 December 2000 Bosnia and Croatia signed an agreement that eliminated customs duties on Bosnian goods entering Croatia and reduced duties on Croatian goods entering the Bosnian market (*IHT*, 20 December 2000, p. 19).

Privatization

According to the Moslem–Croat Federation's privatization law, adopted in October 1997, small privatization was to be followed by the sale of strategic enterprises (electricity, water supply, transportation, mining, forestry, telecommunications and public service, and media). The government would settle its obligations to citizen groups by issuing vouchers that could be used to buy assets offered for sale through auctions and public tenders. The World Bank suggested that small sell-offs start in spring 1998, followed by strategic sectors in summer 1998 and then banks in 1999. In the Republika Srpska some 400 enterprises would be sold. Fifty-five per cent of shares were to go to state-run privatization funds, 30 per cent would be offered to citizens through a voucher scheme and 15 per cent would be sold to strategic investors for cash (*Transition*, 1997, vol. 8, no. 6, p. 24).

At federation level legislation for privatization was finally completed in January 1998. The law establishes privatization certificates as the primary mechanism of ownership transfer. Apartments and small enterprises are targeted for certificate privatization in favour of tenants starting around mid-1998. Large enterprises are to develop individual privatization plans and submit them for approval. Management buy-outs and management–employee buy-outs are expected to play an important role in large privatization (EBRD 1998a: 33).

On 22 July 1998 the tripartite Bosnia-Hercegovina parliament failed to approve a privatization law following objections from Bosnian Serb deputies. UN High Representative Carlos Westendorp decreed the privatization law into effect (*EEN*, 1998, vol. 12, no. 9, p. 4).

Privatization is to be used as a way of paying off a series of government debts to the population arising from the war and the collapse of the former Yugoslavia. Vouchers are to be issued, which can be used either to buy flats or other property or to buy shares in enterprises, either directly or through investment funds. Banks are being specifically excluded from voucher privatization. A percentage of all assets must be bought in cash with vouchers in general being allowed to cover only up to 65 per cent of the purchase price. Voucher privatization is to be used to pay off three sources of state debt. Citizens have claims on the government for so-called frozen foreign exchange deposits. These represent individuals' savings in foreign currency in the old Yugoslav banking system and were seized by Serbia when Yugoslavia disintegrated in 1991. In addition, there are debts representing three years of unpaid wages to about 300,000 former soldiers and policemen during the period of the war. Claims arising from property restitution may also be paid off through vouchers (although no law on restitution has yet been passed). The vouchers, which will be valid for three years, are supposed to be issued in November 1998. They will be awarded according to a points system based both on the claims for unpaid wages, pensions and savings deposits and on the number of years that citizens have previously been in employment. The first phase will cover small-scale privatization of offices, shops, flats and services such as hotels and road maintenance, while the sell-off of stakes in large companies is due to begin in spring 1999. Preparations are less advanced in the Republika Srpska (*FT*, Survey, 21 October 1998, p. iv). 'Because the country has not yet passed a law on restitution for property confiscated by the state, the position of legal claims by those dispossessed after the Second World War is still not clear.' Under the federation system (rules for the Republika Srpska system are not yet in place) citizens pay an extra 35 per cent cash on top of the value of the voucher in small privatization. Vouchers alone are to be used for larger state enterprises. The privatization of state banks has been separated from the voucher programme in recognition of the need for foreign expertise and capital.

A recently passed Federation law required companies to pay 'waiting list' money to workers who were either on a waiting list to join the company in 1991 or would have been eligible for it. The total liability would be KM 600 million to KM 800 million if it could be enforced – unlikely since it would drive nearly every large company into bankruptcy … The new law is now being hastily revised after international protests … The communist-era system gave the unemployed a fictional job with a company, doing nothing for around 30 per cent of the normal wage … Of 15,400 employed in Federation [coal] mines, 2,260 are on 'waiting lists', the lists of temporarily laid-off workers who are paid about 30 per cent of their salaries to remain at home.

(*FT*, Survey, 14 December 1999, pp. 35–6)

The prewar economy of Bosnia and Hercegovina was dominated by around ten large conglomerates responsible for more than half of GDP … Shares in 'socially-owned' enterprises were nationalized during the war and are now owned by the FBH [Federation of Bosnia and Hercegovina] and the RS [Republika Srpska], respectively. However, effective control was retained by management. Public enterprises own the largest banks in both the FBH and the RS and are their largest depositors and borrowers.

(EBRD 1998b: 156)

Federation legislation enabling the financial restructuring, privatization and liquidation of state banks came into force in April 1998. A similar set of laws is being prepared in the RS. The law transfers ownership in state banks from public enterprises to the ministry of finance. The RS embarked on mass privatization in 1996 under a scheme that was criticized by international observers and subsequently cancelled by a new government in early 1998. In June 1998 a new privatization law was passed that is broadly comparable with the FBH law. Privatization in the FBH is set to begin. All non-private shares in the estimated 1,250 enterprises with state, social or mixed ownership are in principle subject to privatization against a mix of cash and vouchers (certificates). Vouchers are being issued for claims against the state, including foreign currency accounts, back wages for the army, restitution claims and general claims based on duration of employment. Documented interest by strategic foreign and local investors takes precedence over voucher privatization. So-called 'strategic' enterprises (approximately 40 per cent of the book value of privatizable assets) are to be subject to a different procedure calling for individual parliamentary approval (EBRD 1998b: 156–7). No enterprise has yet been privatized and no bank has been restructured (EBRD 1999a: 34). A Joint Power Co-ordination Centre was set up in late 1999 to work with the World Bank in preparing an electricity law and to co-ordinate the exchange of electricity between power providers in late 1999. Since the beginning of May 1999 several federation cantons have conducted auctions and tenders for the sale of small-scale assets. Bids under both auctions and tenders must include a cash component of at least 35 per cent, with the remainder payable in 'certificates' (claim accounts). Given the lacklustre demand at the early auctions, the cash requirement is likely to be lowered. Certificates were issued in May 1999 to 1.9 million citizens of the federation, against military back-pay, the value of frozen foreign currency savings (DM 2.4 billion) and 'general claims' against employment history. The RS held its first auctions in July 1999. Large privatization ('privatization through the public offering of shares'), however, continues to be delayed and obstructed. Legal deadlines for ownership revision, preparation of opening balance sheets and presentation by companies of privatization plans have been missed throughout the federation. Preference is to be given to strategic investors in large privatization. Offerings of residual shares can be paid for with certificates, with no minimum cash requirement. The government is encouraging the creation of investment funds, but none have materialized as yet. Foreigners can use certificates only via local intermediaries, but some have been active on the secondary market with certificates quoted at around 30 per cent of their face value. The RS essentially follows the same privatization model but lags behind in preparation.

> The economy is burdened with the pervasive influence of bureaucracy and by the lack of capital and unclear governance in the state sector. Management remains effectively in charge in most enterprises. Delays in the privatization process have limited access to investment finance and given rise to asset stripping (often through the creation of 'joint ventures' between state and private firms). Private businesses generally face a difficult or even hostile tax and administrative environment that has shed little of its socialist legacy. Inconsistent tax treatment tends to distort competition ... The Council of Ministers has wide discretionary powers to grant tax exemptions, a system which is prone to abuse and has contributed to unfair competition. Business legislation in both entities remains a patchwork of sometimes inconsistent laws and regulations, dating back mostly to the Socialist Federal Republic of Yugoslavia and to wartime administrations.
>
> (EBRD 1999b: 198–9)

The first sales under the small privatization scheme began in 1999. Completion of this programme for all state-owned small and medium-sized enterprises is planned for mid-2000. The beginning of large privatization has been delayed. Privatization of the main utilities is not expected to occur until 2001 at the earliest. In December 1999 the US government suspended support for the privatization programme owing to lack of compliance with established privatization law and alleged corruption. 'Slow privatization, insider control and lack of investment finance are delaying restructuring. Asset stripping is widespread, reflecting the weak protection of minority shareholder and creditor rights' (EBRD 2000a: 44).

> Small-scale privatization in the Federation ... [began] in the second half of 1999. Enterprises are being sold either by auction or tender. By May 2000 ... 813 auctions or tenders ... had been held ... for a total of KM 218 million (about 2 per cent of BH GDP), two-thirds of which are to be paid in vouchers. In RS small enterprises are being privatized through a mixture of cash and coupon sales. Vouchers are being issued to citizens based on

registration, which started in January 2000 ... Large, state-owned enterprises continue to dominate the economy in both Entities and progress in their privatization has been slow. However, the pace has increased recently. By August forty large enterprises had been sold in tenders in the Federation and twenty-two in RS.

(EBRD 2000b: 142)

After a slow start privatization has gained momentum over the last six months. Small-scale privatization has made progress in both Entities, particularly in Republika Srpska (RS) where nearly all small enterprises had been offered for sale, and more than half had been sold, by November 2000 ... Some large conglomerates, such as Energoinvest, have also begun preparing for privatization ... In late 2000 the Office of the High Representative imposed a number of amendments to labour and pension laws in both Entities. These amendments are designed to eliminate features of the labour market, such as large unemployment benefit entitlements and the inability to lay off excess labour, that were hindering investment in state enterprises ... A new telecommunications policy, adopted by the state government in November 2000, includes plans for the eventual privatization of the post and telecommunications companies in both Entities. Privatization of the remaining utilities is not expected to occur until the second half of 2001 ... The privatization programme for state-owned banks has also gathered momentum, especially in RS ... Two foreign banks entered the system.

(EBRD 2001a: 52)

Privatization [is] proceeding slowly ... most economic activity remaining in the state sector ... Initiatives to raise minimum capital requirements and to privatize state banks are attracting much-needed strategic investment to the banking sector ... Small-scale privatization is under way. In RS the government is auctioning enterprises ... Citizens are using frozen foreign exchange coupons to purchase these enterprises. In the Federation the process is approximately half-complete ... [enterprises being sold] mainly to management–employee groups and privatization funds. In both Entities the intention is to finish the process by the end of 2002. Large-scale privatization has made some progress but governance problems remain ... Numerous delays [have been encountered] and several transactions were marred by a lack of transparency.

(EBRD 2001b: 122)

In mid-1998, mid-1999 and mid-2000 the private sector accounted for roughly 35 per cent of GDP. This figure had increased to 40 per cent by mid-2001 (EBRD 2001b: 12, 124).

Voucher privatization started in the federation in September 1999 and was due to begin in early 2000 in the Republika Srpska. But only a third of enterprises are being sold this way. The rest depend on cash privatization, which started in the Republika Srpska in July 1999. By mid-September 1999 only ten of the initial batch of 350 enterprises had been sold. Belgium's Interbrew bought the Uniline brewery in 1999 (Business Central Europe 1999: 32).

[Bosnia's] .... privatization programme for large companies [is set to begin], with 1,029 firms to go under the hammer from 1 October [2000]. Some eighty-six strategic companies in the telecoms, energy and transport sectors will be offered to foreign investors through tenders.

(*Business Central Europe*, October 2000, p. 17)

Over eighty large companies were offered to foreign investors in October [2000] and the first one was sold a month later when Germany's Heidelberger Zement bought 51 per cent of Cement Plant Kakanj. The Germans paid DM 55 million for the country's biggest cement maker, with investment guarantees of DM 100 million over the next ten years.

(*Business Central Europe*, December 2000–January 2001, p. 26)

'Bosnia has started a large-scale privatization programme that has already seen its biggest cement plant and its Zenica steel-maker go to foreign investors' (Business Central Europe 2000: 54).

The biggest investors so far have included the Kuwait Investment Agency, which put DM 200 million into the Zenica steel plant and Unis holdings in Sarajevo. Germany's Volkswagen has invested DM 50 million in producing Skoda cars in Sarajevo, while its compatriot Heidelberger Zement paid DM 150 million for a cement plant in Kakanj ... Foreigners should play some part in strengthening the banking sector, with Austrian banks Raiffeisen and Volksbank both entering the market this year.

(p. 36)

[On 30 October 2000 the] Moslem–Croat Federation started a privatization programme under which shares in 550 large companies worth $1.29 billion will be exchanged for vouchers that citizens have received in compensation for losses – such as unpaid salaries – related to the Bosnian war.

(*IHT*, 31 October 2000, p. 15)

(See Petritsch, *The World Today*, 2000, vol. 56, no. 4, p. 24, above.)
Foreign direct investment has been negligible (see Table 1.1).
'A string of ventures have made Slovenia the biggest investor in Bosnia ... [e.g. by] Mercator ... [Slovenia's] biggest retail group ... Pivovarna, Slovenia's biggest brewer ... [and] Softlab, Slovenia's largest software house' (*FT*, 10 July 2001, p. 6).

2 Croatia

POLITICS

Events prior to the general election of 29 October 1995 are dealt with in the Introduction and Overview.

The general election of 29 October 1995

The Sabor (parliament) consists of two houses, the House of Representatives (lower house) and the House of Governors (upper house). The election was for the House of Representatives only.

The last election was held on 2 August 1992 and thirteen parties were represented in parliament. There were 124 seats, half elected on a proportional representation basis and half on a first-past-the-post constituency basis. There was a 5 per cent threshold.

In the October 1995 election the number of seats in the House of Representatives was increased to 127, divided up as follows: eighty MPs on the 'state lists', elected on a proportional representation basis; twenty-eight MPs elected on a first-past-the-post constituency basis; twelve MPs elected by the 'diaspora' (including the preponderant Bosnian Croats); and seven MPs elected by the ethnic minorities (instead of thirteen as before). The seven comprised three MPs elected by the Croatian Serbs (instead of seven), one by the Italians (mainly in Istria), one by the Hungarians (mainly in the north), one by the German-speakers and one by the Slavs (Czechs, Slovaks, Russians and Ukrainians). There was still a 5 per cent threshold for parties, but an 11 per cent threshold was set for alliances.

As expected, the Croatian Democratic Union was victorious, stressing the recent military victories. But the party was disappointed not to win the two-thirds majority in parliament necessary to change the constitution in favour of a stronger presidency. The party did badly in Zagreb and other cities. Opposition parties, although complaining of lack of proper access to the media, successfully played on economic and social problems such as unemployment and on corruption in political life.

The turnout was 65 per cent. Below is the resulting distribution of votes and seats in the House of Representatives:

Croatian Democratic Union: 45.23 per cent of the vote; seventy-five seats. The party won ten of the twelve 'diaspora' seats. Zlatko Mateson became prime minister.

Croatian Peasants' Party: 18.25 per cent of the vote. Leader, Zlatko Tomcic. The party's platform stressed economic and social problems such as unemployment and corruption in political life.

Croatian Social-Liberal Party: 11.55 per cent of the vote. Leader, Drazen Budisa.

Social Democratic Party of Croatia: 9.08 per cent of the vote. Leader, Ivica Racan. Slogan, 'Honesty'.

Croatian Party of Rights: 5.1 per cent of the vote. Extreme right-wing party.

Serbian National Party.

Alliance: the alliance, formed on 28 September 1995, originally included the Croatian Peasants' Party, the Croatian Social-Liberal Party, the Social Democratic Party of Croatia and the Croatian Party of Rights. But these parties decided to run alone. The alliance finally included the Croatian People's Party, the Croatian Independent Democrats, the Istrian Democratic Assembly (which did well in Istria, advocating substantial autonomy), the Croatian Christian Democratic Union and the Croatian Party of Slavonia and Baranja.

Political developments after the October 1995 general election

12 November 1995: Croatia and the Croatian Serbs sign an agreement relating to Eastern Slavonia drafted by Tudjman and Milosevic during the talks in the USA. Eastern Slavonia will return to Croatian control after a transitional term of no more than two years. (The minimum year can be lengthened by up to an additional one year if at least one side requests it.) During the transitional period there will be administration by the United Nations, whose Security Council will decide on the implementation force of peacekeepers and police. Demilitarization will be achieved within thirty days of their deployment. The area will have a multi-ethnic nature, with ethnic Croat refugees allowed to return and ethnic Serbs to remain.

15 January 1996: the UN mandate expires. The UN Security Council authorizes a new force of up to 5,000 peacekeepers (up from 1,600) for Eastern Slavonia, able to call on the support of Nato airpower. For an initial period of twelve months the peacekeepers will supervise demilitarization and try to ensure peace and security.

24 April 1996: the parliamentary assembly of the Council of Europe votes to admit Croatia (its fortieth member). Croatia is required to ratify the European Convention on Human Rights within a year of joining, to recognize the right of citizens to petition the European Court of Human Rights and to abolish the death penalty in peacetime within three years (*IHT*, 25 April 1996, p. 5). (But on 14 May 1996 the Council of Europe's Committee of Ministers postponed

Croatia's entry, the first time that the committee had voted against the parliamentary assembly: *Independent*, 15 May 1996, p. 81. On 5 June the Council of Europe set five conditions for admission, calling for concrete steps to be taken 'as rapidly as possible': the handing over of war crimes suspects; facilitating free elections in Bosnia; allowing the return of Serb refugees; dropping prosecutions against the independent media; allowing the opposition-controlled Zagreb council to elect a mayor: *Guardian*, 5 June 1996, p. 13.)

30 April 1996:

> Zagreb's city council, which appoints the mayor and is dominated by the opposition, a group of seven parties, was tossed out of the door Tuesday [30 April]. The move to dissolve the city council, which took office in October, will ultimately face new elections. And it has triggered an acrimonious power struggle that many say illustrates Mr Tudjman's growing intolerance toward democratic change. The moves have been accompanied by a series of new press laws that make it difficult to criticize the president and government officials ... The president has cited 'national security' in exercising his constitutional veto to keep out all four candidates [for mayor] the opposition has suggested in the last six months. [The president appointed one of his own nominees as mayor.] The government said it was forced to dissolve the city council after the constitutional court, dominated by judges appointed by the president's governing party, the Croatian Democratic Union, ruled that the city budget, submitted by the centre-left opposition majority, was illegal ... But the struggle, Western diplomats said, really centres on the sale of state-owned businesses, many of which have ended up in the hands of close associates of the president. 'This is about patronage and power,' a diplomat said. 'The ruling party has made a lot of money from the privatization of state property. Tudjman is not about to turn over the city administration, that can monitor these sales, to his opponents.'
>
> (Chris Hedges, *IHT*, 3 May 1996, p. 12)

> A whole sequence of laws recently introduced is part of HDZ's [Croatian Democratic Union's] drive to recentralize power, transferring assets and decision-making from local authorities to ministries in Zagreb. The government is removing all the big state-owned firms in the capital from municipal jurisdiction.
>
> (*EEN*, 12 June 1996, vol. 10, no. 12, p. 7)

(Zagreb's dual status as a city and region gave Tudjman the technical power to override the city council in choosing its mayor: *The Economist*, 21 December 1996, p. 44.)

7 May 1996: the Zagreb–Belgrade motorway ('Highway of Brotherhood and Unity') is reopened, although only for international traffic. The Adriatic oil pipeline between the Croatian port of Rijeka and the Serbian town of Pancevo is also reopened (*FT*, 8 May 1996, p. 2).

7 August 1996: Presidents Tudjman and Milosevic meet in Greece and agree to establish diplomatic relations by the end of the month. The statement talks of them being 'ready to proceed to full normalization'.

23 August 1996: foreign minister Mate Granic signs a mutual recognition accord with his Yugoslav counterpart Milan Milutinovic. Ambassadors will be exchanged (i.e. full diplomatic relations formally established) within fifteen days. (This actually occurred on 9 September 1996.) Refugees will be allowed to return.

26 September 1996: two journalists are cleared in court of the charge of defaming President Tudjman. (A new clause in the criminal code allows a maximum sentence of three years for insulting high officials.)

Radio 101 is the last independent radio station. A series of stringent press laws has been passed recently, including one to limit the residency visas of the handful of foreign correspondents based in Croatia to three months. A detailed press law promulgated in October 1996 contains provisions that give the government the power to force newspapers to run corrections or clarifications and sets out the qualifications needed to be a chief editor (Chris Hedges, *IHT*, 9 October 1996, p. 7).

6 November 1996: Croatia becomes the fortieth member of the Council of Europe.

20 November 1996: the government refuses to renew the licence of Radio 101, the last independent radio station, allegedly because the station is 'not objective'. (The licence was later extended to mid-January 1997: *EEN*, 1996, vol. 10, no. 24, p. 8.)

24 January 1997: Radio 101 is granted a five-year broadcasting licence.

13 April 1997: there are both local elections and elections for the upper house. There was a 71 per cent turnout for the local elections. UN observers pronounced the elections to be generally free and fair, although voting in Eastern Slavonia was extended by a day to allow all ethnic Serbs who wished to vote the chance to do so. First-day voting there was poorly organized and the international community was anxious to involve ethnic Serbs in the election before Eastern Slavonia returned to Croatian executive control on 15 July 1997.

The Croatian Democratic Union (CDU) wins 40 per cent of the vote but wins forty-one seats in the sixty-eight-seat Chamber of Deputies (four more than in 1993). The Croatian Peasants' Party wins ten seats, the Social Democratic Party of Croatia five seats, the Croatian Social-Liberal Party five seats, and the Istrian Democratic Forum two seats. The president nominated five seats, two of these being reserved for the Serb minority.

The CDU wins nineteen out of twenty-one counties. The CDU also narrowly controls the Zagreb city assembly, winning twenty-four seats (two short of a majority) to fourteen secured by the Social Democratic Party of Croatia, nine by the Croatian Social-Liberal Party and three by the Croatian Peasants' Party. Two of the three elected members of the Croatian Peasants' Party subsequently defected to the CDU (*FT*, 20 May 1997, p. 3).

'After refusing for two years to recognize the opposition's victory in Zagreb, the Croatian Democratic Union (HDZ) gained control over the Zagreb city council in April by bribing two opposition Peasant Party deputies' (Chris Cviic, *The World Today*, 1997, vol. 53, no. 10, p. 249).

> As for the municipal elections, the CDU predictably did poorly. The urban population deserted it in almost every big town or city, including Split, Rijeka and Osijek. Paradoxically it did better in Zagreb than in 1995 even though its vote dropped from 36 per cent to 34 per cent – simply because in 1995 the opposition had an alliance, whereas this time it contested the elections on an individual party basis.
>
> (*EEN*, 1997, vol. 11, no. 8, p. 3)

In Eastern Slavonia the turnout was around 90 per cent. The newly formed Serb party won eleven out of twenty-eight municipalities, excluding Vukovar where it gained twelve out of twenty-six seats. The CDU also won twelve seats in Vukovar (*The Economist*, 17 May 1997, p. 8). A hardline nationalist Croat party took two seats in Vukovar (*FT*, Survey, 28 May 1997, p. iii).

15 June 1997: Tudjman wins a second five-year term as president (despite reports that he has stomach cancer). He wins 61.42 per cent of the vote, but in a poor turnout of only 57 per cent. Zdravko Tomac (leader of the Social Democratic Party) receives 21.08 per cent of the vote and Vlado Gotovac (leader of the Social Liberal Party) receives 17.7 per cent of the vote. ('Mr Gotovac, a poet who called for the return of ethnic Serbs, was knocked unconscious and hospitalized [during the campaign] by a captain of the presidential guard in the city of Pula. During the assault the officer shouted "Long live Ante Pavelic!" ': Chris Hedges, *IHT*, 17 June 1997, p. 6.)

The head of the OSCE observers concluded that the election 'did not meet the minimum standards for democracies'. 'Croatia has experienced a free but not fair election. While candidates were able to operate freely, the process leading up to the election was fundamentally flawed.' There was also a formal OSCE report: 'The electoral process afforded enormous advantages to the ruling party candidate and limited the ability of the opposition candidates to campaign freely.' The advantages included the degree of state control of the media (especially television) and the disparity in campaign resources. Ethnic Serbs who had fled the country were disenfranchised, while ethnic Croats in Bosnia were allowed to vote.

20 June 1997: the Croatian Social-Liberal Party (CSLP) splits following the suspension of Zagreb city CSLP executive because of its co-operation with the Croatian Democratic Union (*EEN*, 1997, vol. 11, no. 13, p. 6).

14 July 1997: the UN transitional administration in Eastern Slavonia is extended until 15 January 1998 (*EEN*, 1997, vol. 11, no. 14, p. 4).

6 October 1997: ten Bosnian Croats fly from Croatia and surrender to the war crimes tribunal in The Hague.

18 December 1997: parliament approves a constitutional amendment which excludes the 22,000-strong Slovenian minority in Croatia from the register of officially recognized minorities (*EEN*, 1997, vol. 11, no. 24, pp. 6–7).

15 January 1998: the UN transitional administration in Eastern Slavonia comes to an end.

Unemployment is as high as 80 per cent and foreign aid is a fraction of what flows into Bosnia. The UN High Commissioner for Refugees reckons that 15,000 to 20,000 of Eastern Slavonia's 100,000 or so Serbs have left in the past two years. Something like another 30,000 have hedged their bets by moving property to Serbia. The UN transitional administration has concluded agreements with Croatia to encourage the 60,000 Serbs native to Eastern Slavonia to stay. About 40 per cent of jobs in the public sector have been reserved for Serbs, while the Serb community is entitled to half an hour a day of television airtime. The UN administration has persuaded the Serbs to use the Croatian kuna rather than the Yugoslav dinar. In the autumn of 1997 the Serbs boycotted schools to protest against Croatia's curriculum, which teaches that Serbs were aggressors in the war that followed the collapse of Yugoslavia. The UN administration brokered a deal to suspend the teaching of recent history for five years. OSCE is sending 250 monitors, 100 to Eastern Slavonia alone, to encourage Croatia to treat its minorities well. In addition, 180 UN police monitors will remain in Eastern Slavonia, at Croatia's request, to allay foreign suspicions that the local police will mistreat Serbs (*The Economist*, 10 January 1998, pp. 37–8).

> Conflicts between old neighbours, for now, may be limited simply by the low number of returnees who have come or want to come home to crumbled cities like Vukovar … Some, gone for more than six years, have left for good. Other likely returnees drive into Vukovar, only to turn around when they see the bleak prospects. Every factory and nearly every storefront here was reduced to, and remains, rubble. Jobs, except in the open-air market or in a few government offices, are non-existent … But some sense of calm … comes from those trying to look to the future. The Croatian government and communities here, so far, have followed through on promises to establish police, judiciary and school systems that reflect pre-war population splits and, in the last year, voter sentiment. The regional police force is split nearly in half between Serbian and Croatian officers. Judicial appointments have been divvied up between the Serbian and Croatian legal authorities. Schoolbooks are to be available in both the Cyrillic scripts used by the Serbs and the Latin script used by the Croats. UN officials are … saying that many of the 120,000 Serbs in the region still live in eastern Slavonia. They, like many others, are waiting to see if the Croatian government lives up to its promises after the much-heralded transfer date – and if their erstwhile Croat neighbours will return.
>
> (Christine Spolar, *IHT*, 12 January 1998, p. 5)

12 February 1998: the government annuls a decree on the use of state-owned apartments in Eastern Slavonia The decree, adopted in January, allowed the mainly Croat occupants of apartments in Eastern Slavonia who fled during the war to reclaim their property by 15 March (*IHT*, 13 February 1998, p. 6).

19 February 1998: an OSCE spokesman says that Serbs in Eastern Slavonia 'are very much concerned about their future'. 'Recently there have been signs of economic discrimination', e.g. layoffs of Serbs and problems with pensions and social benefits (*FT*, 20 February 1998, p. 2).

'Of the 120,000 ethnic Serbs who lived in the eastern Slavonian enclave two years ago, nearly half have fled, and the number of departures is rising daily, according to relief agencies' (Chris Hedges, *IHT*, 20 March 1998, p. 4).

20 April 1998: a court in Zagreb acquits the former editor of an independent magazine accused of libel by the government. In September 1997 the magazine quoted from a US report which had described the Croatian government as 'corrupted and highly influenced by organized crime' (*FT*, 21 April 1998, p. 2).

4 May 1998: Gojko Susak, the hardline nationalist defence minister, dies of lung cancer.

18 June 1998: Dinko Sakic is extradited from Argentina to Croatia to stand trial for war crimes. He was a commander of the Second World War Jasenovac concentration camp (*FT*, Survey, 7 July 1998, p. iii).

July 1998: parliament has recently approved a comprehensive programme for the return and accommodation of refugees and displaced persons forced to flee their homes in Croatia during the four-year war that followed the collapse of Yugoslavia in 1991. An OSCE report estimates that as many as 200,000 Croatian Serbs fled the country between 1991 and 1995. During the 1995 military operations, around 190,000 people, mainly Croatian Serbs, fled Croatia chiefly to Serbia and the Republika Srpska (*FT*, Survey, 7 July 1998, p. i). Since the handover about 17,000 of the estimated 82,000 Croats displaced in 1991 have returned home. Returning Croats have resorted to violence and intimidation to evict Serbs, despite laws permitting them to remain until their homes can be occupied. Croatia has given citizenship (and in many cases abandoned Serb houses) to Bosnian Croat refugees. There are an estimated 400,000 refugees outside the country, including about 80,000 Serbs living in Bosnia (p. iii).

3 October 1998: Pope John Paul II beatifies Cardinal Alojzije Stepinac, 'one of the most controversial figures in the Balkans – a man denounced as a Nazi collaborator but hailed by many Croats as a national martyr'. The cardinal was tried in 1946 and sentenced to sixteen years in prison on charges of collaborating with the pro-Nazi state established during the Second World War. He died in 1960. Cardinal Stepinac was rehabilitated in 1991, being

> hailed as a hero and a martyr, the victim of communist attempts to suppress the Church and stifle the national aspirations of the Croatian people. Critics of the cardinal say he blessed fascist Croatian soldiers, maintained contacts with the Nazi-backed Ustashe government and carried out its orders to convert Serbs, who are Orthodox Christians, to Roman Catholicism. Admirers say that by allowing Serbs and Jews to convert, he was trying to give them a chance to escape persecution. Croatia's Jewish community, which lost 30,000 members during World War II, said it was grateful to the

archbishop for saving the lives of many. As to the rest of his merits, it said in a statement, 'time will judge'.

(*IHT*, 3 October 1998, p. 2)

The cardinal died under house arrest in 1960. Beatification is the final step before canonization as a saint.

To Orthodox Serbs ... the beatification is a political provocation. They have long viewed Cardinal Stepinac as a wartime sympathizer with the pro-Nazi government of Croatia ... After Germany invaded Yugoslavia in 1941 Ante Pavelic, the leader of the Ustashe, became the head of the pro-Nazi government of newly independent Croatia. Cardinal Stepinac, as archbishop of Zagreb and a fervent anti-communist, initially embraced the Pavelic government as 'God's hand at work'. As evidence mounted of atrocities against Serbs, Jews and other minorities, the archbishop withdrew his support. By 1942 he began denouncing Ustashe excesses, once in a letter to Pavelic and, in 1943, in church homilies and letters to priests. Arrested by Tito's forces in 1946, the archbishop was given a show trial, imprisoned and then put under house arrest in 1951. The Vatican and many historians credit Cardinal Stepinac with saving hundreds of Jews and Serbs, but his critics maintain that by not speaking out more, he in effect supported the Ustashe regime. 'There is no question he saved hundreds of Jews and others,' said Slavko Goldstein, the leader of the Jews in Croatia, who number about 2,000. He described the cardinal's record as mixed. 'He tried to correct some of the worst aspects, but he never condemned the regime as such,' Mr Goldstein said.

(Alessandra Stanley, *IHT*, 5 October 1998, p. 5)

12 October 1998: defence minister Andrija Hebrang resigns.

The HDZ has suffered damaging internal splits in which the hardline, nationalist faction identified with Ivic Pasalic, the president's domestic affairs adviser, has emerged with the upper hand. The struggle for power within the party led to the recent resignation of Hrvoje Sarinic, a former prime minister and head of the presidential office, who was regarded as a leader of the liberal wing of the HDZ, as well as the departures of the defence minister and another key Tudjman aide. They left amid allegations that the military intelligence service had been used to undermine moderates within the HDZ.

(*FT*, Survey, 14 December 1998, p. 25)

3 March 1999: in late January 1999 OSCE reported on human rights in Croatia. The report has not been made public, but it says: 'There has been no progress in improving respect for human rights, the rights of minorities and the rule of law.'

The report ... is filled with damning details – about repression of the media by the Croatian government, about the lack of co-operation with the international war crimes tribunal in The Hague, and above all about its harsh treatment of ethnic Serbs. Only a small percentage of the approximately 300,000 ethnic Serbs forced to flee their homes here during the war have been allowed to return ... The [US] state department, in a human rights report made public last week, described Croatia as 'nominally democratic' but 'in reality authoritarian' ... The European group said that under pressure from the United States and the EU, the Croatian government had made commitments to freedom of the press. But Croatian television, the main source of news for as many as 90 per cent of Croatians, 'remains subject to political control by the ruling party', the report said. On the international war crimes tribunal, the report said the Croatian government had embarked on a campaign to 'encourage distrust and hostility' towards it among the Croatian populace.

(Raymond Bonner, *IHT*, 4 March 1999, p. 9)

'Even today an estimated half of the ethnic Serbs who once lived in Croatia remain refugees beyond its borders' (*IHT*, 28 December 1999, p. 8).

Though Yugoslavia and Croatia resumed diplomatic relations in 1996, only 20,000 of the estimated 300,000 refugees from Croatia have returned to their homes. Denied Yugoslav citizenship, the right to work, vote or own property, they survive on handouts and the charity of local relatives.

(*FT*, 30 December 1999, p. 4)

The [January 2000] election [in Croatia] was seen as a quiet but significant milestone for members of Croatia's slowly returning Serbian community. Before independence they represented 12 per cent of the population, but 100,000 still live in exile in Yugoslavia or in Bosnia.

(*Guardian*, 4 January 2000, p. 10)

4 October 1999: a Croatian court sentences Dinko Sakic (78), the commander of the Jasenovac concentration camp during the Second World War, to the maximum twenty years for war crimes against civilians. Up to 85,000 inmates are estimated to have perished in the camp (*FT*, 5 October 1999, p. 9; *IHT*, 5 October 1999, p. 6).

1 November 1999: Tudjman undergoes an emergency intestinal operation.

24 November 1999:

Bracing for the worst, parliament paved the way on Wednesday [24 November] for transferring some essential powers from the ailing President Franjo Tudjman. Mr Tudjman's doctors acknowledged the leader's condition was grave, and a key aide said he was fighting for his life. A conditional clause on temporary incapacity of the president was supported by eighty-five deputies, giving the motion the necessary two-thirds majority in the 127-seat legislature. The amendment, drafted by Mr Tudjman's Croatian Democratic Union, allows for some presidential powers to be transferred to the speaker of parliament should the cabinet rule that Mr Tudjman is temporarily unfit to perform his duties ... Mr Tudjman was treated in 1996 in a Washington clinic for what American sources said was cancer – a claim he denied. He has been hospitalized in a Zagreb clinic since 1 November, where he has suffered many complications after emergency intestinal surgery. The constitutional amendment gives the government up to thirty days to start the procedure to proclaim him temporarily unable to perform his duties ... [A senior Tudjman aide] hinted that the cabinet could 'very soon' seek the ruling on Mr Tudjman's temporary incapacity from the constitutional court ... If Mr Tudjman is proclaimed unfit, or if he dies, the parliament speaker, Vlatko Pavletic, will assume some of his powers.

(*IHT*, 25 November 1999, p. 6)

Originally, parliamentary elections were scheduled for 22 December [1999] – a pre-Christmas date that seemed designed, in this largely Roman Catholic country, to help his party, since many of its critics, including Croats who also have homes abroad, would be on vacation or out of the country. Mr Tudjman's party is thought to be trying to buy time while the leadership decides who will run for the presidency and when to call parliamentary elections. If Mr Tudjman dies, the parliamentary speaker, Mr Pavletic ... will run the country before new presidential elections within sixty days. Parliament's term is scheduled to expire on 27 January [2000] and new elections should be called by 26 December at the latest, to allow thirty days of campaigning ... Part of the political confusion here stems from the increasing unpopularity of Mr Tudjman's umbrella party, since the economy is stagnant, corruption is visible and unemployment is very high.

(*IHT*, 26 November 1999, p. 7)

Mr Tudjman's ruling Croatian Democratic Union yesterday [24 November] passed a law allowing for powers of the president to be passed to the speaker of parliament in the event of the president being declared 'temporarily incapacitated' ... Hitherto under the Croatian constitution the powers of the president could only be transferred to the speaker of parliament if the president were to die, resign or be declared permanently incapacitated. A presidential election would then have to be held within sixty days ... The president, who was treated for cancer in 1996, has been in hospital since 1 November and has twice undergone surgery. The transfer of power to Vlatko Pavletic, the speaker of parliament, must happen this week to avoid an imminent political crisis in Croatia, as the four-year mandate of the current parliament is due to run out on Saturday [27 November]. The date of the general election, which must be held by 27 January [2000], has still not been set due to the president's illness and has already been postponed once from the favoured date of 22 December [1999] ... The Croatian Democratic Union favours a poll on 28 December, when many expatriate Croats, traditionally strong supporters of the Croatian Democratic Union, would have returned.

(*FT*, 25 November 1999, p. 10)

'Elections must be called a month in advance ... The president was supposed to have signed a decree by last Saturday [20 November] calling for elections to be held on 22 December. He was too ill and they were postponed' (*Telegraph*, 25 November 1999, p. 25).

25 November 1999: the cabinet asks the constitutional court to pass final judgement on whether President Tudjman is 'temporarily incapacitated'. The court has twenty-four hours to decide.

26 November 1999: the constitutional court declares President Tudjman to be 'temporarily incapacitated'. Parliamentary speaker Vlatko Pavletic takes over for an interim but renewable period of sixty days.

The Croatian Democratic Union declares its preference for parliamentary elections to take place on 3 January 2000.

[There is no] post of vice-president ... [and] Mr Tudjman ... never allowed a successor to be named ... Mr Tudjman ran the country through an extensive presidential office of advisers led by Ivic Pasalic, who controls internal security and media matters ... Mr Pasalic is influential but unpopular with the public.

(Steven Erlanger, *IHT*, 27 November 1999, p. 8)

Mr Tudjman's obsessions included his unorthodox view that few Jews and Serbs were killed by the Croatian fascist regime, the Ustashe, during World War II and his conviction that the West wanted to control Croatia ... Croatia, despite its fervent desire to join Europe, has been kept waiting from two of the main waiting rooms for integration: Nato's Partnership for Peace ... and the EU's programme known as Phare ... which provides financial and technical assistance to other post-communist countries.

(Steven Erlanger, *IHT*, 29 November 1999, p. 7)

'He [Tudjman] said fewer than 60,000 Serbs and others died in Croatia's main death camp, Jasenovac, not the 500,000 claimed' (*The Economist*, 18 December 1999, p. 164).

'Among his [Tudjman's] purported historical conclusions were that the number of Serbs and Jews killed at Jasenovac was much smaller than the 700,000 stated in Yugoslav history books' (*The Times*, 13 December 1999, p. 19).

1 December 1999: six main opposition parties formally agree to form a coalition government if they do well enough.

10 December 1999: Tudjman dies of stomach cancer (although this has not yet been officially admitted).

13 December 1999: Tudjman's funeral takes place. The only foreign head of state present was the president of Turkey. The prime ministers of Hungary, Macedonia, Slovenia and Montenegro were present, along with the Croat member of the three-person Bosnian presidency.

21 December 1999: a date is set for the presidential election, namely 24 January 2000.

3 January 2000: a general election is held in which the Croatian Democratic Union (HDZ) is swept from office. The defeat was even more decisive than generally anticipated.

There is a four-year term of office. Fifty-five parties participated. The exact number of seats (around 150) depended on the size of the expatriate turnout.

The turnout is over 78 per cent.

The result of the election in terms of percentage of the vote was as follows: SDP/HSLS, 56 per cent; Group of Four, 12.1 per cent; HDZ, 21.4 per cent; others, 15.9 per cent (*Business Central Europe*, February 2000, p. 14).

There is a complicated system of proportional representation. It is made even more complicated by an eleventh constituency made up of the Croatian diaspora (mostly Bosnian Croats and émigrés) who maintain dual citizenship and can vote in Croatian elections. Minorities are guaranteed another five seats, one for each minority (such as Serbs and Hungarians) (*IHT*, 5 January 2000, pp. 1, 4; *FT*, 5 January 2000, p. 8). 'Around 9 per cent of the Croatian electorate are expatriates' (*Independent*, 3 January 2000, p. 9). Prior to the election the Croatian Democratic Union and the opposition agreed on a new electoral law.

> The agreement, which is already fraying as bitterness between the two sides grows, allows *inter alia* for a reduction in the number of MPs elected by the Croatian diaspora, mainly in Bosnia-Hercegovina – most of whom cast their votes for the HDZ [Croatian Democratic Union] and gave the party twelve seats at the last election in 1995 … Some senior HDZ figures are Bosnian by origin and the party has a grip on the electorate there … For the forthcoming election the number of diaspora MPs is expected to be cut by at least half.
>
> (*FT*, Survey, 9 July 1999, p. 27)

> Much damage has been inflicted on the economy by the tycoon capitalism that emerged after the war. The tycoons' wings have been clipped by the banking crisis, which was partly the result of the reckless expansion and borrowing they indulged in … Growth fell to 2.7 per cent last year [1998]. The central bank blames much of this on a banking crisis that peaked at the end of 1998.
>
> (p. 25)

'The unusual timing [of the election] is seen as politically motivated – designed to coincide with holiday trips home by expatriates, who tend to be disproportionately pro-HDZ' (*FT*, 3 January 2000, p. 4).

The parties and their leaders and platforms were as follows:

Social Democratic Party (SDP): led by Ivica Racan (SDP), a former head of the Croatian Communist Party. Leftist.

Mr Racan says [in an interview that] he will move to cut spending on social services by 17 per cent … [He says that] economic restructuring is something Croatia urgently needs. Mr Racan also promises that an opposition government will co-operate better with the UN war crimes tribunal in The Hague investigating atrocities in the former Yugoslavia, although he said he has his doubts about the tribunal's fairness toward Croatia … Mr Racan also pledges to meddle less in Bosnia than did the Tudjman government … The opposition wants a more powerful parliament and a less powerful presidency, Mr Racan says, a fairer justice system and more open access to state television, which currently operates as a private transmission belt for the governing party, which has run Croatia since independence in 1991. Creating a truly public television service, Mr Racan said, is the coalition's first task … Mr Racan is respected here [Croatia] because of the way he behaved as the last leader of the Croatian Communist Party. People maintain that he could have cracked down on dissent in 1989 and 1990; instead, he threw his support behind Croatia's first multi-party elections in 1990, which led to the sweeping victory of Mr Tudjman and his party. At that time many Croatian Serbs voted for Mr Racan and his party as emblematic of the more multi-ethnic ideals of Yugoslavia. But today, wary about offending the strong nationalist strain in the Croatian electorate, Mr Racan is very careful about criticising the government's footdragging on efforts to allow the return of ethnic Serbs to Croatia … 'We cannot be completely dissatisfied with the return of refugees to Croatia,' Mr Racan said carefully, while saying that that real progress in resettling Croatian Serbs must be 'connected to the rest of the Balkans', meaning Bosnia and Belgrade. But he acknowledged that 'the process has to be faster' in every direction, with Bosnian Croats able to return to Bosnia as well as Croatian Serbs being able to return here.

(Steven Erlanger, *IHT*, 3 January 2000, p. 7)

In interviews Mr Racan has promised media freedom, respect of human rights and more co-operation with the West over Bosnia and with the international tribunal looking into war crimes in the former Yugoslavia … Mr Racan also promises a difficult and politically painful economic restructuring … with a 17 per cent cut in budgetary spending, a reduction of onerous taxes, a more open and honest privatization of state industries and banks, and efforts to reduce unemployment, which is well over 20 per cent. He says he will cut some official salaries in half, including the pay of legislators.

(Steven Erlanger, *IHT*, 5 January 2000, p. 4)

The economy is mired in deep recession. Unemployment is well over 20 per cent. There is a large budget deficit, a $10 billion national debt and declining foreign investment. Further, a fifth of the 4.8 million Croatians are due some kind of government pension from a fund that is virtually bankrupt.

(Steven Erlanger, *IHT* 7 January 1997, p. 5)

Social Liberals (HSLS): led by Drazen Budisa, the opposition's candidate for president. Centrist.

Budisa (4 January 2000): 'Our immediate task is to pull Croatia out of economic crisis, remove anomalies in our democratic system and to lure the country out of international isolation' (*IHT*, 5 January 2000, p. 4).

'The "Opposition Six" is faction-ridden and divided' (*FT*, Survey, 9 July 1999, p. 27). (The 'Opposition Six' refers to the SDP and the HSLS plus the Group of Four.)

Peasant Party.

The conduct of the election was praised as generally calm and orderly by representatives of OSCE. However, concern was expressed over treatment of minorities, biased media coverage of the run-up to the elections and the high numbers apparently voting in Bosnia-Hercegovina.

(*FT*, 5 January 2000, p. 8)

24 January 2000: the first round of the presidential election takes place. Nine candidates take part. The second round will take place on 7 February between Stipe Mesic and Drazen Budisa.

The percentage of the vote won was as follows: Stipe Mesic, 41.6 per cent; Drazen Budisa, 28 per cent; Mate Granic, 21 per cent.

All three main candidates, of the nine who ran, promised an open democratic Croatia, less authoritarian and nationalist, with closer ties to the EU and the USA. All of them also promised to dismantle part of the monarchic, all-powerful presidency that Mr Tudjman left behind him, along with many of its trappings ... Mr Tudjman's aggressive nationalism isolated Croatia from the European mainstream. He was reluctant to co-operate fully with the UN tribunal on war crimes, refusing to hand over some indicted Croats, often citing medical reasons. Also, Zagreb intervened in Bosnia, financing and promoting a separate Bosnian Croat identity despite formal support for the Moslem–Croat federation that Washington demanded. Mr Tudjman's government also put complicated legal and administrative obstacles in the way of Serbs who wanted to return to the homes they had fled in the face of a Croatian military offensive in 1995 that asserted Zagreb's authority. All of Mr Tudjman's likely successors promised to co-operate more fully with the tribunal, to allow Serbian refugees who fled their homes to return more easily and to stop meddling in Bosnia.

These policies will be easier to accomplish in conjunction with a new government, to be led by Ivica Racan, the reformist communist leader who built the opposition coalition in conjunction with Mr Budisa ... In a sense, Croatia's 4 million voters, unlike the pattern in the rest of the Balkans, concentrated on voting for the future, not the past. Croatians voting for Mr Mesic were also seeking a balanced, unthreatening, humorous personality.

(Steven Erlanger, *IHT*, 26 January 2000, p. 7)

Stipe Mesic [a member of the Croatian People's Party] is backed by four centre parties ... Briefly president of Yugoslavia on the eve of its disintegration, he was in Tudjman's party, the HDZ, as speaker of parliament before resigning in 1994 over what he saw as Tudjman's 'meddling' in Bosnia ... Mr Mesic is the only Croat to have given evidence for the prosecution at the war crimes tribunal in The Hague. Married to a Serb, he has campaigned openly for all suspects to be surrendered to the tribunal ... Like Mr Mesic, he [Drazen Budisa] supports a reduction in the powers of the presidency to strengthen government.

(*Guardian*, 25 January 2000, p. 15)

'Mr Mesic served as Tudjman's aide until 1994 when the two split over Croatia's policy in Bosnia-Hercegovina ... [He is] leader of a reform coalition' (*IHT*, 25 January 2000, p. 5). 'Mr Mesic was the last head of Yugoslavia's collective presidency and he served as an adviser to Mr Tudjman until 1994, when they split on Bosnia' (*IHT*, 26 January 2000, p. 7).

Mate Granic is the Croatian foreign minister and candidate of Mr Tudjman's once-dominant Croatian Democratic Union ... The Tudjman party was so badly wounded, after so thoroughly dominating Croatia, that Mr Granic, a moderate in the party, had vowed during the campaign to quit all his party posts should he win the election. He had ignored Western advice to run as an independent and he suffered badly from his connection to a party in bad odour due to economic difficulties, recession, an overvalued currency, high unemployment and widespread corruption.

(Steven Erlanger, *IHT*, 26 January 2000, p. 7)

3 February 2000: US secretary of state Madeleine Albright pays a visit.
6 February 2000:

The new Croatian government is trying to live up to its promises of social equality and justice, with plans to cut officials' salaries by up to 40 per cent and with the arrests of a former cabinet minister and a favoured tycoon ... The prime minister said he would move gradually to bring the overvalued currency, tied to the DM, to a more realistic exchange rate ... He promised that allegations of corruption against former ministers and officials would be pursued, even if the targets, such as the former Tudjman aide Ivic

Pasalic, hold parliamentary seats and official positions. But Mr Racan confirmed that the former government had burned or destroyed many documents ... A former tourism minister, Ivan Herak, is in prison on charges of embezzlement, and Miroslav Kutle, a tycoon from Bosnia, who was close to the Tudjman government, was arrested on Thursday [3 February]. Mr Kutle is considered close to Mr Pasalic, a key figure in the group of businessmen favoured by the old government. Both men are reported to have been involved in a banking scandal. The new interior minister, Sime Lucin, said in an interview that Croatian journalists need no longer worry about their phones being tapped. The new foreign minister, Tonino Picula, said his first foreign visit would be Sarajevo, the Bosnian capital. He intends to show the leaders there that the new Croatian government recognizes Bosnia's independence and wants to work with its officials to make it 'a self-sustaining country'. This is in sharp contrast to Mr Tudjman's support for a separate Croatian entity, including its army, that Mr Racan said cost Zagreb more than $130 million a year. Mr Racan said cutting aid to the Bosnian Croats too radically could risk an expensive wave of immigration to Croatia. But he vowed that all aid would now go through public institutions, mainly the Bosnian government. He also said he would turn over an indicted war criminal, Mladen Naletilic, to the war crimes tribunal in The Hague.

(Steven Erlanger, *IHT*, 7 February 2000, p. 5)

7 February 2000: Stipe Mesic wins the presidential runoff with 56.21 per cent of the vote, against Budisa's 43.79.

'Both candidates are pro-Western, favouring membership of the EU and Nato, and both are part of prime minister Ivica Racan's six-party coalition' (*IHT*, 7 February 2000, p. 5). (It is worth recalling that Croatia does not even belong to Nato's Partnership for Peace programme.)

[Stipe Mesic's] positions are less overtly nationalist than those of his rival Drazen Budisa ... Mr Tudjman's weakened party sees Mr Mesic as the biggest threat to Croatia's interests in Bosnia-Hercegovina, where the party remains strong. Mr Mesic has been blunt on the need to treat Bosnia as an independent state, stop allowing Bosnian Croats to vote in Croatia and stop spending as much as $150 million a year to support the Bosnian Croats and their army. Mr Mesic said: 'I sent a blunt message to the Croats in Bosnia-Hercegovina that they have to turn toward Sarajevo; they must lose all illusions that they will one day be part of Croatia' ... Both Mr Budisa and Mr Mesic were jailed in Tito's Yugoslavia for pro-Croatian activities in the early 1970s, but Mr Budisa is the more ardent nationalist and the more conservative on issues such as drug use and abortion ... Mr Mesic opposed the Tudjman policy ... of financial, moral and military support for a separate Bosnian Croat identity and army in Bosnia ... Mr Mesic said he started to pull away from Mr Tudjman in March 1991 after an infamous meeting between Mr Tudjman and Slobodan Milosevic, then the Serbian president, when the two men agreed to divide Bosnia between them. 'If I left then, I would not be in politics now,' Mr Mesic said, insisting his efforts to change policy from within did not truly fail until three years later ... Both men [Mesic and Budisa] vow to co-operate with Mr Racan and parliament to cut the vast executive powers of the Tudjman presidency ... while wanting to retain the position of commander-in-chief and an important role in foreign policy and domestic oversight.

(Steven Erlanger, *IHT*, 8 February 2000, p. 7)

'Mr Mesic ... says that he wants to remain supreme commander of the army and have responsibility for appointing secret service chiefs' (*IHT*, 9 February 2000, p. 2).

'Stipe Mesic ... immediately invited 300,000 ethnic Serb refugees to return to the country' (*The Economist*, 12 February 2000, p. 4).

'More than 300,000 ethnic Serbs driven out of their homes in August 1995 will be welcome to return ... Stipe Mesic said yesterday [10 February]' (*Independent*, 11 February 2000, p. 15).

'Last month [March] a refugee swap was signed to allow 2,000 Croatian Serbs to return to Croatia and 2,000 Croats to return to Serb-administered Bosnia, the Republika Srpska, by June' (*IHT*, 6 April 2000, p. 4).

Mr Racan's government has a plan for some 16,500 Serb refugees to come back, helped by Western cash for the rebuilding of their homes and the improvement of services. So far, though, the promised money has been slow to come and most of the refugees on the list have yet to return, though several thousand had already done so before the latest plan was announced.

(*The Economist*, 15 July 2000, p. 46)

2 March 2000:

Mate Granic, the former foreign minister ... and Vesna Skare-Ozbolt, a former adviser to Mr Tudjman, quit [the Croatian Democratic Union, founded by Mr Tudjman in 1989] ... to form a centrist party ... after saying they saw no future in a party that had been hijacked by hardliners ... 'The HDZ was and has remained a movement. It has not transformed itself into a modern party,' Mr Granic said.

(*FT*, 3 March 2000, p. 10)

8 March 2000: the new government presents its first budget. 'The budget is nearly balanced – the deficit should be held to 1 per cent of GDP this year [2000]' (*Business Central Europe*, April 2000, p. 49). Defence spending is currently running at 7 per cent of GDP (*Business Central Europe*, February 2000, p. 17).

23 March 2000: President Mesic visits Bosnia (*EEN*, 2000, vol. 12, no. 23, p. 8).

2 April 2000: former foreign minister Mate Granic is elected chairman of the new Democratic Centre Party, largely made up of disaffected former members of the Croatian Democratic Union (*EEN*, 2000, vol. 12, no. 23, p. 8).

10 May 2000: Nato invites Croatia to join its Partnership for Peace programme.

25 May 2000: Croatia formally becomes the twenty-seventh country to sign a Partnership for Peace programme.

June 2000:

> Officials in Croatia's new government say [that there was] a sustained, successful campaign by President Franjo Tudjman and his allies to plunder billions of dollars from the treasury ... during almost ten years of absolute, nationalist rule that ended with Mr Tudjman's death in December [1999]. Over that decade top Croatian officials enriched friends, family members and political allies by manipulating the privatization of state-owned companies and handing out lucrative contracts and suspect loans, government officials now say. State funds were funnelled secretly to Mr Tudjman's political causes, such as support for ethnic Croatian militiamen fighting in neighbouring Bosnia ... The misuse of state money was hidden for years through deceptive accounting practices, World Bank and government officials say. The state accumulated large debts off the books, and there was no treasury ministry to monitor or control how money was spent from the government's 3,000 bank accounts ... It now appears that the officially sanctioned thievery in Croatia ... was greater on a *per capita* basis than any other East European nation undergoing transition, diplomats, officials and foreign experts say ... Mr Tudjman's regime allowed the politically well-connected to acquire big banks and plunder them ... Extensive loan guarantees [were] extended by Mr Tudjman's government ... Unpaid domestic and foreign debt [accumulated]. The government failed to keep up with its pension obligations ... The depth of the problem is surprising because, to the outside world, Croatia's economy had long appeared a model of fiscal discipline. Inflation was low, the currency was stable and there was almost no budget deficit ... The government accumulated huge debts off the books and used deceptive accounting that concealed spending sprees ... President Tudjman secretly ordered the taping of every conversation in his office from 1991 on, generating a trove of documents ... Mr Mesic and his aides were astonished to find more than 14,000 transcripts and 830 audiocassettes ... Certain transcripts were missing and presumably destroyed.
>
> (Jeffrey Smith, *IHT*, 14 June 2000, p. 13)

When the Mesic team began opening up rooms in the presidential palace they found an archive of some 830 tapes and 17,000 transcripts of conversations between Tudjman and just about every single person who had visited him since 1991 ... Tudjman was obsessed with history. That is why he taped everything ... They have revealed that Tudjman's Croatia was rotten to the core; that with his blessing the HDZ elite pillaged every public institution in sight and virtually bankrupted the country … 'There is no serious man who does not claim that Bosnia will fall apart,' said Tudjman [on 8 April 1999]. Tudjman was irritated by the Nato bombings because Croatia had just signed some important business contracts with Serbian industries … He mused about calling for an international conference in which Bosnia would now be formally divided between Serbia and Croatia. The Muslims would be given a small chunk to be called Muslimania and Kosovo would be divided between Serbia and Albania … giving Milosevic some Serbian parts of Bosnia and trading him the southern-most tip of Croatia … [It is] widely believed that much of the most sensitive material was removed in the three weeks between Tudjman's death and the election of the new government … If it is true that sensitive documents were removed, however, those who took them did not have time to smuggle out of the presidential palace the transcripts concerning the wholesale plunder of the economy by Tudjman's entourage … Tudjman kept this artificial economy going by building up a $15.1 billion domestic and foreign debt. At least fifteen banks and other financial institutions are now in a state of collapse … A typical privatization, but one that had more political significance than others, was the takeover of *Vecernji List*, one of Croatia's main daily newspapers. The transcripts … reveal that, using a Virgin Islands-based company set up by the HDZ and funded by money from Croatian banks, Tudjman's party bought the paper illegally … The former barman Miroslav Kutle, now in jail, in exchange for his party loyalty, bought, with no money of his own, 157 companies … None of Kutle's companies, or many of the others handed out to Tudjman's cronies, produced much or succeeded in becoming competitive. In fact the cronies either had no idea how to make money or simply stripped what they had acquired of assets.

(Tim Judah, *New York Review of Books*, 2000, vol. XLVII, no. 13, pp. 20–2)

Secret tape recordings made by the late President Franjo Tudjman of Croatia prove that he and his close circle were directly involved in perpetuating war crimes and stole 1 billion pounds sterling … President Mesic has now handed copies of the transcripts to the War Crimes Tribunal at The Hague. 'The tapes implicate Tudjman's senior military commanders and generals in extensive atrocities and then the subsequent cover-up of these crimes,' he said … Perhaps the most surprising revelation is that … [Tudjman] covered up war crimes at the Bosnian hamlet of Ahmici … In March [2000] at The Hague General Tomas [Tihomir] Blaskic was sentenced to forty-five years. Most of the sentence was for ethnic cleansing of Moslems including at Ahmici. The Tudjman tapes and a Croatian intelligence report back up Blaskic's claims that the Ahmici killers were clandestine Croatian forces under Tudjman's command … One set of tapes show how Tudjman and his cronies skimmed $100 million (69 million pounds sterling) off the top of a near billion dollar sell-off of Croatia's telephone service. Some of the money went into a political slush fund ... The tapes also reveal that Tudjman and his apparent enemy Milosevic ... ignored pledges to respect Bosnia's sovereignty. Even after the signing of the Dayton accord they were still plotting to carve up the region.

(*Independent*, 1 November 2000, p. 16)

28 August 2000:

The Croatian prime minister Ivica Racan ordered an immediate inquiry into the murder of a key witness in war crimes investigations into the murder of Serb civilians in Croatia in 1991. Milan Levar was killed by a bomb outside his home in Gospic, central Croatia, on Monday [28 August]. It was the third attempt on his life ... He was the first and so far only Croat to testify against his compatriots ... Milan Levar was a local official in Gospic when the Serb rebellion against Croatian independence began in the summer of 1991. He participated in the defence of the town ... Levar named high-ranking Croatian army officers in a series of press articles in 1997 and accused them of the 'systematic murder' of Serb civilians ... More revelations about war crimes in Gospic followed, this time from Miroslav Bajramovic, another soldier involved in the defence of Gospic, who described how he took part in the torture and murder of dozens of Serbs. Last year [1999] a Zagreb court convicted Bajramovic and several others of lesser crimes, but dropped the more serious charges for lack of evidence ... In April this year [2000] investigators [from the Hague tribunal] began to search for the graves of an estimated 120 Serbs in the Gospic area.

(*Guardian*, 1 September 2000, p. 13)

12 September 2000:

The Croatian government looks set to hold war crimes trials on its own territory after it emerged that only one of twelve people arrested on Tuesday [12 September] was wanted by the International Criminal Tribunal for Former Yugoslavia ... General Ivan Andabak, the only person arrested at the ICTY's request, was wanted for questioning ... Of the other arrests ten are reported to be in connection with the apparent murder on 28 August of Milan Levar ... Other charges may concern atrocities in Croatia and Bosnia-Hercegovina ... Among those arrested were several generals, according to reports ... The latest arrests follow two last week of those suspected of participating in the Ahmici massacre of Bosnian Moslem civilians in central Bosnia-Hercegovina.

(*FT*, 14 September 2000, p. 10)

'Police in Croatia have arrested sixteen suspected war criminals ... They include three high-ranking officers in the Croatian army' (*Guardian*, 14 September 2000, p. 10).

'General Tihomir Oreskovic ... was among those detained in connection with Mr Levar's assassination ... Authorities in Zagreb simultaneously issued international arrest warrants for two more war crimes suspects ... They are thought to have fled abroad' (*Telegraph*, 14 September 2000, p. 18).

29 September 2000:

> President Stipe Mesic yesterday [29 September] sacked seven generals for complaining that the government was insulting the memory of the country's war for independence by prosecuting alleged war criminals for atrocities committed against Serbs ... The seven Croatian generals ... were among twelve active and retired generals who made their allegations in an open letter published on Thursday [28 September]. They were strong supporters of Tudjman's nationalist government ... They accused Mr Mesic and the government of 'waging a campaign to smear the independence struggle through recent spectacular arrests'.
>
> (*Guardian*, 30 September 2000, p. 19)

24 November 2000: an EU–Balkan summit meeting is held in Zagreb. Albania, Bosnia, Macedonia and Yugoslavia are formally invited. 'The summit also saw Macedonia's signing of the first so-called Stabilization and Association Agreement with the EU – a new kind of agreement intended for western Balkan countries. Croatia also formally started negotiations on such an agreement' (*FT*, 25 November 2000, p. 6). ('[In May 2001] Croatia signed a Stabilization and Association Agreement with the EU, which will liberalize trading terms and increase EU funding': *Business Central Europe*, June 2001, pp. 16, 43.)

December 2000:

> The most damaging quarrels between his [prime minister Ivica Racan's] Social Democrats and their chief coalition partner – the Social Liberals of Drazen Budisa – have been over issues which should not have been so tricky, like constitutional reform. The government succeeded in reducing the president's powers, but marred its victory with internal squabbling.
>
> (Business Central Europe 2000: 37)

'Thousands went on strike to protest against government attempts to hold down public sector wages. The government wants to freeze wages for a year, and then raise them in line with economic growth' (*Business Central Europe*, February 2001, p. 13).

> The December [2000] strikes ... [were by] public sector workers ... The previous government had promised public sector workers an 8.5 per cent salary increase ... Bound by a legal contract, Mr Racan eventually promised to pay up ... A wage freeze was introduced for the public sector. Mr Racan

... had to suspend December's public sector wage freeze just to get unions to come to the table.

(pp. 39–40)

7 February 2001: 'A Croatian court ordered the arrest of General Mirko Norac and his deputy Milan Canic yesterday [7 February], the first time Zagreb has pursued its military leadership for alleged crimes in the 1991 war of independence' (*Guardian*, 8 February 2001, p. 18).

8 February 2001: 'Croatian police yesterday [8 February] began a search for former general Mirko Norac after he failed to hand himself in by an agreed deadline' (*Guardian*, 9 February 2001, p. 16). ('Mirko Norac ... and eleven other generals were sacked ... for publicly criticising the government last year [2000]': *Telegraph*, 15 February 2001, p. 18.)

11 February 2001: 'Around 100,000 nationalists ... [in Split] protest at government attempts to bring alleged war criminals to book ... The Split rally was triggered by a manhunt for ... Mirko Norac ... Tudjman's HDZ followers organized yesterday's [11 February] Split rally' (*Guardian*, 12 February 2001, p. 14).

'Around 100,000 people protested Sunday [11 February in Split] the investigation of [Mirko Norac] ... Three much smaller protests were held elsewhere' (*IHT*, 12 February 2001, p. 4).

21 February 2001: Mirko Norac gives himself up to the authorities for questioning.

> General Norac turned himself in to the authorities ... after the prime minister, Ivica Racan, said he would not be extradited to the Hague war crimes tribunal and that his case would be handled by a Croatian court. Mr Racan spoke shortly after the UN-sponsored tribunal announced that General Norac was not wanted by its prosecutors.
>
> (*Guardian*, 23 February 2001, p. 18)

March 2001: 'Croatia passed a constitutional amendment that will allow its upper chamber of parliament to be abolished when its term expires in April. The upper house can delay but not veto bills, and is dominated by the opposition HDZ' (*Business Central Europe*, April 2001, p. 18).

28 March 2001: 'The upper house of parliament is dissolved' (*EEN*, 2001, vol. 13, no. 4, p. 6).

> In late March the lower house voted to abolish the upper house of parliament ... But the HDZ-dominated Senate refused even to debate the motion ... The upper house's duties won't be abolished but transferred to local government assemblies. Where one-third of local assemblies agree, they can veto a bill and force the lower house to consider their concerns.
>
> (*Business Central Europe*, May 2001, p. 44)

4 May 2001: 'The Croatian police said Friday [4 May] they had arrested seven ethnic Serbs in eastern Croatia on war crimes charges stemming from the 1991 Serbo-Croat war' (*IHT*, 5 May 2001, p. 4).

20 May 2001: local elections are held.

> Croatia's former ruling nationalist party scored surprisingly well in the country's local and regional elections, with official results showing Monday [21 May] that they were leading in a majority of counties. The nationwide polling Sunday [20 May] had been expected … to remove the nationalist Croatian Democratic Union from its last positions of power … But the party, which held power in sixteen out of twenty counties and Zagreb after the 1997 elections, was leading in fourteen of them, defying pre-vote opinion polls. Still, the party will have difficulty forming governments on its own, due to lack of potential coalition partners.
>
> (*IHT*, 22 May 2001, p. 5)

> The government has proved a disappointment for many Croatians … It has appeared timid on many fronts, particularly economic policy. It has failed to make much impact on unemployment … [In] local elections on 20 May … voters … gave a quarter of votes to the once-discredited HDZ but demonstrated their disillusionment by largely staying at home.
>
> (*FT*, Survey, 19 June 2001, p. 39)

'Many … wonder whether the fractious coalition can survive until [general] elections due in two-and-a-half years' time' (p. 41).

'The right-wing Croatian Democratic Union … took first place in local elections and later won three repeat elections' (*EEN*, 2001, vol. 13, no. 5, p. 6).

'Local elections … ended in defeat for the opposition HDZ … It was left holding just two regions, down from sixteen, while the ruling coalition now holds fifteen regions' (*Business Central Europe*, June 2001, p. 16).

4 June 2001:

> Prime minister Ivica Racan … acknowledged Monday [5 June] that problems within his six-party coalition government could lead to early elections … after the Istrian Democratic Party said it was leaving the coalition … The party cited a dispute over its effort to make Italian an official language … The government coalition has challenged the effort in the courts, maintaining that it would require amendment of the Croatian constitution and set a dangerous precedent.
>
> (*IHT*, 5 June 2001, p. 6)

18 June 2001:

> Croatia lost more than 20,000 citizens, including ethnic Serbs, during its 1991–5 war of independence from Yugoslavia, research published yesterday [18 June] shows … The independent … institute of social studies estimated

Croatia's casualties at 20,091. It is the first count to include victims on both sides of the war ... The government count ignored ... about 4,000 ... Serb war casualties.

(*Telegraph*, 19 June 2001, p. 12)

27 June 2001:

Seven governments ... yesterday [27 June] signed an agreement aimed at liberalizing trade in at least 90 per cent of goods trade between them. The move by Albania, Bosnia-Hercegovina, Bulgaria, Croatia, Romania, Macedonia and Yugoslavia marks the latest stage in efforts, under the EU's Stability Pact for South-Eastern Europe, to enhance stability in the region through economic growth. Moldova is expected to join the arrangement shortly. Croatia, Bosnia and Yugoslavia also reached agreement on measures to resettle the remaining 1.2 million refugees and displaced persons in their countries. Initiatives include reconstruction programmes and housing loan schemes.

(*FT*, 28 June 2001, p. 8)

6 July 2001:

The chief prosecutor of the UN war crimes tribunal, Carla del Ponte, disclosed on a visit to Zagreb yesterday [6 July] that two Croats had been indicted for alleged war crimes. Neither she nor the Croatian prime minister, Ivica Racan, disclosed the names of those indicted, and Mr Racan stopped short of clearly saying that the two Croats would be extradited.

(*Guardian*, 7 July 2001, p. 16)

7 July 2001:

Agreement by the government on the extradition of two suspects to the international criminal tribunal caused the resignation of four ministers on Saturday [7 July] ... An emergency cabinet meeting decided to ask the justice ministry to extradite any Croatian citizens wanted by the Hague tribunal, which has issued indictments against two Croatian generals ... On Friday [6 July] Carla del Ponte ... asked [prime minister] Ivica Racan to act on sealed indictments delivered a month ago [12 June] against the two generals for war crimes ... Mr Racan had sent written objections to the indictments ... but she had rejected them ... A report issued last week by the Council of Europe showed continuing institutionalized discrimination against ethnic Serbs wishing to return home.

(*FT*, 9 July 2001, p. 6)

Four members of the cabinet resigned after the government voted to hand over two men, the first citizens of Croatia to be indicted by the Hague tribunal. The decision was carried by nineteen of the twenty-two cabinet ministers ... President Stipe Mesic gave his backing to the government decision in a statement Sunday [8 July] ... The names of the two indicted have not been revealed, but ... [there is speculation] that the court has charged two army generals, Ante Gotovina and Rahim Ademi ... Croatia has handed over a dozen ethnic Croats from Bosnia.

(*IHT*, 9 July 2001, p. 9)

'Four members of the cabinet [members of the Social Liberal Party] resigned, including the deputy prime minister, Goran Granic, resigned in protest, robbing the five-party coalition of its majority. At the same time war veterans threatened mass protests' (*Independent*, 9 July 2001, p. 10).

The four members of the Social Liberal Party who resigned were the deputy prime minister and the defence, economy and technology ministers.

In the past Croatia has co-operated with war crimes investigators in the arrest of Bosnian Croat suspects and has even taken action internally against its own generals suspected of war crimes, but it has never directly agreed to hunt down its Croatian commanders for transfer to The Hague.

(*The Times*, 9 July 2001, p. 10)

[In] Mr Racan's written complaint against the extraditions ... it is believed that he may have asked for the men to be tried at home ... In the past three years Zagreb has extradited twelve Bosnian Croats to face trial at The Hague but no purely Croatian citizens.

(*Guardian*, 9 July 2001, p. 9)

'Franjo Tudjman signed an agreement in 1996 pledging co-operation with the United Nations tribunal' (*Telegraph*, 9 July 2001, p. 10).

'By a majority the cabinet agreed to give way [to the war crimes tribunal] and promptly lost three ministers ... The Social Liberal deputy prime minister stayed on, because he disagreed with his party' (*The Economist*, 14 July 2001, p. 46). ('Five ministers resigned from the coalition government': *Guardian*, 26 July 2001, p. 17.)

9 July 2001: 'Prime minister Ivica Racan said yesterday [9 July] that one of the army generals was willing to surrender voluntarily' (*Independent*, 10 July 2001, p. 10).

13 July 2001:

Tomorrow [15 July] the government faces a parliamentary vote of confidence. The prime minister Ivica Racan's coalition convened the extraordinary session after four cabinet ministers walked out in protest. Yesterday [13 July] the government formally named one of the suspects, General Rahim Ademi, an ethnic Albanian. It said ... that he had agreed to surrender voluntarily in the next ten days. The second suspect is reported to be retired General Ante Gotovina, who has been quoted in the Croatian media as saying in interviews that he does not recognize the court and will not surrender ... [The] Croatian Democratic Union (HDZ) demanded a debate on future co-operation with the tribunal. Croatia enacted a constitutional clause on co-operation ... in 1996, while the HDZ was in power. Its MPs now want the clause changed to prevent suspects said to be wanted purely because of their senior position during the war being handed over ... The government's chance of winning the vote improved significantly on Wednesday [11 July] when Drazen Budisa, leader of the Social Liberal Party (HSLS), resigned. A former presidential candidate, he had made his position to the government's plans clear, prompting the resignation of four HSLS cabinet ministers. Two opinion polls have shown about half the population in favour of co-operation with the Hague [tribunal]: a surprisingly high figure. Up to now most Croatians have ruled out any possibility of their countrymen being guilty of war crimes.

(*Guardian*, 14 July 2001, p. 19)

'General Ademi is still serving as an assistant to the chief inspector of the defence ministry' (*IHT*, 14 July 2001, p. 5).

16 July 2001: '[The] government won a crucial vote of confidence in parliament yesterday [16 July] ... by ninety-three to thirty-six votes, more than the seventy-six needed in the 151-seat chamber' (*Independent*, 17 July 2001, p. 11).

25 July 2001: 'General Rahim Ademi ... turned himself in to the UN war crimes tribunal on Wednesday [25 July]' (*IHT*, 26 July 2001, p. 8).

'The first Croatian to stand trial for atrocities during the four-year Serbo-Croat war flew to The Hague yesterday [25 July]' (*Independent*, 26 July 2001, p. 12).

'General Rahim Ademi ... [was] born in Kosovo of Albanian origin' (*Guardian*, 26 July 2001, p. 17).

9 October 2001:

The Italian and Croatian presidents agreed Tuesday [9 October] that a long-standing dispute over Croatian non-payment of reparations no longer stands in the way of their ties, which they described as excellent ... [The Italian president] who was visiting Croatia, praised the country's stability. He also expressed support for Croatia's efforts to join the EU and Nato.

(*IHT*, 10 October 2001, p. 5)

THE ECONOMY

At first economic reform in Croatia took a back seat, although a market economy was official policy and a new currency (the Croatian dinar) was introduced on 23 December 1991.

There has been real progress in the battle against inflation (after a massively high rate in 1993) and GDP grew in 1994. (See Table 2.1.) Monthly inflation fell from 40 per cent in October 1993 to zero in December 1993 (*Business Central Europe*, October 1994, p. 19). 'Croatia's third stabilization attempt, begun in October 1993, has been more consistently carried through and more successful' (Kraft 1995: 479). Inflation fell from 38.7 per cent a month in October 1993 to 1.4 per cent in November and was actually negative for the following six months. The main ingredients of the stabilization plan have been tight monetary and fiscal policy and a strict incomes policy (p. 480). Unemployment remains very high.

In mid-October 1993 parliament voted to rename the national currency the kuna. (*Kuna* means 'marten', a currency first used in the eleventh century but which also circulated in the period 1941–5, i.e. in the Ustashe period.) The kuna was reintroduced on 30 May 1994 when it replaced the Croatian dinar. In early October 1993 an anti-inflation package was introduced, including a cap on pay increases for public-sector employees. There was also a devaluation of the dinar (*Business Central Europe*, November 1993, p. 15). A managed floating exchange rate regime was introduced at the end of 1993 (Deutsche Bank, *Focus: Eastern Europe*, 1994, no. 108, p. 3). There is now a high degree of current account convertibility, but some capital controls are still in force (EBRD 1994: 21). The kuna has been convertible for current payment transactions in accordance with Article 8 of the IMF statutes since the end of May 1995 (Deutsche Bank, *Focus: Eastern Europe*, 1996, no. 157, p. 16). In practice the floating exchange rate is pegged around the DM. Value-added tax (at a rate of 22 per cent) was introduced at the beginning of 1998 (*FT*, Survey, 7 July 1998, p. i). In April 1998, in response to a domestic credit boom partly financed by foreign borrowing, the central bank introduced new reserve requirements on short-term foreign borrowing and deposits (EBRD 1998b: 160). There is a managed floating exchange rate system (EBRD 1999b: 208).

> The foreign exchange law has been amended, with effect from June 2001 … Individuals will be able to open foreign exchange accounts abroad and banks will be able to offer foreign currency denominated, in addition to foreign exchange indexed loans.
>
> (EBRD 2001b: 130)

All direct price controls have now been removed. Some indirect controls remain, largely through government influence on major enterprises, particularly in the energy sector. A wage freeze is in place for the state sector, supported until November 1994 by a 'social agreement' with unions (EBRD 1994: 21). Some wage controls are still in place for the state-owned sector (EBRD 1995b: 38). The remaining wage controls apply only to the state sector. A bankruptcy law was approved in June 1996, effective from the beginning of 1997 (EBRD 1996b: 145).

Croatia joined the IMF and World Bank on 20 January 1993. Croatia has reached agreement with the Paris Club of official creditors on rescheduling its

Table 2.1 Croatia: selected economic indicators 1990–2000

Economic indicator	1990	1991	1992	1993	1994	1995	1996	1997	1998	1999	2000 (estimate)
Rate of growth of GDP (%)	-7.1	-21.1	-11.7	-8.0	5.9	6.8	6.0	6.5	2.5	-0.4	3.7
Rate of growth of industrial output (%)	-11.3	-28.5	-14.6	-6.0	-2.7	0.3	3.1	6.8	3.7	-1.4	1.7
Rate of growth of agricultural output (%)	-3.2	-7.2	-13.5	4.9	-0.3	0.7	1.3	4.0	10.2	-3.5	2.8
Inflation rate (retail) (%)	609.5	123.0	665.5	1,517.5	97.6	2.0	3.5	3.6	5.7	4.2	6.2
Budget surplus or deficit (% of GDP)[a]		-5.0	-3.9	-0.8	1.2	-1.4	-1.0	-1.9	-1.0	-6.5	-6.9
Unemployment rate (end of year, %)		14.1	17.8	16.6	17.3	17.6	15.9	17.6	18.6	20.8	
Balance of payments (current account, $billion)		-0.589	0.326	0.623	0.854	-1.442	-1.091	-2.325	-1.530	-1.391	-0.399
Foreign direct investment (net, $billion)			0.013	0.102	0.110	0.109	0.486	0.347	0.835	1.445	0.827
Population (million)			4.5	4.6	4.6	4.7	4.5	4.6	4.5	4.5	4.5

Source   Various issues of European Bank for Reconstruction and Development, *Transition Report*; United Nations Economic Commission for Europe, *Economic Survey of Europe*; United Nations, *World Economic and Social Survey*; IMF, *World Economic Outlook*.

Note   [a] General government balance: consolidated central government; excludes privatization revenues (EBRD) foreign debt. The $1 billion debt would be repaid over fourteen years, with repayments starting in 1996. Another $100 million, borrowed after 1992, was to be repaid immediately (*Business Central Europe*, April 1995, p. 51). On 26 April 1996 Croatia reached agreement in principle with the leaders of the London Club of commercial bank creditors, accepting a 29.5 per cent share of the debt of the former Yugoslavia. But creditor banks holding at least two-thirds of the debt had to agree to this arrangement and the Federal Republic of Yugoslavia has raised legal objections (*FT*, 29 April 1996, p. 2; 30 April 1996, p. 2). On 25 July 1997 the IMF withheld a $40 million tranche (of a $486 million three-year loan) because of 'the unsatisfactory state of democracy in Croatia' (*FT*, 31 July 1997, p. 2). On 10 October 1997 the IMF released almost $80 million in loans (*Independent*, 11 October 1997, p. 12). (Croatia decided not to use the IMF's $78 million loan, which had been blocked since July 1997: *IHT*, 14 October 1997, p. 15.) 'The IMF approved a $255 million stand-by loan … after the government agreed to limit wages and spending in order to cut inflation and boost growth. The government also successfully issued a $452 million Eurobond' (*Business Central Europe*, April 2001, p. 18). 'In March 2001 the government signed a stand-by arrangement with the IMF for $256 million' (EBRD 2001b: 130).

During 1991–2 around 30 per cent of fixed assets were damaged or destroyed. The level of industrial production in 1993 was 45 per cent of the maximum achieved in 1987 (Radosevic 1994: 490). War damage has been estimated at $20 billion (*IHT*, 2 July 1994, p. 11). According to government estimates, there was $27.1 billion of direct damage during the war. Some 135,000 houses and apartments were destroyed along with more than 100 bridges and 200 churches (*FT*, Survey, 30 May 1996, p. iv). According to *Business Central Europe* (June 1996, p. 18), only about 10 per cent of fixed industrial capital was destroyed.

The Croatian government maintains that damage caused directly and indirectly by the war total more than $50 billion. As much as 10 per cent of the housing stock (more than 170,000 homes and apartments) was destroyed or damaged. The damage to public utilities and social infrastructure is estimated at $4.2 billion, while the loss in economic output from 1991 to 1996 is put at $22.5 billion. At the height of the war there were over 1.2 million refugees and displaced persons (*FT*, Survey, 14 December 1998, p. 28).

Over 40 per cent of the state budget goes on defence (*IHT*, 12 November 1993, p. 2). The defence budget rose from $1.1 billion in 1994 to an estimated $1.8 billion in 1995, 12.5 per cent of GDP (*The Economist*, 11 November 1995, p. 60). Defence spending is officially recorded at 10 per cent of GDP but is believed to be much higher (*FT*, Survey, 30 May 1996, p. i).

Privatization

According to official estimates, roughly 20 per cent of the economy is in private hands (*Business Central Europe*, September 1993, p. 22). The private sector has seen dynamic growth in services such as retailing (*Business Central Europe*, 1995, p. 15). In mid-1994 the private sector accounted for roughly 40 per cent of GDP

(EBRD 1994: 10). In mid-1995 the private sector accounted for roughly 45 per cent of GDP (EBRD 1995b: 11). A range of 45 per cent to 50 per cent is also mentioned (p. 38). According to official statistics, the private sector is likely to account for 50 per cent of GDP. In addition, a significant proportion of private sector activity may escape the official statistics (EBRD 1996b: 144). In mid-1997 the private sector accounted for roughly 55 per cent of GDP (EBRD 1997b: 14). The grey economy is estimated to be around 25 per cent of GDP (p. 161).

Rough estimates in mid-year of the private sector as a percentage of GDP are provided by the EBRD: 1990, 15 per cent; 1991, 20 per cent; 1992, 25 per cent; 1993, 30 per cent; 1994, 35 per cent; 1995, 40 per cent; 1996, 50 per cent; 1997, 55 per cent; 1998, 55 per cent; 1999, 60 per cent; 2000, 60 per cent; 2001, 60 per cent (EBRD 1999b: 24, 208, and 2001b: 12, 132)

Workers' councils for enterprises have been replaced by management boards (EBRD 1994: 20).

'Most companies were taken into state hands in 1992 as the economy was put on a war footing' (*Business Central Europe*, September 1999, p. 17).

The law on the transformation of enterprises with social capital (passed in April 1991 and going into force in June of that year) required the conversion of almost all socially owned enterprises into joint stock companies. The law allowed workers to buy shares of up to DM 20,000 in book value at a 20 per cent discount to the nominal value plus 1 per cent for every year they have worked. One-third of the remaining shares in each enterprise were to be transferred to two pension funds and the balance was to go to the Croatian Privatization Fund (*FT*, 31 March 1994, p. 32).

The large majority of privatizations have been management or worker buy-outs. Some 200 publicly owned enterprises which had not lodged their proposals for privatization passed completely into the hands of the Privatization Fund. Shares not sold when enterprises were converted were taken up by the Privatization Fund (two-thirds) and the Pension Fund (one-third). Ten per cent of capital was set aside as a provision for restitution claims. Enterprise employees and pensioners receive a discount of up to 50 per cent and have access to an interest-free loan for five years (Deutsche Bank, *Focus: Eastern Europe*, 14 June 1994, no. 108, pp. 5–6). The deadline for the privatization of all socially owned enterprises was originally set for the end of June 1992; all shares not sold by that date (around 50 per cent of the value of all socially owned enterprises) were transferred to three state funds without compensation (United Nations Economic Commission for Europe 1993: 224).

In October 1996 parliament passed the law on compensation for property taken during Yugoslav communist rule, regulating the denationalization of property confiscated or nationalized since 1945. It gives preference to restitution of property where possible (agricultural land, forests, some housing) and provides for compensation in other cases (other housing, developed construction, land) (EBRD 1997a: 28).

Small privatization is now largely complete (EBRD 1994: 20). The privatization of formerly socially owned housing is almost complete (EBRD 1997a: 28).

Writing in late 1994 Bartlett reported that no large social-sector enterprises had been privatized (Bartlett 1996: 162).

There have been 2,877 applications for autonomous privatization, of which well over half (by number; less by value) have so far been privatized. The acceleration of privatization is now a government priority (EBRD 1994: 20). A new privatization ministry was created in January 1995 with the task of accelerating privatization (EBRD 1995a: 54). By mid-1995 about 3,000 applications for autonomous privatization had been received, of which about two-thirds had been approved. Of these a little over 1,000 have been fully privatized (EBRD 1995b: 38). By the end of 1995 about 1,200 of the total 2,750 enterprises had been converted and wholly sold to their employees or management. In a further 900 enterprises the state retained only a minority stake. Ten of the largest enterprises, most utilities and the banks are to be privatized under separate legislation (EBRD 1995b: 38).

By the end of 1995, of the 2,500 enterprises that had entered privatization, 1,145 (mostly small and medium-sized enterprises) had been completely privatized. A further 1,142 enterprises were majority privately owned, while the Croatian Privatization Fund retained a majority stake in about 200 enterprises (including some of the most troubled) (*FT*, Survey, 30 May 1996, p. vi).

Public sector enterprises (the oil company INA, the post office, utilities, healthcare) were to be privatized in the future, but 25 per cent of the capital was to remain in the hands of the government. The large industrial combines, such as the ironworks, were to be restructured and divided into smaller units before being privatized (Deutsche Bank, *Focus: Eastern Europe*, 29 December 1995, no. 145, p. 6). A later report (28 October 1996, no. 165, p. 4) stated that of the 2,548 socially owned enterprises that initially existed, 1,128 had been fully privatized following their conversion into joint stock companies. Most of them were small and medium-sized businesses which were sold to staff (who, under a new law, are able to pay in instalments spread over ten years). In a further 1,317 enterprises the privatization fund is a minority shareholder, while in 103 enterprises (e.g. agricultural enterprises and shipyards) it is a majority shareholder.

By early 1997 over 1,000 out of a total of 2,550 commercialized enterprises had been fully privatized and in another 1,350 the state retained only a minority stake. Most of the fully privatized enterprises are relatively small and the state still accounts for about 40 per cent of the net asset value and of employment in the 2,550 enterprises. The new privatization law also provides guidelines for the sale of large public enterprises, including the oil and gas conglomerate, electricity generation and distribution, television and radio, and telecommunications. It is envisaged that foreign bidding will be permitted for some of these enterprises (EBRD 1997b: 161–2).

Croatia's privatization policy came in for much criticism from some quarters:

1   *EEN* (29 February 1996, vol. 10, no. 5, p. 2) reported that 'Privatization, never a priority for the HDZ [Croatian Democratic Union], has virtually fizzled out'. 'Resources of privatized state firms have disappeared into the

pockets of the chosen few, including members of Tudjman's family' (*EEN*, 31 December 1996, vol. 10, no. 25, p. 6).

2   'His [Tudjman's] privatization policy has succeeded in concentrating vast economic power in the hands of a small oligarchy, while the political and commercial influence of his children evokes the ugly ghosts of regional ruling dynasties from the recent communist past' (Misha Glenny, *The Times*, 7 August 1996, p. 14).

3   'Privatization ... often favours leading members of President Franjo Tudjman's party, the Croatian Democratic Union, at the expense of outside bidders, Western economists say' (Jane Perlez, *IHT*, 21 August 1996, p. 2).

4   Some restructuring was undertaken in late 1994, including the closure of several large plants (EBRD 1995a: 54). But much of the privatization completed by the end of 1995 did not greatly accelerate restructuring. 'In most privatized enterprises the absence of a strong majority owner has inhibited restructuring' (EBRD 1996b: 144–5). The pace of restructuring remains slow (EBRD 1997b: 162).

> Enterprise restructuring is, however, inhibited by poor corporate governance that typically results from the absence of a strong majority shareholder and from large residual state holdings. As a result of a privatization process largely by management and employee buy-outs, small shareholders (mostly employees) own the great majority of shares in privatized companies. The state privatization fund and the state pension fund – the largest shareholders in many majority privatized companies – have not taken an active role in management and enterprise restructuring. Restructuring also remains far from complete in most state-owned companies, including the oil company INA.
>
> (EBRD 1998b: 160)

5   'Industrial restructuring has so far been limited in scope, given industry's incestuous relationship with banks and a privatization scheme biased towards management buy-outs. Those industries that have been restructured are doing well ... Croatian shipyards, for instance' (Business Central Europe 1997: 38).

> Most company shares have been sold, via instalments, to employees. As a result, few firms have received fresh capital or outside shareholders with an interest in pressurizing management to focus on profit. Most have ended up with such an arcane shareholder structure that it is hard for them to restructure at all.
>
> (*Business Central Europe*, February 1998, p. 44)

> Any shares not sold were transferred to the Croatian privatization fund (CPF) and two state pension funds. In practice, the first stage of privatization at most companies amounted purely to a worker buy-out

combined with a transfer of shares to the state. Since none of the industrial companies being privatized were in state hands, Croatia's privatization scheme initially brought about a massive increase in the government's role in industry. The CPF has virtually ignored a 1996 legal amendment which allows it to repossess shares if employees default. Rather, it has lengthened the payment period from five to twenty years ... 1998 looks like becoming yet another wasted year for the country's largely unrestructured corporate base ... Investment funds ... must deposit $2 million in cash and collect at least 100 million voucher points before starting a fund.

(p. 46)

6   'Officials in Croatia's new government say [that there was] a sustained, successful campaign by President Franjo Tudjman and his allies to plunder billions of dollars from the treasury ... during almost ten years of absolute, nationalist rule that ended with Mr Tudjman's death in December [1999]. Over that decade top Croatian officials enriched friends, family members and political allies by manipulating the privatization of state-owned companies and handing out lucrative contracts and suspect loans, government officials now say ... Mr Tudjman's regime allowed the politically well-connected to acquire big banks and plunder them' (Jeffrey Smith, *IHT*, 14 June 2000, p. 13).

When the Mesic team began opening up rooms in the presidential palace they found an archive of some 830 tapes and 17,000 transcripts of conversations between Tudjman and just about every single person who had visited him since 1991 ... Tudjman was obsessed with history. That is why he taped everything ... They have revealed that Tudjman's Croatia was rotten to the core; that with his blessing the HDZ elite pillaged every public institution in sight and virtually bankrupted the country ... [It is] widely believed that much of the most sensitive material was removed in the three weeks between Tudjman's death and the election of the new government ... If it is true that sensitive documents were removed, however, those who took them did not have time to smuggle out of the presidential palace the transcripts concerning the wholesale plunder of the economy by Tudjman's entourage ... A typical privatization, but one that had more political significance than others, was the takeover of *Vecernji List*, one of Croatia's main daily newspapers. The transcripts ... reveal that, using a Virgin Islands-based company set up by the HDZ and funded by money from Croatian banks, Tudjman's party bought the paper illegally ... The former barman Miroslav Kutle, now in jail, in exchange for his party loyalty, bought, with no money of his own, 157 companies ... None of Kutle's companies, or many of the others handed out to Tudjman's cronies, produced much or succeeded in becoming competitive. In fact the cronies either had no idea how to make money or simply stripped what they had acquired of assets.

(Tim Judah, *New York Review of Books*, 2000, vol. XLVII, no. 13, pp. 20–2)

Further developments in privatization

A new privatization law was approved in February 1996. This provides a framework for the privatization of large public enterprises. Vouchers were to be distributed to refugees, war invalids and other displaced persons (perhaps some 300,000 people in total), who could use them to bid for shares either directly or via investment funds. The new law extended the instalment period from five to twenty years. It was envisaged that foreign bidding would be permitted for at least some of the large public enterprises such as the oil and gas conglomerate, the electricity generator, telecoms, and television and radio stations (EBRD 1996b: 144–5). The long-delayed voucher-based privatization programme is under way. Three bidding rounds were scheduled for mid-1998 (EBRD 1998a: 34). While there are few exclusively state-owned enterprises, the state retains significant ownership stakes in many large companies. Only about half of employees in the enterprise sector work in fully private enterprises, roughly a quarter each in new private and fully privatized firms. A further 20 per cent work in firms with minority stakes by the state. The other 30 per cent of the work force is in state-owned enterprises, half of which is accounted for by ten fully state-owned infrastructure companies. More than two years after a privatization law was passed to accelerate the process one of its integral parts, a mass privatization programme, is finally under way. Some 225,000 voucher holders are to acquire shares in 471 firms, either directly or through one of seven competing privatization funds. By mid-1998 the funds had collected about 90 per cent of all vouchers. During three bidding rounds in mid-1998 about 80 per cent of the assets were sold (EBRD 1998b: 160). The long-delayed voucher privatization scheme was implemented in 1998, selling stakes in 471 enterprises. The next step is the consolidation of shares among the seven funds involved in the programme and their listing on the stock exchange (EBRD 1999a: 35). The privatization process has regained momentum. The voucher privatization programme in 1998 has reduced the residual holdings of the Croatian privatization fund by almost half to 17 per cent of the book value of commercialized enterprises covered by the original privatization law of 1991. Another 15 per cent of the equity in these companies is held by the state pension fund. Most stakes held by the two funds are passive minority holdings. Only 5 per cent of commercialized firms covered by the 1991 law (accounting for less than 10 per cent of total book value) are still in majority state ownership. There are a number of large state entities not covered by the 1991 privatization law, accounting for about a quarter of employment in originally state-owned companies. The method of privatization is decided on a case-by-case basis (EBRD 1999b: 206).

The privatization process gained momentum in 1999. However, the privatization fund still manages a portfolio of about 1,900 companies, and the state holds further stakes in companies through the pension fund and through debt–equity swaps in relation to the rehabilitation of banks … The second largest bank in terms of assets (Privedna Banka) was successfully sold to a foreign [Italian] strategic investor … in December 1999.

(EBRD 2000a: 48)

Croatia was to use vouchers (exchangeable for shares or able to be placed in investment funds) instead of cash to compensate some 300,000 victims of the recent war and 4,400 people who were political prisoners under the former communist regime. Vouchers were to be issued in the summer of 1996, with share auctions set to begin in the autumn. The new law also cleared the way for the privatization of state utilities such as telecommunications, the post office and electricity. On offer in the voucher scheme would be assets with a book value just less than half the portfolio of the Croatian Privatization Fund. The 1991 programme allowed employees to spread their payments.

But few have kept up payments and it is hard to find money for the shares. Few people in Croatia have money to buy shares and most shares in privatized companies are trading at a fraction of their book value. Until now the state has not enforced collection of the instalments, but the new privatization law, which sets up the voucher scheme, will allow the state to take shares back if payments are seriously in arrears.

(Gavin Gray, *FT*, 10 April 1996, p. 2)

By 1994 most enterprises had completed their worker buy-outs and the focus shifted to the CPF's burgeoning portfolio. March 1996 saw the completion of a $160 million share issue for the large and profitable Pliva pharmaceutical enterprise, attracting considerable interest abroad and being nearly twenty times oversubscribed. (In April 1996 Pliva became the first East European industrial enterprise to be quoted on the London stock exchange. This followed the successful sale of 31 per cent of its shares. The EBRD holds 11 per cent of shares: Gavin Gray, *FT*, Survey, 30 May 1996, p. v.) The new privatization law also extended the instalment period for worker shareholders to twenty years, while the large number of workers who have defaulted on their instalments would henceforth have their shares confiscated. The voucher scheme for war victims was due to be launched in September 1996 (p. vi).

This week Croatia started the first of three auction rounds of its mass privatization programme. About 500 companies … will be transferred from the Croatian privatization fund to private ownership. Specific categories of people, especially war victims, and seven privatization investment funds are entitled to participate in this programme. Vouchers can be used to bid directly in the auction or be placed in one of the seven privatization funds.

(Deutsche Bank Research, *Emerging Europe Weekly*, Friday 19 June 1998, p. 3)

Most of the coupon holders have invested in the seven privatization funds (*Business Central Europe,* July–August 1998, p. 41).

> The government is nearing completion of another aspect of its sell-off through a voucher privatization scheme ... Stakes ... in 471 formerly socially-owned companies were allocated to investment funds which will be listed on the Zagreb stock exchange early next year [1999] ... The portfolios represent a cross-section of the Croatian economy ... The average stake held by the funds in each company is 29 per cent and each fund is dominated by one or two holdings. The funds have interest in key sectors such as tourism, industry, chemicals, food and agriculture ... The government is finally getting around to the issue of more extensive privatization ... The government has already announced plans for the sales over the next few months of three important commercial banks and, more significantly, of the telecoms operations of HPT, the state-owned post and telecommunications utility.
>
> (*FT*, Survey, 14 December 1998, p. 26)

On 4 September 1999 it was announced that Deutsche Telekom was to acquire a 35 per cent stake in state-owned Croatian Telecom for $850 million. The government planned to sell a further stake of up to 21 per cent in an initial public offering in the second half of 2000. Two tranches of 7 per cent would be offered to current and former employees and to Croatian war veterans, while the government would retain a 30 per cent stake from which dividends would be paid into the state pension fund. Deutsche Telekom would have a option to buy a further 16 per cent stake if the government decides to sell this final 30 per cent (*FT*, 5 October 1999, p. 42; EBRD 2000a: 48).

> The state still retained at the end of 1999 stakes in 1,610 enterprises, of which 851 were loss-making. It held stakes in 329 companies ... The government has begun to liquidate state-owned enterprises held by the privatization fund in an effort to reduce its exposure to losses.
>
> (EBRD 2000b: 150)

> [The government consolidated] state holdings of shares into the privatization fund in 2000 ... During 2001 the government intends to use sales, free distribution for restitution purposes or bankruptcy to reduce the state holding in 327 companies managed by the privatization fund. The government has also committed to beginning the privatization of the oil company, INA ... The government has committed to beginning privatization of the Croatian Energy Company, HEP ... It is also preparing to privatize a further 21 per cent stake in Croatian Telecoms (HT) through domestic and international public offering in the second quarter of 2001. The government is also considering selling a further 16 per cent to Deutsche Telekom, which would then hold a majority stake in the company ... The privatization of the banks that were taken into rehabilitation between 1996 and 1998

is almost complete. The two remaining banks to be privatized are Dubrovacka Banka and Croatia Banka.

(EBRD 2001a: 56)

The privatization of remaining state-held shares is moving forward. By mid-2000 there were 1,852 enterprises in the portfolio of the Croatian Privatization Fund ... By September 2001 the CPF had reduced the number of companies in its portfolio to 1,598 through liquidation, sales of minority stakes and management changes ... In July 2001 the government agreed to privatize a 16 per cent stake ... in Croatia Telecoms ... to Deutsche Telekom. The deal is to be signed later this year and will give Deutsche Telekom, which already owns 35 per cent, a controlling stake in the company. The agreement is controversial ... [requirements including the extension of] the exclusivity period of Croatia Telecoms by two years. The extension is in breach of Croatia's commitment to the WTO to liberalize fixed-line infrastructure from 2003 ... At the end of 2000 the four largest banks accounted for 61 per cent of the total assets of the banking system ... Foreign-controlled banks now account for over 80 per cent of banking assets.

(EBRD 2001b: 131)

'[Some] 85 per cent of bank assets [are] now foreign-owned' (*FT*, Survey, 19 June 2001, p. 40).

Foreign trade

The foreign trade system is liberal. There are no quantitative restrictions on imports. Most imports and exports are tariff-free. An import tax of 10 per cent was introduced as part of the government's macroeconomic stabilization programme in autumn 1993 (EBRD 1994: 21, 109). Most quantitative restrictions have been removed. The new law on trade applies import quotas to less than 1 per cent of tariff items, mainly petroleum derivatives, fertilizers and cement. Export quotas still apply to thirty-five items, mainly timber, crude oil and natural gas. Import licences also apply to items such as some pharmaceuticals and works of art. A new law is transforming almost all the remaining import restrictions into tariffs (EBRD 1996b: 145). The government has recently increased tariffs on agricultural and food products (EBRD 1997b: 162). The bulk of trade is now with the West.

'In July 2000 the WTO general council approved the entry of Croatia, which has committed to reduce agricultural and industrial protection' (EBRD 2000b: 150).

[On 18 September 2000 EU foreign] ministers approved an EU package granting duty-free access to 95 per cent of imports from Albania, Bosnia, Croatia, Macedonia and Montenegro ... The package includes abolition of tariffs on most industrial and farm products to the EU. However, some limits remain on exports of fish products and wine.

(FT, 19 September 2000, p. 10)

On 19 December 2000 Bosnia and Croatia signed an agreement that eliminated customs duties on Bosnian goods entering Croatia and reduced duties on Croatian goods entering the Bosnian market (*IHT*, 20 December 2000, p. 19).

Foreign direct investment

See Table 2.1 for the volume of net direct foreign investment.

Direct foreign investment amounted to $46 million in the period 1990–3 (EBRD 1994: 123). Foreigners and nationals may, subject to reciprocity and usage restrictions, own or lease land (EBRD 1996b: 146).

Net direct foreign investment was $16 million in 1992, $74 million in 1993, $98 million in 1994 and $85 million in 1995 (United Nations Economic Commission for Europe 1996: 149).

In early May 2000 the finance minister announced that the government would exempt reinvested profits from the 35 per cent corporation tax (*Transition*, 2000, vol. 11, no. 2, p. 39).

> The government recently enacted a measure designed to spread the benefits beyond the [eleven] free-trade zones to all of Croatia ... The law establishes a series of tax breaks for investors setting up subsidiaries in the rest of the country – the larger the investment (both in terms of capital and workforce), the bigger the tax break and the longer it applies.
>
> (*IHT*, 19 December 2001, p. 19)

Economic performance

GDP growth turned positive in 1994, but the growth rate declined sharply in 1998 and was actually negative in 1999. (See Table 2.1.) 'The economy slipped into recession by the end of 1998' (EBRD 1999b: 206).

> Croatia's recession ended in the second quarter of 1999, but growth for the full year was −0.3 per cent. The performance of the economy had been negatively affected both by the Kosovo conflict, which lowered tourism revenues significantly, and by the political uncertainty (now resolved) over the succession to President Tudjman.
>
> (EBRD 2000a: 5)

Positive GDP growth was restored in 2000. In 2000 GDP was an estimated 80 per cent of the 1989 level (EBRD 2001b: 59). There was hyperinflation in 1993 (1,518 per cent), but the rise in the retail price level fell sharply the following year and was in single figures thereafter.

3 The Former Yugoslav Republic of Macedonia

POLITICS

Earlier events are dealt with in the Introduction and Overview.

Demographic background

In the 1991 census, boycotted by most Albanians, the official figures showed that the population was split 65 per cent ethnic Macedonian and 21.7 per cent ethnic Albanian.

Likewise, the 21 June–10 July 1994 census was boycotted by most Albanians and to some extent by the Turk and Serb minorities. (All members of ethnic minorities had to complete two forms, one in Macedonian and one in the mother tongue, while all participants had to produce citizenship papers and residence permits.)

Ethnic Albanians claim that they constitute up to 40 per cent of the population. (The largest Albanian party, the Party of Democratic Prosperity, has split. At the congress held on 13 February 1994 the radical wing broke away: *EEN*, 2 March 1994, vol. 8, no. 5, p. 6.)

The final results of the 1994 census were not released until December. The total population was given as 1,936,877, of which Macedonians accounted for 1,288,330 (66.5 per cent) and Albanians 442,914 (22.9 per cent) (in 1953 the respective proportions were 65.59 per cent and 12.45 per cent). But in fact the number of Albanians is closer to 800,000 (40 per cent plus of the population) (*EEN*, 1995, vol. 9, no. 10, p. 2).

According to the 1994 census, the 2 million population was split 67 per cent Macedonian, 23 per cent ethnic Albanian, 4 per cent Turk, 2.3 per cent Gypsy and 2 per cent Serb (*Business Europa*, April–May 1995, p. 8).

> Macedonia has many minority groups, with none representing an overwhelming majority, yet Slavic Macedonians occupy more than 90 per cent of public sector jobs and make up more than 90 per cent of the police force and 90 per cent of the university student population.
>
> (William Walker, *IHT*, 8 June 2001, p. 8)

The Macedonian presidential and parliamentary elections of 16 October 1994

The parties competed for the 120 seats in parliament. There were long delays before the results were published, allegedly due to 'technical' factors (such as inadequate electoral rolls; the official electoral commission admitted that 10 per cent of voters were not on constituency registers, but they were still able to vote). Alleging serious irregularities, the Democratic Party and VMRO (see below) boycotted the second round (which took place on 30 October, when the turnout was only 35 per cent). International observers were far from being entirely happy, but thought the election results should stand. The presidential election was, as forecast, won by the incumbent, Kiro Gligorov, with 52.44 per cent of the registered vote. (There was a high percentage of spoiled votes.) The challenger, Ljubco Georgievski (VMRO), received only 14.5 per cent of the vote.

Pro-Gligorov forces won about 82 per cent of the seats in parliament, with the under-represented opposition threatening civil resistance campaigns. The radical wing of the main Albanian party, the Party for Democratic Prosperity, polled well, gaining the majority of the seats taken by the Albanians. There was concern that Menduh Thaci (see below) was deprived of a parliamentary seat in Skopje on the third ballot by just ten votes after winning comfortably on the first two ballots (Pettifer 1995: 56).

As of the first half of February 1996 the distribution of the 120 seats in parliament was as follows: Social Democratic Party, sixty; Liberal Party, twenty-nine; Party for Democratic Prosperity, twelve (including two MPs who defected from the ethnic Albanian National Democratic Party in 1995); Socialist Party, seven; National Democratic Party, two; Party of Democratic Prosperity of Albania (led by Menduh Thaci and Arben Xhaferi; it is a radical offshoot of the Party for Democratic Prosperity), five; Romanies' Party, two; Moslem Democratic Party–Party for Democratic Action, one; Democratic Party, one; independents, one (*EEN*, 1996, vol. 10, no. 4, p. 7).

Branko Crvenkovski remained prime minister. The Party for Democratic Prosperity joined the Social Democratic Party in government.

The parties and their platforms

Alliance for Macedonia: the governing alliance, led by the Social Democratic Party (which is the party of prime minister Branko Crvenkovski) but also including the Liberal Party and the Socialist Party. In the first round the Alliance gained 32.1 per cent of the vote and twelve seats.

Democratic Party: founded a little over a year before (in 1993), the party was led by Petar Gosev. The party campaigned on a platform of (1) nationalism (it refused to accept the principle of collective rights for the Albanian minority; it was against federalism and the granting of autonomy to ethnic Albanians) and (2) the free market (reduced taxes and faster privatization via vouchers).

The slogan 'With clean hands' signified an anti-corruption stance. In the first round it won only 11.2 per cent of the vote.

Internal Macedonian Revolutionary Organization (VMRO): hardline nationalist party. In the first round it won 14.4 per cent of the vote and fewer than ten seats. It favours privatization (Pettifer 1995: 57).

Party for Democratic Prosperity: the ethnic Albanian party. As a result of the split in February 1994, some hardliners ran as independents in the election (e.g. Menduh Thaci). In the first round it won two seats.

Political developments after the October 1994 general election

6 December 1994: there are reports that Greece has relaxed its embargo, e.g. allowing through fuel for humanitarian purposes.

16 February 1995: ethnic Albanians open a university (in Tetovo) in defiance of government orders.

An Albanian protester has been shot dead, the founder of the university is in prison and Albanian MPs are boycotting parliament (Iso Rusi, *IHT*, 7 March 1995, p. 8).

'He was released four months later on bail … both communities have been careful not to let the situation get out of hand' (Kerin Hope and Anthony Robinson, *FT*, Survey, 7 July 1995, p. 36).

One of the three new deputy prime ministers is from an Albanian party. The unofficial university in Tetovo remains closed, but its lecturers are allowed to teach people in their homes. More Albanians are being accepted at Skopje University, while degrees from Tirana University in Albania are to be recognized (*The Economist*, 6 April 1996, p. 45).

4 September 1995: simultaneous announcements in Washington, Athens and Skopje reveal that the Greek and Macedonian foreign ministers are to meet to take the first steps towards 'the creation of a basis for friendly relations between the two countries'. Only the name of the former Yugoslav republic has yet to be agreed. But other disputes have been resolved. The star of Vergina (a sunburst symbol found on a gold casket in the tomb, unearthed in 1977, of Philip II of Macedonia and also associated with his son Alexander the Great) is to be removed from the Macedonian flag, while sections of the Macedonian constitution considered by Greece to be threatening will be amended. In return Greece will lift its economic embargo and diplomatic relations will be established. (The USA will also establish diplomatic relations with the former Yugoslav republic.) (Greece actually lifted its economic embargo on 15 October 1995.)

13 September 1995: the agreement is signed, taking effect after thirty days.

3 October 1995: President Gligorov, although badly hurt, survives an assassination attempt when a car bomb explodes in Skopje. (He lost his right eye.) Macedonian extremists are suspected. (At first extreme nationalists were blamed, then the Bulgarian mafia: *The Economist*, 6 April 1996, p. 45. 'Gligorov … is convinced, as are other officials, that the impulse came from outside his country and that it was not a personal attack but an effort to destabilize Macedonia and keep it out of Western institutions ... Although they have no proof, important Macedonians point a finger of suspicion at Russia or Bulgaria for the attempted assassination, as part of a strategy to reconstitute a Moscow sphere of influence either among all the Slavs or among the Christian Orthodox which would include Greece and Romania': Flora Lewis, *IHT*, 19 April 1996, p. 8.) Speaker Stojan Andov (of the Liberal Party) becomes acting president. (Gligorov made a good recovery.)

9 October 1995: parliament approves the 4 September agreement.

8 April 1996: the Federal Republic of Yugoslavia and the 'Republic of Macedonia' sign an accord normalizing relations.

June 1996: an association agreement is signed with the EU (*EEN*, 1996, vol. 10, no. 16, p. 4).

1 February 1997: the rector of Tetovo University is released from jail (*EEN*, 1997, vol. 11, no. 3, p. 8).

Mid-February 1997: Slav students begin protests against a government-sponsored law on the enhanced use of Albanian in the pedagogical faculty in Skopje. The protests have since 'turned into organized daily rallies of up to 10,000 people' (*EEN*, 30 March 1997, vol. 11, no. 6, p. 6). 'Hundreds of [Slav] students have been protesting against a law – passed after strong American and EU urging – that lets Albanian be the language of tuition in just one branch of Skopje's university' (*The Economist*, 29 March 1997, p. 54). The government refuses to recognize the self-proclaimed Albanian University of Tetovo set up almost four years ago by the local community, with the support of the Kosovo Albanians (*FT*, Survey, 17 December 1997, p. ii).

19 April 1997: the Democratic Party and the Liberal Party merge to form the Liberal Democratic Party (led by Petar Gosev).

29 May 1997: the foreign, economy and justice ministers are dismissed after a series of scandals that include the collapse of some pyramid investment schemes (*The Economist*, 31 May 1997, p. 4).

(In February 1997 the Tat savings house collapsed amid widespread accusations of corruption and involvement by government officials. In April two modernizers, the deputy prime minister and the foreign minister, were dismissed. The central bank governor was forced to resign and his deputy was placed under arrest on charges of abusing his authority: *FT*, Survey, 17 December 1997, pp. i–ii.)

8 July 1997: parliament passes a law restricting the use of non-Macedonian flags.

(In May 1997 the constitutional court ruled that other countries' flags should not be flown in public. On 8 July parliament approved a new law permitting the flags of ethnic minorities to fly outside municipal buildings only on public holidays: *FT*, Survey, 17 December 1997, p. ii.)

9 July 1997: violence occurs in the ethnic Albanian towns of Tetovo and

Gostivar as police try to prevent the flying of the Albanian national flag. Several people are killed (*EEN*, 1997, vol. 11, no. 14, p. 7).

(The radical mayor of Gostivar insisted on flying the Albanian flag alongside the Macedonian flag outside the town hall. The clashes left three dead and more than 200 injured. But Gostivar quickly returned to calm. Even after the riots the Social Democrats have managed to retain the support of the moderate Albanian Party for Democratic Prosperity. The two parties have co-operated in government since 1992, with the ethnic Albanians holding five cabinet posts. A parliamentary commission has been set up to investigate the Gostivar riots: *FT*, Survey, 17 December 1997, p. ii.)

17 September 1997: the ethnic Albanian mayor of Gostivar is sentenced to thirteen years in jail for not carrying out orders to lower the Albanian flag from public buildings in Gostivar (*EEN*, 1997, vol. 11, no. 18, p. 7). (This was later reduced to seven years: *The Economist*, 7 March 1998, p. 54.) (The mayor of Tetovo received a two-and-a-half-year prison term for a similar offence. The government has defined the region's medieval churches as Macedonian Orthodox. The Orthodox Church in Serbia refuses to accept the new ecclesiastical definitions: Jonathan Steele, *Guardian*, 23 July 1998, p. 12.)

December 1997: the UN Security Council extends the mandates of Unpredep (the UN's preventative force in Macedonia) by nine months until the end of August 1998. But the troops should be withdrawn 'immediately thereafter'. President Gligorov is in favour of extending the mandate beyond August 1998 (*FT*, Survey, 17 December 1997, p. iii).

13 April 1998: Arben Xhaferi, chairman of the Democratic Party of Albanians, announces his withdrawal of the party from parliament (*EEN*, 1998, vol. 12, no. 5, p. 6).

18 October and 1 November 1998: the two rounds of the general election are held.

There are 120 parliamentary seats. Under the new electoral law there is a mix of proportional and first-past-the-post systems (*FT*, 19 October 1998, p. 2).

There were a number of reruns owing to irregularities (*The Economist*, 7 November 1998, p. 56).

The parties in the 1998 general election

Social Democratic Alliance of Macedonia: led by Branko Crvenkovski. It won twenty-nine seats.

VMRO–DPMNE (Internal Macedonian Revolutionary Organization–Democratic Party for Macedonian National Unity): led by Ljubco Georgievski. It won forty-six seats.
   'Mr Georgievski … talked of bringing in $1 billion in foreign investment … [and] of compensating for losses in financial scams' (Business Central Europe 1998: 39).

Democratic Alternative: 'A new, pro-business party founded by Vasil Tupurkovski … a law professor who served as Macedonia's special envoy to the USA. [He has] pledged to bring in $1 billion in foreign investment to reduce unemployment and speed Macedonia's transition to a market economy' (*FT*, 2 November 1998, p. 4). The party won twelve seats.

Democratic Party of Albanians: led by Arben Xhaferi. It won eleven seats.

The VMRO–DPMNE and its coalition allies won sixty-two of the 120 seats. The coalition of Albanian parties won twenty-four seats (*The World Today*, 1999, vol. 55, no. 1, p. 15).

Comments on the election

VMRO–DPMNE has formed an alliance with Democratic Alternative.

> VMRO–DA is close to completing a co-operation agreement with the Democratic Party of Albanians, which would enable it to form a government if it fails to win an outright majority. VMRO, led by Ljubco Georgievski who served briefly as Macedonia's vice-president in the early 1990s, has renounced its nationalist platform since teaming up with Democratic Alternative early this year.
>
> (Kerin Hope, *FT*, 2 November 1998, p. 4)

> The Social Democrats have governed in partnership with the moderate Albanian Party for Democratic Prosperity during six years in power. But Branko Crvenkovski, prime minister, faces criticism over the slow pace of reforms aimed at giving Albanians equal status with Slavs. The more radical Democratic Party of Albanians is fighting the election in alliance with the PDP.
>
> (Kerin Hope, *FT*, 19 October 1998, p. 2)

> VMRO's ... [was] one of the world's first modern-style terrorist organizations ... For people in the southern Balkans VMRO is an acronym redolent of violence. Between the two world wars VMRO's *komitas* [brigands] carried out political assassinations, terrorized villages and exacted tribute on the ground of fighting for an independent Macedonia ... Disbanded under communism, VMRO went underground. But when Macedonia declared independence ... in 1992 it reappeared as VMRO–DPMNE ... [which] revived the dream of uniting western Bulgaria and northern Greece in a Greater Macedonia ... Seven years later, however, VMRO has succeeded in persuading voters that it is a party of peace ... This transformation from nationalist pressure group to centre-right political party owes much to Vasil Tupurkovski, a US-educated international lawyer who founded the DA earlier this year ... [He has] political skills and popularity with young voters ... Mr Tupurkovski has worked especially hard to persuade VMRO to abandon its traditional hostility towards Macedonia's large Albanian minority ... The VMRO–DA coalition is negotiating with the Democratic Party of Albanians, a radical party which used to promote separatism ... Mr

Tupurkovski also helped VMRO underline its break with the past by focusing its election campaign on Macedonia's economic prospects ... [Mr Georgievski stressed the need] to create jobs and opportunities to build small businesses ... [Mr Tupurkovski] has pledged to bring $1 billion in foreign investment, with assistance from ethnic Macedonians in the USA and Australia ... 'Macedonia should become a high-quality agricultural producer and food-processor supplying markets abroad. The way to beat unemployment is to encourage development of family-sized agri-business units' [he said].

(Kerin Hope, *FT*, 3 November 1998, p. 2)

VMRO [is] descended ... from nationalist brigands of the 1920s and 1930s ... But over the past six months it has shed its wild image. Its [32-year old] leader, Ljubco Georgievski, is eloquent about cracking down on corruption and making Macedonia less risky for investors. The DA is run by Vasil Tupurkovski, an American-educated international lawyer, who once headed Yugoslavia's communist youth movement, but now talks about raising money abroad to develop the economy. Mr Tupurkovski ... has helped bring about VMRO's transformation ... [It has made an offer] of a law banning discrimination against Albanians and Macedonia's smaller Turkish and Gypsy minorities.

(*The Economist*, 7 November 1998, p. 56)

Ljubco Georgievski [32, who will be the new prime minister] started negotiating with Arben Xhaferi – whose support he does not need to govern – to see how they could work together ... Last June [1998] ... Alajdin Demiri began a two-year prison sentence for raising an Albanian flag outside the city hall of Tetovo ... When ethnic Albanian politicians began to talk with Mr Georgievski one of his first concessions was that Mr Demiri and another mayor convicted of the same offence be released. According to Mr Xhaferi, they also agreed on a plan to give much more power to local governments and to settle a sometimes violent rallying point for both sides: a university where instruction is in the Albanian language ... Mr Georgievski, at considerable political risk, has agreed to use state funds to support the Albanian-language university, Mr Xhaferi said ... Mr Xhaferi, who in the past has hinted that Albanians here may have to secede in order to secure political rights, now says they must learn to work with Macedonian politicians. Foreign diplomats and Macedonian politicians say even the most radical people here now see that the landlocked country, sandwiched between Serbia, Albania, Greece and Bulgaria, will remain poor and isolated unless its leaders learn to co-operate.

(Mike O'Connor, *IHT*, 1 December 1998, p. 5)

Political developments after the 1998 general election

22 February 1999: a declaration of co-operation is signed by prime minister Georgievski of Macedonia and prime minister Ivan Kostov of Bulgaria. The declaration was signed in two copies in the official languages of both countries.

> Thus Georgievski could claim ... that the Bulgarian side for the first time had agreed to an explicit endorsement of the Macedonian language. Kostov meanwhile was able to tell the Bulgarian public that Macedonian is merely a technical variation of Bulgarian. The Bulgarian side also insisted that the declaration contained an undertaking by the Macedonian side that the Macedonian constitution would never be used as a pretext for interference in the internal affairs of Bulgaria 'to defend the status and rights of persons who are not citizens of the Republic of Macedonia'. This formula is an exact copy of the formula used in the interim agreement between Macedonia and Greece in 1995, and it has the same aim: to prevent Macedonia from using Article 49 of the constitution which obliges the Macedonian state to care for the status and rights of Macedonians in neighbouring states ... In their 'declaration' Bulgaria and Macedonia also included a stipulation that they would prevent the activities of institutions and private citizens that fostered violence or hatism directed at the other side.
>
> (*EEN*, 1999, vol. 12, no. 15, pp. 4–5)

Bulgaria is to donate military equipment. Other agreements included the promotion and protection of investments, trade co-operation, international road traffic and air services (*EEN*, 1999, vol. 12, no. 15, pp. 4–5).

> Bulgaria and Macedonia ... have signed a declaration of principles, which allows them to sidestep the thorny issue of Bulgaria's unwillingness to hitherto recognize the Macedonian language and nationhood ... The formula ... will allow the countries to sign bilateral treaties in the languages recognized by the two countries' constitutions.
>
> (*FT*, Survey, 8 March 1999, p. i)

> Prime ministers Georgievski and Kostov renounced territorial claims upon one another, declared that neither would allow its territory to be used by groups hostile to the other, and noted that the common language of the document they signed was 'Bulgarian, in accordance with the constitution of Bulgaria, and Macedonian, in accordance with the constitution of the Republic of Macedonia'.
>
> (William Pfaff, *IHT*, 9 March 1999, p. 6)

> Georgievski formed a curious coalition between VMRO–DPMNE (with its strong pro-Bulgarian faction in its leadership), the Democratic Alternative of Vasil Tupurkovski (his party representing a bunch of former Yugoslav

apparatchiks that had been left out by the Social Democratic Alliance in the 1990s) and the radical Democratic Party of Albanians … The strongest criticism of the new Macedonian–Bulgarian relationship comes from the SDSM and [President] Gligorov … He said that the amnesty for the Albanian mayors of Tetovo and Gostivar … the recognition of Taiwan and the negotiations with Bulgaria had ignored the institution of the president and had led to the adoption of policies dangerous to Macedonian sovereignty.

> (*EEN*, 1999, vol. 12, no. 15, pp. 4–6)

('Some [money] is coming from Taiwan, which Macedonia has recognized diplomatically. To show its thanks, Taipei is paying $20 million to build Macedonia's first free trade zone': Business Central Europe 1999: 36.)

'Mr Georgievski … has fulfilled an election promise to free the radical mayors of Tetovo and Gostivar' (*FT*, 29 March 1999, p. 2).

12 March 1999: the defence ministers of Macedonia and Bulgaria sign a defence co-operation agreement (*EEN*, 1999, vol. 12, no. 16, p. 10).

25 September 1999: Greece's state-run Olympic Airways begins regular flights between Athens and Skopje (*IHT*, 27 September 1999, p. 2).

13 October 1999: a free trade agreement is signed with Bulgaria (*EEN*, 1999, vol. 12, no. 20, p. 4).

31 October 1999: the first round of the presidential election takes place.

Tito Petrovski came first with 33 per cent of the vote. He is the candidate of the Social Democratic Alliance opposition, the former communists.

> Mr Petrovski's strong showing was seen as a rebuff to the coalition's handling of the nation's laggard economy. Apparently also decisive was the alleged willingness by the ruling coalition to meet many of the ethnic Albanians' demands for more rights.
>
> (*IHT*, 2 November 1999, p. 7)

Boris Trajkovski (VMRO) came second with 22 per cent of the vote. He is the candidate of the governing centre-right coalition (*IHT*, 2 November 1999, p. 7).

'Diplomats said both men were regarded as pro-Western and favoured integration with the EU and better ties with Greece' (*IHT*, 2 November 1999, p. 7).

14 November 1999: the presidential runoff election takes place. The minimum required turnout is 50 per cent plus one vote (*IHT*, 15 November 1999, p. 4).

The election is won by Boris Trajkovski, with 53 per cent of the vote.

> Analysts said broad support from the ethnic Albanian minority … accounted for Mr Trajkovski's victory. The Social Democratic Alliance claimed that electoral fraud was widespread in western Macedonia, where most ethnic Albanians live. Monitors for OSCE said voting procedures were 'generally satisfactory' but said there were irregularities in some western districts.
>
> (*FT*, 16 November 1999, p. 12)

27 November 1999: the supreme court nullifies election results in 230 polling stations (out of 2,793 in total), involving more than 160,000 voters (about 10 per cent of the 1.6 million electorate). Tito Petrovski and the Social Democrats complained about irregularities, mainly in ethnic Albanian-dominated western Macedonia. He lost by 77,000 votes on 14 November. A repeat vote has been set for 5 December 1999 (*IHT*, 29 November 1999, p. 7; *FT*, 29 November 1999, p. 6).

5 December 1999: Boris Trajkovski wins the rerun elections. (He was sworn in on 15 December.)

'Western diplomats said they believed the rerun was generally in order' (*FT*, 7 December 1999, p. 11).

11 March 2000: nationalists hold a meeting to form a new Internal Macedonian Revolutionary Organization (VMRO) in protest at what they regard as Bulgarianization of the ruling VMRO–DPMNE under the premiership of Ljubco Georgievski (*EEN*, 2000, vol. 12, no. 23, p. 9).

25 July 2000: parliament passes a law allowing for higher education in the Albanian language (*EEN*, 2000, vol. 12, no. 24, p. 5). ('The current government, bowing to pressure from OSCE and other international bodies in support of these demands, has agreed to allow the building of a $50 million private university in Tetovo … It will provide higher education in Albanian for up to 2,500 students': *FT*, Survey, 19 February 2001, p. 13.)

('The influx of Kosovar Albanian refugees [during the war in Kosovo] created panic and fears among the Slav majority that the balance of power and population in Macedonia would be changed dramatically. But when the war ended in the summer of 1999 most of the refugees returned to rebuild their shattered homes and lives … The local Albanian community helped by both absorbing some 360,000 Kosovan refugees … and then by calming the Slav majority's fears of being swamped by helping Kosovar families to return home once the bombing stopped … Feuding between the main coalition partners culminated in the exodus of the charismatic politician Vasil Tupurkovski and his Democratic Alternative Party last year [2000]. This led to a reshuffle which opened the door to a stronger government presence for other coalition members, the Liberals and the Democratic Party of Albanians [DPA] led by Arben Xhaferi. As a result, the Albanian community increased its share of power at the central government level, including the deputy premiership and the economics ministry … Bedredin Ibrahimi [is] general secretary of the DPA as well as deputy prime minister … In communist times Macedonia was industrialized but jobs in both the socialized industries and the local administration were overwhelmingly given to Macedonians … The Albanian population, largely excluded from the state sector, was also excluded from the privatization process. It continued to send its young men to work abroad or develop private farming and enterprise, including an informal family-based financial banking system. As a result, Albanians suffered less from the virtual collapse of the state enterprises': Anthony Robinson, *FT*, Survey, 19 February 2001, p. 14.)

24 August 2000: 'Half a dozen MPs from the ruling Internal Macedonian

Revolutionary Organization–Democratic Party for Macedonian National Unity (VMRO–DPMNE) defect to a new breakaway party, the True Macedonian Reform Option' (*EEN*, 2000, vol. 12, no. 25, p. 4).

10 September 2000: 'Local elections are easily won by opposition parties led by the Social Democratic Party of Macedonia. The two ethnic Albanian parties, the Democratic Party of Albanians and the smaller Party for Democratic Prosperity, split irreconcilably' (*EEN*, 2000, vol. 12, no. 25, p. 4).

'International monitors described the ballot as marred by security incidents, irregularities and intimidation' (*IHT*, 12 September 2000, p. 6).

> Flawed local government elections … were marred by violence and criti-cized by international observers for irregularities … VMRO did badly in bigger towns and cities where the effects of an unemployment rate of between 25 and 35 per cent are felt most keenly … At least 3,500 civil servants will be sacked next month [March 2001] under a scheme to reduce overstaffing and create a more professional administration. Some forty loss-making state enterprises that employ more than 10,000 workers face privatization or closure this year [2001]. Planned reforms of the state health service would bring sharp reductions in numbers of medical and hospital staff.
>
> (*FT*, Survey, 19 February 2001, p. 11)

'The forty biggest loss-makers, the state-controlled mines, engineering and other companies account for the bulk of bad loans, non-payment of taxes and inter-enterprise debts' (p. 12).

24 November 2000: an EU–Balkan summit meeting is held in Zagreb. Albania, Bosnia, Macedonia and Yugoslavia are formally invited. 'The summit also saw Macedonia's signing of the first so-called Stabilization and Association Agreement with the EU – a new kind of agreement intended for western Balkan countries. Croatia also formally started negotiations on such an agreement' (*FT*, 25 November 2000, p. 6).

November 2000: on 23 November 2000 the Democratic Alternative, led by Vasil Tupurkovski, left the ruling coalition. On 30 November prime minister Ljubco Georgievski announced a new cabinet following a coalition agreement between the VMRO–DPMNE, the Liberals and the Democratic Party of Albanians (*EEN*, 2001, vol. 13, no. 2, p. 5).

'The Democratic Party of Albanians … became the government's main coali-tion partner after a political shake-up last November [2000]' (*FT*, 2 March 2001, p. 8).

> Last November [2000] the DPA acquired five cabinet portfolios – including the post of deputy prime minister … A new university, sponsored by the international community, is due to open in Tetovo in October [2001] … Some courses will be taught in Albanian as well as English and Macedonian.
>
> (*FT*, 6 March 2001, p. 10)

[There have been] no fewer than five acrimonious cabinet reshuffles. The most recent cabinet upheaval resulted in the departure from the coalition of the Democratic Alternative, led by Vasil Tupurkovski ... The Democratic Alternative was replaced as a coalition partner by the Liberals, with Srgjan Kerim ... taking over the post of foreign minister ... A telephone-tapping scandal is the latest crisis to confront Mr Georgievski. The Social Democrats accuse the interior ministry of using sophisticated electronic equipment provided by the USA for counter-terrorism purposes to tap the mobile phones of senior Macedonian politicians, including Mr Trajkovski and Mr Crvenkovski. Purported transcripts of taped conversations, provided by the Social Democrats, have appeared in Macedonian newspapers.

(Kerin Hope, *FT*, Survey, 19 February 2001, p. 11)

Ethnic Albanian militancy and its ramifications

A new Albanian guerrilla force [exists] in Macedonia ... One senior Macedonian police official ... [said that] armed Albanian groups were active in several villages along Macedonia's northern border [with Kosovo] ... The rebels call themselves the National Liberation Army ... 'The aim [he said] is a greater Kosovo, rather than a greater Albania' ... A group also calling itself the National Liberation Army claimed responsibility last month [January] for an attack on a police station ... near the border with Kosovo ... A spokesman for the Macedonian army ... said the military has had trouble from armed Albanians in the border areas ever since the Kosovo conflict. One soldier was killed and two wounded in 1999 and last summer people ... blew up a transport carrier and two of the army's armoured vehicles ... [he] said ... Arben Xhaferi, leader of the main Albanian political party in Macedonia, which is in the governing coalition, acknowledged that some individuals and small groups could be active but insisted there was no organized campaign.

(*IHT*, 26 February 2001, p. 5)

'The National Liberation Army (NLA) ... emerged only six weeks ago from the village of Tanusevci, just inside the Macedonian border' (*Guardian*, 28 February 2001, p. 15).

'Ethnic Albanians fighting ... include former fighters from the Kosovo Liberation Army' (*FT*, 22 March 2001, p. 8).

'Though many, perhaps most, of the fighters in the new force are from Macedonia, their commanders include some of the hardiest veterans of the Kosovo Liberation Army' (*The Economist*, 24 March 2001, p. 50).

'The National Liberation Army ... says that most of their members are citizens of Macedonia but also veterans of the Kosovo conflict, having volunteered to fight in the Kosovo Liberation Army' (http://news.bbc.co.uk/hi/english ... europe/newsid; 27 February 2001, pp. 1–3).

On 7 March ... the small village of Tanusevci on the Macedonian side of the Kosovo–Macedonian border ... began to reverberate to the sound of mortar and small arms fire. A battle between the self-proclaimed National Liberation Army (UCK – Ushtria Climatare Kombetare) and the Macedonian army claimed the lives of three Macedonians and an undisclosed number of Albanians ... In the late 1990s it [Tanusevci] became an important base for the KLA [Kosovo Liberation Army] and was used both as a transit point for the smuggling of arms and for training rebels ... Last year [2000] Tanusevci became a focal point for the transport of arms to the UCPMB [Liberation Army of Presevo, Medvedja and Bujanovic] rebels in Presevo, only thirty kilometres away. As tensions in the region increased a training base was again set up, this time by the UCPMB ... Tensions erupted in September last year [2000] after an incident in which Macedonian military vehicles were fired upon near the village ... Leaders in Kosovar Albanian society have, almost to a man, refused to associate themselves with the UCPMB or the new UCK ... [for example] Adem Demaci, a former long-time political prisoner and hardline spokesman for the KLA ... [and] Agim Ceku, head of the Kosovo Protection Corps ... There is no doubt that the UCPMB and new UCK movements are related and connected in some way to elements of the formally disbanded KLA. Many guerrillas in Tanusevci openly admit to being former KLA fighters ... Two distinct groups are involved in initiating violence. On the one hand, there are Albanians in southern Serbia and Macedonia who have been disenfranchised and impoverished by the governments in Belgrade and Skopje ... The second group is responsible for financing, arming and organizing the rebellion. This can be divided in two on the basis of motivation. A very small hardcore of veterans is fighting to create a 'Greater Kosovo' that could eventually be added to a 'Greater Albania'. Although much attention has been paid to this ideology in the West, the campaign has attracted very little support amongst Albanians. Some, though, are motivated not by national ideology but by profit. Many entrepreneurs make money from instability, which allows them to control markets and continue their trade in illicit drugs, consumer items and women. The establishment of order in the southern Balkans would be very bad for these people's businesses. It is clear that instability is being caused by a combination of grievance and greed and that the hub for these activities lies inside Kosovo.

(Alex Bellamy, *The World Today*, 2001, vol. 57, no. 4, pp. 10–12)

'About 200 ethnic Albanian guerrillas ... [are] in the border village of Tanusevci' (*Telegraph*, 2 March 2001, p. 17). '[There has taken place] the seizure by up to 100 separatists of the border village of Tanusevci' (*The Times*, 3 March 2001, p. 14). 'There are reportedly about 100 guerrillas occupying [Tanusevci]' (*Independent*, 5 March 2001, p. 13).

'The National Democratic Party ... launched itself last month [February] with a programme for a federal Macedonia' (*Telegraph*, 12 March 2001, p. 11). 'A new Albanian political movement has been unveiled in Skopje. The National Democratic Party advocates an Albanian Macedonian federation ... The party leader [is] Kastriot Haxhirexha' (*Telegraph*, 13 March 2001, p. 16). 'The rebels have formed their own political party' (*IHT*, 23 March 2001, p. 4).

> The rebels, together with the National Democratic Party, a newly formed radical group, want Macedonia to become a federation, with ethnic Albanians taking full control of western Macedonia, where most of the minority lives. 'We have waited ten years for the Albanians to get their rights and it has not happened,' said Fadil Bajrami, a former Democratic Party of Albanians deputy and founder member of the National Democratic Party. 'We see a federation, along the lines of Belgium, as the future in Macedonia' ... Liman Kurtishi [is] a senior member of the new National Democratic Party.
>
> (*FT*, 31 March 2001, p. 8)

'With support from the National Democratic Party, a newly formed radical political group, the rebels want the republic turned into a federation with ethnic Albanians taking control of western Macedonia, home to the majority of Albanians' (*FT*, 2 April 2001, p. 7).

> The clashes are not just a dispute between Albanians and Macedonians. They are also a dispute among Albanians. The established Albanian politicians, as well as those of Kosovo and Albania itself, have all condemned the gunmen ... Apart from four Albanian and two Macedonian MPs, the entire parliament condemned the 'armed groups of extremists' yesterday [18 March] and called for foreign military help. The motion was supported not only by the Albanian party in government but also by the Albanian opposition Party of Democratic Prosperity. So the gunmen operating in the hills above Tetovo represent a minority. That said, it does not follow that a large number of Macedonia's Albanians do not support their goals, as opposed to their violent methods. Before and since independence in 1991 Albanians have regularly criticised the lack of language rights for their community and discrimination in public service jobs. There have been frequent outbursts of nationalism with demands for the right to fly the Albanian flag. Arben Xhaferi, now the leading Albanian moderate in Macedonia, is a jail veteran from flag protests going as far back as 1968. Calls for federalization within Macedonia, which the gunmen seem to be making, have long been canvassed by some Albanians though always rejected by Macedonian politicians on the grounds they would be the first step to secession.
>
> (Jonathan Steele, *Guardian*, 19 March 2001, p. 18)

> In the last week the guerrillas have called for international mediation to secure their aims, which include a division of Macedonia into two federated states composed largely of ethnic Albanians on the one hand and Macedonian Slavs on the other ... The rebels assert they are battling to end

what they call systematic discrimination, saying they want the right to create their own police force, army, schools and parliament in a Macedonian federation of two states.

(R. Jeffrey Smith, *IHT*, 21 March 2001, pp. 1, 6)

[There are] Albanian demands for the recognition of Albanian as a second official language, for more decentralization of local government, for an Albanian-language television station, a change in the preamble of the constitution, an internationally monitored census and for the recognition of an unofficial Albanian-language university ... There has been progress on the university issue and the census.

(*IHT*, 26 March 2001, pp. 1, 8)

'The insurgents' ... demands include the creation of a federal government with separate administrations for Slavs and Albanians' (*FT*, 20 March 2001, p. 10).

Arben Xhaferi ... supports independence for Kosovo but not the creation of a 'Greater Albania' that would unite ethnic Albanians living in three states ... Under his leadership the Democratic Party of Albanians emerged as the dominant ethnic Albanian party, supported by an estimated 80 per cent of the minority ... The ethnic Albanians have achieved a longstanding aim: a university that would teach in the Albanian language. Due to open in October in Tetovo, it will be financed by the EU, European donors and the USA. It will also offer courses taught in English ... Both the Democratic Party of Albanians and the Party for Democratic Prosperity, a smaller ethnic Albanian party, are demanding a change in the preamble of the constitution that makes Macedonians the primary people, as well as immediate approval by parliament of a law decentralizing local government. Local government reform would give ethnic Albanian mayors bigger decision-making powers and allow them to raise funds from local taxes.

(*FT*, 31 March 2001, p. 8)

'A new university, sponsored by the international community, is due to open in Tetovo in October [2001] ... Some courses will be taught in Albanian as well as English and Macedonian' (*FT*, 6 March 2001, p. 10).

'The main promises [made by the government] are to create an Albanian university in Tetovo and establish an Albanian-language television channel' (*Independent*, 21 March 2001, p. 13).

The rebel National Liberation Army (NLA) insists that it is not seeking to break up the Macedonian state but merely to secure equal rights for the Albanians. But in a statement the Tetovo branch of the NLA also said that it would fight if necessary. And its demands include the transformation of Macedonia into a federation.

(Misha Glenny, *The Times*, 21 March 2001, p. 19)

There is no multi-ethnic political party ... Albanians want their language made official, more decentralization, more of a role in the security services, a fair census, a state-funded Albanian-language university and constitutional amendments to put all citizens on an equal footing as constituent peoples in Macedonia.

(Steven Erlanger. *IHT*, 28 March 2001, p. 4)

The guerrillas enjoy widespread support among Macedonia's ethnic Albanians ... Many say they have been treated as second-class citizens by the Macedonian majority ... Rebels interviewed ... said they intended to take over western Macedonia to form a federation within the country. Sceptics say the real objective is joining an enlarged independent Kosovo.

(*Guardian*, 19 March 2001, p. 2)

'Many ethnic Albanians in Macedonia have said they sympathize with the guerrillas' demand for enhanced political and economic rights' (*IHT*, 19 March 2001, p. 7).

'Many believe that what is being played out in Macedonia is the last unresolved issue of the Balkans conflict: the Albanian question – how to reconcile the nationalist aspirations of the Albanian diaspora outside Albania' (Judy Dempsey, *FT*, 24 March 2001, p. 11).

The EU, working in tandem with Nato, has taken the political lead in lining up a solid front on international support behind ... President Boris Trajkovski ... So far ... Javier Solana, the EU's top diplomat ... and his Nato counterpart, secretary-general George Robertson, seem to have worked as a smooth partnership. The crisis in Macedonia has become the first test of a new formula in trans-Atlantic co-operation in which the EU, with a team to head its foreign policy, takes the lead in handling a European security problem and Nato plays a supporting role in small ways inside Macedonia and as a major presence across the border in Kosovo.

(Joseph Fitchett. *IHT*, 23 March 2001, p. 4)

No major party in Albania calls for the creation of a Greater Albania ... In Kosovo, in Macedonia, in southern Serbia, and to a lesser extent in Montenegro, there is an active 'Albanian question'. But the teeth of a relatively few hardliners can be drawn if Albanians feel their rights are represented in the countries in which they live, if they believe that Kosovo will, one day, be independent, and, most important of all if they can prosper in a south-eastern Europe where borders may soon come to mean as much as they do today between Germany, France and Luxembourg.

(Tim Judah, *New York Review of Books*, vol. XLVIII, no. 8, p. 37)

'That phrase "to make borders unimportant" is much heard now in the Balkans from people who want both ethnic unity and an end to fighting' (p. 36).

None of the Nato nations or the other powerful countries involved in the Balkans are ready to endorse a change of borders ... On 26 January 2000 two ethnic Albanian brothers were killed by the Serbian police in Dobrosin ... [a] village just inside the Serbian border. Dobrosin lies in the Presevo Valley, just inside what is called the Ground Safety Zone ... Soon after the brothers were killed Albanian guerrillas calling themselves the Liberation Army of Presevo, Medvedja and Bujanovic (UCPMB) appeared in the village. These are the names of three districts in southern Serbia where there are 100,000 or so Albanians. Politically they were linked to the Popular Movement for Kosovo, the LPK, a tiny party of deeply committed ethnic Albanian nationalists which had, however, been instrumental in creating the Kosovo Liberation Army (KLA) in 1993 ... It seems plausible that until 5 October [2000] ... when Milosevic fell, US troops who control this part of Kosovo's borders may have been less than diligent in choking off supplies to the UCPMB because anything that helped destabilize Milosevic was deemed to be a good thing ... Many of the founder members of the KLA were members of the LPK. Several key members of the LPK were Macedonian Albanians. They included Fazli Veliu, the LPK chairman through much of the 1990s, and Bardhyl Mahmuti, a key organizer and fund-raiser who lived in exile in ... Switzerland. In 1993 a meeting of ethnic Albanian activists took place in Kicevo in western Macedonia ... and there a decision was made to move towards active armed resistance. The result, in August of that year, was the formation of the LPK and in turn the KLA ... After the Kosovo war men like Bardhyl Mahmuti said that the LPK ... should be disbanded ... By contrast, a hard core of LPK members decided to keep the old party alive. These men had a major part in setting up both the UCPMB and the NLA [National Liberation Army]. So did some former LPK men in the Kosovo Protection Corps, which was set up in 1999 as a civil emergency force but absorbed a good part of the former KLA leadership. In Macedonia the political leader of the NLA is Ali Ahmeti, who did so much to arrange supplies for the KLA during the Kosovo war. Ever since the end of the Kosovo war many of the Macedonian Albanian LPK men had been agitating to start a conflict in Macedonia. Many of their old comrades, now in powerful Kosovo parties or even in the civil administration, tried to dissuade them, arguing that a new war would not be in the interests of Kosovo. Bardhyl Mahmuti ... has since called for the NLA to lay down their arms ... In all their official declarations ... the NLA leaders say that they want only rights for Macedonia's Albanians and not the breakup of the state.

(pp. 36–7)

Ethnic Albanian rebel leaders have threatened to broaden their conflict with Macedonia's security forces unless they are involved in negotiations over the country's future. The demands made by political leaders close to the NLA come as an investigation by the *Guardian* showed that the rebels' main political and financial backers are Albanians living in Switzerland. The threats were made by Fazli Veliu, one of the NLA's founders and key political leaders outside Macedonia and Kosovo. Since the end of the war in Kosovo in 1999, he and fellow members of Switzerland's Albanian diaspora have been the catalyst for the creation of the NLA ... Soon after Nato troops entered Kosovo in June 1999, he, along with members of the Kosovo Liberation Army and political exiles in the United States, Germany and Switzerland, was planning the creation of the NLA ... As president of the People's Movement of Kosovo abroad, he [Veliu] had been one of the founders of the KLA.

(*Guardian*, 21 May 2001, p. 10)

A chronology of events

27 January 2001: 'Albanian militants fired a rocket-propelled grenade at a train in Macedonia on Saturday [27 January]' (*The Times*, 29 January 2001, p. 6).

18 February 2001: 'Yesterday [18 February] ethnic Albanian fighters from the newly-formed National Liberation Army suffered casualties a mile short of the Kosovan border after they clashed with a patrol of Macedonian soldiers' (*Telegraph*, 19 February 2001, p. 13). 'Two new Albanian armed groups have sprung up in Macedonia recently, demanding some form of independence for the 500,000 Albanians in the country' (*Telegraph*, 22 February 2001, p. 17).

There are ... two Albanian groups recruiting people for an armed struggle in Macedonia. The first is the National Liberation Army ... [which] in January ... claimed responsibility for a mortar attack on a Macedonian police station which killed one officer and wounded three others ... The second is the Albanian National Army (Armata Kometare Shqipetare) from which less has been heard.

(http://news.bbc.co.uk/hi/english... europe/newsid; 27 February 2001, pp. 1–3)

'[There has been] a recent spate of armed attacks on Macedonian police stations' (*FT*, Survey, 19 February 2001, p. 11).

23 February 2001: '[On 23 February at the Balkan summit in Skopje] President Boris Trajkovski ... and [President] Vojislav Kostunica ... initialled a long-awaited treaty that defines the border between Macedonia and Serbia' (*The Economist*, 3 March 2001, p. 48).

'An agreement settling the border dispute between Yugoslavia and Macedonia signed on 23 February led to stricter patrols, sparking clashes between Macedonian police and ethnic Albanian smugglers' (*FT*, 19 March 2001, p. 10).

26–8 February 2001: there are further clashes between ethnic Albanian militants and Macedonian forces.

1 March 2001:

Macedonia yesterday [1 March] ratified a long-awaited border treaty with Serbia, in spite of tensions over the occupation of a mountain village by ethnic Albanian extremists from Kosovo. The takeover at Tanusevci, close to the border with Serbia, poses the most serious threat to Macedonia's stability since the Kosovo conflict ... The initialling of the border accord by Mr Trajkovski and Vojislav Kostunica ... at last week's Balkan summit in Skopje, may have triggered the guerrillas' move across the border, according to government officials ... The 120-member Macedonian parliament ratified the treaty by eighty-nine to nine votes. Only the Albanian Party for Democratic Prosperity, a small opposition group, voted against ratification on the grounds that political parties in Kosovo were not consulted ... Its rival, the Democratic Party of Albanians ... became the government's main coalition partner after a political shake-up last November [2000].

(*FT*, 2 March 2001, p. 8)

'Last November [2000] the DPA acquired five cabinet portfolios – including the post of deputy prime minister' (*FT*, 6 March 2001, p. 10).

2 March 2001:

[On 2 March] Nato again reassured Macedonia that it was closely monitoring the actions of a force of about 100 ethnic Albanian guerrillas that has occupied the village of Tanusevci on Macedonia's side of the Kosovo border ... The alliance also repeated its commitment to the territorial integrity of the former Yugoslav republic.

(*IHT*, 3 March 2001, p. 2)

4 March 2001: three Macedonian soldiers are killed, two by a landmine and one by sniper fire. Macedonia closes its border with Kosovo.

5 March 2001:

Macedonia said Monday [5 March] that ethnic Albanian guerrilla operations ... were not confined to ... Tanusevci, which is directly on the border with Kosovo ... There are some terrorists operating in the forests around Tanusevci ... [Macedonia] announced that the country was mobilizing army and police reservists ... full mobilization of the police reservists and a partial one for the army ... Earlier Monday Macedonian troops clashed with ethnic Albanian rebels ... while Nato tightened border controls.

(*IHT*, 6 March 2001, p. 6)

'Macedonian troops clashed with ethnic Albanian rebels for the second day running' (*Guardian*, 6 March 2001, p. 13).

Nato yesterday [5 March] started beefing up security along Kosovo's border with Macedonia amid growing concern that the region could face fresh instability if violence by ethnic Albanian extremist groups continues ...

Nato peacekeepers on the Kosovo side of the mountainous border reported seeing seventy to 150 armed men leaving the isolated Macedonian village of Tanusevci.

(*FT*, 6 March 2001, p. 10)

'There were said to be 200 armed rebels in the area, double earlier estimates and the Bulgarian president, Petar Stoyanov, offered to send troops to assist the Macedonian army' (*Independent*, 6 March 2001, p. 17)

'The Bulgarian president offered troops to Macedonia, a move played down by the Bulgarian government' (*The Times*, 6 March 2001, p. 13).

7 March 2001: 'Peacekeeping soldiers securing Kosovo's border with Macedonia opened fire and wounded two [of five] Albanian gunmen Wednesday [7 March]' (*IHT*, 8 March 2001, p. 4). 'US troops ... opened fire when the men pointed weapons at them' (*Independent*, 8 March 2001, p. 14).

'Bulgaria announced that it would begin shipping military equipment to Macedonia this week' (*The Times*, 8 March 2001, p. 14).

8 March 2001:

US-led peacekeepers in southern Kosovo occupied a village on the border with Macedonia on Thursday [8 March] as part of a co-ordinated move with Macedonian military forces through the night and morning to flush out ethnic Albanian rebels from their mountain base ... The operation [involved] some 300 international peacekeepers, most of them American, to occupy Tanusevci ... [which] they found empty and abandoned ... It followed a move on Tuesday [6 March] to secure the village of Mijak, just short of the border.

(*IHT*, 9 March 2001, pp. 1, 4)

(There was confusion as to whether the Kfor troops had crossed into Macedonia. Kfor denied that its forces had done so.)

'The American-led, four-day military operation ... also involved ... Polish, Ukrainian and Lithuanian troops' (*Telegraph*, 9 March 2001, p. 19).

Nato ... decided yesterday [8 March] to let Serb security forces reenter a buffer zone along a part of the Macedonian border ... Lord Robertson, Nato secretary-general said it was 'the first step in a phased and conditioned reduction of [the ground security zone]'.

(*FT*, 9 March 2001, p. 20)

'Nato said yesterday [8 March] Yugoslav forces would within days be allowed to retake the edge of the ground safety zone at the junction of the borders between Kosovo, Serbia and Macedonia' (*Telegraph*, 9 March 2001, p. 19).

'The GSZ [ground safety zone] [is] now exploited by ethnic Albanian extremists as a base for attacking Serb policemen and for crossing between Kosovo and Macedonia to attack Macedonian police' (*FT*, 10 March 2001, p. 7).

'Bulgaria yesterday [8 March] sent a military supplies convoy … to Macedonia' (*Independent*, 9 March 2001, p. 13).

9 March 2001: Macedonia once again closes all border crossings with Kosovo. Heavy fighting leads to the death of one Macedonian policeman.

'Macedonia faces a spreading insurgency with about 300 to 500 armed men active along the mountainous region bordering Kosovo, according to a police official' (*IHT*, 10 March 2001, p. 4).

'They call themselves the National Liberation Army … There are probably fewer than 500 of them' (*Telegraph*, 12 March 2001, p. 11).

12 March 2001: 'Nato and Yugoslavia agreed Monday [12 March] to let Yugoslav troops return to a small section of a buffer area on Serbia's tense border with Kosovo and Macedonia' (*IHT*, 13 March 2001, p. 6). '[The agreement] paves the way for the limited return of Serbian security forces into a sliver of land in the five-kilometre-wide buffer zone [ground safety zone]' (*FT*, 13 March 2001, p. 9).

> A limited number of Yugoslav army and ministry of interior troops [would be allowed] into the buffer zone bordering the Former Yugoslav Republic of Macedonia … an area of the Presevo Valley measuring three miles square up to the border with Macedonia … A [temporary] ceasefire agreement was signed by the commanders of the Liberation Army of Presevo, Medvedja and Bujanovic … [But a] special envoy to Lord Robertson … said it was 'open-ended' and intended to embrace all the Albanian extremist forces including the National Liberation Army operating against the Macedonians special.
>
> (*The Times*, 13 March 2001, p. 21)

Fighting continued between Macedonian forces and ethnic Albanian militants.

13 March 2001: 'In … Skopje [on 13 March] about 10,000 people joined a peace march organized by the DPA … which is the junior partner in the coalition government' (*Telegraph*, 14 March 2001, p. 14).

> Members of Macedonia's biggest ethnic Albanian Party, the Democratic Party of Albanians, marched in central Skopje on Tuesday [13 March]. About 10,000 Albanians called for peace … An estimated 30,000 people, most of them ethnic Albanians, turned out in Skopje … to demonstrate for more rights but also for peace … More militant ethnic Albanians planned to hold a counter-protest Wednesday [14 March] in Tetovo.
>
> (*IHT*, 14 March 2001, p. 5)

Fighting continued between Macedonian forces and ethnic Albanian militants.

14 March 2001: 'Yesterday [14 March] several hundred Yugoslav army soldiers and special police units swept into the buffer zone on Kosovo's boundary with Serbia, close to the Macedonian border' (*Independent*, 15 March 2001, p. 15).

Hundreds of Yugoslav army troops, monitored by international observers, poured into the southern area of Kosovo on Wednesday [14 March] ... into a 5-kilometre (3-mile) buffer zone bordering Kosovo ... Yugoslav troops are allowed to patrol a 25-square-kilometre (10-square-mile) area of the buffer zone in the Presevo Valley region of Serbia ... that is bordered by Kosovo in the west and Macedonia in the south ... Serb actions would be monitored by Nato officials ... The area that Serb soldiers entered Wednesday splits two separate guerrilla groups, one with about 800 rebels in the Presevo Valley and another of perhaps 100 rebels south of there in northern Macedonia.

(*IHT*, 15 March 2001, p. 5)

'Ethnic Albanian guerrillas expanded their insurgency from the countryside to Macedonia's second largest city Wednesday [14 March], battling in a Tetovo suburb with police in an escalation of regional violence' (*IHT*, 15 March 2001, p. 5).

The conflict between rebel Albanians and government troops escalated yesterday [14 March] when fighting spread for the first time from sparsely populated rural areas on the border with Kosovo to the outskirts of Macedonia's second largest city ... Tetovo, twenty-five miles west of ... Skopje. The trouble in the predominantly Albanian community broke out before and during a rally by around 5,000 people chanting slogans in favour of ethnic Albanian fighters and showing their support for rebels fighting Macedonian forces in the north of the country ... The trouble in Macedonia began when about fifteen rebels opened fire with rifles in the Tetovo suburb of Kale north of the city and in the nearby village of Selce.

(*The Times*, 15 March 2001, p. 18)

Last night [14 March] ... fighting between police and ethnic Albanian rebels erupted close to Tetovo, the country's second largest city ... The violence ... marks the spread of the ethnic Albanian insurgency into north-western Macedonia ... Around 200 ethnic Albanian rebels were reported to be involved in the fighting, which is taking place in and around the village of Lavce.

(*Guardian*, 15 March 2001, p. 13)

Fighting broke out [on 14 March] in the village of Lavce in the hills above Tetovo ... [On 15 March] police troops battled with ethnic Albanian rebels on the edge of town ... The support [among ethnic Albanians] for the rebels in these villages and in Tetovo is almost universal.

(Carlotta Gall, *IHT*, 16 March 2001, p. 4)

'Up to 200 [ethnic Albanian] gunmen' [are involved]' (*Telegraph*, 16 March 2001, p. 16).

16 March 2001: mortar shells hit the main square in Tetovo.

'German troops, part of a backup force for the Nato-led peacekeeping mission in neighbouring Kosovo, came under fire in their base in Tetovo. The base is guarded by Macedonian troops' (*IHT*,17 March 2001, p. 4).

> Tetovo, while 80 per cent Albanian, has a police force that is only 10 per cent Albanians among its active officers and 90 per cent Macedonian Slavs. The police chief is Albanian, but he has been sidelined in the operation to combat the rebels.
>
> *IHT*, 17 March 2001, p. 4)

'Rauf Ramadini, the Albanian police commander in Tetovo, was dismissed [on 17 March] and replaced with a Slavic Macedonian officer' (*The Times*, 19 March 2001, p. 13).

'Macedonia estimates that 200 well-equipped and well-trained ethnic Albanian rebels, mostly from Kosovo, are fighting around Tetovo, while another 300 provide logistics support' (*FT*, 17 March 2001, p. 6).

> The Macedonian government says that about 200 National Liberation Army guerrillas are involved in the present fighting ... Some estimates suggest a further 300 men are aiding the guerrillas in the hills ... The rebels probably number less than 400 inside Macedonia.
>
> (*Telegraph*, 17 March 2001, p. 6)

18 March 2001: the Macedonian governments mobilizes army reservists and imposes a night curfew on Tetovo.

> The prime minister ... announced new measures ... including a curfew and restrictions on movement in the Tetovo area ... [A spokesman for the rebels] put the number of local fighters at 2,000, but declined to give an estimate of the total nationwide.
>
> (*IHT*, 19 March 2001, p. 7)

'Ethnic Albanians fighting in Macedonia are ... thought to number no more than 1,000' (*FT*, 22 March 2001, p. 8).

> In a show of unity between politicians from both ethnic communities, the Macedonian parliament ended three days of debate yesterday [18 March] with a condemnation of the gunmen who have been attacking the town of Tetovo. They called for outside military help, but said this should not include troops from neighbouring countries ... The motion called for a 'wider dialogue' among the 'relevant forces' in Macedonia to deal with the country's problems ... The prime minister ... announced new measures ... including a curfew and restrictions on movement in the Tetovo region.
>
> (*Guardian*, 19 March 2001, p. 13)

Apart from four Albanian and two Macedonian MPs, the entire parliament condemned the 'armed groups of extremists' yesterday [18 March] and called for foreign military help. The motion was supported not only by the Albanian party in government but also by the Albanian opposition Party of Democratic Prosperity.

(*Guardian*, 19 March 2001, p. 18)

19 March 2001: Lord Robertson (secretary-general of Nato):

What is necessary ... is to interdict as much of the supplies, the traffic that might be going into Macedonia, so Nato is committed to tightening its controls of the border. Additional troops will be deployed to do that. We are determined that we will starve the limited number of localized extremists from being able to carry out their mischief, and we will take what measures are necessary on the military front ... There is no question of new mandates [to operate within Macedonia]. What is required is the isolation of those who are undermining the democratic process, and we can do that with Kfor on the Kosovo side of the border, cutting off lines of supply ... We will be asking individual Nato members to add to the troops they have in Kosovo in order that more flexibility can be given to the task ... We will not contemplate the changing of borders through violence and we will not contemplate the breakup of the Former Yugoslav Republic of Macedonia and those that seek to do so through whatever means are doomed to failure.

'Nato's 3,000-strong presence in Macedonia is currently limited to logistical support troops ... Around half of the conscript [Macedonian] army is Albanian' (*Independent*, 20 March 2001, p. 13). 'The government has a 15,000-strong standing army' (*The Times*, 22 March 2001, p. 14). 'According to Western estimates, the Macedonian army, 90 per cent of whose officers are ethnic Slavs, have only 20,000 men' (*Guardian*, 22 March 2001, p. 2).

Officially the army has around 15,000 men – including some 1,400 reservists called up last week. Western diplomats put the number of 'combat-capable' soldiers at no more than 1,200 ... Around 30 per cent of the conscripts are Albanian and about 10 per cent are Roma, Turks and other minorities ... The government can also call on 350 special police and 450 gendarmes trained in riot control and paramilitary operations.

(*Guardian*, 26 March 2001, p. 13)

'On the sixth day of hostilities the government deployed tanks and troops in preparation for what it said would be a "final operation" against the ethnic Albanian ... rebels who control the hills above [Tetovo]' (*IHT*, 20 March 2001, p. 1).

20 March 2001:

The government on Tuesday [20 March] postponed its planned military offensive aimed at ending a guerrilla siege of ... Tetovo ... so that civilians could have twenty-four hours to vacate a series of villages occupied by the rebels before a planned artillery bombardment ... The pause was based in part on intelligence information provided by the United States, which has lofted pilotless military reconnaissance over the villages from bases inside neighbouring Kosovo and secretly shared the photographs with the Macedonian army ... The security forces preparing for an offensive near Tetovo are predominantly Macedonian Slavs ... An official said that Macedonia was getting weapons from Greece and Bulgaria, but had not obtained advice from them.

(*IHT*, 21 March 2001, pp. 1, 6)

'A short time after the start of the government offensive, the Macedonian army issued an ultimatum giving the "terrorists" twenty-four hours to cease hostilities or leave Macedonia' (*Independent*, 21 March 2001, p. 13). 'The government ... [told] the rebels they had twenty-four hours to lay down their weapons and surrender or leave Macedonia' (*Guardian*, 22 March 2001, p. 2).

Army units in Tetovo opened fire with tanks for the first time yesterday [20 March] in an attempt to dislodge rebels ... A joint statement from the interior and defence ministries said Macedonian troops would observe a ceasefire from midnight last night to midnight tonight in the town of Tetovo ... 'After the deadline Macedonian security forces will continue using all means against the positions of terrorists until they are completely destroyed,' said the government.

(*Telegraph*, 21 March 2001, p. 15)

The country's two main Albanian parties ... the Democratic Party of Albanians, a minority member of the ethnically mixed government, and the opposition Party for Democratic Prosperity ... [signed a declaration]: 'We call on the groups that have taken up arms on the territory of our state to lay down their arms and return to their homes peacefully. We condemn the use of force in pursuit of political objectives.'

(*Telegraph*, 21 March 2001, p. 15)

[The parties] condemned 'the use of force for political purposes', saying it 'made political dialogue impossible' and blocked Macedonia's hopes of joining the EU ... The two parties urged the government to speed measures it has already agreed on to improve ethnic relations. The main promises are to create an Albanian university in Tetovo and establish an Albanian-language television channel.

(*Independent*, 21 March 2001, p. 13)

'We condemn the use of force for political gains – there is no place for something like that in civilized democratic states,' read the declaration ... 'Violence can be tragic for us as Macedonian citizens and for the entire region,' it said.

(*Guardian*, 21 March 2001, p. 14)

The rebels' call for talks with the government came hours before the army started shelling ... Rejecting the guerrillas' offer, the Macedonian president, Boris Trajkovski, said: 'There will be no negotiations' ... Macedonia's leaders ... were encouraged to take a hard line yesterday [20 March] by Javier Solana, the EU security chief ... The rebels called for negotiations but Mr Solana ... backed the Slav-led government in its refusal to agree to talks. 'Nothing and I mean nothing will be obtained by violent means,' Mr Solana said on a visit to Macedonia ... 'It is a mistake to negotiate with the terrorists and we do not recommend it.'

(*Independent*, 21 March 2001, p. 13)

Javier Solana: 'The terrorists have to be isolated. All of us have to condemn and isolate them' (*Guardian*, 21 March 2001, p. 14). Javier Solana: 'I think it is a mistake in this particular case to negotiate with terrorists. These terrorists have to be isolated' (*FT*, 21 March 2001, p. 10).

'So far nearly 8,000 people have fled their homes in Macedonia to escape fighting' (*Independent*, 21 March 2001, p. 13). 'The United Nations High Commissioner for Refugees says 2,300 ethnic Albanians have gone to Albania and 1,300 into Serbia ... 4,000 were displaced within the country' (*The Times*, 22 March 2001, p. 14).

Since last week about 5,700 Macedonians have crossed into Turkey ... The refugees [are] mostly ethnic Turks and Albanians ... Thousands are also fleeing Macedonia westwards into Albania proper, from where many of them travel to Kosovo.

(*Guardian*, 22 March 2001, p. 11)

'The UN refugee agency said more than 8,000 people, mostly ethnic Albanians, had left their homes since fighting started last month [February]' (*Guardian*, 23 March 2001, p. 15). 'Lord Robertson said [on 23 March] that the UN had estimated that 18,000 ethnic Albanians had left their homes in Macedonia, 11,000 of them displaced inside the country' (*Guardian*, 24 March 2001, p. 17). 'An estimated 22,000 ethnic Albanians have fled from their homes in Tetovo and surrounding villages' (*Telegraph*, 24 March 2001, p. 20).

21 March 2001: Ali Ahmeti (political head of the National Liberation Army):

We, the general staff of the National Liberation Army, announce a unilateral ceasefire and we open the road for dialogue so heads can cool down and to find the best solution. In case our positions are threatened by our opponents then all our forces will be on the move and the conflict would widen. We have repeated constantly and will repeat again that we are for dialogue. We are not for a war that would create rivers of blood between two nations, because the reason for dialogue would be lost in that case. We shall respond to force if fired upon.

' "In order to pave the way for a peaceful solution, the NLA declares an unlimited, unilateral ceasefire," he [Ali Ahmeti] told Kosovo's RTK television, broadcast from Pristina' (*The Times*, 22 March 2001, p. 14).

'Ali Ahmeti, who has identified himself as a rebel leader in Macedonia, was a founder of the KLA and is closely associated with Mr Haradinaj' (*Independent*, 24 March 2001, p. 14). 'Ali Ahmeti ... was a local commander under Mr Haradinaj in western Kosovo and a key figure in organizing the KLA's gun-running and logistics' (*Guardian*, 24 March 2001, p. 17).

'The concession was offered ... in a television broadcast in neighbouring Kosovo ... There was no immediate government reaction to the offer, made public less than five hours before a midnight Wednesday [21 March] deadline was due to expire' (*IHT*, 22 March 2001, p. 1).

> France is to send a battery of pilotless airplanes to join German and US drones already monitoring the border between Kosovo and Macedonia ... Intelligence gathered by the drones will be passed to Kfor commanders and be shared with the Macedonian authorities.
>
> (*IHT*, 22 March 2001, p. 4)

'A police officer was shot and killed when a group of policemen were attacked in the Albanian quarter of Skopje' (*IHT*, 22 March 2001, p. 4).

22 March 2001: 'Macedonian security forces reclaimed some ethnic Albanian rebel positions in mountains overlooking Tetovo yesterday [22 March] after the government came under pressure from EU officials and opposition parties to abandon an all-out offensive' (*Guardian*, 23 March 2001, p. 15).

> Macedonian army units resumed firing on ethnic Albanian insurgent positions outside ... Tetovo yesterday as the EU intensified diplomatic efforts to end the conflict. However, Macedonian forces showed no sign of launching a threatened offensive against the rebels ... During the day two ethnic Albanians were shot dead at a police checkpoint in Tetovo, apparently after attempting to throw a home-made grenade.
>
> (*FT*, 23 March 2001, p. 10)

> Top EU officials urged the Macedonian government ... to exercise restraint against ethnic Albanian militants and to intensify discussions with elected Albanian politicians about political change ... Macedonian police shot and killed two Albanians carrying grenades.
>
> (*IHT*, 23 March 2001, p. 4)

23 March 2001: 'EU leaders received President Trajkovski of Macedonia at their Stockholm summit … They promised to "stand by Macedonia in this critical moment in its history" and urged it to respond to extremist provocations " in a restrained and proper manner"' (*The Times*, 24 March 2001, p. 17).

'EU leaders have a significant carrot to offer: next month [April] the union is to sign a "stabilization and association agreement" with Macedonia that requires it to work for peaceful resolution of its internal conflicts' (*Guardian*, 24 March 2001, p. 17).

Ibrahim Rugova, Hashim Thaci and Ramush Haradinaj (a former senior field commander in the Kosovo Liberation Army and now leader of the Alliance for the Future of Kosovo) sign a statement:

> We, the leaders of the political parties in Kosovo, call on the extremist groups which have taken up arms on the territory of Macedonia to lay them down immediately, and to return to their homes peacefully. We urge the Macedonian government to show restraint and to address and resolve the grievances through peaceful and democratic means.

(The statement was drafted by the EU: *Guardian*, 24 March 2001, p. 2; *IHT*, 24 March 2001, p. 2.)

Javier Solana: 'We now have clear condemnations of violence from the government in Tirana as well as from Albanian political leaders in Skopje and Pristina' (*IHT*, 24 March 2001, p. 2). (Javier Solana is the EU's High Representative for Common Foreign and Security Policy.)

> Under pressure from the EU … Macedonia has continued only sporadic shelling of rebel positions in the mountainous region north of Tetovo that leads to Kosovo … A defence ministry spokesman acknowledged that Macedonian forces had fired Thursday [22 March] on suspected rebel positions in Kosovo. He said rebels had been preparing a cross-border attack.
>
> (*IHT*, 24 March 2001, p. 2)

> Macedonia claimed it had attacked suspected guerrilla positions inside Kosovo for the first time. A defence spokesman … said the army had pounded positions on Thursday [22 March] because guerrillas were preparing a cross-border attack on Macedonian forces.
>
> (*Independent*, 24 March 2001, p. 14)

'There have been signs that the guerrillas may be scaling down the fighting … They … have not responded to sporadic government shelling for several days' (*Guardian*, 24 March 2001, p. 2).

'Lord Robertson said … it was essential … to "marginalize" ethnic Albanian extremists whose objective – as it had been in Kosovo and southern Serbia – was to provoke reaction that would drag in outside forces' (*Guardian*, 24 March 2001, p. 17).

President Vladimir Putin of Russia (attending the summit of EU leaders):

> Today we are witnessing exactly the same situation in Macedonia [as in Chechenia], where nothing has been done to disarm the terrorists … This is creating the conditions to shake Europe at its very heart and allows no confidence about the security of other countries in the region.
>
> *(IHT*, 24 March 2001, p. 2)

'President Vladimir Putin … urged the West to deal with Albanian insurgents in Macedonia in the way Moscow acted in Chechenia, arguing that the use of force is the only way to prevent a destabilization of the region' (*Independent*, 24 March 2001, p. 14).

24 March 2001:

> Two Ukrainian-supplied helicopter gunships arrived in Macedonia on Friday [23 March] and were promptly pressed into action … [on 24 March], firing rockets at guerrilla targets in the hills. Two transport helicopters from Ukraine also flew in and two more are on their way.
>
> *(Guardian*, 26 March 2001, p. 13)

'Two Mi-24 helicopters flown by Ukrainian pilots … blasted the hillside [above Tetovo] with rockets' (*Telegraph*, 26 March 2001, p. 12). '[The] helicopters [were] a gift from Ukraine' (*The Times*, Supplement, 28 March 2001, p. 3).

25 March 2001:

> The [Macedonian] army launched a concerted tank, artillery and infantry offensive at dawn to flush guerrillas out of the hillside positions … Prime minister Ljubco Georgievski said … that the thrust to 'clear the terrain of terrorists' was 'being carried out successfully and already key positions have been taken' … The offensive Sunday [25 March] was the first time they [the Macedonian forces] had attempted a ground assault … Macedonian forces … by nightfall had taken several strategic villages without any apparent loss of life, Macedonian officials said … Mr Trajkovski and the government are under pressure from the West not to use excessive force against the small band of rebels, believed to number fewer that 1,000 and move quickly to address Albanian concerns with elected Albanian representatives … If the operation continues to go well Monday [26 March], the officials said privately, President Boris Trajkovski will consider a rapid call for all-party negotiations on changes to the constitution and the laws to satisfy long-standing Albanian grievances … The opposition Albanian party called for an immediate ceasefire Sunday and said that it would freeze participation in parliament.
>
> *(IHT*, 26 March 2001, pp. 1, 8)

('The Party for Democratic Prosperity, the main Albanian opposition group, has suspended its participation in parliament and urged the Democratic Party of Albanians to pull out of the governing coalition. But leaders from both parties said they were willing to engage in talks over Albanian demands for equal rights': *The Times*, 27 March 2001, p. 16.)

> Macedonian infantry units, backed by tanks and helicopter gunships, yesterday appeared to have successfully driven ethnic Albanian guerrillas from at least some of their key positions outside the northern town of Tetovo ... The push by government forces was their first bid to use a ground offensive ... Prime minister Ljubco Georgievski said ... 'All the information shows that ... we have taken all key points.'
>
> (*FT*, 26 March 2001, p. 8)

'The operation began with airborne troops being dropped on the mountain slopes above the town as a mortar barrage was unleashed' (*The Times*, 26 March 2001, p. 14).

'The guerrillas are thought to have around 800 men' (*Guardian*, 26 March 2001, p. 13). Javier Solana: 'We are talking about 300 to 400 guerrillas' (*IHT*, 26 March 2001, p. 8).

> 'Belgrade's army and police units yesterday [25 March] moved to take control of the Nato-imposed buffer zone separating Kosovo from Serbia proper. The deployments, made with Nato's blessing ... put Serb forces in control of most of the three-mile wide buffer zone ... The Yugoslav deployment of more than 2,000 police and army troops are proceeding carefully under Nato eyes.
>
> (*Guardian*, 26 March 2001, p. 13)

> Hundreds of Yugoslav troops and Serb police occupied much of the buffer zone yesterday [25 March] after Nato commanders allowed them back ... Up to 2,000 members of the joint task force, comprising Yugoslav army troops and Serb special police, occupied most of the territory along the border between Kosovo and Montenegro and the boundary with Serbia proper.
>
> (*Telegraph*, 26 March 2001, p. 12)

'Yugoslav army and Serbian police troops moved into a large section of a buffer zone around ... [Kosovo] on Sunday [25 March] in a Nato-approved operation' (*IHT*, 26 March 2001, p. 8).

26 March 2001:

> Macedonian government forces on Monday [26 March] continued to move carefully through the hills above Tetovo, consolidating their control of villages held by Albanian rebels for nearly two weeks. But after the artillery and infantry assault Sunday [25 March] most of the fighters of the National

Liberation Army ... had abandoned their positions in the night ... Scattered gunfire and explosions could still be heard in the hills ... The operation ... caused few government or civilian casualties ... The secretary-general, George Robertson, and the EU security chief, Javier Solana, came to ... Skopje on Monday night ... They offered support for the Macedonian state, praise for the proportionate military response to the rebels and encourage-ment to act quickly to show Albanians here that progress is possible without the gun ... Lord Robertson ... [said] that Nato and the West would 'continue to isolate these groups, diplomatically and militarily, until they understand that their insurgency cannot and will not succeed' ... On Monday the Nato forces announced that they would form a new group of about 400 British and Scandinavian soldiers to help patrol the border, which is shared by the American and German zones ... Britain announced Monday that it would also provide some unmanned reconnaissance planes to help with intelligence gathering... Government officials promised that there would be aid to villagers to rebuild any damaged houses.

(*IHT*, 27 March 2001, p. 7)

Prime minister ... Ljubco Georgievski ... said the attack with tanks, artillery, infantry and helicopter-borne commandos had secured government control of rebel-held villages and all key positions ... The government said it would try to find a way to compensate for civilian damage.

(*FT*, 27 March 2001, p. 9)

More than 10,000 Kosovo Albanians gathered in Pristina ... yesterday [26 March] for a demonstration ... to mark the twentieth anniversary of a revolt against Serb rule in Kosovo ... which turned into a demonstration of support for ethnic Albanian rebels in neighbouring Macedonia.

(*FT*, 27 March 2001, p. 9)

27 March 2001:

Javier Solana, the EU's foreign policy and security chief, yesterday [27 March] underlined EU support for inter-ethnic dialogue in Macedonia with a high-profile visit to the town of Tetovo, the main centre of the country's ethnic Albanian minority. After talks with local Albanian political leaders ... [he said] 'We think that the fighting is over and that it is time for dialogue ... An important message to the rebels is that the best thing they can do is lay down their weapons and start a political life.' Mr Solana held talks in the town with Arben Xhaferi, leader of the Democratic Party of Albanians, before walking through the town square arm-in-arm with Ismail Murtezan, mayor ... People started trickling back to houses that had been in the line of fire at the foot of the hills above Tetovo. Late on Monday [26 March] Mr Solana and Lord Robertson ... held two hours of talks with the Macedonian leadership. Lord Robertson praised Macedonia for its handling of the weekend assault while calling on the coalition government ... to follow the military action with a political gesture towards the ethnic Albanian minority ... Neither Macedonian Slav nor Albanian newspapers have used the military campaign as an opportunity to libel the other. The Albanian daily *Fakti* called on the rebels to lay down their arms. 'Their desire to consolidate the rights of Albanians could very easily boomerang with destructive effects for the future of Albanians,' read the paper's editorial. The Slav press was also careful not to offend the ethnic Albanian minority. The panic generated by the crisis has increased momentum for talks that would include all political parties to deal with underlying grievances among the Albanian community.

(Irena Guzelova, *FT*, 28 March 2001, p. 8)

'President Boris Trajkovski declared yesterday [27 March] that Macedonia had vanquished the Albanian rebels, arguing that a military offensive had proved the country was able to defend its fragile democracy' (*Independent*, 28 March 2001, p. 13).

28 March 2001:

Security forces launched another operation Wednesday [28 March] against ethnic Albanian rebels, this time in northern Macedonia, close to the border with Kosovo, in a last effort to rout the guerrillas before political talks begin ... Rebels have been fighting in this area since the conflict began in mid-February ... At least several hundred rebels are thought to be operating in the region ... The government claims to have successfully driven back rebels from the region in western Macedonia around the town of Tetovo, the scene of twelve days of fighting. Now it says there remains only a few villages in the north to deal with ... The rebels have pulled back from some of their positions in western Macedonia and some have been caught crossing into Kosovo by international peacekeepers.

(*IHT*, 29 March 2001, p. ii)

A government spokesman says: 'This is our final operation to establish control of this stretch of land. We want to create conditions for continuation of political dialogue' (*Telegraph*, 29 March 2001, p. 18).

'Some members of the Albanian Democratic Party, which is a partner in the coalition government, also denounced the offensive. One member resigned his seat in parliament' (*Telegraph*, 29 March 2001, p. 18). 'There were reports that an Albanian member of Macedonia's parliament had joined the National Liberation Army in protest at the government's actions' (*Independent*, 29 March 2001, p. 14).

29 March 2001:

Fighting between Macedonian security forces and ethnic Albanian rebels in the north of the country spilled over the border into Kosovo on Thursday

[29 March], killing three people and wounding sixteen. One mortar attack narrowly missed a patrol of international peacekeepers and a British television producer [who held both British and Turkish nationality] working for the Associated Press was among those killed. The Macedonian government denied its forces were responsible for the shelling but said it was sending a special commission to investigate the two incidents, in which mortars landed on a cross-border trail and on the village of Krivenik inside Kosovo. Macedonian security forces were continuing their assault on the village of Gracani to try to drive out a group of rebels who seized the village last week. Gracani is just three kilometres (two miles) from the border and the village of Krivenik ... A unit of international peacekeepers was on patrol Thursday when they spotted a group of rebels on the border. As they moved toward them the group came under mortar fire ... The peacekeepers were just 200 to 300 metres from the rebels when the shells landed. Later in the morning Krivenik came under shell fire ... The two dead civilians were said to be villagers from Krivenik ... The attack followed a stepped-up operation Wednesday [28 March] against rebels near the border with Kosovo. The government ... says there are only a few villages in the north to deal with ... Six soldiers and three policemen have been killed since fighting began in mid-January, according to the government. Three civilians have been killed and six wounded in the same period, an interior ministry spokesman said. Civilian casualties [however] may be higher than that.

(*IHT*, 30 March 2001, p. 5)

'A British journalist and a Kosovo Albanian were killed yesterday [29 March] ... The Macedonian army denied responsibility but witnesses said the firing had come from the direction of forces in hot pursuit of Albanian rebel fighters' (*Independent*, 30 March 2001, p. 13).

30 March 2001:

Macedonia said Friday [30 March] that its latest offensive against ethnic guerrillas near the border with Kosovo was over, apart from mopping up operations ... 'The first part of the operation is finished. We have ahead of us just small operations for cleaning up the terrain, especially for mines ... But it is possible that we will see more armed provocations' ... said an army spokesman ... The government also said that it had completed an investigation and determined Macedonian forces were in no way to blame for mortar rounds that killed a British television journalist and two ethnic Albanians ... Government spokesmen suggested that guerrillas had disguised themselves as Macedonian troops to deliberately shell their ethnic kin in order to blacken the name of the Macedonian forces ... Kosovo Albanians held a protest in a Kosovo border town Friday [30 March], blaming Macedonian forces for the fatal cross-border shelling. About 1,000 people marched up to the mountain village of Krivenik.

(*IHT*, 31 March 2001, p. 2)

President Boris Trajkovski (a Methodist by religion):

> There are no more than 300 thugs and criminals and I am sure that most of Macedonia's Albanians do not support them ... I will not allow any division of this country along ethnic lines ... I have ordered an investigation [of the mortar attack] ... and if we are guilty we will accept responsibility.
>
> (*Telegraph*, 31 March 2001, p. 20)

('Western and local analysts say ... the National Liberation Army ... has had as many as 1,500 members': *IHT*, 2 April 2001, p. 2.)

Arben Xhaferi: 'I think the deadline for opening a dialogue is about four weeks ... If we do not get down to negotiations, take decisions and start implementing them, then the people who are in favour of conflict will step up their activities' (*FT*, 31 March 2001, p. 8).

31 March–1 April 2001:

> Macedonia is to begin a broad political dialogue with the leaders of its Albanian community in response to the EU's attempt to defuse the country's crisis, it emerged at the weekend [31 March–1 April]. The EU's foreign policy chief, Javier Solana, who is holding talks in Skopje today [2 April], is expecting to see a 'Europe Committee' or 'round table' designed to resolve the country's bitter inter-ethnic differences and pave the way for a EU–Macedonian agreement next week. Mr Solana and the EU's commissioner for external relations, Chris Patten, are due to meet President Boris Tarjkovski, opposition leaders and leaders of the Albanian parties ... In return Brussels is offering a 'stabilization and association agreement', to be signed in Luxembourg a week today, the first step towards EU membership ... Macedonia says it has now completed the military operation to drive the insurgents out of their mountain hideouts and across the border into UN-governed Kosovo. 'We have accomplished the goal of driving out the terrorists with minimum casualties,' the prime minister, Ljubco Georgievski, said on Saturday [31 March]. 'It was a textbook operation and was praised by the international community for its precision and efficiency.'
>
> (*Guardian*, 2 April 2001, p. 13)

The EU's top foreign policy officials will today [2 April] fly to Macedonia, hoping to kickstart round-table talks among all political parties and begin a reform programme. The initiative ... [followed] intense negotiations with Macedonian political leaders and [was arrived at] in close consultation with Nato ... Its timing is designed to set in train a reform process before next week's meeting of EU foreign ministers in Luxembourg. They intend to sign a stability and association accord with Macedonia – essentially an economic and political incentive for the republic to start reforms in return for eventually negotiating to join the EU ... Mr Solana insisted the EU would not lead the talks [in Macedonia] but would be the 'facilitator'.

(*FT*, 2 April 2001, p. 7)

2 April 2001:

Macedonia's political leaders opened talks yesterday [2 April] to address the country's ethnic tensions, before another visit to Skopje by Javier Solana. [President] Boris Trajkovski ... invited leaders of all political parties to the talks, but the country's main ethnic Albanian opposition party, the Party for Democratic Prosperity, refused to send a representative, saying the meeting was 'badly organized' ... 'We want the meetings to be well prepared with a definite agenda and we want international mediation' ... a PDP spokesman said. The EU has ruled out playing the role of mediator in the talks. However, Mr Solana, accompanied by Chris Patten, external affairs commissioner, hopes to encourage the creation of a committee including representatives of the ethnic Albanian minority, aimed at easing inter-ethnic tensions in Macedonia. Mr Solana sees this as a necessary step to follow up the country's path-breaking stabilization and association agreement with the EU to be signed next week ... The agreement ... will give Macedonia fully liberalized access to EU markets, financial support, political co-operation with the EU and a 'perspective' of eventual EU membership for Macedonia ... The EU expects to spend Euro 40 million ($35 million) on support for Macedonia this year [2001]. It has committed Euro 475 million in assistance to Macedonia since 1992 of which Euro 329 million had been spent by 31 March ... Macedonian security forces exchanged fire yesterday [2 April] with a group of gunmen.

(*FT*, 3 April 2001, p. 8)

3 April 2001:

The authorities reopened a border crossing [at Blace] that had been closed for nearly a month by fighting ... [It] had been closed for the last twenty-five days to all but military traffic and those with special permission ... The army reported no exchanges of fire overnight. Except for small skirmishes on Saturday [31 March] and Monday [2 April], an army spokesman described the past several days as the longest period of calm since guerrillas and Macedonia's military began their face-off six weeks ago ... He said army reservists who had been called up since the fighting began in mid-February were being demobilized, and fresh ones rotated. The army claims it successfully pushed the rebels back across the border into Kosovo.

(*IHT*, 4 April 2001, p. 5)

Guerrillas from Albania are recruiting ethnic Albanians in western Macedonia to open up a second front ... Police said 'uniformed people' had been seen near Debar, a town of 15,000 people split between ethnic Albanians and Macedonian Moslems. Camps used by the Kosovo Liberation Army have been reopened inside Albania, too.

(*Guardian*, 5 April 2001, p. 13)

5 April 2001: UK foreign secretary Robin Cook flies into Macedonia.

Arben Xhaferi ... yesterday [5 April] expressed continuing pessimism over efforts to reduce tensions with the majority Slav community ... The Democratic Party of Albanians and the Party for Democratic Prosperity, a smaller ethnic Albanian party, want a change in the preamble to the constitution that makes the Macedonians the primary people. They also want local government reform to give Albanian mayors bigger decision-making powers ... Mr Xhaferi ... called for an amnesty for those members of the National Liberation Army involved in the fighting around Tetovo ... [The] secretary-general of the Party for Democratic Prosperity said the party had misgivings about joining the new talks aimed at defusing the inter-ethnic tensions.

(*FT*, 6 April 2001, p. 8)

Mr Cook [said] ... 'We want to help Macedonia defeat the terrorists' ... Mr Xhaferi, though a declared opponent of the National Liberation Army, firmly rejected Mr Cook's use of the word 'terrorist'. He said: 'They cannot be terrorists because they have uniforms and a front line – they have not attacked civilians. We have an uprising.'

(*Independent*, 6 April 2001, p. 14)

6 April 2001: 'The Macedonian authorities rounded up thirty-five ethnic Albanians on Friday in a mop-up operation against insurgents ... The men were detained for illegal possession of weapons in several villages near Tetovo ... Seventeen were later released' (*IHT*, 7 April 2001, p. 2).

9 April 2001:

EU foreign ministers yesterday [9 April] signed a political and economic accord with Macedonia ... The 'stabilization and association agreement' holds out the promise of eventual EU membership to Macedonia if it introduces a package of reforms. But ministers refused Macedonia's request to be immediately recognized as an EU candidate ... Following weeks of shuttle diplomacy between Brussels and Skopje, the government finally agreed to the 'Europe Committee' – a round table spanning most of the political spectrum, which was established to open a debate on institutional reform. Supposed to meet in Skopje today [10 April], the committee has been dogged by divisions and suspicion from among ethnic Albanian parties who claim the government is only paying lip service to reforms ... The rival opposition ethnic Albanian Party for Democratic Prosperity did not attend the signing ceremony … in Luxembourg.

(*FT*, 10 April 2001, p. 9)

Macedonia was told yesterday [9 April] to deliver clear concessions to its ethnic Albanian minority by June … Under … the 'stabilization and association agreement' … the EU will open its markets to 95 per cent of Macedonian exports … A series of short-term political priorities was laid down by the EU yesterday, including moves to open a university with an Albanian language element by August, to set up an Albanian language TV channel and to devolve power throughout the country. The Macedonian government has set up a Europe Committee to co-ordinate reform plans and will produce a progress report for the EU's Gothenburg summit in June.

(*Independent*, 10 April 2001, p. 12)

'The Macedonian prime minister, Ljubco Georgievski, promised to meet the June deadline for improved relations between the ethnically Slav majority and the restive Albanian minority' (*Guardian*, 10 April 2001, p. 14).

'International [OSCE] monitors in Macedonia have complained to the government about the arrest and beating of scores of ethnic Albanian civilians, and the vandalizing of dozens of houses, by security forces "cleaning up" after the offensive against Albanian guerrillas' (*Guardian*, 10 April 2001, p. 14).

A British helicopter crashes in Kosovo near the Macedonian border. Two servicemen die. There was no indication that it was other than an accident.

11 April 2001: 'Macedonia … yesterday [11 April] set up a commission to guarantee equal treatment of its ethnic Albanian majority … The commission will also investigate ways to fight organized crime' (*Guardian*, 12 April 2001, p. 14).

A Russian Kfor soldier is shot dead in Kosovo while patrolling the border with Macedonia. Russia blames the Albanian militants.

12 April 2001: US secretary of state Colin Powell visits Macedonia.

14 April 2001: a British Kfor soldier is killed when his vehicle runs over a land mine while patrolling the border with Macedonia.

28 April 2001:

Macedonia sent reinforcements to an area near Kosovo on Sunday [29 April] after eight members of its security forces were killed [on 28 April] in the first serious violence since an ethnic Albanian revolt was quelled last month [March] … Ethnic Albanian demands that the Macedonian constitution be rewritten to guarantee equal status with majority Slavs is unacceptable to the government, which argues that would lead to a *de facto* division of Macedonia. The militants had threatened to strike again unless their demands were met. In the incident Saturday [28 April] the Macedonian government said that the gunmen attacked a four-vehicle patrol between the villages of Selce and Vejce in north-western Macedonia using grenade launchers, hand grenades and automatic rifles. Four policemen and four soldiers died ... Though no new violence was reported police imposed a 10 p.m. to 5 a.m. curfew for Tetovo ... While officials did not name any particular group, Macedonia media pointed the finger of blame at the National Liberation Army ... President Boris Trajkovski ... a Methodist lay preacher ... will arrive in Washington on Monday with an apparent agreement, brokered by US and European diplomats, to avert more fighting and to unite fractious political parties in a coalition government until elections can be held next February.

(*IHT*, 30 April 2001, p. 6)

'Ethnic Albanian rebels, calling themselves the National Liberation Army, said that they had acted in self-defence because government troops moved on their positions' (*FT*, 1 May 2001, p. 8).

30 April–2 May 2001:

Macedonian Slavs smashed and burned shops owned by ethnic Albanians in Bitola, the country's third largest city late on Monday [30 April]. The rioting in Bitola, about 170 kilometres south-west of Skopje, occurred when a group of Macedonians, mostly younger men, targeted about twenty Albanian-owned stores in the business area ... The violence came just hours after the funerals were held in the city for four policemen who were among eight people killed by ethnic Albanian extremists.

(*FT*, 2 May 2001, p. 8)

'Several hundred Macedonians smashed and burnt shops owned by ethnic Albanians in ... Bitola. Restaurants, cafes and bakeries were also hit' (*The Times*, 2 May 2001, p. 12).

After the funerals in Bitola on Sunday [29 April] about 700 Macedonian Slavs went on the rampage, setting fire to about fifty shops belonging to ethnic Albanians and Macedonian Moslems. In Skopje a man eating in an Albanian pizzeria on Tuesday night [1 May] was shot dead and shots were fired at the Albanian embassy.

(*The Times*, 4 May 2001, p. 16)

'Hundreds of Macedonian Slavs torched ethnic Albanian businesses ... early yesterday [1 May] ... Crowds of mostly young men set on fire and destroyed cafes and shops owned by minority ethnic Albanians or Moslem Macedonians' (*Guardian*, 2 May 2001, p. 13).

The wave of rioting ... left one person dead and at least ten shops demolished, the police said Wednesday [2 May]. The police identified the victim ... who was shot by a group of masked assailants ... late Tuesday [1 May] in a suburb of Skopje ... In ethnically mixed Bitola ... at least ten ethnic

Albanian shops were demolished overnight Tuesday and early Wednesday [2 May] in the second round of rioting in the city. The riots in Bitola … broke out early Tuesday [1 May].

(*IHT*, 3 May 2001, p. 7)

Slavs responded with attacks on ethnic Albanian and Moslem-owned shops and properties in Skopje and in Bitola … One ethnic Albanian was killed in Skopje and a machine gun was fired at the Albanian embassy … Tirana, which has condemned the killings of Macedonian servicemen by NLA guerrillas, protested over the embassy shooting.

(*FT*, 3 May 2001, p. 8)

'On Wednesday [2 May] President Boris Trajkovski won backing from President George Bush for the government's strategy of trying to resolve grievances through dialogue' (*FT*, 4 May 2001, p. 6).

3 May 2001:

Government forces launched an offensive against ethnic Albanian rebels Thursday [3 May] after two soldiers were killed and at least one was kidnapped in an ambush … The security forces were returning from a border patrol when they were fired upon before dawn in Vaksince … near the border with Serbia and Kosovo … The army and police opened the attack 'to eliminate the Albanian terrorists' and ordered people in eleven villages near the city of Kumanovo to evacuate … Later Thursday a dusk-to-dawn curfew was imposed in the Kumanovo region. The rebels issued a statement calling for a ceasefire and urging Mr Trajkovski to start talks … The Macedonian government, however, refuses to negotiate with the rebels, whom it views as terrorists trying to carve out an ethnic Albanian state.

(*IHT*, 4 May 2001, p. 5)

'The Macedonian army attacked … Vaksince … with heavy fire, having first warned civilians to leave the area' (*FT*, 4 May 2001, p. 6).

'The defence ministry said that it had sent tanks and armoured personnel carriers to the area after the rebels declared it a "liberated zone" ' (*The Times*, 4 May 2001, p. 16).

'An Ethnic Slav paramilitary group called the Macedonian Revolutionary Organization Todor Alexandrov claims responsibility for several attacks against ethnic Albanians and … against Albanian shops in the town of Bitola' (*EEN*, 2001, vol. 13, no. 5, p. 6).

4 May 2001:

Macedonian government forces unleashed a fresh assault on ethnic Albanian rebels in the country's north. There were unconfirmed reports of civilian casualties … An army spokesman said there were no civilian casualties … Military officials … accused the insurgents of holding 3,500 people –

mostly women and children – as 'human shields' in the towns of Vaksince and Slupcane.

(*IHT*, 5 May 2001, p. 2)

(It was unclear how many civilians stayed of their own free will and how many were coerced into staying.)

A source inside the interior ministry said it was believed that up to 1,500 civilians were still in Vaksince and up to 2,000 in Slupcane ... predominantly women and children ... The authorities issued a new deadline for civilians to leave ... After it expired the shelling began.

(*Independent*, 5 May 2001, p. 16)

5–6 May 2001:

Helicopter gunships, tanks and mortars were used to pound the villages of Slupcane and Vaksince again yesterday [6 May] after the expiry of a deadline for civilians to leave ... A government spokesman said two police checkpoints were attacked by gunmen north of the city of Tetovo. Rebel chiefs said their forces clashed with the army near the village of Shatka, close to the Kosovo border.

(*Guardian*, 7 May 2001, p. 10)

Macedonian troops pounded ethnic Albanian rebel bastions with heavy artillery on Sunday [6 May] as EU and Nato leaders headed here to try to convince the government not to declare a state of war ... The government said late Saturday [5 May] it would launch consultations on whether to declare a state of war, which would give wide-ranging powers to the security forces and the president ... [The president] would be given the ability to rule by decree and appoint a government. A state of war would also give the government the power to seal the borders, ban public gatherings and impose a curfew ... A declaration of war can occur only with the approval of a two-thirds majority of the 120-member parliament ... 'Rather than talk about a state of war, we should discuss a state of peace,' said the EU foreign policy chief, Javier Solana ... At least seven civilians have been killed since the offensive began Thursday [3 May] ... [according to] OSCE.

(*IHT*, 7 May 2001, p. 5)

Most of those [civilians] still under fire refused the offer of a safe escort out of the area from the International Red Cross yesterday [6 May] ... President Boris Trajkovski is known to oppose the move [to declare a state of war] ... There were fears of civil war when the NLA occupied the hills overlooking Tetovo in March. But, although many young Albanians said then that they backed the guerrillas, few joined up and there was no civilian resistance when the Macedonian army forced the rebels into retreat.

(*Independent*, 7 May 2001, p. 12)

'The authorities in Skopje have called on civilians to leave, promising to hold fire for several hours each morning' (*Independent*, 8 May 2001, p. 11).

'Officially only two civilians have been killed in the onslaught but independent Macedonian media put the toll at at least seven civilians and several guerrillas' (*The Times*, 7 May 2001, p. 110).

7 May 2001:

> Macedonian troops pounded ethnic Albanian rebel positions with helicopter gunships Monday [7 May] but government leaders backed away from declaring a state of war. Instead, diplomatic sources said, Macedonian party leaders were close to forming a national unity government in a new tactic to undermine the insurgents … A senior official of the ethnic opposition party said his was the only party that had not consented to join the unity government. He insisted that the party would not do so until shelling of guerrilla-held villages had stopped. State news agencies earlier said a session of parliament that would have debated whether to introduce a state of war on Tuesday [8 May] had been postponed … The EU and Nato … [had] both argued against declaring it.
>
> (*IHT*, 8 May 2001, p. 5)

George Robertson (Nato secretary-general on a visit to Skopje):

> The message today to the government and all the people of this country is they must go back from the brink before further disaster … [The country is] on the brink of an abyss … The international community will not allow democratic institutions to be undermined by the bunch of murderers stuck in the mountains … [The rebels are] a bunch of murderous thugs whose objective is to destroy a democratic Macedonia and who are using civilians as human shields … [Their aim is to provoke] another Balkan bloodbath … There must be support for the government. There must be no support for those who are choosing violence … A downward spiral of violence into another Balkans bloodbath would produce only misery … There must be a support for a grand coalition, a united front against violence … [There would be] aggressive policing of the Kosovo border.

Arben Xhaferi: 'If they proclaim a state of war, we do not want to stay in the coalition' (*Independent*, 8 May 2001, p. 11).

'The rebel NLA again offered a ceasefire in exchange for direct talks with the government' (*Independent*, 8 May 2001, p. 11).

8 May 2001:

Army forces launched punishing assaults on ethnic Albanian rebel strongholds Tuesday [8 May] as Macedonia's political parties attempted to forge a new coalition government ... But a key ethnic Albanian party later said it would not join unless the army called off its offensive ... The new government, whose platform included moving up 2002 parliamentary elections to January from November, was to include the opposition ethnic Albanian Party for Democratic Prosperity ... But ... the party's vice president announced late Tuesday that it would join only if the military stopped its offensive against the rebels ... [The army] confirmed a second army assault late Tuesday on suspected rebel positions in the hills north of Tetovo ... where fighting raged for weeks earlier this year.

(*IHT*, 9 May 2001, p. 7)

9 May 2001: 'Internationally backed efforts to rapidly form an emergency national unity government in Macedonia failed to clear the last hurdle on Wednesday [9 May] when an ethnic Albanian party said it needed more time to decide' (*IHT*, 10 May 2001, p. 7).

Macedonian forces continued to attack rebels in the northern Macedonian hillside village of Slupcane yesterday [9 May] ... [There were] reports that a ceasefire deal between the government and the main Albanian opposition Party for Democratic Prosperity was close ... Under the ceasefire agreement under discussion the army would stop shelling rebel positions in the northeast and give the NLA fighters seventy-two hours to withdraw from the villages they occupied last week. Security forces would then move in ... So far 7,600 ethnic Albanians have fled to Kosovo, the UN High Commissioner for Refugees said, while some 500 mostly Slavs or Roma had moved further into Macedonia.

(*Independent*, 10 May 2001, p. 15)

10 May 2001:

Macedonian and Serbian leaders pledged to work together to fight ethnic Albanian 'terrorists' active on both sides of the border with Kosovo as the Macedonian army continued its assault Thursday [10 May] on rebels in northern villages ... The government again urged civilians to leave Slupcane and two other villages believed to be guerrilla strongholds, but no one was seen leaving the area ... About 8,000 people, mostly ethnic Albanian women, children and old men, have fled across the border since Monday [7 May], the United Nations refugee agency said Thursday. The Macedonian prime minister, Ljubco Georgievski, and his Serbian counterpart, Zoran Djindjic, met Thursday in Skopje and said they had agreed to co-operate in their efforts to contain ethnic Albanian guerrillas who have also been carrying out attacks in Serbia and ... Kosovo. The Macedonian government and Western observers have linked the rebels in Macedonia with members of the former Kosovo Liberation Army.

(*IHT*, 11 May 2001, p. 5)

Mr Georgievski said a 'prolonged ceasefire would allow the terrorists to regroup'. He gave … the Party for Democratic Prosperity … until today [11 May] to make up its mind about joining the coalition ahead of a parliamentary session tomorrow [12 May] to announce the new government. The EU urged the Party for Democratic Prosperity to join the coalition.

(*Independent*, 11 May 2001, p. 15)

Mr Ljubco Georgievski said the army would continue to shell mountain villages held by ethnic Albanian insurgents because laying down arms would allow the guerrillas to resurface elsewhere in the country for a fresh assault. For its part the ethnic Albanian Party of Democratic Prosperity has demanded a total halt to shelling and an international guarantee that a ceasefire will hold before it joins a coalition.

(*FT*, 11 May 2001, p. 10)

11 May 2001:

The opposition ethnic Albanian Party for Democratic Prosperity [PDP] … agreed Friday [11 May] to join a government of national unity … The party, along with the three other main political parties … two Slav and a larger ethnic Albanian group … would form a broad coalition … The rebels swore they would fight on until they were invited to join talks on settling the grievances of the large Albanian minority … The army has extended its daily ceasefire. But … prime minister Ljubco Georgievski … has so far refused the PDP's calls for a longer truce.

(*IHT*, 12 May 2001, p. 2)

(The opposition Social Democratic Party has already agreed to join the coalition government: *The Times*, 9 May 2001, p. 16. 'A coalition government will include ninety-six of the country's 120 MPs': *Guardian*, 12 May 2001, p. 17.)

13 May 2001: 'The Macedonian parliament met Sunday [13 May] to endorse a national unity government … The Macedonian army and police halted their assault Sunday on the rebels' (*IHT*, 14 May 2001, p. 4).

Macedonia formed a new government of national unity, in which all four main parties are represented, in a fresh effort to prevent civil war. The conservative-national VMRO … and the Social Democrats are joined by two ethnic Albanian parties, the DPA and PDP [Party of Democratic Prosperity] … The new government, which was overwhelmingly approved by parliament yesterday evening, can claim to represent almost 90 per cent of the electorate, on the basis of votes cast at the 1998 general election …

One of the first tasks will be to postpone a census from May to October ... Albanians ... argue that the results of the [1994 population census] were rigged and want stricter international controls this time. Macedonian officials argue that Albanians, lured by relative prosperity, have been pouring into the country from Albania and Kosovo and they say that such people should not have the right to citizenship ... On Saturday [12 May] [an] army spokesman ... said that 'about thirty terrorists' were killed ... An NLA spokesman denied his force had suffered any casualties.

(*Guardian*, 14 May 2001, p. 17)

'A one-time Yugoslav army officer who fought the Serbs in Bosnia and Kosovo has taken over as military commander of ethnic Albanian guerrillas in Macedonia ... Gezim Ostreni is a sixty-year-old native of the Debar region of Macedonia bordering Albania' (*Independent*, 14 May 2001, p. 15).

14 May 2001:

Humanitarian workers evacuated dozens of ethnic Albanian civilians from besieged villages in northern Macedonia, ferrying out women, babies and old men ... The rescue mission organized by the International Committee of the Red Cross came after delegates brokered a short break in the fighting ... Aid workers slipped into a handful of villages surrounding the rebel strongholds of Slupcane, Vaksince and Orizare to pull out about 100 ... civilians ... Many of them said they had not been forced to stay.

(*IHT*, 15 May 2001, p. 5)

15 May 2001:

The new unity government of Macedonia ordered troops to briefly stop attacking ethnic Albanian rebels but warned that they will face a full-scale assault in two days unless they clear out of their strongholds in northern villages. The government gave the ethnic Albanian rebels until noon Thursday [17 May] to lay down their arms and leave the northern Kumanovo area villages or face a wide-scale operation ... Until the deadline state troops will respond only when attacked.

(*IHT*, 16 May 2001, p. 5)

'Macedonia's new government admitted it expected more attacks after rebels fired at a security patrol. But it vowed to crush an insurgency, even if it took time' (*FT*, 16 May 2001, p. 10).

16 May 2001: 'The Macedonian authorities have set themselves a deadline – the EU summit in Gothenburg in early June – to see progress in the inter-ethnic talks ... In the hills ... north-east of the capital fighting broke out before dawn yesterday [16 May]' (*Guardian*, 17 May 2001, p. 11).

17 May 2001:

Macedonian government forces held their fire Thursday [17 May], deciding not to enforce a deadline that had been set for the surrender of ethnic Albanian rebels hiding in isolated northern villages. Sporadic clashes … were reported early Thursday before the expiration of the noon deadline. But the front line, near Macedonia's border with Kosovo, remained generally quiet past the deadline.

(*IHT*, 18 May 2001, p. 5)

'President Boris Trajkovski said the ceasefire was working, as ethnic Albanian civilians were leaving the villages' (*Independent*, 18 May 2001, p. 14).
18 May 2001:

Breaking an unofficial ceasefire, army artillery Friday [18 May] targeted rebel positions near the border with Kosovo. But the guns fell silent after six volleys, suggesting that the government was honouring a pledge to act with restraint against ethnic Albanian insurgents. The shells were fired at the villages of Slupcane, Orizare and Vaksince in the Kumanovo region.

(*IHT*, 19 May 2001, p. 2)

21 May 2001:

Heavy fighting raged between Macedonian forces and ethnic Albanian guerrillas Monday [21 May] … Tanks, artillery and combat helicopters were in action against insurgents in a cluster of villages in north-eastern Macedonia … Battles were concentrated on Vaksince and Slupcane and return fire from the village of Vaksince was the heaviest reporters had witnessed in eighteen days of fighting.

(*IHT*, 22 May 2001, p. 5)

'A defence ministry spokesman … said at least 1,000 civilians remain in the northern besieged villages, although hundreds have been evacuated by the International Committee of the Red Cross' (*Independent*, 22 May 2001, p. 13).
22 May 2001:

The area of northern Macedonia occupied by guerrillas of the NLA was reported to be calm yesterday [22 May] … There are fears that the rebels retreating from the Presevo valley [in Serbia] will join the force in Macedonia. Kfor has promised an amnesty for rebels who hand themselves in. They are then released.

(*Independent*, 23 May 2001, p. 15)

23 May 2001:

The echo of artillery fire returned to the hills around … Tetovo yesterday [23 May] as fighting between Albanian rebels and government forces spread on to a second front. The government of Bulgaria called for an international force to be sent to Macedonia to help defeat the rebels ... The Tetovo area has been largely peaceful in recent weeks.

(*Independent*, 24 May 2001, p. 20)

25 May 2001:

The USA and the EU yesterday [24 May] denounced an agreement between Albanian guerrillas and ethnic Albanian political parties in the governing coalition in Macedonia, even though a senior US diplomat negotiated it. The Macedonian government has also expressed its outrage at the deal, under which the rebels agreed to withdraw in return for an amnesty and a veto over political decisions involving ethnic Albanian rights ... The US diplomat, Robert Frowick, is serving as the personal envoy of Mercea Geoana, the Romanian foreign minister and current chairman of OSCE ... The Macedonian army yesterday [24 May] stepped up its attacks on the guerrillas ... The guerrillas reported that seven civilians had been killed.

(*FT*, 25 May 2001, p. 10)

'The US embassy in Skopje condemned the deal and in Brussels Lord Robertson, the Nato secretary-general, said the rebels had no place in negotiations' (*The Times*, 25 May 2001, p. 14).

Ethnic Albanian political leaders ... refused to repudiate the deal ... Nato, the EU and the US embassy in Skopje all denounced the deal ... Some Balkan specialists suspect Mr Frowick was also acting on behalf of the USA, which considers EU efforts to promote dialogue in Skopje are failing to make progress.

(*FT*, 26 May 2001, p. 8)

'Mr Frowick's efforts culminated in a statement signed by the two main ethnic Albanian parties in Macedonia and the NLA. It called for the NLA's rehabilitation, its integration into civilian life and its involvement in round table political talks' (*FT*, 28 May 2001, p. 6).

According to European diplomats, the peace deal called for the rebels to halt fighting in exchange for amnesty guarantees that were made by the ethnic Albanian coalition partners. The rebels would also gain the right to veto future political decisions about the scope of ethnic Albanian rights. The accord was apparently sealed at a meeting Wednesday [23 May] between the leaders of the two ethnic Albanian parties in Macedonia's coalition government and Ali Ahmeti, who is the only known political representative of the NLA ... The leaders of the two [ethnic Albanian] parties [in government], Arben Xhaferi and Imer Imeri ... had so far refused to back away from their decision to negotiate with the guerrillas ... The EU ... urged the two Albanian parties to distance themselves from the rebels and to renounce the secret peace document … The EU defended the Macedonian government's right to use force in suppressing the NLA rebels, but has urged that force be applied with moderation. The United States has also condemned the agreement, insisting that there could be no place at an inter-ethnic negotiating table for the ethnic Albanian fighters known as the NLA … The secretary-general of Nato, George Robertson, echoed that criticism.

(*IHT*, 26 May 2001, p. 2)

'[Under the deal] the guerrillas would not attend talks with Macedonian Slav leaders' (*Guardian*, 29 May 2001, p. 19).

[A] rebel commander … wrote … that six cellars had been hit, killing ten people … Despite repeated appeals to leave, only a few thousand villagers have fled the area of conflict near the Belgrade–Athens highway … The inter-ethnic government coalition of Slavs and Albanians formed 13 May … [was] reeling Thursday [24 May] from revelations that the two ethnic Albanian parties in government had made a secret agreement with the so-called NLA … apparently brokered with the help of a diplomat from OSCE.

(*IHT*, 25 May 2001, p. 5)

'Western intelligence sources estimate that the NLA has 2,000 guerrillas. Rebel commanders claim 6,000 men' (*Guardian*, 25 May 2001, p. 14).
25 May 2001:

About 3,000 … ethnic Albanian civilians … fled Friday [25 May] from rebel-held villages in north-eastern Macedonia as government forces … continued to pound mountainside hamlets … A military spokesman said that as many as 100 ethnic Albanians from southern Serbia were attempting to move into Macedonia with heavy arms.

(*IHT*, 26 May 2001, p. 2)

The Macedonian army continued yesterday [25 May] with an assault launched on Thursday [23 May] on ethnic Albanian villages … There were unconfirmed reports of up to sixty civilian deaths … The United Nations refugee agency reported that more than 2,000 refugees had fled across the border into neighbouring Serbia and others into Kosovo.

(*FT*, 26 May 2001, p. 8)

26–7 May 2001: 'Government forces took the rebel stronghold of Vaksince [on 26 May] and last night [27 May] launched a heavy barrage against the village of Matejce.' There are reports of refugees being beaten by Macedonian forces (*Telegraph*, 28 May 2001, p. 13).
'There were unconfirmed reports that as many as sixty civilians died in the recent fighting. The police said that dozens were likely to have been killed but

insisted that they were all rebels, some of them in civilian clothing' (*IHT*, 28 May 2001, p. 5).

A spokesman for the interior ministry confirmed yesterday [27 May] that the commanding officer of the 'Tigers' police anti-terrorist unit and his deputy had been suspended after they complained that they were being sent into battle without adequate support and had refused to obey orders. The unit had been confined to barracks.

(*The Times*, 28 May 2001, p. 10)

'On Friday [25 May] a commander in the special police forces was sacked for ordering a retreat from a village after three of his men were injured' (*Guardian*, 29 May 2001, p. 8).

28 May 2001:

EU security chief Javier Solana ... failed to persuade political leaders in Macedonia to resume talks Monday [28 May] ... [He] insisted, however, that Macedonian Slav and ethnic Albanian political leaders were 'very close' to resolving a political deadlock ... Speaking ahead of a Nato foreign ministers' conference in Budapest ... George Robertson [said that] ... 'There should be no place at the negotiating table for those who prefer the bullet to the ballot box.'

(*IHT*, 29 May 2001, p. 4)

29 May 2001:

Macedonian leaders declared Tuesday [29 May] that the country's fragile government would remain intact, pledging to resume talks ... Under the agreement brokered by Mr Solana, the deal with the rebels was annulled because the international community had reacted negatively to it, the statement said.

(*IHT*, 30 May 2001, p. ii, supplementary page)

'About 18,000 have fled to Kosovo and the rest of Serbia since fighting resumed a month ago, said ... [a] spokesman to the UNHCR' (*Telegraph*, 30 May 2001, p 15).

'Nato and the EU ... are pressing the government to introduce an amnesty for ethnic Albanian rebels belonging to the NLA' (*FT*, 31 May 2001, p. 10).

'Nato foreign ministers meeting in Budapest urged military constraint' (*Independent*, 31 May 2001, p. 14).

At the first set-piece ministerial meeting between the EU and Nato, Macedonia's government was assured of support for its statehood and promised that no one expected it to treat with Albanian gunmen. It was also told to be 'proportionate' in its response to violence and take due regard for civilian life. The [foreign] ministers called for a progress report, by the end of June, on a set of reforms designed to reassure Macedonia's ethnic Albanians.

(*The Economist*, 2 June 2001, p. 45)

31 May 2001:

In a major policy shift prime minister Ljubco Georgievski said Thursday [31 May] that Macedonia could rewrite its constitution to upgrade the position of the ethnic Albanians ... The government said earlier that such constitutional changes would lead to a division of Macedonia into a part dominated by Albanians and another by Slavs ... Mr Georgievski said the constitution might be rewritten to declare the ethnic Albanians a constituent nation and their language official.

(*IHT*, 1 June 2001, p. 5)

Albanian would 'most probably' be declared a second official language and the Macedonian Orthodox Church would lose its privileged place in the constitution ... The Macedonian government is offering an amnesty to the ethnic Albanian gunmen ... The amnesty was offered by President Boris Trajkovski ... All except those who organized the insurgency or killed Macedonian police or soldiers would qualify, and a safe corridor would be provided for them to retreat to Kosovo ... The government originally described the NLA as 'invaders from Kosovo'. The change has come after pressure from Nato and ... Javier Solana.

(*Guardian*, 1 June 2001, p. 13)

1 June 2001:

President Boris Trajkovski ... offered an amnesty Friday [1 June] to ethnic Albanian militants if they lay down their weapons ... [The] offer came as the fighting moved to Tetovo ... Eight rebels were killed Friday in fighting with troops just outside Tetovo ... an army spokesman said ... Arben Xhaferi said after a meeting with Mr Trajkovski ... the plan involved demilitarizing the rebels and reintegrating them into society ... Imer Imeri said the plan included an amnesty for those who have not committed criminal acts or organized the rebellion. A special corridor reportedly would be formed with the help of Nato to allow the more radical militants to cross into neighbouring Kosovo.

(*IHT*, 2 June 2001, p. 9)

3 June 2001:

Army helicopters pounded northern rebel positions and ground troops fought insurgents at close quarters Sunday [3 June] as the president prepared to discuss his peace offer with leading politicians in the government coalition. Military officials said troops used their 'entire combat arsenal, including the helicopters' to respond to rebel attacks from the northern villages of Matecje and Slupcane. President Boris Trajkovski called a meeting Sunday of key Albanian and Slav political leaders. He was expected to discuss an amnesty offer if rebels ended the three-month insurgency.

(*IHT*, 4 June 2001, p. 7)

Ljubco Georgievski said in a television interview late Sunday [3 June] that the broad-based coalition government ... may be a failure. 'The government is barely functioning,' Mr Georgievski said. Soon after he spoke fresh clashes erupted just outside of Tetovo ... Macedonian troops clashed with rebels near [Tetovo] ... early Monday [4 June], just hours after the country's prime minister suggested that early elections may be needed to end a political impasse and the ongoing ethnic Albanian insurgency.

(*IHT*, 5 June 2001, p. 5)

6 June 2001:

Macedonia threatened to declare a state of war Wednesday [6 June] after five soldiers were killed in a rebel ambush the night before [5 June] ... One of the men killed was an ethnic Albanian – Albanians also serve in the army and police ... [On 6 June] a gunman opened fire on the office of President Boris Trajkovski in a drive-by attack. No one was wounded ... The president came under criticism for the first time from members of his own party over the handling of the conflict ... It criticized Mr Trajkovski for not carrying through with a promise to first fight the rebels and then progress to talks ... Prime minister Ljubco Georgievski ... called for full military mobilization and emergency powers.

(*IHT*, 7 June 2001, pp. 1, 4)

'Gunmen fired two shots at the Macedonian president's office in Skopje Wednesday evening ... No one was injured' (*IHT*, 8 June 2001, p. 4).

Declaring a state of war would give President Trajkovski emergency powers to rule by decree. But war can only be declared with the support of a two-thirds majority in parliament ... The EU quickly intervened to urge Macedonia not to declare war.

(*FT*, 7 June 2001, p. 9)

Mr Georgievski wanted to declare a state of war in April, but backed down under pressure from the EU and Nato ... Already Slavs and Albanians will not venture into each other's areas in Skopje ... The military's most elite troops – its force of about fifty commandos – refused to obey when they were ordered to storm a village, saying they could not complete the mission without heavy casualties.

(*Independent*, 7 June 2001, p. 12)

One of the dead was an ethnic Albanian conscript … A spokesman for … prime minister Ljubco Georgievski … also called for a declaration of loyalty by the Albanian political leaders … Mr Georgievski has also rowed back on a speech he made last week which offered to change the constitution and give Albanians more rights. He now says he was speaking 'cynically' to show what pressure Macedonia was under from the international community and what 'blackmail' it faced from the Albanian parties … [The army has acquired] from Ukraine four Russian-made helicopter gunships … The two main Macedonian parties are already jockeying for votes in early elections due in January [2002]. Suggesting that the election should be advanced to this September [2001], Mr Georgievski started to blame the Social Democrats – even before the latest ambush – for not letting him order former military action.

(*Guardian*, 7 June 2001, p. 12)

7 June 2001:

Macedonian Slavs in a southern town [Bitola] smashed dozens of houses and shops belonging to ethnic Albanians before ending their rampage early Thursday [7 June]. The police said about 100 houses were damaged and a mosque was set on fire in the riots that began Wednesday in Bitola … Thousands of Macedonian Slav rioters rampaged in Bitola despite a dusk to dawn curfew. Ten homes – including one owned by the deputy health minister, an ethnic Albanian – were set on fire. Three of the slain soldiers came from the city … [Bitola has] a mixed community of Slavic Christians, Slavic Moslems and ethnic Albanians. The Albanians, at about 3 per cent, are Bitola's smallest group … Sporadic clashes with the rebels continued early Thursday on two fronts, near … Tetovo … and near Kumanovo.

(*IHT*, 8 June 2001, p. 4)

The Human Rights Watch organization accused Macedonian police yesterday [7 June] of taking part in riots it said were clearly aimed at forcing ethnic Albanians to flee the southern city of Bitola … Many [Albanians] … fled [Bitola] after the first round of riots … after eight Macedonian police and soldiers were killed in April.

(*Independent*, 8 June 2001, p. 17)

8 June 2001:

The Macedonian government intensified its offensive against ethnic Albanian rebels on Friday [8 June], ignoring a rebel offer for a ceasefire …

Albanian rebels ... offered a unilateral ceasefire from midnight Thursday, asking for political dialogue and amnesty for their fighters ... The rebels ... even appeared in uniform in an outlying suburb of Skopje ... Hundreds of people were fleeing homes in the Skopje suburb of Aracinovo ... Prime minister Ljubco Georgievski withdrew his call for a declaration of war ... [but] continued his fighting talk on Friday: 'Macedonia must mercilessly confront the terrorists. Any delay would only mean a deepening and spreading of the fighting. Without destroying them first, it is not possible to start a political dialogue' ... President Boris Trajkovski said he was preparing a peace plan to present to parliament that would offer a partial amnesty to rebel fighters to persuade them to withdraw and end the conflict ... Mr Trajkovski's peace plan ... appears to offer an amnesty to rebel fighters but not their leaders ... 'Local leaders put under pressure to join the rebel groups have to be given the chance to pull out. This plan gives them the chance to lay down their arms and reintegrate into society,' said Mr Trajkovski.

(*IHT*, 9 June 2001, p. 2)

'Local radio reported that thirty masked guerrillas entered the village of Aracinovo, just 10 kilometres from the capital' (*FT*, 9 June 2001, p. 14).

'Rebels took up positions within range of the airport' (*Telegraph*, 9 June 2001, p. 23).

9–10 June 2001:

[After] the takeover of ... Aracinovo ... 10 kilometres (six miles) east of Skopje ... a rebel commander ... Hoxha ... said in an interview Saturday [9 June] that his battalion had brought a number of 120mm artillery pieces ... and might fire them at the nation's largest petroleum refinery, the capital and its airport unless the military stopped its indiscriminate shelling of nearby ethnic Albanian villages where the rebels are based ... The rebels issued their threats as Javier Solana ... obtained a government promise to begin a cross-ethnic dialogue on political reform within two weeks.

(*IHT*, 11 June 2001, p. 2)

'The rebel commander said: 'I have given an ultimatum to Georgievski. He has until tomorrow morning to stop the bombardments. I will attack police stations, the parliament – everything I can – with 120mm mortars' (*Guardian*, 11 June 2001, p. 11).

'Albanian rebels killed a Macedonian soldier ... yesterday [10 June] ... The UN said about 7,000 people had crossed the border into ... Kosovo ... over the previous forty-eight hours. That brought the total in Kosovo from Macedonia to 29,000 since ... February' (*FT*, 11 June 2001, p. 9).

'The UNHCR estimated that at least 10,000 people ... had crossed since Friday [8 June]' (*Guardian*, 11 June 2001, p. 11).

11 June 2001:

Macedonia's government and ethnic Albanian rebels both declared brief
ceasefires on Monday [11 June] for the first time in their four-month conflict
... [The president's] national security adviser ... said the government's
action was an effort to alleviate what he called two humanitarian disasters –
water shortages in the city of Kumanovo and food shortages in the villages
affected by fighting ... [He] denied that the government was reacting to the
rebels' threat to bombard Skopje unless the army stopped attacking villages
north-east of the capital ... The rebels responded by declaring a twenty-
four-hour ceasefire of their own, running until mid-day Tuesday [12 June].
It was the first time that both sides officially declared concurrent ceasefires
since the conflict started.

(*IHT*, 12 June 2001, p. 5)

12 June 2001:

Macedonia's government on Tuesday [12 June] gave formal backing to a
Nato-endorsed peace plan to end an ethnic Albanian insurgency as a fragile
ceasefire appeared to hold ... The plan ... endorsed by the EU and Nato ...
envisages disarming the insurgents and negotiating a lasting settlement
between the majority Slav population and the ethnic Albanian minority ...
[But a problem is] the government's refusal to negotiate with the rebels ...
Hours after that [the rebels'] deadline there were no reports of major
clashes. But the truce was disrupted overnight, when rebels fired on a police
truck ... They later said the attack was a mistake ... Tuesday afternoon
Kumanovo [still] had no water and vehicles carrying ... food [were] turned
back to Skopje, apparently because checkpoint troops objected to reporters
in the convoy.

(*IHT*, 13 June 2001, p. 6)

Government officials accused ethnic Albanian politicians of trying to gain
political capital out of the convoy by insisting that journalists should be
allowed to accompany it ... [One of the government officials] said the NLA
had demanded the presence of journalists to prove that they had not cut off
the water supply [from a reservoir] ... Yesterday [12 June] the government
announced that an elite unit of soldiers and police would soon be ready for
action ... The NLA says it will refuse to endorse any peace plan unless it is
involved in the talks, a condition ruled out by Skopje ... The UNHCR says
that more than 20,000, mainly ethnic Albanian women and children, have
entered Kosovo since Friday [8 June].

(*Guardian*, 13 June 2001, p. 12)

Aid agencies attempted to ferry supplies to civilians ... Ethnic Albanian
guerrillas said they would extend a brief truce beyond a noon GMT dead-

line, provided the army held fire to allow the first big relief convoy access ...
Rebels said they would allow taps to be turned on at a reservoir behind their
lines only after emergency aid was delivered ... A rebel commander ... said
his men were acting in self-defence when they fired machine-guns at
policemen.

(*Independent*, 13 June 2001, p. 15)

'Leaders of Macedonia's main political parties are to meet in the southern
town of Ohrid this week ... to try to agree political changes' (*FT*, 13 June 2001,
p. 9).

'The Macedonian army's chief of staff resigned yesterday [12 June] ...
[because of what he described as the] "bad morale of his troops" and because
he felt personally responsible for the loss of twenty-six young soldiers' (*The Times*,
13 June 2001, p. 16).

13 June 2001:

Nato secretary-general George Robertson is scheduled to travel to Skopje ...
on Thursday [14 June] to discuss the plan ... The leaders of all four major
Macedonian political parties will then confer about it at a lakeside retreat
this weekend. The heart of the plan would be a proposed joint statement by
the political leaders on the substance and timetable for changes meant to
elevate the status of Macedonia's ethnic Albanian minority ... Among the
pledges being considered is a proposed amendment to the Macedonian
constitution that would help grant equal status to Albanians and the
majority Slavs. The constitution's preamble now describes the country as a
home to Slavic Macedonians. Officials also said the plan could include a
series of new government commitments to rebuild towns destroyed by
fighting, construct new schools and permit expanded international monitoring of the Macedonian police and army. These forces have been
implicated frequently in human rights abuses and the president ...
appointed a new joint commander Wednesday [13 June] ... The plan being
drawn up is similar to another one drawn up last month [May] that was
signed in Prizren, Kosovo, by the rebel's political director, Ali Ahmeti. That
plan was drafted by an American diplomat, Robert Frowick, and the editor
of a leading Kosovo newspaper, Veton Surroi, in consultation with the
leaders of Macedonia's ethnic Albanian political parties ... According to
officials familiar with its contents, it called for a ceasefire followed by a
month-long period of rebel disarmament, plus a government-approved
amnesty for former fighters. The arms were to be handed over to local
politicians and international officials, who would in turn pass them along to
the government. Police and army forces would reestablish control of rebel-
held territory under international supervision ... Low-level skirmishes are
continuing ... On Wednesday [13 June] ... government officials and rebel
leaders continued to wrangle about the repair of damaged pumps that
supply water to ... Kumanovo. The rebels, who control the territory where

the pumps are situated, have offered safe passage to repair crews only if the government fulfils certain conditions, such as allowing journalists to visit the war-damaged areas now blockaded by government forces, officials said. The government refused ... On Tuesday night [12 June] assailants ... shot and killed ... an ethnic Albanian activist.

(*IHT*, 14 June 2001, p. 4)

14 June 2001:

Macedonia officially asked Nato on Thursday [14 June] to help disarm ethnic Albanian guerrillas ... while pledging to discuss Albanian demands to change the country's constitution ... But the government rejected as 'absolutely unacceptable' a rival plan by the NLA calling for a general amnesty, a place in reform talks and the chance to join the army and police. Mr Trajkovski asked George Robertson to send Nato troops to oversee the disarmament of the NLA, whose members, under his proposal, will be given an amnesty only if they are Macedonian citizens and did not help organize the escalating rebellion ... Mr Trajkovski said a round of political talks with the four parties, two Slav and two ethnic Albanian, in the unity coalition would start immediately in Skopje ... Mr Robertson said the Macedonian army would extend its ceasefire for the duration of the weekend talks ... Mr Robertson said there was no place at the bargaining table for the rebels ... Fighting flared in the north-west.

(*IHT*, 15 June 2001, p. 5)

'The Macedonian government yesterday [14 June] asked Nato to consider monitoring a voluntary disarmament programme for the rebels ... The rebels have also called for a Nato deployment in Macedonia' (*FT*, 15 June 2001, p. 7).

'[The] conflict has already displaced about 70,000 people and reduced five villages to ruins, though it has claimed relatively few lives – perhaps two or three dozen' (*The Economist*, 16 June 2001, p. 51).

15 June 2001:

Yesterday [15 June] rebel commanders offered to extend a unilateral ceasefire by another twelve days ... The number of violations of the three-day-old ceasefire are mounting ... A key rebel demand is that Nato deploys peacekeepers throughout Macedonia to monitor the implementation of any deal.

(*Telegraph*, 16 June 2001, p. 20)

'Ethnic Albanian rebels yesterday extended a twelve-day truce with Macedonian forces until 27 June ... Meanwhile coalition government parties ... began a two-day summit in parliament in Skopje to try to reach a peace deal' (*FT*, 16 June 2001, p. 9).

The NLA said the ceasefire would be extended to 27 June 'to create conditions for dialogue' ... Government officials said each side was preparing for constitutional reforms, including wider use of the Albanian language and changes to the constitution's preamble mentioning Albanians as a minority and not as one of two 'founding peoples' ... Prime minister Ljubco Georgievski remains a wild card. Mr Georgievski has expressed support for the peace plan, but as his political power has weakened he has adopted a more radical tone. He is suspected of supporting the formation of paramilitary groups and the arming of Macedonian Slav reservists in recent days.

(*IHT*, 16 June 2001, p. 2)

President George W. Bush (speaking in Poland): 'America's role is important, and we will meet our obligations. We went into the Balkans together, and we will come out together. Our goal must be to hasten the arrival of that day' (*IHT*, 16 June 2001, p. 4).

16 June 2001: 'The EU has agreed to appoint a special envoy to Macedonia to oversee implementation of political reforms' (*FT*, 18 June 2001, p. 6).

17 June 2001: 'Negotiations in Macedonia ended a third day of talks with no word on whether a deal ... was any closer' (*IHT*, 18 June 2001, p. 4).

Macedonia allowed food supplies into areas held by ethnic Albanian rebels while politicians remained locked away for a third day yesterday [17 June] ... After five days of haggling over terms, the government let aid agencies ferry food and medicines late on Saturday night [16 June] to civilians holed up behind civilian lines in exchange for access to a reservoir to reconnect a town's water supply after eleven days without.

(*FT*, 18 June 2001, p. 6)

18 June 2001: 'Macedonia yesterday [18 June] reestablished diplomatic relations with mainland China, just two years after switching ties to Taiwan ... leaving the island's government with just twenty-eight diplomatic partners and only one – the Vatican – in Europe' (*IHT*, 19 June 2001, p. 12).

20 June 2001:

The Nato allies announced Wednesday that they were prepared to send up to 3,000 troops to Macedonia ... for a limited time ... to help disarm ethnic Albanian rebels once a peace agreement is reached that ensures a cessation of hostilities ... The disarmament force would be a 'coalition of willing nations' answering a call for assistance by the Macedonian government. It would not require a United Nations Security Council mandate ... Despite Nato's announcement, the prospects for a quick peace appeared dim as ... President Boris Trajkovski said in Skopje that peace talks between Slav and ethnic Albanian representatives had reached an impasse ... because of what he described as unreasonable demands by the ethnic Albanians. 'They have dramatically changed their standpoint, practically asking for a two-nation state ... They have no sincere intention of conducting a dialogue and finding effective and acceptable political solutions,' he said ... Mr Trajkovski ... said the ethnic Albanian negotiators appear to be holding out 'in the expectation that the international community will intervene and support their unrealistic political demands, which would included cementing terrorist positions in temporarily occupied territories'.

(*IHT*, 21 June 2001, pp. 1, 6)

'The [Nato] operation involves ... a battalion of 3,000 to 5,000 soldiers' (*FT*, 21 June 2001, p. 9).

The breakdown of talks coincided with fresh outbreaks of fighting early yesterday [20 June] between rebels and government forces around the rebel-held town of Aracinovo, three miles from Skopje. There were also clashes around Slupcane ... Yesterday the Albanian political parties appealed for international mediation.

(*Telegraph*, 21 June 2001, p. 18)

Many guerrillas are known to be veterans of the Kosovo Liberation Army ... Some rebels are suspected of trying to foment a broader conflict to further nationalistic aims of carrying out a Greater Albania that would unite ethnic communities from Kosovo, Macedonia and Albania itself.

(*IHT*, 21 June 2001, p. 6)

21 June 2001: 'A government official ... said the logjam was over ethnic Albanian demands for a federal structure for Macedonia' (*IHT*, 22 June 2001, p. 5).

Government sources said yesterday [21 June] that deadlock was due to the Albanian leader Arben Xhaferi insisting on a federal structure for Macedonia ... Sporadic fighting between government troops and the NLA guerrillas continued yesterday ... Bulgaria confirmed yesterday [21 June] that its army special operations units ... were conducting an exercise near the Macedonian border.

(*Guardian*, 22 June 2001, p. 14)

'Nato sources said the ethnic Albanians in Macedonia appeared to be hoping that an intervention force would be sent to police a division of the country' (*The Times*, 22 June 2001, p. 17).

'The present blockage arises from demand from the ethnic Albanian parties which want to lay down a series of policy areas within which they would have a veto' (*Independent*, 22 June 2001, p. 13). 'The Albanian side demanded the right to veto all laws ... The constitution says Macedonia is the nation-state of the Slav majority' (*Independent*, 23 June 2001, p. 15).

22 June 2001:

> Macedonian forces launched a heavy offensive Friday [22 June] against Albanian rebel positions just north of Skopje ... The main offensive was aimed against the settlement of Aracinovo, five miles (eight kilometres) from the city centre ... The military also turned their guns against villages further north ... As commander-in-chief of Macedonian forces, the president would have ordered today's military operation ... The renewed fighting caused another surge of refugees fleeing into Kosovo. The United Nations refugee agency said 1,450 Albanians had crossed into Kosovo from Thursday, bringing the total since February to more than 50,000 ... Nato's secretary-general, George Robertson, denounced renewed fighting.
>
> (*IHT*, 23 June 2001, pp. 1, 4)

24 June 2001:

> Javier Solana ... said the two sides had agreed a ceasefire ... Both the government official and the rebels confirmed a limited ceasefire ... A rebel spokesman ... said that fighters in Aracinovo had received orders to pull ... [out of Aracinovo on condition] that Nato observers are deployed in Aracinovo and that the Macedonian army does not enter the town ... Immediately after the ceasefire was announced a delegation of Nato and Western representatives headed into the besieged town.
>
> (*IHT*, 25 June 2001, p. 7)

'Local NLA commanders have agreed to pull back their forces on condition that they are allowed to take all their weapons with them ... Villagers left behind will have their safety guaranteed by foreign observers from OSCE and other international bodies' (*The Times*, 25 June 2001, p. 10).

'A group called Macedonian Paramilitary 2000 threatened imminent vigilante attacks on Albanians' (*Guardian*, 25 June 2001, p. 10).

25 June 2001:

> Ethnic Albanian militants pulled out of ... Aracinovo ... Monday [25 June] under a Nato-brokered deal ... Buses headed out of Aracinovo carrying rebels ... The alliance then sent at least four trucks to the village to take out weapons belonging to the rebels ... The EU told the country's foreign minister ... Ilinka Miteva ... not to count on new financial aid unless the government and ethnic Albanian opponents settle their differences ... The EU ministers appointed former defence minister François Leotard of France as resident envoy to Macedonia, reporting to the EU foreign affairs chief, Javier Solana.
>
> (*IHT*, 26 June 2001, p. 7)

Nato and EU officials yesterday [25 June] escorted four buses carrying ethnic Albanian rebels out of the village of Aracinovo near Skopje under the terms of a ceasefire brokered by Javier Solana ... Nato also sent four vehicles into the village to collect weapons left behind by the rebels ... US troops in four-wheel-drive vehicles and armoured personnel carriers deployed in the area after the rebel withdrawal ... The buses were expected to carry the rebels to other rebel-held villages near the Kosovo border.

(*FT*, 26 June 2001, p. 6)

Albanian guerrillas, accompanied by American Kfor troops, withdrew from a strategic village while keeping hold of their weapons. They were not compelled to leave the country but merely to move back into the hills ... On Monday [25 June] Macedonian demonstrators ... demanded the resignation of President Trajkovski ... They burnt the flag of the EU.

(*The Times*, 27 June 2001, p. 14)

'The crowd included armed police reservists and soldiers' (*The Times*, 30 June 2001, p. 16).

'The ceasefire brokered by the EU allowed several hundred rebels to move from the village of Aracinovo ... to Nikustak, four miles further north' (*Guardian*, 27 June 2001, p. 18).

'About 250 Albanian rebels ... [were evacuated] from ... Aracinovo in buses belonging to American Kfor troops' (*Independent*, 28 June 2001, p. 1). 'On Monday [25 June] up to 500 rebels left the area, accompanied by a US army escort' (*Guardian*, 28 June 2001, p. 12). 'More than 300 guerrillas ... were bused by the US army out of the village' (*Telegraph*, 28 June 2001, p. 18). 'Nato peace-keepers extricated 300 militants' (*IHT*, 29 June 2001, p. 9). '[The] president allowed 350 ethnic Albanian guerrillas to retreat from a village without surrendering their arms' (*FT*, 30 June 2001, p. 2).

Aracinovo was now a demilitarized zone ... Last night [25 June] at least 3,000 nationalist demonstrators, some throwing stones, gathered in front of President Boris Trajkovski's residence in Skopje to demand his resignation. They were angry that he appears to have abandoned the military opposition to the rebels.

(*Telegraph*, 26 June 2001, p. 11)

'Protesters ... [were] backed by police and army reservists' (*Telegraph*, 27 June 2001, p. 13).

'The police ... did not intervene to stop the storming of Parliament on Monday [25 June]' (*Independent*, 28 June 2001, p. 3).

'On Monday night [25 June] more than 5,000 Macedonian Slavs marched through the streets of the capital, protesting Western involvement in the conflict, firing guns in the air and occupying the parliament building for several hours'

(*IHT*, 27 June 2001, p. 5). 'Demonstrators burned pictures of ... Javier Solana and the flag of OSCE' (*IHT*, 28 June 2001, p. 8).

'A Slav paramilitary group known as the Lions began to daub menacing graffiti on the walls of Skopje. Albanian businessmen were threatened with death. Civilians with criminal links started to appear with guns from the government's arsenal' (*The Economist*, 30 June 2001, p. 44).

'A heavy exchange of fire began around the town of Tetovo' (*Guardian*, 26 June 2001, p. 10).

26 June 2001:

> President Boris Trajkovski on Tuesday [26 June] warned Macedonians of the danger of civil war and appealed to his security forces for support after young armed reservists led a riot outside parliament to protest an evacuation plan for ethnic Albanian insurgents ... Fresh fighting erupted following fierce protest by nationalists enraged over the evacuation of ethnic Albanian rebels by Nato troops, including Americans. Macedonian troops fired ... at three rebel-held villages in the Kumanovo area, north-east of Skopje.
>
> (*IHT*, 27 June 2001, p. 1)

Boris Trajkovski:

> The shooting in the parliament building could have easily thrown us into civil war. I can understand the anger but not bursts of fire ... [The aim is to] eliminate the terrorists from Macedonia ... with as little loss of human life as possible. We are not fighting against one another. This is what the enemy wishes. If we accept that way defeat will be inevitable.

'More than 100,000 people have been displaced by the conflict so far' (*FT*, 27 June 2001, p. 10).

27 June 2001: 'Government forces launched fresh attacks on Albanian rebels' (*Independent*, 28 June 2001, p. 1).

'There was confusion over the exact role of the police. Under the Nato-brokered withdrawal Aracinovo is meant to become a demilitarized zone' (*Guardian*, 28 June 2001, p. 12).

> Numerous arrests and police beatings of ethnic Albanians have been reported ... since Albanian rebels ... began their insurgency ... President George W. Bush ... signed an executive order [on 27 June] barring Americans from any transactions involving the property of any known [ethnic Albanian] rebel leaders. In a separate proclamation Mr Bush also restricted their entry to the USA.
>
> (*IHT*, 28 June 2001, p. 4)

'[On 28 June] President Boris Trajkovski ... and other officials appealed to European leaders to follow Mr Bush's lead' (*IHT*, 29 June 2001, p. 9). ('President

George. W. Bush's administration announced in June that it was freezing the assets of people it considered to be supporting ethnic Albanian rebels in Macedonia or southern Serbia ... Five of the names on the list were those of senior officers of the Kosovo Protection Corps, the civilian force that was set up after the war in Kosovo to absorb the Albanian guerrilla fighters of the KLA. The head of the corps, Agim Ceku, a former general and partner of Nato who was not on the list, said he would resign. The five officers were eventually suspended, pending investigation. They remain on the list, which bans them from entering the United States and freezes their assets ... Mr Ceku, the commander of the corps and former chief of staff of the KLA, said he wanted to see the evidence': *IHT*, 7 August 2001, p. 4.)

> Seven governments ... yesterday [27 June] signed an agreement aimed at liberalizing trade in at least 90 per cent of goods trade between them. The move by Albania, Bosnia-Hercegovina, Bulgaria, Croatia, Romania, Macedonia and Yugoslavia marks the latest stage in efforts, under the EU's Stability Pact for South-Eastern Europe, to enhance stability in the region through economic growth. Moldova is expected to join the arrangement shortly. Croatia, Bosnia and Yugoslavia also reached agreement on measures to resettle the remaining 1.2 million refugees and displaced persons in their countries. Initiatives include reconstruction programmes and housing loan schemes.
>
> (*FT*, 28 June 2001, p. 8)

28 June 2001:

> Government troops fought ethnic Albanian rebels Thursday [28 June] ... The EU envoy, François Leotard ... narrowly avoided being declared persona non grata before starting his mission when he said the Macedonian government should talk to the rebels. He later clarified his comments to make it clear that the EU's position remained unchanged: negotiations should be held with the political leaders of the ethnic Albanians ... but not with the guerrillas.
>
> (*IHT*, 29 June 2001, p. 9)

'François Leotard, the EU's envoy ... on the eve of his arrival on 27 June, proposed ... that the Slav-led government should ... negotiate with the rebels ... He was obliged to backtrack within twenty-four hours' (*The Economist*, 30 June 2001, p. 44).

'Mr Leotard caused alarm on Wednesday [27 June] when he contradicted the EU's position' (*FT*, 30 June 2001, p. 2).

29 June 2001: 'Nato ambassadors yesterday [29 June] rubber-stamped plans for a 3,000-strong force that would be employed in Macedonia after a political settlement' (*FT*, 30 June 2001, p. 2).

Macedonia will demobilize police reservists who have been fighting ethnic Albanian rebels to give peace negotiations a chance, the interior minister said Friday [29 June] ... Ljube Boskovski, whose ministry is in charge on internal security forces, also said some troops might be withdrawn from their positions around the capital, Skopje, as a sign of goodwill amid fresh international efforts at peace ... There have been widespread accusations that forces under Mr Boskovski's ministry, particularly the reservists, were behind recent rioting in Skopje when thousands of demonstrators stormed parliament ... The region near the Kosovo border where fighting has been concentrated was quiet Friday [29 June].

(*IHT*, 30 June 2001, p. 4)

1 July 2001:

Heavy shelling and machine-gun fire erupted around ... Tetovo and near a village [Radusa] north-west of Skopje on Sunday evening [1 July] after a weekend of calm ... The fighting began as the newly arrived US envoy, James Pardew, and ... François Leotard began talks with Macedonian politicians.

(*IHT*, 2 July 2001, p. 5)

2–3 July 2001: 'Sporadic fighting is continuing in several regions ... An estimated 105,000 people have been displaced by the fighting, including more than 65,000 who have fled into neighbouring Kosovo' (*IHT*,4 July 2001, p. 4).

5 July 2001:

Macedonia announced an open-ended ceasefire with Albanian rebels yesterday [5 July], which could pave the way for a peace deal and the deployment of a Nato [3,000-strong] force ... Nato's secretary-general [George Robertson] said ... 'Nato has not made a decision on the date for helping in Macedonia. That will be determined by the progress in the political dialogue and the ceasefire. We will have to make an assessment of when the circumstances are right. That is when there is a durable ceasefire and a sustainable political settlement' ... The Macedonian defence minister said the ceasefire, brokered by Nato and the EU, would take effect from midnight last night ... The ceasefire agreement was signed by Pande Petrevski, Macedonia's chief of general staff, and Ali Ahmeti for the NLA.

(*Independent*, 6 July 2001, p. 11)

'The deal consists of two linked agreements, one between the NLA and Nato, the other between the Macedonian authorities and Nato. The NLA has signalled that it would be prepared to disarm, but only after a political–constitutional settlement' (*Guardian*, 6 July 2001, p. 11).

The Macedonian government and the NLA yesterday [5 July] signed separate, open-ended ceasefires, brokered by Nato ... However, in the hours before the ceasefire was due to take hold renewed fighting was reported. The ceasefires reflect Nato's decision to negotiate directly with the NLA, previously branded 'terrorists' by both Nato and the EU.

(*FT*, 6 July 2001, p. 6)

'Ethnic Albanian rebels and the Macedonian army signed separate ceasefire deals with Nato ... Nato and Macedonian government officials said the ceasefire was part of a deal under which a political agreement would be published by 15 July' (*Telegraph*, 6 July 2001, p. 21).

'Thursday evening [5 July] intense fighting raged in ... Tetovo ... Fighting was also reported near villages ... in the north of the country' (*IHT*, 6 July 2001, p. 1).

6 July 2001:

A truce between Macedonian forces and ethnic Albanian rebels appeared to be holding yesterday [6 July], but one person was killed when Yugoslav troops fired on suspected guerrillas trying to cross into Serbia ... Sporadic firing between rebels and the Macedonian army was reported around ... Tetovo ... In another incident gunmen fired at a convoy of German Nato troops in Macedonia.

(*The Times*, 7 July 2001, p. 18)

The rebels, members of the NLA, number from 1,000 to 1,500. Operating in loosely co-ordinated groups, they are fighting on two broad fronts, one a string of ethnic Albanian villages to the north-east of Skopje and the other the Tetovo region in the west. Many fighters polished their skills in the Kosovo conflict and many are from Albania ... Many were born in Macedonia. On paper the Macedonian army numbers 16,000, with several thousand additional police troops. Military experts say the two forces have no more than 2,500 well-trained fighters between them, far too few to fight effectively on both fronts at the same time. The chronic weaknesses of the forces is, in part, a fluke of history. When Yugoslavia broke up in the early 1990s, and Macedonia and other republics declared independence, the federal government in Belgrade removed its troops and weapons. Macedonia had to build up a new military force from scratch ... As the insurgency spread, Macedonia went on a small buying spree in Ukraine, acquiring a small fleet of MI-24 helicopter gunships, MI-8 helicopters equipped with rocket launchers, Sukhoi 25 attack planes and BM-21 truck-mounted rocket launchers.

(Michael Gordon, *IHT*, 7 July 2001, p. 5)

9 July 2001:

Macedonia's crumbling four-day-old ceasefire suffered a further setback when the Macedonians deployed civilian paramilitaries in action against

Albanian rebels for the first time. A rebel commander said about thirty plain-clothes paramilitaries attacked Albanian positions in the town of Tetovo and in the nearby village of Poroj. A Nato spokesman said 'intense' fighting had followed.

(*Telegraph*, 10 July 2001, p. 12)

10 July 2001: 'Macedonia will win aid worth more than 50 million euros from the EU if it implements a settlement between its Slav and ethnic Albanian citizens, Chris Patten, the external relations commissioner, pledged yesterday [10 July]' (*Guardian*, 11 July 2001, p. 14).

Mr Patten pointed to the 42 million euros that had already been earmarked for Macedonia and said Brussels was also considering 'a package of more than 50 million euros, including substantial budgetary assistance, tied to specific uses, if – but only if – there is a political agreement that is implemented'.

(*Independent*, 11 July 2001, p. 11)

12 July 2001: 'François Leotard ... said Thursday [12 July] that talks ... were gathering pace after weeks of deadlock ... Meanwhile, overnight clashes between government forces and guerrillas strained the ... truce' (*IHT*, 13 July 2001, p. 5).

This week the rebel NLA set up roadblocks in and around Tetovo, in effect taking control of many suburbs and surrounding villages ... The rebels claim the government is sending armed civilians to do the shooting. Certainly, it is using Serbian, Ukrainian and Bulgarian mercenaries. If it is using civilians, that is new ... Nato has warned the rebels that any attack on Skopje, or the capital's airport, might be taken as an attack on itself ... The Slav side is split. The hawks are led by the prime minister, Ljubco Georgievski, backed by the interior minister, who controls the heavily militarized police force. The doves, under President Boris Trajkovski, believe these hardliners instigated the recent violent protests outside the parliament building ... The hawks are also believed to be backing paramilitary organizations ready to attack civilian Albanians if the rebels kill too many policemen or soldiers, or occupy too much more territory.

(*The Economist*, Saturday 14 July 2001, p. 44)

18 July 2001:

Prime minister Ljubco Georgievski said the draft [proposal by the United States and the EU] was a 'blatant violation of Macedonia's internal affairs' that would mean 'carving up the country' ... Mr Georgievski accused the West of siding with the Albanian insurgents. He said the rebels received 'logistical support from the so-called Western democracies … What we have on the table is a document tailored to break up Macedonia.'

(*IHT*, 19 July 2001, p. 5)

'Ljubco Georgievski denounced Western peace proposals as "interference" in his country's affairs and accused the West of supporting Albanian terrorists before talks with the EU and US envoys' (*Independent*, 19 July 2001, p. 13).

Ljubco Georgievski: 'That package actually represents a serious interference in the internal affairs of Macedonia … [and a] *de facto* federalization of Macedonia … [The US and EU envoys were trying] to break up Macedonian institutions' (*Guardian*, 21 July 2001, p. 16).

19 July 2001:

Negotiations between Macedonian and Albanian leaders were at a standstill Thursday [19 July], a day after the Macedonians bluntly rejected a Western-backed peace proposal, and experts from both sides are expected to take over from politicians. Tentative agreement on expert-level talks to be held Friday [20 July] was reached with the help of … François Leotard … and James Pardew … Both Mr Trajkovski and a Western diplomat said experts, not political leaders, are expected to meet Friday. They said the political negotiations were stalled after the Macedonians rejected the final compromise accepted by the Albanian negotiators … Both ethnic Albanian parties involved in the peace process stayed away from Thursday's meeting among Macedonian parties, Mr Trajkovski and the two Western envoys.

(*IHT*, 20 July 2001, p. 5)

Ethnic Albanian political leaders in Macedonia yesterday [19 July] walked out of talks … The Macedonian representatives accused Western mediators of supporting ethnic Albanian rebels fighting the government. Javier Solana … postponed a trip to Macedonia after two bomb blasts in Skopje. Three Macedonians were seized overnight and accused of being spies by ethnic Albanian guerrillas near the border with Kosovo, police said.

(*The Times*, 20 July 2001, p. 15)

[There was] a rejection by Slav politicians of reforms granting the ethnic Albanian minority extensive language rights … The talks … broke down amid recriminations by Ljubco Georgievski … He accused the international community of imposing a political settlement … [There are] fears among Macedonian Slavs that if they grant generous language rights to the ethnic Albanians it will only be a matter of time before Albanian becomes the country's second official language … Macedonians, who speak a south-Slav language similar to Serb … have been trying to establish the legitimacy of the republic and their language … It is the extent to which the Albanian language can be used that has irked the Slavs. The negotiators proposed that, on the local level, a minority language could be used officially if 20 per cent or more of the population spoke it.

(Judy Dempsey, FT, 20 July 2001, p. 8)

'The negotiators, led by James Pardew ... and François Leotard ... have proposed giving the Albanian language a semi-official status' (Judy Dempsey, *FT*, 25 July 2001, p. 6).

The wide-ranging negotiations, which have made major progress on constitutional changes, increased representation for Albanians in the public services and more power for local authorities, have stalled on a single issue: recognition of Albanian as a second official language. 'What we have on the table is a document to break up Macedonia,' said prime minister Ljubco Georgievski, referring to Western proposals and, in particular, the place of language. Arben Xhaferi ... said [that] 'Macedonia would be the only case in history where a war will start because of linguistic disputes' ... for ethnic Albanians the ability to speak Albanian in parliament, to read it in the country's laws, to use it to address a bureaucrat, in short to make it official, is the absolute test of their standing ... But for Macedonians ... the Albanian language is an enemy at the gate ... Macedonians believe that language is a stalking horse for their country's disintegration. They argue it would create a new constitutional order in which the state would eventually be federalized under the guise of Western-imposed multiethnicity. They point to a history of ethnic Albanian ambivalence toward Macedonia, including demands for 'territorial autonomy' and, more recently, 'internal self-determination'. Bilingualism will breed not bury separatism, they argue. For ethnic Albanians that fear misses the point. Macedonians, they argue, need not abandon but must relegate their national pride and the ascendance of their language before a new civic concept of equality ... Although ethnic Albanians are the largest minority, representing 23 per cent to 33 per cent of the population ... there are many minorities here. Roma, Turks, Vlachs, Serbs and others together make up 10 per cent of the population. This is not just a country of Macedonians and Albanians, they say, and the Macedonian language unifies this diverse state. Moreover, the other minorities are almost universally hostile to the ethnic Albanian campaign for greater civil rights, which they view as coercive, non-democratic and exclusionary.

(Peter Finn, IHT, 21 July 2001, p. 4)

Albanians ... want Albanian to be used in parliament and government institutions when requested. The proposed deal, brokered by the EU and Nato, also calls for Albanian to become an official language in areas where Albanians are a majority and for greater Albanian representation in the country's police force.

(Irena Guzelova, FT, 27 July 2001, p. 7)

20 July 2001: 'On Friday [20 July] Western and local legal experts met to discuss the issue [of the Albanian language], but there were no negotiations between leaders of the political parties' (*IHT*, 21 July 2001, p. 2).

> Two European ceasefire monitors and their local interpreter were killed when their Land Rover hit a land mine and plunged down a ravine near [Tetovo] ... The monitors were the first officials killed in the six-month old conflict. The monitors – a Norwegian and a Slovak – accompanied by an ethnic Albanian from Macedonia, were reporting on conditions on the ground by the EU monitoring mission, a long-standing programme in Macedonia, which in recent days has been observing compliance with a Nato-brokered ceasefire that went into effect on 5 July ... The EU has 100 monitors in the former Yugoslav countries, including twenty-five in Macedonia ... The NLA now maintains checkpoints on the edge of the city, just a few hundred metres from government forces. The area where the three men were killed, a few kilometres south-west of Tetovo, was just on the edge of previous military activity and a dividing line between the rebels and government forces ... The Macedonian government immediately charged that the NLA had planted the land mine, an accusation rejected by the rebels. The ethnic Albanian army countered that the mine was planted by the Macedonian army.
>
> (*IHT*, 21 July 2001, p. 2)

> The deputy head of the EU mission in Sarajevo ... said the monitors had been investigating NLA movements ... No evidence has emerged that the vehicle was targeted deliberately, but the increased presence of the guerrilla army around and inside Tetovo has alarmed international officials. Groups of NLA gunmen now man checkpoints within 200 metres of the Macedonian army in Tetovo.
>
> (*Guardian*, 21 July 2001, p. 16)

22 July 2001:

> Ethnic Albanian rebels launched an infantry attack Sunday [22 July] on government forces in the Tetovo area ... the defence ministry said ... A ministry spokesman said that the rebels had opened infantry fire ... on Macedonian army positions ... The Macedonian forces ... returned fire ... The clash ended after about two hours ... The latest orders from the general staff ... said government troops should respond if under direct attack or if the rebels approached them to within less than 200 metres (660 feet).
>
> (*IHT*, 23 July 2001, p. 4)

'Western sources said the army responded disproportionately to a few rounds of incoming fire from NLA positions' (*The Times*, 23 July 2001, p. 10).

23 July 2001:

Security forces and ethnic Albanian rebels engaged in fierce small-arms and mortar battles in Monday [23 July] in and around … Tetovo … It was the second day of fighting in Tetovo … Government forces were also reported to have shelled rebel positions in several villages in the mountains north of Tetovo … Monday's battles were the most serious breach yet of a Nato-brokered ceasefire that went into effect on 5 July. On Sunday [22 July] international observers helped to restore the ceasefire after a two-hour battle, but they were unable to stop Monday's battle … A government spokesman … said the rebels had fired fifty mortar rounds at the army general staff headquarters in the city and had advanced to within 760 metres (half a mile) of the town's centre … The fighting seemed to indicate that both sides had used the eighteen-day ceasefire to reinforce their positions and were prepared for intense fighting if the talks broke down and the ceasefire completely dissolved. Meanwhile, an international observer, who asked not to be identified, said: 'We have evidence that there is a growing tendency for ethnic Albanians to proceed with forms of ethnic cleansing used elsewhere in the Balkans that up to now have not been used here. They are trying to drive Macedonians from traditional ethnic Albanian villages with intimidation, beatings and warnings.'

(*IHT*, 24 July 2001, p. 5)

A senior police official in Tetovo said the rebels had taken the city's football stadium and were within 50 metres of government troops trying to keep them away from the city centre. A government spokesman said an eleven-year-old girl was killed … Macedonian television reported … [that] a soldier was killed yesterday in a separate clash near Mavrovo, about 45 miles south-west of Skopje.

(*Independent*, 24 July 2001, p. 13)

24 July 2001:

The government on Tuesday [24 July] accused Nato and international peace mediators of backing ethnic Albanian rebels. A government spokesman said American and EU envoys had wrongly blamed Macedonia for wrecking a ceasefire and sparking vicious fighting between security forces and rebels in Tetovo that left two dead on Monday … Western diplomats denied that … James Pardew and François Leotard had accused Macedonia of firing first … [The government spokesman] also asserted that Nato countries were directing the NLA with the goal of making Macedonia an international protectorate … Diplomats have been struggling to keep talks alive while voicing suspicion that hardline elements in the government would rather return to fighting than make unpalatable compromises need to secure peace … As darkness began to fall fighting erupted again in Tetovo

... after a day of relative calm ... Macedonia ordered the closing of its border crossings into ... Kosovo. In Skopje crowds of people who said the guerrillas had forced them from their village homes during fighting on Monday [23 July], staged an angry protest outside parliament.

(*IHT*, 25 July 2001, p. 4)

Macedonian refugees pushed out of their villages by rebels ... [were] joined by other Macedonians from Skopje ... Hundreds went on an anti-Western rampage, stoning the US, British and German embassies, trashing a McDonald's and a British Airways office and setting cars ablaze.

(*IHT*, 26 July 2001, p. 8)

('The Macedonian government shut the border with Kosovo last week, temporarily halting Nato supply convoys to ... Kfor ... The restriction was lifted within hours ... Kfor depends on supplies transported overland from the main logistical base in the Greek port of Salonika': *Telegraph*, Thursday 2 August 2001, p. 15. 'Since the end of the Kosovo war in 1999 there have been about 4,000 Nato troops [Kfor Rear] based in Macedonia, in addition to intelligence and training personnel stationed there since the early 1990s, when Nato signed the Partnership for Peace with the republic. Kfor Rear provides essential military, transport, food supplies and logistics backup for the 40,000 Kfor troops in Kosovo': *FT*, 7 August 2001, p. 6.)

Even as EU and US diplomats yesterday [24 July] tried to revive political negotiations, the NLA was consolidating its grip in the north of the country around Tetovo, while security forces were responding with heavy bombardments. Moreover, some members of the Macedonian government and the media are increasingly critical of the international mediators, spreading rumours [denied by Nato] that Kfor ... is providing the NLA with equipment ... The latest upsurge in fighting took place north of Tetovo, where large swathes are under the control of the NLA and where civilians are often intimidated or kidnapped.

(*FT*, 25 July 2001, p. 6)

In Skopje 300 Macedonian refugees from Monday's fighting near Tetovo protested outside parliament, calling on the security forces to recapture their villages. The crowd attacked a passenger van carrying three ethnic Albanians ... but it escaped. Some Macedonians are convinced that Nato is helping the NLA as it did the KLA in Kosovo.

(*Guardian*, 25 July 2001, p. 15)

'On Tuesday night [24 July] demonstrators from the majority Slav population ... attacked the British, German and American embassies and set fire to vehicles belonging to UN and EU agencies' (*Telegraph*, 26 July 2001, p. 18).
'On Tuesday night [24 July] the rebels reached the heart of the city for the

first time, with reports of gunfire in the main square ... [There are] uncon-firmed reports of rebel attacks south of Tetovo' (*Independent*, 26 July 2001, p. 12).

[There are] growing anti-Western sentiments within some sections of the Macedonian government and increased calls by hardline nationalists to renew fighting against the rebels ... Ljubco Georgievski sent a letter to President Boris Trajkovski on Tuesday [24 July] urging him to order a mili-tary strike to drive the rebels back.

(*IHT*, 26 July 2001, p. 1)

25 July 2001:

Nato has won the agreement of Macedonian government forces and ethnic Albanian guerrillas to reinstate a ceasefire ... Under the deal ... the NLA guerrillas would retreat from territory they have occupied since the truce took effect on 6 July. This would allow displaced Macedonian villagers to return ... The government ... in return said its forces would exercise restraint around ... Tetovo ... Some government ministers, including Ljubco Georgievski, the prime minister, have accused Nato, the EU and OSCE of siding with the rebels. This has been strongly denied by all three ... Lord Robertson ... and Javier Solana ... prepared to embark today [26 July] on a crisis mission to Macedonia.

(*FT*, 26 July 2001, p. 6)

[The deal calls for] the ethnic Albanian rebels to withdraw from the road from Tetovo to the Kosovo border and from a dozen Macedonian Slav villages they had captured earlier this month. In return the Macedonian government said its army would exercise restraint.

(*FT*, 27 July 2001, p. 7)

A mob of about 500 hurled stones at the parliament building in Skopje ... Last night [25 July] there were more anti-Western demonstrations in Skopje. Refugees were joined by local residents in a protest outside ... parliament demanding government strikes against the rebels ... A deadline for rebel forces to withdraw from the Tetovo area by midday passed without action from Macedonian troops.

(*Telegraph*, 26 July 2001, p. 18)

Thousands fled ... Tetovo yesterday [25 July] after the government warned Albanian rebels to withdraw from the city or face a full-scale offensive ... At least eleven civilians have been killed ... The government gave the guerrillas an ultimatum to withdraw from Tetovo by noon yesterday ... America said yesterday it has secured a commitment from Ukraine, which has sent attack helicopters and pilots, to stop supplying arms to Macedonia.

(*Independent*, 26 July 2001, p. 12)

Wednesday [25 July] was relatively calm compared with the last three days of intense fighting in and around Tetovo and rioting Tuesday [24 July] in Skopje. But maintaining the peace has been complicated, some international observers said, by numerous rebel violations of the 5 July ceasefire. The rebels have used the last three days to fortify their positions and claim new territory in violation of the truce, international observers said. The rebels are also said to have used the truce to push thousands of Macedonians out of areas under rebel control. Over the last six months of the conflict tens of thousands of people have fled in advance of violence and the arrival of soldiers or rebels of different ethnic backgrounds ... On Wednesday hardline government officials kept up their complaints ... Western officials said that many of the accusations reflected a deep split between moderates and hardline nationalists within the government.

(*IHT*, 26 July 2001, pp. 1, 8)

26 July 2001:

For the second day running Tetovo was quiet. There were sporadic shots ... Ethnic Albanian guerrillas had [begun] to pull out of ... [a number of] villages ... Talks between Macedonia's ethnic Albanian and Slav political leaders are expected to resume today [27 July] in ... Tetovo ... President Boris Trajkovski highlighted the symbolic significance of the decision to resume talks in ... Tetovo.

(*FT*, 27 July 2001, p. 7)

President Boris Trajkovski: 'Tetovo is the symbol of joint ethnic life ... the melting pot of Macedonia.'

Ethnic Albanian forces ... began to withdraw from their positions as Lord Robertson ... and Javier Solana ... arrived in Macedonia ... The breakdown in talks led to fierce fighting earlier this week ... around Tetovo, with 10,000 Macedonians fleeing their homes in the city and nearby villages.

(*Telegraph*, 27 July 2001, p. 19)

Javier Solana: 'The political process is back on track. The ceasefire is back on track. Ninety-five per cent of those things that were to be negotiated are already agreed. The remaining 5 per cent must be agreed in the coming days.'

The ceasefire officially began at 6 a.m. and as the day progressed there were no reports of fighting ... The two sides engaged in fierce gun and mortar exchanges earlier this week, killing at least thirty people ... The truce was holding although rebel forces apparently did not fully vacate all of the areas they had agreed to leave as part of the new ceasefire accord by a 1 p.m. Thursday [26 July] deadline ... Some of Thursday's deadlines were apparently behind schedule ... Some refugees ... also reportedly were having difficulty returning ... The interior ministry announced that it was charging eleven ethnic Albanians with war crimes. One was the man who signed the new ceasefire on behalf of the rebels, Ali Ahmeti, the political leader of the NLA.

(*IHT*, 27 July 2001, p. 1)

'In this week's fighting eleven civilians ... have been killed ... There were plans for 800 ethnic Slavs who fled the fighting to be bused back to their homes' (*Independent*, 27 July 2001, p. 13).

'On Thursday [26 July] the government sent three buses of Macedonians back to their homes, but most returned to the capital for fear of the Albanian rebels' (*IHT*, 28 July 2001, p. 2).

27 July 2001:

The front line in Tetovo ... continued to run through the town ... The rebels were supposed to have withdrawn ... They appeared to have dismantled a few checkpoints, but part of Tetovo was still under rebel control ... News came yesterday morning [27 July] that the ... new round of peace talks ... had been postponed because of 'security concerns' in Tetovo.

(*Independent*, 28 July 2001, p. 13)

Western diplomats shuttled between the main political leaders in Macedonia on Friday [27 July], laying the groundwork for direct talks ... [on] Saturday [28 July] in the south of Macedonia next to Lake Ohrid ... which has been largely unaffected by the conflict ... The renewed talks were to have taken place in Tetovo ... but government officials said the atmosphere was too fragile for full talks in Tetovo. Defence officials accused the rebels of some thirty-one incidents of gunfire overnight, and this evening there were reports of small arms fire inside Tetovo as well as a possible skirmish in a nearby village.

(*IHT*, 28 July 2001, p. 2)

28–9 July:

Interior minister Ljube Boskovski escaped an ambush Sunday evening [29 July] as his car was sprayed with bullets on the main highway linking Skopje ... to Tetovo. The attack occurred ... as the car, also carrying journalists from state-run television, passed near the village of Grupcin on Mr Boskovski's way to visit refugees returning to their homes. The ambush came as government and ethnic Albanian leaders held a second day of peace talks in the south-western city of Ohrid.

(*IHT*, 30 July 2001, p. 10)

Macedonian government and ethnic Albanian political leaders convened yesterday [29 July] for the second successive day in the lakeside retreat of

Ohrid ... The status of the Albanian language remains a sticking point, as does an Albanian demand to let local leaders appoint their own police force. Negotiators were working on a compromise under which the Albanian tongue would become official only in areas where ethnic Albanians make up more than 20 per cent of the population ... A few thousand Slav villagers, thrown out of their homes in the most recent rebel advance, demonstrated outside parliament on Saturday night [28 July] ... The West organized a series of confidence-building measures and escorted bus-loads of refugees of both ethnic groups back to a couple of villages. But none felt secure enough to remain.

(*FT*, 30 July 2001, p. 5)

The guerrillas were reported to have shelled a government military barracks yesterday [29 July] ... One Macedonian political observer said the guerrillas were acknowledged to have been the victors in last week's fighting. NLA guerrillas captured some Tetovo suburbs and nearby villages.

(*Telegraph*, 30 July 2001, p. 11)

30 July 2001:

The Macedonian prosecutor's office ... ordered the detention of eleven ethnic Albanian guerrilla leaders, including the rebels' political chief, Ali Ahmeti. The order came as the prosecutor opened an investigation of the rebel NLA. The rebels are not included in the peace talks ... Progress was reported Monday [30 July] in the peace talks between Macedonian and ethnic Albanian political leaders ... [but] the main sticking point remained the extent of using Albanian as an official language in public. According to a draft peace proposal, Albanian would become an official language in areas where ethnic Albanians make up 20 per cent or more of the population. However ... there was still disagreement over how such a rule should be carried out, including its application on the local level ... Last week ... 8,000 or more Slavs fled the fighting ... On Saturday [28 July] the government escorted about 350 Macedonians back to three villages ... but most of them ... decided it was not safe.

(*IHT*, 31 July 2001, p. 4)

Talks on a draft peace plan ... [were] edging forward 'millimetre by millimetre', according to François Leotard ... There were doubts about the circumstances surrounding the attempted 'assassination' of Mr Boskovski on Sunday [29 July] ... Nationalists are angry at what they see as an attempt by Nato and the EU to place the guerrillas on a par with the Macedonian government ... [There are] parliamentary elections in November ... The guerrillas are not directly involved in the peace talks, but they have an effective veto on the outcome.

(*Telegraph*, 31 July 2001, p. 13)

They [the rebels] have taken advantage of a Nato-brokered ceasefire to move into villages surrounding Tetovo right under the noses of Western observers and government forces. Last week, virtually overnight, they seized most of Tetovo itself ... Thousands of civilians from both communities have fled their homes into the safety of areas dominated by their own ethnic group. The UNHCR estimates that 30,000 refugees are displaced inside Macedonia and that more than 76,000 Albanians fled across the border to Kosovo to escape government shelling. Just over 17,000 have returned in the past week. Between 7,000 and 8,000 Macedonian Slavs have over the past couple of weeks escaped the rebel advance. An OSCE report documents kidnappings, disappearances and beatings of ethnic Slavs and of Albanians employed by official bodies, which it says are 'consistent with an attempt to ethnically cleanse the area' ... Ordinary Slavs blame Nato for not adequately disarming KLA members after the war with Serbia, allowing the KLA to foment the rebellion in neighbouring Macedonia ... Ljube Boskovski, the hardline interior minister, is accused of distributing thousands of arms to locally formed self-defence units ... Some in Macedonia's current government may also have a political interest in prolonging the crisis. Vladimir Milcin, head of the Open Society Institute in Skopje, recently accused Ljubco Georgievski, prime minister, of using Slav nationalism to deflect public opinion from a series of financial scandals that have beset his VMRO–DPMNE party.

(*FT*, 31 July 2001, p. 8)

'The rebels are ignoring the deal and occupying part of Tetovo' (*Independent*, 31 July 2001, p. 11).
  1 August 2001:

Western officials declared a breakthrough Wednesday [1 August] in Macedonia's peace talks, breaking an impasse on the contentious issue of the use of the Albanian language ... [But] the deal goes into effect only if there is progress on ethnic Albanian demands for broader autonomy for local police departments ... Albanian would now be accepted as an official language in areas where 20 per cent of the population is ethnic Albanian ... Albanian will also be acceptable in parliament ... The talks adjourned until Friday [3 August] ... Defence minister Vlado Buckovski ... pledged Wednesday to ignore minor provocations by ethnic Albanian insurgents ... He threatened 'adequate military response if need be' in case of major violations of the shaky truce ... The gesture came amid reports that five ethnic Albanian rebel officers died over the weekend [29 July] in the north-western town of Gostivar – the worst single blow to the movement so far.

(*IHT*, 2 August 2001, p. 5)

James Pardew:

This is a significant development in the negotiating process … [Language] has always been the toughest issue and now we have both parties agreeing. It is conditional until the entire framework agreement and all its annexes are agreed. That means that nothing is completed until everything is completed. The language issue now we can set aside.

2 August 2001: Macedonia's national day.

The prime minister, Ljubco Georgievski, expressed his hope that talks … could end with a plan to avert a new Balkan war. 'But signing that document while our territories are occupied by terrorists would be a shameful agreement for Macedonia. We must take back our occupied territories because we cannot close our eyes to the fact that we are talking under the threats of guns,' he said at a monastery [in southern Serbia] where Macedonia agreed in August [on 2 August] 1944 to become part of Yugoslavia … 'All the Albanian extremists in Kosovo, southern Serbia, Macedonia and Montenegro have only one goal, the creation of a Greater Albania … Unfortunately today we have a strong and decisive people but indecisive leadership,' prime minister Georgievski said.

(*IHT*, 3 August 2001, p. 4)

Ethnic Albanian rebels have over the past few days continued to strengthen their control over north-western Macedonia despite a renewed ceasefire. International observers said the rebels had set up checkpoints along the roads that link the villages between the mainly Albanian town of Tetovo and Gostivar, some 30 kilometres south. Clashes between the two sides have also continued.

(*FT*, 3 August 2001, p. 5)

3 August 2001:

Peace negotiators tried Friday [3 August] to bridge differences … over sharing power in the country's police force as insurgents clashed again with government forces and gained more territory. The rebels were said to have carried out fourteen armed attacks overnight against government troops near … Tetovo, gaining almost complete control of a key road in the area … linking Tetovo with neighbouring Kosovo … On the agenda Friday were demands that the ethnic Albanian population … be better represented in the police, that local police departments have greater authority and that Albanians independently elect local police chiefs in areas where they live.

(*IHT*, 4 August 2001, p. 4)

5 August 2001: 'A breakthrough was reached Sunday [5 August] in the Macedonian peace negotiations with an agreement on changes in the police force' (*IHT*, 6 August 2001, p. 1).

> The number of ethnic Albanians in the police force should in the future reflect the country's ethnic mix ... Currently ethnic Albanians make up only 5 per cent of the 6,000 policemen ... In return the Skopje government would retain central control of the police ... The plan also envisions the deployment of dozens of international police experts to help carry out the reform ... Macedonians ... have agreed to the expanded use of the Albanian language, set a minimum of minority votes to pass laws in parliament and have marked funds for Albanian language higher education.
>
> (*IHT*, 7 August 2001, p. 4)

'Javier Solana ... yesterday [5 August] ... made a personal appearance at peace talks. Mr Solana was accompanied by Anatoli Zlenko, Ukrainian foreign minister ... There was only sporadic shooting overnight ... Ethnic Albanians ... make up ... only 6 per cent of the police' (*FT*, 6 August 2001, p. 7).

'It is believed the compromise agreed by Mr Solana means 500 new Albanian police officers will be appointed in Macedonia, and trained by Western police, with a second batch of 500 some time in the future' (*Independent*, 7 August 2001, p. 9). 'When the crisis began the Macedonian air force consisted of four helicopters – one of which crashed into a ski resort in the first few weeks' (*Independent*, 6 August 2001, p. 10).

6 August 2001: talks stall on the questions of disarming the NLA (especially the timing) and an amnesty for ethnic Albanian insurgents (*IHT*, 7 August 2001, p. 4; *FT*, 7 August 2001, p. 1; *The Times*, 7 August 2001, p. 10; *Independent*, 7 August 2001, p. 9; *Guardian*, 7 August 2001, p. 11; *Telegraph*, 7 August 2001, p. 14).

'Over the past few days there have been skirmishes north of Skopje. But Nato officials said the scale of the fighting was low' (*FT*, 7 August 2001, p. 1).

7 August 2001: 'Yesterday [7 August] police killed five ethnic Albanians in a raid on a [one-storey] house in Skopje ... in a run-down Albanian quarter ... saying they had plotted attacks in the capital' (*FT*, 8 August 2001, p. 5).

'Macedonian police shot dead five ethnic Albanian gunmen, including a guerrilla commander ... Police displayed an arms cache they said came from the house' (*Telegraph*, 8 August 2001, p. 13).

> The interior ministry claimed the five men killed were members of the NLA, planning to begin a campaign of 'urban terrorism' ... There were inconsistencies between the official version of the events and the evidence at the scene ... The police said they had arrested thirty men.
>
> (*Independent*, 8 August 2001, p. 11)

'Interior ministry officials claimed the group was planning to attack police officers in the capital' (*Guardian*, 8 August 2001, p. 11).

The Ohrid talks appeared once again to be on track ... The Macedonians dropped demands for a quick disarming of the rebels ... However, as night fell negotiators in Ohrid were still haggling over constitutional issues ... Despite a ceasefire conflict and violence continued in various degrees. The rebels of the NLA still control northern roads and fire on Macedonian soldiers and police. Macedonian forces seem mostly to be in a defensive crouch except for the raid Tuesday [7 August] ... President Trajkovski has ordered troops to prepare to clear roads held by rebels, in case peace talks fail.

(*IHT*, 8 August 2001, p. 5)

'The Macedonian negotiators dropped their insistence that the rebels start disarming immediately' (*The Times*, 8 August 2001, p. 13).

The deal looked close to being agreed on Sunday [6 August] before the Macedonian side made unexpected new demands at the eleventh hour for the rebels to disarm before the deal was finalized ... But last night [7 August] there were reports that the Macedonians were softening on the issue ... Ukraine is to suspend exports of heavy weapons to Macedonia.

(*Independent*, 8 August 2001, p. 11)

The deal gives Albanians greater rights in return for the complete disarmament of the NLA ... On Monday [7 August] talks ... broke down after the Macedonian leaders presented new demands calling for the NLA to disarm before any changes were undertaken. But late yesterday [7 August] ... the Macedonians dropped their demands ... Constitutional experts were preparing the final details of the deal ... The details of an amnesty designed to ensure that the guerrilla group supports the agreement had also been worked out ... [but it does not seem] the amnesty would extend to all members of the guerrilla army.

(*Guardian*, 8 August 2001, p. 11)

'The agreement calls for ... parliament ... [to ratify it] within forty-five days ... There are reports that a faction of the NLA, calling itself the Albanian National Army, has condemned the agreement and is vowing to fight on' (*IHT*, 13 August 2001, p. 1).

8 August 2001:

Leading politicians in Macedonia ... [initialled] ... a deal Wednesday [8 August], the Macedonians evidently surmounting their bitterness over an Albanian rebel ambush on an army convoy that killed ten soldiers ... The rebel attack ... west of Skopje [on the road to Tetovo] ... inflicted the highest one-day toll on the army in the six-month-old conflict ... The political leaders only initialled the accord and formal signing is not scheduled until Monday [13 August] ... On Wednesday evening a small group of protesters marched on the US embassy in Skopje to express unhappiness at US pressure to reach a settlement. The government placed a curfew on the town of Prilep to head off possible unrest there, because eight of the ten dead soldiers were from the area ... After word of the ambush reached Ohrid ... the political party headed by prime minister Ljubco Georgievski suspended its participation. But a few hours later Mr Georgievski agreed to initial the agreement ... Combat erupted in Tetovo.

(*IHT*, 9 August 2001, pp. 1, 5)

'Ljubco Georgievski ... had earlier withdrawn his party from political talks ... He was followed by members of the other main Macedonian Slav group, the Social Democratic Party' (*Guardian*, 9 August 2001, p. 11).

The worst day of violence yet also saw an Albanian civilian killed ... Last night [8 August] hundreds of angry Macedonians gathered outside the EU's office in Skopje, calling for arms ... Angry crowds of ethnic Macedonians began gathering in Skopje to protest at the killing of the soldiers.

(*Independent*, 9 August 2001, p. 10)

'In Skopje several hundred people gathered in the evening outside parliament ... Demonstrators also blocked the main roads' (*FT*, 9 August 2001, p. 5).

'The deal includes an agreement by the Macedonian government to grant an amnesty to the Albanian rebels, except for those suspected of committing war crimes' (*The Times*, 9 August 2001, p. 11).

'The political and military parts of the package are skilfully synchronized so that parliament has to pass the laws needed to enshrine the offers of greater rights to the Albanians in the same period as the guerrillas complete their handover of weapons' (*Guardian*, 11 August 2001, p. 18).

9 August 2001: 'Albanian rebels battled government forces for control of ... Tetovo ... A policeman was killed ... A rebel commander said his fighters were in control of "half of the city"' (*Independent*, 10 August 2001, p. 12).

[There was] heavy fighting between government forces and rebels in and around the city of Tetovo. A Macedonian policeman was killed ... The army chief of staff, Pande Petrovski, resigned yesterday [9 August], taking responsibility for the soldiers' deaths. His deputy, Metode Stamboliski, was appointed in his place ... Albanian homes in the Skopje suburb of Saraj were attacked by a Macedonian mob ... A Slav nationalist mob went on the rampage in the early hours ... in Skopje's commercial centre ... In Tetovo many houses belonging to Slavs who had previously fled the city were burnt down by the rebels ... President Boris Trajkovski ... [said]: 'The national security council supports the most energetic offensive measures aimed at eliminating the threats posed to Macedonian security forces and citizens of Macedonia.'

(*Telegraph*, 10 August 2001, p. 20)

10 August 2001:

> Escalating fighting … is threatening the planned signing of a peace deal …
> Fighting flared throughout north-western Macedonia on Thursday night [9
> August] and continued yesterday [10 August]. In the worst incident an army
> truck hit two anti-tank mines some 10 kilometres from Skopje, killing eight
> soldiers … Heavy fighting was also reported north of Skopje …
> International observers reported three more government soldiers killed …
> James Pardew … condemned the rebel attacks.
>
> (*FT*, 11 August 2001, p. 8)

'Seven government soldiers were killed when their truck hit a land mine …
about 10 kilometres north of … Skopje … Government forces and rebels also
traded gunfire early Friday on the outskirts of Tetovo' (*IHT*, 11 August 2001, p.
1). 'An eighth Macedonian soldier died late Friday night [10 August]' (*IHT*, 13
August 2001, p. 4).

> At least seven Macedonian soldiers were killed in a land mine explosion …
> The Macedonian army has been steadily losing ground to the rebels …
> Rebels and security forces fought an intense battle on Thursday [9 August]
> for control of Tetovo, most of which has been in rebel hands since earlier
> fighting … Minority groups are being 'ethnically cleansed' – Macedonians
> intimidated into leaving Tetovo in rebel hands, Albanians threatened and
> warned to flee government-held areas … A little known rebel group called
> the Albanian National Army yesterday [10 August] claimed responsibility
> for the killings of ten Macedonian soldiers ambushed on Wednesday [8
> August] … This second group has been known in Macedonia since at least
> last year [2000], when it claimed responsibility for murdering three
> Macedonian police officers.
>
> (*Independent*, 11 August 2001, p. 12)

> At least seven Macedonian soldiers were killed yesterday [10 August] by
> landmines … A new group calling itself the Albanian National Army said
> that it had carried out the attack in 'revenge' for the deaths of five ethnic
> Albanians in a police raid on a house in Skopje on Wednesday [8 August]
> … Earlier government helicopter gunships and Su25 Frogfoot ground attack
> aircraft bought from Ukraine flew over the city of Tetovo after overnight
> clashes. The aircraft have flown over Macedonia before but have never
> dropped bombs … Yesterday [10 August] witnesses said Su25s had bombed
> rebel-held areas on Thursday [9 August] night … The defence ministry
> denied the account.
>
> (*The Times*, 11 August 2001, p. 11)

'Half of … Tetovo fell to … the NLA … on Wednesday [8 August]'
(*Telegraph*, 11 August 2001, p. 19).

'A curfew [for Skopje] was announced for 9 p.m.' (*Guardian*, 11 August 2001, p. 13).

'On Friday night [10 August] hundreds of Slavic Macedonian demonstrators returned to the centre of Skopje, some marching on the US embassy to protest what they say is Western bias in favour of the Albanians' (*IHT*, 13 August 2001, p. 4).

11 August 2001: 'On Saturday [11 August] the government reported that the insurgents were continuing to attack army positions in the northern village of Radusha in fighting that it said was aimed at control of Skopje's water reservoir' (*IHT*, 13 August 2001, p. 4).

> The Macedonian population is left to square accounts of heavy rebel losses with the fact that, if anything, they are expanding their sphere of influence. Government officials also claimed Saturday that a large force of several hundred ethnic Albanian rebels had crossed from neighbouring Kosovo ... The charge was denied by Nato.
>
> (*IHT*, 13 August 2001, p. 1)

(Other reports mentioned a figure of 600 guerrillas claimed to be crossing from Kosovo.)

12 August 2001:

> Macedonia's government yesterday [Sunday 12 August] called a unilateral ceasefire ... that started at 7.30 p.m. local time, following a weekend of the heaviest fighting seen so far, which moved to within three miles of the outskirts of Skopje ... Government officials said rebels attacked a police station in the village of Ljuboten, some three miles from Skopje's outskirts.
>
> (*FT*, 13 August 2001, p. 6)

13 August 2001: political leaders sign the peace accord ('framework document') in Skopje in a low-key ceremony attended by George Robertson and Javier Solana.

The peace accord includes the following elements:

1   amendments to the introduction of the constitution to delete reference to Macedonian Slavs as the only 'constitutional' people and to make Macedonia a 'civic society' of all its ethnic groups;
2   the creation of a 'double majority' system in parliament, requiring that half of the lawmakers voting on a measure must come from at least one minority group for it to be enacted;
3   Albanian becomes the second official language in communities where ethnic Albanians comprise more than 20 per cent of the population;
4   state-funded higher education in the Albanian language is to be provided where ethnic Albanians comprise more than 20 per cent of the population

(previously the state funded only lower education in Albanian in such communities);

5   there is to be proportional representation of ethnic Albanians in the constitutional court and of Albanians and other minorities in government administration and the police;

6   calls for ethnic Albanian police commanders in communities where ethnic Albanians form a local majority;

7   broader authority is to be given to local governments;

8   provision for a census later in the year to establish the exact ethnic composition of the population;

9   equal status is given to the Orthodox, Moslem and Catholic faiths;

10 an amnesty is to be granted to militants who have not committed crimes during clashes with government forces.

Parliament has forty-five days to pass the reforms from the day the president presents them to parliament. (The reforms were presented on 16 August.)

George Robertson:

> [The accord is a] remarkable moment for the history of Macedonia. This day marks the entry of Macedonia into modern, mainstream Europe ... Clearly, there has to be a sustainable ceasefire and clear indications from the insurgents that they mean business in terms of disarming completely and handing over their weapons and ammunition to the Nato troops when they come.

('Operation Essential Harvest' to collect weapons voluntarily surrendered by the ethnic Albanian rebels was scheduled to last a maximum of thirty days and was to involve around 3,500 British-led Nato troops.)

'In a letter to President Trajkovski Lord Robertson stressed that a deployment of 3,500 Nato troops to collect arms from the Albanian rebels required further agreements, including an amnesty for many of the rebels' (*FT*, 14 August 2001, p. 5).

> The EU and Nato have proposed measures which would free all rebels from the prospect of prosecution unless they have been indicted by the UN's International Criminal Tribunal for the former Yugoslavia. But the Macedonian government thinks this too lenient and wants a start to disarmament before any amnesty.
>
> (*Independent*, 14 August 2001, p. 9)

'EU officials also promised a donors' meeting to consider aid for Macedonia, while the European Commission is set to approve a Euro 50 million package to support the agreed reforms' (*FT*, 14 August 2001, p. 5).

> [On 14 August the EU] held out the prospect of Euro 30 million in extra aid ... 'inextricably linked to the agreement's implementation'. The Euro 30

million ... would come from a Euro 5.5 billion fund for the Balkans for 2000–2006 and would be on top of Euro 42 million earmarked for the country this year. The Commission ... is also looking at disbursing Euro 10 million in grants and Euro 40 million in credits. The Commission intends to hold a donors' meeting in conjunction with the World Bank once the Macedonian parliament enacts the agreement, which it is scheduled to do by the end of September.

(*FT*, 15 August 2001, p. 5)

'Despite the ceasefire ... there was heavy fighting overnight in the north' (*IHT*, 14 August 2001, p. 1).

The number of civilians and ethnic Albanians rebels killed in recent fighting is not known with certainty. ('At least nineteen government soldiers and as many rebels have died in fighting since ... last Wednesday [8 August]': *Telegraph*, 14 August 2001, p. 13.)

'Most of Tetovo is under rebel control' (*Telegraph*, 14 August 2001, p. 13).

After the Milosevic government of Serbia was unseated, these Albanian fighters ... KLA forces on the ground in Kosovo ... moved on to Macedonia, where the territories bordering Kosovo are also mainly populated by ethnic Albanians. It was the US army's refusal to properly police this zone and its frontier that allowed the Albanian militants to mount their new drive into Macedonia. This contributed to the impression, now widespread in Macedonia, that the United States secretly backs the Albanians against the Macedonian Slavs. The American army actually is merely afraid to expose its soldiers to danger.

(*IHT*, 25 August 2001, p. 4)

14 August 2001:

Nato officials reported progress Tuesday [14 August] in preparations for a mission to disarm insurgents in Macedonia despite sporadic outbreaks of fighting and allegations of summary killings of ethnic Albanians that threatened to undermine a peace agreement. The political leader of the ... NLA, Ali Ahmeti, signed an agreement to turn over weapons to Nato soldiers after receiving assurances of an amnesty and of political reforms ... The Nato officials said that a status-of-forces agreement had been reached between the alliance and the Macedonian government, and that later in the day the rebel forces declared how many weapons they intended to turn in. Officials of Nato were working with the Macedonian government to get them to accept that figure, estimated at 2,000 weapons ... Under the deal President Boris Trajkovski was offering an assurance that rebels would not be prosecuted ... Only those liable for prosecution at the UN war crimes tribunal would be excluded from the amnesty ... An amnesty law has to be approved by the Macedonian parliament ... Ethnic Albanians accused Macedonian troops on Tuesday of summarily executing at least nine ethnic Albanian civilians in the village of Ljuboten, near Skopje, this week and of burning and looting houses in the village ... [A source] said that the bodies of five men ... had been found.

(*IHT*, 15 August 2001, p. 5)

Although there are factions among the Albanian fighters, their civil representatives agreed on Tuesday [14 August] ... to turn over their weapons ... estimating that they would have about 3,000 weapons to turn over ... [The] status-of-forces agreement specifying the role of the Nato force and what local laws would apply to Nato soldiers ... was signed on Wednesday [15 August].

(*IHT*, 16 August 2001, p. 1)

Nato officials said that the Macedonian government had vowed, in a status-of-forces agreement, defining Nato's mission to 'strictly abide by international human rights standards and accept OSCE and EU monitoring' after the arms collectors go ... Nato is putting their faith in the peace deal holding and also in an expanded monitoring force of OSCE observers who will train Macedonian police.

(*Guardian*, 18 August 2001, p. 2)

'Nato officials ... maintained a ceasefire was "broadly holding"' (*FT*, 15 August 2001, p. 5).

The discovery of the bodies of five men ... in Ljuboten ... a village five miles north of Skopje ... prompted the accusation of war crimes [committed] by the Macedonian police ... Local people ... deny that they were members of the NLA ... The men were all killed on Sunday [12 August] ... The ministry of the interior, the department responsible for the police operation, described the dead men as 'terrorists'.

(*Guardian*, 15 August 2001, p. 10)

'The killing [took place] on Sunday [12 August] of about ten Albanian villagers in Ljuboten ... They died when Macedonian security forces allegedly raided the village' (*FT*, 17 August 2001, p. 14).

'The Albanian National Army, a rebel group ... rejected the peace deal' (*The Times*, 15 August 2001, p. 11).

'Western intelligence experts confirmed that the Marxist–Leninist terrorist group [the Albanian National Army], which has about 200 members and unlike the NLA does not wear uniform, has existed for some time' (*Telegraph*, 20 August 2001, p. 8).

15 August 2001: Nato approves the first phase of Operation Essential Harvest, the advance party comprising around 400 British troops.

The Macedonian government formally approved an amnesty for the NLA yesterday [15 August], although anyone who refused to hand over his weapons or 'had committed serious crimes which could be prosecuted by the International Tribunal for the former Yugoslavia' would not be pardoned.

(*The Times*, 16 August 2001, p. 10)

The Macedonian defence ministry said on Wednesday [15 August] that there was still fighting in … Tetovo, in surrounding villages and in the Kumanovo area, north of Skopje. There was no report of casualties. About 100 people have been killed since fighting began in February, but about thirty of them were killed in the past two weeks … But the country seemed relatively quieter on Wednesday … President Boris Trajkovski will be presenting a package of constitutional reforms to the Macedonian parliament … Under the peace agreement President Trajkovski is to ask his parliament to amend the preamble of the constitution so that it no longer implies that Slavic Macedonians have preeminent status … Parliament has forty-five days to pass [all] the reforms.

(*IHT*, 16 August 2001, pp. 1, 6)

'Less than 100 have died since the rebels began their campaign six months ago' (*Telegraph*, 16 August 2001, p. 12). 'War-related deaths have been below 200 … The conflict has displaced tens of thousands' (*Telegraph*, 21 August 2001, p. 18).

'Over 100,000 people … have been displaced since March' (*IHT*, 17 August 2001, p. 5). 'More than 150,000 people have been displaced from their homes, 100 have died and property has been severely damaged' (*IHT*, 18 August 2001, p. 4). 'In the last six months more than 125,000 people from the two principal ethnic groups have been forced from their homes' (*IHT*, 27 August 2001, p. 6).

'At least 200 people have been killed and 100,000 displaced' (*The Economist*, 18 August 2001, p. 11).

'Some 300 Macedonians have already died and 100,000 have been "ethnically cleansed"' (*The Times*, 22 August 2001, p. 12).

Ali Ahmeti: 'If we give up 2,000 or 2,500 weapons, Albanians gain a big percentage in the police force and in the army …. [If that happens] there is no need for keeping weapons' (*IHT*, 17 August 2001, p. 6).

'The NLA is believed to number between 2,500 and 3,000 fighters, and Nato estimates the number of weapons turned in would be in this range' (*FT*, 16 August 2001, p. 4).

'British defence sources estimate there are up to 3,000 members of the NLA armed with weapons numbering in the low thousands … The Macedonian defence ministry says there are up to 8,000 rebels, possessing at least 8,000 weapons' (*Guardian*, 16 August 2001, p. 2).

'Nato's operation [is] to start collecting "one weapon" from each member of the 2,500 to 6,000-strong ethnic Albanian NLA' (*The Times*, 22 August 2001, p. 11).

'The Macedonian army has suggested 8,000 guns. The NLA figure is 2,500. Unofficial Nato estimates suggest 4,000 to 5,000' (*Guardian*, 22 August 2001, p. 10).

(There was widespread scepticism about the proportion of actual weapons that would be handed over.)

('Most Macedonians believe that the rebels are not really fighting for greater political and cultural rights for Albanians ... Rather, the majority believes that Ali Ahmeti's real goal is to unite all ethnic Albanians in the region who now live here, in Serbia, Montenegro, Greece and in Albanian itself into one unified state': *IHT*, 17 August 2001, p. 6.)

16 August 2001: 'A Macedonian police officer was killed by a sniper at a checkpoint near Tetovo ... Police blamed ethnic Albanian rebels for the attack' (*The Times*, 17 August 2001, p. 10).

> Yesterday [16 August] there were reports of sporadic shooting in ... Tetovo and a checkpoint in the north was attacked ... on Wednesday [15 August]. However, before the shooting of the policeman [on 16 August] Nato officials judged the ceasefire was generally holding.
>
> (*Independent*, 17 August 2001, p. 15)

> The US government is planning to finance an intense political advertising and lobbying campaign in the next forty-five days here [in Macedonia] to secure parliamentary passage of a peace deal ... that is regarded with deep scepticism by Macedonian political parties and the Macedonian public ... All twenty-five ethnic Albanian members of parliament are expected to support the deal, whose ratification requires eighty votes to amend the constitution ... [in] the 120-member parliament.
>
> (*IHT*, 17 August 2001, pp. 1, 6)

17 August 2001: the first Nato soldiers (Czech, French and British) in the advance party arrive.

'One diplomat ... said the ceasefire was "looking pretty good" despite the killing of a Macedonian policeman and an Albanian civilian in Tetovo since Thursday [16 August] and some sporadic shooting near rural villages' (*IHT*, 18 August 2001, p. 5).

18–19 August 2001:

> Macedonian and Nato officials said Sunday [19 August] there had been no fighting overnight, for the first time since Macedonian and ethnic Albanian political leaders signed a peace accord last Monday [13 August]. But there was some gunfire Sunday night ... [On 19 August there] was a small anti-Western protest by angry members of the Macedonian majority. The demonstrators, who blame Nato for failing to stop guns and guerrillas flooding into Macedonia from neighbouring Kosovo, have barricaded the main [Kfor] supply route into [Kosovo].
>
> (*IHT*, 20 August 2001, p. 1)

'A small protest by 150 Macedonians closed the main road linking Macedonia and ... Kosovo ... The blockade [was] manned by protesters demanding help for villagers who fled villages occupied by the rebels' (*FT*, 20 August 2001, p. 7).

'Macedonian forces and rebels exchanged sustained gunfire yesterday [19 August] near the village of Neprosteno in the north-west ... [There was] a blockade of the road into Kosovo by Slav refugees who had fled from the area now controlled by the NLA' (*Telegraph*, 20 August 2001, p. 8).

20 August 2001: '[There has been] overnight skirmishing between rebels and security forces 40 kilometres (25 miles) west of Skopje ... The defence ministry announced it was ready to pull back front-line forces and stop warplane and helicopter flights over areas of confrontation' (*IHT*, 21 August 2001, pp. 1, 5).

The ceasefire faltered again late on Sunday [19 August] when rebels and security forces waged gun battles punctuated by mortar explosions in villages outside Tetovo, 40 kilometres west of Skopje. But conflict zones have been quiet by day over the past week and although no night has passed without some skirmishing, the frequency and severity of violations have diminished.

(*FT*, 21 August 2001, p. 6)

'Sporadic fighting in Neprosteno ... an Albanian village to the east of Tetovo ... followed heavy shelling overnight' (*Guardian*, 21 August 2001, p. 2).

21 August 2001:

After hearing a favourable report from General Joseph Ralston, commander of Nato forces in Europe ... Nato ministers decided Tuesday [21 August] to send a full 3,500-soldier task force into Macedonia ... However, the decision was issued 'under silence' until mid-day Wednesday [22 August], meaning it can be rescinded if any of the nineteen member countries objects by then ... General Joseph Ralston ... told Nato's ruling council that 'the ceasefire is generally holding, with incidents declining both in intensity and numbers' ... General Ralston apparently emphasized that the danger of waiting, and perhaps seeing the ceasefire unravel, was greater than the danger to Nato troops of going in immediately ... Fighting has not stopped – sniper and mortar fire were exchanged in a village near Tetovo and an explosion rocked an Orthodox church ... An explosion Tuesday [21 August] ripped apart a fourteenth century monastery [St Atanasie and the Holy Virgin in the village of Lesok in the north-west], one of the most revered Orthodox buildings in Macedonia and was one of the few attacks on religious buildings in six months [of fighting] ... Neither the Macedonian Slavs, who are Orthodox, nor the ethnic Albanians, who are Moslem, have made religion an overt part of the conflict here.

(*IHT*, 22 August 2001, p. 4)

An explosion ... badly damaged a church within an Orthodox monastery in the village of Lesok ... There have been few such attacks on religious buildings so far ... although a mosque in the central town of Prilep was set on fire by Macedonian protesters in an attack a fortnight ago ... Several mosques in rebel-held villages north of Kumanovo have also been badly damaged after months of shelling by government forces.

(*Guardian*, 22 August 2001, p. 10)

Huge planeloads of arms from Ukraine and Russia are being delivered secretly at night ... as part of a buildup of arms by the government, according to Western defence sources ... Under pressure from the EU ... Ukraine, Skopje's main arms supplier, had agreed to consider suspending arms shipments to Macedonia.

(*The Times*, 22 August 2001, p. 11)

22 August 2001:

Nato on Wednesday [22 August] formally gave the go-ahead to its full 3,500-soldier mission ... as a mid-day deadline passed without objections from any of the member countries ... Macedonia's government Wednesday claimed that the country's rebels have 85,000 weapons – far more than the 2,000 the militants have said they would hand over to Nato's disarmament mission.

(*IHT*, 23 August 2001, p. 1)

George Robertson: 'There are risks involved ... Members of the alliance have agreed to send their troops because we know the risks of not sending them are far greater.'

The Nato task force commander, General Gunnar Lange, from Denmark, said he had intelligence reports that new shipments of weapons were already on their way to the rebels from Kosovo ... The rebels say they have a total of 2,000 guns, but the Macedonian interior ministry claims the figure is 85,000.

(*Independent*, 23 August 2001, p. 12)

Nato officials conceded that they did not expect the guerrillas to hand over all their weapons, but they were looking for a total of at least 2,500. The Macedonian government's ... estimates have fluctuated wildly from an initial 8,000 to more than ten times that figure.

(*Guardian*, 23 August 2001, p. 11)

The Macedonian interior ministry caused a storm by suggesting that there were more than 80,000 [weapons]. It later clarified this to say that the figure included grenades and landmines. The Macedonian ministry of defence has put the total at 8,000 ... The parliamentary speaker, Stoyan Andov, a Macedonian hardliner close to the prime minister and the interior minister, has said he will only put ratification of the peace accord on the agenda when one third of NLA weapons have been given up.

(*Guardian*, 24 August 2001, p. 2)

'The Macedonian government is insisting that since there are about 7,000 rebels, they must hand over at least 7,000 guns' (*The Economist*, 25 August 2001, p. 37).

24 August 2001:

> Nato announced a deal on Friday [24 August] with ethnic Albanian rebels on the number of weapons the insurgents are to surrender ... But it was unclear whether the government would accept the figure. Major General Gunnar Lange, the Nato [task force] commander ... refused to confirm the figure. But Western diplomats said the two sides had settled on about 3,000 weapons ... Nato hopes to start the mission on Monday [27 August] and collect about a third of the arms by the end of the week. The rebel NLA initially said it had just 2,000 weapons ... Nato officials have played down the dispute over weapons figures, arguing that the point of the mission is to build trust – to persuade the ethnic Albanian and Macedonian sides to use the arms handover as their first mutual confidence-building measure. The peace accord envisions a staggered process in which a cache of weapons is handed over in exchange for political steps by the government. The weapons are to be handed over in three stages. The number must be accepted by the government.
>
> (*IHT*, 25 August 2001, p. 2)

'In the town of Blace ... about fifty people have been blocking Nato trucks from the main route to Kosovo for nearly a week' (p. 1).

> The agreed [between Nato and the NLA] inventory of arms – about 3,500 ... was presented to President Trajkovski yesterday [24 August] for his approval ... Western defence sources said the important issue was not the numbers but the fact that the NLA was giving up a significant capability.
>
> (*The Times*, 25 August 2001, p. 16)

> Nato has settled on ... a little more than 3,000 weapons [that] need to be collected ... Western diplomats said ... Ethnic Albanian guerrillas are expected to give up a third of their weapons by the end of next week as a result of the agreement between rebel commanders and Nato officials ... Despite the Nato presence there is still no ceasefire.
>
> (*Guardian*, 25 August 2001, p. 17)

'The NLA insisted that it had only about 2,300 weapons ... Western intelligence assessments put the figure at up to 5,000 ... The compromise figure ... is thought to be between 3,000 and 4,000' (*Telegraph*, 25 August 2001, p. 22).

25–6 August 2001: sporadic fighting is reported.

> Nato on Sunday [26 August] issued a breakdown of the 3,300 weapons it expects ethnic Albanian rebels to voluntarily turn over to the alliance for

destruction beginning Monday [27 August]. But ... Macedonian prime minister Ljubco Georgievski labelled the overall number 'humiliating' and threatened to respond to an explosion that killed two Macedonians early Sunday. The explosion ripped through a Macedonian-owned hotel in Celopek, 10 kilometres (six miles) south ... of Tetovo and just across a river from rebel-held territory. A barman and a waiter were killed in the explosion, which occurred in the hometown of Macedonia's hardline interior minister, Ljube Boskovski ... Major General Gunnar Lange ... said ... Sunday that the 3,300 weapons say they have are 'very close to our own numbers' ... The rebels also plan to hand over 110,000 rounds of ammunition, he said.

(*IHT*, 27 August 2001, pp. 1, 6)

Major General Gunnar Lange: 'On Friday [24 August] we presented the government ... a figure of 3,300 weapons that the so-called NLA had declared to voluntarily hand over to Nato' (*FT*, 27 August 2001, p. 4).

'Prime minister Ljubco Georgievski yesterday [26 August] repeated his view that the figure of 3,300 was a "ridiculous" total ... He estimated the true figure was closer to 60,000 weapons' (*The Times*, 27 August 2001, p. 9).

'The prime minister claims that the rebels have at least 60,000 weapon ... But the weapons handovers were always intended to be a gesture, not a complete disarmament, as Nato officials privately concede' (*Independent*, 27 August 2001, p. 11).

'Prime minister Ljubco Georgievski insists the size of the rebel arsenal is closer to 60,000' (*IHT*, 30 August 2001, p. 5).

'Britain is providing 1,900 of the 4,500-strong Nato force' (*Independent*, 28 August 2001, p. 8).

27 August 2001: weapon collection begins.

A British soldier dies from injuries received the previous day. He was struck on the head by a piece of concrete thrown by youths (seemingly Slav Macedonian) from a road bridge. The object broke the windscreen of the vehicle the soldier was in at the time.

There are many reports of a widespread anti-Nato atmosphere among Slav Macedonians encouraged by elements of both the government and the media.

'[Nato] has been consistently demonized as an ally of the rebels' (*IHT*, 28 August 2001, p. 4). '[There is] widespread suspicion among Slav Macedonians that the package was forced on the country at gunpoint ... [The] population has become deeply suspicious of the United States, the EU and Nato' (*IHT*, 31 August 2001, p. 5).

There has been a venomous anti-Western campaign orchestrated by hardline ministers in the Macedonian government. For months Ljubco Georgievski, the prime minister, and Ljube Boskovski, have publicly savaged Nato for allegedly backing the ethnic Albanians ... Attacks on foreigners have become commonplace. The nationalist local media have further stirred feelings, accusing Nato of illicitly arming Albanian rebels and preventing the government from using force to crush them.

(*Telegraph*, 28 August 2001, p. 8)

Many ethnic Macedonian Slavs now feel ... hatred ... for anybody with any apparent connection with Nato or Nato countries ... Macedonian Slavs see it [the peace accord] as a sell-out and resent the deployment of 4,500 Nato soldiers'... Among the most resentful are the 67,000 Macedonian Slavs who the Skopje government estimates have fled their homes.

(*FT*, 28 August 2001, pp. 1–2)

Sections of the Slav population and the Macedonian government feel betrayed. They abandoned their traditional allegiance to the Serbs during the 1999 Kosovo conflict and backed Nato. They expected a reward. Instead, they were pressed to sign a peace deal that they regard as tilted toward the ethnic Albanians.

(*FT*, editorial, 29 August 2001, p. 14)

28 August 2001: the collection of weapons proceeds smoothly and amicably.

It emerged yesterday [28 August] that the Nato force is prepared to take on tasks outside its remit of collecting weapons. British soldiers escorted Macedonian Slavs through territory occupied by ethnic Albanian armed groups to the village of Lesok, where a church was blown up last week. The soldiers kept watch on the surrounding hillsides as the worshippers prayed outside the ruins and then helped them return safely to Skopje.

(*FT*, 29 August 2001, p. 2)

'A Nato liaison team negotiated a rebel withdrawal so that Tuesday's service ... could go ahead and British soldiers provided a sense of security for the Macedonians, who fled here in July, homes and businesses aflame at their backs' (*IHT*, 29 August 2001, p. 1). 'But senior Nato officials insist that the British teams were in the area because it was near a weapons-collection site and that Macedonian civilians should not expect the alliance's soldiers to watch over their activities in the future' (*IHT*, 3 September 2001, p. 5).

29 August 2001: George Robertson (on a visit to Macedonia):

It is not just the number of weapons that matter. It is the fact that the so-called NLA is handing over these weapons and disbanding as an organization. I hope the people of Macedonia will see these weapons coming out of Macedonian politics and will draw the right lesson. There is a moral obligation behind this political framework agreement. Just as I expect the insurgents to deliver on their commitments, I expect the Macedonian members of parliament also to recognize their responsibilities.

The German parliament overwhelmingly approves the deployment of up to 500 German soldiers with the Nato task force.

30 August 2001:

> In the first part of the three-step process, Nato formally informed Mr Trajkovski on Thursday [30 August] that the NLA had turned in one-third of its 3,300 weapons, clearing the way for the first parliamentary vote ... Mr Trajkovski said he planned to write to OSCE to ask formally for up to 150 monitors, who will watch the return of Macedonian security forces into the areas now held by the guerrillas ... Far fewer rebels were visible Thursday in the Tetovo area.
>
> (*IHT*, 31 August 2001, p. 6)

The British foreign secretary, Jack Straw, visits Macedonia.

'Two British counter-insurgency advisers would help the Macedonian government in forming a new anti-terrorist unit and "rapid reaction force for emergencies" ' (*The Times*, 31 August 2001, p. 10).

'A bomb destroyed an Albanian shop in Skopje yesterday [30 August] ... but no one was hurt' (*Independent*, 31 August 2001, p. 12).

31 August 2001: President Trajkovski (in his address to parliament): 'This agreement is not perfect, but no agreement is. It is the best we have at the moment and it has some positive aspects. The alternative is war.'

> Mr Trajkovski's plea for support [for the peace accord], which opened a debate on whether to adopt reforms to promote and protect minority rights, was delayed by six hours by hundreds of protesting Macedonians, who blocked entrances to parliament and denounced the process as a sellout at gunpoint. About 500 demonstrators blocked the parliament doors and scuffled with some lawmakers ... Many Macedonians are sceptical about the rebels' pledges and Nato's role in the peace process, which they fear will lead to the partition of their country along ethnic lines.
>
> (*IHT*, 1 September 2001, p. 2)

'Mr Trajkovski requested the return of a United Nations peace force stationed in the country in the 1990s. He called for international recognition of Macedonia as the country's name ... In three days ... 1,470 weapons ... [were] collected' (*Telegraph*, 1 September 2001, p. 20).

'The majority of the angry crowd outside parliament were refugees who fled from occupied areas of the country. Most say they were forced out at gunpoint' (*Independent*, 1 September 2001, p. 12).

'Although the protesters were few in number, their view that the accord has been imposed by the West and is unnecessary is shared by large parts of the country's Macedonian Slav majority' (*Guardian*, 1 September 2001, p. 15).

1–2 September 2001:

> The Macedonian parliament will reopen debate Monday [3 September] on a
> peace plan after a two-day delay … Stojan Andov, the parliament speaker,
> suspended the debate Saturday [1 September] … Mr Andov had insisted on a
> presidential guarantee that everyone who fled the fighting could return home
> safely. Up to 120,000 people remain displaced by the fighting, according to
> the UN refugee agency. President Boris Trajkovski gave Mr Andov 'assur-
> ances that the existing problems would be overcome', a presidential statement
> said Sunday … A firebomb early Sunday [2 September] destroyed a tea
> house in an ethnic Albanian district of Skopje … Other bomb attacks
> damaged an Albanian home and a car belonging to a Macedonian firm.
>
> (*IHT*, 3 September 2001, p. 4)

'The Albanian barricade … trapped a group of Macedonian refugees in the
Albanian-dominated foothills' (*IHT*, 3 September 2001, p. 5).

'Mr Andov suspended the debate, which began on Friday [31 August], after a
rebel roadblock prevented a group of Macedonians passing through … [An]
estimated 69,000 Macedonians [have been] displaced by the fighting' (*Guardian*,
3 September 2001, p. 11).

'[Mr Andov] was reported to have relented after the Albanians decided … to
dismantle a road barricade that had trapped displaced Macedonians revisiting
their homes' (*Telegraph*, 3 September 2001, p. 11).

> Islamic 'holy warriors' came to various countries to the mountains of
> central Bosnia … They volunteered for the Bosnian army … The muja-
> hadin [is] the secretive movement of Islamic volunteer fighters who have
> been operating in the Balkans for the better part of a decade … Several
> thousand of the warriors first appeared in Bosnia in 1992 … [They were]
> estimated to number 3,000 to 5,000 … Under the Dayton Peace Accords
> the mujahadin were meant to leave Bosnia, but a number married local
> women … Others left for Albania where they helped train the rebels who
> became known as the KLA. This year [2001], according to Western diplo-
> mats, the fighters have appeared once more, now on the side of Albanian
> rebels in Macedonia.
>
> (*IHT*, 3 September 2001, p. 8)

'The Dayton peace agreement that ended the war ordered all foreign soldiers
to leave the country. But an undisclosed number remained there, obtaining
Bosnian citizenship as members of the army or by marrying Bosnian women'
(*IHT*, 13 September 2001, p. 6).

3 September 2001: James Pardew:

> I cannot judge at this point whether the security of civilian monitors would
> be adequate [without military protection]. All I can say is that those

responsible for deploying monitors are raising security as an issue … I am not pushing an agenda here. But security after disarmament is an issue being raised as we try to raise the number of monitors.

(*FT*, 4 September 2001, p. 10; *IHT*, 4 September 2001, p. 1)

Violence has virtually stopped … Under the peace deal the international community, including Nato, OSCE and the EU, has pledged to deploy monitors. Their main role will be to observe the return of the Macedonian security forces to guerrilla-held areas … The EU and OSCE are currently planning to increase their numbers from about fifty to about 100.

(*FT*, 3 September 2001, p. 10)

'At present there are about fifty [OSCE] monitors in Macedonia' (*The Times*, 3 September 2001, p. 13).

'OSCE is preparing to send 150 peace monitors and the EU has promised thirty' (*IHT*, 6 September 2001, p. 4).

'Parliament resumed debate of crucial constitutional amendments Monday [3 September] after a two-day suspension … Daily skirmishes between the police and guerrillas continue to endanger the peace process' (*IHT*, 3 September 2001, p. 5).

'In the front-line villages of north-western Macedonia … kidnappings, beatings and shootings remain a regular feature of life' (*Telegraph*, 3 September 2001, p. 11).

5 September 2001: Human Rights Watch (based in New York):

The evidence available to us indicates that the attack on Ljuboten had no military justification and was carried out for purposes of revenge and reprisal … During a Sunday [12 August] house-to-house attack police forces shot dead six civilians. One man was killed by police as he tried to close the door to his home when police entered the yard. Two men were summarily executed by police after they were taken out of the basement in which they were hiding … It is imperative that an independent, impartial and credible investigation is conducted into the role of [interior] minister Boskovski, as well as the role of those under his authority, in the events in Ljuboten. Serious abuses were committed in Ljuboten and those responsible for ordering, committing or condoning those abuses must be brought to account.

Human Rights Watch said interior ministry police had shot dead six civilians in Ljuboten. Three more died in random shelling and another villager was fatally shot as he tried to flee … The action by Macedonian security police in Ljuboten [took place] between 10 and 12 August.

(*The Times*, 6 September 2001, p. 12)

6 September 2001:

Macedonia's parliament yesterday [6 September] voted overwhelmingly in favour of starting work on political reforms … By a margin of ninety-one to nineteen, well over the required two-thirds majority, deputies approved the drafting of amendments to the constitution aimed at granting greater rights to the ethnic Albanian minority ... Yesterday's vote, after nearly a week of debate, only begins the legislative process. Detailed clause-by-clause discussions will now take place following a final vote, for which a two-thirds majority will again be required. However, yesterday's vote will trigger a fresh round of disarmament by the guerrillas.

(*FT*, 7 September 2001, p. 9)

'In parliament legislators made lengthy and highly critical speeches of the government and of the Western-mediated plan ... Thursday's vote represents the first of three parliamentary sessions to approve the peace plan' (*IHT*, 7 September 2001, p. 7). 'Members of Macedonia's security council rejected a proposal Thursday [6 September] to allow any international military force to take over after Nato's thirty-day operation' (*IHT*, 8 September 2001, p. 5).

7 September 2001: weapons collection resumes. The second stage involves a further third of the agreed weapons total.

9 September 2001:

EU foreign ministers will back a Nato-led force to protect up to 200 monitors in Macedonia when Nato's 'Essential Harvest' operation ends ... There is still disagreement over whether a force, were it agreed, should be backed by a UN mandate. There is also uncertainty about whether the Macedonian government would agree to another Nato mission without UN consent ... At an informal meeting of EU foreign ministers ... Britain alone rejected the need for a UN mandate – a view it shares with the United States ... The EU believes a UN mandate would have international legitimacy and allow non-Nato countries to participate in a mission whose scope and duration has still to be decided. The willingness to send another Nato-led force reflects the view within the EU that Macedonia is still unstable after months of fighting. The fear is that any 'security vacuum' [the term used by EU foreign ministers] could be exploited by either side, making the monitors vulnerable to attack ... Support for a Nato-led force puts paid to a proposal by François Leotard, the EU's special envoy in Macedonia, that the EU could lead a force to protect monitors who will assist in the return of refugees to villages where control is contested. It was confirmed yesterday [9 September] that Mr Leotard had, a few days ago, handed in his resignation ... EU diplomats insisted that ... [his] resignation, which is effective from 8 October, had nothing to do with the proposal.

(*FT*, 10 September 2001, p. 1)

Diplomats made clear that million of euros of assistance could be at risk if Skopje refused to allow troops to protect [150–200] unarmed observers from the EU and OSCE ... Behind the scenes EU diplomats said they feared that the Slav-dominated government would crack down on rebels ... once the

disarmament mission has finished … Over the weekend … [it was reported] that government troops and rebels exchanged fire in the western Tetovo area.
(*Guardian*, Monday 10 September 2001, p. 10)

10 September 2001: a spokesman for the government (in response to the EU suggestion) : 'We have nothing against Nato forces being part of an international force with a UN mandate with a mission to protect Macedonia's borders with Kosovo and Albania' (*IHT*, 11 September 2001, p. 7).

'More than 36,000 ethnic Albanian refugees have crossed the border from Kosovo into Macedonia and another 45,000 remain in Kosovo … Virtually none of the 30,000 or so Macedonian Slavs has returned' (*FT*, 11 September 2001, p. 8).

13 September 2001:

Nato said Thursday [13 September] it had collected more than two-thirds of the declared arsenal of ethnic Albanian guerrillas … despite a threat to disarmament by Macedonian paramilitaries. Separately, Macedonia's parliament indefinitely put off debate on whether to seek a referendum on civil rights reforms benefiting the large Albanian minority … A referendum [is sought] by nationalist foes of the reforms.

(*IHT*, 14 September 2001, p. 10)

Nato says it has recovered 2,135 of its target 3,300 NLA weapons … The announcement came in spite of two threats to the peace process: one from the Macedonian parliament, which put on hold a debate on civil rights reforms benefiting ethnic Albanians, the other from paramilitaries who appeared to be trying to disrupt the disarmament … [A] Nato spokesman said some disarmament had been disrupted by Macedonian paramilitaries harassing demobilized NLA men near ceasefire lines north of Tetovo.

(*The Times*, 14 September 2001, p. 11)

[The arsenal collected by Nato] includes few serious items: ground-to-air missiles, rocket- and grenade-launchers, snipers' rifles. The rebels have buried many others, Nato suspects … Slav-Macedonian civilian police reservists have not had to hand in the 10,000 or so Kalashnikovs that … interior minister Ljube Boskovski … and his friends gave out in the spring … His ministry's legitimate anti-terrorist police, the Tigers, are recruiting hard. But only 10 per cent of those drawn by its colourful advertising are accepted. The rest go off to join the Lions and other dubious groups … Last week British paratroopers had to save a senior ethnic Albanian policeman from a Lions gang … In provincial towns they [the Lions] and those like them are extorting money from businesses, buying off local police and other officials, and chasing out of town those who might support President Boris Trajkovski and others trying to build peace.

(*The Economist*, 15 September 2001, p. 42)

14 September 2001:

The Nato secretary-general, Lord Robertson, flew to Skopje yesterday [14 September] for crisis talks aimed at calming the demands of Macedonian MPs for a watering down of the country's fragmented peace agreement. He also hoped to overcome opposition to Nato's tentative plans to keep troops in the country to prevent a new drift toward civil war. President Boris Trajkovski ... has said that foreign troops must have a UN mandate and are needed only to seal the border with Kosovo ... Macedonian hardliners, who have been forming armed paramilitary units, want all foreign troops to leave so that they can have a free hand to deal with [ethnic Albanian] gunmen. Although the ceasefire is holding, about 22,000 Macedonians have fled from mixed towns and villages since the peace agreement was signed last month. By contrast ... almost 35,000 displaced ethnic Albanians have gone home, according to the UN High Commissioner for Refugees. This imbalance, coupled with the increasingly nationalistic tone of the local media, is strengthening the widespread majority Macedonian view that the peace agreement is biased in favour of the Albanian minority and is a step towards partition ... Pressure is also growing on MPs to put the peace agreement to a referendum ... Nato said on Wednesday [12 September] that two thirds of the estimated Albanian arsenal of around 3,500 weapons had been given up, although it admitted that about a third of the Kalashnikov rifles handed in were unserviceable ... Leaders of the two biggest Macedonian parties supported ... the peace agreement ... but are giving MPs a free vote.

(*Guardian*, 15 September 2001, p. 17)

'Macedonian radio reported an exchange of fire overnight between rebels and security forces around the villages of Ratae and Zilce near ... Tetovo' (*Independent*, 15 September 2001, p. 19).

17 September 2001:

The Macedonian government said Monday [17 September] that it would accept a small Nato security force ... 'Macedonia will request that Nato authorize another small-scale mission' after the weapons collection by the alliance is completed, said a presidential adviser ... [He] added that the government would ask OSCE to increase its monitoring presence ... Government attempts to prolong the fragile peace came after an outburst of violence and amid potential threats to the country's internationally backed peace plan posed by attempts to put the plan to a referendum ... The referendum proposal, brought by the small New Democracy Party, needs a simple majority of sixty-one votes in the 120-seat parliament to pass. Branko Crvenkovski, leader of the pro-Western Social Democratic Alliance, has warned that his party could pull out of the fragile government coalition if parliament voted for the referendum ... The police in the village of Zilce, about seven kilometres (four miles) north-east of Tetovo, exchanged fire with ethnic Albanians in the neighbouring village of Semsevo Sunday [16 September].

(*IHT*, 18 September 2001, p. 9)

18 September 2001:

The Macedonian parliament wrestled with a referendum motion ... With many of the majority Macedonian electorate opposed to concessions to the ethnic Albanian minority, the pact could unravel if put to a referendum. Meanwhile tension was growing in the north after battles between Macedonian forces and ethnic Albanians. A standoff developed in the village of Zilce ... Angry Macedonians blockaded a road to prevent police units in the village from being replaced by army units.

(*IHT*, 19 September 2001, p. 8)

Macedonian MPs ... considered putting it [the peace plan] to a referendum ... Italy's foreign minister in Skopje ... said: 'A delay of some months to organize and carry out a referendum seems to us to be a very serious danger for the political stability we are trying to reach' ... Nato sources said yesterday [18 September] that the leader of the NLA, Ali Ahmeti, told them his fighters would continue to surrender their weapons even if the Macedonian government stalled on implementing political concessions.

(*Telegraph*, 19 September 2001, p. 12)

19 September 2001:

Macedonian legislators on Wednesday [19 September] put off the start of changes crucial to peace with Albanian guerrillas in order to debate whether to submit the deal to a referendum ... An assembly session scheduled Wednesday to give conditional approval to fourteen amendments was cancelled ... Deputies insisted that a vote on whether to hold a referendum should come first. 'Two months would be needed to organize a referendum and this would put us in a difficult situation,' Javier Solana said ... The rebels have turned in two-thirds of their declared arsenal to Nato troops and say they will surrender the rest even if parliament has not yet reciprocated.

(*IHT*, 20 September 2001, p. 9)

20 September 2001:

Nato resumed collecting weapons from the ethnic Albanian rebels yesterday [20 September] in the final phase of its mission despite footdragging by lawmakers ... Parliament was expected to discuss the [constitutional] amendments before the last of the weapons were collected. After hours of uncertainty over whether it would convene, the session finally began on Wednesday [19 September]. The discussion was also delayed by a proposal by the small New Democracy Party to put the constitutional amendments to a referendum ... [As regards] the tense standoff with people in the villages of Zilce and Ratae, who refused to allow police units to be replaced by the army ... by yesterday the army had moved in to take their place ... An explosion outside Skopje yesterday damaged an ethnic Albanian-owned gas station.

(*Independent*, 21 September 2001, p. 18)

24 September 2001:

Macedonia's parliament on Monday [24 September] approved in principle fifteen constitutional amendments ... Hours before the vote state security forces at a checkpoint shot and killed an ethnic Albanian ... Nationalist legislators vow to weaken some of the draft clauses ... before they are ratified next month. The agreement could unravel if the assembly votes to put the changes to a referendum, an issue it planned to debate on Tuesday [25 September]. Ethnic Albanians said that altering the reforms or submitting them to a plebiscite would renew the conflict. A Nato spokesman said that the rebels had turned in 92 per cent of their declared 3,300-weapon stockpile to alliance troops, with three days left in their mandated thirty-day disarmament period ... On Monday ... the draft amendments were passed by simple majorities, sometimes well short of the two-thirds margin that they will need for final ratification. The most controversial change would replace the reference to 'national state of Macedonian people' in the constitution's preamble with 'a state of its citizens'. Another important change would require legislation affecting culture, language and education to be passed with the support of at least half the minority deputies in parliament. Final ratification would clear the way for legislation to decentralize power, add ethnic Albanians in the police force in proportion to their one-third presence in the population and to allow some official use of their language.

(*IHT*, 25 September 2001, p. 9)

An ethnic Albanian man was shot dead and another wounded when they failed to stop at a checkpoint. The shootings happened [near] ceasefire lines in the mountainous Rasce area, north of Skopje, where there is a large concentration of security forces protecting the capital's water supply. It was believed to be the first killing directly related to Macedonia's ethnic conflict since a Western-mediated truce was reached in mid-August.

(*Independent*, 25 September 2001, p. 14)

Nato was last night [24 September] making final preparations for sending in a follow-up contingent after the German government last week agreed to lead the operation – the first time it has done so in the Balkans. The operation, called Amber Fox, will consist of between 1,000 and 1,100 soldiers, including French and Italian troops ... The troops' primary function will be to protect about 150 civilian monitors drawn from OSCE and the EU ... The monitors' main task is to see that refugees are allowed to return to their towns and villages and to oversee implementation of reforms designed to give more rights to the Albanian minority ... More than 50,000 ethnic Albanian refugees have returned from Kosovo.

(*FT*, Tuesday 25 September 2001, p. 12)

The alliance has agreed to provide a much smaller follow-on force, ostensibly to protect international monitors who will observe the implementation of the peace deal. The real reason is more probably that the international community believes a symbolic Nato presence alone will do much to prevent further fighting.

(*Independent*, 27 September 2001, p. 16)

26 September 2001: 'Nato declared an end to its weapons collection mission on Wednesday [26 September]' (*IHT*, 27 September 2001, p. 5).

The mission gathered in a total of 3,875 weapons ... [above the declared total of] 3,3000 ... A total of 397,625 items of ammunition, including mines and explosives, were also given up by the rebels ... Last night [26 September] the UN Security Council unanimously supported its [the follow-up force's] deployment.

(*Telegraph*, 27 September 2001, p. 23)

Major General Gunnar Lange (commander of Nato forces in Macedonia): 'No matter what else happens from this point on, during the past thirty days the violence dramatically declined in Macedonia and a real commitment has been shown to end the fighting for good ... [The KLA] has promised to disband.'

27 September 2001:

Germany was preparing Thursday [27 September] to take command of a Nato mission for the first time after the nineteen-nation alliance ordered the deployment of 1,000 soldiers to safeguard civilian observers ... Germany cleared the final hurdle for the three-month Nato deployment when the Bundestag overwhelmingly approved the mission, called 'Amber Fox' ... Germany will provide 600 of the 1,000-strong force. Already 450 German soldiers are on the ground ... The troops will be deployed solely to protect 280 civilian observers who will monitor the terms of a 13 August peace agreement ... Nato rushed to fill a potential security vacuum early Thursday by issuing an activation order to extend a military presence after the expiration on Wednesday [26 September] of a thirty-day Nato mandate to collect weapons from Albanian rebels ... It could be extended beyond that 'depending on the situation in the country' Nato said ... The late-night Nato decision ... was delayed Wednesday on last-minute objections by the Macedonian government over the duration and size of the Nato presence ... The three-month mission got off to an auspicious start as ... ethnic Albanian rebels announced they had disbanded in accordance with the ... peace agreement.

(*IHT*, 28 September 2001, p. 4)

'NLA leader Ali Ahmeti told reporters he favoured displaced Macedonians returning to their homes and that state security forces could move into areas previously held by rebels as long as they had Albanians in their ranks' (*FT*, 28 September 2001, p. 12).

Ali Ahmeti (leader of the NLA):

> The signal has been given to all former fighters that they should reintegrate as civilians of this country ... Last night at midnight the NLA was formally disbanded and all the former fighters have become ordinary citizens of this country once again ... We want all the displaced people to return to their homes, whatever their background ... For us it is of key importance to have an amnesty for our fighters, for them to reintegrate into society.
> (*IHT*, 28 September 2001, p. 4; *Guardian*, 28 September 2001, p. 18; *The Times*, 28 September 2001, p. 19)

'In the last few days police checkpoints leading up to rebel-held areas have been dismantled, enabling people to visit nearby Tetovo for the first time in months' (*Guardian*, 28 September 2001, p. 18).

28 September 2001:

> More than 55,000 of Macedonia's war refugees have returned home but repatriating the rest will depend in part on setting up ethnically mixed police patrols ... the UN High Commissioner for Refugees, Ruud Lubbers ... said Friday [28 September]. About 97,000 people remain displaced.
> (*IHT*, 29 September 2001, p. 7)

3 October 2001:

> There are fears that the peace process could break down if government forces go ahead with a plan to retake areas under the control of Albanians rebels today [4 October]. A rebel commander [a known hardliner called Leka] yesterday [3 October] warned of war if security forces tried to enter the territory while Western officials reacted with anger and concern when the Macedonian interior minister, Ljube Boskovski, yesterday announced the move to retake rebel-held areas, ignoring calls to wait until a Western-brokered peace deal was implemented and a promised amnesty for the rebels agreed. 'Tomorrow [4 October] is D-Day for Macedonia when our security forces will return to occupied territory,' Mr Boskovski said ... yesterday ... Gunfire still rings out across the front line and many rebels are still in position, though out of uniform ... Parliament has stopped meeting

to debate the measures since Nato hailed its mission as a success and started to pull out some troops. Parliament refuses to resume sessions until the rebels account for several missing ethnic Macedonians.

(*Independent*, 4 October 2001, p. 16)

'Ljube Boskovski said the police would start returning to former guerrilla areas today [4 October], without the prior agreement of the Western peace monitors' (*Guardian*, 4 October 2001, p. 19).

4 October 2001: 'The Macedonian police entered a few ethnic Albanian villages on Thursday [4 October] but backed off from others that it intended to retake in the country's former war zones as Western officials warned the government against moves that could reignite violence' (*IHT*, 5 October 2001, p. 4).

Macedonian security forces took control of three ethnic Albanian villages but backed off several others after meeting resistance ... The EU's ... commissioner for external affairs, Chris Patten ... said Thursday [4 October] that a donors' conference scheduled for 15 October to consider resumption of financial aid to Skopje was 'absolutely inconceivable' unless the situation improved.

(*IHT*, 6 October 2001, p. 2)

Macedonian police units moved towards areas recently held by ethnic Albanian guerrillas ... drawing strong criticism from EU politicians. Units ... patrolled three villages close to the NLA's old frontline near the north-western town of Gostivar ... The police did pull back from other former rebel-held areas elsewhere ... The EU external affairs commissioner, Chris Patten ... said parliament had broken its promise to complete the [ratification] process by last week ... The donors' conference due on 15 October had been postponed, he added.

(*Guardian*, 5 October 2001, p. 18)

5 October 2001:

American and European officials ... apparently succeeded Friday [5 October] in pressuring the Macedonian police to suspend an effort to retake control ethnic Albanian areas ... Javier Solana ... and ... Chris Patten met with the rival sides in Skopje. They demanded that Macedonia honour the accord ... As an apparent result the police said they would stop entering ethnic Albanian-populated villages and that any future restoration of government authority in the contested areas would be carried out in co-operation with Nato, the EU and OSCE.

(*IHT*, 6 October 2001, p. 5)

Macedonian security forces pulled back from positions close to the old front-line with the NLA yesterday [5 October], amid fierce international criticism

... Ratification [of the peace accord] is already twelve days behind schedule ... The Hague tribunal will next week be sent a list of alleged war crimes committed by the Macedonian army and police, accompanied by a request that it investigate the hardline interior minister, Ljube Boskovski ... Eyewitness accounts of alleged killings, kidnappings, torture and the systematic destruction of mosques [have been] gathered by the European Council of Humanity (ECHAC), which carried out similar work in Kosovo and East Timor ... ECHAC says the police, army and paramilitary groups have been using the war with the NLA as an excuse to launch a systematic campaign to force ethnic Albanians out of the country ... adding that during May and June there was a deliberate policy of shelling civilian targets ... While alleged NLA crimes received coverage earlier this year [2001], the ECHAC report contains the first claims of widespread abuses by the army and police ... ECHAC says it will produce a second collection of eyewitness accounts alleging abuse and crimes by the NLA.

(*Guardian*, 6 October 2001, p. 19)

6–9 October 2001:

The Macedonian government is expected to decree an amnesty ... on Tuesday [9 October] ... for up to 3,000 former NLA guerrillas who disarmed ... But ... legislation [needed] to improve the civil rights of minority Albanians remained on hold over Skopje's demand for the release of twelve Macedonians said to have been abducted by guerrillas.

(*IHT*, 8 October 2001, p. 7)

A planned amnesty for former ethnic Albanian gunmen was thrown into disarray yesterday [9 October], with Albanian politicians saying a government statement has not gone far enough to ensure that those who rebelled will be safe ... The Macedonian cabinet announced an amnesty on Tuesday [9 October] ... The Macedonian government declared that there will be no arrests of former NLA gunmen who have given up their weapons ... unless they are charged with any war crimes by the Hague tribunal ... But the pledge, framed by President Boris Trajkovski's office, caused ethnic Albanians to doubt the cabinet's intentions because it listed a series of incidents for which former guerrillas would still be prosecuted. These included several ambushes of security forces and the bombing of a hotel ... The second largest Albanian party in the government, the Democratic Prosperity Party ... is demanding that the amnesty be enshrined in law, passed by the parliament ... One senior Western diplomat expressed alarm at the new conditions laid down by the government, but later expressed his hope that they 'would be ironed out shortly'. Nato officials stressed their belief that only the Hague tribunal would have the right to prosecute former guerrilla fighters for war crimes.

(*Guardian*, 10 October 2001, p. 10)

A statement by President Boris Trajkovski said: 'I hereby confirm my intention to grant amnesty to members of the so-called National Liberation Army who have voluntarily handed over their weapons' ... However, representatives of the ethnic Albanian community boycotted a key meeting of parliament on Tuesday [9 October], protesting an apparent attempt by majority Slavs to revise some provisions of the peace agreement ... Slavs were trying to retain references to the Macedonian Orthodox Church and the Macedonian people in the constitution.

(*IHT*, 10 October 2001, p. 6)

'Constitutional reforms to improve the civil rights of minority Albanians remain on hold over demands for the release of fourteen Macedonians allegedly abducted by guerrillas' (*FT*, 10 October 2001, p. 13).

11 October 2001: 'The police Thursday [11 October] reported discovery of a weapons cache in rebel-held territory ... An ethnic Albanian official accused the authorities of intentionally raiding villages ahead of a government-declared amnesty to arrest former rebels' (*IHT*, 12 October 2001, p. 6).

12 October 2001:

Nato on Friday [12 October] praised ethnic Albanian rebels for accepting a government-declared amnesty ... The NLA said Thursday [11 October] they welcomed ... the move ... The rebels also reiterated earlier demands by ethnic Albanian politicians that the amnesty be passed into law by parliament and called for the release of all ethnic Albanians detained for participating in the six months of clashes.

(*IHT*, 13 October 2001, p. 5)

16 October 2001: President Trajkovski (in a letter to parliament): 'If these unacceptable efforts go on, I shall consider them a form of dictate and will have to reconsider my role [in the peace process].'

President Boris Trajkovski on Tuesday [16 October] condemned 'certain groups of deputies' for 'continuing to block' constitutional amendments ... It was unclear whom Mr Trajkovski blamed for the stalled peace process – hardline Macedonian deputies bent on changing the amendments or ethnic Albanian lawmakers boycotting parliament ... But some blame Mr Trajkovski for the delay. The law calls for the president to review all the amendments and pass them on to parliament ahead of any vote in the legislature. Instead of presenting parliament with all fifteen amendments for enactment as a package – as called for by the ethnic Albanian side – he has forwarded only nine. This led ethnic Albanian deputies to boycott key parliamentary meetings, fearing a plot by the Macedonians to introduce changes in some of the amendments, particularly one, still withheld by Mr Trajkovski, that would make all ethnic groups equal under the law ... Also Tuesday parliament postponed a debate on whether the peace deal should be put to a national referendum ... Delayed reforms have led the EU to postpone an international donors' conference originally set for 15 October.

(*IHT*, 17 October 2001, p. 6)

17 October 2001:

The UN High Commissioner for Refugees says that at least 60,000 people have yet to move back to areas they left when ethnic Albanian rebels took over. The people still displaced are from both Macedonia's main communities, the Slav majority and Albanian minority ... The government estimates that 44,000 people, almost two-thirds of them Slavs, are still displaced within the country. The UNHCR says that almost 20,000 ethnic Albanians are in Kosovo and Serbia ... None of the fifteen promised amendments to the constitution have been passed.

(*Guardian*, 18 October 2001, p. 20)

18 October 2001: George Robertson and Javier Solana visit Macedonia and express concern about the progress of legislation.

21 October 2001:

President Boris Trajkovski ... approved Sunday [21 October] a plan for the deployment of ethnically mixed police units to areas seized by ethnic Albanian rebels ... [He] accepted the plan after weekend talks with Nato and EU representatives resulted in 'slight modifications' to an initial plan.

(*IHT*, 22 October 2001, p. 5)

22 October 2001:

Macedonian police units reentered former guerrilla areas yesterday [22 October] in an internationally guided scheme ... Twelve policeman dressed in blue with sidearms only, drove in patrol cars into five villages flanked by monitors and liaison experts from Nato, OSCE and the EU. The police units, comprising six Macedonians and six ethnic Albanians, made token patrols, but only through primarily Macedonian districts, and left after three hours. The five villages were designated 'low-risk' areas at the start of the pilot project for reintroduction of state organs in areas seized by ethnic Albanians.

(*FT*, 23 October 2001, p. 12)

'The Macedonian police began returning to villages in the north of the country Monday [22 October] in the first phase of a plan to reestablish government control over an area seized by ethnic Albanian guerrillas' (*IHT*, 23 October 2001, p. 9).

'While yesterday's visit lasted only a few hours, the patrols are expected to resume twenty-four-hour operations within a week. If they are successful more villages could follow suit' (*Guardian*, 23 October 2001, p. 16).

23 October 2001:

> The authorities on Tuesday [23 October] blamed ... ethnic Albanian rebels for a blast that destroyed a police station in the contested north-west. The blast late Monday [22 October] at a building that served both as police station and municipal office in Tearce, 35 kilometres (20 miles) north-west of Skopje, came just hours after the country's first ethnically mixed police units patrolled the village.
>
> (*IHT*, 24 October 2001, p. 4)

5 November 2001: 'A key ethnic Albanian party demanded revision Monday [5 November] of a part of the Western-brokered peace agreement ... The Party for Democratic Prosperity said it could not accept one of the fifteen constitutional amendments' (*IHT*, 6 November 2001, p. 7).

12 November 2001:

> Western envoys were yesterday [12 November] trying to patch up Macedonia's fragile peace process after three policemen were killed [on Sunday 11 November] by ethnic Albanian rebels ... in an ambush outside the ethnic Albanian village of Trebos in the north-west ... in former rebel-held territory ... The police ... were sent over the weekend to secure the site of an alleged mass grave, which the government claims holds the bodies of thirteen Macedonian Slavs kidnapped during this summer's fighting ... Western diplomats blamed the interior minister, who is known as a hardliner, for provoking the violence ahead of a crucial vote in parliament to ratify August's peace accord ... One Western envoy ... said Mr Boskovski had disregarded previously agreed procedures before moving into the site of the alleged grave. Government forces also arrested seven former rebels, saying they had been discovered with weapons supposed to have been handed in ... An offshoot of the disbanded NLA calling itself the Albanian National Army claimed responsibility for the deaths. As expected yesterday's parliamentary session [arranged for 13 November] was cancelled [on 11 November]. During the afternoon [of 12 November] police units began to withdraw from Trebos. Nato, the EU and OSCE also secured the release of thirty-nine ethnic Macedonian civilians who were temporarily held by ethnic Albanians.
>
> (*FT*, 13 November 2001, p. 14)

> About 100 people [were] abducted or taken hostage [on Sunday 11 November] ... All the captives were released ... The abductions followed the deployment Sunday of a strong police force ... A Western diplomat ... said the large size of the force was an unnecessary provocation by Macedonian authorities ... The police deployment Sunday [11 November] came after police found ... [weapons] in a vehicle at a checkpoint near Tetovo ... The Albanian National Army claimed responsibility [on 12

November]. The statement said the killings were a response to the arrests of the ethnic Albanians.

(*IHT*, 13 November 2001, p. 3)

'A new front line was promptly drawn just outside the village [of Trebos] (*The Economist*, 17 November 2001, p. 46).

14–15 November 2001:

Ethnic Albanian gunmen and Macedonian police forces remained in a tense standoff Thursday [15 November] around several villages in western Macedonia ... Nato peacekeepers deployed more troops and armour into the besieged villages on Wednesday [14 November] to try to prevent the situation from worsening ... Diplomats and mediators have criticized the interior minister, Ljube Boskovski, saying that he provoked the new crisis by sending police units into the western district against the advice of Nato peacekeepers and international monitors. Even President Trajkovski has come under fire in the local media for approving the police operation, although on Wednesday he denied ordering it. The incident on Sunday [11 November] began when the police arrived to investigate reports of a mass grave that was said to contain the bodies of missing Slavic Macedonian villagers. But after a meeting with Nato officials Wednesday, an interior ministry spokesman ... said that the police would pull out of the area and that the grave would be investigated later with international monitors.

(*IHT*, 16 November 2001, p. 4)

16 November 2001:

Macedonia's parliament adopted constitutional changes on Friday [16 November, the vote being taken in the early hours] ... Lawmakers first voted separately on each of the fifteen amendments ... The chamber then voted overwhelmingly in favour of amending the constitution as a whole to incorporate the changes ... The preamble to the constitution had been the most contentious issue. In the final version all four major parties – two Macedonian and two ethnic – agreed to define the republic as comprised of 'all citizens' of 'the Macedonian people, as well as citizens living within its borders who are part of the Albanian people', among others ... President Boris Trajkovski declared an amnesty for the former guerrillas on Friday hours after parliament ratified the reforms ... All former ethnic Albanian guerrillas, including about 120 detainees and convicts, would be covered by the amnesty, except those indictable by the United Nations war crimes tribunal ... Despite the breakthrough the situation remained tense around ... Tetovo, where a new group of ethnic Albanian militants announced a state of 'highest alert' and warned Macedonian forces to keep their distance ... The Albanian National Army declared 'all predominantly Albanian areas restricted for Macedonian forces ... All such forces will be attacked without warning if they try to enter Albanian areas' ... The police reported scattered shooting in the area late Thursday [15 November] and early Friday ... Nato forces remained stationed in the area, creating a buffer zone between Macedonian forces and rebels in control of three villages, Palatica, Semsovo and Trebos.

(*IHT*, 17 November 2001, p. 3)

'A fifty-strong rebel group, the self-styled Albanian National Army, declared a "war for liberation" ... The ANA claimed that militants had been involved in the killings of eleven Macedonian soldiers and three police' (*The Times*, 17 November 2001, p. 20).

A new group calling itself the Albanian National Army ... announced a 'war for the liberation of all Albanian territories in former Yugoslavia' and said it had been involved in clashes in Macedonia. But it admitted having only a few dozen members and a senior NLA figure said it was 'not worth commenting on them'.

(*Guardian*, 17 November 2001, p. 18)

21 November 2001:

Macedonia's main moderate party walked out of the country's national unity government yesterday ... Branko Crvenkovski ... leader of the Social Democratic Alliance of Macedonia (SDSM) ... [said] 'It is true that the international community has urged us to remain in the government. But we cannot act as babysitter for Georgievski and Boskovski and clean up their dirty work' ... The Unity government was formed in May ... The small Liberal Democratic Party – the SDSM's coalition partner, which holds only one seat in parliament – also left the government. Of the sixteen cabinet seats, the SDSM had three (defence, foreign affairs and a deputy premier-ship), while the LDP had the health ministry ... Mr Crvenkovski said ... his party could no longer be used as an alibi for the 'catastrophic ruling' of their rivals. Early elections are on schedule for January next year [2002] ... Investigators found human body parts yesterday at an alleged mass grave in north-western Macedonia ... Carla del Ponte, the UN war crimes prose-cutor, visited Macedonia on Tuesday [21 November] and said the tribunal was launching investigations into the state security forces and ethnic Albanian guerrillas.

(*Independent*, 22 November 2001, p. 18)

Leaving the government was seen by many as a party strategy to win votes in elections early next year from people who are critical of the government's handling of the peace process. The party did not want to be used to excuse 'a catastrophic economic policy, crime, corruption, political party feudalism.

These things even escalated during the conflict. We cannot be babysitters and clean up a dirty job' ... said Branko Crvenkovski ... The SDSM had long said it would return to opposition once the country's peace deal ... was passed by parliament ... There was some confusion as to whether human remains had been found ... [during] the excavation of an alleged mass grave near ... Tetovo ... The operation took place near the villages of Trebos and Dzepciste and was observed by a team from the Hague international war crimes tribunal for former Yugoslavia. The Macedonian interior ministry alleged that up to twelve civilians who went missing ... were buried at the site.

(*Guardian*, 22 November 2001, p. 18)

26 November 2001:

Elite police forces have largely withdrawn from entrances to territory inhabited by former guerrillas, defusing tension ... The special forces blockaded the Tetovo Valley two weeks ago after ethnic Albanian gunmen killed three policemen ... In Skopje's parliament majority Macedonians and minority ethnic Albanians agreed on postponing early elections to April from the 27 January [2002] date prescribed by the peace settlement. A formal vote on the issue will be held on Tuesday [27 November]

(*IHT*, 27 November 2001, p. 6)

28 November 2001:

Macedonia said Wednesday [28 November] that it would seriously consider seeking a three-month extension of the Nato military mission ... President Boris Trajkovski said ... that he would give 'strong consideration' to the extension of the mission, which is scheduled to end on 26 December.

(*IHT*, 29 November 2001, p. 8)

THE ECONOMY

Net financial transfers from the federal government of the former Yugoslavia had been of the order of 5 to 7 per cent of GDP (United Nations, *World Economic and Social Survey*, 1996, p. 33).

The Yugoslav dinar was withdrawn in April 1992 and replaced by coupons. A new currency, the denar, was introduced in May 1993. The denar has been floating since the beginning of 1994. There is near full current account convertibility except for citizens wishing to holiday abroad. Controls remain on the capital account. The liberalization of the foreign trade regime is well advanced (EBRD 1994: 25, 109). Officially the denar has been floating since the beginning of 1994, but in practice it has remained closely aligned to the DM. Import licensing and quantitative import restrictions have been removed for all but 4 per cent of import categories (remaining restrictions applying mainly to chemicals, steel and some foodstuffs). Auctions are held for imports still subject to quotas (EBRD 1996b: 151). All residual quantitative restrictions on imports were removed in November 1996 (EBRD 1997a: 29). The exchange rate of the denar has been more or less stable for the past year (*Business Europa*, April–May 1995, p. 11). The denar was devalued by 14 per cent in July 1997 (EBRD 1997b: 169). The denar was devalued by 16 per cent in July 1997, falling from twenty-seven to thirty-one denars to the DM (*FT*, Survey, 17 December 1997, p. ii). There is a *de facto* peg of the exchange rate to the DM (EBRD 1999b: 218). In June 1996 an association agreement was signed with the EU.

The first stabilization package was introduced in April 1992 and the second in the autumn of that year. But a third one was needed, introduced in December 1993 and this time sponsored by the IMF, and inflation was brought down to quite low levels by March 1994 (Kraft 1995: 485). There has been heavy reliance on wage and price controls, e.g. in April 1993 wages were frozen for six months at 125 per cent of their March level (p. 487).

The January 1994 reform programme, worked out with the IMF and the World Bank, was designed to bring inflation down from its current annual rate of 350 per cent to 70 per cent by the end of the year, reduce the budget deficit from 13.5 per cent of GDP to 6.6 per cent, start large-scale privatization and introduce a bank restructuring scheme (*Business Central Europe*, February 1994, p. 18; Deutsche Bank, *Focus: Eastern Europe*, 1994, no. 103, p. 5). A rigorous incomes policy has been in force since the end of 1993 (EBRD 1994: 25). Wage control was extended until the end of 1996 (EBRD 1996b: 151). A tough incomes policy has 'helped to keep the rise in nominal incomes below the rate of inflation by freezing wages in the state sector and in enterprises with more than 30 per cent social capital' (United Nations Economic Commission for Europe 1996: 167). A six-month wage freeze introduced after the 14 per cent devaluation in July 1997 affected all budgetary entities and all enterprises that were not fully privately owned. It lapsed at the end of 1997. The unemployment rate stood at 36 per cent, according to a 1997 labour force survey, though the true rate is most likely lower due to activities in the informal sector. In January 1998 the government implemented a programme to stimulate employment involving concessions on social security contributions (EBRD 1998b: 166).

Liberalization of the price system is advanced, although a 'notification requirement' remains for milk, municipal rents, water, central heating and vehicle insurance (EBRD 1994: 25). There have been further moves towards cost recovery in the prices of electricity and oil derivatives (EBRD 1995a: 56). About 80 per cent of prices in the retail price index are free of controls. Price controls apply, for example, to flour, bread, electricity and oil derivatives (EBRD 1995b: 42). About 90 per cent of prices in the retail price index are free of controls, including all retail prices for basic goods (with the exception of bread). But guaranteed base prices for agricultural products remain for wheat, sugar, sugar beet, sunflower oil and tobacco. There have been large increases in the prices of electricity and oil derivatives, but further increases are required to bring them to cost recovery levels (EBRD 1996b: 151). The government envisaged that in 1997 there would be guaranteed base prices only for wheat, lamb, beef and tobacco (EBRD 1997a: 29). The government has introduced important reforms in agricultural prices. The price cap on bread has been abolished and guaranteed prices for products such as sugar beet and sunflower oil have been eliminated. Guaranteed prices for tobacco and wheat are now set below 70 per cent of world prices, although procurement prices for tobacco were increased sharply in early 1999 (EBRD 1999b: 218). 'The government continues to regulate the domestic price of oil and oil products' (EBRD 2000b: 162).

> Conflict and violence during 2001 have threatened macroeconomic stability and prospects for growth ... In order to finance increased military expenditure, in June 2001 the government introduced a tax on financial transactions. The tax will apply throughout the second half of 2001 ... After five years of government control the prices of bread and flour were liberalized in October 2000 ... The government continues to control the prices of most utilities and miscellaneous items such as oil, mail and motor insurance.
>
> (EBRD 2001b: 146)

On 24 October 1996 the London Club of bank creditors reached agreement in principle with Macedonia on repaying its share of the former Yugoslavia's commercial bank debt of $5.6 billion. (The debt arose from the 1988 rescheduling agreement, called the New Financing Arrangement.) Macedonia would take on 5.4 per cent of the principal and 3.65 per cent of the interest, i.e. some $280 million in total (*FT*, 25 October 1996, p. 3). Agreement was reached on 26 March 1997, with Macedonia issuing new bonds totalling $228.7 million in exchange for its share of the total Yugoslav debt of around $5.6 billion in principal and interest (*FT*, 27 March 1997, p. 2).

In August 1999 the IMF agreed a new loan of $19 million to help offset the recent sharp fall in exports (EBRD 1999b: 218).

> The government has used funds from the budget to repay savers who lost money in the collapse of the pyramid scheme operated by the TAT savings house, controlled by businessmen and local government officials in the southern Macedonian town of Bitola ... [The central bank] has overseen the repayment of about DM 700 million, although 'only a small amount' was returned in cash. Depositors used their frozen savings to purchase shares in companies being privatized or to acquire state-owned apartments and plots of land.
>
> (*FT*, Survey, 20 February 2001, p. 12)

[On 18 September 2000 EU foreign] ministers approved an EU package granting duty-free access to 95 per cent of imports from Albania, Bosnia, Croatia, Macedonia and Montenegro ... The package includes abolition of tariffs on most industrial and farm products to the EU. However, some limits remain on exports of fish products and wine.

(*FT*, 19 September 2000, p. 10)

In April 2001 FYR Macedonia became the first country in south-eastern Europe to sign a Stabilization and Association Agreement with the EU ... [There is] emphasis on regional co-operation ... FYR Macedonia has immediate free axis to EU markets (except for agriculture and fisheries), while it agrees to eliminate its own tariffs on EU goods over a maximum of ten years. For textiles and steel, the country's biggest exports, the liberalization timetable is less than ten years. Import quotas on agricultural and fishery products were abolished on both sides when the agreement was signed but there is no timetable for further tariff liberalization in these sectors.

(EBRD 2001b: 146)

Privatization

Rough estimates in mid-year of the private sector as a percentage of GDP are provided by the EBRD: 1990, 15 per cent; 1991, 15 per cent; 1992, 15 per cent; 1993, 35 per cent; 1994, 35 per cent; 1995, 40 per cent; 1996, 50 per cent; 1997, 50 per cent; 1998, 55 per cent; 1999, 55 per cent; 2000, 55 per cent; 2001, 60 per cent (EBRD 1999b: 24, 220, and 2001b: 12, 148).

Private activity, including that in the informal sector, probably accounts for 25–40 per cent of GDP (EBRD 1994: 24). The private sector, taking into account the informal sector, probably accounts for 45 to 55 per cent of GDP (EBRD 1996b: 150).

Under the federal programme during 1990–1 privatization was greater in Macedonia than in all the other ex-Yugoslav republics combined; the principal participants were enterprise employees who received 'internal' shares (Koevski and Canning 1995: 5, 33). The Law on the Transformation of Enterprises with Social Capital was passed in June 1993. The 1,517 enterprises in the first stage of privatization accounted for over 50 per cent of total corporate assets. A total of 414 enterprises, such as public utilities, were excluded from the first stage (pp. 9–11). Although the process was to take place on a commercial basis (i.e. privatization by sale), there were to be discounts available to present and former employees, citizens were able to use the hard currency deposits frozen in 1990, and former owners (or their heirs), whose property was confiscated by the communists, were to be compensated. The Pension Fund was to receive 15 per cent of enterprise equity (pp. 9, 13). 'The privatization strategy of the Macedonian government is a multi-track, "commercial" one, aiming to establish a durable pattern of responsible ownership, with active core shareholders (e.g. banks) providing corporate control' (p. 1). 'The new, multi-track privatization scheme emphasizes the creation of a durable pattern of responsible ownership, with dominant "insider" control groups ... Foreign investors are given equal treatment' (p. 33). To encourage at least a 51 per cent stake (varying) initial payments could be followed by a period of up to five years to pay off the remainder (pp. 11–12, 33). Small and medium-sized enterprises were free to choose their privatization method(s). Small enterprises could choose from public auction, competitive tender or direct agreement with an interested buyer. (Employees would have the opportunity to buy the enterprise outright by paying an amount equivalent to 51 per cent of the value of the enterprise and undertaking to pay the remainder in instalments over five years.) The options facing medium-sized and large enterprises were essentially the same, including public auction or tender, direct acquisition and management buy-outs. Large enterprises, however, would have to select an appropriate method in consultation with the Privatization Agency (pp. 11–12). The initiative for commencing privatization rested with the enterprise (i.e. the workers' councils or the boards of directors), but enterprises failing to meet the prescribed deadlines would be privatized by the agency (the deadlines for presenting privatization plans being December 1994 for small and medium-sized enterprises and December 1995 for large ones). Overall, progress has so far been slow, but may be expected to gather momentum from the beginning of 1995 (p. 33).

Writing in March 1995, Pettifer (1995: 57) mentioned the 'almost total lack of progress' in the area of privatization.

According to Bartlett (1996: 163), the main approach is direct sales. Small and medium-sized enterprises can be bought (1) by anyone outright or in instalments over five years, or (2) through an employee buy-out of at least 51 per cent of capital.

It has been revealed that privatization has been completed in 145 small and medium-sized enterprises (of which only six are actually management buy-outs); of these 145 enterprises 110 are small ones which became completely employee-owned (*Business Europa*, April–May 1995, p. 9).

In 1994 eighty-four large enterprises were privatized. A draft law on restitution was in preparation (EBRD 1995a: 56). Over 90 per cent of small enterprises are already privately owned. The 1989 bankruptcy law is still in force (EBRD 1994: 24). By mid-1995 about 120 enterprises had been privatized, primarily through management buy-outs (EBRD 1995b: 42). More than half of the enterprises (representing at least half of the former state assets in the enterprise sector) have been privatized through management and employee buy-outs (p. 23). As of July 1996, 838 of the 1,217 enterprises covered by the law on transformation (passed in June 1993) had been privatized, mainly through employee buy-outs, or had become subject to liquidation proceedings. In most cases the only bidders were management and employees. It was the intention to raise the total number of privatized enterprises to 1,150 by spring 1997 using this framework. In addition, the privatization (through the transfer of shares to employees and management) of about 400 enterprises has been initiated under a law which existed before the breakup of Yugoslavia. In April 1996 a law enabling the privatization of agro-kombinats (controlling 15 per cent of total agricultural land) was passed. Over 95 per cent of all enterprises are privately owned, almost all being small (less than twenty employees). A special restructuring programme was introduced in 1994 to restructure the twenty-five largest loss-making enterprises. These included utilities, agro-kombinats, mines and textile, chemical and electrical machinery enterprises (EBRD 1996b: 150–1). By mid-1997 about 1,000 of the 1,217 enterprises covered by the law on transformation of social capital (passed in June 1993) had been privatized. The main method was by management and employee buy-out (MEBO). 'The style of privatization by MEBO, not effectively changing ownership, resulted in poor corporate governance and most companies are not in a position to self-finance or attract new capital' (EBRD 1997b: 169). The government has continued to make progress in its privatization programme. By the end of 1997 almost all enterprises designated in 1993 for privatization had completed the process, representing more than three-quarters of all enterprises. Management and employee buy-out remains the most common method, however, and progress on improving corporate governance is slow (EBRD 1998a: 35). By mid-1998 roughly four-fifths of all 'socially owned' enterprises identified for privatization had been privatized, mostly through management and employee buy-outs. However, most of these are small and medium-sized enterprises. There are a number of large loss-making industrial enterprises with majority state ownership which are being restructured and are to be sold to strategic investors or otherwise liquidated. The government is also preparing international tenders for stakes in telecoms, energy and the oil refinery.

> Improvements in corporate governance have been slow. This is due in part to the prevalence of management and employee buy-outs in the privatization process, which can act as a hindrance to enterprise restructuring. As of March 1998 enterprises sold to outsiders accounted for less than 15 per cent of employees in privatized enterprises ... Financial discipline has been weakened by continued lending of banks to loss-making enterprises with a poor debt service record and by an ineffectual bankruptcy law inherited from the former Yugoslavia ... A new bankruptcy law became effective in May 1998 ... Foreign investors have been deterred by high political risk in the region. Their participation in the privatization process amounted to less than 2 per cent of equity privatized.
>
> (EBRD 1998b: 166–7)

The situation has greatly improved in 1998, facilitated by an improved economic climate and greater emphasis on sales to outsiders in privatization. Several large foreign investments have been included or are at an advanced stage of preparation, including the sale of state shares in a steel company to a strategic investor. It is planned to privatize infrastructure on a case-by-case basis. The intention is to sell at least one-third of Macedonian Telecommunications to an international strategic investor (EBRD 1998b: 166–7). The privatization of agriculture has lagged behind the rest of the economy. But the pace has increased in 1998. By May 1998, 70 per cent of all agricultural enterprises had been privatized (representing about 40 per cent of employment in the sector). The rest are scheduled for privatization by the end of 1998. After some initial delays substantial progress is being made on the restructuring of the large agro-kombinats (EBRD 1998b: 166). Application of the new bankruptcy law, which became effective in May 1998, is proceeding very slowly, particularly with regard to large enterprises. By the end of June 1999 small privatization was largely complete with 1,458 enterprises sold. Of the 250 or so enterprises still to be sold, only seventy-one have not yet started the process. Large privatization has been slow. Bank privatization has proceeded gradually. The privatization of the agricultural sector has proceeded more slowly than that in manufacturing or services. But by the end of 1998, 323 agricultural enterprises had been sold (representing about 15,000 employees). Three large agricultural kombinats were privatized in late 1998 (representing 15 per cent of all kombinats), with each being split into a number of smaller companies. Most privatizations in agriculture have been sales to existing managers and farmers (EBRD 1999b: 213–19).

> Extensive use of management–employee buy-outs has resulted in poor corporate governance and improvement is slow. New bankruptcy procedures are not yet being implemented effectively ... Large-scale privatization has been slow to take off ... Large-scale privatization of loss-making companies has been slow. Of the twelve large companies targeted by the government for privatization, only three had found investors by March 2000 ... The largest bank, Stopanska Banka, was fully privatized in early 2000 [April] through the sale to a strategic investor, the National Bank of Greece, and with the participation of the EBRD and IFC. Only one bank, the Macedonian Development Bank, has majority state ownership ... The government is preparing key strategic sectors such as telecommunications for privatization and is aiming to attract the interest of foreign investors ... The government is trying to identify strategic foreign investors to participate in the privatization of the power utilities ... Privatization of the agricultural sector has proceeded steadily and more than three-quarters of agricultural land is privately owned. The law on agricultural land passed in 1999 abolished restrictions on land ownership and gave impetus to the enlargement of existing farms. Full privatization of the sector is expected by the end of 2000.
>
> (EBRD 2000a: 54)

The privatization of large-scale enterprises has accelerated ... The privatization programme continues to move forward. By May 2000 1,572 enterprises had been privatized and a further 138 enterprises were in the process. Significant progress has been made in the agricultural sector, where 394 companies are now privatized (compared with 323 at the end of 1998) and a further thirty-two are in the process. Meanwhile, a programme to sell or liquidate twelve large, loss-making enterprises launched in 1998, has accelerated recently ... By August 2000 nine of these enterprises had found either private investors, had been sold to workers or liquidated, with the three remaining enterprises scheduled for sale or closure by the end of March 2001. A new list of forty loss-making state-owned companies has been drawn up, with a target of sale or liquidation by the end of 2001 ... Inter-enterprise arrears are estimated to have risen by 63 per cent in 1999. This rise reflects a number of factors, including the way in which the privatizations were carried out (mostly management–employee buy-outs), the absence of hard budget constraints and effective bankruptcy procedures and the weak enforcement of creditor and shareholder rights ... At the end of 1999 the share of total bank capital in the country that was privately owned reached 77 per cent.

(EBRD 2000b: 162–3)

Progress has been made on large-scale privatization, but several large loss-makers remain in state hands ... By the end of 2000 more than 1,600 enterprises had been privatized, with a further 126 companies in the process of privatization. The government has drawn up an action plan, with assistance from the World Bank, to privatize forty large, loss-making enterprises by June 2002. Each enterprise will be treated on a case-by-case basis, and will be either financially restructured and fully privatized or closed ... Although privatization is nearing completion, corporate governance needs to be improved ... The government sold 51 per cent of the fixed-line telecommunications company, Macedonian Telecommunications (MT), in early 2001. Of the six companies that originally made bids, Matav of Hungary won the tender. MT continues to have a monopoly in fixed-line and other telecommunications services, and no date has been set for ending it.

(EBRD 2001a: 64)

Over the past two years ... FYR Macedonia ... has been one of the fastest reforming countries, with significant progress being made on privatization, banking reform and institutional reform ... [But] the increased uncertainty [caused by fighting] has led to a slowdown in reform.

(EBRD 2001b: 28)

By the end of June 2001 1,646 companies had been privatized since the start of the programme in 1993 ... Sixty-five per cent of the privatized enterprises are small, 19 per cent are medium-sized and the remaining 16 per cent are large. Privatization in the agricultural sector is nearly complete with 418 companies privatized. Attention is now focussed on forty large loss-making enterprises scheduled for privatization or closure by the end of 2002 ... Strategic investors [are being sought]. The internal ethnic conflict has led to a delay in the programme. However, in June 2001 the government announced the liquidation of five of these enterprises (with 7,000 employees) ... Despite a new bankruptcy law, inter-enterprise arrears have continued to mount.

(p. 146)

'At the end of 2000 ... the share of privately-owned bank capital had risen to 83.5 per cent' (p. 147).

So far some 250 enterprises have been privatized (*FT*, Survey, 7 July 1995, p. 34). Managers and employees have taken control of half the 1,200 companies slated for disposal by mid-1996. Only six companies have been sold to buyers from abroad. The Skopje stock exchange was to open on 28 March 1996 (*FT*, 25 March 1996, p. 2). Almost 900 of the 1,200 manufacturing and service enterprises on the privatization agency's list of disposals are now privately owned. Most processing of agricultural products is still carried out by some 200 agro-kombinats, state conglomerates which control some 30 per cent of farmland. Some have diversified into hotels, transport and tourism. In 1997 their assets were to be split up and sold. Processing facilities, livestock and agricultural assets would be offered for sale, with preference given to bids from managers and employees. State landholdings would not be put up for sale. Instead, the agro-kombinats' holdings would be made available on five-year leases. Private farmers produce about 75 per cent of agricultural output on fragmented holdings with an average size of 2.8 ha (*FT*, Survey, 15 November 1996, p. ii).

The privatization agency announced that 130 enterprises had been privatized by July 1995 (*Business Central Europe*, September 1995, p. 19). By the end of 1995, 604 privatization deals had been completed and a further 396 were in process, out of a total of 1,216 non-agricultural enterprises subject to eventual privatization. Restructuring of the main loss-making enterprises is also under way. In 1995 twenty-three large enterprises (accounting for 45 per cent of total equity and 55 per cent of overall losses) were broken down into 130 smaller units, some of which were closed (*Business Central Europe*, May 1996, p. 74).

On 21 April 1998 parliament passed a law which allowed restitution of land and assets expropriated since 1945 (*EEN*, 1998, vol. 12, no. 6, p. 7).

In June 2000 the Macedonian government placed the following advertisement in the Western media (e.g. *The Economist*, 24 June 2000, p. 158):

The Privatization Council of the Republic of Macedonia, chaired by the prime minister, announces the initiation of a mass privatization programme and invites investment firms, fund groups and banks to submit applications to form and manage privatization funds in conjunction with its mass voucher privatization programme. The funds will provide a vehicle for Macedonian citizens to invest privatization vouchers they will be receiving from the government in a portfolio of professionally managed Macedonian securities ... Privatization funds will be permitted to acquire these vouchers by advertising and soliciting Macedonians who will exchange them for units of the fund. With these units the funds will bid for shares of 222 medium-sized and nineteen of the largest companies which will be auctioned by the government ... After one year the privatization funds will be authorized to convert themselves into investment funds, pay dividends to shareholders and list their shares on stock exchanges ... Foreigners may own up to 100 per cent of privatization fund management companies and are entitled to generous management fees.

'Some forty loss-making state enterprises that employ more than 10,000 workers face privatization or closure this year [2001]' (*FT*, Survey, 19 February 2001, p. 11). 'The forty biggest loss-makers, the state-controlled mines, engineering and other companies account for the bulk of bad loans, non-payment of taxes and inter-enterprise debts' (p. 12).

Foreign direct investment

'Beyond 1990 it appears that, due to regional instability and doubts with regard to the nature and internal stability of the fledgling Macedonian state, foreign investment effectively ceased ... current legislation does not permit land ownership by foreigners (Koevski and Canning 1995: 14). Net direct foreign investment was $5 million in 1994 and $11 million in 1995 (United Nations Economic Commission for Europe 1996: 149). Macedonia has attracted little direct foreign investment. Greece estimates that Greek companies account for about half the $70 million to $80 million attracted to date. The European Bank for Reconstruction and Development puts the total at $76 million in the period 1989 to 1996 (*FT*, Survey 1997, 17 December 1997, pp. iii–iv). Foreigners are prohibited from owning land (EBRD 1996b: 151).

Greek companies are increasingly active. Hellenic Petroleum SA is investing $190 million in Okta, Macedonia's main energy company. This is the largest foreign investment to date. As part of the deal it has agreed to build a 220-kilometre (138-mile) pipeline to carry crude oil from Salonica, in northern Greece, to Skopje, and to double Okta's annual refining capacity. The state-controlled National Bank of Greece is close to acquiring Stopanska Banka, Macedonia's leading bank, while Alpha Credit Bank, Greece's largest private bank, is to buy Creditna Banka, a private Macedonian bank (*IHT*, 23 October 1999, p. 13).

On 10 November 1999 Greece and Macedonia launched a $90 million project to build a 220-kilometre oil pipeline from the northern Greek port of Thessaloniki to Skopje. It will link refineries controlled by Hellenic Petroleum, the partly privatized Greek energy group, in Thessaloniki and Skopje. The pipeline, due to be completed in 2001, is being constructed by a joint venture between Hellenic and Meton-Etep, a private Greek construction company. Elpet-Balkaniki, the joint venture, has already acquired a 54 per cent stake in Okta, the state-controlled Macedonian refinery. Hellenic has taken over management and plans to modernize the refinery (*FT*, 11 November 1999, p. 14).

Foreign investment increased sharply in 1998, rising from $18 million in 1997 to well over $100 million. But several planned deals were postponed in the first half of 1999 (EBRD 1999b: 219).

Foreign investment levels, though low, are good by historical standards. Greeks are prominent ... The National Bank of Greece has grabbed 40 per cent of a fragmented market by buying a majority in Stopanska Banka ... Slovenia's Nova Ljubljanska Banka bought 25 per cent of Skopje-based Tutunska Bank. The ferro-nickel – one of the twelve loss-makers – went to [a French company].

(Business Central Europe 2000: 38–9)

Matav [is] the Hungarian telecommunications company ... [It was] privatized only in 1993 and [is] now majority-owned by Deutsche Telekom of Germany ... [Its] acquisition announced just before Christmas [2000] and expected to close this month [January 2001] ... [of] a 51 per cent stake in MakTel, the monopoly Macedonian carrier .. signifies a new phase of Matav's evolution ... The Macedonian acquisition [is] through a consortium in which Matav holds an 87.4 per cent stake.

(*FT*, 3 January 2001, p. 26)

'A consortium led by ... Matav bought 51 per cent of Macedonia's state telecoms group, MakTel' (*Business Central Europe*, February 2001, p. 12).

Austria's Erste Bank pulled out of its planned acquisition of Stopanska Banka ... Last year [2000] the National Bank of Greece, the country's biggest banking group ... paid DM 117 million for 68 per cent of Stopanska, a loss-making state-owned group, and took over management ... As part of the deal with Stopanska, the government agreed to take over about Euro 100 million in non-performing debt, much of it owed by four big loss-making state enterprises that were formerly shareholders in the bank ... The EBRD and the International Finance Corporation, the World Bank's private sector lending arm ... each hold 11 per cent of Stopanksa ... Alpha Bank, Greece's biggest private bank, followed suit by acquiring 65 per cent of Kreditna Banka, a profitable private bank, for DM 18 million ... Slovenia's Nova Ljubljanska Bank agreed to pay DM 40 million for 80 per cent of Tutunska Banka, another profitable private bank.

(*FT*, Survey, 19 February 2001, p. 12)

'Deutsche Telekom-controlled Matav of Hungary ... [has taken a] 51 per cent controlling stake in the mobile and fixed line telecoms operator ... MakTel' (p. 12).

Under a package agreement announced during the Kosovo conflict, Hellenic Petroleum, the state-controlled Greek oil refining group, acquired a majority stake in Okta, Macedonia's only refinery, and undertook to finance a 230-kilometre pipeline ... to carry crude oil to Macedonia from the northern Greek port of Thessaloniki ... due to be completed by this year end [2001].

(p. 14)

'There is an underlying consensus about the current government's pledge to discuss and draw up the telecoms windfall spending with the international financial institutions and seek the advice of foreign, especially the US and EU, embassies' (p. 12). 'Before signing its recent loan agreements with the World Bank and the IMF, the pro-market coalition government ... agreed to discuss and vet all projects with the international financial institutions. The list includes the EBRD and the IFC' (p. 11).

'[The] government has managed ... to attract about $250 million in investment from Greece' (*The Economist*, 3 March 2001, p. 51).

(See Table 3.1 for the small volume of net foreign direct investment.)

Economic performance

Economic performance was generally pretty grim in the first half of the 1990s. Though poorly enforced, Macedonia's participation in sanctions on the Federal Republic of Yugoslavia did not help. But GDP growth turned positive in 1996. (See Table 3.1.) 'FYR Macedonia's economy was affected more severely [than Bulgaria's] by the Kosovo crisis, both through trade effects and the influx of large numbers of refugees. Nevertheless, the economy made a strong recovery in the second half of the year [1999]' (EBRD 2000a: 5). In 2000 GDP was an estimated 77 per cent of the 1989 level (EBRD 2001b: 59). There was hyperinflation in 1992 (1,664 per cent). Consumer prices were more or less stable in 1997–9. The inflation rate rose to just under 10 per cent in 2000. Fighting in 2001 had an adverse effect on the economy.

Pettifer (1995: 56) saw the situation thus: after admission to the IMF in December 1992 and to the World Bank in December 1993 substantial aid was mobilized. When an agreement on economic reconstruction was signed in February 1994 a standby loan of $80 million was arranged. Inflation has been reduced and the denar stabilized, but at considerable cost in terms of lost output and high unemployment. GDP in 1994 was only about 65 per cent of its 1992 level and unemployment stands at between 20 per cent and 30 per cent of the total work force.

More than 40 per cent of the workforce is unemployed or on forced leave from factories that have shut down (Kerin Hope, *FT*, 14 October 1994, p. 2).

Unemployment has been pushed up from around 25 per cent to an estimated 30 per cent of the labour force and at times during 1994 to as much as 40 per cent (Koevski and Canning 1995: 2).

Per capita income fell from $2,200 in 1990 to $1,600 in 1994. Unemployment is officially 20 per cent but at least another 10 per cent of workers are on unpaid leave (Business Central Europe 1995: 42).

'The local economy is in a pitiful state with little prospect of recovery in the foreseeable future ... Unemployment in Macedonia has risen inexorably over the past year to over thirty per cent' (*EEN*, 14 August 1996, vol. 10, no. 16, p. 4).

According to the Ministry of Development, the unemployment rate was about 24 per cent in December 1995, compared with 37 per cent officially

Table 3.1 FYR Macedonia: selected economic indicators 1990–2000

Economic indicator	1990	1991	1992	1993	1994	1995	1996	1997	1998	1999	2000 (estimate)
Rate of growth of GDP (%)	-9.9	-7.0	-8.0	-9.1	-1.8	-1.2	1.2	1.4	2.9	2.7	5.1
Rate of growth of industrial output (%)	-10.6	-17.2	-16.0	-14.3	-9.7	-8.9	5.0	2.9	4.5	-2.5	
Rate of growth of agricultural output (%)	-10.2	17.6	0.4	-20.4	7.8	2.3	-2.9	0.0	3.9	0.3	
Inflation rate (consumer, %)	608.4	114.9	1,664.0	338.4	126.5	16.4	2.5	1.5	0.6	-1.3	9.2
Budget surplus or deficit (% of GDP)[a]		-3.6	-9.8	-13.4	-2.7	-1.0	-1.4	-0.4	-1.8	0.0	1.0
Unemployment rate (end of year, %)[b]	22.9	24.5	26.2	27.7	30.0	35.6	38.8	41.7	41.4	47.0	
Balance of payments (current account, $billion)	-0.400	-0.262	-0.019	-0.015	-0.180	-0.222	-0.289	-0.277	-0.309	-0.135	-0.279
Foreign direct investment (net, $million)			0.0	0.0	24.0	12.0	12.0	18.0	175.0	27.0	169.0
Population (million)			2.2	2.2	1.9	2.0	2.0	2.0	2.0	2.0	2.0

Source Various issues of European Bank for Reconstruction and Development, *Transition Report*; United Nations Economic Commission for Europe, *Economic Survey of Europe*; United Nations, *World Economic and Social Survey*; IMF, *World Economic Outlook*.

Notes:

[a] General government balance: includes the state, municipalities and extrabudgetary funds (EBRD)
[b] Registered unemployment: the data recorded on employment covers only the social sector in agriculture, hence unemployment rates are biased upwards (United Nations Economic Commission for Europe). Unemployment rates based on a labour force survey are as follows: 1996, 31.9%; 1997, 36.0%; 1998, 34.5%; 1999, 32.4%; 2000, 32.1% (EBRD 2001a: 65).

reported (United Nations Economic Commission for Europe 1996: 86). Most enterprises are working at less than half their capacity (p. 168).

The official figure for unemployment is close to 40 per cent. But this is criticized for failing to take sufficient account of the growing private sector. The ministry of finance puts the unemployment rate at between 22 and 24 per cent (*FT*, Survey, 15 November 1996, p. iii). Unemployment is officially estimated at more than 30 per cent. Western financial officials estimate that the grey economy is at least equivalent to 20 to 30 per cent of GDP and could be as much as 40 per cent (*FT*, Survey, 17 December 1997, p. ii).

(See Table 3.1 for figures on unemployment provided by the EBRD.)

'[On 12 March 2002] international donors approved a $515 million aid package for Macedonia ... more than double the amount expected ... the European Commission and the World Bank organized the one-day pledging conference to reward authorities ... and ethnic Albanian leaders for respecting a peace deal' (*FT*, 13 March 2002, p. 10).

4 Slovenia

POLITICS

Earlier developments are dealt with in the Introduction and Overview.

6 March 1995: Italy lifts its veto on Slovenia having an association agreement with the EU. (Negotiations on associate status began on 15 March; Slovenia and the EU initialled a trade and political co-operation agreement on 15 June 1995.) The dispute was about the property rights of Italians who fled from the Istrian peninsula after the Second World War. Italy demanded that the property rights of Italian citizens who left the territory of Slovenia after 1945 should be restored. This contradicts the stipulations of the 1975 Osimo Treaty and of the Rome Agreement of 1983, which provides for fair indemnity for such property. The Slovene government has undertaken to submit to parliament legislation harmonizing its laws with those on property rights in force in the EU member states. Under present Slovene law foreign physical persons can inherit property (including land) and can acquire and own buildings (but not land), while foreign-owned legal persons are allowed to acquire all kinds of business-related property (Anton Bebler, *The World Today*, May 1995, vol. 51, no. 5, p. 98). In 1975 Italy and Yugoslavia signed a treaty which agreed compensation for property losses and all other outstanding issues (*FT*, Survey, 6 April 1995, p. 35). The promise to the EU does not mean that Italians will be allowed to claim back their property or to take part in auctions of real estate. (The Italian government insists that property should be returned if still under the control of the Slovenian state. Otherwise, if the property is for sale, former Italian owners should be given preferential purchase rights: *FT*, Survey, 26 March 1996, p. i.)

On 4 February 1998, Italy accepted $62 million from Slovenia in compensation for property seized from ethnic Italians who fled after the Second World War. (Some 21,000 Italians left the country.) This confirmed the validity of the Osimo and Rome agreements, under which the former Yugoslavia agreed to pay a total of $110 million in compensation. Slovenia's share is $62 million (*FT*, 6 February 1998, p. 2).

1 February 1996: the fourth and final minister (for economics) from the Associated List of Social Democrats resigns from the government. (The loss of fourteen seats reduced the government coalition to forty-five out of the ninety seats in the Chamber of Representatives.)

(According to *EEN*, the Associated List left the coalition government on 26 January 1996 following the sacking of the economics minister. On 30 January three other Associated List ministers resigned: 1996, vol. 10, no. 14, p. 5.)

10 June 1996: an association agreement is signed with the EU. An exchange of letters is annexed to the agreement: (1) Slovenia will allow all EU citizens to buy land and property, on a reciprocal basis, within four years of the agreement being ratified, and (2) any EU citizens who have previously 'permanently resided on the present territory of the Republic of Slovenia for a period of three years' will be allowed to buy property immediately the agreement is ratified (*FT*, 10 June 1996, p. 2).

25 June 1996: Slovenia becomes the tenth associate member of the Western European Union (WEU).

July 1996: Davorin Kracun is appointed foreign minister, the replacement for Zoran Thaler, who lost a vote of no confidence on 16 May (*EEN*, 18 July 1996, vol. 10, no. 14, p. 5).

The 10 November 1996 general election

The election was for the ninety seats in the National Assembly. The turnout was 72 per cent. The voting system is a complicated mixture of first-past-the-post and proportional representation. Two seats are reserved for the ethnic Hungarian and Italian minorities. There was a 3.5 per cent threshold. (See Table 4.1.)

Table 4.1   Slovenia: the general election of 10 November 1996

	Seats	*Vote (%)*
Liberal Democratic Party	25	27.05
Slovene People's Party	19	19.48
Social Democratic Party of Slovenia	16	16.12
Christian Democrats	10	9.0
Associated List of Social Democrats	9	9.5
Democratic Party of Retired People	5	4.31
Slovene National Party	4	3.22
Hungarians	1	
Italians	1	
Total	90	100

Information on some of the parties is as follows:

Associated List of Social Democrats: the party is against giving property back to families of those suspected of collaborating with Italy and Germany during the Second World War (*The Economist*, 2 November 1996, p. 58).

Slovenian Spring: a coalition comprising: (1) the Slovene People's Party; a rightist party, led by Marjan Podobnik, with strong support in the countryside; (2) the Christian Democrats (led by Lozje Peterle); (3) the Social Democratic Party of Slovenia (led by Janez Jansa; a centre-right party which wishes to restore land and property to the Roman Catholic Church) (*Independent*, 9 November 1996, p. 14). (The Slovene People's Party 'preaches "family values" tinged with green': *The Economist*, 2 November 1996, p. 58).

Slovene National Party: led by Zmago Jelincic. Neo-fascist party.

Political developments after the November 1996 general election

8 December 1996: the referendum on the voting system attracts a turnout of only 37 per cent. None of the proposals for changing the current mixed proportional and constituency system gets anywhere near the required 50 per cent plus one vote (*EEN*, 1996, vol. 10, no. 25, pp. 7, 9).

8 January 1997: the stalemate over the hung parliament (forty-five seats for the government coalition and forty-five seats for the opposition) is broken when a Christian Democrat MP defects to the former.

27 February 1997: parliament endorses (by fifty-two votes to thirty-seven) a coalition government comprising the Liberal Democratic Party, the People's Party (which fought the election as part of Slovenian Spring) and the Democratic Party of Retired People. 'The coalition … has forty-nine seats in the ninety-seat lower chamber of parliament, and can expect support from the Hungarian minority MP and the Italian one as well as from the independent MP Ciril Pucko' (*EEN*, 1997, vol. 11, no. 4, p. 1).

> Premier Janez Drnovsek's new coalition government is expected to have a smooth run in the foreseeable future, assuming it can continue to rely on parliamentary support from the one Hungarian and one Italian minority MP as well as on all or some of the Slovenian National Party's four MPs.
>
> (*EEN*, 13 March 1997, vol. 11, no. 5, p. 9)

March 1997: Borut Pahoris elected leader of the Associated List of Social Democrats.

8 July 1997: Nato's secretary-general Javier Solana Madriaga:

> Today the heads of state and government have agreed to invite the Czech Republic, Hungary and Poland to begin accession talks with Nato … We

affirm that Nato remains open to new members ... We will review the process at our next meeting in 1999. With regard to aspiring members, we recognize with great interest and take account of the positive developments toward democracy and the rule of law in a number of south-eastern European countries, especially Romania and Slovenia.

(A majority of the sixteen Nato countries, led by France, supported the inclusion of Romania and Slovenia in the first wave of invitations. But the USA was adamant that only three countries would be invited to become members of Nato in the first wave.)

14 July 1997: parliament endorses the amendment to Article 68 of the constitution to allow foreigners to purchase land.

16 July 1997: the European Commission recommends that Slovenia opens negotiations (along with Cyprus, the Czech Republic, Estonia, Hungary and Poland) in early 1998 for entry to the EU. (The invitation was formally approved at an EU summit on 13 December 1997, formal negotiations for membership beginning on 31 March 1998. Slovakia, Latvia, Lithuania, Bulgaria and Romania were to be given special EU aid to help them meet the conditions necessary for membership negotiations to begin.)

Concern has been expressed about the effectiveness of the coalition government.

> It means less emphasis on market reforms ... Introducing EU-friendly reforms will be the main challenge for the government in 1998 and 1999 ... The other challenge ... will be to keep crony politics in check. In recent years a string of high-profile public officials have become directors of companies they helped to privatize. Now there is a growing sense of the coalition parties focusing more on dividing the spoils than on governing ... The other great concern is that government spending, previously kept firmly under government control, is soaring ... The central bank is opposed to too much foreign money entering the country, through either loans or the stock market ... Consequently, industrial production is at a near standstill ... The banking system ... is only slowly opening up ... Companies, often owned by their own management, are jealous of their independence.
>
> (Business Central Europe 1997: 30)

31 July 1997: foreign minister Zoran Thaler resigns (effective September). (He resigned 'partly in protest at the workings of the coalition government ... ostensibly because of his frustration with parochial local politics': *EEN*, 1997, vol. 11, no. 15, pp. 1, 3.)

23 November 1997: Milan Kucan wins a second five-year term as president, with nearly 56 per cent of the vote. Janez Podobnik (speaker of parliament) comes second with 18 per cent of the vote.

17 April 1998: Slovenia, Hungary and Italy agree to establish a new joint peacekeeping brigade under Italian command as from January 1999 (*EEN*, 1998, vol. 12, no. 6, p. 9).

November 1998:

> The EU's negative progress report of November 1998 shook Slovenia ... The EU's criticisms centred on the country's slow progress in adopting the *acquis communautaire*, or EU legislation. That failure stems from Slovenia's weak government: it is a divided three-party coalition, with a parliamentary majority of just one vote. Decision-making is therefore as slow as economic and legislative reform.
>
> (Business Central Europe 1998: 30)

21 June 1999: President Clinton becomes the first US president to visit Slovenia.

19 September 1999: the Pope visits Slovenia.

13 October 1999: the European Commission recommends that EU leaders at the December 1999 meeting in Helsinki allow Bulgaria, Latvia, Lithuania, Malta, Romania and Slovakia to begin accession negotiations in 2000.

The 'principle of differentiation' for entry date will apply to each of the twelve candidates, reflecting differing states of readiness for EU entry. A 'fully flexible, multi-speed accession process' is envisaged. 'Each country will be able to proceed on merit, including the possibility for those which join the negotiations from 2000 to catch up with the others.' The European Commission thinks that existing EU members should undertake internal reforms by the end of 2002: 'Whether the first accessions can take place as from 1 January 2003 will then depend entirely on the speed with which the applicant countries can make progress on meeting the criteria.'

Latvia has made good political progress but falls short of international standards on the protection of the linguistic rights of minorities. (Estonia is also criticized as regards linguistic rights.) Latvia has made 'significant and sustained progress' towards meeting market economy criteria and in regards to its ability to withstand competitive pressures. Latvia has a good chance of catching up with the group led by Hungary, with Lithuania not far behind. Latvia joins Malta and Cyprus, Hungary, Poland, Estonia and Slovenia in having functioning market economies. Lithuania could become a functioning market economy in 2000 if it pushes ahead with promised reforms.

Malta and Cyprus have already met the economic terms set by the EU, being able to cope with competitive pressures and market forces in the EU. Hungary and Poland come next in economic terms, followed by Slovenia, Estonia and then the Czech Republic. Hungary, Poland, Estonia and Slovenia have improved their ability to cope with competitive pressures and market forces 'in the medium term' (meaning more than one year from 2000). Hungary is the closest of the Eastern European countries to meeting the criteria on a market economy with the capacity to withstand competition within the EU.

(*FT*, 14 October 1999, pp. 1, 10; *IHT*, 14 October 1999, p. 5; *Guardian*, 14

October 1999, p. 14; *Independent*, 14 October 1999, p. 18; *The Times*, 14 October 1999, p. 21; *Telegraph*, 14 October 1999, p. 20.)

11 January 2000: the party leaderships of the Social Democratic Party and the Slovenian Christian Democrats approve a draft agreement for an electoral agreement (*EEN*, 2000, vol. 12, no. 22, p. 6).

29 January 2000: the leaders of the Slovenian Christian Democrats (led by Lozje Peterle) and the Slovenian People's Party (led by Marjan Podobnik) sign a formal opposition coalition agreement (*EEN*, 2000, vol. 12, no. 22, pp. 4, 6).

15 March 2000: the Slovenian People's Party announces its intention to leave the ruling coalition government following its merger with the Slovenian Christian Democrats. Nine SPP ministers resign from the cabinet (*EEN*, 2000, vol. 12, no. 23, p. 11).

8 April 2000:

> The government collapsed when the National Assembly refused to approve a new cabinet sought by prime minister Janez Drnovsek, a Liberal Democrat. Parliament, which has ninety members, voted fifty-five to thirty-one on Saturday [8 April] to reject Mr Drnovsek's request for ratification for a cabinet reshuffle after his junior partner, the People's Party [headed by deputy prime minister Marjan Podobnik], pulled out of the government ... The conservative People's Party quit the government to join forces with the opposition Christian Democrats ... Parliament has thirty days to elect a new prime minister or give a confidence vote to the current prime minister ... If no candidate wins enough parliamentary support President Milan Kucan must bring forward the next election.
>
> (*IHT*, 10 April 2000, p. 4)

15 April 2000:

> Slovenia's opposition has agreed on a candidate to replace Janez Drnovsek as prime minister ... The newly formed conservative Slovenian People's Party and the centre-right Social Democrats agreed late on Saturday [15 April] to nominate Andrej Bajuk ... But the two parties hold just forty-four seats out of ninety in parliament ... Mr Drnovsek's centre-left coalition lost a no confidence vote last week after the conservative People's Party quit the government to merge with the opposition Christian Democrats, forming the Slovenian People's Party and leaving Mr Drnovsek without a majority.
>
> (*FT*, 17 April 2000, p. 6)

7 June 2000: parliament narrowly approves a new government under a new prime minister, Andrej Bajuk.

Bajuk is an Argentine-Slovene banker (*Business Central Europe*, June 2000, p. 15).

'Parliament ... finally elected, by a margin of one vote, a right-wing government led by Andrej Bajuk, a recently returned émigré ... The 7 June success was down only to two maverick independent MPs who switched sides' (*FT*, Survey,

11 July 2000, p. 35). Fifty-seven-year-old Andrej Bajuk is vice-president of the new party, which is called the SKD (Christian Democrats) + SLS (People's Party) Slovene People's Party. His parents fled Slovenia in 1945.

> They went to South America to escape recriminations for their wartime support for Slovenia's Nazi German and Italian fascist occupiers against the communist-led partisans. Some fear that the aggressive political style of his government risks reopening the long-running left–right divisions symbolized by Mr Bajuk's own life story. Many fears concern Janez Jansa, the defence minister and leader of the junior coalition Social Democratic Party, seen as the government's most powerful figure. The worries prompted Milan Kucan, the president, to warn about the dangers to national unity – and the EU accession process – at a 22 June press conference to mark the ninth anniversary of Slovenia's referendum on independence from Yugoslavia ... His warning came after Mr Bujak spent his first Sunday in office at a commemoration for more than 10,000 Slovenian anti-communist fighters massacred by communists after being handed back by the allies at the end of the Second World War ... The country tried to heal the national divisions in 1991 with a conciliation ceremony where both sides recognized the horror of wartime events.
>
> (*FT*, Survey, 11 July 2000, p. 35)

> From April to June [2000] the country endured a spell of political uncertainty ... Many have seen the subsequent two months of wrangling as a waste of scarce parliamentary time. The EU has sounded concerned about the effects of the hiatus on passage of legislation for membership ... The president ... [has been concerned] by the new government's conduct. With only months to govern, and a business backlog to clear, it has concentrated on replacing heads of a wide variety of state-influenced organizations with its own appointees.
>
> (*FT*, Survey, 11 July 2000, p. 35)

25 July 2000: parliament passes a constitutional amendment providing for a greater element of proportional representation in elections (*EEN*, 2000, vol. 12, no. 24, p. 7).

26 July 2000: Andrej Bajuk and Lozje Peterle resign as deputy chairmen of the ruling Slovene People's Party–Slovene Christian Democrats coalition in protest at the passing of the election law changes (*EEN*, 2000, vol. 12, no. 24, p. 7).

27 July 2000: president Milan Kucan announces that a general election is to be held on 15 October 2000.

> The announcement was made a day after Slovenia's ruling parties, the conservative People's Party and the centre-right Social Democrats, declared their coalition agreement dead after falling out over a new electoral law ...

Andrej Bajuk, the prime minister, said on Wednesday [26 July] he would remain in office until the election but intended to form a new party in the next few weeks.

(*FT*, 28 July 2000, p. 8)

Parliamentary elections on 15 October are expected to be won by Liberal Democracy of Slovenia following the end of July break-up of the ruling alliance (Social Democracy of Slovenia together with the Christian Democrat People's Party) after parliament on 25 July passed a constitutional amendment changing the electoral law in favour of proportional representation.

(*EEN*, 2000, vol. 12, no. 24, p. 4)

31 July 2000: premier Andrej Bajuk and Christian Democrat leader Lozje Peterle (foreign minister) announce the formation of a new party, the New Slovenia–Christian People's Party, which is to hold its inaugural congress on 4 August (*EEN*, 2000, vol. 12, no. 24, p. 7).

26 September 2000: the Social Democratic Party (headed by former defence minister Janez Jansa) and the New Slovenia–Christian People's Party (headed by Andrej Bajuk) sign an agreement for an electoral compact (*EEN*, 2000, vol. 13, no. 1, pp. 7–8).

15 October 2000: a general election is held.

The Liberal Democrats (Liberal Democracy of Slovenia), led by Janez Drnovsek, win 36.3 per cent of the vote and thirty-four of the ninety seats in parliament.

Janez Drnovsek returns as prime minister. Liberal Democracy of Slovenia is back in coalition government with its erstwhile partners the United List of Social Democrats with eleven seats and the Democratic Party of Pensioners of Slovenia, the new Party of Youth of Slovenia and Zmago Jelincic's Slovenian National Party, all with four seats. Neither ... Janez Jansa's Social Democratic Party nor ... Andrej Bajuk's New Slovenia made any inroads of consequence, winning respectively fourteen and eight seats ... Bajuk's government initially was concocted from the Social Democratic Party and the then recently married Slovenian People's Party and the Christian Democrats. It ended up with only the Social Democratic Party and New Slovenia. Worst of all Bajuk and his colleagues began to appoint their cronies and supporters to top management positions in state-owned companies.

(*EEN*, 2000, vol. 13, no. 1, p. 10)

8 November 2000: despite some familiar concerns expressed in the latest EU assessment, Slovenia remains a front-runner for membership.

The EU's report on Slovenia (*Progress Towards Accession*, 8 November 2000, pp. 81–2):

Public administration is another area requiring attention. Little progress has been achieved in this respect ... The denationalization process remains slow ... Slovenia can be regarded as a functioning market economy and should be able to cope with competitive pressure and market forces within the Union in the near term, provided that it completes the remaining reforms that would increase competition in the economy. Continued macroeconomic stability, with fiscal and external balances under control, has provided the basis for steady growth. Some steps to assure the medium-term sustainability of pension reform have been taken. The legal and institutional framework for a market economy is largely in place. However, implementation of this framework can be improved. Furthermore, the state still has considerable influence in certain areas of the economy. In particular, the continued dominance of the financial sector by state-owned banks holds back development and competition. The slow progress on privatization and rigid business conditions are keeping foreign direct investment inflows at a low level ... Slovenia should continue eliminating the remaining administrative restrictions to capital movement.

15 November 2000: 'Liberal Democracy of Slovenia, the United List of Social Democrats, the Slovene People's Party–Christian Democrats and the Democratic Party of Pensioners sign a governing coalition agreement' (*EEN*, 2001, vol. 13, no. 2, p. 6). '[A] new governing coalition led by premier Janez Drnovsek's Liberal Democracy of Slovenia [was] installed in mid-December' (p. 4).

13 November 2001: the EU publishes its reports on enlargement.

The EU publishes its progress reports on the twelve EU applicants for EU membership with which negotiations have begun. There are thirteen applicants in all (including Cyprus, Malta and Turkey), but negotiations have not yet begun with Turkey.

'The EU is heading for a "big bang" enlargement of up to ten countries that could take place as early as 2004 after negotiations are wrapped up by the end of next year [2002]' (*FT*, 14 November 2001, p. 12).

As many as ten new members could join the EU in a 'big bang', according to a report from the European Commission yesterday [13 November] ... Diplomats had previously believed that an advance guard of a few countries ... would make up the first wave of entrants, with others joining later in stages.

(*Independent*, 14 November 2001, p. 20)

'The Commission said candidates which were ready should be able to conclude their talks by the end of next year and take part as members in the European Parliament elections in June 2004' (*Guardian*, 14 November 2001, p. 19). '[The Commission said that] significant progress [had been made], providing "a sufficient basis for up to ten new member states in 2004" ' (*IHT*, 14 November 2001, p. 7).

Günter Verheugen (EU enlargement commissioner): 'The aim of achieving the first accessions before the European Parliament elections in 2004 remains a demanding one. But it is not a utopian dream; it is a realistic and feasible challenge' (*FT*, 14 November 2001, p. 12).

> Behind yesterday's carefully worded document lie highly political considerations, and the position of Poland is pivotal. Its progress has been overtaken by others but Poland enjoys the powerful support of Germany, which, for historical reasons, sees enlargement as politically impossible without the Poles. If Poland is admitted the Commission knows it will have great difficulty in turning down small countries that have made rapid progress, including Slovakia, Latvia and Lithuania. There are also concerns over the creation of barriers between neighbours by excluding Slovakia and admitting the Czech Republic or letting in Estonia but blocking ... Latvia and Lithuania.
>
> (*Independent*, 14 November 2001, p. 20)

> Although the EU's report cannot say so, since it restricts itself to technical assessments of readiness, the political logic points increasingly to a 'big bang' enlargement. That is because it is widely felt, particularly in Germany, that a first batch of new members that excluded the biggest candidate, Poland, would not be worth having. And since Poland is a relative laggard in the negotiations, an enlargement that excluded the Poles would probably have to include quite a few others that might not, under strict criteria, have been in the first intake. A similar logic also suggests that it would be hard to admit one Baltic state but not all three – or the Czech Republic without Slovakia.
>
> (*The Economist*, 17 November 2001, p. 41)

'[After the 11 September terrorist attacks on the United States the Commission said that] a strong and united Europe is more important than ever before to ensure peace, security, freedom and prosperity for all its citizens' (*FT*, 14 November 2001, p. 12).

'The ten new members would add some 75 million people to the EU's present population of 375 million' (*The Economist*, 17 November 2001, p. 41). 'The fifteen-nation EU could soon ... [see] its population expanded from 370 million to 450 million' (*Independent*, 14 November 2001, p. 20). '[The EU] structural (regional) and agricultural funds account for 80 per cent of the EU's annual budget' (*FT*, 14 November 2001, p. 12).

> The conditions – that entrants have a functioning market economy and are able to withstand competitive pressure and market forces inside the EU – are met only by Cyprus and Malta ... The Czech Republic, Estonia, Hungary, Latvia, Lithuania, Poland, Slovakia and Slovenia are functioning market economies and, according to the Commission, [these eight coun-

tries] should be able to cope with competitive pressure and market forces [within the EU] 'in the near term' provided they follow EU policy recommendations. Bulgaria is 'close to being a functioning market economy' and with hard work should cope with competitive pressure in the medium term. Romania meets neither criterion ... difficulties are 'severe' ... but, for the first time, has made some progress.

(*FT*, 14 November 2001, p. 12)

[As regards the first eight countries, the Commission says that] while there are 'substantial differences' between their performance in bringing their laws and economies into line with the EU ... if efforts continue these should be able to cope with 'competitive pressure and market forces within the Union in the near term.'

(*Independent*, 14 November 2001, p. 20)

'[Of all the twelve negotiating countries] Cyprus is the most advanced in the negotiations and Romania the least. Poland is sixth' (*Guardian*, 14 November 2001, p. 19). 'The Commission said all the [thirteen] candidate countries, with the exception of Turkey, met the political requirements. Romania and Bulgaria failed to make it mainly on economic grounds' (*IHT*, 14 November 2001, p. 7).

'Malta and Slovenia received excellent reports for their economic and legislative progress' (*IHT*, 14 November 2001, p. 7).

Overall public administration reform [in Slovenia] has progressed over the previous year. However, the laws on civil servants and public agencies still remain to be adopted. They are an important part of the framework legislation for public administration reform providing for the independence of the civil service and status of public agencies. The efforts in this area should be continued ... Slovenia is a functioning market economy. Provided that it implements the remaining reforms to increase competition in domestic markets, it should be able to cope with the competitive pressure and market forces within the Union in the near term ... Remaining restrictions to capital movements are progressively being removed, in the context of managed exchange rates. However, the persistent inflation, linked to widespread indexation ... remains a concern. Labour markets are not sufficiently flexible ... The authorities should now progress with the implementation of the announced structural reforms and privatization in a number of essential sectors such as banking and insurance ... Slovenia has made good overall progress in transposition and implementation of the *acquis* ... Slovenia ... has now met its commitment on transformation of the duty free shops ... Slovenia's administrative capacity for the implementation of the *acquis* has been enhanced ... In the area of reinforcement of the administrative and judicial capacity (including the management and control of EC funds) the priorities have been met partially. It should now focus especially on the remaining short-term priorities, especially related to control of

EC funds. Slovenia has also made good progress in implementing a number of the medium-term priorities. It should speed up its preparations in the area of economic and social cohesion and ensure fulfilment of priorities in the areas of the economic criteria, internal market, agriculture, and employment and social affairs.

(*Progress Towards Accession*, 13 November 2001, pp. 91–3)

The reports came out too late to include in Volume II, which covers Eastern Europe (*Eastern Europe at the Turn of the Twenty-first Century: A Guide to the Economies in Transition*). The following summaries from the actual reports highlight some of the remaining problems:

The judicial system [in Bulgaria] remains weak ... Corruption has continued to give serious cause for concern ... Roma continue to suffer from widespread social discrimination ... Bulgaria is close to being a functioning market economy. It should be able to cope with competitive pressure and market forces within the Union in the medium term, provided it continues implementing reform and intensifies the reform effort to remove persistent difficulties.

(*Progress Towards Accession*, 13 November 2001, pp. 96–8)

The government [of the Czech Republic] has taken steps to improve the functioning of the central and regional administration. However, it is regrettable that the Czech Republic continues to lack a civil service act for its public administration; this is essential for establishing independence, professionalism and stability ... Some additional measures to fight against corruption and economic crime have been taken. Nonetheless, corruption and economic crime remain a serious cause for concern ... Increased efforts are necessary to better fight the persistent trafficking of women and children ... Further efforts to combat widespread discrimination [against Roma] are needed.

(*Progress Towards Accession*, 13 November 2001, pp. 104–5)

Corruption ... remains a problem [in Hungary]... In the area of public service media, a solution needs to be found regarding the composition of the supervisory boards of trustees ... It will be important to enhance efforts to fight against widespread discrimination [against Roma] ... Together with recent non-transparent fiscal practices, the uncertainty of the pension system and the delays in the reform of the health care system have raised some concern about the continuation of consolidation and the medium-term sustainability of public finances ... Some of the provisions laid down in the law on Hungarian minorities living in neighbouring countries [the Status Law] apparently conflict with the prevailing European standard of minority protection ... The Law ... is currently not in accordance with the principle of non-discrimination laid down in the Treaty.

(*Progress Towards Accession*, 13 November 2001, pp. 98–100)

Corruption [in Poland]... remains a source of concern ... Growth experienced a significant slowdown starting in the second half of last year [2000] ... The sharp decline in growth reflects in large part problems in the macroeconomic policy mix – the co-ordination of fiscal and monetary policy. Already high unemployment has risen further and the budget deficit is on a rising path ... The authorities should speed up privatization and restructuring in some key areas, such as in some traditional industries or in agriculture ... Further measures need to be taken to improve Poland's infrastructure and the response of the labour markets to changing economic conditions ... In the agriculture sector ... the substantial transformation which is needed in terms of policy, legislation and structures has not yet taken place.

(Progress Towards Accession, 13 November 2001, pp. 104–6)

Corruption [in Romania] remains a serious problem that is largely unresolved. Other particular concerns are the lack of progress in carrying out a strategic reform of the public administration and the need to further guarantee the independence of the judiciary ... Efforts to improve the actual living conditions in childcare institutions should continue ... The Roma strategy has not yet been implemented; anti-discrimination legislation has been adopted but it is not yet operational; and the demilitarization of the police has not yet started ... Romania has made progress towards establishing a functioning market economy and although it would not, in the medium term, be able to cope with competitive pressure and market forces within the Union, it has taken measures that would allow it to develop its future capacity, provided that it keeps to the engaged economic reform path ... The recent privatizations demonstrate a new commitment towards the establishment of a functioning market economy. However, there are still serious economic imbalances with high inflation and a widening current account deficit, in a difficult social environment. The still fragile macroeconomic environment, the uncertain legal framework and the poor administrative capacity hinder the development of the private sector. Large parts of the enterprise sector have yet to start restructuring or are still in the early stages ... Enterprises' financial discipline should be established by halting the accumulation of inter-enterprise arrears and the provision of state support to inefficient ventures ... A further priority is to accompany enterprises' restructuring and privatization with the establishment of sound legal and institutional foundations of the functioning market economy ... Restructuring of the [agricultural] sector has barely begun.

(Progress Towards Accession, 13 November 2001, pp. 101–3)

Corruption [in Slovakia] remains a serious cause for concern ... As regards the Roma minority ... it will be important to improve efforts to fight against widespread discrimination ... As regards nuclear energy, Slovakia should implement its decommissioning commitments, and continue to ensure a high level of nuclear safety.

(*Progress Towards Accession*, 13 November 2001, pp. 92–4)

THE ECONOMY

Slovenia aspires to a normal Western political and economic system and prospects there are by far the brightest in the former Yugoslavia. (See Table 4.2). Growth turned positive in 1993 and the annual rate of inflation peaked in 1990. But unemployment remains a problem, although perhaps not as great as the official figures may suggest. The unemployment rate is 14.8 per cent. But according to ILO (International Labour Organization) calculations, unemployment peaked at 9.1 per cent in 1993. 'The unemployment figures should be taken with a pinch of salt. Many of the allegedly unemployed are working in Slovenia's thriving "shadow economy", now estimated to be worth 30 per cent of the official one' (*IHT*, Survey, 6 April 1995, pp. 13, 11). The unemployment rate hovers around 13 to 14 per cent, but it is only about 7.5 per cent using the ILO method (*Transition*, January–February 1996, vol. 7, no. 1, p. 9).

There is a liberal foreign trade regime and the economy is quickly being integrated into the world economy, e.g. it became a member of the IMF in January 1993 and the World Bank in February; a trade and co-operation agreement was signed with the EU in April 1993; an association agreement was signed with the EU on 10 June 1996 (see above). According to *IHT* (Survey, 6 April 1995, p. 11), in 1994 more than 70 per cent of exports went to the EU; the EU supplied a near-equal amount of imports. Germany is a particularly important trading partner. On 23 February 1995 Slovenia signed a free-trade pact with the four remaining EFTA countries (Iceland, Liechtenstein, Norway and Switzerland). The pact would come into force on 1 July 1995 as far as the four were concerned, but Slovenia was to have a seven-year transition period. As of January 1996 Slovenia becomes a member of the Central European Free Trade Agreement (Business Central Europe 1995: 33). 'The EU … now accounts for 60 per cent of the total [exports]' (*FT*, Survey, 9 July 2001, p. 11).

On 9 June 1995 a tentative debt agreement was reached with Western commercial banks, with the signing perhaps taking place in September. Slovenia was to be responsible for 18 per cent of the former Yugoslavia's total debt of $4.65 billion owed to the banks. Slovenia had already secured debt rescheduling with the Paris Club of creditor governments (*FT*, 12 June 1995, p. 2). On 28 February 1996 the Slovenian parliament approved the agreement with the London Club, Slovenia taking over 18 per cent of the former Yugoslavia's total debt to the commercial banks. The total debt was valued at $5.58 billion (of which $4.4 billion represented principal), but certain secondary market transactions were to be deducted. Slovenia was the first of the former Yugoslav states to finalize an agreement and was released from the 'joint and several liability' clause in the 1988 agreement. But the Federal Republic of Yugoslavia threat-

Table 4.2 Slovenia: selected economic indicators 1990–2000

Economic indicator	1990	1991	1992	1993	1994	1995	1996	1997	1998	1999	2000 (estimate)
Rate of growth of GDP (%)	-4.7	-8.9	-5.5	2.8	5.3	4.1	3.5	4.6	3.8	5.2	4.6
Rate of growth of industrial output (%)	-10.3	-12.4	-13.2	-2.8	6.4	2.0	1.0	1.0	3.7	-0.5	6.2
Rate of growth of agricultural output (%)	1.6	-3.3	-6.7	-4.2	4.2	1.6	1.1	-2.9	3.1	2.3	
Inflation rate (consumer, %)	549.7	117.7	207.3	32.9	21.0	13.5	9.9	8.4	8.0	6.1	8.9
Budget surplus or deficit (% of GDP)[a]	-0.3	2.6	0.3	0.6	-0.2	-0.3	-0.2	-1.7	-1.4	-0.9	-1.3
Unemployment rate (end of year, %)[b]				9.1	9.1	7.4	7.3	7.1	7.6	7.4	7.2
Balance of payments (current account, $billion)	0.526	0.190	0.926	0.192	0.574	-0.100	0.031	0.012	-0.147	-0.783	-0.612
Foreign direct investment (net, $billion)	-0.002	0.041	0.113	0.111	0.131	0.183	0.188	0.340	0.250	0.144	0.110
Population (million)		2.0	2.0	2.0	2.0	2.0	2.0	2.0	2.0	2.0	2.0

Source   Various issues of European Bank for Reconstruction and Development, *Transition Report*; United Nations Economic Commission for Europe, *Economic Survey of Europe*; United Nations, *World Economic and Social Survey*; IMF, *World Economic Outlook*.

Notes:

[a] General government balance: includes the state, municipalities and extrabudgetary funds; excludes privatization revenues (EBRD)
[b] Based on labour force surveys consistent with ILO definitions (EBRD 2001a: 65).

ened legal action to halt the deal, demanding a general agreement on the debt and on the estimated $2 billion of gold and hard currency assets frozen around the world (*FT*, 1 March 1996, p. 2; 13 March 1996, p. 2; 30 April 1996, p. 2; Deutsche Bank, *Focus: Eastern Europe*, 1996, no. 153, p. 5). 'The EU ... now accounts for 60 per cent of the total [exports]' (*FT*, Survey. 9 July 2001, p. 11).

A new (convertible) currency, the tolar, was introduced on 8 October 1991 and a floating exchange rate adopted. Convertibility is full for current account purposes and the remaining restrictions on the capital account are to be phased out (EBRD 1994: 37, 109). By the end of 1994, 98 per cent of imports were free from restrictions. The government is committed to further trade liberalization and to the elimination of all non-tariff barriers (EBRD 1995a: 64). (Non-tariff barriers are still substantial in sectors such as telecommunications and electrical equipment: EBRD 1997b: 201.) On 1 September 1995 the tolar became externally convertible in accordance with the provisions of Article 8 of the IMF.

To counter exchange rate appreciation the central bank increased quantitative controls on the capital account (EBRD 1998a: 41.) Capital account restrictions were introduced in early 1997. In October 1998 further restrictions were introduced on portfolio flows, forcing foreign investors to hold Slovenian shares for at least seven years (EBRD 1998b: 190–1).

> Recent actions taken by the central bank to curb foreign capital inflows ... have been justified on the grounds that the rising wave of capital inflows, in particular of foreign portfolio investment, was undermining the conduct of monetary policy ... The introduction of expensive custody accounts and associated regulations has been effective for the moment in choking off the flow of foreign portfolio investment.
>
> (Kevin Done, *FT*, Survey, 28 April 1997, p. i)

> With a view to harmonization with EU requirements the central bank has substantially reduced restrictions on capital inflows ... On 1 February 1999 the central bank substantially reduced restrictions on capital account inflows that had been in place since 1995. Some restrictions remain on portfolio investments of less than four years' duration, but under the new rules any portfolio investment in excess of 10 per cent of the company's shares is now defined as foreign direct investment and as such is exempt from any restriction. Purchases of debt instruments (private issues only) and shares issued by domestic companies on the primary market are also exempt. In addition, restrictions on financial credits have been completely relaxed. However, the central bank has the power to reintroduce a non-interest-bearing deposit requirement for a two-year period (regardless of maturity of credit) on a percentage of the financial credit, ranging from zero per cent to 30 per cent.
>
> (EBRD 1999a: 43–4)

The foreign exchange operations law passed in March 1999 and the implementing regulations adopted in July and September 1999 are significant steps towards full liberalization of capital flows. The main achievements of the legislation are the complete liberalization of inward and outward direct investments and the significant liberalization of credit operations and securities transactions. The law and its implementation so far leave restrictions for the most part only on the inflow of short-term capital (EBRD 1999b: 266).

> While restrictions of inward and outward direct investments were lifted in 1999, restrictions on portfolio flows remained in the form of fiduciary accounts. Under this system a foreign portfolio investor could only purchase securities through a brokerage or a bank, debited to the fiduciary account opened at the bank. Upon purchase a bank had to pay a premium for the purchase of the right to buy foreign currency, unless the buyer of securities renounced the right to sell them within a certain period. Effective from July 2001 foreign portfolio investments for all long-term securities (shares and bonds) are no longer subject to these obstacles, although some restrictions remain for investments in short-term securities of less than six months.
>
> (EBRD 2001b: 194)

On 1 September 1999 capital controls were relaxed. 'The rule change allowed foreigners to hold stocks for one year rather than four years before selling them back into the domestic market without facing custody charges' (*FT*, 10 November 1999, p. 54). Slovenia reduced the amount of time foreigners must hold Slovenian stocks from four years to one year (*IHT*, 9 November 1999, p. 8). 'An easing of foreign currency controls means that top Slovenian corporate customers can seek loans elsewhere in Europe' (*FT*, Survey, 11 July 2000, p. 36).

> [The abolition of] restrictions on foreign portfolio investments ... became effective on 1 July [2001]. Foreigners had previously been banned from selling back Slovenian securities to domestic buyers for six months after their initial purchase (or forced to pay a quarterly fee equal to 0.2 per cent of asset value).
>
> (*FT*, Survey, 9 July 2001, p. 12)

'Both monetary and fiscal policy have supported stabilization and wage pressure has been kept to a manageable level' (Kraft 1995: 474). The Bank of Slovenia Law, passed immediately after the declaration of Slovene political independence, established the independence of the central bank. The bank was not allowed to extend loans to the government for more than 5 per cent of the budget (p. 475). Incomes policy has also played a role in the stabilization effort, e.g. a wage freeze was introduced in February 1993 (pp. 478–9). A tight monetary and fiscal policy has been supplemented by wage controls in the battle against inflation (*Guardian*, 23 January 1993, p. 37). Collective tripartite contracts between the government, employers and trade unions provide the legal basis for determining wages. A law was passed in April 1994 levying a 50 per cent tax on wages above a defined level. But this and other attempts to control wage increases have met with limited success. Price liberalization was almost complete by mid-1994. Regulated prices include electricity and natural gas (EBRD 1996b: 175). In September 1996 the employers' representatives cancelled the tripartite agreement governing nationwide pay scales and conditions of employment. But previously agreed pay scales were to remain in place until March 1997 (EBRD 1997a: 33). The employers proposed a series of reductions in non-wage allowances and this led to strikes in late 1996. After the 1996 social agreement expired in May 1997, parliament adopted a minimum wage law (EBRD 1997b: 202). The new wage act adopted in mid-1997 changed the rules for public sector and minimum wage indexation. Full indexation to retail prices on a quarterly basis was replaced by an annual partial indexation to consumer prices (EBRD 1998b: 190). The replacement of the 20 per cent sales tax by VAT, scheduled for January 1998, has been postponed until July 1999 (EBRD 1998b: 191). In 1997 administered prices still accounted for about 28 per cent of the retail price index and 20 per cent of the consumer price index. But price liberalization has intensified since mid-1997. Price controls for bread, milk and pork have been removed, while flour, sugar and oil products are still controlled. Prices for petrol and diesel oil have been raised significantly (EBRD 1998b: 190). A new VAT law and a law on excise duties were adopted in December 1998 and implemented in July 1999. An agreement among domestic banks was initiated in 1995, with the backing of the central bank, in an attempt to lower deposit interest rates and to curb aggressive rate-setting for market share. The banks abandoned this practice in early 1999 (EBRD 1999b: 266).

> Incomes policy has long played an important role in establishing the framework for setting wages in both the public and private sectors. The social partners – the government, employers and labour unions – agree annually to a formula under which wages are adjusted to inflation … Inflationary pressures have persisted in the current year [2001] … due in part to the almost full indexation of nominal wages, pensions and interest rates.
>
> (EBRD 2001b: 194–5)

At the beginning of June 1997 a collective wage agreement was signed by employer associations and the majority of trade unions. Incomes were to rise by no more than 85 per cent of the increase in retail prices, instead of the 100 per cent under the old agreement introduced in 1990 and renewed in 1993 (Deutsche Morgan Grenfell, *Focus: Eastern Europe*, 5 September 1997, p. 52).

'Slovenia … is the only one of the EU candidate countries that has still not introduced VAT (value-added tax) – after several delays the government is now aiming for 1 July 1999 … and it has been slow to grasp the nettle of pension reform' (Kevin Done, *FT*, Survey, 18 May 1998, p. iii).

> Slovenia has one of the world's most generous pay-as-you-go pension systems, but demographic trends with an aging population mean the system is unsustainable … Publication of a White Paper on pension reform

provoked the biggest demonstrations seen in Slovenia since independence, and the protests have forced the government to ... make the changes less radical.

(p. i)

'Already last year [1997] the need to finance the growing deficit in the pension system helped to push the consolidated budget into a deficit for the first time of 1.1 per cent of GDP' (p. iii).

In May 2000 Slovenia and the EU reached agreement on partial liberalization of trade in agricultural products ... A law on customs tariffs, which was adopted in July 2000 and will come into effect in January 2001, will harmonize most external tariffs with those in the EU.

(EBRD 2000b: 210)

Privatization

The Restitution and Denationalization Law of 1991 was designed in part to appease the Catholic Church, which was the largest landowner before the Second World War and derived a large income from its extensive hardwood forests. The law stipulated that claimants must have been Yugoslav citizens as of 9 May 1945. In December 1995 parliament imposed a three-year moratorium on the restitution of properties of more than 200 ha.

Over the past year a number of Italian, Austrian and German families whose estates had been expropriated in the 1940s have lodged claims for restitution. Worried at the prospect of the return to private hands of another 15 per cent or so of the country's woods, premier Janez Drnovsek's ruling Liberal Democracy of Slovenia has encouraged popular fears that the old landed aristocracy would get back their lands for nothing ... Generally there is public hostility to the idea that the landed grandees might turn the budding bourgeois state back into a plutocracy.

(*EEN*, 18 January 1996, vol. 10, no. 2, p. 8)

Under the 1993 law land and buildings can be returned to the former owners (EBRD 1994: 36, 65).

Slovenia has restituted farmland (Swinnen 1999: 640).

Slovenia has based its restitution policy on the citizenship of the land's owner in 1945. If this person was Slovenian and the heirs have a different citizenship, they are still restituted the land ... [Slovenia and Poland] have transferred the state farmland into a state fund responsible for privatizing the land and managing its use during transition. However, while Poland is selling most of this land, Slovenia is restituting most of its farmland to former owners. The main explanation is that most of the former owners in

Slovenia were Slovenian citizens, while in Poland the state farms are mostly located in West Poland and use land which before World War II was owned by Germans … But Slovenia is also restricting restitution to domestic citizens. It excludes land formerly owned by Italian citizens from the restitution process … Under pressure from the Italian government the Slovenian government is considering possible compensation (in value) to the former owners.

(p. 647)

The privatization law was finally passed on 11 November 1992 after much controversy and included practically all possible methods of privatization (Zizmond 1993: 902–3). The law was amended in June 1993. The roughly 2,700 enterprises involved in the programme were to submit their proposals by the end of 1994. The basic approach is to distribute the share capital as follows: 10 per cent to a restitution fund (to compensate for seized property); 10 per cent to a staff pension fund; 20 per cent to employees in exchange for vouchers; 20 per cent to a development fund (at a later date these shares will be sold to investment funds, which, in turn, will sell units to the population in exchange for vouchers, allocated according to age); the remaining 40 per cent can be purchased by employees (at a 50 per cent discount on the purchase price, with payment spread over four years) or sold at auction or by tender. Enterprises are free to choose the privatization method. In the case of a proposal (which must be approved) to sell the entire share capital to a foreign investor, the revenue raised will be allocated to the funds.

The number of socially owned enterprises involved was 1,500–1,800, lower than the original number of 2,600, which had been inflated by factors such as double registrations (Deutsche Bank, *Focus: Eastern Europe*, 8 November 1994, no. 119, p. 3).

Privatization of socially owned enterprises is governed by the December 1992 law. The government aimed to privatize a total of 1,549 enterprises concerned. The sale was to take place through mass privatization involving the issuing of 'ownership certificates' to all Slovene nationals. They are exchangeable for either enterprise or investment funds shares. Enterprises can distribute a maximum of 20 per cent of the shares to incumbent employees free of charge. A further 40 per cent is transferable to three state-run funds (20 per cent to the development fund, 10 per cent to the pension fund and 10 per cent to the restitution fund set up to compensate individuals for previous nationalizations). The remainder may be sold to management/employees or to outsiders. The expectation was that most enterprises would be privatized by the end of 1996. Large public utilities are still either majority or wholly publicly owned. Banks are to remain majority state-run in the short term. Action has been taken to break up large 'socially managed' enterprises into smaller units. The bankruptcy law, which became effective in 1994, is being enforced. A development fund is involved in the restructuring of ailing enterprises with a view to ultimate privatization (EBRD 1996b: 175). Employees own a majority stake in enterprises representing 44 per cent of the book value of privatized enterprises (EBRD 1997a: 33). By June 1997, of the initial 1,594 enterprises eligible for privatization, 1,400 had their privatization plans approved. Of these over 1,000 were privatized. There is majority insider control in 65 per cent of privatized enterprises. But these account for only 16 per cent of the total equity of the 1,594 enterprises. Large capital-intensive enterprises have tended to choose other privatization options, such as public offerings on the stock market (EBRD 1997b: 201). The privatization of socially managed enterprises was completed by mid-1997. But large public enterprises are still majority state-owned, as are the two large banks and several large conglomerates (EBRD 1998a: 41).

Restructuring has preceded privatization and Mira Puc (managing director of the Agency for Restructuring and Privatization) commented as follows: 'Conditions are different in each country. The political conditions here would make it impossible to do it [privatization] all through the state like in Germany, because all managers here believe they already own the companies' (*FT*, Survey, 12 April 1994, p. 32). The Development Fund has already sold about thirty companies (p. 32).

Since the privatization process is just getting under way, the private sector currently accounts for about 15 per cent of GDP and 20 per cent of employment (Deutsche Bank, *Focus: Eastern Europe*, 17 December 1993, no. 95, pp. 3–4).

Rough estimates in mid-year of the private sector as a percentage of GDP are provided by the EBRD: 1990, 15 per cent; 1991, 15 per cent (EBRD 1999b: 24, 268); 1992, 30 per cent; 1993, 40 per cent; 1994, 45 per cent; 1995, 50 per cent; 1996, 55 per cent; 1997, 60 per cent; 1998, 60 per cent; 1999, 60 per cent; 2000, 60 per cent; 2001, 65 per cent (EBRD 2001b: 12, 195).

By some estimates the underground economy accounts for around 7 per cent of GDP (Deutsche Bank, *Focus: Eastern Europe*, 8 November 1994, no. 119, p. 4).

Almost all small trade and service activity is operated by the private sector (EBRD 1994: 36, 65). 'Local economists reckon that the grey market is worth a third of GDP, as local wideboys try to avoid the high tax burdens' (*Business Central Europe*, June 2000, p. 17).

Large privatization has been slow, but it is likely to become comprehensive by the end of 1995 (EBRD 1994: 36, 65). By the end of 1994 over 92 per cent of the enterprises that had been earmarked for privatization under the mass privatization programme had submitted plans to the agency. About 40 per cent of them had completed the first phase of privatization and were awaiting registration by the courts (EBRD 1995a: 64). By mid-1995, 215 enterprises had been formally privatized. Another 478 had obtained ministerial approval for their privatization plans but were awaiting court approval. The programme was expected to be completed by the end of 1995 (EBRD 1995b: 58). Only twenty-seven socially managed enterprises have not presented their privatization plans. They are mostly non-viable enterprises that will have to be restructured or closed down. By the end of 1996 privatization plans had been completed or were being implemented for enterprises representing over 95 per cent of the total share capital in the trade and industry sectors. It is expected that privatization will be concluded by mid-1997 (EBRD 1997a: 33). By July 1997 the privatization agency had approved 1,420 privatization programmes for the roughly 1,600 remaining 'socially managed' enterprises. By July 1998, 90 per cent of these privatization programmes had reached the final stage. The remaining 180 enterprises have either been liquidated or transferred to the state development fund for restructuring. But some large loss-making enterprises in the metal and oil sectors were not included in the original privatization law and are still fully or majority state owned. The government plans to keep at least 51 per cent of Telekom Slovenije. The energy sector is almost fully state owned, except for the oil and gas sectors where the state is a minority shareholder (EBRD 1998b: 190–1). 'While privatization of socially (i.e. employee) managed enterprises is nearly complete, progress has been very slow in privatizing large firms' (EBRD 1999a: 24).

> The state still owns more than 50 per cent of total assets in the economy, including two large banks, fixed-line telecoms, energy, ports, highways and large enterprises in the steel and aluminium sectors. Little progress has been made recently in privatizing these assets, although the privatization programme for the telecoms sector has been approved.
>
> (p. 44)

While the privatization of 'socially owned' enterprises (mostly small and medium-sized enterprises) is now complete, there has been little progress in large privatization. A number of large enterprises in the aluminium, steel and oil sectors are still in the rehabilitation process led by the Slovene development corporation and other state agencies. A programme for steel sector privatization was initiated in 1998, aiming at providing significant concessions to employees and at attracting strategic investors. Although by law employees had an option to acquire up to 20 per cent of the shares, this option was used only up to 11 per cent. With the capital increase provided by institutional investors this share has been further diminished. So far only one steel company has been privatized and that was in May 1999. Under the June 1999 law on the First Pension Fund unused vouchers issued for the privatization of socially owned enterprises and held by the privatization investment funds can be exchanged for shares in remaining enterprises and banks. The holders of shares in the privatization investment funds also have the option of exchanging their shares for pension vouchers, which in turn can be sold or exchanged for pension policy provided by the newly established First Pension Fund (EBRD 1999b: 266).

> While the privatization of socially (i.e. employee) managed enterprises is nearly complete, the pace of large-scale privatization remains slow. An estimated 50 per cent of the country's assets are still state-owned, either directly or indirectly through pension and restitution funds ... The pace of bank privatization remains slow ... Changes to the company law and the foreign exchange law in 1999 removed the remaining legal obstacles to the non-

financial sectors. However, the company law requirements of heavy workers' representation on the supervisory board of large companies inhibits effective corporate governance ... The new insurance act adopted in January 2000 has removed all restrictions on foreign direct investment in the area of insurance.

(EBRD 2000a: 78)

While the majority of the 'socially owned' enterprises (mostly small and medium-sized enterprises) had been privatized by the end of 1998, the state still holds shares in around 180 mainly large companies (eighty with a majority interest and 100 with a minority interest). These shares were transferred to the state-owned Slovene development corporation with a mandate to liquidate or privatize the enterprises ... Privatization in the banking sector advances, but does not aim to attract strategic investors.

(EBRD 2000b: 210)

The government has recently initiated a steel restructuring programme ... The privatization of up to 25 per cent of the dominant fixed-line operator, Telecom Slovenije (ST), is high on the government's agenda ... The government plans to move forward with the privatization of ... Nova Ljubljanska Banka and Nova Kreditna Banka Maribor ... The market ... is currently dominated by the two state-owned banks.

(EBRD 2001a: 88)

At mid-2001 the state still held shares in around 200 mainly large companies ... In November 2000 the government began to restructure four major steel companies ... In February 2001 Austrian mobile telephony operator Mobilkom ... [became] the first foreign investor to hold a controlling stake in a telecommunications company ... The government is planning to reduce its 65 per cent share in Telecom Slovenia ... the state-owned fixed-line monopoly ... to less than 50 per cent through public offerings and sales to a strategic investor ... In May 2001 Société Générale (France) successfully acquired a 96.5 per cent stake in SKB, the third-largest bank in terms of assets. Privatization plans are moving forward for the two largest banks.

(EBRD 2001b: 194)

The first public offering was made in February 1994. Only a handful of enterprises have been privatized so far (*Business Central Europe*, May 1994, p. 21). The first share-for-voucher auction, involving fifty of the 2,000 enterprises in the mass privatization programme, was planned for December 1994 (*Business Central Europe*, October 1994, p. 15). Sixty of the 1,350 enterprises in the programme were to take part in the first auction on 7 December 1994. A second auction was expected in early February 1995, followed by further auctions every two months (*Business Central Europe*, December 1994–January 1995, p. 53). Investment funds took part in the first real share auction on 8 March 1995. Over 65 per cent of enterprises were scheduled for privatization by the end of 1995 (*Business Central Europe*, April 1995, p. 20). The privatization deadline has been extended to the end of 1996 and most enterprises have opted for management–employee buy-outs (Business Central Europe 1995: 33). Out of around 1,500 enterprises going through privatization, just 666 have had their programmes signed off by the privatization agency. Around 240 are ready and 200 have not even had initial approval (*Business Central Europe*, September 1996, p. 31). 'Most of the 1,500 formerly socially-owned companies were sold in 1998, but fifty to sixty are still held by the Slovenian development fund ... More big sales are planned for 2000, including Telekom Slovenije, power plants and possibly some steel factories' (Business Central Europe 1999: 28). 'The government has been slow to sell off state property. In fact more than half of economic assets are still state-owned. And even such firms as have been sold have been reluctant to restructure' (Business Central Europe 2000: 30). 'In February [2001] ... the government announced a comprehensive sell-off of bank, utilities and heavy industry ... The emphasis has now shifted to bringing in strategic investors' (*Business Central Europe*, April 2001, p. 51).

Only forty-nine of the 300 top Slovenian companies are privately owned (*Transition*, July–August 1994, vol. 5, no. 6, p. 20).

Up to now privatization has made little headway. Of the 1,500–1,800 socially owned enterprises (originally put at 2,600 and inflated partly by double registrations) only about 700 have applied to the Agency for Privatization. Of the roughly 350 approved cases only something like seventy to a hundred have actually initiated the process to date. Less than ten enterprises have completed privatization. The bulk of privatization is on the basis of management and employee buy-out. One of the first enterprises to pass into private hands under the ownership scheme is the Lek pharmaceutical and chemical company (Deutsche Bank, *Focus: Eastern Europe*, 8 November 1994, no. 119, p. 3).

Gavin Gray (*FT*, Survey, 1995, p. 36) stated that by the end of 1994 more than 1,300 of the socially owned enterprises had drawn up plans for privatization (another source put the number at 1,350: *IHT*, 6 April 1995, p. 11). Mira Puc believed that most of them would be in private hands by early 1996. Only steel, postal services and a few other strategic industries would be owned by the state. The role of the privatization agency was to check that the submitted plans conformed with the law.

Privatization has been sluggish: 230 of the 300 largest enterprises are still not privatized. Of the 1,300 'socially owned' enterprises that submitted privatization or restructuring programmes only about 300 have been approved. But by the end of 1996 only a handful of strategic industries (e.g. the postal service and steel) should remain unprivatized (*Transition*, January–February 1996, vol. 7, no. 3, p. 9).

Slovenia's privatization policy has been heavily criticized in some quarters:

1   'Slovenia's privatization programme not only fails to improve corporate governance – control of companies remains with management, where it has

always been – it also results in minority shareholders being treated with contempt. And foreign investors are avoiding the country until the mess is sorted out.' (Apart from some hundred 'no-hope cases' which were nationalized, enterprises chose their own method of privatization, from about six, after the start of the process in 1992. 'Most, predictably, went for a predominantly management–employee buy-out option, so that control of Slovene industry will be little changed.') In around 80 per cent of privatized companies managers and employees have accumulated the maximum 60 per cent of shares allowed by the law. 'In another 10 per cent of companies insiders own 50 to 60 per cent ... Even these figures probably understate the degree of insider control. Some of Slovenia's biggest and capital-rich companies were too expensive for insiders to gain a majority. These companies, around 100 in total, have opted to privatize by offering their shares to the general public in return for ownership certificates. Supermarket chain Mercator and drug-makers Lek and Krka have more than 50,000 owners. With big-company ownership so widely dispersed, management calls the shots' (*Business Central Europe*, September 1996, p. 31).

> The exception to MBO privatization is the 100-odd companies privatized through the stock exchange ... Slovenia's fund managers are employed by state-owned banks, and so will be no more distant from politics than their notorious Czech cousins. The stock exchange will stagnate as they sit on their holdings, ruining it as a source of capital and hence of corporate discipline.
>
> (p. 7)

> There are still the utilities, a couple of big banks and several other sectors that remain firmly in state hands. But let that pass. Of 1,340 industrial companies slated for privatization, more than 1,000 have passed from workers' control through the mill of voucher privatization, complete with investment funds, to – well, in most cases, workers' control. Quite literally, in the case of 70 per cent of them, mostly small and medium-sized ... Even in the bigger firms, workers and managers kept their say ...[Funds] have not exercised much corporate governance ... If employers number over 1,000 they get half the supervisory board seats. And ... that is in addition to anyone employee shareholders vote in.
>
> (*Business Central Europe*, September 1997, p. 34)

2   'Barely half of state industry has been privatized and its new owners are mainly managers and workers ... Companies have been slow to revamp themselves' (*The Economist*, 2 November 1996, p. 58).

3   Anthony Robinson (*FT*, 6 April 1995, p. 35) argues that:

The attempt to privatize the economy ran into resistance. This led to the adoption in most cases of privatization through a form of management or worker buy-out. In effect, privatization Slovene-style means that workers and managers generally retain ownership through the issue of free or discounted shares in their enterprise ... Most 'socially owned' enterprises are expected to be privatized by the end of this year [1995], using variants of the free or discounted share-offer formula. But in the meantime enterprise managers have been unable to resist demands for higher wages and have been unwilling to invest.

4   'The surprise was that about two-thirds of the population decided to invest all or some of their vouchers in the [investment] funds which ended up with 56 per cent of the vouchers issued ... In the best cases funds – which have begun to build up holdings in companies by trading stakes between themselves – are beginning to exercise some much needed corporate governance ... But others are taking advantage of the lack of transparency and market information – the vast majority of the newly privatized companies are not listed – by buying shares from individuals at low prices and selling them on for large profits' (Virginia Marsh, *FT*, Survey, 18 May 1998, p. iii).

5   'Privatization through management and employee buy-outs has effectively perpetuated the Yugoslav system of "social management" of enterprises. This entails high labour representation on supervisory boards and disproportionate control by managers and employers *vis-à-vis* outside shareholders. Most enterprises have undergone little restructuring. The existing ownership structures are likely to prevail for some time as shares cannot be sold on the secondary market for at least two years after privatization. Also, share purchases of more than 25 per cent of a company are subject to approval by the securities market agency ... Foreign direct investment has been discouraged by excluding foreigners from the privatization process' (EBRD 1998b: 190). 'However, existing ownership structures are changing slowly, with some consolidation of ownership through takeovers and mergers. The ban on selling shares in privatized enterprises on the secondary market for at least two years after privatization is in most cases no longer in effect' (EBRD 1999b: 267).

6   'The Slovene privatization process was the result of political compromise and negotiations, typical of the previous self-managed system ... Priority was given to the management and employees, who selected the transformation method ... The preference for employee buy-outs was given with the internal distribution of the enterprises' shares via vouchers and the internal buy-outs at a discount. During the mass privatization the enterprises' shares were mostly distributed among internal owners and government funds, while the public offering of shares was limited. The privatization investment funds, mostly run by banks, were established to collect the "citizens' ownership certificates" and thus buy the shares of enterprises distributed to government funds and other shareholders (e.g. employees) ... Unlike some

Central and Eastern European countries (e.g. Hungary), Slovenia has been much more reluctant to allow foreign ownership and since "real" owner-ship changes have not been substantial insider-owners are still in the majority ... The privatization of the Slovene former "socially-owned" enterprises did not generally bring new and different managers ... Managers in the former "socially-owned" enterprises ... remain a domi-nant force' (Bojnec 1999: 90–1). 'The majority of employment is still in "socially-owned" enterprises, while the majority of gross profits and total revenues is generated by private enterprises and those with mixed owner-ship; this implies that private enterprises are more efficient than "socially-owned" enterprises' (p. 71).

7 '[A] challenge ... will be to keep crony politics in check. In recent years a string of high-profile public officials have become directors of companies they helped to privatize. Now there is a growing sense of the coalition parties focusing more on dividing the spoils than on governing' (Business Central Europe 1997: 30).

Further developments in privatization

While more than 2,000 companies were privatized, many remain under state influence via government-controlled banks and investment funds ... The state retained considerable influence via two state-controlled funds, the pensions and property restitution funds, which received substantial alloca-tions of stock, and state-controlled banks, which bought stock. Management changes were rare and restructuring took a back seat ... More than half the economy has stayed under direct government control. including the biggest banks and the telecoms utility. With consistently low public sector deficits, the government has been under little financial pressure to privatize ... But the lack of structural reform is beginning to cause problems ... The govern-ment has responded with its biggest privatization programme, which is planned to include the two largest banks, the telecoms operator and a number of big industrial enterprises ... such as the troubled Slovenke Zelezarne steelworks ... [and] Talom, the aluminium producer ... [The] finance minister wants to complete the programme by the end of next year [2002] ... Just as most other central European countries are reaching the final stages of their privatization programmes, Slovenia is starting to sell its largest companies ... According to a new privatization law passed in April [2001], the emphasis will be on securing good strategic investors ... The next twelve to eighteen months should see the privatization of the two biggest banks, the dominant insurance company, the telecoms utility and a string of industrial assets, including the national steelworks and the Adriatic port of Koper ... In April [2001] Société Générale took over SKB [bank] with its 10.2 per cent market share ... The privatization of the two largest institutions, Nova Ljubljanska Banka (NLB) and Nova Kreditna Banka

Maribor (NKBM) is under way ... NLB [has] a market share of 43 per cent ... NKBM has a 12 per cent market share.

(FT, Survey, 9 July 2001, pp. 11–12)

[As regards] the return of private property nationalized in the 1940s by the communists to prewar owners or their heirs ... although Slovenia passed, a decade ago, one of the most generous schemes, 40 per cent of the cases still remain to be settled. Among them is a large claim from the church for the return of extensive forests and rural estates.

(p. 13)

Foreign direct investment

The volume of direct foreign investment has been relatively low. (See Table 4.2.) But obstacles are gradually being removed.

Direct foreign investment amounted to $275 million in the period 1990–3 (EBRD 1994: 123). Foreigners cannot own land (EBRD 1996b: 176). Net direct foreign investment was $-$2 million in 1990, $41 million in 1991, $113 million in 1992, $112 million in 1993, $86 million in 1994 and $144 million in 1995 (United Nations Economic Commission for Europe 1996: 149).

'Cumulative foreign direct investment is an unimpressive $2.7 billion, with only $50 million added during 2000' (Business Central Europe 2000: 30).

The constitution did not allow the sale of land to foreigners (*FT*, 6 April 1995, p. 35). This was the case until 14 July 1997. 'A widespread fear of selling out to foreigners continues to deter foreign investment' (Kevin Done, *FT*, Survey, 18 May 1998, p. iii).

All sectors are open to foreign investors operating through joint ventures. But wholly owned foreign companies are restricted in certain fields, such as military equipment, transport and communications (*IHT*, Survey, 6 April 1995, p. 12). A new company take-over law was introduced in July 1995, designed to place foreign and domestic investors on an equal footing. Share purchases that add up to a greater than 25 per cent interest in a company were to be subject to investigation (*Business Europa*, July–August 1995, p. 46).

Under the association agreement with the EU foreign banks were to be able to open branches in Slovenia as of mid-1998 (EBRD 1998a: 26, 41). Foreign banks are not allowed to open branches and no new foreign-owned banks have been licensed since 1994 (EBRD 1998b: 191).

A new banking law was adopted on 20 February 1999. It allows the entry of foreign bank branches, although it discriminates against them by allowing the central bank to ask for a deposit (either cash or financial assets) as a guarantee for the settlement of liabilities arising from their banking operations in Slovenia.

(EBRD 1999a: 44)

The first foreign bank branch was approved in June 1999 (EBRD 1999b: 265).

Under the February 1999 reciprocity law EU nationals who have permanent residence in Slovenia for at least three years may now purchase Slovene property (EBRD 1999b: 267).

> Changes to the company law and the foreign exchange law in 1999 removed the remaining legal obstacles to the non-financial sectors. However, the company law requirements of heavy workers' representation on the supervisory board of large companies inhibits effective corporate governance ... The new insurance act adopted in January 2000 has removed all restrictions on foreign direct investment in the area of insurance.
>
> (EBRD 2000a: 78)

'Potential investors still face rules which require them to make an offer for a company's whole share capital if they buy as little as 25 per cent. In big companies workers' representatives have to be given half the board seats' (*FT*, Survey, 11 July 2000, p. 36).

Economic performance

Slovenia is a really bright spot in the former Yugoslavia, although problems remain. GDP growth turned positive in 1993. (See Table 4.2.) In 1998 GDP was an estimated 4 per cent in excess of the 1989 level. The figure for 1999 was 9 per cent (EBRD 2000a: 4, and 2000b: 65). The figure for 2000 was 14 per cent in excess (EBRD 2001b: 59). The annual rate of inflation peaked in 1990 (549.7 per cent), but it did not reached single figures until 1996.

The unemployment rate hovers around 13 per cent to 14 per cent, but it is only about 7.5 per cent using the ILO method (*Transition*, January–February 1996, vol. 7, no. 1, p. 9).

'Income per person is on the same level, by some measures, as in Greece, the poorest EU state' (*FT*, Survey, 11 July 2000, p. 35). 'Growth was 4.9 per cent last year [1999], taking GDP per head to more than $10,000 a year. In purchasing power, the country's GDP per person has been ahead of Greece's in many recent years' (p. 36).

5 The Federal Republic of Yugoslavia: Montenegro

Statistical, historical and political background

Area, 5 per cent of the former Yugoslavia. Population (1989), 0.7 million (3 per cent of the Yugoslav total); 69 per cent Montenegrins, 13 per cent Moslems and 6 per cent Albanians. Contributed 2 per cent of Yugoslav GNP. Index of *per capita* income, 73 (Yugoslav average = 100). The 1991 census gave a population of 616,327, of which Montenegrins accounted for 61.8 per cent, Slav Moslems 14.6 per cent, Serbs 9.3 per cent and Albanians 6.6 per cent (*EEN*, 1995, vol. 9, no. 10, p. 4).

'Seven out of ten [Montenegrins] follow the Orthodox Christian religion, divided .... by a schism between its Serbian and Montenegrin branches' (*FT*, Weekend, 15 July 2000, p. xviii).

The capital was known as Titograd before the name was changed to Podgorica. On 29 December 1993 the Montenegrin parliament reinstated Cetinje as the capital, although Podgorica was to remain the seat of government.

Independent in 1799, Montenegro was first a prince-bishopric (1799–1851), then a principality (1851–1910) and finally a kingdom (1910–18), under inter- mittent Russian patronage. Montenegro is poor and mountainous (its name means 'black mountain'). The December 1990 election produced a win for the Communist Party, which became known as the Democratic Party of Socialists in June 1991. The president was Momir Bulatovic. Montenegro supported Serbia as the threat of disintegration grew. A referendum held on 1 March 1992 attracted a turnout of 66 per cent, and 96 per cent voted to remain part of Yugoslavia. On 27 April 1992 Serbia and Montenegro declared a new Federal Republic of Yugoslavia, with 44 per cent of the area and 39 per cent of the population of the old one. (Montenegro accounts for only about 5 per cent of the population, GNP and assets of the Federal Republic of Yugoslavia: *The Economist*, 23 July 1994, p. 42.) The 31 May 1992 general election is discussed in the chapter on Serbia. There were also elections on 20 December 1992 (see below). Bulatovic won 43 per cent of the votes in the first round of the Montenegrin presidential election, with Branko Kostic (who favours close ties with Serbia) winning 24 per cent. In the second round, held on 10 January 1993, Bulatovic was re-elected with 63.3 per cent of the votes (the latter securing 36.7

per cent). The distribution of seats in the eighty-five-seat Montenegrin assembly was as follows: the Democratic Party of Socialists, forty-six; the People's Party, fourteen; the Liberal Alliance, thirteen; the Serbian Radical Party, eight; the Social Democratic Party of Reformists, four.

For a while Bulatovic distanced himself from Milosevic and an attempt to declare Montenegrin independence was not out of the question (an 'attempt' because Serbia could well have resisted such a move with force of arms). For example, the then federal prime minister Milan Panic survived a vote of no confidence on 4 September 1992 with the help of Montenegrin MPs. Even more dramatically, on 2 November 1992 Panic survived by the narrowest of margins another vote of no confidence only when (having lost decisively in the lower house) Montenegrin representatives in the upper house (where they have an equal share of seats) supported him. Montenegrin parliamentarians tried to save Yugoslav president Cosic when he was dismissed on 1 June 1993 (see below). Montenegro favoured allowing UN monitors along the Serbia–Bosnia border to enforce the sanctions which were supposed to be (but never were) imposed on the Bosnian Serbs after 8 May 1993 (and Montenegro would have welcomed a mission from the CSCE). President Bulatovic visited Albania on 20 September 1993. On 31 October 1993 the Autocephalous Montenegrin Orthodox Church was re-established despite resistance from the Serbian Orthodox Church (the two having been merged in 1920). The new patriarch is Antonije Abramovic, who lived in Canada for over forty years.

POLITICS

3 November 1996: in the republican election in Montenegro (see Table 5.1) the parties were as follows:

Democratic Party of Socialists: led by Milica Pejanovic-Djurisic.

People's Accord: an alliance between the pro-Serb People's Party (led by Novak Kilibarda) and the pro-Montenegrin independence Liberal Alliance of Montenegro (led by Slavko Perovic).

Accord is a marriage of convenience for the sake of democracy in Montenegro. Divisive issues such as the sovereign/territorial status of Montenegro and the Church are not discussed. The joint election platform emphasizes only a handful of issues upon which there is agreement: a new electoral law providing for 100 per cent proportional representation (at present there is a 100 per cent constituency first-past-the-post system); depoliticization of the police; freedom of the press with parliamentary control over state media; and rapid privatization ... the speeches are devoted mostly to criticism of the 'criminals' in power.

(*EEN*, 1996, vol. 10, no. 20, pp. 1–2)

Social Democratic Party.

Party of Democratic Action: Moslem party.

Democratic Alliance: ethnic Albanian party.

Democratic Union: ethnic Albanian party.

Table 5.1   Montenegro: the republican election of 3 November 1996

	Seats
Democratic Party of Socialists	45
People's Accord (made up of People's Party, 10 seats, and Liberal Alliance of Montenegro, 9 seats)	19
Party of Democratic Action	3
Democratic Alliance	2
Democratic Union	2
Total	71

5 December 1996: Montenegrin President Momir Bulatovic publicly criticizes the rigging of local elections in Serbia (*EEN*, 1996, vol. 10, no. 24, p. 8).

6 December 1996: Montenegro issues a statement: 'The annulment of democratic elections belongs to the practice of totalitarian regimes ... absolutely undemocratic' (*IHT*, 7 December 1996, p. 5; *FT*, 7 December 1996, p. 2). (On 29 December 1996 the Montenegrin prime minister, Milo Djukanovic, sent a letter of support to students in Belgrade: *EEN*, 1996, vol. 10, no. 25, p. 9.)

21 February 1997: prime minister Milo Djukanovic: 'There is no question that Milosevic's policy is not the policy for the future of the people of Serbia and Yugoslavia.' Milosevic is an 'incompetent politician' and should be removed from 'any office in Yugoslavia's political life'. (On 24 March 1997, after he himself was criticized for such remarks, Djukanovic was forced to resign as deputy chairman of the Democratic Party of Socialists: *EEN*, 1997, vol. 11, no. 6, p. 1. Djukanovic: 'I believe that Yugoslavia ... should be a country of deep reforms, a developed democracy, and integrated in the world economy ... President Bulatovic feels that we do not have the right to show much initiative, and that we should have great respect for Slobodan Milosevic. However, a passive stance such as this will only lead to an unconditional acceptance of Yugoslavia the way Mr Milosevic and Serbia see it ... Not only can Montenegro be an equal member of the federation, but thanks to its reformist ideas it can also become the leader of the federation': *Moscow News*, 19 June–2 July 1997, p. 4.)

11 July 1997: Bulatovic is replaced as chairman of the Democratic Party of Socialists by Milica Pejanovic-Djurisic. Djukanovic is now the party candidate in the forthcoming Montenegrin presidential election (*EEN*, 1997, vol. 11, no. 14, p. 1).

5 October 1997:

> The 5 October presidential elections, monitored by ninety OSCE observers, are thought to have been broadly fair. Premier Milo Djukanovic, contrary to opinion poll predictions that he would beat the incumbent president Momir Bulatovic, trailed the latter by 145,337 votes to 147,609. The other six candidates won about 13,000 votes between them ... Turnout was a respectable 67 per cent ... Djukanovic is careful not to espouse secession of Montenegro from the Yugoslav federation, stressing rather the need for Montenegro to have proper and equal status within the Yugoslav federation, free of Belgrade's yoke.
>
> (*EEN*, 1997, vol. 11, no. 19, pp. 1–2)

(When Bulatovic left the Democratic Party of Socialists in spring 1997 he took with him seventeen MPs who formed a separate parliamentary faction. The People's Party also split, with party chairman Novak Kilibarda keeping the alliance of five MPs: p. 2.)

19 October 1997: Djukanovic wins the rerun presidential election with 174,745 votes to Bulatovic's 169,257. The turnout is 75 per cent. OSCE concludes that there were 'imperfections and infractions'. '[But] Preliminary results of the election reflect the will of the electorate. Generally, the elections at the polling station level were well-conducted.'

Bulatovic (whose term as president expires on 15 January 1998) disputed the result, accusing Djukanovic of changing electoral lists and being involved in cigarette smuggling. In return, Djukanovic accused Bulatovic of embezzlement.

14 January 1998: riot police break up a demonstration in Podgorica by pro-Bulatovic supporters claiming electoral fraud. There are injuries on both sides. (This was the third day of demonstrations.)

15 January 1998: Milo Djukanovic is sworn in as president.

> Milosevic is trying to exert pressure on Montenegro with an economic blockade. According to the Montenegrin government, border controls have gone up between Montenegro and Serbia, and Serbia is now importing goods through the Greek city of Salonika rather than the Montenegrin port of Bar.
>
> (*The Economist*, Survey, 24 January 1998, p. 14)

5 February 1998: the national accord between the People's Party and the Liberal Alliance of Montenegro is dissolved following prolonged disagreements (*EEN*, 1998, vol. 12, no. 2, p. 8).

21 April 1998: Momir Bulatovic presides over the inauguration of the new Socialist People's Party of Montenegro formed out of the pro-Bulatovic wing of the Democratic Party of Socialists (*EEN*, 1998, vol. 12, no. 5, p. 6).

18 May 1998: Yugoslav prime minister Radoje Kontic (a Montenegrin) is dismissed after a vote of no confidence is passed in both federal houses of parliament. 'Formally, Mr Kontic was accused of incompetence in running the country's economy. But Mr Djukanovic said Mr Kontic was punished for refusing to impose a state of emergency in Montenegro when Mr Bulatovic lost presidential elections there in October' (*IHT*, 19 May 1998, p. 6). The Montenegrin parliament deems the removal of Kontic to be illegal.

19 May 1998: Montenegro's parliament votes not to recognize the new Yugoslav government headed by Momir Bulatovic.

20 May 1998: Bulatovic's premiership is ratified by both houses of the federal parliament, although the only Montenegrin representatives present belong to Bulatovic's party.

The Montenegrin chairman of the federal parliament justice committee accused Montenegrin federal deputies of the Bulatovic faction in parliament of committing treason by voting against Kontic (*EEN*, 1998, vol. 12, no. 6, p. 8). The Montenegrin parliament replaced the six Montenegrin MPs in the Chamber of Republics (the upper house) with new ones, passing a special binding resolution requiring the six MPs to abide by the instructions of the Montenegrin parliament (p. 2).

The Montenegrin parliament has announced that it will no longer respect the laws promulgated by the federal parliament, that it will not recognize the new prime minister and that it will ignore the dictates of Milosevic. Milosevic has begun to undermine the Montenegrin government. He has halted pension payments and federal funds to Montenegro. Milosevic has banned Djukanovic from assuming his constitutional role in the federal government and publicly humiliated him, refusing to invite him to the ceremony commemorating the establishment of Yugoslavia or allow him to take his seat in the federal defence council (Chris Hedges, *IHT*, 29 May 1998, p. 2).

31 May 1998: in the general election Djukanovic's coalition To Live Better won a more convincing victory than generally expected. The coalition (comprising the Democratic Party of Socialists, the Social Democratic Party and the People's Party) could also rely on the support of the Liberal Alliance of Montenegro and the ethnic Albanian MPs.

OSCE observers thought that the election was 'generally well conducted' (*FT*, 2 June 1998, p. 2) and that it was 'a significant improvement' on earlier polls (*Independent*, 2 June 1998, p. 16). But there was concern about Djukanovic's use of the media in Montenegro and of anti-Djukanovic bias in much of the media in Serbia (*Guardian*, 2 June 1998, p. 12).

The percentage of the vote won was as follows:

To Live Better: 49.5 per cent.

Socialist People's Party: 36.07 per cent. (Led by Momir Bulatovic.)

Liberal Alliance of Montenegro: 6.2 per cent. The party has openly called for secession from the Federal Republic of Yugoslavia (*IHT*, 2 June 1998, p. 5).

Moslem Party of Democratic Action: there has been a split between a faction led by Harun Hadzic and one led by Rifat Veskovic (*EEN*, 1998, vol. 12, no. 6, p. 2).

12 June 1998: President Djukanovic of Montenegro suggests that Montenegro will withdraw its nationals from the Yugoslav army if the latter becomes involved in the war in Kosovo (*EEN*, 1998, vol. 12, no. 7, p. 8). Djukanovic advocates granting Kosovo a substantial degree of autonomy and calls for the inclusion of OSCE mediators in the talks. Djukanovic: 'Montenegro will not be dragged into internal conflicts on Yugoslav territory. If a conflict flares up we will recall our army recruits from Kosovo' (*Business Central Europe*, June 1998, p. 20).

16 June 1998: the Montenegrin parliament approves a law which deprives Bulatovic's Socialist People's Party of representation in the federal parliament (*FT*, 18 June 1998, p. 3).

Parliament passes a new law of Montenegrin representation in the federal Chamber of Republics. Henceforth all Montenegrin deputies to the chamber will be elected on a majority basis rather than on a proportional representation basis. As a result the party of former president Momir Bulatovic loses all its chamber deputies (*EEN*, 1998, vol. 12, no. 7, p. 8).

17 June 1998: the Montenegrin parliament resolves that Montenegrin national servicemen should be withdrawn from Kosovo and that the 'contact group's' 12 June recommendations for Kosovo be implemented (*EEN*, 1998, vol. 12, no. 7, p. 8).

23 July 1998: the government resolves unilaterally to issue export and import licences independently of the federal government (*EEN*, 1998, vol. 12, no. 9, p. 5).

3 August 1998: the government of Montenegro suspends all contacts with the Yugoslav government until federal prime minister Momir Bulatovic steps down. A member of the cabinet says that a referendum on Montenegro's secession from the Federal Republic of Yugoslavia is possible (*IHT*, 4 August 1998, p. 7).

11 August 1998: last week the Montenegrin government refused to reinforce Serb forces in Kosovo. In addition, a statement from the Montenegrin parliament that conscripts from Montenegro should not be asked to fight in Kosovo appears to have been respected (Jonathan Steele, *Guardian*, 12 August 1998, p. 13).

24 November 1998:

> Political reformers in Montenegro continue to find ways to irritate the leaders of Serbia, in recent weeks by printing newspapers and magazines banned by the Serbian authorities and smuggling them under cover of darkness to Belgrade by bus, train and plane ... Already Montenegro has halted its transfer of tax revenue to the federal government, which it claims has not been legally constituted since May. During the conflict this summer in Kosovo ... senior Montenegrin officials publicly discouraged teenagers from reporting for the Yugoslav military draft. In recent weeks the government announced plans to open its own 'liaison' offices in five foreign capitals, including Washington, and is considering a separate Montenegrin currency. The Montenegrin president, Milo Djukanovic, has become one of the fiercest critics of the Yugoslav president, Slobodan Milosevic, having

denounced his refusal to grant autonomy to Kosovo's ethnic Albanian majority and accused him of stifling freedom and economic reform ... The government in Podgorica has taken over the tasks of licensing mass media, levying customs duties and approving imports and exports from its territory ... In addition, Montenegro has diverted $1 million in federal taxes to fund its pensions because Belgrade has not made payments for the past four months. It has begun to negotiate its own trade deals with the West, having won permission to tap international loan funds under a partial exemption from the sanctions that was brokered by with US help. It has licensed a radio station to begin transmitting into Serbia ... Last week, in a bid to reassert its jurisdiction over the media, Serbia levied a $300,000 fine against the publisher of *Monitor*, a Montenegrin magazine that illustrated an article about Serbia with an advertisement by a student group calling for national resistance. Montenegrin officials said that the fine will not be enforced. Mindful of the historical affection that many Montenegrins retain for the Yugoslav federation, Mr Djukanovic and his ministers have cast themselves as supporters of a reformed Yugoslavia, not of its further breakup ... A referendum held in the early 1990s, when other Yugoslav republics voted to secede from the federation, showed overwhelming support for continued union. But a poll taken several weeks ago found the population deeply divided, with about 30 per cent favouring each side and the remainder undecided or uninterested. Mr Djukanovic said independence must be supported by two-thirds of the population to prevent such a move from causing social unrest.

(R. Jeffrey Smith, *IHT*, 28 November 1998, p. 7)

January 1999:

Montenegro neither recognizes the federal Yugoslav government nor partici-pates in any of its decision-making, nor pays taxes or other dues to the Yugoslav government ... One by one the Montenegrins have taken over federal competencies. Last autumn [1998] the ministry of trade began to issue its own import and export licences; customs began to be levied by the Montenegrin government and paid directly into the Montenegrin exchequer; in mid-January Montenegro and Croatia unilaterally opened two border crossings despite the strong opposition of Belgrade. Within a few weeks the airports will be nationalized and taken out of the hands of the Serbian airline JAT. The introduction of a currency board in Montenegro, with a peg to the DM, is expected before the end of March if not before. The federal army – in the form of the Second Army based in Podgorica – is the only federal institution that the Montenegrin administration does recognize.

(*EEN*, 1999, vol. 12, no. 14, p. 2)

4 March 1999: Montenegro announces that it is unilaterally abolishing visa requirements (*Independent*, 5 March 1999, p. 14).

13 April 1999: president Milo Djukanovic of Montenegro rejects the idea that Yugoslavia should join the union of Russia and Belarus (*EEN*, 1999, vol. 12, no. 16, p. 10).

18 April 1999: the Yugoslav military prosecutor opens criminal proceedings against deputy prime minister Novak Kilibarda of Montenegro for allegedly 'undermining' Yugoslavia (*EEN*, 1999, vol. 12, no. 16, p. 10).

20 April 1999:

> The Yugoslav army yesterday [20 April] took the first steps towards seizing control in the republic of Montenegro by ordering the Montenegrin government to place its police force under military command. The order brought an instant rebuff from Milo Djukanovic, the democratically elected Montenegrin president. 'It is out of the question that the ministry of the interior could be subordinated to the Yugoslav army,' Mr Djukanovic said ... The Yugoslav federal army headquarters stepped up the pressure when it delivered a letter on Monday night [19 April] to the Montenegrin prime minister ordering him to place the republic's police directly under military command ... Tension also increased yesterday when forces of the second corps of the Yugoslav army moved to close the Debeli Brijeg border point near Herceg Novi – the only border crossing between Montenegro and Croatia ... Mr Djukanovic said the [Montenegrin] police had not given up the post ... Croatia's ambassador to the UN ... demanded that Yugoslavia withdraw its troops from the area, part of the UN-monitored demilitarized zone.
>
> (*FT*, 21 April 1999, p. 1)

'Croatia [has complained] about an incursion by up to 300 Serbian troops into a UN-monitored demilitarized zone in the disputed Prevlaka peninsula, between Croatia and Montenegro' (*FT*, 22 April 1999, p. 2).

> Serbian forces were reported [by Croatia's official news agency] to have crossed via Montenegro into the peninsula of Prevlaka, a finger of Croatia that has been a demilitarized zone under UN control since the end of fighting in Bosnia three years ago ... The incursion would mark the first time that President Slobodan Milosevic of Yugoslavia has challenged the territorial lines that emerged from the Dayton peace accords on Bosnia.
>
> (*IHT*, 21 April 1999, p. 1)

'The Yugoslav army is blocking access to Montenegro from Croatia, directly challenging the [Montenegrin] government's authority in an area declared a demilitarized zone by the UN' (*The Times*, 22 April 1999, p. 25).

21 April 1999: the Montenegrin government rejects the Yugoslav army demand that the Montenegrin interior ministry be put under army command (*EEN*, 1999, vol. 12, no. 16, p. 10).

22 April 1999: 'Montenegro's border with Croatia was operating normally after the Yugoslav army closed it for two days, although the army has kept a post inside the border and is denying access to foreigners without valid Yugoslav visas' (*FT*, 23 April 1999, p. 2).

26 April 1999:

> EU foreign ministers yesterday [26 April] decided to toughen sanctions against Yugoslavia and start preparations on a stability pact for south-east Europe to bring peace, order and democracy to the Balkans after the war … The ministers decided the ban on the sale of oil and petroleum products, formulated last week, should enter into force no later than Friday [30 April] and agreed seven further measures to be adopted quickly. The sanctions partly targeted the family and associates of Slobodan Milosevic and partly closed loopholes in measures agreed last year [1998] to halt export credits and investment flows to Yugoslavia … Mr Milosevic, his associates and senior officials of the Yugoslav and Serbian governments are subjected to a travel ban. An existing freeze on Serbian and Yugoslav funds abroad was extended to cover individuals linked to the two governments. In a further loophole-closing measure, the ministers agreed a 'comprehensive' flight ban between the EU and Yugoslavia.
>
> (*FT*, 27 April 1999, p. 2)

(The USA later tightened its sanctions on Yugoslavia but granted concessions to Montenegro. 'Washington has made the crucial pledge that ships carrying oil bound for Montenegro will be exempt from the planned embargo on Serbia': editorial, *New York Times*, in *IHT*, 6 May 1999, p. 8.)

15 May 1999:

> The Yugoslav army, made up mostly of Serbs, has set up checkpoints on eastern and western Montenegrin border crossings, which give it control of all access routes … Early Saturday [15 May] the army blocked the eastern border to Albania, preventing Kosovo Albanian refugees from crossing into Albania, separating men from the convoys and taking them to unknown destinations.
>
> (*IHT*, 17 May 1999, p. 6)

'Federal Yugoslav troops have replaced Montenegrins who normally guard the border with Albania' (*FT*, 17 May 1999, p. 2).

> The Yugoslav army put checkpoints on the border between Montenegro and Bosnia-Hercegovina in an attempt to stop recruits and reservists leaving the country, a source close to the Montenegrin police said. The source said only 20 per cent of recruits and reservists from [Montenegro] … has accepted military call-up.
>
> (*The Times*, 17 May 1999, p. 9)

20 May 1999:

Montenegrin officials are reporting that Yugoslav soldiers have thrown up a barrier around Montenegro, setting up checkpoints at all the main border crossings. Local men of a fighting age were allowed to leave Montenegro only if they had special dispensation from the army. One official said Serbia had effectively taken control of the border.

(*FT*, 21 May 1999, p. 2)

21 May 1999:

Hundreds of residents of Cetinje, Montenegro's historic capital and symbol of its independence, yesterday [21 May] gathered to protest at the arrival of some 1,300 Yugoslav army reservists. The army's provocative move came a day after it had blocked Montenegro's frontiers, confiscating Italian aid and turning back trucks carrying supplies because the drivers had no federal Yugoslav visas ... The mayor of Cetinje ... told reporters that the army had trained artillery on the town and set up checkpoints on surrounding roads ... 'The regime in Belgrade wants to install the Yugoslav army as a dictatorship power in Montenegro,' Mr Djukanovic said in an interview on Thursday [20 May] ... Mr Djukanovic controls the police while Mr Milosevic controls the army. Local analysts say there may be 10,000 police and 20,000 army troops.

(*FT*, 22 May 1999, p. 2)

Thousands of residents of Cetinje took to the streets yesterday to protest against the deployment of Yugoslav army reservists and heavy artillery units to the city and the sensitive border with Serbia ... On Thursday [20 May] the Montenegrin president, Milo Djukanovic, accused federal army forces of trying to usurp the powers of his administration ... Local officials say that earlier this week around 1,200 Serb reservists unexpectedly arrived in the region, with artillery and tanks trained on the small town. The government estimates that more than 20,000 Yugoslav troops are stationed across Montenegro.

(*Guardian*, 22 May 1999, p. 4)

'The Yugoslav army has seized control of all major roads into Montenegro, blocking imports of raw materials, confiscating much-needed humanitarian aid and preventing Westerners from entering Yugoslavia's smaller republic, authorities here said Thursday' (*IHT*, 22 May 1999, p. 4).

2 July 1999:

The Nato secretary-general, Javier Solana, said Friday [2 July] the alliance would take action if President Slobodan Milosevic of Yugoslavia tried to provoke a conflict in Montenegro ... Mr Milosevic, still firmly in control of his army, is sending reinforcements into Montenegro, according to General Wesley Clark ... General Clark said [Thursday 1 July] Nato intelligence had detected recent reinforcements into Montenegro, as well as efforts by Mr Milosevic to put ethnic Serbs and political allies of Mr Djukanovic's opponent into positions of authority there.

(*IHT*, 3 July 1999, p. 5)

The Nato secretary-general, Javier Solana, said Friday [2 July] that there had been no buildup of Serbian troops in Montenegro through transfers from Kosovo ... The Kosovo peace agreement reached in June guaranteed that Serbia would not deploy withdrawing troops into Montenegro, and stipulated that Nato would take action if the accord was not respected, he added. Mr Solana also said that he would not favour Montenegro's becoming independent from its partnership with Serbia to make up federal Yugoslavia ... Earlier on Friday Mr Solana told reporters in Sarajevo that Nato would take action if President Slobodan Milosevic of Yugoslavia tried to provoke a conflict in Montenegro. Meanwhile, the Montenegrin president, Milo Djukanovic, said that his republic was waiting patiently for Serbia's reply to its proposal to redefine their partnership, but would go it alone if Serbia held to its 'retrograde' stance. Montenegro this week proposed to Belgrade a redefinition of relations between the two republics, ensuring more autonomy for pro-Western Montenegro ... 'We are convinced this new formula can satisfy the requirements of Montenegro and ensure the survival of the Yugoslav federation,' the Montenegrin leader has said. Mr Djukanovic has pledged to hand over anyone indicted by the UN tribunal in The Hague for war crimes in Kosovo, a Belgrade newspaper reported Friday ... 'Montenegro will hand over to the international tribunal anyone indicted for war crimes who happens to be in the territory of Montenegro,' the independent daily *Blic* quoted Mr Djukanovic as declaring at a rally in Niksic on Wednesday evening [30 June].

(*IHT*, 3 July 1999, internet)

9 July 1999:

In Belgrade on Friday [9 July] the official news agency Tanjug announced that representatives of Mr Milosevic's Socialist Party and Mr Djukanovic's party would meet this week [the week starting 1 July] to discuss Montenegro's demands ... In a 26 May ultimatum to Belgrade ... Montenegro called for the withdrawal of Yugoslav army troops, control over its own economy and the right to conduct its own foreign policy. But the Yugoslav army is flexing its muscles, setting up periodic roadblocks in an attempt to block shipments of goods into Montenegro because the republic's government ... is refusing to pay federal customs duties or taxes to Belgrade.

(*IHT*, 12 July 1999, p. 4)

'The negotiating platform that aims to redefine Montenegro's constitutional arrangements with Serbia ... includes a potentially explosive demand for Montenegrin control of Yugoslav army units based on its territory' (*FT*, 12 July 1999, p. 2). 'Among Montenegro's demands, expected to be adopted as official policy later this month [July], are its choice as federal prime minister, control over the Yugoslav army in Montenegro and adoption of its own currency board financed by the West' (*FT*, 14 July 1999, p. 2).

14 July 1999: talks begin between Montenegro and Serbia on redefining their relationship.

President Milo Djukanovic of Montenegro:

> I want first of all to see Montenegro as a democratic country, economically developed and integrated into Europe. If Montenegro can achieve this in its present status as a member of the Yugoslav federation then that is good. If that should prove impossible, however, then the issue of independence will be imposed as an inevitable alternative.
>
> (*IHT*, 15 July 1999, p. 6)

5 August 1999: the government of Montenegro approves a draft proposal to redefine relations with Serbia. If Serbia rejects the proposals a referendum on independence will be held in Montenegro. The draft includes the following proposals:

1   the name Federal Republic of Yugoslavia to change to Association of the States of Montenegro and Serbia (Commonwealth of Montenegro and Serbia);
2   the federal Yugoslav government to be replaced by a six-member 'council of ministers';
3   the current two-chamber Yugoslav parliament to be replaced by a single house, with an equal number of seats for Montenegro and Serbia; the one-chamber assembly will choose the federal president (both republics having a veto);
4   Montenegro to have its own defence ministry and army command; Montenegrin recruits to serve only in Montenegro and troops on Montenegrin soil will no longer be commanded from Belgrade; the creation of a defence council chaired by the presidents of Montenegro and Serbia; a unanimous decision will be necessary to declare war or a state of emergency. Command over federal defence to alternate between Montenegro and Serbia every two years;
5   Montenegro to have its own foreign ministry and policy;
6   Montenegro to have its own (convertible) currency.
   (*IHT*, 6 August 1999, p. 4; *FT*, 6 August 1999, p. 2; *Telegraph*, 7 August 1999, p. 14; *Guardian*, 7 August 1999, p. 13; *The Economist*, 14 August 1999, p. 32)

The Montenegrin prime minister, Filip Vujanovic, says the draft will allow Montenegro to 'secure democratic and economic development' and join

European and world institutions without 'harming' Serbia. Vojislav Seselj says the Yugoslav army will intervene if Montenegro tries to secede. President Djukanovic of Yugoslavia has said that Serbia would be given as much as six weeks to accept or reject the proposal (*IHT*, 6 August 1999, p. 4). Vojislav Seselj: 'If anyone tries to secede we will use all measures to protect the integrity of the state' (*Business Central Europe*, September 1999, p. 45).

> Djukanovic's coalition government is divided on the issue [of independence]: his major coalition partner, the Social Democratic Party, advocates outright independence, while the smaller partner, the National Party, with the exception of its maverick leader, Novak Kilibarda, is for some kind of link with Serbia. These divisions, mirrored to some extent in Djukanovic's own party, have enabled the president to remain on the fence and avoid antagonizing his international backers.
>
> (Roberts 1999: 13)

> About one-third of Montenegro's 680,000 people favour retaining an alliance with Serbia – that is they support Mr Milosevic and the Yugoslav federation, opinion surveys show. Others want complete independence just as firmly ... The Yugoslav government never answered a Montenegrin proposal last August [1999] to restructure the constitutional relationship between the two republics. Mr Djukanovic had promised to hold a referendum on independence if the proposal was not answered in six weeks, but now, nine months later, he says there is no hurry.
>
> (*IHT*, 25 May 2000, pp. 1, 5)

'Nearly a third of Montenegro's population view themselves as Yugoslavs' (Irena Guzelova, *FT*, 19 September 2000, p. 10).

'Mr Djukanovic broke from Mr Milosevic in 1997 ... About 35 per cent to 40 per cent of Montenegro's 650,000 people support union with Serbia' (Steven Erlanger, *IHT*, 19 September 2000, p. 6).

12 August 1999: the federal government is reshuffled. Momir Bulatovic remains prime minister. Seven ministers are dismissed and twelve new ones (five from the Radical Party) brought in, making a twenty-seven-strong cabinet. All the new ministers are on a list of 308 senior officials and businessmen barred from travelling to the West. There are no representatives of Montenegro's ruling Democratic Socialist Party and earlier talks with Vuk Draskovic's Serbian Renewal Party were not successful.

25–6 October 1999: there are talks between Montenegro's Democratic Party of Socialists and Serbia's Socialist Party and its allies (including the Yugoslav United Left and the Radical Party).

'The Serbian delegation yesterday [25 October] was led by Vojislav Seselj, leader of the Radical Party and a deputy prime minister. Before the talks he warned that separation would lead to a "bloody war" and provoke another Nato intervention' (*FT*, 26 October 1999, p. 12).

The talks did not yield results (*FT*, 30 October 1999, p. 5).

29 October 1999: the Montenegrin parliament adopts a law granting nationals the right to hold Montenegrin as well as Yugoslav citizenship (*FT*, 30 October 1999, p. 5).

Parliament passes a citizenship law requiring all applicants to have lived in Montenegro for ten years consecutively prior to the application (*EEN*, 2000, vol. 12, no. 21, p. 6).

24 November 1999: Montenegro declares the airports in Podgorica and Tivat to be its property.

8 December 1999: the Yugoslav federal air traffic directorate closes Golubovei airport in Podgorica and suspends traffic. The Yugoslav army takes control for twelve hours in a standoff with Montenegrin police. Objections were made to the building of a hangar in the military part of the airport for helicopters and aircraft for the Montenegrin government and police. (Air traffic resumed the following day.)

6 March 2000:

> Measures include a new pro-Belgrade media offensive in the republic and the setting up of a special forces unit ... A pro-Serbian television station loyal to the United Yugoslav Left, the party of Mr Milosevic's wife, Mirjana Markovic, has begun broadcasting Belgrade's propaganda using military transmitters. A paramilitary unit has also been set up within the Yugoslav army in Montenegro. The Seventh Military Police battalion is made up of pro-Milosevic Montenegrins, local sources say, and their numbers have been increased from 400 to 900 trained saboteurs and special forces.
>
> (*Telegraph*, 7 March 2000, p. 23)

28 March 2000:

> President Milo Djukanovic ... accused Mr Milosevic of recruiting a special army battalion to be used to overthrow the government of Montenegro ... Last weekend [25–6 March], under pressure from Belgrade, Mr Djukanovic said, his government agreed to allow Yugoslav army troops to join Montenegrin police at border posts facing Albania and ... Kosovo ... Montenegro has no security or economic guarantees from the West ... Mr Djukanovic said he opposed the creation of a special military police unit within the Yugoslav Second Army based in Podgorica and numbering about 1,000 men, Montenegrins led by Serbs who are loyal to Mr Milosevic. 'They are in fact a paramilitary unit and their party association is unanimous,' he said. 'They are devoted to Mr Milosevic. Over 50 per cent of them have criminal records. They are not being retained to protect the country but to overthrow the government.'
>
> (*IHT*, 29 March 2000, p. 6)

'Mr Milosevic has as many as 20,000 soldiers posted inside Montenegro and on its borders, including paramilitary forces believed to be far better trained and equipped than Montenegro's growing police force of some 15,000' (*IHT*, 25 May 2000, p. 5).

25 April 2000: a memorandum of understanding and co-operation is signed with Albania during a visit by the Albanian foreign minister (*EEN*, 2000, vol. 12, no. 23, p. 7).

May 2000: 'In May the Montenegrin police and Yugoslav army staged joint military exercises to show tensions had eased since December [1999] when there was a tense stand-off between the two at Montenegro's main airport' (*FT*, 2 June 2000, p. 8).

31 May 2000: Goran Zugic, President Djukanovic's security adviser, is assassinated (shot dead).

11 June 2000: local elections are held in the capital Podgorica and in the coastal town of Herceg Novi. OECD observers were satisfied. The turnout was 75 per cent.

> Mr Djukanovic is hoping his governing For a Better Life coalition, a three-party alliance, will defeat the main anti-independence SNP [Socialist People's Party] – and the pro-independence Liberal Party – and so keep his options open on the highly contentious independence issue … The Yugoslav Army – the only remaining federal body in the republic wielding any clout – has contributed to tension in the republic by holding high-profile military exercises. Podgorica was yesterday [9 June] awash with speculation after a Russian newspaper reported that Mr Milosevic plans to create a new Yugoslavia made up of eight cantons, in which Montenegro would have equal status as regions within Serbia … At the same time members of Montenegro's pro-Yugoslav party, the SNP, are increasingly unhappy with Belgrade's dominance of their party.
>
> (Irena Guzelova, *FT*, 10 June 2000, p. 6)

About one-third of the electorate live in Podgorica. The total population of Montenegro is a little over 600,000 (*FT*, 13 June 2000, p. 10).

The two local elections involve about a third of the electorate (*Independent*, 13 June 2000, p. 16).

The result reflected the political divisions in Montenegro as regards relations with Serbia:

1   In Podgorica the fifty-four seats were split as follows: For a Better Life coalition, twenty-eight (a gain of one); the pro-Milosevic Yugoslavia Coalition, twenty-two seats (a loss of one); the Liberal Alliance, four.

2   In Herceg Novi the thirty-five seats were split as follows: Yugoslavia Coalition, nineteen (a gain of six); For a Better Life coalition, fourteen; the Liberal Alliance, two.

Voters in Herceg Novi, where many Serb refugees from Bosnia live, opted to vote for the pro-Yugoslav SNP, giving the party control of its first municipality in Montenegro's more prosperous south. Some voters said they were dissatisfied with corruption scandals involving the ruling parties.

(*FT*, 13 June 2000, p. 10)

The pro-Serb forces tend to be concentrated in inland cities closer to the Serbian border but Herceg Novi has always had a high proportion of Serb migrants from Bosnia and Hercegovina. Since the collapse of Tito's Yugoslavia the new headquarters of the Yugoslav navy are nearby ... A leader of the pro-Belgrade block said that ... his party, already strong in the north, now held one-third of Montenegro's twenty-one municipalities.

(*Guardian*, 13 June 2000, p. 15)

Many are not surprised with the outcome in Herceg Novi, which is home to many retired Yugoslav Army officers. The town also has a big Serbian refugee population that fled the wars in Croatia and Bosnia ... Mr Djukanovic has warmed relations with neighbouring Croatia, reopening a border crossing and broadening co-operation with the nearby Croatian resort of Dubrovnik ... Herceg Novi's new mayor ... based his campaign on promises to oppose such co-operation.

(*Independent*, 13 June 2000, p. 16)

'The result was a heavy blow for the Liberal Alliance, which provoked the elections by pulling out of government-led local coalitions, hoping to improve its showing and press for anti-corruption measures and an early independence referendum' (*IHT*, 13 June 2000, p. 5).

The result was generally greeted with relief within Montenegro and in the West. It was felt that a more one-sided outcome would have been destabilizing.

'About a third of Montenegrins firmly support independence; a third want no loosening of ties with Serbia; the remainder are in the middle' (*The Economist*, 15 July 2000, p. 29).

The United States and its allies have pursued a strategy similar to the 'strategic ambiguity' that the United States employs toward China with regard to Taiwan. The West has offered Montenegro just enough support to give Milosevic pause about invading the republic, but has refrained from a blanket security guarantee that might embolden Milosevic to separate so definitely from Belgrade as to provoke a war.

(Editorial, *Washington Post*, in *IHT*, 10 July 2000, p. 8)

6 July 2000: the Montenegrin government, parliament and president rejected the federal constitutional changes of July 2000. President Milo Djukanovic said that Montenegro would not take part in the federal elections (later set for 14 September 2000).

On 6 July 2000 both houses of the Yugoslav parliament approved two consti-tutional changes, requiring the direct election through a popular ballot of the Yugoslav president and the upper house of parliament. They also allow two four-year terms for the president and raise the threshold for impeachment.

> The effect will be to give Mr Milosevic a very good chance of remaining in power past July of next year [2001], when his current one-year term expires. Until now the federal president was elected by both houses of the federal parliament and could only serve one four-year term, while the upper house of the federal parliament was itself elected by the republic parliaments. The changes also put the federal government in charge of organizing elections, instead of the two republics, Serbia and Montenegro.
>
> (Steven Erlanger, *IHT*, 7 July 2000, pp. 1, 8)

'The upper chamber has, until now, given both republics in the federation equal weight ... The move to elect deputies directly annuls the balance stipulated in the 1992 constitution' (*Independent*, 7 July 2000, p. 13). 'Henceforth it [Montenegro] will have no more weight than its share of Yugoslavia's population – about 7 per cent' (*The Economist*, 15 July 2000, p. 45). 'The new election rules, intended to put into effect constitutional changes pushed through this month [July], were overwhelm-ingly adopted [on 24 July] by both houses of the Federal Assembly' (*IHT*, 25 July 2000, p. 2). 'On Monday [24 July] the Yugoslav parliament went ahead with the adoption of new electoral laws allowing candidates to be elected by a simple majority' (*Independent*, 28 July 2000, p.13). (For details, see Serbia.)

On 8 July 2000 the chairman of the supreme court declared that Yugoslavia no longer existed. On 10 August the government resolved unilaterally to take over federal insurance companies in Montenegro (*EEN*, 2000, vol. 12, no. 24, p. 5).

(The impact on Montenegro of the Kosovo crisis and the October 1999 Serbian Revolution are dealt with in the chapter on Serbia.)

28 December 2000: 'President Milo Djukanovic outlined a hardline stance on independence on Thursday [28 December], jettisoning Yugoslavia as it is now constituted. His proposal prompted the People's Party to leave the coalition government' (*Guardian*, 30 December 2000, p. 13).

> The tiny National [People's] Party withdrew from President Djukanovic's fragile parliamentary coalition ... The seven National Party deputies ... say they left because of his efforts to achieve independence from Belgrade ... Dragan Soc, the National Party leader and justice minister ... said that the party had second thoughts about a Montenegrin government proposal to revise radically the Yugoslav federation ... The defection left Mr Djukanovic without a majority in the seventy-eight-seat parliament ... The president's Democratic Socialist Party has thirty seats, while a third member of his Live Better coalition, the Social Democratic Party, has five seats.
>
> (*The Times*, 30 December 2000, p. 26)

'The People's Party leaves the ruling coalition after the government sets out its pro-independence stance' (*EEN*, 2001, vol. 13, no. 2, p. 5).

20 February 2001: 'President Milo Djukanovic ... yesterday [20 February] called an early general election' (*Telegraph*, 21 February 2001, p. 15). 'Parliamentary elections are announced for 22 April' (*EEN*, 2001, vol. 13. no. 3, p. 5).

24 February 2001: the Socialist People's Party elects Predrag Bulatovic as its new chairman, replacing Momir Bulatovic (*EEN*, 2001, vol. 13, no. 3, p. 5).

24 March 2001: '[The] opposition Socialist People's Party and People's Party forms the "Together for Yugoslavia" electoral alliance' (*EEN*, 2001, vol. 13, no. 4, p. 7). ('The Serb People's Party joined the alliance on 25 March': p. 7.)

12 April 2001: a statement is issued by the 'contact group': 'We support a democratic Montenegro within a democratic Yugoslavia' (*IHT*, 13 April 2001, p. 4).

'The six-nation "contact group" for the former Yugoslavia ... said they would deprive Montenegro of political and financial support if it split from Yugoslavia' (*FT*, 21 April 2001, p. 5).

'The "contact group" on the Balkans – the USA, Britain, Germany, France, Italy and Russia – warned Montenegro ... that it would cut off aid to Montenegro if it pursues the goal of independence' (*Guardian*, 21 April 2001, p. 15).

22 April 2001: a general election is held for the seventy-seven seats in parliament. There is an extremely high turnout. Pro-independence parties win a much slimmer majority of seats than expected.

A minimum of forty-six seats (a two-thirds majority) is needed to change the constitution.

'If the pro-independence parties win Sunday's election, his [Djukanovic's] supporters hope to hold a referendum by 13 July ... Montenegro already has its own foreign and monetary policy and the only remaining functioning federal institutions are the army and air traffic control' (*FT*, 21 April 2001, p. 5).

> If Mr Djukanovic wins an absolute majority of the parliamentary seats it could give him a comfortable position for holding a referendum on 13 June – the same day in 1878 the tiny kingdom won international recognition ... [There are] reports by Montenegrin officials that Belgrade has reintroduced custom barriers between the two republics abolished after ... Slobodan Milosevic was ousted.
>
> (*FT*, 23 April 2001, p 6)

'Although the Yugoslav army has an estimated 15,000 to 20,000 troops stationed in Montenegro, both the army and the federation's civilian leadership have said they would not intervene to block its separation' (*IHT*, 24 April 2001, p. 5).

> Opponents of Mr Djukanovic ... [claim] that he has allowed the country to become a paradise for cigarette smuggling .. Italian investigators and

newspapers have linked Mr Djukanovic's administration to an organized tobacco smuggling ring ... Italian investigators believe that transit fraud could account for as much as 60 per cent of Montenegro's GDP, which totalled $700 million in 1999 ... To call an independence referendum he [Djukanovic] will have to look for more backers for the necessary two-thirds majority in the seventy-seven-member parliament ... Carla del Ponte, the chief prosecutor at the war crimes tribunal in The Hague, handed over sealed indictments last week containing names of Montenegrin officials who took part in bombing operations around Dubrovnik in 1991. It is believed that Mr Djukanovic could be among them, as he was the prime minister of Montenegro at the time.

(*Independent*, 21 April 2001, p. 13)

('[There are] persistent allegations of Montenegro's role as a haven for organized crime – including the smuggling of arms, prostitutes and, especially, cigarettes ... According to investigators into the Italian Mafia, 50 per cent of the Montenegrin GDP can be traced back to the smuggling ... Italian investigators say dozens of criminals in Montenegro enjoy state protection': *FT*, 10 August 2001, p. 7. President Djukanovic wrote to deny the allegations: *FT*, 15 August 2001, p. 5.)

Mr Djukanovic ... envisions a loose union of Serbia, Montenegro and neighbouring nations to pursue free trade, joint participation in peace-keeping and a common currency, the euro ... Italian and other officials have expressed concern about alleged links between Mr Djukanovic's government and organized crime, including a lucrative trade in cigarette smuggling.

(*IHT*, 23 April 2001, p. 10)

President Milo Djukanovic's pro-independence coalition ... [won] thirty-six of parliament's seventy-seven seats against the pro-Yugoslav bloc's thirty-three ... Mr Djukanovic could take a parliamentary majority by teaming up with the small Liberal Party. The Liberals want to leave Yugoslavia and would insist upon an immediate referendum as the price of their support. That is a more extreme position than Mr Djukanovic's. He wants an independent Montenegro, but then plans to form another union with Serbia as an equal partner ... Polls suggest that up to 60 per cent of Montenegrins support independence. But equally, the government lacks a mandate to push for full independence, and would risk international isolation if it did so. And besides, Mr Djukanovic knows that, even if he wins a referendum, he lacks the two-thirds majority needed to ratify the result in parliament.

(*Business Central Europe*, June 2001, p. 42)

The Victory for Montenegro coalition, led by Milo Djukanovic, won 42.05 per cent of the vote and thirty-six seats. The uncompromisingly secessionist Liberal Alliance won 7.65 per cent of the vote and six seats. The three ethnic

Albanian parties won 2.6 per cent of the vote and two seats. The pro-independence camp is supported by the Social Democratic Party.

The anti-independence Together for Yugoslavia coalition, comprising the Socialist People's Party (led by Predrag Bulatovic) and the Serb People's Party, won 40.67 per cent of the vote and thirty-three seats.

'Mr Djukanovic's pro-independence parties won 54 per cent of the vote and the pro-Yugoslav alliance 40.6 per cent' (*FT*, Survey, 10 July 2001, p. 14). 'Around 60 per cent of voters want independence' (p. 13).

'The preliminary assessment of OSCE [was] that the voting had been "pluralistic, accountable and transparent"' (*IHT*, 24 April 2001, p. 5).

'Despite the presence of around 3,000 monitors, there were reports of irregularities' (*Guardian*, 23 April 2001, p. 13).

'The state media are strictly under his [Djukanovic's] control' (*Independent*, 24 April 2001, p. 13).

20 May 2001: 'The ruling Democratic Party of Socialists turns down the coalition proposals of the Liberal Alliance of Montenegro' (*EEN*, 2001, vol. 13, no. 5, p. 7).

22 May 2001: 'The constitutional court rules that a referendum on independence would be validated by a simple majority rather than a two-thirds majority' (*EEN*, 2001, vol. 13, no. 5, p. 7).

30 May 2001: 'Filip Vujanovic ... was asked to form a minority government. The hardline secessionist Liberal Alliance is said to have agreed to support it in return for a referendum on independence from Yugoslavia being arranged within six months' (*The Times*, 31 May 2001, p. 10).

July 2001:

> [The] new government ... aims to hold a referendum on independence by next January [2002]. But ... Milo Djukanovic has recently implied that he might be more flexible on the issue than he was. He gets on well with Zoran Djindjic [the prime minister of Serbia], who says he is willing to talk about a new Yugoslav federation in which Serbia and Montenegro are both independent in all but name.
>
> (*The Economist*, 7 July 2001, p. 49)

Milo Djukanovic:

> We propose new democratic relations between our two independent states which should be applicable to relations between all the former Yugoslav states. It would be based on free trade, the euro as a common currency and visa-free travel. We also propose the demilitarization of Serbia and Montenegro with joint command of the reduced army ... I managed to cut our foreign debt by $170 million to $340 million by secondary market operations.
>
> (*FT*, Survey, 10 July 2001, p. 13)

'Montenegro ... shares only an army and flight control system with Belgrade' (*FT*, Survey, 10 July 2001, p. 14).

19 September 2001: 'Montenegro's pro-independence leaders refused to attend inaugural talks in Belgrade on the future of Yugoslavia ... [They] object to the inclusion in the talks of Dragisa Pesic, the federal prime minister who is a Montenegrin opposition official' (*Guardian*, 20 September 2001, p. 17).

THE ECONOMY

There were heavy falls in GDP in the Federal Republic of Yugoslavia between 1990 and 1993. (See Table 5.2.) But the economy grew in 1994. The GDP growth rate fell sharply in 1998 and turned heavily negative in 1999. Positive growth returned in 2000. In 2000 the level of GDP in the Federal Republic of Yugoslavia was still only 47 per cent of the 1989 level (EBRD 2001b: 59). Table 5.2 shows the conquering of hyperinflation, although inflation began to rise again in 1998. (See Serbia for details.)

> Since the introduction of UN sanctions, local industry has either closed or cut production to 20 per cent or less of capacity. The huge KAT aluminium plant in the Zeta valley, which once produced nearly half the republic's foreign exchange earnings, works at 20 per cent capacity ... its large, modern commercial fleet (once responsible for 25 per cent of foreign exchange earnings) is stranded or impounded around the world. The tourist industry, aside from its Yugoslav clients, is virtually dead. Unemployment is high but hard to quantify (well over 15 per cent).
>
> (*EEN*, 15 March 1995, vol. 9, no. 6, p. 3)

'For the first time since the Second World War Montenegrins' wages are higher than Serbians' (*The Economist*, 14 December 1996, p. 44).

> Montenegro initially launched its privatization process in the early 1990s by transferring state-owned capital to a number of state funds. By the end of 1995 these funds had become majority shareholders in about 350 compa- nies. A new privatization plan in Montenegro was approved in 1998 and led to the establishment of a privatization council. The plan, which has yet to be implemented, targets about 300 enterprises, most of which will be priva- tized either by a mass voucher scheme or by international tender.
>
> (EBRD 2000b: 9)

'Montenegro has had a privatization plan since 1998, but implementation is slow' (EBRD 2001a: 62). 'But the recent political changes ... are giving a new impetus to the process' (p. 28).

Table 5.2 The Federal Republic of Yugoslavia: selected economic indicators 1990–2000

Economic indicator	1990	1991	1992	1993	1994	1995	1996	1997	1998	1999	2000 (estimate)
Rate of growth of GDP (%)	-7.9	-11.6	-27.9	-30.8	2.5	6.1	7.8	10.1	1.9	-15.7	5.0
Rate of growth of industrial output (%)	-11.7	-17.6	-22.4	-38.2	1.3	3.8	7.6	9.5	3.6	-22.5	10.9
Rate of growth of agricultural output (%)	-7.0	9.7	-17.8	-3.2	6.0	4.2	1.5	7.3	-3.2	2.7	-19.7
Inflation rate (consumer, %)	593.0	121.0	9,237.0	116.5×10^{12}	3.3	78.6	94.3	21.3	29.5	37.1	60.4
Budget surplus or deficit (% of GDP)				-28.0		-4.3	-3.8	-7.6	-5.4	-8.3	-1.0
Unemployment rate (end of year, %)		21.0	24.6	23.1	23.1	24.6	25.8	25.8	25.1	26.5	27.3
Balance of payments (current account, $billion)					-0.400	-1.000	-1.670	-1.564	-0.660	-0.764	-0.680
Foreign direct investment (net, $billion)								0.740	0.113	0.112	0.025

Source Various issues of European Bank for Reconstruction and Development, *Transition Report*; United Nations Economic Commission for Europe, *Economic Survey of Europe*; United Nations, *World Economic and Social Survey*; *Business Central Europe*; *Financial Times*.

> Privatization in Montenegro has been more advanced than that in Serbia, although progress has slowed down in recent years. The government plans to accelerate the process via tender privatization of fifteen to twenty large enterprises … a mass voucher privatization programme for 240 medium-sized companies, a batch sale privatization of thirty-three companies and liquidation of about thirty companies.
>
> (EBRD 2001b: 143)

In mid-2000 the private sector's share of (Yugoslav) GDP was roughly 40 per cent (p. 144).

Montenegro objected to a new company law drawn up by the Serbian Socialist Party, which argued that the proposed law would prevent the new bourgeoisie from grabbing state assets. The Montenegrin government, in contrast, believed that the law as drafted would slow down privatization and effectively reintroduce 'self-management' (*EEN*, 28 April 1995, vol. 9, no. 9, p. 5). Montenegro hoped to complete the privatization of all 'socially owned' enterprises by the end of 1995 (*EEN*, 24 August 1995, vol. 9, no. 17, p. 2). 'Montenegro has privatized 90 per cent of industry, whereas in Serbia industry remains 90 per cent state-owned' (*EEN*, 15 March 1996, vol. 10, no. 4, p. 4). The government says that it will accelerate the privatization of large enterprises and will introduce voucher privatization in which every citizen will receive a voucher worth around DM 5,000. The government has offered majority stakes in six large enterprises to foreign purchasers (*EEN*, 23 January 1998, vol. 12, no. 1, p. 3).

The Montenegrin solution has been to transfer majority ownership to three state-managed funds, with employees retaining a minority holding. Ten per cent of an enterprise's shares are allocated to the workers, who have the right to purchase an additional 30 per cent at a discounted rate (usually between 15 and 20 per cent of the full price). The remaining 60 per cent is split between three state-managed funds. The development fund receives 36 per cent, the pension fund 18 per cent and the unemployment fund 6 per cent. The funds are required to sell their entire stake within five years of the restructuring of a enterprise, with a minimum 20 per cent sold each year. By mid-1996 this first phase, begun in 1991, was almost complete with 96 per cent of enterprises transferred from social ownership to the funds and employees. 'The next stage – finding buyers – is proving more formidable' (*Business Europa*, September–October 1996, p. 17).

Montenegro has 'privatized more quickly than he [Milosevic] has … A foreigner was recently allowed to buy a state brewery … [But] Montenegro's privatization is still pretty tentative, and still pretty much an affair for insiders' (*The Economist*, 14 December 1996, p. 44).

The process of privatization is well under way. Foreign companies can take majority shareholdings in enterprises by buying stakes held by government institutions, mainly the development fund. Of the 350 'socially owned' enterprises that were effectively nationalized by the state, eighty-five have been sold to domestic investors while just one big enterprise (a brewery) was taken over by a Belgian company in 1997 (*FT*, Survey, 27 January 1998, p. 14).

The first phase of privatization is now all but complete, with majority stakes in 90 per cent of enterprises transferred to one of three state-managed funds (the minority stakes are held by employees). The development, unemployment and pension funds must sell an annual minimum 20 per cent stake in each of their enterprises, with the aim of completing the process within five years. More than 80 per cent of small and medium-sized enterprises are in private hands, with large enterprises to follow. Majority stakes in six big enterprises, including tobacco and aluminium, are to be sold by international tender (*Business Central Europe*, February 1998, p. 25).

There has been criticism of the government's decision to sell 'without a public bidding process, an aluminium plant that provides half of the country's legitimate income' (R. Jeffrey Smith, *IHT*, 28 November 1998, p. 7). A Swiss-based company is taking over the management of an aluminium plant (KAP) in Montenegro that would in effect give it control of half of the economy. The five-year contract 'conducted in secret without an open tender could involve a local trading company with close ties to Montenegro's ruling circles'. The contract to run the bankrupt enterprise specifies an annual payment. The foreign company can set a timetable for privatization in which it would have the right of first refusal and can sell any asset without government approval. Montenegro is believed to have the largest reserves in Europe (excluding Russia) of bauxite (the raw material for aluminium). Government officials estimate that KAP consumes 60 per cent of Montenegro's electricity output and is the largest customer of the republic's railways and of the port of Bar. 'As a result, the plant accounts for more than half Montenegro's economy and foreign exchange earnings' (Guy Dinmore, *FT*, 8 December 1998, p. 2).

> Aluminium and tourism are the mainstays of the ... economy ... High taxes on legal employment have distorted competition, pushing more than 40 per cent of the economy into the shadows and encouraged illegal and criminal activities, such as smuggling cars and cigarettes in response to trade sanctions on Yugoslavia ... More than 40,000 people work in 350 loss-making state enterprises and a further 42,000 work in the bloated public sector. A World Bank study estimates that another 15,000–25,000 workers are on waiting lists or unpaid leave ... Thus far the only big privatization by a foreign strategic investor was the purchase of Niksic brewery by Interbrew of Belgium in 1997. The pace is about to quicken, however. Telekom Montenegro is already out to tender. Three types of privatization under way include open tenders for big companies, batch privatization (under which investors are offered a bundle of enterprises of varying quality) and mass privatization through vouchers organized by PriceWaterhouseCoopers under contract from USAID ... The aluminium sector with its under-capitalized bauxite mines, worn out railways and 1972-vintage aluminium smelter alone accounts for an estimated 53 per cent of GDP when suppliers such as the electricity corporation and the port of Bar are included. But KAP, the aluminium company, which accounts for more than 70 per cent of

Montenegro's export earnings, ran up accumulated losses of $157 million over the last few years. The debt was recently rescheduled over fifteen years and Swiss-based Glencore won a controversial management contract ... At current levels of output and world prices, KAP is probably paying its way. But its years of heavy losses and non-transparent transactions drained the economy, imposed heavy losses on the railways, electricity company and other creditors.

(*FT*, Survey, 10 July 2001, pp. 14–15)

George Soros ... yesterday [2 June 2000] announced the founding of Euromarket Bank, the first international bank in Montenegro ... His not-for-profit development corporation, the Soros Economic Development Foundation, would invest DM 7 million in the bank's DM 11.2 million initial capital. Other investors are DEG, the German development bank, with DM 3 million; SKB Bank, the largest private bank in Slovenia, with DM 600,000; and Futura Investment, a private investment bank, with DM 600,000.

(*FT*, 3 June 2000, p. 10)

Montenegro plans to introduce the DM as its second currency this week ... newspapers and officials reported Monday [1 November] ... Citizens would receive their salaries and pensions in marks beginning Tuesday [2 November] ... The move, which must still be approved by the Montenegrin government, is considered an interim step before the introduction of a separate currency. The Yugoslav dinar would be allowed in the interim.

(*IHT*, 2 November 1999, p. 7)

On 2 November 1999 Montenegro decided to make the DM legal tender alongside the dinar. The change would be implemented the day after it was published in the official gazette, so basic goods such as bread, milk, petrol and power would be priced in DMs from 4 November onwards. Prime minister Filip Vujanovic: 'I believe this mechanism will protect us from [Belgrade's] destructive monetary policy which is threatening to turn into chaos.' The DM fetches almost seventeen dinars on the black market, compared with an official rate of six. 'Many companies as well as individuals already flout a ban on its use in transactions' (*Independent*, 3 November 1999, p. 13).

Food staples, pensions, utility bills and other government-regulated prices would be set in DMs from 4 November (*Telegraph*, 3 November 1999, p. 14).

The Montenegrin government yesterday [2 November] decided to make the DM its official currency in a bid to shield its economy from rising inflation and a fall in the Yugoslav dinar. The decision to adopt the DM is the first step towards launching an independent monetary system ... The next move will be to legalize the use of other currencies in business transactions. In the final stage the republic will launch its own currency, the Montenegrin marka, which will trade side by side with the DM.

(*FT*, 3 November 1999, p. 10)

Montenegro has launched its new currency, the marka. It would trade along-side the DM against which it would trade at par. Both currencies would be legal tender and all government transactions would be carried out in either of them. Businesses would be free to use the currency of their choice. A currency board (governed by one Montenegrin and four other nationals from the G7 countries) would back the system and the number of markas would equal the total value of foreign currency reserves. The reserves would be held in either DMs or euros (*FT*, 30 October 1999, p. 5). (On 5 January 2000 a Montenegrin official said that he expected the Yugoslav dinar to be gradually phased out by the end of that month: *IHT*, 6 January 2000, p. 13.)

Ljubisa Krgovic (the central bank governor):

> Introduction of the DM was the biggest reform and move to date. It enabled us to set up our own central bank, and we are moving now to reform the banking system and replace ZOP, the centralized clearing system inherited from Yugoslavia. The demise of ZOP means the end of a govern-ment monopoly. It will be replaced by competition between the banks.
>
> (*FT*, Survey, 10 July 2001, p. 14)

> The Yugoslav national bank in Belgrade has hit back by blocking all payments between the two republics. Some 18,000 pensioners living in Montenegro who get their pensions from Belgrade have had their payments blocked; 8,000 military employees and 2,000 civil servants are in the same boat. To make matters worse, Serb police this week stopped dozens of trucks with fresh food from crossing into Montenegro ... Montenegrin busi-nessmen owed money by firms on either side of the border have no way of getting it back.
>
> (*The Economist*, 4 December 1999, pp. 48, 51)

'Montenegro abolished the Yugoslav dinar in November 2000, leaving the DM (Euro) as the sole legal tender in the republic' (EBRD 2001b: 20).

> The prices of staple consumer goods, i.e. bread and milk, were partially liberalized over the past year. Both bread and milk increased in price by nearly 60 per cent in January [2001] and a further 100 per cent in August. Post and telecommunications charges were raised by nearly 100 per cent in June 2001. Further liberalization is planned for 2001 on controlled prices of items such as transportation, telecommunications and municipal services.
>
> (p. 142)

'The Montenegrin government has prepared a tax action plan' (p. 142).

> Serbia has imposed a full economic blockade on Montenegro ... The embargo, which local newspapers said came into effect at the weekend [4–5 March], will further tighten the economic noose on Montenegro, which

traditionally relies heavily on Serbian exports ... Since Serbia began blocking wheat exports last year [1999] the Montenegrin government has been forced to import from Slovenia and Croatia, which are considerably more expensive.

(*Telegraph*, 7 March 2000, p. 23)

'Serbia ... largely sealed the border between the republics this month [March], preventing any trade between Serbia and Montenegro' (*IHT*, 18 March 2000, p. 4).

'Yugoslavia's newly democratic government has already abolished Milosevic-era trade barriers against Montenegro' (*Business Central Europe*, June 2001, p. 42).

Chris Patten, the EU commissioner for external relations, became the first Western politician to visit ... [Montenegro] since the Kosovo conflict ... Mr Patten ... promised yesterday [10 March] to boost planned help of Euro 60 million by a further Euro 5 million to fund infrastructure projects ... As part of Yugoslavia, Montenegro cannot receive significant aid from most international institutions. Mr Patten's Euro 5 million package will avoid being channelled through the government by going to specific projects, including a bridge at Mora and a road linking the capital with its airport.

(*Independent*, 11 March 2000, p. 14)

On 8 May 2000 EU finance ministers decided to provide Euro 20 million of special assistance, the money being allocated before by-elections in two Montenegrin cities on 11 June (*FT*, 9 May 2000, p. 10).

European foreign ministers ... approved [on 18 September 2000] an EU package granting duty-free access to 95 per cent of imports from Albania, Bosnia, Croatia, Macedonia and Montenegro ... The package includes abolition of tariffs on most industrial and farm products to the EU. However, some limits remain on exports of fish products and wine.

(*FT*, 19 September 2000, p. 10)

'The EU agreed to ... allow Croatia, Bosnia and Albania to export 95 per cent of their industrial and agricultural products to EU countries duty free. Montenegro will be allowed to export aluminium' (*The Times*, 19 September 2000, p. 14).

'Over the last three years the EU and USA delivered DM 450 million in aid, with a further DM 280 million pledged for this year [2001]' (*FT*, Survey, 10 July 2001, p. 13).

6 The Federal Republic of Yugoslavia: Serbia

POLITICS

Political developments prior to Dayton

In July 1990 the Serbian League of Communists and the Socialist Alliance merged to form the Serbian Socialist Party (SSP), with Slobodan Milosevic appointed chairman. Milosevic was born in Serbia, but is of Montenegrin descent. (He was born in 1941 of mixed Montenegrin and Serbian parentage: *EEN*, 1997, vol. 11, no. 1, p. 3.) He convincingly won the December 1990 Serbian presidential election with 65 per cent of the vote. Vuk Draskovic of the Party for Serbian Renewal came an unexpectedly poor second, with only 16 per cent. The SSP convincingly won the December 1990 Serbian parliamentary election on a platform of Serbian nationalism, a strong federation and promises of economic security (the party being lukewarm on economic reform in general). On 27 April 1992 Serbia and Montenegro declared a new Federal Republic of Yugoslavia. The 31 May 1992 general election in the new Yugoslavia was formally boycotted by the Serbian opposition and by the Albanians of Kosovo. The turnout was 55 per cent in Serbia and 57 per cent in Montenegro. The 138 seats in the House of Deputies were allocated as follows: the SSP, seventy-three; the ultra-nationalist Serbian Radical Party, thirty-three; the Montenegrin Socialist Democratic Party, twenty-three; the Democratic Community of Hungarians of Vojvodina, two; the League of Communists Movement, two; and independents, three. Dobrica Cosic became president and the émigré Milan Panic (a wealthy businessman in the USA) was appointed prime minister in July. Internal opposition began to grow all the same. Anti-war demonstrations took place. (There were earlier ones about economic conditions and government control of the media.) On 24 May 1992 opposition parties and prominent intellectuals formed the Democratic Movement of Serbia and the Serbian Orthodox Church issued a critical statement. But most opposition politicians, perhaps not surprisingly, curried nationalist favour while ethnic Serbs were fighting in other parts of the former Yugoslavia.

In the Serbian presidential election of 20 December 1992 Milosevic (56.32 per cent of the vote) comfortably beat the main contender Panic (34.02 per cent of the vote). (The electoral commission initially declared Panic to be ineligible to stand on the grounds that he had not lived long enough in Yugoslavia, but this decision was overruled by the supreme court.) In the Serbian parliamentary election the Serbian Socialist Party (SSP) led by Milosevic remained the largest party in the 250-seat Serbian National Assembly with 101 seats. The extreme nationalist Serbian Radical Party led by Vojislav Seselj made great strides to come second with seventy-four seats. The DEPOS (Democratic Movement of Serbia) opposition alliance won a disappointing forty-nine seats, with other parties as follows: Democratic Union of Hungarians in Vojvodina, nine; Democratic Party, seven; Citizens of Kosov-Methija, five. The Albanians in Kosovo boycotted the election as did most Moslems in the Sanjak (which straddles Serbia and Montenegro). In the words of the CSCE observers in Serbia, 'the electoral process was seriously flawed'. Examples of wrongdoing included: media manipulation; at least 5 per cent of (mainly young) voters excluded from the electoral register; some given two votes (mainly married women registered under their married and maiden names); unsealed ballot boxes; and a lack of voting secrecy. On 21 October 1993 Milosevic dissolved parliament and called a new election for 19 December 1993 (though not for the presidency) in order to thwart a vote of no confidence proposed by the Serbian Radical Party.

The general election did take place on schedule, on 19 December 1993, with some reruns on 26 December owing to irregularities. All parties played the nationalist tune and played on the collective paranoia of the whole world seeming to be against Serbia. Draskovic openly advocated a 'Greater Serbia' and even criticized Milosevic for supporting the Owen–Stoltenberg proposals. The Socialist Party won 123 seats, just three short of an absolute majority. DEPOS won forty-five seats and the Serbian Radical Party thirty-nine. The Serbian Unity Party (founded on 3 November 1993 by Zeljko Raznatovic, also known as 'Arkan') did surprisingly poorly, winning only one seat. (Six of the forty-five DEPOS MPs went over to Milosevic soon after the election: *The Economist*, 23 July 1994, p. 42.)

Post-Dayton Serbia

22 February 1996: France and the Federal Republic of Yugoslavia restore diplomatic relations at the ambassador level.

7 August 1996: Presidents Milosevic and Tudjman meet in Greece and agree to establish diplomatic relations by the end of the month. (This actually occurred on 9 September 1996.) The statement talks of them being 'ready to proceed to full normalization'.

23 August 1996: foreign minister Milan Milutinovic signs a mutual recognition accord with his Croatian counterpart Mate Granic. Ambassadors will be exchanged (i.e. full diplomatic relations formally established) within fifteen days. Refugees will be allowed to return.

29 September 1996: Dragoslav Avramovic, the former governor of the central bank, agrees to lead a coalition of opposition parties called Zajedno ('Together').

(But he had to step down on 9 October, seemingly on health grounds. He is in his late seventies.)

1 October 1996: the UN Security Council votes fifteen to nil to lift trade, travel and transportation sanctions permanently. This is in line with the Dayton accords, which made the lifting automatic ten days after declaring 'free and fair' elections. But the so-called 'outer wall' of sanctions (admittance to international institutions such as the UN, the IMF and the World Bank) remain until other conditions are met, such as compliance with the war crimes tribunal, resolution of the Kosovo problem and resolution of the debt/assets problem with the other countries of the former Yugoslavia.

3 October 1996: Milosevic and President Izetbegovic of Bosnia-Hercegovina meet in Paris and pledge to establish full diplomatic relations.

10 October 1996: the Federal Republic of Yugoslavia and Germany sign a treaty to repatriate some 135,000 refugees over the next three years, starting in December 1996. Most of the refugees are ethnic Albanians from Kosovo (*IHT*, 11 October 1996, p. 5).

3 November 1996: Yugoslav (federal) elections are held. (See Table 6.1.)

The federal parliament (Chamber of Citizens) has 138 seats. Serbia is allocated 108 seats and Montenegro thirty seats. There were only a few foreign observers (*FT*, 5 November 1996, p. 2). 'Though monitoring of the elections was wholly inadequate, there was no major fraud, certainly not enough significantly to have changed the results' (*EEN*, 1996, vol. 10, no. 22, p. 3).

Table 6.1   The Federal Republic of Yugoslavia: the federal election of 3 November 1996

	Party	*Seats*
Serbia	Serbian Socialist Party, Yugoslav United Left, New Democracy Party	64
	Together (Zajedno)	22
	Serbian Radical Party	16
	Party of Vojvodina Hungarians	3
	Coalition Vojvodina	2
	Party of Democratic Action	1
Montenegro	Democratic Party of Socialists	20
	People's Accord (between Liberal Alliance of Montenegro and the People's Party)	8
	Social Democratic Party	1
	Party of Democratic Action	1
	Democratic Alliance	0
	Democratic Union	0

The parties in the 3 November 1996 federal election were as follows:

Serbian Socialist Party: the president is Slobodan Milosevic and the chairman is Zoran Lilic.

Mr Milosevic needs a majority in the federal parliament to make changes in the constitution of Yugoslavia, now comprised of Serbia and Montenegro. Next year he will complete two terms as president of Serbia, and is expected to become leader of Serb-led Yugoslavia. He wants to make this latter post the most powerful one in the country and for this he will need to change the constitution. The success of Mr Milosevic's coalition will be helped by the six-year boycott of official institutions in Serbia by ethnic Albanians in the province of Kosovo.

(Laura Silber, *FT*, 2 November 1996, p. 2)

Under the Serbian constitution he cannot be elected for a third term [as Serbian president]. He might try to amend the constitution, should the presidency of Yugoslavia not be forthcoming, but to do that he needs a two-thirds majority in the Serbian parliament. For the presidency of Yugoslavia he needs a simple majority in the federal parliament.

(Dessa Trevisan, *The Times*, 4 November 1996, p. 15)

'The [federal] parliament, politically irrelevant, along with the ineffectual offices of the federal presidency and prime ministry, is, however, seen as the next stepping stone in Mr Milosevic's drive to retain control of a country that he has run for the last nine years' (Chris Hedges, *IHT*, 4 November 1996, p. 5). It is claimed that no matter what title he has, Milosevic intends to run the Federal Republic of Yugoslavia.

When Mr Milosevic's term expires at the end of 1997, he can ... use a two-thirds majority in the federal parliament to amend the constitution and transfer his power to the post of federal president. But even if he fails to receive a two-thirds majority on Sunday [3 November], he can be appointed as the federal prime minister by the federal president and retain power through that office.

(Chris Hedges, *IHT*, 4 November 1996, p. 5)

Yugoslav United Left: led by Ljubisa Ristic and Mirjana Markovic (Milosevic's wife). Allied to the Serbian Socialist Party.

New Democracy Party: led by Dusan Mihailovic. Allied to the Serbian Socialist Party.

Together (Zajedno): an alliance between the Serbian Renewal Movement (led by Vuk Draskovic), the Democratic Party of Serbia (led by Zoran Djindjic), the Democratic Party (led by Vojislav Kostunica) and the Civic Alliance of Serbia (led by Vesna Pesic). Despite the resignation (on health grounds) of Dragoslav Avramovic as coalition leader on 9 October 1996, the leaders 'say that they will stick to Avramovic's liberal economic programme entailing privatization, an open economy and the reestablishment of relations with the international financial community' (*EEN*, 1996, vol. 10, no. 21, p. 2). 'A disparate grouping of liberals and Serb nationalists who freely admit entering a temporary marriage of convenience in an attempt to break the left-wing monolith' (Julian Borger, *Guardian*, 2 November 1996, p. 17).

Zoran Djindjic has shifted position many times. He was a student anarchist in the 1970s, an anti-nationalist in the 1980s and a Serb nationalist as recently as September 1996. He supported Karadzic during the war (John Pomfret, *IHT*, 31 December 1996, p. 2).

Vesna Pesic always opposed the ethnic wars (*Independent*, 6 December 1996, p. 16). She said:

Only complete freedom of expression and legal equality of all political factions can enable solutions to be established which will not be questioned afterwards, a crucial question for the Balkans This is especially true for Kosovo, which is tearing Serbia apart from within. Traumas and new potential conflicts can only be avoided by establishing a state of law and respect for basic human rights – in other words, democracy.

(*Guardian*, 1 January 1997, p. 9)

Party of Democratic Action: led by Razim Lajiic.

Serbian Radical Party: led by Vojislav Seselj.

17 November 1996: the second round of the local elections is held, the first having been held on 3 November. (Serbia's municipal governments own television and radio stations, magazines and newspapers: *IHT*, 29 November 1996, p. 8.)

The Zajedno alliance claimed to have won elections in fifteen of the eighteen largest cities or towns in Serbia, including Belgrade (the result in the capital being initially accepted by the electoral commission). But the electoral commission or local courts began to declare results invalid. (Zajedno victories were reversed in all but one city: *IHT*, 6 December 1996, p. 9.) In Belgrade, for example, a local court called for fresh elections in thirty-three of the sixty seats won by Zajedno (out of 110 in total). According to *The Economist* (30 November 1996, p. 60), Milosevic 'is using courts and local electoral committees, both under his party's thumb, to reverse the results'. 'Courts controlled by the regime annulled the vote' (*IHT*, 29 November 1996, p. 8).

The annulments led to massive demonstrations by supporters of opposition parties and by students (with their chants including 'red bandits'). The largest number of demonstrators in Belgrade at one time may have been as high as 250,000 and in Nis up to 40,000.

Thirty-two protestors have been arrested, mostly students (*IHT*, 6 December 1996, p. 9).

26 November 1996: the Montenegrin opposition National Accord alliance holds a rally in Podgorica in support of opposition demonstrations in Serbia against Milosevic. Further demonstrations are planned (*EEN*, 1996, vol. 10, no. 24, p. 8).

27 November 1996: some fresh elections are boycotted by Zajedno. (In twelve towns where Zajedno gains were annulled the coalition took part in a further round of voting and won. But in Belgrade, Nis and Kraljevo, Zajedno boycotted the poll reruns and took their cases to the courts: *Guardian*, 9 December 1996, p. 2.)

2 December 1996: the scheduled opening of parliament is postponed.

3 December 1996: the independent radio B-92 (whose news programme has been jammed) is closed down. A student-run radio is also closed.

Five supreme court judges criticize their colleagues for approving the annulment of local elections, accusing them of political subservience. (They were supported the following day by some ninety court judges.)

4 December 1996: the Socialist Party leader in Nis (the second largest city) resigns.

5 December 1996: the government promises to lower electricity prices and to pay arrears on pensions and student grants. (Arrears covered pensions, salaries, student grants and social welfare: *IHT*, 16 December 1996, p. 7.)

The two radio stations are allowed to resume broadcasting.

The information minister resigns on grounds of conscience, his 'liberal concepts' being clearly at odds with those of colleagues (*Independent*, 7 December 1996, p. 11).

The supreme court is to review the annulment of local election results in Belgrade.

Montenegrin President Momir Bulatovic publicly criticizes the rigging of local elections in Serbia (*EEN*, 1996, vol. 10, no. 24, p. 8).

6 December 1996: EU foreign ministers refuse to grant trade concessions to the Federal Republic of Yugoslavia.

Montenegro issues a statement: 'The annulment of democratic elections belongs to the practice of totalitarian regimes ... absolutely undemocratic' (*IHT*, 7 December 1996, p. 5; *FT*, 7 December 1996, p. 2). (On 29 December 1996 the Montenegrin prime minister, Milo Djukanovic, sent a letter of support to students in Belgrade: *EEN*, 1996, vol. 10, no. 25, p. 9. In contrast, President Tudjman of Croatia 'now has only kind words for him [Milosevic]. According to Tudjman, "foreign elements" were plotting to destabilize and overthrow the governments in Serbia, Croatia and Bosnia, partly by organizing simultaneous demonstrations in the three capitals': pp. 5–6.)

7 December 1996: the supreme court rejects five of the forty-six appeals relating to Belgrade. This alone deprives Zajedno of their majority (leaving them with fifty-five out of 110 seats), but, in addition, is interpreted by Zajedno as a prelude to a rejection of the other forty-one appeals.

10 December 1996: the supreme court of the Federal Republic of Yugoslavia rejects the appeals against the annulments.

Nato foreign ministers 'strongly deplore' the annulment of local elections in Serbia.

11 December 1996: an organized group of workers joins the demonstrations for the first time. Workers down tools in six factories in Belgrade, one in Nis and one in Mladenovac (*IHT*, 12 December 1996, p. 9).

12 December 1996: riot police turn away student demonstrators attempting to march to the district of Belgrade (Dedinje) where Milosevic lives. (This is the second attempt since the demonstrations began: *IHT*, 13 December 1996, p. 5.)

13 December 1996: Milosevic talks of 'threatening political terrorism' but declares that he will allow a 'respected' delegation from OSCE to 'assess all the facts'. OSCE declines on the grounds that it will be unable to verify the local election results.

15 December 1996: a district court in Nis orders the electoral commission to reconsider its annulment. Nis district court's ruling effectively orders the electoral commission to reverse its decision on the victors of twenty-six of the seventy seats on the Nis municipal council (*IHT*, 16 December 1996, p. 7).

16 December 1996: a court in Smederevska Palanka orders the local electoral commission to award control of the municipal council to Zajedno. (But on 18 December 1996 the commission confirmed a Socialist Party victory.)

The largest and most influential union (Alliance of Independent Trade Unions of Yugoslavia) verbally supports the smaller union Nezavismost over wages, working conditions and the electoral dispute (*IHT*, 17 December 1996, p. 6).

17 December 1996: Milosevic meets student leaders.

18 December 1996: students are again prevented from marching to the Dedinje district where Milosevic lives.

20–1 December 1996: an OSCE delegation, led by former Spanish prime minister Felipe Gonzalez, visits Serbia.

The first of the pro-Milosevic demonstrations takes place (this one outside Belgrade).

22 December 1996: the Union of Free Cities and Municipalities of Serbia is formed, with 'shadow' municipal governments being set up.

24 December 1996: Milosevic organizes a rally in Belgrade (many were bused in) but only 30,000–100,000 turn up (instead of the expected 500,000). In his address Milosevic says: 'Strong Serbia is not to the liking of some powers abroad and that is why they are trying to break it up with the help of domestic traitors.' Rival demonstrators clash and one anti-Milosevic demonstrator is so badly injured that he later dies (apparently after being trampled by demonstrators fleeing a police charge); another is critically injured when he is shot by a supporter of Milosevic. Riot police club anti-Milosevic demonstrators and use tear gas against them.

Michael Dobbs (*IHT*, 31 December 1996, p. 5) comments on Milosevic's speech:

Such rhetoric does not impress the urbanized elite ... But it plays well in the countryside, which has always been the backbone of Mr Milosevic's support. Even in the cities public opinion is deeply divided. Many people remain apathetic. For every citizen of Belgrade who has taken part in the protests, at least five or six have stayed at home ... By contrast, in Czechoslovakia's 'velvet revolution' of 1989, within four days, 90 per cent of the population was in the streets. While talk of Mr Milosevic's imminent demise appears premature, he has nevertheless suffered a major political setback ... The small New Democracy Party, which forms a coalition with the ruling Socialist Party, has called on Mr Milosevic to recognize the results of the 17 November election. The leaders of Montenegro ... are also distancing themselves from the Milosevic regime.

The Serbian privatization minister confirms his resignation (*EEN*, 31 December 1996, vol. 10, no. 25, p. 9). The information minister has also resigned (p. 2).

25 December 1996: anti-Milosevic demonstrations again take place.

26 December 1996: demonstrations that lead to the 'obstruction of normal traffic' in Belgrade are banned. But a small student demonstration succeeds in marching and Zajedno supporters hold a brief rally. (Note that daily separate demonstrations have typically been held by students and Zajedno supporters, the former being the first to take place.)

President Izetbegovic says of the demonstrations in Croatia and Serbia: 'Both situations are creating a good environment so Bosnia-Hercegovina can stand on its own feet. Serbia will be preoccupied with itself for a long time and not with Bosnia-Hercegovina because of internal economic and social reasons' (*The Times*, 27 December 1996, p. 10).

Despite the Dayton accord ... it has been evident for some time that the chance for real peace will come only when the war leaders have been ousted ... If the change can be effected peaceably in Serbia – suddenly a miraculous chance – it will be felt then in Zagreb and Sarajevo. The whole vicious circle could be reversed in the direction of hope.

(Flora Lewis, *IHT*, 5 December 1996, p. 8)

27 December 1996: Felipe Gonzalez delivers the OSCE verdict on the municipal elections: 'It is my opinion that both the authorities and all political forces in Yugoslavia must accept and abide by the results of the local elections of 17 November.' All should 'comply with the will expressed at the polls by the citizens'. Although the Socialist Party and its allies won a majority of the votes, the opposition won in twenty-two disputed municipalities (nine in Belgrade and thirteen other towns and cities). (Thus OSCE supported Zajedno's claims with the exception of Pozega.)

Celebrating demonstrators clash with riot police. Two foreign television crews are attacked.

28 December 1996: the funeral of Predrag Starcevic (who died on 24 December) takes place. Large numbers of his fellow anti-Milosevic demonstrators turn out.

In Nis the electoral commission ignores a local court and the OSCE recommendation. The electoral commission awards nine of the twenty-six council seats to the Socialist Party and orders fresh elections for the remaining seats.

29 December 1996: demonstrators are prevented from marching by riot police.

An actor reads out a letter purported to have been written by some army officers representing military units (including a paratroop brigade) in six towns: 'The truth is the most important thing, regardless of how dark it is. Serbia should stand together with countries where it is possible to live honestly, happily and in a satisfactory way ... We are firmly with the people.' The troops will not fire on demonstrators even if ordered to do so (*IHT*, 30 December 1996, p. 6; 31 December 1996, p. 5).

'Although the ambivalence of the underpaid Serb army may concern him, he [Milosevic] has so far retained the loyalty of Serbia's 80,000 police force' (Anthony Lloyd, *The Times*, 3 January 1997, p. 14). 'Military personnel are habitually paid late; longstanding resentment at the diversion of resources to Milosevic's 100,000-strong police force ... is coming to a head' (*EEN*, 31 December 1996, vol. 10, no. 25, p. 2).

31 December 1996: demonstrators celebrating the arrival of the new year use whistles, alarm clocks (to warn Milosevic that he has little time left) and bells (to symbolize the passing of his regime).

In his new year speech Milosevic says that 1996 has been a good year despite some 'internal and external interference'. He promises that 1997 will bring economic reform, increased investment and a rise in wages.

1 January 1997: the opposition have decided that there will be no protests on New Year's Day, although students march on Belgrade television to denounce its virtual blackout on news of the protests (*IHT*, 3 January 1997, p. 1).

2 January 1997: an emergency meeting of the council of the Serbian Orthodox Church issues the following statement (signed by, among others, Patriarch Pavle):

> He [Milosevic] has already set us against the whole world and now wants to pit us against each other and trigger bloodshed just to preserve power. The Serbian Orthodox Church strongly condemns the falsifying of people's votes, the stifling of political and religious freedoms, and especially the beating up and murder of people on the streets.

The statement calls on the government to 'respect the results' of the local elections held on 17 November. 'This is the only way of restoring our people's faith in a peaceful and better future.' The statement accuses the regime ('Communist, Godless and Satanic') of 'bringing the country and the nation to complete collapse and making people beggars', and of 'betraying' the Serbs of the Krajina and Bosnia.

The stinging rebuke by the Orthodox bishops contrasted with a generally passive and even approving stance by the Church toward the Milosevic government in the past, and with the Church's failure to condemn the three-and-a-half-year war in Bosnia-Hercegovina ... The Church ... has given tacit support to the political aims of both the Krajina and the Bosnian Serbs.

(Michael Dobbs, *IHT*, 3 January 1997, p. 1)

In December 1996 'Patriarch Pavle refused to receive and bless a delegation of protesting Belgrade students' (Julian Borger, *Guardian*, 3 January 1997, p. 9).

On 23 December 1996 Patriarch Pavle sent a letter of support to demonstrating students (*EEN*, 1996, vol. 10, no. 25, p. 9).

3 January 1997: Serbia responds to OSCE in a letter signed by foreign minister Milan Milutinovic. The letter concedes that the opposition coalition won the election in three provincial towns and 'nine municipalities in Belgrade' (out of sixteen). The outcome in Nis remains 'unclear'. But it makes no mention of the ruling Belgrade city council (which is made up of members delegated from the sixteen municipal councils and elects the mayor). (There was an error in Felipe Gonzalez's report, in which reference is made to 'nine municipalities in Belgrade' instead of 'eight Belgrade municipalities plus the city assembly': *IHT*, 4 January 1997, p. 7.) (The Socialist Party is confirmed the winner in six of the disputed towns: *Guardian*, 4 January 1997, p. 13.)

The concessions are regarded as inadequate by OSCE and the domestic opposition.

4 January 1997: it is rumoured that the mayor of Belgrade has offered to resign. (He stayed on. But he later called on the government to respect the initial vote count: *IHT*, 14 January 1997, p. 2.)

5 January 1997: demonstrators clog the centre of Belgrade with a slow-motion parade of vehicles.

Dragoslav Avramovic publicly joins the demonstrators.

6 January 1997: demonstrators march to St Sava's Cathedral for midnight mass to celebrate the Orthodox Christmas Eve.

Yugoslav army chief of staff Momcilo Perisic meets student representatives. The army then issues a statement: 'General Perisic underlined the Yugoslav army's special interest in seeing that all current problems are overcome within the legal institutions of the system in a manner deployed in democratic countries.'

There is an explosion (possibly caused by a grenade) on the grounds of the party headquarters of the Yugoslav United Left (led by Mirjana Markovic) (*IHT*, 8 January 1997, p. 7).

7 January 1997: Serbia's supreme court recognizes the opposition's victory in the town of Lapovo (*IHT*, 8 January 1997, p. 7).

8 January 1997: the government acknowledges the opposition's victory in Nis.

9 January 1997: the supreme court announces that the opposition won in Vrsac (one of the six towns described on 3 January as having been won by the Socialist Party).

Riot police withdraw after a long standoff with students in Belgrade.

10 January 1997: fifty-two members of the Serbian Academy of Sciences and Art sign an open letter to Milosevic calling for recognition of the local elections results (*Guardian*, 11 January 1997, p. 14).

11 January 1997: representatives of government and students meet. The government issues a statement saying that the will of the citizens 'must be fully respected' (*IHT*, 13 January 1997, p. 1).

13 January 1997: the local electoral commission in Nis refuses to concede the opposition victory.

14 January 1997: the Belgrade electoral commission recognizes that Zajedno won sixty seats on the 110-seat Belgrade city council (twenty-three going to the socialist coalition, ten awaiting a final decision and the remainder going to other parties). The Nis electoral commission recognizes the opposition victory there.

15 January 1997: the mayor of Belgrade is dismissed.

16 January 1997: OSCE again urges acceptance of all the local election results.

A car bomb seriously injures the (ethnic Serb) dean of the University of Pristina (Kosovo). The major of Pristina (of the Serbian Socialist Party) blames 'Albanian terrorists' who 'receive support in Belgrade from those who have been trying to destabilize Serbia for months'. (Zajedno leaders condemned the bombing and denied any involvement. They said the Serbian government wanted to divert attention from the demonstrations in Serbia and find an excuse to impose emergency measures. The media in Albania have reported that the radical Liberation Army of Kosovo had claimed responsibility for the bombing: *IHT*, 21 January 1997, p. 4.)

17 January 1997: a court rejects the Socialist Party's appeal against the Nis electoral commission's pronouncement.

20 January 1997: the Belgrade municipal court, as a result of appeals from the Socialist Party and the Serbian Radical Party, issues a statement: 'The decision of the [Belgrade] electoral commission [on 14 January] is suspended until the Supreme Court decides [which court should rule on the matter].'

The supreme court rules in favour of the Socialist Party in Sabac.

Patriarch Pavle addresses demonstrators in Belgrade: 'Your sentiment of truth and justice and respect for the freely expressed will of the people is shown in peaceful ways worthy of you and your ancestors.'

21 January 1997: the supreme court rules in favour of the Socialist Party in Smederevska Palanka.

Taxi drivers join demonstrators in Belgrade.

Some demonstrators are injured when riot police use batons.

23 January 1997: attention turns to Kragujevac, where the opposition victory has not been disputed. Police occupy the local radio and television station to prevent new management taking over. Riot police use force to unblock the main road to Belgrade.

24 January 1997: agreement is reached, with Radio Kragujevac broadcasting only commercial and entertainment programmes until a court makes a final decision (probably in February). The television station will stay off the air until then.

27 January 1997: the First Municipal Court overrules the 14 January judgement of the Belgrade electoral commission regarding Belgrade city council.

Zajedno formally takes control in Nis.

Patriarch Pavle leads a large religious ceremony through Belgrade in celebration of St Sava (the thirteenth-century founder of the Serbian Orthodox Church).

30 January 1997: Zoran Lilic, president of the Federal Republic of Yugoslavia: 'The results of the elections should be recognized ... everywhere the opposition won by the will of the people' (*Independent*, 1 February 1997, p. 15).

Former Yugoslav president Borisav Jovic thinks that the opposition victories in the local elections should be recognized (*Guardian*, 31 January 1997, p. 14).

2 February 1997: there are clashes between riot police and demonstrators.

3 February 1997: there are further clashes.

Patriarch Pavle appeals to the police 'to protect law and order and not those in power, who are sinking deeper and deeper, not knowing what they are doing' (*IHT*, 4 February 1997, p. 5).

4 February 1997: Milosevic writes to prime minister Mirko Marjanovic:

> In keeping with its constitutional competence, I propose that the Serbian government submit to parliament a draft emergency law which will proclaim as final, results of a part of local elections in Serbia in keeping with the findings of the OSCE mission. I wish to stress that the state interest of improving relations of our country with the OSCE and the international community far exceeds the importance of any number of council seats in a handful of towns. I believe that the election disputes ... especially in Belgrade ... have inflicted great damage on our country at the internal and international level and that this is the final moment for the problem to be resolved in the highest institutions of our republic, the government and the national assembly.

Opposition leaders vow to continue demonstrating until control of local councils is actually achieved, until state control of national television and radio is ended, and until those responsible for the police attacks and for falsifying the election results are punished.

The independent BK television station claims that the state-controlled network is to end the contract under which it provides transmitters (because of alleged non-payment of broadcasting fees).

The mandate of Belgrade city council expires.

6 February 1997: the three leaders of Zajedno, invited to talks in France with the French prime minister, say that they will end the demonstrations and begin discussions on wider issues once parliament passes the emergency law.

11 February 1997: the emergency law is passed by parliament. The parliamentary session is boycotted by Zajedno, whose leaders state that demonstrations will continue until the local councils are actually handed over.

'The Socialists reshuffled the government, creating a ministry to take powers away from local councils. A new hardline minister for information ... was also appointed' (*The Times*, 12 February 1997, p. 14).

12 February 1997: student leaders vow to continue demonstrations until other conditions are met, such as the dismissal of the rector of Belgrade University.

15 February 1997: Zajedno leaders call for a halt to demonstrations, but threaten to resume them if state controls on the media are not relaxed by 9 March 1997.

21 February 1997: Zoran Djindjic is elected mayor of Belgrade.

26 February 1997: the Zajedno leaders visit the UK.

7 March 1997: the rector of Belgrade University offers his resignation to the university council. Students end their demonstrations.

9 March 1997: Zajedno organizes a rally in Belgrade to commemorate the pro-democracy riots of six years ago. The rally is also in support of media freedom.

7–9 April 1997: the Carnegie Foundation in New York hosts talks on Kosovo attended by Serbian opposition leaders and several senior Kosovo representatives (*EEN*, 1997, vol. 11, no. 7, p. 5).

11 April 1997: a gunman kills Radovan Stojicic in a restaurant. (Stojicic was deputy interior minister and head of Milosevic's security apparatus.)

23 June 1997: the executive committee of Montenegro's Democratic Party of Socialists endorses Milosevic's candidacy for the Yugoslav presidency, but rejects proposals for constitutional change to allow for the direct election of the Yugoslav president (*EEN*, 1997, vol. 11, no. 13, p. 7).

> The ruling Democratic Party of Socialists in Montenegro, which is now dominated by the strongly anti-Milosevic premier Milo Djukanovic, will clearly not agree to any changes in the existing Yugoslav constitution. So Milosevic's power will have to rely on his *de facto* status as Serbia's leading, most powerful politician. In Serbia his writ still runs more or less unchallenged, especially since the opposition alliance Zajedno has now formally collapsed largely thanks to the ambition and erratic nature of the Serbian Renewal Movement leader Vuk Draskovic and his wife Danica ... The 100,000-strong police force is effectively his [Milosevic's] own praetorian guard ... The transformation of Serbia from being a regional power to a tawdry tin-pot dictatorship with little future for at least a generation is one of the most remarkable aspects of recent Balkan history. The fact that Milosevic, as the architect of Serbia's downfall, survives at all is a reflection of the degradation of the state as well as the unfortunate lack of a credible opposition ... Milosevic has engineered the virtual collapse of the armed forces so that he cannot physically be challenged or subjected to a military coup.

(pp. 1–2)

15 July 1997: Milosevic is elected president of the Federal Republic of

Yugoslavia for (one only) four-year term. He ran unopposed, the lower house of the federal parliament voting eighty-eight for and ten against and the upper house voting twenty-nine for and two against.

23 July 1997: Milosevic is sworn in as federal president and steps down as Serbian president. (Milosevic has recently closed down six independent radio stations and two television channels: *FT*, 24 July 1997, p. 2.)

20–1 September 1997: parliamentary and presidential elections take place.

The elections were boycotted by the Democratic Party of Serbia (led by Zoran Djindjic) and the Civic Alliance of Serbia (led by Vesna Pesic).

There are 250 seats in parliament. The three-party ruling coalition, including the Yugoslav United Left led by Mira Markovic (Milosevic's wife) won 110 seats, thus losing its majority in parliament. The neo-fascist Radical Party, led by Vojislav Seselj and advocating a 'Greater Serbia', saw a big increase in their seats to eighty-two. The Serbian Renewal Party, led by Vuk Draskovic, won forty-five seats. Five smaller parties won thirteen seats.

OSCE observers talked of a 'climate of mistrust' and of their 'serious concerns'. The 'process leading to the election was flawed', although 'technical' polling on election day was lawful in most places. There were cases where ballot papers were not numbered and there was bias in the media. In its formal report OSCE concluded that the elections were 'fundamentally flawed', with widespread potential for vote-rigging and bias in the state media in favour of the governing Socialists. The Socialists failed to allow other parties full access to the vote count. There were also several irregularities in Kosovo (*IHT*, 10 December 1997, p. 7).

The turnout was 57.5 per cent. The presidential election had to go to a second round (on 5 October 1997). Zoran Lilic, the former president of the Federal Republic of Yugoslavia and a protégé of Milosevic, won 35.7 per cent of the vote. Vojislav Seselj (leader of the Radical Party) won 27.28 per cent of the vote, while Vuk Draskovic (leader of the Serbian Renewal Movement) won 20.64 per cent.

30 September 1997: in a vote inspired by Vuk Draskovic's Serbian Renewal Movement, Zoran Djindjic is voted out of office as mayor of Belgrade by the city assembly. (A number of demonstrations followed but these were easily controlled by the riot police.)

> The Serbian Renewal Movement, now in unholy alliance with the Socialists in Belgrade, sold city-owned flats dirt-cheap to its loyalists and showed its reverence for media freedom by sacking the staff of Studio B, a television station owned by the government of Belgrade … Belgrade has no mayor.
>
> (*The Economist*, Survey, 24 January 1998, p. 14)

5 October 1997: the turnout for the second round of the presidential election is only 48.97 per cent and thus below the minimum 50 per cent necessary for the vote to stand. Seselj wins 49.1 per cent of the vote and Lilic 47.9 per cent.

24 October 1997: Zoran Todorovic is assassinated. '[He was] the third and

highest-ranking member of Mr Milosevic's circle to be shot fatally this year ...
Opposition politicians were quick to seize on the killing as a sign of the links
between political power and crime in Yugoslavia.' Todorovic was director of
Beopetrol (which has a virtual monopoly on oil imports) and secretary-general of
Mira Markovic's Yugoslav United Left (*IHT*, 25 October 1997, p. 2).

7 December 1997: the third round of the presidential election takes place.
Although the turnout is 51 per cent, the pro-Milosevic candidate Milan
Milutinovic (who is foreign minister of the Federal Republic of Yugoslavia) does
not win a large enough percentage of the vote (41.5 per cent to Seselj's 33 per
cent) for the vote to stand.

('If Mr Seselj loses on 21 December 1997, Mr Milosevic can consolidate. He
has already put Dragan Tomic, a loyal apparatchik, back as speaker of Serbia's
parliament, which makes him acting president': *The Economist*, 13 December
1997, p. 48.)

21 December 1997: the fourth round of the presidential election produces a
result, with Milutinovic winning 59 per cent of the vote to Seselj's 37.5 per cent.
The turnout is 50.53 per cent. The Radical Party claims widespread fraud and a
turnout below the minimum necessary 50 per cent.

OSCE describes the elections as 'fundamentally flawed', especially in Kosovo
where the elections were boycotted by the ethnic Albanians (*FT*, 22 December
1997, p. 2; *IHT*, 23 December 1997, p. 10).

'The authorities organized massive electoral fraud in Kosovo. Although the
Albanians were clearly observing their usual boycott, a phantom army of
Albanian voters had, according to official figures, turned out to vote for the pres-
idential candidate supported by Milosevic' (Thomas 1998: 118).

22 December 1997: Serbian Renewal Movement–Together is constituted as a
new party under the chairmanship of Velimir Ilijc. The main opposition leaders
apart from Vuk Draskovic attend the inaugural ceremony (*EEN*, 1998, vol. 11,
no. 25, p. 8).

23 February 1998: in recognition of Milosevic's positive attitude towards the
new government in the Republika Srpska, the USA announces that it is willing
to allow the Federal Republic of Yugoslavia to take part in the Southern Europe
Co-operation Initiative (a regional trading group proposed by the USA), to
increase its diplomatic representation at the UN and to open a consulate in New
York. In addition, JAT (the Yugoslav airline) will be able to obtain landing rights
for charter flights in New York (*FT*, 24 February 1998, p. 2). (On 5 March 1998
the USA withdrew the concessions because of the Kosovo crisis.)

(The US special envoy to the Balkans, Robert Gelbard, describes the Kosovo
Liberation Army, as 'without question, a terrorist group': *IHT*, 11 March 1998,
p. 6.)

5 March 1998: the USA withdraws the 23 March concessions granted to the
Federal Republic of Yugoslavia.

24 March 1998: in Serbia the Radical Party joins the Socialist Party and the
Yugoslav United Left in a coalition government. Vojislav Seselj becomes one of
five deputy prime ministers. The coalition has 187 of the 250 deputies.

The KLA has been active in the Kosovo region since April 1996. Last November [1997] its fighters repelled a foray into the area by Serbian police and effectively established a 'liberated zone' in the Drenica region. The move against the Albanian insurgents coincided with delicate negotiations over the formation of a new Serbian government ... During January and February [1998] lengthy talks took place over a new government between Milosevic's Socialists and the Serbian Renewal Movement headed by the former opposition leader Vuk Draskovic. It became increasingly clear, however, that Milosevic was unwilling to share power with the erratic and unpredictable Vuk Draskovic. When the fighting began, Belgrade-based analysts speculated that it had been launched to 'create a psychology and illusion of acute threat'. This atmosphere of crisis allowed Milosevic to create a new alliance with his former adversary Vojislav Seselj.

(Thomas 1998: 118)

9 April 1998: Yugoslav deputy prime minister Danko Djunic resigns, citing a lack of progress in reforming the economy. He headed the Yugoslav team in talks with the London Club of commercial creditors (*FT*, 11 April 1998, p. 2). (A report in June 1997 stated that the reformist Djunic had recently been appointed deputy prime minister in overall charge of economic reform: *FT*, 23 June 1997, p. 2.)

Kosovo: the background to war

It is unfortunate for the Albanian majority that Serbs claim Kosovo to be the 'cradle' and spiritual centre of Serbian Orthodox civilization before the Turkish conquest. The Ottomans defeated the Serbs at the Battle of Kosovo Polje in 1389. (The word *Mehotia*, which Serbs use in the term 'Kosovo-Mehotia', means 'land of monasteries'.)

Kosovo was the poorest area in the former Yugoslavia. In 1981 Kosovo had an unemployment rate of 27.3 per cent (compared with a national average of 12.6 per cent) and an index of social product per head of 26.8 (Yugoslav average = 100) (McFarlane 1988: 60). Before the war Kosovo's population was around the 2 million mark and, owing to rapid population growth and a net outflow of Serbs, over 90 per cent Albanian. There was Albanian agitation for autonomy in the late 1960s and for republican status after the death of Tito in May 1980. In March 1989 Kosovo's autonomy was reduced, in March 1990 Serbia took control of the police, and on 5 July 1990 Serbia dissolved Kosovo's government and parliament (in response to an earlier statement of Albanian deputies, which declared 'an independent and equal union within the Yugoslav federation with the same contractual status as the other republics'). On 28 September 1990 Serbia promulgated a new republican constitution, which annulled the status of both Kosovo and Vojvodina under the 1974 federal constitution (which was not itself altered).

Compared with the wars in Bosnia and Croatia, Kosovo escaped relatively unscathed for a long time. 'Some 150 have died in ethnic violence' (*FT*, 3 September 1996, p. 2). But the situation deteriorated over time. On 25 December 1992 former US president George Bush wrote to Milosevic and the chief of staff of the Yugoslav army in these terms: 'In the event of conflict in Kosovo caused by Serbian action, the United States will be prepared to employ military force against the Serbs in Kosovo and in Serbia proper.' On 24 November 1993 the International Helsinki Federation for Human Rights (IHF) published a worrying report entitled *From Autonomy to Colonization: Human Rights Violations in Kosovo 1989–1993*.

> The methods of harassment range from verbal insults and meaningless identity checks in the street to arbitrary detention and torture or ill-treatment – not infrequently with fatal consequences, including death – and summary shootings of demonstrators or killing of unarmed individuals ... The region has been placed under virtual colonial control which has resulted in a total marginalization of the Albanian majority in Kosovo. The entire province has been gradually Serbianized ... The IHF is deeply concerned that the Serbian oppressive policies carried out in Kosovo aim at a permanent change in the demographic structure of the region.
>
> (*FT*, 3 September 1996, p. 2)

The Serbian parliament adopted legislation providing cash incentives for Serbs to settle in Kosovo, while restrictions were imposed on freedom of movement for ethnic Albanians, on the use of the Albanian language and on the holding of property.

The Dayton accords of 1995 essentially ignored Kosovo.

'Serbs are prohibited from selling land to Albanians ... The education agreement is in abeyance in part because the Serbs have understandable misgivings about blessing schools that issue diplomas stamped "Republic of Kosovo" ' (*The Economist*, Survey, 24 January 1998, pp. 14–15). 'Though prohibited by law from buying property from Serbs, the Albanians manage to buy up land and houses at high prices from a dwindling Serb community that sees no future in the impoverished province' (Guy Dinmore, *FT*, Survey, 27 January 1998, p. 15).

> The minority Serbian population there [in Kosovo], radicalized by tense relations with the Albanian majority, invariably voted for supporters of Milosevic or other ultra-nationalist candidates. With little backing for more moderate Serbian opposition parties and the Albanians boycotting the polls, Kosovo regularly elected to parliament a solid bloc of pro-Milosevic candidates. Knowing that Kosovo provided an unfailing core of loyal parliamentary supporters, Milosevic felt little incentive to engage in serious dialogue with the Albanian political leadership on territorial compromise, short of independence.
>
> (Thomas 1998: 118)

Although Milosevic hopes to gain public support for his government from renewed nationalist strife in Kosovo, this is doubtful strategy. The demonstrations in Pristina on 19 March [1998] showed that Kosovo Serbs could still be brought out onto the streets to support the government. In northern and central Serbia, however, the attitudes of the population are characterized by political apathy and social and economic exhaustion ... While most Serbs would maintain that Kosovo should remain part of the Serbian state there is little enthusiasm for renewed warfare.

(p. 120)

Owing to discrimination and sackings the ethnic Albanians of Kosovo ran a 'second economy', i.e. they set up their own structures, such as education establishments and a health service.

On 24 May 1992 the Albanians managed to run their own unofficial presidential and parliamentary elections, with Ibrahim Rugova becoming president and the Democratic League of Kosovo being the successful party. Rugova, the leader of the Democratic League of Kosovo, proposed a UN protectorate. (The then president of Albania, Sali Berisha, refrained from stirring the nationalist pot, but nevertheless expressed the opinion that Kosovo should be under UN control and declared a neutral zone.) Although a consistent believer in non-violence, Rugova's advocacy has changed from greater autonomy to outright independence.

He [Ibrahim Rugova] insists on Gandhiesque peaceful means ... But on the central goal he is quite unyielding: self-determination for his people, statehood for the republic [of Kosovo] which he claims already exists. His main rival, Adem Demaci ... might be prepared to settle for slightly less than Rugova: a republic within a very loose confederation with Serbia and Montenegro. But he wants more dramatic protest actions to achieve it. He has called on his followers to imitate the student and opposition demonstrators in Belgrade. That is the Kosovar Albanian mainstream. But in the past year there have also been a number of terrorist attacks, with responsibility claimed by a Kosovo Liberation Army. Are these the work of impatient young radicals ... or are they actually secretly encouraged by ... Milosevic [who] might in desperation play the Kosovo card, provoking a terrorist assault or armed rising, which he could then heroically suppress?

(Timothy Garton Ash, *The Times*, 19 March 1997, p. 18)

Adem Demaci believes that the Federal Republic of Yugoslavia should comprise three republics, namely Serbia, Montenegro and Kosovo (*The Economist*, 29 March 1997, p. 54).

His compromise solution is a confederation of three equal entities – Serbia, Montenegro and Kosovo. That would first mean Serbia restoring the autonomy and self-rule that were taken away by ... Milosevic in 1989 ...

Ibrahim Rugova … is a passionate believer in Gandhi-style non-violence … Rugova's objective, Kosovo's independence, has remained elusive … Unlike Mr Rugova, Mr Demaci has endorsed these attacks [by the Kosovo Liberation Army] as justified … No advocate of violence himself, he has denounced Rugova's passivity and inflexible ethnic nationalism.

(Dusko Doder, *IHT*, 26 March 1998, p. 8)

Ibrahim Rugova (11 March 1998):

I insist that the best, the optimal and most viable solution and the best for the region and the neighbouring countries – Albania, Serbia, Macedonia and the rest – would be an independent Kosovo with all guarantees for the local Serb population and Serb interests in Kosovo.

(*Guardian*, 12 March 1998, p. 14)

Details were released on 20 September 1998 of an interim solution to the status of Kosovo proposed by Rugova's negotiating team. Kosovo was envisaged as 'temporarily part of Yugoslavia, as an independent entity equal to the other two republics [Serbia and Montenegro] in the federation'. Kosovo would have its own parliament, government and courts as well as its own police and an independent central bank, but would share the market and a common economy with the rest of Yugoslavia. Control of Kosovo's borders could remain in the hands of the Yugoslav army and federal customs authorities. If negotiations failed to come up with a lasting solution to Kosovo's status during a three-year interim period, Kosovo's residents would vote on the proposals in a referendum. The United States had recently released details of a proposal for a three-year interim solution restoring the autonomy enjoyed by Kosovo until 1989 (*IHT*, 21 September 1998, p. 6).

The Kosovo Liberation Army (KLA) argued that aeons of non-violence had not worked.

The armed movement [Kosovo Liberation Army] was organized six years ago to fight for independence and closer affiliation with Albania, the guerrillas said … The rebel group carried out its first attack in 1993, but it was not until the middle of last year [1997] that it began to mount regular and sustained assaults. In the last few months the rebels have overrun more than a dozen police stations, carrying away scores of automatic weapons. They have attacked many police patrols and checkpoints and claim responsibility for the assassination of more than fifty Serbian policemen and officials, as well as of ethnic Albanians suspected of collaborating with the Serbian authorities … Ibrahim Rugova, while calling for an independent state, has condemned the use of force.

(Chris Hedges, *IHT*, 3 March 1998, p. 5)

The Kosovo Liberation Army (KLA) appeared in April 1996 and started to act publicly in 1997 (*Guardian*, 16 March 1998, p. 10). 'The KLA has been active in the Kosovo region since April 1996. Last November [1997] its fighters repelled a foray into the area by Serbian police and effectively established a "liberated zone" in the Drenica region' (Thomas 1998: 118).

'Ethnic Albanian rebels overran eleven Serbian police stations in September 1997, armed with weapons from Albania and 'ready to wage a secessionist war' (Chris Hedges, *IHT*, 20 October 1997, p. 5). Four Serbian police officers and five civilian officials were killed recently. More than thirty people, Albanians and Serbs, have been killed in rebel attacks.

> For the first time since the attacks began nearly eighteen months ago, the rebels have pushed back the Serbian authorities far enough to carve out remote mountain sanctuaries, which they use as bases for their attacks … The rise of the guerrilla movement appears to mark a dangerous crumbling of support in Kosovo for the non-violent civil disobedience campaign led by Ibrahim Rugova.
>
> (Chris Hedges, *IHT*, 20 October 1997, p. 5)

The ambushing of Serb police patrols in Kosovo on 27–8 February 1998 left four policemen dead. On 28 February 1999 up to 3,000 ethnic Albanians commemorated the anniversary of what they regard as the start of the war in Kosovo, when Serb forces attacked a car containing KLA members.

> The situation in the province has steadily deteriorated. Until recently the Albanians of Kosovo followed the advice of their self-proclaimed president, Ibrahim Rugova, and restricted themselves to peaceful protests. But the last eighteen months have witnessed the emergence of the Kosovo Liberation Army, a shady group that has claimed responsibility for dozens of attacks on Serbian police officers and civilians. It has also killed Albanians accused of collaborating with the Serbs … Rugova, a moderate, is fast losing support among his people.
>
> (Misha Glenny, *IHT*, 10 December 1997, p. 8)

On 23 February 1998 the US special envoy to the Balkans, Robert Gelbard, described the Kosovo Liberation Army, as 'without question, a terrorist group' (*IHT*, 11 March 1998, p. 6).

'The ethnic Albanian Kosovo Liberation Army, which began as a ragtag, peasant resistance movement, has after eight months of fighting, become a high-tech, mobile guerrilla force, and come next spring [1999] it expects renewed fighting.' Adem Demaci is the KLA's general political representative (*IHT*, 2 January 1999, p. 2).

'Only a year ago the rebels [the KLA] numbered no more than 2,000, but they are now estimated to have as many as 17,000 fighters' (*IHT*, 7 June 1999, p. 7).

'The rebel group [is] said to include 10,000 hardened fighters and 30,000 irregulars who joined after being driven from their homes this spring' (*IHT*, 22 June 1999, p. 1).

On 13 August 1998 the KLA named for the first time its own political representative. Adem Demaci was head of the Parliamentary Party of Kosovo, had spent twenty-seven years as a political prisoner and is believed to have close ties with militants based in Switzerland (*FT*, 17 August 1998, p. 3). Demaci resigned as chairman of the Parliamentary Party of Kosovo (*EEN*, 1998, vol. 12, no. 10, p. 8).

On 21 February 1999 Suleiman Selimi was appointed KLA overall commander.

'There are 6,000 to 10,000 Albanian partisans inside Kosovo, alliance officials estimate ... Nato says there are about 40,000 Yugoslav soldiers and interior ministry police officers in Kosovo' (*IHT*, 25 May 1999, p. 1). ('Hashim Thaci, the KLA's thirty-year-old political leader and prime minister of the provisional government agreed at the Paris peace talks in March [1999] ... said the KLA had around 20,000 armed soldiers inside Kosovo': *FT*, 27 May 1999, p. 2. 'In Washington US officials said the KLA was growing ... The KLA had grown from around 5,000 troops in March [1999] to nearly 17,000': *FT*, 29 May 1999, p. 3.)

'The rebel group [is] said to include 10,000 hardened fighters and 30,000 irregulars who joined after being driven from their homes this spring' (*IHT*, 22 June 1999, p. 1).

The Liberation Army of Presevo, Medvedja and Bujanovic (UCPMB)

The goal there [Kosovo's eastern border with the rest of Serbia] is to prevent armed Albanians, some of them in uniform, from attacking targets inside Serbia, especially in the five-kilometre-wide (three-mile-wide) demilitarized zone, where Serbian troops are not allowed to enter, although the police are ... Such armed groups [are] offshoots of the supposedly dismantled KLA ... US troops have now built watchtowers along the border with Serbia, near the towns of Bujanovic, Presevo and Medvedja, which have majority Albanian populations and which more radical Albanians refer to as 'eastern Kosovo'. Armed Albanians wearing uniforms with shoulder patches like those of the KLA, but representing an organization dubbed the Liberation Army of Presevo, Medvedja and Bujanovic [UCPMB], have been seen in the demilitarized zone. In response, the government of Yugoslavia put four more militarized police units into the area. The entry is also known as an entry point for drug smuggling.

(*IHT*, 29 February 2000, p. 5)

The Liberation Army of Presevo, Medvedja and Bujanovic ... [is named after these] towns inside Serbia that have majority ethnic Albanian populations ... [The UCPMB call the area] 'Eastern Kosovo', where at least 70,000 Albanians live in the arc from Medvedja in the north to Presevo in the south ... The Albanian fighters say their group came into being on 26 January [2000] when two local farmers [brothers] ... were killed by the Serbian police.

(*IHT*, 3 March 2000, p. 4)

More than 500 well-armed ethnic Albanians are active in the rugged hills of the no-man's-land around Presevo, and their numbers are growing thanks to a well-financed recruiting campaign throughout Kosovo, US military officials said. The guerrillas include elements of the now-disbanded KLA.

(*IHT*, 16 March 2000, p. 4)

'Yugoslavia's southern border districts are 80 per cent Albanian' (*Telegraph*, 3 March 2000, p. 18).

US peacekeeping troops in Kosovo were holding nine men in detention Thursday [16 March] after raiding border villages and strongholds of ethnic Albanians thought to be involved in a cross-border insurgency against Serbian police officers. Troops discovered twenty-two crates of ammunition and weapons, as well as uniforms and equipment for a number of guerrillas in several different sites along the 28-kilometre (17-mile) border. Helicopters and hundreds of infantry soldiers took part in simultaneous dawn raids Wednesday [15 March] ... The operation came after secretary of state Madeleine Albright, her spokesman, James Rubin, and Nato's supreme commander, General Wesley Clark, all warned Albanians not to start an insurgency beyond Kosovo's border in southern Serbia, where some 70,000 Albanians live ... The UN secretary-general, Kofi Annan ... speaking after US peacekeepers raided command posts of ethnic Albanian militias, said at a news conference: 'It is clear that it is the Albanians who are now the cause of these provocations.'

(*IHT*, 17 March 2000, pp. 1, 4)

'On Wednesday US soldiers raided villages in south-eastern Kosovo, seizing weapons and ammunition evidently being used by Albanian fighters to strike at Serbs across the border' (*IHT*, 18 March 2000, p. 4). ('[But] elements within the organization – the Liberation Army of Presevo, Medvedja and Bujanovic, which is composed largely of former KLA members – seem determined to continue their challenge to Serbian forces in the Presevo Valley ... These militiamen have continued to wear uniforms and conduct training exercises with AK-47 assault rifles in and around the village of Dubrosin, which lies in the neutral zone between US forces in Kosovo and Yugoslav forces in Serbia proper. In addition, some members of the militia group have continued to cross back and forth between the US-patrolled area of the area of Kosovo and the neutral zone, where they undergo training ... It now appears that the organization is internally divided. The leaders who met with US officials and Hashim Thaci ... have been unable thus far to make good on their promises': *IHT*, 29 March 2000, p. 5.)

'The guerrillas ... [demand] the region's reunification with Kosovo, from which it was separated only in the 1950s' (William Pfaff, *IHT*, 17 March 2001, p. 10).

> The south-east borders of Kosovo were changed by Tito ... in order to remove the Presevo Valley from Kosovo ... After World War II the fledgling 'Macedonian' state to the south needed a secure road link with Serbia that did not run through Moslem Albanian areas in Kosovo known for their nationalist feeling.
>
> (James Pettifer, *The World Today*, 2001, vol. 57, no. 7, p. 18)

Refugees after the start of the bombing campaign

The start of the Nato bombing campaign on 24 March 1999 was accompanied by a sharp increase in 'ethnic cleansing' and in the number of ethnic Albanian refugees.

> During Monday's session [19 July 1999] Nato diplomats scrutinized other weaknesses in alliance strategy, including a failure to anticipate that Nato bombing would provoke Yugoslav and Serbian forces to escalate the brutal expulsion of ethnic Albanians and thus heighten a humanitarian catastrophe that the alliance was seeking to prevent. Nato officials said they were caught offguard by the extent of the Belgrade government expulsion campaign, even though 'Operation Horseshoe' – as the Yugoslav army called it – was known to have been conceived by Mr Milosevic and his advisers in October [1998].
>
> (William Drozdiak, *IHT*, 21 July 1999, pp. 1, 4)

> Mr Milosevic and his government are attempting to solve their Kosovo problem by producing a basic demographic change in the province through deporting its Albanian population, the overwhelming majority. According to German government sources, this programme for purging Kosovo of its Albanian population was prepared at the end of last year [1998] under the codename 'Horseshoe'. Its initial purpose was to defeat or neutralize the KLA, in rebellion against Serbia. In terms of Serbia's internationally recognized, if abusive, sovereignty over Kosovo, this was a legitimate objective. The government's experience in operations against the KLA during the fall of 1998, which displaced 300,000 people, proved unsatisfactory, since the displaced Kosovars eventually returned home and the KLA's resistance to the Serbs resumed. Horseshoe was designed to produce a permanent solution, and was launched even before the Rambouillet discussions in February [1999], which the Serbian leadership did not take seriously.
>
> (William Pfaff, *IHT*, 15 April 1999, p. 6)

The bombings were indeed the trigger for most of the ethnic cleansing. The campaign had already begun, directed at Albanian villages thought friendly to the KLA. A plan, 'Operation Horseshoe', had been prepared in Belgrade for the full-scale expulsion and murder of Kosovo Albanians, and it was ordered into action during the hours following the start of the bombings. But ethnic cleansing was clearly a result, as well as the cause, of the Nato bombing campaign.

(William Pfaff, *IHT*, 8 July 1999, p. 8)

In early 1999 there were clear signs of preparation for an intensification of this campaign: a build-up of Serb forces, the introduction of paramilitaries to the region and a new integration of police and military units, designed specifically for operations against the civilian population. The new wave of expulsions which started after 24 March [1999] was well organized and systematic. What happened after the bombing began, therefore, was probably a speeded-up version of what would have happened anyway. Of course, the 'what if' questions of history can never be answered with certainty; but one thing here is quite clear: if Nato had not intervened and if hundreds of thousands of Albanians had been driven out of Kosovo in the spring and summer of 1999, those refugees would still be in exile today.

(Noel Malcolm, *Telegraph*, 24 March 2000, p. 28)

Events prior to Nato's bombing campaign

Early demonstrations included one forcibly dispersed in Pristina over education on 13 October 1992, but the Albanians feared massive reprisals if such demonstrations became widespread.

On 17 July 1995 sixty-nine ethnic Albanian former policemen were sentenced to prison terms ranging from one to eight years for allegedly forming an illegal police force (bringing the total convicted to eighty-five).

On 2 September 1996 agreement was reached to end the ethnic Albanian boycott of schools, which had begun in 1990. Ethnic Albanian students would move from the parallel (underground) system operating from private houses to educational establishments in Kosovo. On 7–9 April 1997 the Carnegie Foundation hosted talks in New York on Kosovo attended by Serbian opposition leaders and several senior Kosovo representatives (*EEN*, 1997, vol. 11, no. 7, p. 5).

On 16 January 1997 a car bomb seriously injured the (ethnic Serb) dean of the University of Pristina (Kosovo). The mayor of Pristina (of the Serbian Socialist Party) blamed 'Albanian terrorists' who 'receive support in Belgrade from those who have been trying to destabilize Serbia for months'. (Zajedno leaders in Serbia condemned the bombing and denied any involvement. They said the Serbian government wanted to divert attention from the demonstrations in Serbia and find an excuse to impose emergency measures. The media in Albania have reported that the radical Liberation Army of Kosovo had claimed responsibility for the bombing: *IHT*, 21 January 1997, p. 4.)

On 1 October 1997 riot police broke up a peaceful protest in Pristina by Albanian students demanding Albanian-language education in state educational institutions. The events were repeated on 30 December 1997 and 4 January 1998 in Pristina and elsewhere.

Rugova had banned street demonstrations, but the 1 October demonstration was 'the first public defiance of his authority'. The roughly 3,000 students of the underground Albanian university, formed in 1989, were 'demanding that Pristina University be returned to ethnic Albanian control'. 'The university is now run by Serbs who refuse to hold classes in Albanian, and all its 18,000 students are Serbs' (Chris Hedges, *IHT*, 20 October 1997, p. 5).

The ambushing of Serb police patrols in Kosovo on 27–8 February 1998 left four policemen dead. There was a subsequent Serb offensive in Kosovo, primarily in the Drenica area and the village of Prekaz in particular. (Among the fatalities during the 5–6 March offensive was Adem Jashari, who, according to the Serbian government, was the leader of the KLA.) There were varying estimates of the total number killed. As of 10 March 1998 the Serbian government's figures were six Serb policemen and forty-six ethnic Albanians dead. Unofficial estimates put the number of Albanians killed at least eighty, including women and children (*IHT*, 18 March 1998, p. 4, 23 March 1998, p. 5, and 24 March 1998, p. 1). 'In the indiscriminate killings by hundreds of heavily armed Serbian police and military units last month [March], more than half of the victims were women and children ... The Serbs, rather than hunt down armed groups, blasted villages into rubble' (Chris Hedges, *IHT*, 7 April 1998, p. 6).

On 2 March 1998 Serb riot police used violent methods to disperse a large-scale demonstration in Pristina.

The 'contact group' of countries (the USA, Russia, France, Germany, the United Kingdom and Italy) met in London on 9 March 1998 (and agreed to meet in Washington on 25 March). Although Russia was represented by its deputy foreign minister, foreign minister Yevgeni Primakov was contacted by telephone. The six countries agreed to ask the United Nations Security Council to impose a comprehensive arms embargo on the Federal Republic of Yugoslavia and also agreed to stop supplying equipment that could be used for internal suppression and terrorism. The five Western countries agreed to deny visas to those responsible for repression in Kosovo and to halt government-financed export credits for trade and investment (including funding for privatization, the proceeds of which are considered to be used to finance the Milosevic regime). (Russia said it would reconsider these points if the repression continued.) Yugoslav assets abroad would be frozen by the five countries after 25 March 1998 if the repression continued. The 'contact group' condemned the 'unacceptable use of force' by Serbia and the 'deplorable' actions of the Serbian police. It also condemned the 'terrorist actions' of the Kosovo Liberation Army (KLA) and agreed that Kosovo should be granted autonomy but not independence.

The six countries issued a statement which said that within ten days Milosevic should take 'rapid and effective steps to stop the violence and engage in a commitment to find a political solution to the issue of Kosovo through dialogue'. Special police units should be withdrawn from Kosovo. Access to Kosovo should be allowed to OSCE, the International Committee of the Red Cross, 'contact group' diplomats and the UN High Commissioner for Refugees. Milosevic should commit himself publicly 'to begin a process of dialogue'. The international war crimes tribunal in the Hague should consider extending its enquiries to Kosovo. There should be an international peacekeeping force in Macedonia after the mandate of the current force ends in August 1998 (*IHT*, 10 March 1998, pp. 1, 6; *Independent*, 10 March 1998, p. 9; *Guardian*, 10 March 1998, p. 2; *FT*, 10 March 1998, p. 1).

On 10 March the Serbian government offered an 'open dialogue' with 'responsible' Albanian representatives from Kosovo.

Ibrahim Rugova (11 March 1998):

> I insist that the best, the optimal and most viable solution and the best for the region and the neighbouring countries – Albania, Serbia, Macedonia and the rest – would be an independent Kosovo with all guarantees for the local Serb population and Serb interests in Kosovo.
>
> (*Guardian*, 12 March 1998, p. 14)

On 11 March Nato refused Albania's request for Nato troops to patrol its border with Yugoslavia. But Nato said it would help in other ways.

A Serbian delegation arrived in Pristina on 12 March 1998 offering 'the highest level of autonomy'. The Albanians did not respond, saying that they had been given no warning or invitation and that they wanted an outside mediator. Ibrahim Rugova: 'This offer is not at all serious. It was made just to ease outside pressure on Serbia.' ('Leaders of Serbia's ethnic Albanian majority have refused to meet Serb republic representatives because to do so would endorse their subordination to that republic. They have demanded to negotiate instead with the Yugoslav federation and with foreign mediators present': *FT*, editorial, 27 April 1998, p. 21.)

An Albanian demonstrator was shot dead in Pec on 18 March by Serbian police.

On 22 March 1998 Ibrahim Rugova, the only candidate, won the presidential election. There were also parliamentary elections (130 seats) in the self-proclaimed Kosovo Republic. Serbia deemed the elections illegal but did not interfere.

Ethnic Serbs demonstrated in Pristina on 23 March 1998 against an agreement on education. Ethnic Albanian students would be able to return to state educational institutions in phases by 30 June 1998. Serbs and Albanians would be taught in (respectively) morning and afternoon shifts in their own languages with different curricula. Albanians would have access to dormitories and dining rooms by the end of September 1998 (*FT*, 24 March 1998, p. 2; *The Times*, 24 March 1998, p. 14).

On 24 March the Serbian government claimed that one Serb policeman had been killed in an attack by the KLA and that four Albanians had been killed in retaliatory action.

On 25 March 1998 the 'contact group' agreed to extend the deadline for compliance of their demands (including the full withdrawal of special police units and unconditional dialogue with ethnic Albanians).

> We expect President Milosevic to implement the process of unconditional dialogue and take political responsibility for ensuring that Belgrade engages in serious negotiations on Kosovo's status. If Belgrade fails to meet the London benchmarks and if the dialogue does not get under way within the next four weeks we shall take steps to apply further measures.

US secretary of state Madeleine Albright: 'Mr Milosevic … must embrace dialogue publicly, enter it without preconditions, accept outside participation and take political responsibility for making it work.' The 'contact group' countries would try to reach agreement on the terms of an arms embargo by 31 March (*IHT*, 26 March 1998, pp. 1, 4; *FT*, 26 March 1998, p. 3; *Telegraph*, 26 March 1998, p. 19).

On 31 March 1998 the UN Security Council imposed an arms embargo on the Federal Republic of Yugoslavia. A resolution condemned the 'excessive force' used by Serbia and urged 'the authorities in Belgrade and the leadership of the Kosovar Albanian community to enter into a meaningful dialogue on political status issues'. The outcome of a dialogue should include 'an enhanced status for Kosovo which would include a substantially greater degree of autonomy and meaningful self-administration'.

Serbian president Milan Milutinovic flew to Pristina on 7 April and offered a dialogue with ethnic Albanians. The latter refused desiring foreign mediation and the removal of Serbian special police units from Kosovo.

The Yugoslav army (involved in the fighting) claimed on 23 April that twenty-three 'terrorists' had been killed in clashes while attempting to cross from Albania into Kosovo. The army also said: 'The international community should stop Albania in its activities in training, infiltrating and illegally arming the terrorists' (*IHT*, 25 April 1998, p. 1).

On 23 April 1998 a referendum was held in Serbia, posing the question: 'Do you accept foreign representatives taking part in resolving the problems of Kosovo and Metohija?' The turnout was 73.05 per cent and foreign representation was rejected by 94.73 per cent of those who voted.

On 29 April 1998 the 'contact group' agreed to freeze Yugoslav assets held abroad. But Russia dissented from a threat to block new foreign investments if Serbia did not sign up to a framework of talks on Kosovo by 9 May. (The ban on investment was implemented on 9 May. But on 18 May the 'contact group' declared that the ban on foreign investments 'will not be put into effect'.)

Milosevic and Rugova met in Belgrade on 15 May 1998 (persuaded by Richard Holbrooke). They agreed that their negotiating teams should meet in Pristina on 22 May.

Milosevic … has now essentially banned the voices he fears most, Yugoslavia's independent radio and television stations … The ban was disguised as a normal licensing decision … Of thirty-eight independent radio and television stations that broadcast news in the Yugoslav republics of Serbia and Montenegro, thirty-five were shut down. Only three were granted new licences. Those are two television stations and the radio station B-92, known internationally as the leader and organizer of the independent media. Those stations are now required to pay licensing fees of $12,000 to $15,000 a month, which will quickly put them out of business. All the other outlets granted frequencies either do not broadcast news or are pro-Milosevic. Mr Milosevic's wife, son and daughter now each own a broadcast station.

(Editorial, *New York Times*, in *IHT*, 25 May 1998, p. 8)

The federal government has denied frequencies to local independent radio and television stations that have irritated the authorities by rebroadcasting news bulletins of Belgrade's B-92 radio station. B-92 itself has been given a frequency but at an exorbitant fee that it cannot afford and says it will not pay (*FT*, 28 May 1998, p. 2).

A law was passed on 26 May 1998 which allowed the government to appoint directly the rector, deans and management board of Belgrade University. There were student demonstrations and the rector resigned in protest (*FT*, 28 May 1998, p. 2).

On 28 May 1998 Nato foreign ministers agreed various measures, including the following:

1   The issuing of a joint statement: 'The status quo is unacceptable. We support a political solution which provides an enhanced status for Kosovo, preserves the territorial integrity of Yugoslavia and safeguards human and civil rights of all inhabitants of Kosovo, whatever their ethnic origin.'
2   Military exercises in and training for Albania and Macedonia.
3   An increase in the size of the UN force in Macedonia from 800 to its original size of 1,050. A continued military presence will be necessary after the expiry of the UN mandate on 31 August 1998.
4   Nato should 'consider the political, legal and, as necessary, military implications of possible further deterrent measures'. Plans will be commissioned for possible preventative deployments on the borders with Kosovo.

On 4 June 1998 Rugova called off talks due the following day, blaming the Serb assault.

On 8 June the EU strongly condemned Serbia for 'a campaign of violence going far beyond what could legitimately be described as a targeted anti-terrorist operation'. The EU banned new investment in Serbia (Montenegro being excluded from the ban). (The main effect was on the $1 billion investment by Italian and Greek companies in Serbian telecommunications: *FT*, 9 June 1998, p. 2; *The Times*, 9 June 1998, p. 17.) The USA also imposed a ban.

Nato secretary-general Javier Solana (11 June 1998): 'President Milosevic has gone beyond the limits of tolerable behaviour ... We have to show that we are ready to back up international diplomacy with military means.' Nato foreign ministers announced that air exercises would be held in Albania and Macedonia 'as quickly as possible' and that plans had been drawn up to 'halt or disrupt' the violence in Kosovo.

On 12 June 1998 the foreign ministers of the 'contact group' (including Russia) condemned the 'massive and disproportionate use of force'. They made four demands of Milosevic: 'immediate action' to end the repressive action by Serb military forces against the civilian ethnic Albanian population in Kosovo and the withdrawal of 'security units used for civilian repression' (i.e. special police and the army); unimpeded access for international monitors and observers; measures to help refugees return home; and 'rapid progress' in talks with the Albanian leadership. If the demands were not met there would be 'moves to further measures to halt the violence and protect the civilian population, including those that could require the authorization of a United Nations Security Council resolution'. 'Kosovo Albanian extremists' were warned to refrain from violent acts.

The USA, the UK, Germany, France, Italy, Canada and Japan banned flights to their countries by Yugoslav air companies.

Action would be postponed until Milosevic met Yeltsin in Moscow on 15–16 June.

On 15 June 1998 Nato held air exercises in Albania and Macedonia along the border with Kosovo (Operation Determined Falcon). The EU banned flights by Yugoslav air companies to all EU countries. The opposition Democratic Party, Social Democracy, Democratic Alternative and Civic Alliance of Serbia agreed to form an alliance (*EEN*, 1998, vol. 12, no. 7, p. 8).

Holbrooke restarted his mediating role on 23 June 1998 when he met Milosevic. The following day he met members of the Kosovo Liberation Army (later complaining about the lack of a clear chain of command).

On 29 June the EU banned flights by Yugoslav carriers.

By the beginning of July 1998 the American position had changed as a result of the increasing strength of the Kosovo Liberation Army (as well as its human rights violations, including killings and kidnappings) and the military restraint shown by the Serbs. The USA began putting greater emphasis on its calls for restraint by the KLA. The USA also began calling for a ceasefire before the withdrawal of Serb forces.

The KLA has seized about a third of Kosovo in the last few months (*IHT*, 4 July 1998, p. 10). On 11 September 1998 a US official (who asked not to be identified) said that Nato had not taken any action because of US intelligence failures. In the second half of July 1998 intelligence officers thought that the KLA could achieve an independent Kosovo and thus spread separatism and Albanian nationalism. In addition, there was an underestimation of Serbian capabilities, especially the morale of regular army units in Kosovo (Joseph Fitchett, *IHT*, 15 September 1998, p. 10).

On 2 July 1998 the US announced the formation of a monitoring unit, comprising US, Russian, Austrian and Polish diplomats (*Independent*, 3 July 1998, p. 14).

Richard Holbrooke began a fresh series of talks in the region on 3 July 1998.

The diplomats (accredited in Yugoslavia and agreed in the 16 June 1998 talks between Milosevic and Yeltsin) began their patrols in Kosovo on 6 July 1998.

The 'contact group' met on 8 July 1998 and issued a statement:

> Although the primary responsibility for the situation in Kosovo rests with Belgrade, the 'contact group' acknowledges that armed Kosovo Albanian groups also have a responsibility to avoid violence and all armed activities. The 'contact group' reiterated that violence is inadmissible and will not solve the problem of Kosovo. Indeed, it will only make it more difficult to achieve a political solution. The 'contact group' also concluded that all concerned on the Kosovo Albanian side should commit themselves to dialogue and a peaceful settlement and reject violence and acts of terrorism. The 'contact group' insisted that those outside the Federal Republic of Yugoslavia who are supplying financial support, arms or training for armed Kosovo Albanian groups should cease doing so immediately. It is clear that the Kosovo Albanian team for all these talks must be fully representative of their community in order to speak authoritatively.

On 8 August 1998 the 'contact group' presented plans for a constitutional settlement that would give the People of Kosovo control of their own internal affairs, control over their own security and real autonomy (*Guardian*, 10 August 1998, p. 11).

The 'contact group' put forward the following proposals: Kosovo should be given broad autonomy as a 'special part' of Serbia or a 'constituent unit' of the Federal Republic of Yugoslavia; 'Kosovo would be obligated not to secede unilaterally and Belgrade would be obligated not to alter Kosovo's status unilaterally; Kosovo should have 'constitutionally protected significant legislative, executive and judicial powers, including control of local police'; Kosovo should have its own taxation, flag and emblems and 'international relations in particular areas'. The 'contact group' expressed 'its willingness to provide political, economic, technical and other support for the implementation of such an agreement' (*FT*, 13 August 1998, p. 2).

Serbian sources said Sunday (16 August 1998) that advancing units had taken control of Junik, the main rebel stronghold in south-western Kosovo. Junik, near the border with Albania, was known as the organizational, logistical and weapons distribution centre for the Kosovo Liberation Army.

> With its offensive, the government has regained control of major roads and pushed rebel fighters from many areas. The main ethnic Albanian political party says 159 villages and hamlets that were controlled by the rebels are now back under government authority, but most of the residents have fled.

Once civilians leave an area, the police often loot and then burn homes, farms and businesses ... Before the offensive, rebel forces controlled as much as 40 per cent of the province. Their support had swelled dramatically since a police drive in March ... Now government officials contend that the rebels have been beaten. But this is not conventional war, or even standard guerrilla warfare, because the Kosovo Liberation Army is not nearly as much an army as it is a movement.

(Mike O'Connor, *IHT*, 17 August 1998, p. 5)

A five-day Nato exercise in Albania began on 17 August, involving troops from eleven Nato countries, Russia, Albania and Lithuania (*IHT*, 18 August 1998, p. 5).

On 4 September 1998 US special envoy for Kosovo, Christopher Hill, charged that EU governments were indifferent to Kosovo while being absorbed in 'discussions over a united Europe', content to 'toast themselves' on forging a so-called 'united Europe' that conveniently left out the Balkans (*IHT*, 7 September 1998, p. 8; *The Times*, 7 September 1998, p. 11; *Guardian*, 7 September 1998, p. 12). (Two days later EU foreign ministers angrily rejected the claims made by Christopher Hill.)

Former US presidential candidate Bob Dole and US assistant secretary of state John Shattuck visited Kosovo on 5–6 September 1998. Dole: 'American and European leaders have pledged not to allow the crimes against humanity which we have witnessed in Bosnia to occur in Kosovo. But, from what I have seen this weekend, such crimes are happening' (*IHT*, 8 September 1998, p. 7).

President George Bush warned the Serbian leader, Slobodan Milosevic, that the United States was prepared to use military force against Serb-instigated attacks in Kosovo. When he took office President Clinton repeated this warning. Yet at this moment ... Serbia is engaged in major, systematic attacks on the people and territory of Kosovo ... The primary victims of Serbian attacks are civilians. Humanitarian workers are denied access and are often harassed and attacked ... This is a war against civilians, and we know who is responsible: Slobodan Milosevic ... The United States and its Nato allies must press for a ceasefire and withdrawal of Serbian police and military by a certain date. It must back this with an ultimatum to use major force immediately and effectively ... American officials have pledged not to allow the crimes against humanity that we witnessed in Bosnia to be repeated in Kosovo. From what I have seen, such crimes are already occurring.

(Bob Dole, *IHT*, 15 September 1998, p. 8)

On 6 September 1998 EU foreign ministers agreed to halt commercial flights by Yugoslav airlines. (At first the UK said that it could not enforce the ban for a year because of an agreement reached in 1959. But it changed its mind on 16 September and the ban became immediate.) (On 30 October 1998 Serbia retaliated against EU countries that had barred the Yugoslav carrier JAT. A levy was imposed on every passenger flying with airlines from offending EU countries and landing fees were increased: *FT*, 31 October 1998, p. 4.)

> The EU's confusion coincided with a major Yugoslav and Serbian offensive in Kosovo ... The UN said this week that up to 700 people had been killed in the six-month struggle ... In addition, an estimated 265,000 people have been driven from their homes because of Belgrade's scorched-earth policy against the separatists.
>
> (Barry James, *IHT*, 11 September 1998, p. 6)

On 23 September 1998 the UN Security Council approved (with China abstaining) a France–UK resolution demanding an immediate ceasefire, an end to 'all action by security forces affecting civilians', the immediate withdrawal of 'security units used for civilian repression' and 'rapid progress on a clear timetable' for peace talks. 'Further action and additional measures' would be taken in the event of non-compliance. The situation in Kosovo 'constitutes a threat to peace and security in the region'. The resolution referred to 'enforcement provisions' of Chapter 7 of the UN Charter. (Under the UN Charter a Chapter 7 resolution is militarily enforceable: *IHT*, 24 September 1998, p. 7. 'Chapter 7 of the UN Charter [is] that part of the treaty which envisages the use of force in order to stop a situation which may threaten international security': *Newsbrief*, 1998, vol. 18, no. 10, p. 74.) The resolution demanded that the promises Milosevic made to President Yeltsin of Russia in June 1998 be kept. (The promises included allowing EU observers into Kosovo, guaranteed access to aid agencies and the safe return of refugees.) 'Immediate steps to avert an impending catastrophe' should be taken. The resolution also demanded that the Kosovo Albanian leadership condemn all terrorist action.

Evidence came to light on 29 September 1998 of a massacre (on 26 September) of at least sixteen ethnic Albanian civilians (men, women and children) in the village of Gornje Obrinje, allegedly committed by Serbian forces. The following day there were reports of another massacre having taken place on 26 September of fourteen ethnic Albanian men in the village of Golubovac near the town of Kijevo. There were also reports of the killing of at least four ethnic Albanian men after a returning civilian convoy had been stopped at the village of Vraniq on 28 September.

Richard Holbrooke met with Slobodan Milosevic on 5 October 1998 to make clear what had to be done to ward off Nato military action. Holbrooke: 'Significant military forces, regular forces and military uniformed police remain in Kosovo.' A Nato official said (on 7 October) that there were still 14,000 Serbian troops in Kosovo and 11,000 special police. Though the 25,000 total was less than the 36,000 stationed there ten days ago, there was evidence that troops were digging in for the winter (*FT*, 8 October 1998, p. 2). Before February 1998 there were 12,500 troops in Kosovo and about 6,500 special police, US officials said. After the build-up and a partial withdrawal there were still 18,000 troops and 11,000 special police (*IHT*, 10 October 1998, p. 2).

An agreement between Holbrooke and Milosevic was announced on 13 October 1998, although Nato's threat to use air strikes to ensure compliance remained in force. The agreement included the following:

1   An international team of 2,000 unarmed monitors ('compliance verifiers'; 'verification monitors'; 'verification force'; 'verification mission') from OSCE, backed up by Nato reconnaissance flights over Kosovo. (The Kosovo Diplomatic Observer Mission was made up of US, EU and Russian military experts: *IHT*, 5 October 1998, p. 1. William Walker is the US ambassador heading the OSCE verification mission.)

    ('Neither Belgrade nor Nato wanted allied forces on the ground': Joseph Fitchett, *IHT*, 15 October 1998, p. 8.)
2   The maintenance of the ceasefire.
3   The withdrawal of Serb heavy weapons and the return of Serb security forces (soldiers and special police) to where they were before March 1998. (It was not clear which forces were to be withdrawn from Kosovo and which merely to barracks.)

    'What the West has now accepted is an arrangement under which most of Mr Milosevic's soldiers and police – 19,000 out of 29,000 according to one White House official – will remain ... Some number of them are now meant to return to their garrisons' (editorial, *Washington Post*, in *IHT*, 15 October 1998, p. 10). 'Albanians complain that the Holbrooke deal allows the Yugoslav president to keep 20,000 police and soldiers in Kosovo' (*Independent*, 21 October 1998, p. 11).
4   The police force to be run by local authorities in Kosovo and to reflect the ethnic composition of the local population.
5   Aid agencies to work unhindered.
6   The return of refugees to their homes.
7   Elections (monitored by OSCE) to take place within nine months.
8   The international war crimes tribunal was to send a mission but was not to have jurisdiction on Yugoslav territory, i.e. permission would be needed to extradite suspects.
9   The 'main elements' of an agreement on political autonomy to be reached by 2 November 1998 (*IHT*, 15 October 1998, p. 6).

Holbrooke said that he hoped Yugoslavia would agree to 'the creation most importantly of a political process that gives the people of Kosovo autonomy and self-determination'. But 'a statement from Mr Milosevic's office ... said only that the agreement would guarantee Kosovo's autonomy within Serbia ... Mr Milosevic made no mention of autonomy, much less of self-determination in a television broadcast to the nation' (*IHT*, 14 October 1998, p. 4). Holbrooke: 'The first time in history that a military organization claimed the right of military intervention in a sovereign country to protect the population of that country against its own leaders' (*IHT*, 5 November 1998, p. 10).

A spokesman for the KLA: 'We insist on full independence. We cannot live with

Serbia. We agree to a three-year transition period that would lead to self-determination.' He said that a KLA truce would continue (*IHT*, 14 October 1998, p. 4).

(The UN Security Council formally endorsed the Kosovo peace agreement on 24 October and gave Nato a mandate to protect unarmed monitors.)

'As with Bosnia, Kosovo has once again sharpened tensions between the United States and the EU over security issues, revealing a European incapacity to mount a concerted response to a crisis in Europe without American leadership' (Roger Cohen, *IHT*, 11 November 1998, p. 7).

Two independent newspapers in Serbia were closed down on 14 October 1998 until further notice for allegedly spreading 'fear, panic and defeatism' and undermining 'the people's readiness to safeguard the territorial integrity and sovereignty of Serbia'. The two newspapers were *Danas* (*Today*) and *Dnevni Telegraf* (*Daily Telegraph*) and they were alleged to have failed to comply with a decree controlling the media during the crisis, e.g. the decree banned the unauthorized transmission of foreign broadcasts and reproduction of foreign news items. (Two radio stations in Serbia have been closed over the past week: *FT*, 15 October 1998, p. 2.) (*Danas* was later printed in Montenegro, but sales were banned in Serbia: *Independent*, 5 November 1998, p. 17.) Another independent newspaper, *Nasa Borba*, was closed the following day for as long as the threat of Nato attack persisted (*IHT*, 16 October 1998, p. 11).

On 16 October 1998 Nato extended the deadline for withdrawing forces (originally 0500 GMT on Saturday 17 October) by ten days (to 7 p.m. GMT or 8 p.m. local time on Tuesday 27 October) in order to allow OSCE time to make the necessary arrangements, i.e. until 27 October. Javier Solana: 'We are still at some distance from full compliance. According to our information, and our information is good, many army and special units remain in Kosovo.' 'Nato estimated that 17,000 troops and 11,000 police were in Kosovo a couple of weeks ago and US officials said they had seen no evidence of forces being pulled back in large numbers' (*IHT*, 17 October 1998, p. 4). 'Nato's supreme commander, General Wesley Clark, has told President Milosevic of Yugoslavia that he must remove another 4,500 army and police troops from Kosovo ... 7,500 police and soldiers have left the province over the past two weeks' (*The Times*, 22 October 1998, p. 17). 'A Nato official said yesterday [23 October] Mr Milosevic still had a total of 25,000 troops and police in the province, or 10,000 more than there were in March' (*FT*, 24 October 1998, p. 2).

There were reports of outbreaks of fighting.

On 16 October 1998 the Bundestag voted in favour of committing German fighter planes to any Nato air strikes, the vote being 503 to 63 with 18 abstentions. 'It was the first time Germany had approved the possible use of force outside Nato territory without a United Nations mandate' (*IHT*, 17 October 1998, p. 2).

'U2 planes began [on 18 October] their mission shortly after General Clark signed the deal with Yugoslavia's military leaders on Thursday evening [15 October] authorizing penetration of Yugoslav airspace by Nato planes' (*Guardian*, 19 October 1998, p. 11).

On 20 October 1998 the Serbian parliament passed a new information law forbidding publication or dissemination of information that might threaten the territorial integrity of the country (*EEN*, 1998, vol. 12, no. 12, p. 9).

> The Serbian government lifted a ban on several independent newspapers Wednesday [21 October], a day after it imposed a law restricting their work … But some of the editors … warned that the new law made it impossible to work … The three newspapers were banned last week … The government also evicted a Belgrade radio station from its premises and shut down a number of provincial media outlets. The new information law also bans broadcasts of Serbian-language programmes by foreign media.
>
> (*IHT*, 22 October 1998, p. 5)

> Two prominent Belgrade independent editors and a publisher were summoned to court on Friday [23 October] for criticism of President Slobodan Milosevic … The three face fines … for allegedly 'trying to undermine the constitutional order' … The media law bans the broadcast or republication here of materials in the Serbo-Croatian language from foreign media sources … The *Evropljanin* article … denounced him for introducing 'dictatorship' and leading the country into political, economic and social chaos.
>
> (*IHT*, 24 October 1998, p. 5)

(Fines were imposed.)

'Four Serbian journalists, who had launched their own, overt press attack on Mr Milosevic, were yesterday [23 October] out on trial for sedition … The four [are] accused editors of the Serbian magazine *The European*' (*FT*, 24 October 1998, p. 2). 'Harsh legislation targeting the Serbian media drove the owner of an independent daily newspaper to close his publication … The owner and editor-in-chief of NT Plus said he decided to halt publication after receiving anonymous telephone threats of legal action' (*IHT*, 28 October 1998, p. 5).

> Nato officials said Monday [26 October 1998] that the alliance had obtained written commitments from Slobodan Milosevic to cut back the military presence in Kosovo and to lift roadblocks by noon Tuesday [27 October], just ahead of the alliance's deadline to proceed with air strikes … Key provisions include the departure of all extra units of the special military police, leaving under 5,000 men. Regular Serbian forces are to be kept to a ceiling of 10,000 men, all in barracks that they will leave only after giving prior notice to the [OSCE] monitors … Heavy weapons, down to mortars, are to be stored … A sole exception to the curbs will be 1,500 border guards, on patrol against arms smuggling and also conducting normal frontier functions in Kosovo … Some observation posts will remain, but no more roadblocks.
>
> (*IHT*, 27 October 1998, p. 6)

On 27 October Nato deemed Serbian compliance to be sufficient not to commence air strikes.

> Serbia's chief of secret police [Jovica Stanisic] ... has been dismissed [28 October 1998] after losing a political struggle against hardliners heading a campaign of internal repression ... Over the past two years [he] was widely credited with blocking hardline factions led by Mira Markovic, wife of Mr Milosevic, and the ultra-nationalist Radical Party chief, Vojislav Seselj ... Also at risk is General Momcilo Perisic, chief of staff of the federal Yugoslav army, who last week expressed his opposition to the confrontation with Nato ... A tough new media law has led to the closure of four independent newspapers and one magazine.
>
> (*FT*, 29 October 1998, p. 2)

> The daily *Vijesti*, published in Montenegro ... linked the dismissal [of Jovica Stanisic, head of the public and state security department] and that of Milorad Vucelic, vice-president of Serbia's ruling Socialist Party, with the Kosovo issue ... Belgrade commentators saw the security chief as the leading pragmatist in Mr Milosevic's entourage and a man who in the past had shown resistance to President Milosevic's authoritarian excesses on the political front. There is speculation that he objected to the rise of extremist Serbian nationalist leaders now allied with Mr Milosevic. The Yugoslav president has been using the right this month to spearhead his drive against dissent in Serbia – and not only in the independent media but also at Belgrade University ... So far this month the government has shut down three newspapers.
>
> (*Guardian*, 29 October 1998, p. 17)

On 4 November 1998 Louise Arbour (chief prosecutor for the international war crimes tribunal) and her team were denied visas for a fact-finding visit to Kosovo. 'Ms Arbour said the Milosevic–Holbrooke talks had led to confusion about the war crimes tribunal's jurisdiction, which she said was clear. A UN Security Council resolution in 1993 gave the tribunal jurisdiction across all of former Yugoslavia' (*Guardian*, 9 November 1998, p. 13).

> A court in Belgrade has imposed [9 November 1998] the maximum fine on the owners and chief editor of an independent newspaper after finding them guilty of breaching Serbia's restrictive new information law ... Following a trial Sunday [8 November] against the *Dnevni Telegraf* paper, the court ruled that its publishing company and chief editor ... must pay 1.2 million dinars ($120,000) for 'publishing information inciting destruction of the constitutional order'. The verdict against the newspaper, known for its criticism of President Milosevic's regime, was handed down a day after it resumed publication following weeks of government bans, court trials and police raids. In its first edition Saturday [7 November] *Dnevni Telegraf* ran an

ad paid for by a Belgrade university student group that called for the abolition of the government.

(IHT, 10 November 1998, p. 5)

On 10 November the Serbian police impounded all 100,000 copies of *Dnevni Telegraf* after the newspaper failed to pay the fine (*IHT*, 11 November 1998, p. 7).

On 13 November 1998 Nato approved an 'extraction force' ('joint guarantor'). Deployed in Macedonia and commanded by the French, it would be used if necessary to rescue the 2,000 OSCE verifiers (*The Times*, 14 November 1998, p. 18).

Some details of the plan for Kosovo proposed by the USA were published on 18 November, proposals which would essentially restore the pre-1989 level of autonomy. The US proposals would cover an interim period of three years, after which Kosovo's final status would be determined (*FT*, 19 November 1998, p. 2; *IHT*, 19 November 1998, p. 10.)

On 24 November 1998 General Momcilo Perisic was dismissed as head of the armed forces. He was replaced by General Dragoljub Ojdanovic.

President Slobodan Milosevic has dismissed the chief of the army, General Momcilo Perisic, in what observers said was a continuing purge of the military ... Senior army officers are reported to be unhappy with Milosevic's having agreed to Nato's surveillance of Kosovo. General Perisic's dismissal follows the dismissal of the Yugoslav air force commander, General Ljubisa Velickovic, on 30 October. Three days earlier the chief of Serbia's security service, Jovica Stanisic, had been dismissed.

(IHT, 26 November 1998, p. 5)

Slobodan Milosevic of Yugoslavia has conducted an extraordinary purge of his innermost circle, dismissing the leaders of the army, the air force and the intelligence service, as well as one of his most trusted political commissars ... The purge, conducted in the wake of Mr Milosevic's agreement 13 October to pull troops out of Kosovo, culminated last week with the dismissal of Momcilo Perisic, the long-serving army chief of staff and an architect of the war in Bosnia ... The purges began shortly after the departure from Belgrade of the US envoy, Richard Holbrooke, who persuaded Mr Milosevic to agree to international observers in Kosovo, and were preceded by the closing of independent newspapers and academic dismissals at Belgrade University. The removal of General Perisic on Tuesday [24 November] was perhaps the least surprising. He publicly criticized Mr Milosevic last month [October] for allowing what is left of Yugoslavia to become a pariah state ... General Perisic, who led the Yugoslav National Army during the atrocities in Bosnia, was reported to have opposed the use of soldiers against ethnic Albanian citizens in Kosovo during the summer offensive there ... What was surprising was General Perisic's decision to fight back. On Thursday night [26 November] the general taunted Mr Milosevic with a statement saying he had been dismissed illegally and hinting that he was prepared to lead Yugoslavia down a different path. 'I was replaced without consultations, in an inadequate and illegal way,' the general said in a statement issued through an independent news agency. 'This establishment does not like officials with high personal integrity who use their own heads. I am still at the disposal of the army, the people and the state.'

(Jane Perlez, *IHT*, 30 November 1998, pp. 1, 9)

General Perisic, a native of Montenegro, is reported to have the backing of that republic's president, Milo Djukanovic, a former Milosevic ally who has turned against the Yugoslav president and has won US support for his stand. General Perisic was replaced by General Dragoljub Ojdanovic, a member of Mirjana Markovic's political party who was commander of one of the army's corps most active in the savage 1991 fight to wrest the city of Vukovar from Croatia, officials said. The first senior officer to be removed was Jovica Stanisic, the head of state security services. Mr Stanisic, who knows all the dirty secrets of Mr Milosevic's rule, was replaced by a senior police patrol officer, Rade Markovic, a loyalist of Miss Markovic's (though not related) and a member of her party, known as the Yugoslav Left. Along with Mr Stanisic, a dozen top operational officers of the security service were forced into retirement or removed. Mr Milosevic next dismissed Milorad Vucelic, the deputy leader of Mr Milosevic's Socialist Party, who served as the president's political disciplinarian. The head of the air force, General Ljubisa Velickovic, who protested Mr Milosevic's agreement to allow Nato surveillance flights over Kosovo, was also removed.

Mr Milosevic has carried out purges before, but never to this extent, and he has never so obviously filled vacancies with loyalists of his wife ... A critical factor governing how long the government will survive is the economy ... [which] continues to decline ... So far Mr Milosevic has managed to manipulate the currency so that he can pay about three-quarters of the annual state pensions due and keep the police and army paid. With help from Russia, which provides natural gas even though Yugoslavia is late in its payments, and with deals like a recent oil purchase from Libya, Mr Milosevic is able to provide energy for the long-suffering people.

(Jane Perlez, *IHT*, 30 November 1998, pp. 1, 9)

James Rubin (US state department spokesman, 30 November 1998): 'Milosevic has been at the centre of every crisis in the former Yugoslavia over the past decade. He is not simply part of the problem. He is the problem. We have no illusions about Milosevic and do not see him as a guarantor of stability.'

Serbia's crackdown on the independent media has taken a further disturbing twist after the government told *Ekonomska Politika*, a highly respected and formerly privately run weekly, it was imposing a new editor-in-chief ... *Ekonomska Politika* first learnt of its nationalization in a government decree published on 14 November which ordered its ownership transferred to the state-run Borba publishing house ... This week the EU declared it would deny visas to nineteen politicians and establishment figures in Serbia responsible for the media law.

(*FT*, 18 December 1998, p. 4)

Kosovo's main Albanian-language daily, *Bujku*, was not allowed to publish on 18 November (*Independent*, 19 December 1998, p. 16).

'Kosovo's crumbling truce appeared to collapse entirely on Christmas Eve after Serbia sent ... tanks into Podujevo in search of Albanian fighters from ... the Kosovo Liberation Army' (*Independent*, 26 December 1998, p. 5). 'Sporadic fighting continued around the north Kosovo town of Podujevo yesterday [25 December] as William Walker, the senior international official in the province, blamed Serbs and Albanians' (*The Times*, 26 December 1998, p. 19).

A sustained Christmas Eve assault in northern Kosovo by Serbian forces and sporadic clashes with separatist guerrillas on Friday [25 December] threatened a tenuous two-month ceasefire .. Thursday's [24 December] attack, which diplomats said was the worst violation since the ceasefire went into effect, came after eleven days of combat and assassinations in which, international monitors say, the two sides have shown that they do not intend to solve their differences peacefully. 'Both sides have gone looking for trouble and they have found it,' said William Walker [the US diplomat who heads the OSCE monitors] ... There are about 600 monitors in Kosovo now and the plan is to have about 2,000 in place by the end of January [1999].

(*IHT*, 26 December 1998, pp. 1, 5)

Safety worries have made OSCE member states reluctant to send volunteers to the monitoring force, originally intended to be 2,000-strong but cut back to 1,500 last week by OSCE's incoming chairman, the Norwegian foreign minister Knut Vollebaek ... The observers – originally deployed to verify Mr Milosevic's troop withdrawal – have an ill-defined peacekeeping role thrust upon them.

(Chris Bird, *Guardian*, 11 January 1999, p. 2)

The eventual maximum number of verifiers has been reduced from 2,000 to 1,600 because of the difficulty of getting qualified people to do the job (*IHT*, 27 January 1999, p. 6). 'The OSCE mission has gone beyond its mandate of monitoring a ceasefire and partial withdrawal of government forces' (*FT*, 14 January 1999, p. 3). 'Overstepping its formal mandate, the OSCE team has negotiated local truces and inspected mass graves' (*The Economist*, 16 January 1999, p. 46).

It was discovered on 16 January 1999 that forty-five ethnic Albanian citizens (including three women and a child) had been killed the day before, allegedly by Serbian forces, in the village of Racak. (On 17 March 1999 the team of Finnish forensic scientists declared Racak a 'crime against humanity' but the word 'massacre' was not used.)

> The Yugoslav government on Monday [18 January 1999] declared the head of the international truce-monitoring team in Kosovo to be persona non grata and ordered him to leave the country within forty-eight hours … Serbian forces continued shelling rebels … and Serbian border guards turned back Louise Arbour, chief prosecutor of UN war crimes tribunal, when she tried to enter Kosovo from Macedonia … The Yugoslav statement said the government had 'examined the activities of William Walker, head of the Kosovo verification mission of OSCE, and determined that they were in flagrant contradiction with the arrangements of the OSCE mission agreement'. 'His activities are greatly exceeding the mandate of mission leader as defined by the OSCE mission agreement,' the statement added … Mr Walker, after visiting … Racak … said it was 'a horrendous and very, very serious event in obviously some sort of execution fashion'. The mutilated bodies were found Saturday [16 January] in a gully outside the village. Most had been shot at close range in the head and stomach … New fighting to the north and south of Pristina raised fears that the three-month-old, US-negotiated peace agreement was near collapse.
>
> (*IHT*, 19 January 1999, pp. 1, 5)

General Wesley Clark (commander of allied forces in Europe) and General Klaus Naumann (chairman of Nato's military committee) met Milosevic on 19 January 1999. William Walker received a twenty-four hour extension of the expulsion order. 'On Monday [18 January] he had been given two days to leave the country after he bluntly blamed Serbian forces for the massacre of ethnic Albanians at Racak' (*IHT*, 20 January 1999, p. 1).

'Nato's two top generals yesterday [19 January] warned Yugoslavia's president that his countries faced air strikes unless he complied fully with his commitments on Kosovo. They also demanded he reverse his decision to expel the chief international observer from the province' (*FT*, 20 January 1999, p. 2). 'The traditional pro-Serb sympathies of Moscow did not prevent it joining the chorus of Western denunciation of the Walker expulsion' (p. 18).

> 'Although I am not a lawyer,' he told reporters, 'from what I personally saw I do not hesitate to call the event [at Racak] a massacre, obviously a crime very much against humanity. Nor do I hesitate to accuse the government security forces of responsibility' … Mr Walker readily admits his mission has gone beyond its mandate. Instead of 'observing' or 'verifying' his monitors have mediated an end to local clashes, brokered ceasefires and started to investigate the disappearance of hundreds of missing civilians … OSCE, the UN and even Russia … rallied behind the American … In his previous

Balkans post ... [William Walker was] the last UN transitional administrator in eastern Slavonia ... His main role in that period, from 1997 to 1998, was to protect the interests of the Serb community in eastern Slavonia and persuade them to stay.

(*FT*, 23 January 1999, p. 11)

On 21 January William Walker defied the expulsion order. 'OSCE's fifty-four member states agreed in Vienna that the entire mission of 800 unarmed observers would leave Kosovo if Mr Walker were forced out ... Finnish forensic experts were yesterday [21 January] allowed to start examining the corpses' (*FT*, 22 January 1999, p. 2).

On 22 January Walker's expulsion order was suspended ('frozen').

International monitors who discovered the bodies of forty-five ethnic Albanians shot execution-style have concluded in their official report that the attack in the Kosovo village was an act of revenge by Serbian forces for the killing of four of their men. The report, which has not been made public, described a scene of bodies with wounds from gunshots at close range and in some cases at 'extremely close range' in the front, back or top of the head. The monitors ... were on the scene immediately before and after the massacre.

(*IHT*, 23 January 1999, p. 4)

What we are attempting is unprecedented in scope and effort and requires maximum flexibility on our part. We are designing as we proceed. Under the auspices of OSCE we are in Kosovo to keep the two sides apart until a political solution can be reached ... [The] mission reports on ceasefire violations and tries to keep isolated clashes from spiralling into broader conflict ... In my reaction to the massacre I blamed the government's security services. Critics have said that I reacted hastily and wondered if the victims were in fact battle casualties. After a week of reviewing what we know, let me restate my position. The Racak villagers were unquestionably killed by units of the Serbian security services. Neither I nor any of those who accompanied me saw any signs of a two-sided battle ... [The] expulsion order has been 'frozen' and I have been asked many times if that means that I may still be expelled. I can only say that I have received assurances that it won't happen.

(William Walker, *IHT*, 27 January 1999, p. 6)

A troop and police attack on [Racak] ... was carried out at the order of senior officials of the Serbian-led Belgrade government, who then orchestrated a cover-up attempt after an international outcry, according to Western intercepts of telephone conversations. Angered by the slaying of three policemen in Kosovo, the officials ordered government forces to 'go heavy' on 15 January ... A high-ranking political figure in Belgrade and a senior commander of security operations in Kosovo sought to cover up what had taken place.

(*IHT*, 29 January 1999, p. 10)

'The recorded conversations have connected Nikola Sainovic, the Yugoslav deputy prime minister and General Sreten Lukic, Kosovo's senior police commander, to the Racak massacre … On the tapes General Lukic is initially told to "go heavy" against Racak' (*The Times*, 29 January 1999, p. 17).

UN secretary-general Kofi Annan:

> The international community should have no illusions about the need to use force when all other means have failed. We may be reaching that point once again in the former Yugoslavia … Let me ask only that we all – particularly those with the capacity to act – recall the lessons of Bosnia.

The 'contact group' officials met in London on 22 January 1999 and 'set the goal of early negotiations on a political settlement with direct international involvement'. They condemned the 'mass murder' in Racak.

On 18 January 1999 Serbian Renewal Movement chairman Vuk Draskovic was appointed Yugoslav deputy prime minister for international relations (*EEN*, 1999, vol. 12, no. 14, p. 7).

> A set of principles [was] endorsed Friday [22 January 1999] in London by the 'contact group' … Officials say the principles include effective self-government for the Kosovar Albanians – their own political, legal, judicial and police powers – in parallel structures to the existing Serbian ones. The point is to provide a form of political autonomy within the Yugoslav federation, but without independence, with the final status of Kosovo to be decided at least three years later through some form of referendum.

(*IHT*, 25 January 1999, p. 6)

The 'contact group' issued a statement in London on 29 January 1999, 'summoning representatives of the Yugoslav and Serbian governments and of the Kosovo Albanians' to a conference starting no later than 6 February in Rambouillet (the chateau) near Paris. A maximum of three weeks was given for the achievement of a negotiated settlement. The representatives were expected to make adequate progress on a deal involving 'substantial autonomy' (though not independence) for Kosovo within seven days and to conclude the deal by no more than seven days after that. The conference was to be co-chaired by the British and French foreign secretaries (Robin Cook and Hubert Vedrine). They would be helped by three international observers, the US envoy Christopher Hill, the EU envoy Wolfgang Petritsch and a Russian official.

> The draft peace plan for Kosovo effectively removes the Serbian government's authority over the province … The plan gives sweeping powers to

the head of the new international monitoring mission [Kosovo Verification Mission], including the right to remove and appoint officials in the administration and judiciary. The monitoring mission, run by OSCE, will also supervise elections in Kosovo within nine months and set up its own broadcasting network ... The status of Kosovo ... is not defined under the plan, but for an interim period of three years the territory ... will be granted 'a high degree of self-government'. The Kosovo government will have the option of holding posts in the government of Serbia and the Federal Republic of Yugoslavia ... The head of the Kosovo Verification Mission will supervise implementation of the agreement and, for an undefined transitional period, have the power to shut down existing institutions.

(*FT*, 2 February 1999, p. 1)

According to the draft, the head of the Kosovo verification team ... would have authority over both Belgrade and the ethnic Albanian leaders in ensuring the proper implementation of the peace settlement ... It was envisaged that the head of the OSCE team in the province would have similar powers to those of Carlos Westendorp, the High Representative in Bosnia ... However ... the peace plan would leave foreign and defence matters, as well as financial strategy, to Belgrade and sovereignty of the province would not be affected. The OSCE verification team has 1,070 members operating in Kosovo. That will rise to 1,600 and will reach the originally proposed 2,000 level once a peace settlement is approved. The final 400 verifiers will be legal experts and police officers.

(*The Times*, 3 February 1999, p. 11)

'The government of Yugoslavia ... will control foreign, defence, trade, monetary and fiscal policy' (*IHT*, 3 February 1999, p. 5).

The revised draft ... states that all paramilitary groups, including the KLA, would be dismantled within three months of the agreement being signed. The new plan also instructs Serbia to reduce its police force strength in Kosovo to 2,500 immediately, from the current level estimated at around 10,000. The head of the international monitoring mission in Kosovo will set a timetable for the remaining police to leave as the territory puts together a new force reflecting its ethnic makeup ... The federal army is to be scaled down to just 1,500 confined to three garrisons and patrols along the border with Albania and Macedonia.

(*FT*, 6 February 1999, p. 2)

The sixteen-strong ethnic Albanians delegation included the following:

1   Ibrahim Rugova.
2   Rexhep Qosja. '[He] heads the United Democratic Movement in opposition to Mr Rugova. He aspires to a "Greater Albania". Members of his delegation

have close ties to the KLA and could emerge as a political wing' (*FT*, 6 February 1999, p. 2).

3   Veton Surroi. Independent. He is the publisher of *Koha Ditore*, the largest circulation newspaper in Kosovo (*IHT*, 11 February 1999, p. 10).

4   Hashim Thaci. He is head of the KLA political directorate.

5   Azem Syla. 'He could be the top military commander of the KLA' (*FT*, 6 February 1999, p. 2).

6   Jakup Krasniqi. 'An important KLA official ... He is part of the rebels' directorate that holds together a network of warlords' (*IHT*, 11, February 1999, p. 10).

7   Xhavid Haliti. 'A key organizer for the rebels ... He has been based in Tirana ... and appears to have been in charge of overseeing the arms flow over the northern Albanian mountains into Kosovo' (*IHT*, 11 February 1999, p. 10).

8   Bujar Bukoshi. 'Based in Germany ... [He] has been the major fund-raiser for the money coming from Albanians living abroad' (*IHT*, 11 February 1999, p. 10).

(There are five KLA representatives altogether.)

The thirteen-strong Serbian and Yugoslav delegation includes the following:

1   Ratko Markovic, deputy prime minister of Serbia.

2   Nikola Sainovic, federal Yugoslav deputy prime minister.

3   Another deputy prime minister and representatives of Kosovo's various ethnic groups, including Albanians, Moslem Slavs, a Turk, a Gypsy and an Egyptian.

President Milan Milutinovic of Serbia joined the talks on 11 February.

The Rambouillet talks started on 6 February 1999. (There were reports of fighting continuing in Kosovo throughout the talks.)

On 14 February foreign ministers in the six-nation 'contact group' decided to extend the peace conference for another week, setting a firm deadline for noon on Saturday 20 February. On 20 February the talks were extended until 23 February (2 p.m. GMT). The sticking points were the Serbian objections to a Nato-led peacekeeping force and ethnic Albanian demands for a referendum on Kosovo's future status after three years. (There were reports on 20 February of fighting in Kosovo.)

> The Kosovo talks plunged into crisis as secretary of state Madeleine Albright said Sunday [21 February] that both Serbians and ethnic Albanians were refusing key points in the peace plan ... 'We had never said that there would be bombing of the Serbs if there was a no answer also from the Albanians' ... The ethnic Albanian delegation balked Saturday [20 February] ... Mrs Albright also berated him [Milosevic] for refusing to discuss the plan for Nato forces ... The international political blueprint for Kosovo ... was

accepted by Serbia's president, Milan Milutinovic ... The Kosovo delegation insisted that the plan should include a referendum on Kosovo's future status, which would virtually guarantee a vote for independence ... Western governments ... have insisted that the peace plan not prejudge the province's final status ... After a three-year period of autonomy Kosovo would get international support in negotiating its future status with Belgrade ... The Kosovar delegation ... seemed ready to accept the deal earlier in the week ... Air strikes against Serbia are 'not going to help' provide stability in Kosovo if the ethnic Albanians refuse to accept the autonomy offer at Rambouillet, Robin Cook, Britain's foreign secretary, said.

(*IHT*, 22 February 1999, pp. 1, 4)

On 23 February 1999 the peace talks were suspended until 15 March 1999, when a 'peace implementation conference' would be convened (in Paris as it turned out).

International mediators said that there was a 'consensus' on a political agreement on autonomy for Kosovo, but neither side signed any agreement. The ethnic Albanian delegation said that it needed to hold 'technical consultations' with its 'political and military' base in Kosovo. The document did not refer to a referendum after three years. Instead, there was reference to 'taking into account the political will of the local population' and the 1975 Helsinki Final Act. The Serbs said that that they were ready to 'discuss the scope and character of an international presence'.

Under the terms of an agreement cobbled together less than two hours before the talks ended Tuesday [23 February] the ethnic Albanians said they supported the agreement 'in principle' but need until 15 March to discuss the terms inside Kosovo and gauge popular reaction ... The chief opponent of the accord is Adem Demaci, a KLA political spokesman who initially opposed the negotiations and urged the commanders who took part to reject the draft accord ... After hearing Mr Demaci's arguments various military commanders telephoned ... to raise objections. These calls had a particular impact on Hashim Thaci ... Mr Thaci attempted to pressure other delegates to oppose the deal and raised objections up to the last few minutes of the talks ... His efforts came as a surprise to Western diplomats ... US officials assigned part of the blame for the failure to achieve a final settlement to Adem Demaci ... who refused to attend the talks .... Mr Demaci met Friday morning [19 February] in Slovenia with Mr Thaci and encouraged him to take a hardline tack ... It was Hashim Thaci ... who surprised Western diplomats by refusing to give his unconditional approval to the accord ... The result has been to defer by at least three weeks a Western plan to gain the ethnic Albanians' approval and use it as a lever to pressure the Belgrade government and its Serbian counterpart into also saying yes – a strategy that would be backed up by the threat of Nato air strikes.

(R. Jeffrey Smith, *IHT*, 25 February 1999, pp. 1, 6)

The ethnic Albanian delegation ... yesterday [24 February 1999] announced the formation of a 'provisional government' to be headed by the rebel KLA ... The KLA news agency Kosovapress said the delegation had agreed to set up a new provisional government, made up equally of the two main ethnic Albanian parties and the KLA and led by a prime minister to be chosen by the rebel group.

(*FT*, 25 February 1999, p. 2)

Veton Surroi, who played a moderating role within the sixteen-strong Kosovo Albanian delegation, accused Adem Demaci ... of trying to block the proposed agreement ... Mr Surroi's comments confirmed the impression created at Rambouillet that there are deep divisions within the KLA ... Mr Demaci ... appears to have engineered the appointment of Suleiman 'Sultan' Selimi as the first overall military commander of the KLA ... Mr Demaci has also attacked an agreement made within the delegation to form a 'provisional government' headed by a prime minister from the KLA, which will hold office until elections take place nine months after a peace accord is signed.

(Guy Dinmore, *FT*, 26 February 1999, p. 2)

US intelligence reported that Serbian troops, backed by scores of tanks, were massing just across the [Kosovo] border ... Secretary of state Madeleine Albright and General Wesley Clark said that Nato was ready to retaliate if the Serbian forces struck ... Serbian military strength in Kosovo has already risen to 'more than double' the levels accepted by Belgrade in October [1998] in a deal to avert Nato air strikes. Supposedly limited to 10,000 army troops and 11,000 paramilitary police, the Serbs now have more than 25,000 troops and police in Kosovo plus a growing force of 7,500 troops backed with 200 tanks just north of the province, a Nato official said.

(*IHT*, 26 February 1999, pp. 1, 4)

On 25 February 1999 China used its veto to block a resolution that called for the renewal of Unpredep in Macedonia until 31 August 1999. (On 27 January 1999 Macedonia established diplomatic relations with Taiwan.) The 1,100-member UN Preventative Deployment Force (Unpredep) included about 360 troops from the USA, 640 from Scandinavia and about fifty from Indonesia. It was originally set up in 1992 to deter the spread of fighting from other parts of the former Yugoslavia. Despite plans in 1998 to phase it out, the force was retained and strengthened owing to the fighting in neighbouring Kosovo. Macedonia provided logistical support for civilian monitors in Kosovo and was a base for Nato operations in the region. China's veto meant that there would be a technical phase-out period of at least a month during which time alternative arrangements would be made. The force could be made part of Nato or a separate monitoring group patrolling borders (*IHT*, 26 February 1999, p. 5).

On 1 March 1999 Hashim Thaci was named as head of a provisional ethnic

Albanian government until a peace accord was signed and elections were held for a Kosovo parliament (*IHT*, 4 March 1999, p. 6). The following day Adem Demaci announced his resignation as political representative of the KLA. 'Sources close to the rebels said Mr Demaci had been dismissed by regional commanders meeting in their central Drenica stronghold at the weekend' (*FT*, 3 March 1999, p. 2).

Holbrooke met Milosevic on 10 March 1999 but did not succeed in persuading him to accept Nato troops.

The peace talks reconvened in France (this time in Paris) on 15 March 1999. (Heavy fighting was reported in Kosovo. Nato sources said that there were at least 15,000 Yugoslav army and 20,000 Serbian police forces in Kosovo: *Guardian*, 16 March 1999, p. 14.)

The ethnic Albanian delegation said that it was willing to sign the agreement.

Politically, the proposals involved a three-year period of autonomy. Kosovo would remain part of Serbia, which would control its economy, money, defences and foreign relations (William Pfaff, *IHT*, 11 February 1999, p. 8). Self-government would centre on elected bodies:

1   A hundred-seat assembly controlling taxes and budgets representing all communities.
2   Parliament to elect a president, who will name a prime minister.
3   Thirty local councils responsible for such issues as law enforcement, schools, medical care and land use. This system will accommodate the Serbs, estimated at 5 per cent of the population of Kosovo.

(*IHT*, 12 February 1999, p. 10)

Kosovo would have its own judiciary.

The whole arrangement would be reviewed in three years. The draft peace plan said that 'an international meeting' would be held after three years 'to determine a mechanism for a final solution to Kosovo on the basis of the will of the people' and other factors (*FT*, 16 March 1999, p. 3). An international meeting would take account of the 'will of the people' and the 'opinions of relevant authorities' (*IHT*, 16 March 1999, p. 8).

The political plan was to be enforced by a Nato-led force (Kosovo Peace Implementation Force or Kfor) comprising around 28,000 troops. Yugoslav armed forces would have to leave the province except for 1,500 border guards, who would have to stay in their frontier positions under rules enforced by Nato troops. They would be confined to a five-kilometre zone bordering Albania and Macedonia. Yugoslav paramilitary police would be limited to 2,575. They would stay for one year only, operating under the direct control of the international verification commission. By the end of the year a 3,000-member new local police force would have been trained. These men, then in the KLA, would be required to surrender their heavy weapons to storage depots under Nato supervision and would be banned from carrying light weapons or wearing insignia (*IHT*, 11 February 1999, p. 8, and 12 February 1999, p. 10). The Rambouillet timetable would remove all special police after a year and all army after six months, except for 1,500 border troops (*FT*, 1 April 1999, p. 2).

'Under an annex of the Rambouillet accords that were to govern the behaviour of the purely Nato forces, they were to be given full access to go anywhere they wanted in the Federal Republic of Yugoslavia and will be immune from any legal process' (*IHT*, 5 June 1999, p. 4). The annex says: 'Nato personnel shall enjoy, together with their vehicles, vessels, aircraft and equipment, free and unrestricted passage and unimpeded access throughout the FRY, including associated airspace and territorial waters' (*IHT*, 11 June 1999, p. 7). ('In the crucial weeks before Nato bombing began, [Madeleine] Albright telephoned Milosevic to suggest a meeting in Geneva, at which time the [US] administration was prepared to discuss changes in the Rambouillet accords that the Serbs had rejected. These previously undisclosed contacts show clearly that the West offered Milosevic every reasonable opportunity to resolve the Kosovo crisis diplomatically': James Rubin, former US state department spokesman, *FT*, Weekend, 30 September 2000, p. i. 'Albright, in fact, made two rare and unpublicized telephone calls to Milosevic, one before Rambouillet and one prior to the bombing. She offered, for the first time since the crackdown on Kosovo began, to meet him … Albright called Milosevic a second time while the talks were in progress. During this conversation she offered to meet him face to face, saying they could discuss the critical question of Nato peacekeepers at such a meeting. She suggested they meet in Geneva, after the Rambouillet conference concluded … Albright clearly signalled in that second phone call that the US was prepared to be flexible in reaching an agreement … Some observers have pointed to inflexibility in the wording of the military annex prepared for Rambouillet as the reason the Serbs balked. This is nonsense. The Serb delegation was told time and time again that the document was negotiable': James Rubin, *FT*, Weekend, 7 October 2000, pp. i, ix.)

'According to Pentagon officials in Washington, President Milosevic has now deployed up to 18,000 troops into Kosovo … while between 16,000 and 21,000 are waiting just across the border' (*Independent*, 18 March 1999, p. 15). '[There are] reports that Milosevic has moved 30,000 to 40,000 troops into or close to Kosovo' (*IHT*, 18 March 1999, p. 8). 'Some 30,000 to 40,000 Serbian troops continued deploying in and around Kosovo on Thursday [18 March]' (*IHT*, 19 March 1999, p. 1). President Clinton [22 March 1999]: 'More than 40,000 Serb security forces are poised in and around Kosovo, with additional units on the way.'

'On Wednesday [17 March] Serbia shut down two Albanian-language newspapers … In the past week or so … the judiciary have handed down six separate verdicts against the independent media' (*IHT*, 19 March 1999, p. 6).

On 18 March 1999 representatives of the ethnic Albanian delegation signed the agreement. Russia's mediator, Boris Mayorsky, refused to sign as a witness.

The talks in Paris were called off on 19 March 1999. The 1,380 OSCE verifiers prepared to leave the following day.

'Yugoslavia's decision to reject an international plan … led to the collapse of the peace talks in Paris last week. It also signalled the start of a major new offensive by nearly 40,000 Serbian soldiers and security forces based in and around Kosovo' (*IHT*, 22 March 1999, p. 6).

On 22 March Richard Holbrooke began fresh talks with Milosevic, but by the following day it was clear that the mission had failed.

On 23 March 1999 the Yugoslav government declared a state of 'immediate threat of war'. 'Milosevic yesterday [23 March] sacked the second most powerful figure in the Yugoslav army, General Alexander Dimitrijevic, the head of military security' (*FT*, 24 March 1999, p. 1). Russian prime minister Yevgeni Primakov, on his way to a visit to the USA, turned around in mid-flight over the Atlantic after a telephone discussion with US Vice-President Al Gore. A US official said: 'The Vice-President could not assure Primakov that bombing would not take place while he was here.'

Nato's seventy-eight-day bombing campaign

Nato began missile and air attacks on 24 March 1999. Among the first targets were Serbian air defences (Operation Allied Force). (A decision to launch air strikes has to be made unanimously, but afterwards no single Nato member can call a halt although objectors can withhold use of their military forces: *FT*, 30 March 1999, p. 2. The most commonly quoted figure is that the USA provided about 80 per cent of the planes involved in the bombing campaign. The technological gap between the USA and Europe was exposed.)

'The decision by Nato to attack a sovereign nation for the first time in its fifty-year history represents a momentous transformation for a defensive alliance conceived to protect Western Europe from an invasion by the Soviet Union' (*IHT*, 24 March 1999, p. 1).

'The war with Serbia to stop tyranny and ethnic cleansing in Kosovo was a milestone ... It was the first war that was not for conquest, or defence or the imposition of political power, but to assert standards of behaviour' (Flora Lewis, *IHT*, 18 March 2000, p. 8).

German planes took part in combat for the first time since the end of the Second World War.

Russia suspended co-operation with Nato and participation in the Partnership for Peace programme.

The government of Montenegro declared that it would not recognize the declaration of an 'imminent state of war' and other decisions made by the federal government. The declaration was a prelude to a state of war or emergency, which would give sweeping powers to the federal government (*FT*, 25 March 1999, p. 2).

> Nato gave unusual written assurances Wednesday [24 March] to five countries neighbouring Serbia that the alliance would consider any military strikes against them by Belgrade's forces to be 'unacceptable'. Allied officials said that they had given the assurances after Albania, Bulgaria,

Macedonia, Slovenia and Romania had expressed concern about threats to their own safety ... Officials said that Mr Solana's letters had gone out before Yugoslavia warned Romania, Albania, Hungary, Bulgaria and Macedonia not to support Nato bombing raids or the ethnic Albanian rebels in Kosovo.

(*IHT*, 25 March 1999, p. 5)

Nato's bombing campaign was highly controversial, of course. For one thing, Nato did not seek a UN Security Council resolution to approve the bombing campaign because both Russia and China would have opposed it. Instead, Nato argued that humanitarian considerations outweighed the usual considerations of state sovereignty.

(It was discovered on 16 January 1999, for example, that forty-five ethnic Albanian citizens, including three women and a child, had been killed the day before, allegedly by Serbian forces, in the village of Racak. On 17 March 1999 the team of Finnish forensic scientists declared Racak a 'crime against humanity' but the word 'massacre' was not used.) (Serbia's sovereignty over Kosovo in the context of the disintegration of the former Yugoslavia, however, has been challenged.) Nato also argued that its actions were in the spirit of previous resolutions (on 31 March 1998 and 23 September 1998). (Note also that on 26 March 1999 the Security Council rejected by twelve votes to three – including Russian and China – a Russian resolution calling for an immediate cessation of bombing and a return to negotiations.)

With reservations about aspects such as the height at which Nato planes flew, the bombing campaign was both justified and successful. (Criticisms relating to civilian casualties are dealt with below, under the section on the toll.) It was clearly a mistake to openly declare at the start that a ground invasion was not going to happen (although it is not difficult to appreciate both the domestic political constraints operating and the differences of opinion among Nato members on the issue). There is no doubt that the start of the bombing campaign was accompanied by a rapid acceleration of the 'ethnic cleansing' of ethnic Albanians. But what critics fail to appreciate is what would have happened if Nato had simply been bluffing. Milosevic would have had a clear run to carry out what he had always intended to do. Human rights violations would have run riot. It is worth remembering two points:

1   On 24 November 1993 the International Helsinki Federation for Human Rights (IHF) published a worrying report entitled *From Autonomy to Colonization: Human Rights Violations in Kosovo 1989–1993*. 'The IHF is deeply concerned that the Serbian oppressive policies carried out in Kosovo aim at a permanent change in the demographic structure of the region.'

2   ' "Operation Horseshoe" ... was known to have been conceived by Mr Milosevic and his advisers in October [1998]' (William Drozdiak, *IHT*, 21 July 1999, p. 4).

According to German government sources, this programme for purging Kosovo of its Albanian population was prepared at the end of last year [1998] under the codename 'Horseshoe' ... Horseshoe was designed to produce a permanent solution, and was launched even before the Rambouillet discussions in February [1999].

(William Pfaff, *IHT*, 15 April 1999, p. 6)

The bombings were indeed the trigger for most of the ethnic cleansing. The campaign had already begun, directed at Albanian villages thought friendly to the KLA. A plan, 'Operation Horseshoe', had been prepared in Belgrade for the full-scale expulsion and murder of Kosovo Albanians, and it was ordered into action during the hours following the start of the bombings. But ethnic cleansing was clearly a result, as well as the cause, of the Nato bombing campaign.

(William Pfaff, *IHT*, 8 July 1999, p. 8)

Nato's bombing strategy was and still is criticized for starting the campaign with just a few selected and publicized targets in the hope that Milosevic would use this as a cover for capitulating. But he did not. Factors in his decision included the hope that the stresses and strains among Nato members would bring the campaign to a premature halt, and the openly declared unwillingness of Nato to commit ground troops for an invasion of Kosovo. On 27 March 1999 Nato announced that phase two of the bombing campaign was to begin, including attacks on Serbian ground forces in Kosovo (which were not at all decisive and led to far fewer losses in Serbian troops and armaments than initially thought by Nato). It was only when Nato attacked infrastructure and other economic and communications targets within Serbia itself that Milosevic started to buckle. The targets included power stations, oil refineries, bridges, party and government buildings, television stations and allegedly dual civilian/military factories (e.g. cars and armaments). They were considered to be legitimate military targets because they helped the war effort and because they struck at the economic power of Milosevic and his cronies. Other factors affecting Milosevic's capitulation included the build-up of Nato forces in countries such as neighbouring Albania and Macedonia (there to look after refugees) coupled with Nato announcing that no options were ruled out. (President Clinton, for example, in an article published in the *IHT* on 24 May 1999, stated that: 'While I do not rule out other military options, we are pursuing our present strategy.') Nato secretary-general Javier Solana played a crucial role in maintaining cohesion among Nato members. General Wesley Clark from the USA, Nato's supreme allied commander in Europe, proved to be a dogged and highly intelligent leader (although controversial in some ways, e.g. the row with Britain's first head of Kfor, General Mike Jackson, about the Russian takeover of Pristina airport before the entry of Kfor troops into Kosovo). (Among the three new Nato members Poland was the most supportive, Hungary was next and the Czech Republic was by far the least enthusiastic. The governments of countries seeking future Nato membership, such as Albania, Bulgaria, Croatia, Romania, Slovenia and Slovakia, actively assisted Nato despite varying degrees of enthusiasm among their populations.)

Javier Solana took charge of the EU's foreign and security policy on 18 October 1999, a newly created post of co-ordinator (high representative of the EU's common foreign and security policy). He has combined this role with that of secretary-general of the WEU. George Robertson (formerly Britain's foreign secretary and now Lord Robertson) replaced Solana as Nato secretary-general on 14 August 1999. On 8 October 1999 General Klaus Reinhardt (Germany) replaced General Sir Michael Jackson (UK) as head of Kfor.

In November 2001 Ibrahim Rugova drew parallels between Nato's bombing campaign and the bombing of targets in Afghanistan by the United States (aided by the United Kingdom) after the 11 September 2001 terrorist attacks in New York and Washington:

> To describe it as a war against Islam … is as senseless as describing the Nato air campaign [against Milosevic] as a war against Orthodox Christianity … Some people in Nato countries criticised their governments for intervening. Fortunately for us they were ignored … We knew that if the bombing stopped Milosevic would win and we would all pay a dreadful price … When Milosevic refused to capitulate after only a few days of bombings, the critics queued up to say the military campaign was flawed and failing … [Then came] Slobodan Milosevic's sudden capitulation in 1999 … [The rapid collapse of the Taleban [in Afghanistan] after weeks of bombing reminds me of [that sudden capitulation] … Another criticism of the Nato air campaign in Kosovo at the time was that it created rather than averted a humanitarian crisis there. People are today saying the same thing about the military campaign in Afghanistan. But in Kosovo, as in Afghanistan, what many people failed to realise is that the humanitarian crisis had begun much earlier … [In both cases] military action was the only way to create the conditions for resolving the humanitarian crisis … Without Nato's intervention and determination [in Kosovo] hundreds of thousands would still be living in tents all over Europe … More than $1.5 billion has been invested in Kosovo's future by the international community over the past two years – more than $750 for each person here. The uncomfortable reality is that military force is sometimes necessary to protect human rights and enforce the rule of law … Military force brought an end to four years of suffering in Bosnia. It reversed the ethnic cleansing that had begun in Kosovo on a massive scale in 1998. And Nato forces have delivered many of those indicted for war crimes in the former Yugoslavia to The Hague.
>
> (*Telegraph*, 20 November 2001, p. 24)

(The following section deals with the major criticisms of Nato's bombing campaign.)

The toll

German foreign minister Joschka Fischer has recounted that when he went to Belgrade shortly before Nato started bombing, Mr Milosevic told him: 'I am ready to walk on corpses and the West is not. That is why I shall win.'

(Flora Lewis, *IHT*, 4 June 1999, p. 8)

'[The bombing campaign ended with] the lack of a single allied casualty in combat' (*IHT*, 11 June 1999, p. 1).

Only two Nato planes were shot down, although one was a US stealth bomber. Both pilots were rescued. (Two US pilots were killed in a training accident involving Apache helicopters.)

Nato estimates that 5,000 Yugoslav servicemen have been killed in the air campaign. The Yugoslav military command has admitted to only 1,800 dead (*FT*, 4 June 1999, pp. 1–2).

'Some 5,000 Serbian troops were killed and 10,000 wounded, the alliance estimates ... The Serbs contend that 1,500 civilians were killed during the bombing' (*IHT*, 7 June 1999, p. 9).

'At 50,000 the number of Serbs [troops] to be withdrawn is 10,000 higher than Nato originally estimated' (*FT*, 11 June 1999, p. 21).

[US] defence secretary William Cohen and General Henry Shelton, the chairman of the joint chiefs of staff ... provided the most detailed accounting to date of what allied planes had destroyed: 450 artillery pieces, 220 armoured personnel carriers, 120 tanks, more than half of Yugoslavia's military industry and 35 per cent of the country's electric power. The officials said allied warplanes had flown 35,000 missions, including just under 10,000 bombing runs, dropping 23,000 bombs and missiles.

(*IHT*, 12 June 1999, p. 5)

Nato officials acknowledged Tuesday [22 June] that the alliance knocked out a good deal less Serbian military equipment in Kosovo than had been thought ... As they were counted through Nato checkpoints the Serbian force of nearly 47,000 men seemed less demoralized than allied accounts had led people to believe ... One important factor in discrepancies in wartime damage counts was the elaborate measures taken by Serbian commanders in using decoys.

(*IHT*, 23 June 1999, p. 1)

The only official tabulation of Serbian withdrawals has come from William Cohen, the [US] defence secretary, who said Monday [21 June] that about 47,000 troops and nearly 800 military vehicles – tanks, armoured personnel carriers and apparently mobile artillery – had been withdrawn from Kosovo.

(p. 4)

In the two weeks since Nato forces arrived in Kosovo alliance officials have scaled back their initial estimates of the damage inflicted by the seventy-eight-day air campaign ... The supreme commander of Nato, General Wesley Clark, said last week that the alliance had, for example, destroyed 110 of the roughly 300 tanks ... But that number was less than the 150 tanks Nato believed it had destroyed in the waning days of the war ... As the Serbs pulled out over eleven days, Nato commanders counted 220,000 tanks, 300 armoured personnel carriers and 308 artillery batteries ... There were also 47,000 soldiers and police who left the province.

(*IHT*, 29 June 1999, p. 4)

Serb forces claim to have lost only thirteen tanks (*FT*, 19 July 1999, p. 2).

At least 10,000 Albanians have perished at Serb hands in Kosovo in a wave of killing that 'beggared belief', a [UK] foreign office minister said yesterday [17 June] ... 'Tragically our estimates of the numbers of innocent men, women and children killed will almost certainly have to be revised upwards.'

(*Telegraph*, 18 June 1999, p. 1)

'At least 10,000 Kosovar civilians are now believed to have been murdered in 100 massacres by Serb forces between 25 March [1999] ... and 10 June [1999]' (*Independent*, 18 June 1999, p. 3).

The Yugoslav army chief of staff, General Dragoljub Ojdanovic, said Wednesday [21 July 1999] that 524 Yugoslav soldiers were killed during and after the eleven-week-long Nato bombing campaign against Yugoslavia ... General Ojdanovic said that thirty-seven soldiers were still listed as missing ... On 10 June ... President Slobodan Milosevic said that the army had lost 462 soldiers and 114 Serbian policemen had been killed.

(*IHT*, 22 July 1999, p. 5)

(Slobodan Milosevic, in a television address: 'From 24 March [1999] until today [10 June 1999] 462 Yugoslav army soldiers and 114 police were killed.')

'Mass graves scattered across Kosovo contain an estimated 11,000 bodies, the interim administrator for the UN, Bernard Kouchner, said Monday [2 August]' (*IHT*, 3 August 1999, p. 5).

General Wesley Clark said Thursday [16 September 1999] that only twenty-six actual [tank] wreckages had been found by allied troops ... but Nato commanders insisted that they had confirmed evidence of ninety-three Serbian tanks being destroyed by allied warplanes, most of which were taken away by Serbian forces ... That figure – fewer than the 110 previously claimed by alliance spokesmen or the 122 total announced by the Pentagon at the war's end ... Nato airstrikes had hit 153 armoured personnel carriers ... 339 military vehicles were hit and 389 artillery pieces or mortars.

(*IHT*, 17 September 1999, p. 5)

[Nato has been] dogged by accusations that the [air] campaign destroyed only thirteen tanks ... Nato's strike assessment team said it found evidence of twenty-six tank 'catastrophic kills' ... adding that another sixty-seven strikes had been confirmed ... The alliance said that 110 tanks had been hit, against ninety-three it accounts for now. Nato also said it hit 210 armoured troop carriers, compared with 153 now accounted for, and 449 artillery pieces or mortars, as opposed to 389 verified ... Nato flew 35,000 sorties [in total].

(*Independent*, 17 September 1999, p. 16)

(More than 3,000 separate bombing missions were flown over Kosovo: *Guardian*, 17 September 1999, p. 16.)

General Clark also argued that this 'battle-damage beancounting' was only part of the story. What it failed to show was the extent to which the Yugoslav military had to keep its tanks and other assets hidden and inoperative to avoid them being hit.

(*The Times*, 17 September 1999, p. 17)

('Some have claimed that Nato cannot fight a modern war and cite the Kosovo campaign, saying "no war by committee" ... [But] the problems in the campaign were less a function of war by committee than a result of divisions within the US government': Wesley Clark, *IHT*, 2 February 2002, p. 6.)

An internal United States air force report ... logs only fifty-eight accurate strikes, compared with the 744 'confirmed' by Nato at the end of the war ... The new figures were compiled by a special investigation team from the US and other Nato air forces ... They found that while the US top brass boasted that Nato forces had disabled 'around 120 tanks', 'about 220 armoured personnel carriers (APCs)' and 'up to 450 artillery and mortar pieces' in seventy-eight days of bombing, the true figures were probably less than one-tenth of that. According to the investigation, Nato hit just fourteen tanks, eighteen APCs and twenty artillery and mortar pieces. These figures are much closer to the losses admitted by Serb forces ... Completed last summer [1999] the report's existence was never made public and it was superseded by a second report, more to the liking of Nato and the Pentagon.

(*Independent*, 8 May 2000, p. 12)

When the air campaign was over last year [1999] General Wesley Clark wanted to know what had happened. According to *Newsweek*'s report in late

June he sent a thirty-man team, mostly from the US Air Force, to investigate ... General Clark ... sent the team back to check the targets on the ground, rather than from helicopters ... The US Air Force then produced a report of its own, based on cockpit videos or flashes detected by satellites, which backed its own claims of success. But General Clark's British and German deputies, and also the CIA, warned him not to believe the air force figures ... We also know that General Clark was forced into early retirement, apparently because he insisted that ground intervention was the only sure way to get Serbia's capitulation. His offence seems to have been to attempt to introduce realism into plans drafted to please officials afraid of casualties.

(William Pfaff, *IHT*, 11 May 2000, p. 8)

General Sir Michael Jackson said that the Yugoslav army had 20,000 soldiers, 400 tanks and 200 artillery pieces in Kosovo. In addition there were 20,000 special police (*The Times*, 11 May 2000, p. 20).

On 10 November 1999 the first figures for Kosovo were given by the International Criminal Tribunal for the Former Yugoslavia. Carla del Ponte (chief prosecutor) said that so far 2,108 bodies had been exhumed. No breakdown by nationality was given. Carla del Ponte:

This figure does not necessarily reflect the total number of actual victims, because we have discovered evidence of tampering with graves. There are also a significant number of sites where the precise number of bodies cannot be counted ... The figures themselves may not tell the whole story, and we would not expect the forensic evidence in isolation to produce a definitive total.

'She said that 11,334 Albanians had been reported as missing and believed dead' (*IHT*, 11 November 1999, p. 4). 'The UNHCR said it believed the total was not lower than 4,600, based on painstaking interviews with refugees' (*The Times*, 11 November 1999, p. 25).

Nato officials conceded last night [17 August] that their wartime estimates of the number of Kosovo Albanian civilians massacred by Serb forces might have been too high. They were reacting to findings by forensic experts for the International Criminal Tribunal in The Hague who are preparing to complete their work in Kosovo after exhuming about 3,000 bodies. Not all the dead can be proved to be victims of murder or execution ... During the Nato airstrikes ... Nato officials talked of 100,000 missing and said at least 10,000 had been killed.

(*Guardian*, 18 August 2000, p. 1)

United Nations forensic investigators searching for the bodies of ethnic Albanians killed by Yugoslav army and paramilitary forces in Kosovo now expect the final toll of confirmed killings to be between 4,000 and 5,000. This is half the total estimated during Nato's seventy-eight-day bombing campaign ... Two figures were frequently quoted: 100,000 missing and 10,000 murdered by the Serbs.

(*The Times*, 19 August 2000, p. 13)

'The [US] State Department has estimated that 10,000 Kosovar Albanians were killed this year in the Serbian campaign to force the ethnic Albanian population from its homeland' (*The Times*, 11 December 1999, p. 4).

On 6 February 2000 a report was issued by Human Rights Watch (based in New York). It estimated that at least 500 civilians had been killed by Nato during the seventy-eight-day bombing campaign. The report said that: 'Human Rights Watch has found no evidence of war crimes ... [But] the investigation did conclude that Nato violated international humanitarian law' (*Independent*, 7 February 2000, pp. 1, 3; *IHT*, 8 February 2000, p. 7). Nato may have breached the Geneva Convention in five areas:

1   Air attacks using cluster-bombs (which spray bomblets over a wide area) near populated areas. The UK continued to use them even after the USA stopped in mid-May.
2   Attacks were made on targets of questionable military legitimacy. 'Nine incidents were a result of strikes on non-military targets that Human Rights Watch believes were illegitimate', including Radio Television Serbia in Belgrade, the New Belgrade heating plant and seven bridges that were neither on major transportation routes nor had military functions. Bridges were bombed during daylight hours when civilians were most likely to be crossing them.
3   Nato did not take adequate measures to warn civilians of strikes.
4   Nato took insufficient precautions when attacking mobile targets. Convoys were struck without knowing with certainty that they were made up of Yugoslav forces. Seven incidents were the result of attacks on convoys or transportation links. These raise the question of whether the fact that the pilots were flying at high altitudes may have contributed to civilian deaths.
5   Nato caused excessive civilian casualties by not taking sufficient measures to verify that targets did not have concentrations of civilians.

The report estimates that one-third of the number of lethal episodes and half the casualties could have been avoided if Nato had strictly followed the rules.

Belgrade claims that Nato bombing killed 5,000 civilians. A Nato report does not include a death toll for enemy soldiers or for civilians (*Independent*, 7 February 2000, pp. 1, 3; *IHT*, 8 February 2000, p. 7).

In Belgrade a war crimes tribunal included in its indictment the names of 503 civilians, 240 soldiers and 147 politicians killed during the Nato bombing campaign (*Independent*, 19 September 2000, p. 12; *Guardian*, 19 September 2000, p. 17).

Human Rights Watch … [says that] of the approximately 500 Yugoslav citizens killed in Serbia and Kosovo by Nato bombs, half died unnecessarily because of Nato violations of humanitarian law and practice … [The organization] has criticized Nato in four areas: the use of cluster bombs, 'inherently indiscriminate weapons', near civilian areas; the deliberate bombing of targets with little or no military significance, including the television station, Belgrade's heating plant, bridges, some factories and other infrastructure; the bombing of targets, like the Varvarin bridge, during the daytime, when civilians would be at a market, and the failure to take sufficient precautions to identify mobile targets before bombing.

(*IHT*, 8 June 2000, p. 5)

On 2 June 2000 chief war crimes prosecutor Carla del Ponte said:

I am now able to announce my conclusion, following a full consideration of my team's assessment of all complaints and allegations, that there is no basis for opening an investigation into any of those allegations or into other incidents related to the Nato bombing … Although some mistakes were made by Nato, I am very satisfied that there was no deliberate targeting of civilians or unlawful military targets by Nato during the bombing campaign.

(*IHT*, 3 June 2000, p. 1; *Guardian*, 3 June 2000, p. 21)

On 7 June 2000 Amnesty International published a report highly critical of Nato.

[The report accused Nato] of committing serious violations of the rules of war, unlawful killings and – in the case of the bombing of Serbia's television headquarters – a war crime … The Amnesty report … states that 'Civilian deaths could have been significantly reduced if Nato forces had fully adhered to the rules of war' … Amnesty records that Nato aircraft flew 10,484 strike missions over Serbia and that Serbian statistics of civilian deaths in Nato raids range from 400–600 up to 1,500. It specifically condemns Nato for an attack on a bridge at Varvarin on 30 May last year [1999], which killed at least eleven civilians. 'Nato forces failed to suspend their attack after it was evident that they had struck civilians,' Amnesty says. When it attacked convoys of Albanian refugees near Djakovica on 14 April and in Korisa on 13 May, 'Nato failed to take necessary precautions to minimise civilian casualties'. The report says Nato repeatedly gave priority to pilots' safety at the cost of civilian lives … Of the Nato destruction of the train at Gurdulica bridge on 12 April … Nato had not, Amnesty adds, 'taken sufficient precautionary measures to ensure there was no civilian traffic in the vicinity of the bridge before launching the first attack'.

(*Independent*, 7 June 2000, p. 17)

Amnesty International said Wednesday [7 June] that Nato had violated international law in its bombing over Yugoslavia by hitting targets where civilians were sure to be killed. In particular, the human rights group said that Nato's bombing of Radio Television Serbia, on 23 April 1999, 'was a deliberate attack on a civilian object and as such constitutes a war crime'. Sixteen people died ... Nato has defended the bombing as an attack of the 'propaganda machine' of President Slobodan Milosevic ... In some cases, Amnesty said, Nato failed to take sufficient precautions to minimize civilian casualties. The number of civilian deaths from Nato air strikes 'could have been significantly reduced if Nato forces had fully adhered to the laws of war during Operation Allied Force', the report said. Amnesty also condemned a Nato attack on a bridge at Varvarin on 30 May 1999, in which at least eleven civilians died. 'Nato forces failed to suspend their attack after it was evident that they had struck civilians', the report said, and it criticized Nato for ordering its pilots to fly so high that they could not take proper precautions against bombing civilians. In particular, the report criticized the bombing of civilian convoys of Albanian refugees near Djakovica on 14 April and Korisa on 13 May.

(*IHT*, 8 June 2000, p. 1)

In the 195 sites examined last year [1999] the number of bodies found has been less than initially reported to the tribunal [in The Hague] – in part because of apparent Serbian tampering with the graves. But the investigators have 300 sites to examine this year [2000] and in just three weeks have exhumed 160 bodies ... Some 3,500 people are listed as still missing since the war by the International Committee of the Red Cross. The tribunal exhumed 2,108 bodies last year, 70 per cent of them identified. There is no final count of the dead from the war, although statisticians from the University of Bordeaux in France have estimated of what they know that about 9,000 people died in the eighteen months beginning in February 1998, when fighting erupted between the KLA and Serbian security services. The war crimes tribunal has reports of more than 11,000 bodies in 500 graves, but generally the actual number of bodies found has been lower than that reported.

(Carlotta Gall, *IHT*, 16 May 2000, p. 9)

What about all the murders that have taken place under the nose of the Nato forces? Well, the statistics for the first eight months of the Nato occupation of Kosovo are as follows: 457 people were killed, of whom 176 were Albanians, 157 were Serbs, and 124 were 'others' (or unidentified). There is quite a contrast here with the number of people murdered by Serb forces up until early June last year. Careful analysis of eye-witness reports of those killings has come up with 11,334 victims – a figure which is likely to be an under-estimate, as it does not include people led away by the Serb forces and never seen again ... In the previous twelve months ... before 24 March

1999 ... Serb forces had driven more than 300,000 Albanians out of their homes – homes which, in many cases, they then looted and burnt. Roughly 2,000 people had been killed, some of them in massacres such as the one at Racak where forty-five civilians were murdered.

(Noel Malcolm, *Telegraph*, 24 March 2000, p. 28)

There have been 507 murders altogether [in Kosovo], with the rate falling from forty a week last summer [1999] to about five, a level comparable to European cities, Kfor says. But this has been achieved only with the departure of 200,000 Serb refugees, leaving just 100,000 in the province.

(*FT*, 24 March 2000, p. 10)

Carla del Ponte ... said yesterday [26 January 2001] ... [that] Slobodan Milosevic should be investigated for the deaths of sixteen Serbian state television employees killed by Nato bombs in Belgrade in 1999 ... She claimed that Mr Milosevic had been warned of the air strike on the television station.

(*The Times*, 27 January 2001, p. 16)

'The former head of Serbian state television ... Dragoljub Milanovic ... was arrested yesterday [13 February 2001] on suspicion of knowing in advance of the Nato air raid that killed sixteen of his staff in April 1999' (*Independent*, 14 February 2001, p. 16).

'Nato's bombing of Serbian state television ... in 1999 ... was not illegal, the European Court of Human Rights ruled yesterday [19 December 2001]. It said Nato could not be responsible for actions abroad' (*Independent*, 20 December 2001, p. 14).

A chronology of events

On 27 March 1999 a US F-117A stealth fighter was shot down. The pilot was rescued.

On 1 April 1999 three US soldiers on duty in Macedonia were taken prisoner by the Yugoslav army. (They were released on 2 May 1999 after talks between Milosevic and a group of US clergymen led by Jesse Jackson.)

Also on 1 April 1999 Yugoslav state television showed a meeting between Milosevic and Rugova. On 5 May Ibrahim Rugova and his family flew to Rome as guests of the Italian government. 'Ibrahim Rugova ... said Monday [17 May 1999] that he was effectively a prisoner while in Belgrade and that his call there for an end to Nato air strikes was done merely to help his family' (*IHT*, 18 May 1999, p. 7).

Ibrahim Rugova ... says he was acting under duress when he backed Slobodan Milosevic's call for an end to Nato air strikes ... Mr Rugova ... [said] that the agreement had no meaning and that he had only signed it 'to gain some freedom for my family'. Rugova and his family ... have settled in Bonn.

(Guardian, 18 May 1999, p. 5)

'Nato warned President Slobodan Milosevic [on 2 April] it would intervene if he attempted a coup against his reformist opponents in Montenegro ... Javier Solana ... said the alliance had "plans to stop" any attempt to unseat Milo Djukanovic, the Montenegro president' (*FT*, 3 April 1999, p. 1).

('The [US] state department said last week that Washington was "highly concerned" that Mr Milosevic would provoke violence in Montenegro in order to give the estimated 12,000 Yugoslav troops based in the republic an excuse to take over an elected government that has declared itself neutral in the conflict over Kosovo': *IHT*, 6 April 1999, p. 1.)

Phase three started when the interior ministry building in Belgrade was attacked on 3 April 1999. Other infrastructure/economic targets followed, including government and party buildings, power stations, oil refineries, bridges and television stations and civilian/military factories (e.g. cars and armaments). They were considered legitimate targets because they helped the war effort and because they struck at the economic power of Milosevic and his cronies.

> Nato leaders and officials [3–4 April 1999] continued to rule out a ground invasion of Kosovo, or using any ground forces that would have to 'fight their way in'. But plans are being studied for the Western alliance to send an 'escort force', which might have to number 60,000 or more, into Kosovo to protect returning refugees. This would happen only after Yugoslav forces had withdrawn – or had been driven – from the region. But it might occur before any peace deal was signed. First signs of the shift came from Javier Solana, Nato secretary-general, late on Saturday [3 April], which appeared to toughen the alliance's demands ... To end the bombing, Mr Solana said, Yugoslavia had to 'stop all repressive and combat activity and withdraw its forces from Kosovo, and accept arrangements in which all refugees can return safely to Kosovo under protection of an international security force' ... Officials had to 'clarify' that the statement reflected the secretary-general's view and had not been adopted by Nato. But it is understood to have reflected the views of informal discussions between the five Nato countries that are also members of the 'contact group', co-ordinating the international community's response to the Yugoslav crisis.

(FT, 5 April 1999, p. 2)

'Nato officials said Sunday [4 April] that the alliance ... would commit allied ground troops to help neighbouring countries cope with a growing ethnic Albanian exodus from Kosovo ... [There are] roughly 350,000 refugees now in Albania and Macedonia' (*IHT*, 5 April 1999, p. 1). 'More than 200,000 people ... [fled] to Albania' (p. 8).

On 7 April 1999 Nato said that five questions had to be answered affirmatively by Milosevic for bombing to stop:

1   Is he ready for a verifiable cessation of all military activity?
2   Is he ready to withdraw troops, police and paramilitary units from Kosovo?
3   Is he ready to accept the deployment of an international security force?
4   Will he permit the unconditional return of all refugees and unimpeded access for humanitarian aid?
5   Will he accept a political agreement based on the Rambouillet peace agreement?

> Unidentified gunmen on Sunday [11 April] shot and killed a well-known opposition publisher outside his apartment in Belgrade. The publisher, Slavko Curuvija, the owner of the *Dnevni Telegraf* and the news biweekly *Evropljanin*, was shot as he returned home ... In the widespread crackdown by President Slobodan Milosevic against the independent media, *Dnevni Telegraf* and *Evropljanin* were heavily fined last year [1998] for breaching Serbia's restrictive information law, passed in October [1998], and then banned. Mr Curuvija reregistered them in Montenegro ... They were printed in Croatia, but their distribution in Serbia was widely curtailed.
>
> (*IHT*, 12 April 1999, p. 8)

'On Sunday [11 April] [Albania's] foreign minister ... said his government had "now decided to give Nato the rights to control all our air spaces, ports and any other kind of military infrastructure in Albania" ' (*IHT*, 12 April 1999, p. 1).

On 12 April 1999 a joint statement was issued by nineteen Nato foreign ministers. The foreign ministers insisted that air strikes would continue until Mr Milosevic acceded to five conditions:

1   Ensure a verifiable stop to all military action and the immediate ending of violence and repression.
2   Agree to the stationing in Kosovo of an international military presence.
3   Ensure the withdrawal from Kosovo of the military, police and paramilitary forces.
4   Agree to the unconditional and safe return of all refugees and displaced persons, and unhindered access to them by humanitarian aid organizations.
5   Provide credible assurance of his willingness to work on the basis of the Rambouillet accords in the establishment for Kosovo in conformity with international law and the charter of the United Nations.

'The Nato statement went further than the Rambouillet documents in demanding the withdrawal of all Serbian military forces from Kosovo' (*IHT*, 12 April 1999, p. 6).

'Nato is united in not planning a hostile invasion, saying it would only send ground troops into a "permissive environment" ' (*FT*, 13 April 1999, p. 2).

On 14 April 1999 President Yeltsin of Russia appointed Viktor Chernomyrdin as his special envoy on the Kosovo crisis.

On 18 April Belgrade broke off diplomatic relations with Albania.

'Romania agreed Tuesday [20 April 1999] to a Nato request to open an air corridor for [Nato] bombers, subject to parliamentary approval' (*FT*, 22 April 1999, p. 2).

'The Bulgarian prime minister, Ivan Kostov, said Wednesday [21 April 1999] that he had agreed to a Nato request and cut off an oil pipeline to Yugoslavia' (*IHT*, 23 April 1999, p. 4).

On 22 April 1999 Romania's parliament voted to grant a Nato request for unrestricted use of its airspace. The vote was 225 to twenty-one, with ninety-nine abstentions. Slovenia said it would allow Nato forces to cross its territory if ground troops were sent in (*FT*, 23 April 1999, p. 2).

Nato celebrated its fiftieth anniversary on 23 April 1999. (Nato was actually founded on 4 April 1949.) Of the forty-three governments invited to attend the Nato summit only Russia declined the invitation, in protest at the Nato bombing of Yugoslavia.

The three-day Nato summit ended on 25 April 1999. 'The Nato spokesman said the alliance had given security assurances to the frontline states. He said two of the seven countries, Romania and Slovenia, had granted access to their air space, while a parliamentary vote was expected tomorrow [27 April] in Bulgaria on the same issue' (*FT*, 26 April 1999, p. 1). Slovakia's prime minister, Vladimir Dzurinda:

'If ground troops will be necessary, we will always stay on the side of Nato ... Milosevic cannot win. It would be a very dangerous precedent' ... Mr Dzurinda noted that his government had opened Slovak air space to Nato warplanes and had agreed to give the Western alliance ground access along a rail and highway corridor as well.

(*IHT*, 26 April 1999, p. 5)

'Nato's fiftieth anniversary communiqué: "Milosevic must withdraw from Kosovo his military, police and paramilitary forces." The key word "all" is missing' (Charles Krauthammer, *IHT*, 3 May 1999, p. 8).

On 25 April the Bulgarian parliament approved the use of Bulgarian airspace to Nato planes (*EEN*, 1999, vol. 12, no. 16, p. 9).

Vuk Draskovic (Yugoslav deputy prime minister, 25 April 1999):

'People who lead this country must say clearly where we stand ... They must say what will be left of Serbia in twenty days if the bombing continues ... [Yugoslav leaders must] stop lying to the people and finally tell them the truth. The people should be told that Nato is not facing a breakdown, that Russia will not help Yugoslavia militarily, and that world public opinion is against us ... The obligation of all leaders of our country is to face the people every day and explain to them through the media the truth, the reality, and on the basis of that reality we must be ready for very urgent and very brave moves toward approaching a compromise and peace based on the Charter of the United Nations.' He [Draskovic] later added that everything was negotiable except that Kosovo must remain part of Serbia.

(*FT*, 27 April 1999, p. 2)

'On the vital question of how the UN force would be composed, Mr Draskovic indicated that while having Nato nationals on such a force was not desirable, it would be up to the UN to decide' (*FT*, 28 April 1999, p. 2).

On 28 April 1999 Yugoslav deputy prime minister Vuk Draskovic was dismissed 'because of his recent public statements which were in contradiction with the positions of the federal government and jeopardising the respect of the federal government'. 'The ouster ... came three days after Mr Draskovic said the government would entertain a peace deal calling for a UN presence that would include Nato countries' (*IHT*, 29 April 1999, p. 1). 'Earlier this week Mr Draskovic ... proposed that a UN-led peacekeeping force, including Nato representatives, be allowed into Kosovo' (*FT*, 29 April 199, p. 1).

What may have irked Mr Milosevic more than the suggestion that international troops could come into Kosovo was Mr Draskovic's statement that war crimes could have been committed in the province, and that a special commission should be set up to investigate ... Mr Draskovic courted trouble earlier in the airstrikes campaign when he lambasted the killing of the newspaper editor Slavko Curuvija as a cowardly act. 'Those who ordered and committed the murder have taken arms against Serbia more destructive than all the bombs of Nato. Let Slavko be the first and last victim of those who want to initiate a mad circle of fratricidal murder,' Mr Draskovic said ... Mr Draskovic was first arrested in 1985 and jailed in 1991. Two years later he went on hunger strike.

(*The Times*, 29 April 1999, p. 19)

Vuk Draskovic's comments in a later interview:

We cannot yield any piece of our sovereignty under the flag of Nato. However, we are members of the UN and OSCE. Their flag is our flag, too. And under these flags are also the forces of the Nato countries. But we cannot accept Nato alone. The best way to obtain Serbian agreement would be to register any implementation force under the flag of the UN or OSCE, which would include the full involvement of Russian troops and other European countries that are not members of Nato. Serbia will never accept an independent Kosovo. The full territorial integrity of Serbia and Yugoslavia must remain intact ... We Serbs must choose the way of Europeanization.

(*IHT*, 4 May 1999, p. 8)

The British foreign secretary [29 April] yesterday challenged Slobodan Milosevic to air a 'startlingly frank' interview given to the BBC by Vuk Obradovic, a former general and leader of the small opposition Social Democratic Party. The interview was censored by the Yugoslav military.

(*FT*, 30 April 1999, p. 2)

Mr Obradovic, a former general, is the president of the country's Social Democratic Party ... A BBC spokesman said that Mr Obradovic told Mr Simpson: 'President Milosevic is a problem of the democratic forces in Serbia who we are going to get rid of' ... Earlier this week Mr Obradovic gave his view of the president [Milosevic] to *The Guardian*: 'His political initiative is over ... He should leave on his own now. And if he does not, we will make him leave.'

(*Guardian*, 30 April 1999, p. 3)

Vuk Obradovic, president of the Social Democratic Party and once a rising star in the Yugoslav army ... was quoted in the Italian newspaper *La Repubblica* as saying: 'Milosevic should resign – especially because it is clear that he will fall anyway.'

(*Independent*, 20 April 1999, p. 4)

On 2 May 1999 a US F-16 was shot down over Serbia. The pilot was rescued.

'Using a new US weapon for the first time in combat, Nato knocked out electricity in Belgrade and most of Serbia on Monday [3 May] by causing short circuits that took Yugoslav technicians hours to repair' (*IHT*, 4 May 1999, p. 1).

'Hungary reaffirmed [on 3 May] its policy of allowing Nato forces unrestricted use of air space and airfields after a proposal by socialist MPs that Hungary should allow no direct strikes from its bases' (*FT*, 4 May 1999, p. 2).

'Bulgaria's parliament yesterday [4 May] approved a request by Nato to use the country's airspace for launching attacks against Yugoslavia' (*FT*, 5 May 1999, p. 20).

On 6 May 1999 foreign ministers of the G8 countries adopted the following general principles on the political solution to the Kosovo crisis:

1   Immediate, verifiable end of violence and repression in Kosovo.
2   Withdrawal from Kosovo of military, police and paramilitary forces.
3   Deployment in Kosovo of effective international civil and security presences, endorsed and adopted by the United Nations, capable of guaranteeing the achievement of the common objective.
4   Establishment of an interim administration for Kosovo to be decided by the Security Council of the United Nations to ensure conditions for a peaceful and normal life for all inhabitants in Kosovo.
5   The safe and free return of all displaced persons and unimpeded access to Kosovo by humanitarian aid organizations.

6   A political process towards the establishment of an interim political framework agreement providing a substantial self-government for Kosovo, taking full account of the Rambouillet accords and the principles of sovereignty and territorial integrity of the Federal Republic of Yugoslavia and the other countries of the region. Also the demilitarization of the UCK (Kosovo Liberation Army).

7   Comprehensive approach to the economic developments and stabilization of the crisis region.

In order to implement these principles the G8 foreign ministers instructed their political directors to prepare elements of a UN Security Council resolution.

The G8 presidency would inform the Chinese government of the results of the meeting.

On 7 May 1999 the Chinese embassy in Belgrade was bombed. Nato described the bombing as a 'terrible accident', an explanation which China did not accept. It was the result of 'faulty information' as regards targeting, mistaking the building for the federal directorate of supply and procurement (a military office). (It was later revealed that an outdated map had been used and that personnel formerly used to check targets had been switched to finding new targets.) Three Chinese journalists were killed. Angry demonstrations followed in China, including three days of mob attacks on US and UK embassies. On 10 May China suspended co-operation with the USA on stopping proliferation of weapons of mass destruction, and discussions about human rights and high-level military contacts. (On 30 July 1999 the USA agreed to pay $4.5 million to the families of those killed and wounded when the Chinese embassy in Belgrade was bombed. The money would be given to the Chinese government, which would decide how to divide the funds among the three people killed and twenty-seven injured. No mention was then made of compensation for the embassy building. The Chinese foreign minister and the US secretary of state met on 24 July and senior trade negotiators from China and the USA resumed bilateral talks on 26 July. On 16 December 1999 it was announced that the USA had agreed to pay $28 million by way of compensation for the embassy building, while China agreed to pay $2.87 million for damage caused to US diplomatic buildings in China during demonstrations: *IHT*, 17 December 1999, p. 4. An announcement was made on 9 April 2000: 'The CIA has fired one intelligence officer and reprimanded six managers, including a senior official, for errors that led to the US bombing of the Chinese embassy in Belgrade … The Yugoslav arms agency … was the only target chosen by the CIA … According to the CIA, an intelligence officer … obtained the correct address of the Yugoslav Federal Directorate of Supply and Procurement … But the detailed two-year-old map used for targeting did not show the numbers of the buildings on that street, so the officer used the numbering of buildings on parallel streets … A cross-check of various databases listing sensitive sites, such as schools, hospitals and embassies, failed to catch the error because the data had not been updated after the Chinese embassy moved there from another part of Belgrade in 1996': *IHT*, 10 April

2000, pp. 1, 5. A spokesman for the Chinese foreign ministry said on 10 April: 'The Chinese embassy in Yugoslavia has unmistakable markings and is also clearly indicated on US maps. The US claim that it did not know its exact location does not hold water. It is hard for people to believe that the bombing was the fault of several officials whose mistake was not corrected in a review process. The Chinese government strongly demands a comprehensive and thorough investigation into its bombing of the Chinese embassy in Yugoslavia, bring the perpetrators to justice and give the Chinese government and people a satisfactory explanation': *FT*, 11 April 2000, p. 12; *IHT*, 11 April 2000, p. 5.)

'The Serb announcement [on 10 May] to reduce troops in Kosovo to levels prior to the Nato air campaign would cut troop numbers from a Nato-estimated 40,000 to around 30,000' (*FT*, 12 May 1999, p. 2). 'Yugoslavia said Monday [10 May] it was ordering a partial withdrawal of its 40,000 soldiers and police forces in the province, apparently aiming for a level of around 12,000 troops' (*IHT*, 12 May 1999, p. 6). 'Government troops could be reduced to about 12,000, that is the number of soldiers normally responsible for security in Kosovo' (*IHT*, 13 May 1999, p. 5).

In May 1999 there were reports of anti-Milosevic demonstrations in the Serbian towns Krusevac and Aleksandrovac, mainly by women and children related to reservists. Those taking part numbered around 3,000 and 1,000 respectively. Further demonstrations took place in these towns and others (such as Pancevo, Cacak and Raska). Reservists themselves also took part in the demonstrations.

> In Krusevac [on 17 May] more than 3,000 demanded an end to the Kosovo fighting and called for the return of men sent from the town to fight ... Protesters chanted: 'We want sons, not coffins' ... In Alexandrovac 1,000 people ... tried to stop troops from returning to the front.
> (*The Times*, 19 May 1999, p. 1)

> Anti-war demonstrations have erupted in towns in southern Serbia ... the industrial town of Krusevac and nearby Aleksandrovac. Local journalists said the protests were triggered by the return of the bodies of ten reservists killed in Kosovo just as more conscripts were due to go to the front. Demonstrations began on Monday [17 May] and continued yesterday [18 May] ... Many of the protesters, about 3,000 in Krusevac and 1,000 in Aleksandrovac, were women and children.
> (*FT*, 19 May 1999, p. 1)

> Anti-war protests yesterday [19 May] spread to the northern industrial city of Pancevo [in Serbia], where ... several hundred people, many of them women, demonstrated against the mobilization of reservists ... [A Nato spokesman] said troops probably heard about the 'forceful measures' being used by police to break up the families' demonstrations against conscription.
> (*FT*, 20 May 1999, p. 2)

'Citing a Montenegrin newspaper, Reuters reported Thursday [20 May] that about 1,000 Serbian army troops had deserted from their posts in Kosovo and joined anti-war demonstrations in two southern Serbian towns' (*IHT*, 21 May 1999, p. 1).

> A group of about 400 reservists arrived Wednesday [19 May] in Aleksandrovac and Krusevac, their hometowns, claiming they would not go back ... Hundreds of deserters also arrived in Krusevac ... Women in Krusevac and Aleksandrovac organized street protests, demanding their sons be allowed to return home from army service in Kosovo ... Hundreds of mothers, wives and sisters of conscripted soldiers and reservists sent to Kosovo were reported to have taken part in demonstrations in Krusevac and Aleksandrovac on Wednesday [19 May]. The women's protests reportedly began after the bodies of seven soldiers were brought back to Krusevac on Friday [14 May] ... Three were brought back to Aleksandrovac ... Demonstrations have also been reported in Cacak, not far from Belgrade ... Large numbers of reservists have been called up in southern Serbia.
>
> (p. 5)

> About 1,000 reservists rushed back to their hometowns in southern Serbia after hearing reports that police had maltreated their relatives – mostly mothers – holding anti-war protests ... In the central city of Cacak the local council is under opposition control. The mayor has objected to the army placing troops and equipment close to civilian areas and several hundred people this week demonstrated for an end to the war ... The Yugoslav army is built around a small core of professionals and a large mass of first-time conscripts and reservists.
>
> (*FT*, 21 May 1999, p. 2)

> Anti-war protests ... continued in Krusevac yesterday [24 May] where, residents said, up to 2,000 reservists and their relatives rejected orders for the conscripts to return to Kosovo ... Residents in Raska said their families demanded mobilization from Mr Milosevic's northern hometown of Pozarevac instead. There were also unconfirmed reports that anti-war protests by Serbs had spread for the first time to Kosovo, in the central town of Lipljan, which has been hit heavily by Nato.
>
> (*FT*, 25 May 1999, p. 2)

> Protests have begun again in towns and villages in Yugoslavia as army reservists, supported by their mothers, wives and other family members, have resisted orders to go back to Kosovo ... The unrest appears to be spreading in the region. As crowds appeared back on the streets in Krusevac and Aleksandrovac, protests by reservists and their families were also reported in the town of Raska, close to the border with Kosovo ... A resident who watched the protest Sunday [23 May] ... estimated that perhaps

as many as 2,000 people demonstrated for several hours in the city [Krusevac] centre Monday [24 May] and the same number Sunday [23 May] ... The reservists ... are not refusing outright to serve in Kosovo, residents who described the protests say, but are asking that other reservists do a tour of duty first. Many accuse the local authorities, and in particular the governing Socialist Party, of showing favouritism and allowing young men with connections to avoid being ordered into active service.

(*IHT*, 26 May 1999, p. 9)

President Clinton (in an article published in the *IHT* on 24 May 1999): 'While I do not rule out other military options, we are pursuing our present strategy.'

The Nato allies approved plans Tuesday [25 May 1999] to send at least 20,000 additional troops to Albania and Macedonia as part of an augmented peacekeeping force ... The expanded presence, which is expected to reach nearly 50,000 allied soldiers within weeks [raising the size of their ground forces to between 45,000 and 50,000], seems likely to fuel a controversial debate about the prospects of launching an invasion ... While the allies say that their soldiers will enter ... [Kosovo] only to enforce a peacekeeping mandate, top Nato political and military leaders have sought recently to foster ambiguity about the force's eventual mission ... 'All options remain open,' secretary-general Javier Solana said ... Nato officials said there are about 14,000 troops employed in Macedonia and 8,000 more in Albania, where they have been helping to care for nearly 90,000 refugees ... Britain has been the leading advocate of increasing the alliance's ground presence so that Nato troops would be in a position to enter Kosovo even without the consent of the Belgrade government, once Yugoslav forces have been sufficiently battered by sustained bombing raids. Germany, Greece and Italy have objected to any consideration that the alliance might send an invasion force into Yugoslav territory in the absence of permission from the Belgrade government or the UN Security Council.

(*IHT*, 26 May 1999, p. 10)

Nato approved plans to prepare an expanded force (Kfor Plus) of about 48,000, (compared with the previous figure of 23,000) to implement a peace agreement (*FT*, 26 May 1999, p. 2).

On 27 May 1999 the UN's International Criminal Tribunal for the former Yugoslavia indicted Slobodan Milosevic (and four others), the first time that this has happened to a sitting head of state. The charge: 'The accused planned, instigated, ordered, committed or otherwise aided and abetted in a campaign of terror and violence directed at Kosovo Albanian citizens.'

Louise Arbour (chief prosecutor):

On 22 May I presented an indictment for confirmation against Slobodan Milosevic and four others, charging them with crimes against humanity –

specifically murder, deportation and persecutions, and with violations of the laws and customs of war. The indictment was confirmed on 24 May ... The following accused are jointly indicted: Slobodan Milosevic, president of the Federal Republic of Yugoslavia; Milan Milutinovic, president of the Republic of Serbia; Nikola Sainovic, deputy prime minister of the FRY; Dragoljub Ojdanovic, chief of the general staff of the armed forces of the FRY; and Vlajko Stojiljkovic, minister of internal affairs of the FRY ... This indictment does not represent the totality of the charges that may result from our continuing investigations of these accused, nor does it represent our final determination of the responsibility of others in relation to the same events. The present indictment is based exclusively on crimes committed since the beginning of 1999 in Kosovo. We are continuing to develop an evidentiary base upon which I believe we will be able to expand upon the present charges. We are actively investigating other incidents in Kosovo, as well as the role of the accused, or of some of them, in Croatia and Bosnia ... There is a credible basis to believe that these accused are criminally responsible for the deportation of 740 Kosovo Albanians and the murder of 340 Kosovo Albanians.

Russia has agreed to tell Slobodan Milosevic that Nato forces must be at the core of an international force in postwar Kosovo ... Western diplomats said. Until now Moscow has never challenged Mr Milosevic's position of accepting a lightly armed peacekeeping force, including Russian forces and troops from neutral nations, but excluding units from Nato countries that have fought against Serbia.

(*IHT*, 29 May 1999, p. 1)

Russian envoy Viktor Chernomyrdin and Finnish president and EU envoy Martti Ahtisaari flew to Belgrade on 2 June 1999 after extensive talks in Bonn at an EU summit (with US deputy secretary of state Strobe Talbott in attendance) which resulted in an international peace plan to be presented to Slobodan Milosevic. Martti Ahtisaari: 'It is neither negotiations nor an ultimatum. It is making an offer for peace and spelling out in no uncertain terms what the conditions are.'

Speaking Thursday evening [3 June] in Cologne, where he was briefing the fifteen EU leaders upon his return from Belgrade, Mr Ahtisaari agreed that it was necessary for everybody to communicate the same message to Belgrade. 'To me it was absolutely vital that there would be no doubt and no misunderstanding about what was being discussed,' he said. When he presented the peace package in Belgrade on Wednesday evening [2 June], Mr Ahtisaari made a point of reading the entire document aloud. The Finnish president said there was never any question of negotiating with Mr Milosevic. 'My role was to answer questions about the document, and there were plenty of them,' he said, the most pointed being whether he could improve on the conditions that the paper laid out. 'I had to say that it was the best offer the international community was in a position to make,' Mr Ahtisaari said. Rather than say more, he urged Mr Milosevic to discuss the terms with members of his government and deliver his decision at a meeting the following day.

(*IHT*, 5 June 1999, p. 4)

The Yugoslav government and Serbian parliament accepted the international peace plan brought by Martti Ahtisaari and Viktor Chernomyrdin on 3 June 1999. (Note that the footnote mentioned in point 10 below was not voted upon: *IHT*, 8 June 1999, p. 8.)

The text of the document was as follows:

1   The immediate and verifiable end of violence and repression in Kosovo.
2   The verifiable withdrawal from Kosovo of all military, police and paramilitary forces according to a rapid time schedule. [Note the word 'all'.]
3   Deployment in Kosovo, under the aegis of the United Nations, of effective international civilian and security presences.
4   The international security presence with substantial Nato participation must be deployed under unified command and control and authorized to establish a safe environment for all people in Kosovo and to facilitate the safe return to their homes of all displaced persons and refugees.
5   The establishment of an interim administration for Kosovo as part of the international civilian presence under which the people of Kosovo can enjoy substantial autonomy within the FRY (Federal Republic of Yugoslavia) to be decided by the Security Council of the United Nations. The interim administration to provide transitional administration while establishing and overseeing the development of provisional democratic self-governing institutions to ensure conditions for a peaceful and normal life of all inhabitants in Kosovo.

    [On 2 June 1999 Bernard Kouchner, the French health minister, was named as the special representative of the UN secretary-general (SRSG) for Kosovo, the head of the UN civil administration in Kosovo (UNMIK). Bernard Kouchner arrived in Kosovo on 15 July 1999.]
6   After withdrawal an agreed number of Yugoslav and Serbian personnel will be permitted to return to perform the following functions: liaison with international civil mission and international presence; marking/ clearing minefields; maintaining a presence at Serb patrimonial sites; maintaining a presence at key border crossings.
7   Safe and free return of all refugees and displaced persons under the supervision of the UNHCR and unimpeded access to Kosovo by humanitarian aid organizations.
8   A political process towards the establishment of an interim political

framework agreement providing for a substantial self-government for Kosovo, taking full account of the Rambouillet accords and the principles of sovereignty and territorial integrity of the FDY and the other countries of the region, and the demilitarization of the UCK (KLA). Negotiations between the parties for a settlement should not delay or disrupt the establishment of democratic self-governing institutions.

9   A comprehensive approach to the economic development and stabilization of the crisis region. This will include the implementation of a Stability Pact for South-Eastern Europe with broad international participation in order to further promotion of democracy, economic prosperity, stability and regional co-operation.

10   Suspension of military activity will require acceptance of the principles set forth above in addition to agreement to other, previously identified, required elements, which are specified in the footnote. A military–technical agreement will then be rapidly concluded.

Withdrawal: Procedures for withdrawals, including the phased, detailed schedule and delineation of a buffer area in Serbia beyond which forces will be withdrawn.

Returning personnel: Equipment associated [with] the returning personnel; Terms of reference for their functional responsibilities; Timetable for their return; Delineation of their geographical areas of operation; Rules governing their relationship to international security presence and international civil mission.

Other required elements:

Rapid and precise timetable for withdrawals meaning, e.g. seven days to complete withdrawal; air defence weapons withdrawn outside a 25 km mutual safety zone within forty-eight hours.

Return of personnel for the four functions specified above will be under the supervision of the international security presence and will be limited to a small agreed number (hundreds not thousands).

Suspension of military activity will occur after the beginning of verifiable withdrawals.

The discussion and achieving of a military–technical agreement shall not extend the previously determined time for completion of withdrawals.

A second footnote refers to the composition of the international force:

It is understood that Nato considers an international security force with 'substantial Nato participation' to mean unified command and control and having Nato at the core. This in turn means a unified Nato chain of command under the political direction of the North Atlantic Council in consultation with non-Nato force contributors. All Nato countries, partners and other countries will be eligible to contribute to the international security force. Nato units will be under Nato command. It is understood that Russia's position is that the Russian contingent will not be under Nato command and its relationship to the international presence will be governed by relevant additional agreements.

('The radical Party and its leader, deputy prime minister Vojislav Seselj, voted against the proposals in parliament, and Mr Seselj vowed to quit the government the day after Nato troops entered Kosovo': *IHT*, 4 June 1999, p. 2.)

On 8 June 1999 foreign ministers of the G8 countries agreed on a draft resolution to be presented to the UN Security Council. The following sequence of events was envisaged: (1) signature of the military–technical agreement; (2) verifiable start of the Serb military withdrawal; (3) a pause in Nato bombing; (4) adoption of the resolution by the UN Security Council; (5) deployment of peacekeeping forces; (6) formal end of the Nato air campaign upon completion of the Serb withdrawal. Events 2, 3 and 4 were meant to be almost simultaneous. This would allow fulfilment of the demand by Russia and China for a halt in bombing before the passing of the resolution.

Key portions of the draft resolution were as follows:

The Security Council:

Demands in particular that the Federal Republic of Yugoslavia put an immediate and verifiable end to violence and repression in Kosovo and begin/complete verifiable phased withdrawals from Kosovo of all military, police and paramilitary forces according to a rapid timetable, with which the deployment of the international security presence in Kosovo will be synchronized. [Note that an aim here was to avoid a vacuum which the KLA might try to fill. Another aim was to prevent withdrawing Yugoslav troops taking revenge on ethnic Albanians.]

Confirms that after the withdrawal an agreed number of Yugoslav and Serb military and police personnel will be permitted to return to Kosovo to perform the functions in accordance with Annex 2.

Decides on the deployment in Kosovo, under UN auspices, of civil and security presences, with appropriate equipment and personnel as required.

Requests the secretary-general to appoint in consultation with the Security Council a special representative to control the implementation of the civil presence, and further requests the secretary-general to instruct his special representative to co-ordinate closely with the international security presence to ensure that both presences operate towards the same goals and in a mutually supportive manner. [The tasks of the 'special representative' include 'promoting the establishment, pending a final settlement, of substantial autonomy and self-government in Kosovo': quoted in *IHT*, 14 June 1999, p. 8.]

Authorizes member states and relevant international organizations to establish the international security presence in Kosovo as set out in point 4 of Annex 2. ['All necessary means' implies that military action may be used if necessary, as laid out under Chapter 7 of the UN charter. Chapter 7 authorizes the Security Council to intervene against a sovereign state in the interests of international peace.]

Decides that the responsibilities of the international security presence to be deployed in Kosovo will include: demilitarizing the Kosovo Liberation Army (KLA); establishing a secure environment in which refugees and displaced persons can return home in safety; supervising de-mining until the international civil presence can take responsibility for this task; border-monitoring duties.

Authorizes the secretary-general to establish an international civil presence in Kosovo in order to provide an interim administration under which the people of Kosovo can enjoy substantial autonomy.

Demands full co-operation by all concerned, including the international security presence, with the International Criminal Tribunal for the former Yugoslavia.

Demands that the KLA and other armed Kosovo Albanian groups end immediately all offensive actions and comply with the requirements for demilitarization as laid down by the head of the international security presence.

Decides that the civil and security presences, established for an initial period of twelve months, are to continue thereafter unless the Security Council decides otherwise.

Annex 1:

Petersberg Principles, 6 May 1999 (excerpts):

The G8 foreign ministers adopted the following general principles on the political solution to the Kosovo crisis:

Deployment in Kosovo of effective international civil and security presences, endorsed and adopted by the United Nations, capable of guaranteeing the achievement of the common objectives.

The safe and free return of all refugees and displaced persons and unimpeded access to Kosovo by humanitarian aid organizations.

A political process towards the establishment of an interim political framework agreement providing for a substantial self-government for Kosovo.

Annex 2 (3 June 1999 agreement):

Agreement should be reached on the following principles to move toward a resolution of the Kosovo crisis:

Verifiable withdrawal from Kosovo of all military, police and paramilitary forces according to a rapid time schedule.

Deployment in Kosovo, under UN auspices, of effective international civilian and security presences.

The international security presence with substantial Nato participation must be deployed under unified command and control.

Establishment of an interim administration for Kosovo as part of the international civilian presence under which the people of Kosovo can enjoy substantial autonomy.

After withdrawal an agreed number of Yugoslav and Serbian personnel will be permitted to return to perform the following functions: liaison with international civil mission and international presence; marking/clearing minefields; maintaining a presence at Serb patrimonial sites; maintaining a presence at key border crossings.

Safe and free return of all refugees and displaced persons.

A political process towards the establishment of an interim political framework agreement providing for a substantial self-government for Kosovo, taking full account of the Rambouillet accords and the principles of sovereignty and territorial integrity of the Federal Republic of Yugoslavia and the other countries of the region, and the demilitarization of the KLA.

Suspension of military activity will require acceptance of the principles set forth above in addition to agreement to other, previously identified, required elements.

Rapid and precise timetable for withdrawals; air defence weapons withdrawn outside a 25 km mutual safety zone within forty-eight hours.

Return of personnel for the four functions specified above will be under the supervision of the international security presence and will be limited to a small agreed number (hundreds not thousands).

Suspension of military activity will occur after the beginning of verifiable withdrawals.

The discussion and achieving of a military–technical agreement shall not extend the previously determined time for completion of withdrawals.

The exact relationship with Russian forces will be the subject of negotiations between Nato and Russia.

On 9 June 1999 the military–technical agreement was signed on behalf of Nato by Lieutenant-General Michael Jackson (the British general in charge of the allied rapid reaction force and of Kfor). Two Yugoslav generals signed on behalf of the FRY. (Dragoljub Ojdanovic, chief of the general staff of the armed forces of the FRY, did not attend the talks because he has been indicted as a war criminal by the international court.) Concessions to the Yugoslav military included an extension in the time allowed for the withdrawal of their forces from seven to eleven days. The buffer zone in Serbia is now five kilometres for Yugoslav forces, while there is a twenty-five-kilometre no-fly zone.

A formal suspension of Nato bombing was announced on 10 June 1999 after a start to the Yugoslav withdrawal had been verified. (But Nato air strikes actually stopped when the military–technical agreement was signed.) This was followed by the UN Security Council approving the resolution (with only minor amendments) by fourteen to zero, with China abstaining.

> Nato military commanders were caught by surprise Friday [11 June 1999] when Russia sent the first foreign peacekeeping troops into Yugoslavia … A Russian convoy consisting of about fifty vehicles and up to 200 soldiers crossed the Yugoslav border from Bosnia early in the day … The battalion was drawn from some 1,300 Russian soldiers who are based in the northern Bosnian town of Ugljevik … The US deputy secretary of state Strobe Talbott … reversed course in mid-air and flew back to Moscow Friday after hearing about the Russian troop movement … Foreign minister Igor Ivanov … said the Russian soldiers were preparing to assume positions along the northern rim of Kosovo but did not plan to enter Kosovo without co-ordinating their moves with allied commanders … Russia insists on having its own sector, preferably in the north where Serbian religious shrines and many of the province's Serb inhabitants are located. But Nato commanders fear that a Russian sector would quickly lead to the *de facto* partition of Kosovo … Nato military authorities have divided the Kosovo map into five sectors that would be controlled by allied forces from Britain, France, Italy, Germany and the United States.
>
> (*IHT*, 12 June 1999, pp. 1, 4)

> It was confirmed yesterday [14 June] that Moscow had tried to fly additional troops from Russia into Kosovo on Friday evening [11 June] … Hungary's prime minister said he had rejected a request from Moscow to allow six aircraft, containing 600 paratroops, to use Hungarian air space. Bulgaria said yesterday [14 June] it had also refused access to Russian military aircraft.
>
> (*FT*, 15 June 1999, p. 4)

'So far Bulgaria, Romania and Hungary ... have resisted Russian requests to use their airspace, saying that they are waiting clarification about the disposition of the peacekeeping force' (*IHT*, 16 June 1999, p. 1)

The Russian troops arrived at Pristina airport in the early hours of Saturday 12 June, while Nato forces did not start moving into Kosovo until dawn. The Russian troops were welcomed by ethnic Serbs and Nato forces by ethnic Albanians. The Russian forces blocked off the airport, which led to a standoff with Nato forces. Russia's move was generally seen as a response to not being allocated a separate sector and as an attempt to divide Kosovo into Serbian and ethnic Albanian parts.

It was unclear who had issued the orders for the rapid advance of Russian troops. Russian foreign minister Igor Ivanov told reporters that the movement of the troops was 'something of a surprise for me' (*IHT*, 14 June 1999, p. 10). 'Igor Ivanov ... admitted his ministry had not been informed about the move' (*FT*, 14 June 1999, p. 2). 'Nato officials did note that Russia had broken an agreement [relating to Sfor in Bosnia] by sending its troops from Bosnia' (*FT*, 16 June 1999, p. 2).

> Sir Michael Jackson balked at carrying out an order from Nato's supreme commander, General Wesley Clark, to send a force to seize the airport ahead of the Russians ... General Jackson said: 'No, I'm not going to do that. It's not worth starting World War Three.'
>
> (*IHT*, 11 September 1999, p. 1)

> General Jackson's resistance to General Clark [comes] under a little-known Nato procedure that allows a Nato officer to consult his national commanding officer if he wishes to disobey an order from a superior Alliance officer of another nation ... General Jackson's reservations won the day when senior military commanders in Britain and the United States decided together to rescind the order.
>
> (*IHT*, 14 September 1999, p. 4)

(British prime minister Tony Blair, although a strong advocate of Nato bombing and the use of ground troops if necessary, was against the use of British troops to seize Pristina airport.)

On 15 June 1999 a statement was issued by the Holy Synod of the Serbian Orthodox Church:

> Every sensible person has to realise that numerous internal problems and the isolation of our country on the international scene cannot be solved or overcome with this kind of government and under the present circumstances. Faced with the tragic situation in our nation and our country we demand that the current President of the country and his government resign in the interest of the people and their salvation so that new officials acceptable at home and abroad can take responsibility for the people and

their future as a national salvation government ... We also appeal to our brothers in Kosovo to stay in their homes and not to leave their relics ... [The Church is] convinced that the final justice is with our Lord and not in the hands of an instrumentalized court in The Hague.

The church was generally associated with Serbia's expansionist wars in the nineties, but its bishops turned against the regime after the 1995 Bosnian peace deal which they saw as a sell-out ... The church is particularly associated with Kosovo; the seat of the Orthodox patriarch is in Pec and the present Patriarch, Pavle, is a former bishop of the diocese of Prizren.

(Marcus Tanner, Guardian, 16 June 1999, p. 2)

In the frankest admission by a senior cleric of Serb atrocities committed against Moslem Albanians, Bishop Artemije of Kosovo spoke of the 'evil' committed by Serbs. But he insisted that there was no collective guilt and reiterated the Church's demand that Yugoslav president Slobodan Milosevic resign. 'We Serbs have lived in great pain and compassion at what was happening to our Albanian neighbours. We were sorry for every innocent victim,' said Bishop Artemije in Gracanica monastery.

(FT, 29 June 1999, p. 1)

Late Friday [18 June 1999] the US secretary of defence, William Cohen, reached an agreement with Russian officials, including the defence minister, Marshal Igor Sergeyev, to add 3,600 Russian troops to the peacekeeping force, which will ultimately total more than 50,000. Russia will deploy troops in the American, German and French sectors and control the grounds of Pristina airport, while leaving air control to Nato forces.

(IHT, 21 June 1999, p. 5)

The agreement provides that the Russian troops will operate within the US, German and French sectors of Kosovo, plus Pristina's airport in the British sector ... British forces will direct air traffic ... With no separate Russian sector there will be no obvious geographic basis for partition. Russian troops will serve under Russian commanders, who in turn will report to the top Nato officers of their sectors.

(p. 8)

Russian troops will not have to apprehend people accused of committing war crimes (*IHT*, 1 July 1999, p. 5).

Moscow would control its own soldiers, but would co-ordinate all activities with the respective national commanders of the sectors, who in turn would answer to Nato's chief commander in Kosovo, British General Mike Jackson

... Britain has committed about 13,000 troops, France 9,000, Germany 8,000 and the USA 7,500.

(*IHT*, 19 June 1999, p. 1)

Negotiators for Nato and the Kremlin agreed on terms Monday [5 July 1999] for deploying peacekeepers in Kosovo ... But neither side would disclose details of the negotiations ... The nature of the compromise that allowed Monday's agreement was not clear ... Russian officials said ... that a Russian liaison at Nato headquarters in Belgium would continue to work on other points of the deployment ... A workable formula for the operation seemed to have been devised last month. The accord stated that Russian troops would not serve under a direct Nato command, but instead would accept – and by and large execute – Nato orders issued through a liaison. But after the signing Moscow began arguing that its troops should be allowed to follow Russian orders, not Nato's, according to Western officials.

(*IHT*, 6 July 1999, pp. 1, 4)

Javier Solana said Sunday [20 June 1999] that all Serbian troops and police had left Kosovo province in compliance with the agreement signed 9 June and that he was, therefore, officially terminating Nato's bombing campaign against Yugoslavia ... Yugoslav forces completed their pullout eleven hours before the midnight deadline.

(*IHT*, 21 June 1999, p. 5)

'Lieutenant-General Sir Mike Jackson, the Kfor commander, had reported Kosovo clear of all uniformed Yugoslav forces – except for a few stragglers – by 1 p.m. local time yesterday [20 June] ... eleven hours ahead of the deadline of midnight local time' (*FT*, 21 June 1999, p. 1).

The G8 countries met in Cologne on 18–20 June 1999, although President Yeltsin of Russia made an appearance only on the final day. 'Mr Clinton and other leaders adamantly refused to channel reconstruction funds to Serbia as long as Mr Milosevic remained in office' (*IHT*, 21 June 1999, p. 1).

The Cologne declaration, however, opens the way for immediate humanitarian aid to the entire Balkan region, conditioning 'reconstruction' aid to democratic reforms in Serbia. The eight leaders endorsed the creation of a 'stability pact' for the Balkans, an initiative of the EU.

(p. 6)

'The leaders affirmed their strong support for the EU-led stability pact for the reconstruction of south-east Europe ... There were no specifics on how much money would be involved, although it was accepted that Europe should pay the lion's share' (*FT*, 21 June 1999, p. 3). ('President Clinton said [in Bonn] Monday [21 June] that humanitarian assistance for Yugoslavia could include electricity to keep hospitals running and prevent people from freezing in the winter': *IHT*, 22

June 1999, p. 7. Clinton: 'It's important ... that the Serbs not freeze to death and that hospitals should not be forced to close. But building bridges so they can go to work? I don't buy that.')

On 21 June 1999 Nato and the KLA announced a detailed demilitarization agreement drawn up by Nato officers and KLA commanders. The agreement is signed by Lieutenant-General Sir Michael Jackson and Hashim Thaci.

1   Effective immediately:

All hostile acts by the KLA will cease, including firing of weapons, use of explosive devices, placing of mines, use of barriers or checkpoints. The conducting of other military, security or training activities will cease.

The KLA will not attack, detain or intimidate any civilians in Kosovo or confiscate or violate their property.

The KLA agrees not to conduct any reprisals, counterattacks or unilaterals in response to violations of the accord.

The KLA ceases movements of 'armed bodies' into neighbouring countries. (This applies to movements to and from countries such as Albania and Macedonia.)

2   Within four days of signing:

The KLA will close all fighting positions, entrenchments and checkpoints on roads, and mark minefields and booby traps.

A joint implementation commission will be established with representatives from the KLA and Nato-led forces.

3   Within seven days:

The KLA will establish secure weapons storage sites to be verified by Nato forces. The storage sites apply to all weapons except for pistols and licensed hunting shotguns.

The KLA will clear minefields and booby traps and vacate fighting positions. The KLA members will assemble in authorized locations agreed by Nato commanders. Kfor permission will be needed to leave these areas. ('The rebels have agreed to carry weapons only in the designated assembly areas, with only commanders and their bodyguards permitted to be armed outside these': *IHT*, 30 June 1999, p. 4. 'Members are supposed to be confined to barracks, and if they venture out must not carry weapons or wear uniforms or insignia ... Commanders [however] are still allowed to wear their uniforms and carry pistols when on official business. They can also be accompanied by three bodyguards each': *IHT*, 1 July 1999, p. 10.)

4   Within thirty days:

All KLA members not of 'local origin' to withdraw.

The KLA to store in registered sites all prohibited weapons. The KLA members will no longer be permitted to carry prohibited weapons, including all automatic rifles, and any weapon 12.7 mm or larger, and all missiles, mines, grenades or other explosives. Once these weapons are stored they will be under the joint control of the KLA and Nato for sixty days, after which Nato will assume complete control. No weapons will be carried within 1.5 miles of main roads and principal towns and cities as well as the border.

5   Within ninety days:

The KLA will have completed the process of demilitarization and will stop wearing military uniforms or KLA insignia. Kfor permission will be needed to train and parade. (Nato military commanders originally proposed that the KLA stop wearing their uniforms or other insignia within thirty days.)

The agreement allows for the 'formation of an army in Kosovo on the lines of the US National Guard in due course as part of a political process designed to determine Kosovo's future status'. It will have a core of 4,000 professionals plus reservists.

Clause 8 of the agreement threatens 'military action as deemed appropriate' by the commander of Kfor for any KLA member in breach of the agreement.

Hashim Thaci, the KLA's political head, said yesterday [21 June 1999] that under the deal the movement would transform itself into a national guard. The agreement also offers 'special consideration' to KLA fighters in the formation of civilian administration and the police force 'in view of the expertise they have developed'.

(FT, 22 June 1999, p. 3)

The paragraph says the international community should take full account of the KLA's contribution during the Kosovo crisis. There should be recognition that the KLA is 'committed to propose individual current members to participate in the administration and police force of Kosovo, enjoying special consideration in view of the expertise they have developed'.

(FT, 23 June 1999, p. 3)

The agreement reached early Monday [21 June] to disband the KLA included – at the insistence of its commanders – a pledge by the Nato allies to consider letting the rebels form a provisional army for Kosovo modelled on the United States National Guard ... Some Nato allies, particularly

Germany, opposed including the pledge in the final document ... The rebel group [is] said to include 10,000 hardened fighters and 30,000 irregulars who joined after being driven from their homes this spring.

(*IHT*, 22 June 1999, p. 1)

General Jackson took pains to emphasize the document signed Monday was 'a unilateral undertaking' on the part of the rebels ... He insisted that it was not a formal pact with Nato like the one with the Yugoslav generals that laid out the deadlines for withdrawing their troops, underscoring the sensitivity of appearing to endorse the creation of a provisional army.

(p. 7)

'The National Guard analogy removes the implication of Kosovo sovereignty, as American states have them' (*IHT*, 24 June 1999, p. 10). 'The US National Guard ... [is] a citizens' militia which can use heavy weapons' (*The Economist*, 26 June 1999, p. 49).

'The success of the KLA in assuming civil power in much of the province – with international community administrators yet to arrive – is a foretaste of troubles to come' (William Pfaff, *IHT*, 24 June 1999, p. 10).

A human rights investigator for Amnesty International said that hundreds of detainees were certainly being held in Serbia ... The peace deal with Slobodan Milosevic ... failed to include a clause guaranteeing the International Committee of the Red Cross access to all prisons to ensure that Kosovo Albanians did not disappear into Serbian jails.

(*IHT*, 25 June 1999, p. 7)

On 29 June 1999 there took place the first of a series of anti-government demonstrations organized by the Alliance for Change, an umbrella group of around thirty opposition parties. Demands included the resignation of Milosevic and early elections. (On 12 June 1999 the main Serbian opposition parties, excluding Vuk Draskovic's Serbian Renewal Movement, had met in Herceg Novi in Montenegro with representatives of the ruling Montenegrin Democratic Party of Socialists to form the Alliance for Change, composed of around thirty parties and movements. The meeting was attended in part by some senior foreign emissaries, including US envoy Robert Gelbard: *EEN*, 1999, vol. 12, no. 18, p. 9.)

'The Nato secretary-general, Javier Solana, said Friday [2 July] the alliance would take action if President Slobodan Milosevic of Yugoslavia tried to provoke a conflict in Montenegro' (*IHT*, 3 July 1999, p. 5).

The Kosovo peace agreement reached in June guaranteed that Serbia would not deploy withdrawing troops into Montenegro, and stipulated that Nato would take action if the accord was not respected, he added. Mr Solana also said that he would not favour Montenegro's becoming independent from its partnership with Serbia to make up federal Yugoslavia.

(*IHT*, 3 July 1999, internet)

'The international community made clear yesterday [13 July 1999 in Brussels] it would provide economic support to Montenegro, but reiterated that Serbia ... would get only humanitarian aid while President Slobodan Milosevic remained in power' (*FT*, 14 July 1999, p. 2).

Efforts to dislodge Slobodan Milosevic from power were bolstered last night [12 July 1999] when ... He [Vuk Draskovic] told the BBC that his party will hold its first mass demonstration on Saturday [17 July] in the central Serbian town of Kragujevac ... Mr Draskovic runs the widely-watched Studio B television station.

(*Guardian*, 13 July 1999, p. 2)

'Ibrahim Rugova ... returned here [Pristina on 15 July 1999] ... Mr Rugova received a warm welcome from a cheering crowd' (*IHT*, 16 July 1999, p. 4).

Barely hours after returning home, Ibrahim Rugova ... left again for Italy [on 15 July] ... His unexpected departure put a cloud over the first session [on 16 July] of the UN-appointed [advisory] Kosovo Transitional Council ... The UN had delayed the session by several days to allow Mr Rugova to attend, but he instructed his party, the Democratic League of Kosovo (LDK), to boycott it.

(*Guardian*, 17 July 1999, p. 17)

'The Alliance for Change ... attracted 10,000 people to a rally in the town [of Kragujevac] on Thursday [15 July]' (*Guardian*, 17 July 1999, p. 17).

The Serbian parliament ... formally repealed on Thursday [15 July] a decree in effect during the Nato air campaign against Yugoslavia, which banned residents from gathering in public places. It also repealed other decrees, including those that allowed the police to conduct searches without a warrant, those that expanded police powers without a warrant, those that expanded police powers and those that limited the freedom of movement of people suspected of undermining the country's defence.

(*IHT*, 16 July 1999, p. 4)

On 17 July some 20,000 people in Kragujevac attended the first rally organized by Vuk Draskovic's Serbian Renewal Movement (*IHT*, 19 July 1999, p. 4).

On 23 July 1999 Russia ended its boycott on contacts with Nato, attending a meeting in Brussels. (On 16 February 2000 the new Nato secretary-general, George Robertson, visited Russia. 'A joint statement issued after George Robertson, Nato secretary-general, met Vladimir Putin ... said the two sides aimed to intensify their contacts and become a cornerstone of European security': *FT*, 17 February 2000, p. 12.)

On 24 July 1999 Vuk Draskovic spoke at a rally in Nis attended by around 25,000 people.

> This will be Mr Draskovic's last mass rally for some time, senior aides said Saturday [24 July] … His aides say he will hold no more meetings for at least several weeks … Mr Draskovic is concentrating instead on trying to choose a transitional government of experts agreed on by most or all opposition parties, and then trying to push Mr Milosevic to empower that government and finally to step aside after new elections … The Alliance for Change demands Mr Milosevic's resignation first, before any transitional government.
>
> (*IHT*, 26 July 1999, p. 4)

> The KLA has taken sweeping control in Kosovo, establishing a network of self-appointed ministries and local councils, seizing businesses and apartments and collecting taxes and customs payments in the absence of a strong international presence … The KLA's swift move to take power has been aided by the squabbling and ineffectiveness of the moderate opposition, along with a disorganized UN administration that is short on personnel and awaiting the police that member countries promised to send to help to maintain order … The United Nations is planning to deploy a police force of 3,100, but it has only 156 officers in Kosovo at the moment.
>
> (Chris Hedges, *IHT*, 30 July 1999, p. 1)

> In the first wild weeks since the end of Nato's bombing campaign … there has been an administrative vacuum in which only the supporters of the KLA have been able to impose any sense of organization at street-level in towns and villages across Kosovo.
>
> (*FT*, 2 August 1999, p. 3)

> Organized gangs are taking advantage of the UN's failure to police the province … A Nato spokesman admitted yesterday [1 August] a 'law and order vacuum' has been created by a long delay in deploying UN civil administrators and an expected 3,000-strong police force … Western diplomats in Pristina say gangs, some of which are suspected of having links to the KLA, are taking apartments, real estate, businesses, fuel supplies and cars from Kosovo Albanians and Serbs, who have little recourse to justice … While the UN plans to deploy 3,125 international police, only 400 have arrived … According to a UN police commander … there are three main types of organized criminal gangs in Kosovo: Russian, Albanian and those linked to the KLA.
>
> (*Independent*, 2 August 1999, p. 9)

The stability pact for south-east Europe (Balkan Stability Pact) was endorsed at a summit meeting held in Sarajevo on 30 July 1999 attended by representatives from some forty countries. Serbia was not invited, but Dragoslav Avramovic represented the Serbian political opposition and President Djukanovic of Montenegro also attended. The assembled leaders agreed to find ways of helping Montenegro while 'respecting Yugoslavia's sovereignty and territorial integrity'.

On 30 July 1999 Ibrahim Rugova returned to Kosovo from Italy with his family, saying that he intended to stay.

> An independent group of experts Monday [2 August 1999] outlined a plan for the formation of a transitional government to lead Yugoslavia out of economic misery and prepare for new elections. The group called for a major rally to be held in the capital Belgrade on 19 August in support of the idea. An independent economist [Mladjan Dinkic] said the head of the Serbian Orthodox Church, Patriarch Pavle, and all opposition leaders and independent figures, including the former army chief General Momcilo Perisic, would be invited to attend ... The so-called Stability Pact for Serbia, which details a plan for an interim government, has been drafted by a still-anonymous group of prominent Serbs ... It says both the ruling parties and the opposition should agree to give up their aspirations to power for one year, when free and fair elections would be held.
>
> (*IHT*, 3 August 1999, p. 5)

> Mladjan Dinkic is the thirty-five-year-old leader of the Group 17 organization of independent Yugoslav economists and an up-and-coming politician ... The creation of a transitional government is at the heart of a new 'pact for the stability of Serbia', a document drawn up by a group of economists and academics in response to the regional stability pact unveiled by world leaders in Sarajevo ... According to the draft released yesterday [3 August], the transitional government would have a one-year mandate.
>
> (*Guardian*, 4 August 1999, p. 13)

> The head of Serbia's Orthodox Church and the country's main opposition leaders [including Zoran Djindjic and Vuk Draskovic] agreed on Monday [10 August 1999] to join a mass anti-government rally in Belgrade on 19 August ... Opposition leaders and a group of independent economists met the head of the Serbian Orthodox Church, Patriarch Pavle, and other Church dignitaries in its Belgrade seat.
>
> (*IHT*, 10 August 1999, p. 5)

'Patriarch Pavle, the church leader, met with opposition leaders Monday [9 August] and the two sides agreed to form a transitional government of experts that would prepare for elections within a year and democratic and economic reforms' (*IHT*, 11 August 1999, p. 4).

The 19 August rally is being organized by independent economists, Mladjan Dinkic and Predag Markovic, the creators of the stability pact for Serbia ... The authors of the stability pact for Serbia and others [such as Zoran Djindjic] ... insist that Mr Milosevic must step down before any transition government can take over ... But Mr Draskovic ... is arguing for a transitional government that includes some sort of power-sharing deal with Mr Milosevic.

(*IHT*, 12 August 1999, p. 5)

On 11 August 1999 the Serbian Orthodox Church, after a meeting of its highest body, the Holy Synod, called for the resignation of Yugoslav president Slobodan Milosevic and Serbian president Milan Milutinovic. There was also a call for a transitional 'government of [non-party] experts' to prepare fresh elections and democratic and economic reforms (*IHT*, 12 August 1999, p. 5).

The leader of the largest opposition party and an influential former army general Tuesday [17 August 1999] pulled out of a major anti-Milosevic rally scheduled for Thursday [19 August]. Vuk Draskovic ... said he would not participate in the rally because of the actions and behaviour of the Alliance for Change ... Momcilo Perisic ... said he did not support a transitional government of experts, one of the aims of the rally, but early elections for a new government. That puts Mr Perisic closer to Mr Draskovic, who also favours early elections ... Mr Djindjic, the Alliance for Change generally and the Clinton administration want Mr Milosevic to resign as a first step and for him to be delivered, perhaps within six months, as a war criminal to The Hague. They want a transitional government of experts to serve for one year to prepare fresh elections. The Alliance does not call for early elections. Mr Draskovic ... has proposed either new, internationally supervised elections to replace Mr Milosevic, or a transitional government, to be negotiated with the regime, that would render Mr Milosevic a figurehead.

(*IHT*, 18 August 1999, p. 2)

Vuk Draskovic unexpectedly addressed the crowd on 19 August 1999.

Mr Draskovic ... called for elections under international supervision. Referring to Mr Milosevic's pariah status internationally, Mr Draskovic said 'Serbia is in jail.' 'We are in jail,' he said, because Serbia 'is led by those who are totally isolated by the world' ... But he also denounced other opposition parties for making 'unrealistic' plans for 'some transitional governments' that no one will recognize. Such criticism, however, was not well received. As Mr Draskovic left the speaker's stand he was booed and jeered by many in the crowd.

(*IHT*, 20 August 1999, pp. 1, 4)

On 21 August 1999 Ibrahim Rugova attended a meeting of the multi-ethnic advisory transitional council, but Hashim Thaci did not.

Nato and UN officials have agreed to the formation of a civilian emergency force from the remnants of the KLA ... tentatively called the Kosovo Corps ... Although Nato sees the Kosovo Corps as a civilian force, the rebel army's officers see it as a potential core of a future national army ... [There is a] 19 September deadline for complete demilitarization of the 9,000 KLA troops ... The new force is expressly civilian and is intended to cope with national emergencies such as forest fires, earthquakes, mountain rescue and reconstruction. Nevertheless, it will have 3,000 members, with a military structure formed from the core commanders and brigades of the present KLA.

(*IHT*, 4 September 1999, p. 2)

'Composed of 3,000 regulars and 2,000 part-timers, this force [the Kosovo Corps] would be used for emergency relief, infrastructure rebuilding and ceremonial duties' (*FT*, 9 September 1999, p. 2).

Leaders of the KLA accepted [on 21 September 1999] the plan to transform the ethnic Albanian rebel organization into a civil defence group after a personal appeal by General Wesley Clark ... and after winning a concession from Nato on the group's name. The agreement came Monday night [20 September] ... Negotiations between Nato and the KLA revealed fundamental differences between the two sides over the rebel group's future ... The accord was reached after top KLA officials, including all but one of the rebel army's regional commanders, won agreement from Nato to call the new ethnic Albanian group 'the Kosovo Protection Corps'. The group, which Nato had wanted to name 'the Kosovo Corps', will oversee humanitarian assistance and disaster assistance ... General Sir Michael Jackson gained a renewed promise from the KLA leadership that the rebel group would officially cease to exist at midnight Tuesday [21 September] ... The new head of the Kosovo Protection Corps ... will be Agim Ceku, the KLA chief of staff.

(*IHT*, 22 September 1999, p. 5)

The United Nations administration in Kosovo announced yesterday [3 September] that it was dropping the Yugoslav dinar and that from today [4 September] all official dealings would be in German marks. The UN is also to set up a customs service at the border with the Former Yugoslav Republic of Macedonia ... All currencies would be legal tender, but the province would use the German mark as its preferred currency ... The Yugoslav currency, until now the only currency officially accepted, was still valid but its use would be discouraged. All taxes would be collected in marks and not sent to Belgrade. The decree merely legalizes the existing situation. In Kosovo, as in much of the Balkans, the mark is the main currency in daily use.

(*The Times*, 4 September 1999, p. 19)

EU foreign ministers [meeting on 5–6 September 1999] agreed to ease sanctions on Kosovo and Montenegro imposed during the recent Kosovo conflict, but failed at a weekend meeting … to reach a common position on Serbia. The ministers were unable to agree an 'energy for democracy' initiative … The initiative would have provided Serb municipalities controlled by opponents of Slobodan Milosevic with fuel … The meeting agreed, however, that Kosovo and Montenegro should be exempted from the oil embargo and ban on commercial flights.

(*FT*, 6 September 1999, p. 2)

'The EU announced Monday [6 September] the lifting of oil and flight embargoes on Kosovo and Montenegro' (*IHT*, 7 September 1999, p. 6).

The deadline for decommissioning KLA weapons expired on 19 September 1999. Kfor was generally satisfied that this would be met. But the KLA and Kfor said that they were to delay signing a demobilization agreement from the morning to midnight on 19 September. Later on it was announced that the deadline for signing the demobilization agreement would be shifted by forty-eight hours from midnight on 19 September to midnight on 21 September.

Serb leaders in Kosovo yesterday [22 September 1999] pulled out of the United Nations' civilian advisory body, protesting against the creation of … Kosovo Protection Corps … The Yugoslav government and Russia have already criticised the ethnic Albanian dominance of the force. The Serb leaders say they will continue to stay in contact with the international administration, despite leaving the transitional council.

(*FT*, 23 September 1999, p. 2)

Only about 3,000 people attended a demonstration in Belgrade on 23 September 1999. Zoran Djindjic: 'If there is no support, no energy, we'll say people in Serbia do not want to go to the streets to demand their rights. We'll say we are not the people they want as leaders' (*FT*, 24 September 1999, p. 2).

On 30 September 1999 leaders of the Alliance for Change and the Serbian Renewal Movement met to try to resolve differences about early elections.

On 3 October Vuk Draskovic was involved in a car accident. A lorry swerved into three cars. He was only slightly injured, but three of his bodyguards and his brother-in-law were killed. Draskovic: 'It was an obvious assassination attempt.' (Another theory is gang warfare. Draskovic's brother-in-law was director of the board for municipal building sites in Belgrade, generally recognized as a corrupt source of rich pickings.)

Mr Draskovic was shocked by what he perceived as an assassination attempt on 3 October, when a truck swerved into his car, killing his brother-in-law, and then struck the car behind him, killing three of his bodyguards. The police have not found the truck's driver or its current owner, lending credibility to Mr Draskovic's immediate charges of an attempted political hit by the Milosevic regime.

(Steven Erlanger, *IHT*, 15 October 1999, p. 6)

The opposition parties said Thursday [7 October 1999] they had agreed on the most important conditions for early elections. 'Following a constructive discussion, participants have agreed on all important issues concerning election conditions and election laws,' said a statement ... Another session would be held next week. The conditions agreed on Thursday include a proportional voting system, a revision of election lists, and the presence of domestic and foreign observers at all stages of the voting process. The statement also said the opposition would demand new electoral commission members, the replacement of a restrictive media law, and new laws governing political parties and international rules for the campaign.

(*IHT*, 8 October 1999, p. 2)

The EU agreed Monday [11 October 1999] to supply heating oil to two Serbian cities led by the opposition, despite strong objections by the United States and the failure of Serb opposition leaders to turn up in Luxembourg for a meeting with EU foreign ministers ... The ministers agreed to ship some 25,000 tonnes of heating oil and 1,000 tonnes of diesel fuel to the cities of Nis and Pirot in a $5.3 million programme, paid for by the EU, called 'energy for democracy' ... The foreign ministers also lifted an air embargo on Montenegro and Kosovo ... But they left intact the ban on flights to and from Serbia proper.

(*IHT*, 12 October 1999, pp. 1, 10)

(It was not until 6 December 1999, however, that the Serbian authorities allowed the oil through.) ('Initiatives have included heating oil and bitumen for road-building to opposition-controlled councils': *Telegraph*, 19 September 2000, p. 16.)

On 14 October 1999 opposition parties published a joint document specifying the conditions needed for early elections. These included a proportional voting system, revision of election lists, the presence of domestic and foreign observers, and a free media (*FT*, 15 October 1999, p. 10).

'The political leadership that emerged from the KLA is suffering a collapse of its support in the province, according to voter surveys, interviews with ordinary ethnic Albanians and even senior figures in the former rebel movement' (Peter Finn, *IHT*, 18 October 1999, p. 10).

'Nightly street demonstrations ... have all but fizzled out' (*IHT*, 21 October 1999, p. 5).

On 28 October 1999 most opposition parties except the Serbian Renewal Movement signed an agreement on electoral co-operation (*EEN*, 2000, vol. 12, no. 21, p. 6).

Leaders of the Alliance for Change visiting the USA met with the US secretary of state on 3 November 1999. '[US] Secretary of state Madeleine Albright ... pledges to lift economic sanctions in exchange for clean elections that, US officials say, would inevitably force Mr Milosevic from power' (*IHT*, 5 November 1999, p. 7).

> The Yugoslav government has dismissed a US proposal for a partial suspension of sanctions in return for early elections, saying that the offer would prove meaningless once President Slobodan Milosevic has been reelected. Spokesmen and media outlets ... assert that the Americans would only recognize a vote that the government loses ... Mrs Albright announced in Washington on Wednesday [3 November] that the United States would suspend sanctions on oil deliveries and flights to Belgrade if Mr Milosevic held early, free and fair elections.
>
> (*IHT*, 6 November 1999, p. 4)

> The chief UN administrator in Kosovo [Bernard Kouchner] signed a power-sharing agreement on Wednesday [15 December 1999] with Kosovo's ethnic Albanian leaders, creating a governing body aimed at bolstering political stability in the province ... [The agreement] envisages the formation of an interim administration. No representatives of the dwindling Serbian community were present at the signing. The new body, in which the UN administrator will act as governor, is to be established immediately. It is expected to absorb all existing administrative structures and be in operation by 31 January [2000] ... Under the agreement ... the three ethnic Albanian leaders – Ibrahim Rugova, Hashim Thaci and Rexhep Qosja – are to work with the UN, the EU, OSCE and the UNHCR ... The new body will comprise fourteen departments intended to function like government ministries. The departments will be devoted to rebuilding the war-shattered province. Some will deal with trade, finance and the economy ... The addition of the Kosovo leaders to the decision-making administration indicated a tacit recognition by the UN that, after six months, it could not administer the province effectively without their participation.
>
> (*IHT*, 16 December 1999, p. 6)

'The agreement creates an interim governing body until elections are held ... Kosovan Serb leaders refused to sign the agreement' (*Guardian*, 16 December 1999, p. 17).

Daily opposition rallies in Belgrade ended on 18 December 1999 after dwindling attendance (*EEN*, 2000, vol. 12, no. 21, p. 6). (The numbers were by then down to a few hundred.)

> In the absence of a strong international police force in Kosovo and facing a rise in crime, the commander of Nato peacekeeping troops in the province [General Klaus Reinhardt] has ordered his soldiers back out onto the streets in force ... He says the 1,800-member UN police force is not able to cope

... Over the weekend [18–19 December] a marked increase of troops was evident.

(IHT, 22 December 1999, p. 4)

The UN has provided only 1,700 of the 4,000 policemen it promised. Bernard Kouchner believes that a force of 6,000 officers is necessary (*Guardian,* 6 December 1999, p. 12; *Independent,* 7 December 1999, p. 13).

On 10 January 2000, after a meeting organized by the Serbian Renewal Movement, seventeen opposition parties agreed to join forces. They demanded early elections at all levels by the end of April 2000 or demonstrations would begin in March. (The document was not signed by former chief of staff General Perisic's Movement for a Democratic Serbia: *EEN,* 2000, vol. 12, no. 22, p. 6.)

On 15 January 2000 Zeljko Raznatovic (known as Arkan) was shot dead in Belgrade's Intercontinental Hotel. A friend and a bodyguard were also killed. Intense speculation surrounded the assassination: was it a gangland killing or one ordered by Milosevic to ensure that Arkan would never be able to reveal what he knew about Milosevic's role in the Balkan wars?

On 7 February 2000 Yugoslav defence minister Pavle Bulatovic was shot dead in a Belgrade restaurant. He was a Montenegrin and represented the pro-Serbia Democratic Party of Socialists in Montenegro. There was intense speculation as to the likely motive.

On 14 February 2000 the EU suspended the commercial flight ban on Serbia for six months but added about 180 names to the list of over 600 people subject to visa bans and financial restrictions.

On 10 March 2000 Serbia and Russia signed a free trade agreement (*EEN,* 2000, vol. 12, no. 23, p. 10).

A spy in Nato provided the Serbs with top-secret details of allied bombing raids against Yugoslavia last year [1999], including targets to be hit and precise flight paths, according to high-level US sources. An internal classified report drawn up for senior US defence officials concludes that the Serbs had access to Nato's daily orders for air raids and reconnaissance flights during the first two weeks of the allied bombing campaign, which began on the night of 24 March [1999].

(Guardian, 9 March 2000, p. 1)

The report was drawn up by James McCarthy, a retired US air force general (*Guardian,* 11 March 2000, p. 1). Nato officials denied that a spy had been involved.

Nato's air war in Kosovo suffered from poor security in its initial weeks, but there is still no reason to believe that allied operations were betrayed to Belgrade by a spy, according to US officials ... Officials also denied that a secret US report ... indicated the existence of a spy.

(IHT, 11 March 2000, p. 2)

In a continuing crackdown on the independent media in Serbia, officials shut down another small television station on Thursday [16 March] and seized its transmission equipment for unspecified violations of the law. A station in Cuprija was shut down last week, while Belgrade's Studio B this week had to pay a $245,000 bill that was suddenly demanded by the government. Independent newspapers like *Danas* and *Glas Javnosti* have recently faced heavy fines, and a popular evening paper, *Vecernji Novosti*, was brought back under strict government control.

(IHT, 17 March 2000, p. 5)

The head of the locally-based Humanitarian Law Fund ... estimates that 1,400 ethnic Albanians are still being held in Serbian jails ... Most of them were arrested between March and June 1999, during Nato's air campaign ... Flora Brovina ... a prominent Kosovo Albanian poet and humanitarian worker ... was sentenced to twelve years in prison last December [1999].

(Guardian, 18 March 2000, p. 17)

More than 1,400 ethnic Albanians remain incarcerated in prisons in Serbia, many of them facing trumped-up charges of 'terrorism'. Most of them ... were rounded up by Serb security forces in Kosovo in swoops which began in 1998 when the KLA began its uprising. Many were locked up during ... Nato air strikes ... Those recently jailed included ... the poet and physician Flora Brovina ... The Belgrade-based Humanitarian Law Centre ... says 2,050 Albanian prisoners ... were transferred to Serbia by June [1999]. Around 600 have been freed ... No UN resolution or agreement signed by Belgrade and Nato takes them into account.

(Independent, 18 March 2000, p. 16)

Serbian lawyers are reaping exorbitant sums to arrange the release of Albanians from prisons in Serbia, in what appears to be a ransom racket supported by the government of the Yugoslav president, Slobodan Milosevic ... The exact number of Albanian detainees in Serbia is unclear. The Serbian ministry of justice has published a list of almost 2,300 names and the International Committee of the Red Cross has registered about 1,700 detainees. But Albanian human rights groups in Pristina claim there may be secret prisons and the number could be as high as 7,000.

(Guardian, 23 March 2000, p. 20)

Thousands of people gathered here in the biggest protest yet against a clampdown by the Yugoslav authorities on opposition media. The protest in Kraljevo, central Serbia, on Saturday [18 March] came after the authorities dismantled the main transmitter of the opposition-run local television station late Friday [17 March], the third closure of a local station last week [the week beginning 13 March] ... Earlier last week Serbian police and telecommunications inspectors broke into television stations in Pirot, southern Serbia, and Pozega, western Serbia, closing them down. Several hundred people protested in Pirot on Saturday night [18 March] for the third night. Kraljevo television officials said that unlike the other stations that were closed down they had received no notice about irregularities or outstanding debts.

(*IHT*, 20 March 2000, p. 6)

In recent weeks Mr Milosevic's government has cracked down on local media, particularly on television and radio stations affiliated with municipal governments opposed to him. The transmission equipment of some of them has been confiscated, purportedly for non-payment of fees and taxes; others have been fined for allegedly objectionable content.

(*IHT*, 25 March 2000, p. 1)

Independent media outlets have received crippling fines and town councils controlled by the opposition have had their powers stripped away. Last weekend the telecommunications ministry dismantled the transmitters at TV Kraljevo, a local TV station in the centre of Serbia. The station was the seventh to have its transmission suspended in less than a month. At the beginning of March armed men broke into Belgrade's opposition-controlled TV station Studio B, commandeered its transmitters and beat a technician and a guard ... [Some] 10,000 people demonstrated against the closure of TV Kraljevo ... The state-controlled media portray opponents to the regime as enemies of the state ... Bakers and dairy producers who raise prices and defy wide-ranging price controls are often attacked as agents of the West ... Groups of reservists have launched protests against a new wave of call-ups to the army and some local politicians are still willing to voice opposition.

(*FT*, 24 March 2000, p. 23)

At an EU summit held on 24 March 2000 Javier Solana (the EU's high representative for foreign policy) and Chris Patten (the EU's external relations commissioner) were given overall control over the EU's Balkan aid programme after they had presented a critical report. ('The EU's Balkan aid has amounted to nearly $9 billion since 1991': *The Times*, 25 March 2000, p. 15.)

European Union aid efforts in the Balkans are being hampered by poor co-ordination between a plethora of international bodies, slow decision-making and bad presentation ... A joint report from Javier Solana, the EU's foreign policy representative, and the European Commission, presents a frank picture of their shortcomings ... 'EU assistance has been massive, but has suffered from a lack of visibility due to dispersion over various programmes and inadequate co-ordination between EU and member state programmes,' the report concludes. 'The effectiveness of our policies suffers from the multiplicity of institutions and frameworks in the region, from complex and lengthy procedures for policy formulation.' The report says the EU and its member states have been the biggest Balkan donor, providing Euro 9 billion since 1991. But the number of institutions, including UNMIK, the UN mission in Kosovo, and the EU-led Balkan stability pact, is a problem. 'The effectiveness of the [EU's] policies is affected by the plethora of actors involved,' it warns. 'Division of labour is too ad hoc and there is a high degree of duplication.' The report also says the EU has failed to integrate assistance provided by its central institutions with that from individual member states and to publicize the two as a coherent whole. 'EU assistance has had a positive impact, but it is often criticised for being too slow, bureaucratic and insufficiently targeted. Nothing would do more for the image of the EU in the region than being able to deliver on promises rapidly and efficiently,' it says.

(*FT*, 23 March 2000, p. 14)

A controversial report by Mr Solana and Mr Patten ... was highly critical of Europe's efforts. Their joint document concluded that the West is having 'considerable difficulties' in Kosovo, that ethnic violence is 'at high levels' and that the UN's administration is dogged by 'insufficient personnel and resources'.

(*Independent*, 25 March 2000, p. 14)

On 24 March 2000 Nato secretary-general George Robertson and General Wesley Clark visited Kosovo on the first anniversary of the start of the bombing campaign. But they did not visit Mitrovica as intended. (There were reports of a possible Serbian plot to assassinate the two, leading to changes in the itinerary: *The Times*, 28 March 2000, pp. 1, 3; *IHT*, 29 March 2000, p. 6.)

A two-day conference, hosted by the EU and the World Bank, was held in Brussels on 29–30 March 2000 to discuss the financing for construction projects throughout the Balkans.

Up to Euro 1.7 billion will be pledged today [30 March] for Balkan reconstruction ... The bulk of the schemes will be on a shortlist of thirty-five 'quick start' projects that Western donors want to begin over the next twelve months. They include roads, railways, ports and bridges to underpin the strategy of encouraging trade among Balkan countries. One project will see the upgrading of the Blace border post in Macedonia ... Another is the construction of a new bridge over the Danube between Romania and Bulgaria. The conference ... is expected to pledge a total of Euro 1.787 billion to the Stability Pact for South-Eastern Europe.

(*Independent*, 30 March 2000, p. 15)

'Balkan countries stand to get nearly $2 billion to build or repair roads, bridges, power connections and other infrastructure' (*Guardian*, 30 March 2000, p. 12).

The EU is spearheading an increase in planned financial aid for the region, including Euro 1.8 billion to be spent in the next twelve to eighteen months ... Projects worth a further Euro 2.7 billion were in preparation for later ... Chris Patten, the European commissioner for external relations ... announced the EU would give Euro 530 million to the quick start package, a first instalment on a Euro 12 billion six-year programme for the region, including Euro 5.5 billion for the western Balkans ... Bobo Hombach, the stability pact's special co-ordinator ... forecast individual states would roughly match the EU's Euro 530 million. Mr Patten's six-year total includes Euro 2.3 billion for Serbia, which will not be awarded unless the country rids itself of President Slobodan Milosevic. But it does include a small amount for Montenegro ... However, the World Bank cannot help Montenegro because it is not a sovereign state.

(*FT*, 30 March 2000, p. 9)

The [stability] pact's economic centrepiece is a network of 'stabilization and association' agreements between the EU and all Balkan states to promote mutual free trade. These are planned to pave the way for eventual EU membership for the Balkans. But that could take many years. To deliver more rapid aid the pact's authors plan loans and grants for infrastructure and other schemes. Because most of the money will be drawn from existing aid programmes, the pact's main aim is to co-ordinate what is already in the pipeline from the EU, the World Bank, the EBRD and national governments ... The pact's biggest financial elements include 130 regional investment schemes, worth about Euro 11 billion, including roads, railways and electric power projects. Attention will focus on a list of more than Euro 1 billion in 'quick start' schemes that Bobo Hombach, the pact's co-ordinator, wants to implement in the next few months. About two-thirds of the value will be in infrastructure projects and of the rest Euro 290 million in support for the private sector, including small business ... The signs are that many countries, including the UK, will simply redirect existing Balkan aid programmes. Germany is the exception, promising an extra DM 1.2 billion. The USA has promised up to $350 million, but the amount of new money is unclear and is linked to the size of the EU contribution. The European Commission is increasing its Balkan aid by about Euro 300 million to Euro 1.3 billion a year.

(*FT*, 20 March 2000, p. 22)

International leaders this week pledged at a conference in Brussels Euro 2.4 billion to be spent on projects which start within the next year. The money ... will go to projects scrutinized and co-ordinated by the World Bank and European Investment Bank.

(*FT*, 31 March 2000, p. 18)

[On 2 April 2000] Serb leaders [decided] to end a six-month boycott of the province's main postwar institutions. Members of Kosovo's Serb National

Council agreed to send representatives to two multi-ethnic bodies set up by the United Nations administration in charge of the territory ... [But] the representatives will only be observers and their participation will be reviewed after three months.

(*IHT*, 3 April 2000, p. 6)

'A split [has occurred] in the leadership of the province's Serbian population, with the Mitrovica representatives opposing a decision by other leaders to join a UN-sponsored joint administration for Kosovo' (*IHT*, 6 April 2000, p. 4). A Serb representative attended a session of Kosovo's interim government on 11 April (*IHT*, 12 April 2000, p. 4).

A peaceful anti-Milosevic demonstration (calling for early elections), which was held in Belgrade on 14 April 2000, attracted a larger crowd than expected (in excess of 100,000 by most estimates). The demonstration was a combined effort by opposition parties. Vuk Draskovic and Zoran Djindjic not only attended but also shook hands. The student organization Otpor ('Resistance') also took part.

('The student-based Serbian resistance movement Otpor ... the name means "resistance" ... is a broadbased movement, not a political party ... The movement was created in October 1998 by around twenty activists – mainly students, some young professionals – who cut their teeth in the anti-Milosevic protest movement of 1996–7 ... Otpor sprung to life when Milosevic moved to neutralize the universities as centres of revolt. In 1998 the government drew up a Universities Law that made the deans and rectors appointees of the regime. In addition, it called on university professors to sign contracts that many viewed as crude pledges of party loyalty ... When the law came into force universities saw a wave of academic firings and resignations': Gillian Sandford, *The World Today*, 2000, vol. 56, no. 8, p. 32.)

On 18 April 2000 Eurocorps (providing about 350 officers out of a total headquarters staff of around 1,000) is put in command in Kosovo. Lieutenant General Juan Ortuno of Spain takes over from General Klaus Reinhardt of Germany.

(Eurocorps was set up in 1995 by France and Germany, with its headquarters in Strasbourg. Spain, Belgium and Luxembourg later joined.)

Seven members of a group calling itself the Serb Liberation Army went on trial yesterday [24 April 2000, in the Serbian city of Nis] on charges of plotting an armed takeover of Yugoslavia and the assassination of President Slobodan Milosevic. The alleged conspirators, six civilians and a soldier, were all from Krusevac, an opposition stronghold. They were arrested last December [1999] on charges of forming a terrorist organization and have since been indicted for plotting to kill Mr Milosevic and his army chief, General Nebojsa Pavkovic ... The group, known as Osa or 'Wasp' ... first surfaced last October [1999] ... It later claimed responsibility for the apparent assassination attempt against Vuk Draskovic ... [But one defen-

dant said the claim] had only been for promotional purposes … The group
is the second to have been arrested for plotting to overthrow the Serbian
leader. Last November [1999] Yugoslav authorities claimed they had broken
up a group known as Pauk or 'Spider', which they said had links with
French intelligence. A government minister claimed they also had a range of
plans to try to kill Mr Milosevic.

(*Telegraph*, 25 April 2000, p. 14)

On 25 April 2000 Zika Petrovic, head of Yugoslav Airlines (JAT), was assassinated in Belgrade. He was a close friend and ally of Milosevic and a member of
Mira Milosevic's Yugoslav United Left Party.

On 3 May 2000 General Joseph Ralston became Supreme Allied
Commander, Europe. He replaced General Wesley Clark.

'Opposition leaders … cancelled a planned rally in Mr Milosevic's hometown
[of Pozarevac] on Tuesday [9 May] after officials detained opposition figures
and blocked access to the city' (*IHT*, 10 May 2000, p. 4). 'Serb police yesterday
[9 May] blocked demonstrators from entering Pozarevac … to attend a protest
over last week's arrest of three opposition activists' (*FT*, Wednesday 10 May
2000, p. 10).

But around 100 members of the Youth Resistance Movement, Otpor, and
other anti-Milosevic activists slipped past the cordon to interrupt a hastily
convened counter-meeting set up by officials … The incident that sparked
this crisis happened last week in Pozarevac, when three members of the
Otpor movement became involved in a fracas with bodyguards of
Milosevic's son Marko. They were arrested … [The three were] released,
but yesterday they were arrested again.

(*Guardian*, 10 May 2000, p. 14)

'Two young Otpor activists and a lawyer had been badly beaten in …
Pozarevac by bodyguards working for the president's son, Marko … Otpor
started as a student response to a restrictive law on universities in October 1998'
(*IHT*, 23 May 2000, p. 10).

On 13 May 2000 Bosko Perosevic, the head of the Vojvodina provincial
government and a member of the Socialist Party, was shot dead. Police arrested
a solitary gunman and said that he was a member of Otpor and the Serbian
Renewal Party (*Telegraph*, 15 May 2000, p. 7).

The government announced that the fifty-year-old killer was an Otpor
activist and a supporter of Vuk Draskovic's Serbian Renewal Movement,
suggesting that both groups were in the pay of Western intelligence agencies
… It [a possible new law on terrorism] could be used against opposition
politicians and also against independent journalists, whom the government
accuses of working for Nato and the 'enemies of the state'.

(Steven Erlanger, *IHT*, 23 May 2000, p. 1)

On 15 May 2000 up to 25,000 opposition supporters attended an anti-Milosevic demonstration in Belgrade. Both Zoran Djindjic and Vuk Draskovic attended the rally (*IHT*, 16 May 2000, p. 9). Around 30,000 attended the rally (*Guardian*, 16 May 2000, p. 15). The opposition demonstration failed to attract more than 10,000 people (*EEN*, 2000, vol. 12, no. 23, p. 10).

> The Serbian government Wednesday [17 May] seized ownership and control of the main opposition television station, Studio B, which it accused of advocating an uprising against the authorities. Studio B, which belongs to the city of Belgrade, also provided a frequency for the independent radio station B2-92, which was also effectively silenced ... Studio B was controlled by the Serbian Renewal Party of Vuk Draskovic ... Since December [1999] its broadcasts have frequently been jammed and it has also been one of the main targets of an increasing series of fines and lawsuits aimed at the independent media ... The official charge against the station ... was that Studio B had called for a violent overthrow of the constitutional order and incited people to riot ... The police ... locked the offices of B2-92 and Radio Indeks, which are also in the building, as well as the offices of the largest independent newspaper, *Blic*.
>
> (Steven Erlanger, *IHT*, 18 May 2000, p. 5)

'A government statement said the moves were a response to frequent media demands for "the toppling of the constitutional order and rebellion against a legally elected government" ... On Monday [15 May] police detained at least twenty student activists' (*Telegraph*, 18 May 2000, p. 22).

> Studio B is controlled by local authorities in the capital, and run by the biggest opposition party, the Serbian Renewal Movement ... B2-92 has used some Studio B frequencies after the original B-92 was taken over by the government during the Nato air raids last year [1999].
>
> (*Independent*, 18 May 2000, p. 14)

'Studio B was run by Belgrade City Hall, currently controlled by the Serbian Renewal Party' (*IHT*, 19 May 2000, p. 8).

> Police arrested and later released more than fifty members of ... Otpor as well as members of opposition parties ... Russia has authorized a credit worth $102 million to Yugoslavia and committed itself to deliver oil and oil derivatives worth $32 million ... The UN war crimes tribunal in The Hague yesterday [17 May] demanded an explanation from Russia as to why it allowed ... indicted war criminal Dragoljub Ojdanovic ... now [Yugoslav] defence minister, to visit Moscow.
>
> (*FT*, 18 May 2000, p. 10)

(The Yugoslav defence minister visited Russia on 10–12 May 2000. Russia has a legal obligation under UN resolutions to enforce an international arrest warrant against a wanted war criminal.)

('The glaring frailty of the formal opposition's top leadership ... was highlighted in May when there were violent clashes between police and protestors in Belgrade over the forceful closure of the country's leading non-government media. While youngsters including Otpor members as young as seventeen were being teargassed and beaten in the streets, not a single opposition leader was to be seen': Gillian Sandford, *The World Today*, 2000, vol. 56, no. 8, p. 34.)

Arrests and anti-Milosevic demonstrations followed.

There was a student demonstration on 26 May 2000.

> The Serbian education ministry ... had banned all gatherings at universities. The order served notice that the summer term was to end immediately, a week early, and students would be allowed to enter universities only to sit their exams.
>
> (*Independent*, 27 May 2000, p. 16)

About 10,000 attended an opposition rally in Belgrade on 27 May (*IHT*, 29 May 2000, p. 9).

On 1 June 2000 the Serbian government took over the opposition-run Belgrade city transport company (*EEN*, 2000, vol. 12, no. 23, p. 10).

On 4 June 2000 the Serb National Council decided to suspend its participation as observer in the Interim Administrative Council and other joint bodies in Kosovo until after a UN Security Council meeting to review its resolution. The Serbs were protesting against the recent spate of killings and demanded that the Security Council implement more stringent security measures (*IHT*, 5 June 2000, p. 5). The Serbs demanded the establishment of 'functional self-rule' in areas occupied by Serbs (*Guardian*, 5 June 2000, p. 15).

'After a meeting this week, Albanian leaders promised them [the Roma] security, and a Roma representative has joined the interim government' (*Guardian*, Saturday 10 June 2000, p. 21).

Li Peng (chairman of China's National People's Congress) visited Serbia on 11–13 June 2000.

On 15 June 2000 Vuk Draskovic was shot at and slightly injured at his holiday home in Montenegro. He blamed agents sent by Milosevic. A number of suspects were arrested by Montenegrin police, who claimed the suspects came from Serbia.

> The regulation, signed by the UN chief here [in Kosovo], Bernard Kouchner, is intended to prevent the publication or broadcasting of personal details about people who might become targets of Albanian or Serbian vigilantes ... [It] provides for the fining, suspension or closing of print or broadcast media ... Mr Kouchner issued the regulation after an Albanian-language newspaper, *Dita*, published an article on 27 April [2000] accusing two Serbs ... of being 'paramilitaries' ... [One] still lived in

Kosovo and worked as a translator for the United Nations. The paper published his address and photograph. Three weeks later he was found murdered ... Mr Kouchner shut down the paper for eight days ... The publisher of *Dita* justified the publication of the information by saying that the system of justice in Kosovo was not working and that there had been no punishment for people accused of war crimes. As soon as the suspension ... [he] republished the article. Mr Kouchner then issued his regulation on 17 June covering broadcast and print media, appointing a temporary news media manager ... Appeals are subject to a board appointed by Mr Kouchner ... [The publisher of *Dita*] tested it [the regulation] on 26 June, publishing the names of two Serbs ... accused of attacking ethnic Albanians.

(*IHT*, 14 July 2000, p. 2)

Moderate Serbs are to resume co-operation with ethnic Albanians and UN representatives by returning to the interim UN-controlled government of the province. The decision depends on the implementation of UN commitments to send anti-terrorist police to Serb areas targeted by ethnic Albanian extremists and to admit more Serbs to the Albanian-dominated Kosovo police force.

(*Guardian*, 26 June 2000, p. 14)

On 29 June 2000 the Yugoslav parliament was meant to discuss a new anti-terrorism law. But it was withdrawn.

The proposals were hastily withdrawn, with the official explanation that 'further discussions and consultations' were needed, after Vojislav Seselj, leader of the Serbian Radical Party, announced that his MPs would not vote for it ... Analysts believe that Mr Seselj was against the law because it would target both him and his party ... Rumours have been circulating in Belgrade for some time that President Milosevic would like to get rid of the neo-Fascist Mr Seselj.

(*Independent*, 1 July 2000, p. 16)

Terrorism is defined as 'acts that threaten constitutional order in the country'. Suspects could be detained without charge for thirty days, compared with the seventy-two hours under existing legislation. Prison terms ranging from five years to life would apply for 'acts that threaten constitutional order' or 'create a feeling of insecurity and fear among citizens'. Prison terms would apply for activities against the state or just the intention to commit them (*Independent*, 29 June 2000, p. 14; *Telegraph*, 29 June 2000, p. 17; *IHT*, 29 June 2000, p. 4).

On 6 July 2000 the Yugoslav parliament approved two constitutional changes, requiring the direct election through a popular ballot of the Yugoslav president and the upper house of parliament. They also allow two four-year terms for the president and raise the threshold for impeachment. The lower house passed the changes by ninety-five to seven, while the vote in the upper house was twenty-seven to zero.

> The effect will be to give Mr Milosevic a very good chance of remaining in power past July of next year [2000], when his current one-year term expires. Until now the federal president was elected by both houses of the federal parliament and could only serve one four-year term, while the upper house of the federal parliament was itself elected by the republic parliaments. The changes also put the federal government in charge of organizing elections, instead of the two republics, Serbia and Montenegro. The changes make Mr Milosevic's election plans less dependent on Montenegro's agreement ... Even if Mr Djukanovic decides that Montenegro should boycott the federal elections, they will now take place anyway, and Mr Milosevic's allies in Montenegro, who attract at least 30 per cent of the vote, will win seats ... Serbia's divided democratic opposition, most of which already boycotts the parliament and thus could not vote against the changes, seemed caught by surprise.
>
> (Steven Erlanger, *IHT*, 7 July 2000, pp. 1, 8)

'Opinion polls show Mr Milosevic remains Serbia's most popular politician' (Irena Guzelova, *FT*, 7 July 2000, p. 8). 'In a poll in May [2000] nearly 40 per cent of Serbs agreed that their leader, while imperfect, was better than any of his foes' (*The Economist*, 15 July 2000, p. 45). 'Recent opinion polls in Yugoslavia have indicated that more than two-thirds of the electorate favours Mr Milosevic's ouster. The problem is that ... the polls also indicate that each of his potential political opponents is even less popular than he is' (*IHT*, 31 August 2000, p. 9). 'An opinion poll has suggested that Vojislav Kostunica, a university professor who is more moderate that Mr Milosevic but no friend of Nato, might win 42 per cent of the vote as a united opposition candidate, against 28 per cent for Mr Milosevic' (*The Economist*, 5 August 2000, p. 44).

'The upper chamber has, until now, given both republics in the federation equal weight ... The move to elect deputies directly annuls the balance stipulated in the 1992 constitution' (*Independent*, 7 July 2000, p. 13).

'Henceforth it [Montenegro] will have no more weight than its share of Yugoslavia's population – about 7 per cent' (*The Economist*, 15 July 2000, p. 45). 'The changes reduced the role of Montenegro from that of an equal partner in the federation, with a 50 per cent say in the House of Republics, to a minor partner with a symbolic 6.5 per cent say corresponding to its share of the electorate' (*IHT*, 15 August 2000, p. 8).

'The new election rules, intended to put into effect constitutional changes pushed through this month [July], were overwhelmingly adopted [on 24 July] by both houses of the Federal Assembly' (*IHT*, 25 July 2000, p. 2).

> Under the new rules ... Mr Milosevic can win by gaining a simple majority of votes cast, no matter how low the turnout ... Appointees [of Mr

Milosevic] will have complete control of the procedures for both presidential and municipal elections to be held the same day.

(*IHT*, 31 July 2000, p. 9)

'On Monday [24 July] the Yugoslav parliament went ahead with the adoption of new electoral laws allowing candidates to be elected by a simple majority' (*Independent*, 28 July 2000, p. 13).

On 7 July 2000 the Montenegrin government issued a draft resolution for consideration by the Montenegrin parliament:

> The latest changes represent a classic constitutional destruction. They are illegal, illegitimate and unacceptable ... By doing this the illegitimate federal parliament is trying to create a unitary state, scrapping the statehood and sovereignty of the Republic of Montenegro ... The parliament invites citizens of Montenegro, citizens and democratic forces of Serbia and the international community to help resolve problems in relations between Montenegro and state authorities of Serbia and the federation peacefully.

> The draft resolution ... urged the Yugoslav Army not to allow itself to be abused by politicians [This week Montenegro accused Mr Milosevic of using the army units based in the republic to stir tensions and pave the way for a coup; the only remaining federal institution in the republic is the Yugoslav army], and it called on the international community to help resolve the crisis peacefully. The resolution applies to all political and legal acts adopted by the federal Yugoslav parliament without the participation of the representatives of the Montenegrin authorities, it said ... The draft resolution said the constitutional changes denied Montenegro the principle of equality with Serbia, laid down by the 1992 constitution ... The draft urged the Montenegrin interior ministry, political parties and institutions to work toward a peaceful solution ... Montenegro's pro-Western leadership has slowly been concentrating power in the republic in what is known as 'creeping independence'.

(*IHT*, 8 July 2000, pp. 1, 4)

'Pro-Western Montenegrin authorities said the changes are an illegal attempt to annul the republic's statehood' (*IHT*, 10 July 2000, p. 4).

The resolution was passed by the Montenegrin parliament on 8 July 2000.

President Milo Djukanovic of Montenegro (10 July 2000):

> It is evident that Yugoslavia no longer exists. Instead of two equal states – Montenegro and Serbia – we have a one-state model ... [Montenegro] has practically left the constitutional and legal system of Yugoslavia ... Milosevic's dilemma was Yugoslavia or The Hague ... He chose to destroy Yugoslavia.

President Djukanovic says that Montenegro will not take part in federal elections scheduled for autumn 2000 (*Guardian*, 11 July 2000, p. 15).

[On 24 July 2000] the federal parliament in Belgrade ... reshuffled electoral districts in Serbia so that voters from Kosovo ... can cast their ballots in two districts in Serbia proper. International officials in Kosovo ... have just completed registering voters for the polls expected in October. While around a million ethnic Albanians registered, barely a thousand Serbs did.

(*Guardian*, 25 July 2000, p. 12)

Fewer than 1 per cent of Kosovo's Serbs will be able to take part in the province's municipal elections this autumn after violent intimidation by Belgrade hardliners prevented them from registering to vote ... OSCE ... announced yesterday [24 July] at the close of the registration process that fewer than 1,000 Serbs, out of an estimated 105,000 who remain in the province, would be eligible to vote because of threats delivered by representatives of the Belgrade regime ... More than a million Kosovo Albanians have registered to vote, out of an estimated 1.2 million people of all ethnicities on the electoral register ... Potential Serb voters in Kosovo were threatened with a variety of measures ... said [the head of the OSCE joint registration task force], including long-term persecution should they return to Serbia, arrest on espionage charges, random violence and suspension of pensions.

(*Independent*, 25 July 2000, p. 12)

(Local elections in Kosovo were later fixed for 28 October 2000.)
A military court in Nis (Serbia) sentences a journalist, Miroslav Filipovic, to seven years in prison for espionage and spreading false information. 'Miroslav Filipovic, a reporter for the independent Belgrade daily *Danas*, was the first journalist prosecuted for espionage ... The court ruled that Mr Filipovic gathered confidential military information for foreign organizations between May 1999 and May 2000' (*IHT*, 27 July 2000, p. 6).

Miroslav Filipovic was arrested in May [2000] after writing articles, including one in *The Independent*, detailing Serbian army atrocities against Kosovo Albanians during last year's Nato bombing campaign. He worked for the independent Belgrade daily *Danas* ... but also wrote for the [London-based] Institute for War and Peace Reporting (IWPR) and the French news agency Agence France-Presse (AFP) ... The stories [also] dealt with the organization and restructuring of activities in Serbia and in ... Montenegro ... [and] the conduct of Yugoslav army troops in predominantly Moslem villages in ... Sandjak.

(*Independent*, 27 July 2000, p. 13)

The European Commission has authorized the release of up to $22.7 million to pay for the clearing of the Danube of debris from bridges destroyed by Nato bombing. EU finance ministers recently decided to pay as much as 85 per cent of the cost of the project (*IHT*, 27 July 2000, p. 6).

On 27 July 2000 President Milosevic announced that parliamentary, presidential and local (Serbian) elections would be held on 24 September 2000.

> Vuk Draskovic told Radio B2-92 of Belgrade after surviving an assassination attempt in mid-June [2000] that he had no interest in the elections ... The spokesman for his party says the movement will neither participate in the elections nor support any candidate.
>
> (*IHT*, 31 July 2000, p. 9)

'Vuk Draskovic ... has said that he will boycott the election if Montenegro does' (*The Economist*, 5 August 2000, p. 44).

'Vuk Draskovic ... said his party will not contest the parliamentary and presidential elections unless Montenegro is involved. The party ... will [however] take part in the local elections' (*Telegraph*, 4 August 2000, p. 11).

'Yugoslav authorities announced [on 31 July] that four Dutchmen were arrested in Montenegro for allegedly plotting to kidnap or assassinate Mr Milosevic and ... Radovan Karadzic' (*IHT*, 4 August 2000, p. 5).

> [Yugoslav] information minister Goran Matic said the four men ... were assassins sent by Western intelligence agencies ... The group was arrested ... at the border between Montenegro and Serbia 'right before the G8 summit in Okinawa' which began on 21 July ... One of the men shown on the film said he and his friends were looking for people indicted by the United Nations war crimes tribunal ... Washington has offered a reward of up to $5 million to anyone giving information leading to the arrest of Mr Milosevic, Ratko Mladic ... and Radovan Karadzic.
>
> (*IHT*, 1 August 2000, p. 8)

> The Yugoslav army on Thursday [3 August] announced the arrest in Montenegro of two Britons and two Canadians, accusing them of possessing weapons and explosives ... The arrest of the men [had occurred] near the Montenegrin–Kosovo border sometime Monday night [31 July] or Tuesday morning [1 August] ... The army said the four men were employees of the Nato-led forces in Kosovo and were suspected of training pro-Western secessionists in Montenegro ... to commit 'terrorist actions' ... These charges were rejected by their employers, who said the men were simply returning from a weekend in Montenegro to Kosovo ... and were not carrying arms or explosives ... Belgrade has accused the West of training the Montenegrin police in preparation for a secession by Montenegro ... The two Britons work in Kosovo training local police at the police academy, said their employer, OSCE ... [whose] spokeswoman ... said that the two men were unarmed and were on a 'weekend excursion' to Montenegro ... [One of the two Canadians] is the owner of ... a construction company

based in Calgary and had been running its Pristina office for a year, where the company has some twenty contracts, mostly with the Nato-led peace-keeping forces ... [The other Canadian is] his nephew ... The two Canadians ... had also gone to Montenegro from Kosovo, employees of their company said.

(*IHT*, 4 August 2000, p. 5)

'The Serbian authorities recently alleged that Britain's SAS special forces were training Montenegrin police in preparation for its secession from Yugoslavia' (*FT*, 4 August 2000, p. 8).

OSCE forbade its staff Friday [4 August] to travel to Montenegro after two British police officers and two Canadians were arrested by the Yugoslav army on suspicion of spying and training secessionist forces ... Montenegro ... does not require Westerners to obtain Yugoslav visas, but the Yugoslav army in Montenegro, which is loyal to Mr Milosevic, does not recognize the waiver and considers anyone without a visa to be in the country illegally.

(*IHT*, 5 August 2000, p. 4)

'Montenegro ... has waived the federal rules requiring visitors to obtain visas to travel to Yugoslavia and they are not required for anyone intending to stay for less than thirty days' (*Telegraph*, 9 August 2000, p. 8).

On 6 August 2000 Vuk Draskovic's Serbian Renewal Party announced that it would put forward its own presidential candidate, the mayor of Belgrade Vojislav Mihajlovic.

The announcement was made at the start of two days of meetings involving sixteen opposition parties to decide whether to present a united front against President Milosevic ... Other opposition parties back Vojislav Kostunica, leader of the centre-right Democratic Party of Serbia.

(*IHT*, 7 August 2000, p. 6)

The decision ... goes against the wishes of the fifteen remaining opposition parties – which last weekend agreed to unite behind one candidate, widely expected to be Vojislav Kostunica, a moderate nationalist who favours democratic change. Opinion polls show that if Serbia's fractious opposition were to unite behind one candidate they could beat Milosevic. A recent poll showed that if all the parties gathered behind Mr Kostunica he would win 42 per cent of the votes, 14 [percentage] points over Mr Milosevic ... Opposition leaders accuse Vuk Draskovic ... of working behind the scenes with Mr Milosevic ... The fifteen remaining parties meet today [7 August] to decide what their next step will be. They now hope that Mr Mihajlovic's relative obscurity will stop him from attracting votes away from their joint candidate. Mr Mihajlovic is not known outside Belgrade ... Any number of candidates are permitted to stand in the presidential elections, but the winner must gather more than 50 per cent of the votes to take office. Failing that there will be a second round of voting between two candidates. Opposition leaders outside the Serbian Renewal Party hope they will be able to get through to this stage – leaving Mr Kostunica to run against Mr Milosevic.

(*FT*, 7 August 2000, p. 7)

'Mr Kostunica's own Democratic Party of Serbia started life as a nationalist group for those who thought Mr Djindjic too pro-West' (*FT*, 4 October 2000, p. 8).

Until yesterday [6 August] Mr Draskovic had said that his party planned to boycott the presidential and local elections on 24 September ... Vojislav Kostunica is a moderate nationalist who heads the Democratic Party of Serbia ... Many view Mr Draskovic's undermining of united opposition efforts as a sign that he is ready to make a deal with the regime ... Mr Mihajlovic ... is the grandson of General Draza Mihajlovic, the commander of the World War Two royalist and nationalist chetnik movement in Serbia. General Mihajlovic was sentenced to death by Tito's victorious partisans for his alleged co-operation with the German occupation army. Mr Draskovic ... has written a book about him.

(*Independent*, 7 August 2000, p. 11)

'Vuk Draskovic ... called Mr Kostunica a man "who frightens many citizens of Serbia, as his policies are in fact the same as those of Slobodan Milosevic"' (*Telegraph*, 7 August 2000, p. 1).

In a recent opinion poll [Vojislav Kostunica] was backed as a united opposition candidate by 42 per cent, against 28 per cent for Mr Milosevic. Mr Draskovic has opposed Mr Kostunica, arguing that his nationalist views would put him at odds with the world and frighten many Serbs 'as his policies are the same as those of Mr Milosevic'.

(*The Times*, 7 August 2000, p. 13)

On 7 August 2000 fifteen opposition parties formally named Vojislav Kostunica as their presidential candidate.

Vojislav Kostunica, a constitutional lawyer, was dismissed from the Belgrade University law faculty in 1974 for defending a senior professor jailed for criticizing the Tito government. In 1989, when the Serbian leader, Slobodan Milosevic, tried to co-opt intellectuals and was offering to rehire those who had been dismissed, only Mr Kostunica refused ... Mr Kostunica [is] a moderate nationalist, anti-communist and democrat ... and polls suggest that Mr Kostunica, fifty-six, ought to be able to win ... Mr Kostunica expects widespread vote stealing and even raises the possibility that Mr

Milosevic will postpone these elections by creating some military 'emergency' ... For the Yugoslavs Mr Kostunica's virtues are many: a reputation for modesty, honesty and principle, a belief in democracy, a career untainted by any previous co-operation with the Milosevic regime, a clear patriotism and sense of nationhood, and a nuanced but sharply critical stance toward the United States and the Western countries that bombed Serbian targets last year [1999] ... Mr Kostunica's patriotism, his criticism of the war crimes tribunal in The Hague as a political instrument, his support for Serbs in Kosovo and his scepticism toward the West made him a good choice for a democratic opposition accused over and over again by Mr Milosevic of being traitors in the pay of Washington and Nato ... He [Kostunica] ... thinks there must be a counterbalance to US power, that the war crimes tribunal in The Hague is an instrument of US political goals rather than a model of legal justice, and that Washington too often insists on supporting politicians who do not have realistic support.

(Steven Erlanger, *IHT*, 5 September 2000, pp. 1, 4)

Mr Kostunica ... said he would favour a form of state 'truth commission' of independent historians and experts to examine the crimes and victims of all parties to the Yugoslav wars ... Mr Kostunica ... sees The Hague war crimes tribunal for Yugoslavia as 'an instrument of American policy and not of international law'. He criticizes the tribunal for refusing to examine the possibility of war crimes by Nato leaders for the bombing of civilian targets ... And he has said he will not turn Mr Milosevic ... over to The Hague for trial. Mr Kostunica refuses to be explicit now over whether he would turn over Radovan Karadzic and Ratko Mladic, two key Bosnian Serb leaders indicted by the tribunal. They might be the price for what Mr Kostunica wants: a reentry to European institutions like the Council of Europe and OSCE, and the restoration of Yugoslavia as a respected member of the United Nations.

(Steven Erlanger, *IHT*, 30 September 2000, pp. 1, 5)

'He and his party believed that the Serbian question was central, and he supported the efforts of Radovan Karadzic for self-determination of the Serbs in Bosnia. Mr Kostunica condemned ethnic cleansing however' (Steven Erlanger, *IHT*, 9 October 2000, p. 11).

'Kostunica ... was fired from Belgrade University for opposing Tito's 1974 constitution as unfair to the Serbs' (Timothy Garton Ash, *New York Review of Books*, 2000, vol. XLVII, no. 18, p. 10).

'Mr Kostunica ... has taken many positions at odds with those of Western countries, He said he would seek the withdrawal of Nato troops from Kosovo. And he promised not to co-operate with the international war crimes tribunal in The Hague' (R. Jeffrey Smith, *IHT*, 23 September 2000, p. 5).

'Vojislav Kostunica ... declared last week that, if elected, he would not extradite Mr Milosevic ... Mr Kostunica said that he would accept a pro-independence referendum in Montenegro but expected the majority of Montenegrins to want to stay within the union' (*Telegraph*, 9 September 2000, p. 16).

'Reiterating a campaign pledge, Mr Kostunica said he would not extradite ... [Milosevic] or his aides to the UN war crimes tribunal ... He called the court "a political institution" ' (*IHT*, 26 September 2000, p. 4).

> Aged fifty-six, he [Kostunica] is a lifelong anti-communist, a moderate Serb nationalist and an economic liberal. He was among Belgrade University staff who were sacked in 1974 for opposing constitutional changes which gave Yugoslavia's republics and Kosovo substantial autonomy. After the death of Tito ... he co-authored the first book which was allowed to be published advocating a multi-party system. Six years later he refused to take his job back at the university when Serbia's new leader, Mr Milosevic, offered it. Instead, Mr Kostunica took up the political fight against Mr Milosevic and joined other friends in forming the Democratic Party. They were elected to the federal parliament. Three years later the party split over whether to co-operate with Mr Milosevic, and Mr Kostunica took the radicals with him to form the Democratic Party of Serbia. Although a strong supporter of the rights of Serb minorities during Yugoslavia's dissolution, he was never involved in paramilitary activities ... One of his main promises is to change the Serbian constitution towards a parliamentary system. He then says he will resign after eighteen months and hold new elections ... While he says he would accept an independent Montenegro, he has irritated its government by accusing it of being afraid of democracy in boycotting the elections.
>
> (*Guardian*, 8 September 2000, p. 16)

> Together with Zoran Djindjic he helped found Serbia's first and largest opposition party, the Democratic Party, but found it insufficiently nationalist and, in 1992, split and set up his own smaller Democratic Party of Serbia ... Mr Kostunica supported the Serb cause in the Croatian and Bosnian wars of the early 1990s. He attacked Mr Milosevic for signing the 1995 Dayton Accords.
>
> (*FT*, 30 September 2000, p. 15)

'Mr Kostunica opposed ... Bosnia's Dayton peace accord' (*FT*, 12 October 2000, p. 8).

> [On 12 August 2000 there were reports that] President Slobodan Milosevic has adopted a military doctrine to protect Yugoslavia's 'constitutional order' ... A leading analyst said it was basically a reorganization of the military that would shift the focus towards tackling 'internal enemies' ... The military would be brought under a unified command with less emphasis on the military police, which would be responsible for controlling domestic critics of Mr Milosevic.
>
> (*IHT*, 14 August 2000, p. 6)

President Slobodan Milosevic is the head of the country's army under a new military doctrine adopted this month [August] ... The president of the republic commands the Yugoslav army in wartime and in peacetime as supreme commander. Until the change the president's command had been based on decisions by the supreme defence council, which he heads. The council has not met since the October 1997 election of Milo Djukanovic ... [as] president of Montenegro.

(*IHT*, 23 August 2000, p. 6)

On 18 August 2000 a bomb exploded in a building in Pristina, used by OSCE, local Serbian authorities and local political parties (including Serbian, Bosnian and ethnic Albanian).

'Serbia's single largest opposition party decided Thursday [24 August 2000] to run candidates in next month's parliamentary elections in Yugoslavia, dropping a boycott threat. But the Serbian Renewal Party said it would contest the vote independently' (*IHT*, 25 August 2000, p. 7).

On 25 August it was announced that for the first time Mirjana Markovic (Milosevic's wife) would run as a candidate in the forthcoming federal elections, specifically as a candidate for the lower house of parliament (*Guardian*, 26 August 2000, p. 20).

Also on 25 August it was announced in the independent media that former Serbian president Ivan Stambolic had disappeared in mysterious circumstances (*Telegraph*, 30 August 2000, p. 12).

Mr Stambolic repeatedly said he would not run in the presidential election on 24 September, but he recently attacked Mr Milosevic in two blistering interviews broadcast in Serbia and Montenegro and may have been reconsidering ... He had helped to promote Mr Milosevic in the Communist Party until the latter took a nationalist turn in 1987 and organized an internal coup against him. His absence from politics since then has given him an image of being above the intrigues and in-fighting of the opposition parties.

(*Guardian*, 5 September 2000, p. 13)

On 28 August 2000 Yugoslav and Russian trade ministers signed a bilateral free trade agreement in Belgrade (*EEN*, 2000, vol. 12, no. 25, p. 4).

On 4 September 2000 police raided the headquarters of Otpor.

The United Nations grudgingly agreed yesterday [4 September] that Kosovo residents could vote in the presidential and parliamentary elections, as the region remains recognized as a province of Serbia ... Referring to Yugoslavia as a whole, OSCE said the framework for the polls fell short of accepted standards of freedom and fairness.

(*Guardian*, 5 September 2000, p. 13)

In a concession to President Slobodan Milosevic the UN administrator for Kosovo announced yesterday that he would allow the holding of Yugoslav elections in the Serbian province ... Bernard Kouchner warned that the Yugoslav presidential, parliamentary and local elections called for 24 September would not be free, fair, democratic or non-violent, and did not comply with any international standards ... Officials from Mr Milosevic's party announced Serbs would be able to vote in 500 polling stations, a claim derided by Dr Kouchner.

(*Independent*, 5 September 2000, p. 13)

When President Milosevic runs for reelection ... he will be backed by many of this province's [Kosovo's] population ... Serbs and Albanians ... for different motives, are hoping that the disgraced Milosevic regime will remain in power ... The Albanians will be spectators at the election, since they do not recognize Yugoslavia's sovereignty over Kosovo ... Their backing for the regime is widespread albeit deeply cynical ... The argument goes that the longer the Serbian nationalist leader stays in power the longer the West will continue its huge military and economic commitment to Kosovo ... For the Serb population the benefits of keeping Milosevic in power are also practical ... They rely heavily on the centralized government in Belgrade. 'The main reason that Milosevic remains strong here [in Kosovo] is that salaries for teachers, health workers and pensioners are still being paid by Belgrade,' said Father Sava, an Orthodox Serb priest who is an outspoken Milosevic critic.

(Richard Beeston, *The Times*, 13 September 2000, p. 17)

'A Belgrade analyst said [that] "Mitrovica is generally pro-Kostunica" ... Mr Kostunica is backed by Oliver Ivanovic, leader of the northern Kosovo Serbs' (*Telegraph*, 15 September 2000, p. 16).

People expect there will be widespread electoral fraud ... Most of the manipulation is expected to happen in Kosovo ... There are 900,000 Kosovars, most of them Albanians, on the electoral list. Few are expected to vote, but independent experts say at least 300,000 votes from the province could be recorded in favour of Mr Milosevic. In the 1997 Serbian presidential elections 200,000 Albanians 'voted' for Mr Milosevic's right-hand man, Milan Milutinovic, despite a boycott by Albanians ... When the UN mission in Kosovo agreed to let elections go ahead it made no arrangements for monitoring them and banned them from being held in public buildings.

(*FT*, 14 September 2000, p. 8)

[In Montenegro] President Milo Djukanovic has decided to boycott the elections ... The current situation seems to serve both Mr Milosevic and Mr Djukanovic, with the boycott protecting the Montenegrin's political base while effectively handing Mr Milosevic control over the new federal parliament ... [There is the argument] that Mr Djukanovic is betting on Mr Milosevic's remaining in power, which is likely to produce an independent Montenegro in the next few years – the same bet being made by Kosovo's Albanians. If Mr Milosevic is beaten by the candidate of Serbia's democratic opposition, Vojislav Kostunica, it will be harder to get Western support for the further breakup of Yugoslavia ... While Mr Djukanovic's government has officially discouraged the state media from reporting on the campaign, the president is allowing Montenegrins to vote in the election, trying to avoid an open conflict with the 35 per cent to 40 per cent of the population that favours unity with Serbia.

(Steven Erlanger, *IHT*, 13 September 2000, p. 11)

Mr Djukanovic broke from Mr Milosevic in 1997 ... About 35 per cent to 40 per cent of Montenegro's 650,000 people support union with Serbia ... There are fears in the capital, Podgorica, that Mr Milosevic will manipulate pro-Serbian feelings ... and use the army – and a special paramilitary grouping called the Seventh Battalion ... to foment what could become a civil war.

(Steven Erlanger, *IHT*, 19 September 2000, p. 6)

At first negotiations between Mr Djukanovic and his pro-Serbian opponents about a procedure for allowing some citizens to vote in regular polling booths went quite well. But ... the opposition suddenly rejected the oversight of polls by Montenegro's security forces ... As a result of this deadlock the pro-Serbian camp in Montenegro will simply run its own ballots ... with no restrictions on multiple voting or other forms of fraud.

(*The Economist*, 16 September 2000, p. 63)

The Montenegrin government says it will permit elections to be held in its territory, but will urge its supporters to boycott them ... Nearly a third of Montenegro's population view themselves as Yugoslavs ... Montenegro is in the process of establishing a large and well-armed force of special police and there are some 10,000 police or more in active service ... The Yugoslav army has stepped up border patrols and, except for one crossing, has closed the border with Bosnia ... Recently SNP [the pro-Yugoslav Socialist People's Party] and government members started a series of talks designed to reduce tensions.

(Irena Guzelova, *FT*, 19 September 2000, p. 10)

On 7 September 2000 Greek foreign minister George Papandreou met Slobodan Milosevic in Belgrade.

On 14 September 2000 Vojislav Kostunica travelled to Kosovo as part of his campaign. A rally in Mitrovica was disrupted by pro-Milosevic supporters.

On 8 September 2000 former Yugoslav president Zoran Lilic confirmed that he had resigned from all Socialist Party of Serbia posts (*EEN*, 2000, vol. 12, no. 25, p. 5).

> His [Milosevic's] colleagues in the Socialist Party are still reeling from the blow administered recently by Zoran Lilic, a former Yugoslav president and long-time adviser to Mr Milosevic. Mr Lilic has resigned from the Socialist Party ... The Lilic resignation follows last week's announcement by the ultra-nationalist Vojislav Seselj that his party, the Radicals, would not back Mr Milosevic in the event of a run-off in the presidential elections ... The Serbian government has refused to allow any Western observers into the country to monitor the elections but has invited teams from Russia, India and China.
>
> (*The Times*, Friday 15 September 2000, p. 17)

> Key supporters seem to be abandoning the president. Ivan Stambolic, Mr Milosevic's former mentor, was kidnapped this month, after rumours surfaced that he planned to stand for the opposition in the parliamentary elections. Zoran Lilic, a senior party figure, has resigned unexpectedly. Belgrade analysts say this highlights tensions between the Socialists and the JUL [United Yugoslav Left], the smaller left-wing party run by Mira Markovic, Mr Milosevic's powerful wife.
>
> (*FT*, 22 September 2000, p. 22)

> Serbia's ultra-nationalist Radical Party ... said yesterday [13 September] that it was cutting all ties to the regime ... The Radical's presidential candidate, Tomislav Nikolic, cited unacceptable corruption in the group around Mr Milosevic's wife and electoral malpractice by the ruling Socialist Party ... Feuds within the ruling coalition have festered for months. Analysts say that relations between the Socialists, the Radicals and the United Yugoslav Left – the three parties which make up the ruling coalition in both the Serbian and Yugoslav parliaments – have worsened dramatically. At issue is the economic and political influence of leading members of the United Yugoslav Left, the party founded and run by Mr Milosevic's wife, Mirjana Markovic. Though extremely unpopular the United Yugoslav Left has a stranglehold on top state jobs. Socialist officials are furious that up to 40 per cent of joint candidates put forward for federal seats by the regime are from the United Yugoslav Left.
>
> (*Telegraph*, 14 September 2000, p. 18)

> Vojislav Kostunica ... would almost certainly win a free and fair ballot ... But the elections will be neither free nor fair ... The electoral laws are seriously flawed and have been designed to facilitate fraud. There will be no proper international observation ... Freedom of media and freedom of association are simply not met. Last week the country's electoral commission ordered what is left of the independent media to stop distributing what they

described as 'political propaganda for the opposition'. The latter is constantly harassed, its campaign rallies banned, its grass-roots activists arrested and beaten. Mr Milosevic's immense propaganda machine is portraying his political opponents as traitors and fascists. Ludicrous tales of their alleged plots with the Nato aggressor are revealed daily, to fuel the collective paranoia and prepare the ground for future, more radical measures against the opposition. If, against all odds, it happens to win ... The most likely outcome is still a fraudulent victory for Mr Milosevic ... [whose] original term comes to an end in July 2001.

(David Russell-Johnston, president of the Parliamentary Assembly of the Council of Europe, *IHT*, 18 September 2000, p. 8)

'The Yugoslav constitution is so ambiguous it could allow Mr Milosevic to serve out his term until next July, even if the opposition wins' (*Guardian*, 21 September 2000, p. 2).

'Recent changes [have been] made by Mr Milosevic and his supporters to the Yugoslav constitution ... The new provisions would allow him to remain in office until the end of his four-year term next summer' (*IHT*, 23 September 2000, p. 5).

On 18 September 2000 EU foreign ministers published a 'message to the Serbian people':

We reaffirm that a choice leading to democratic change will entail radical change in the EU's policy with regard to Serbia. We will lift the sanctions against the Federal Republic of Yugoslavia; we will support the necessary economic and political reforms by providing Serbia with aid for its reconstruction and support reintegration ... into the international community.

(*Guardian*, 19 September 2000, p. 17)

European foreign ministers ... said they would lift sanctions against Belgrade and bring Yugoslavia back into the diplomatic fold if the democratic opposition won the elections this Sunday [24 September] ... Voting for democratic change would result in a radical change in policy, including a generous aid package and an acceleration in trade ... EU governments would ask their parliaments to send 'witnesses for democracy' to monitor the elections. Other international organizations declined to send observers, arguing that the conditions for a fair election are absent ... Ministers approved an EU package granting duty-free access to 95 per cent of imports from Albania, Bosnia, Croatia, Macedonia and Montenegro ... The package includes abolition of tariffs on most industrial and farm products to the EU. However, some limits remain on exports of fish products and wine.

(*FT*, 19 September 2000, p. 10)

The EU agreed Monday [18 September] to lift sanctions against Belgrade if the opposition in Yugoslavia emerged victorious in the elections on Sunday

[24 September] ... The United States said Saturday [16 September] it, too, would be willing to lift sanctions if the opposition won power.

(*IHT*, 19 September 2000, p. 6)

'The Clinton administration ... has made a ... statement that "when a democratic transition takes place, we will take steps to remove sanctions"' (*IHT*, 23 September 2000, p. 5).

Foreign ministers ... promised to lift sanctions, provide aid and bring the country back into the international community if its electorate seized the chance to 'repudiate clearly and peacefully the policy of Milosevic' ... The EU also agreed to ... allow Croatia, Bosnia and Albania to export 95 per cent of their industrial and agricultural products to EU countries duty free. Montenegro will be allowed to export aluminium.

(*The Times*, 19 September 2000, p. 14)

'If there was "a choice leading to democratic change" the EU would lift sanctions against the Federal Republic of Yugoslavia. Economic aid will also be made available' (*Independent*, 19 September 2000, p. 12).

In Belgrade a war crimes trial starts against fourteen Western leaders involved in the Nato bombing campaign. The indictment names 503 civilians, 240 soldiers and 147 policemen killed in the Nato raids (*Independent*, 19 September 2000, p. 12; *Guardian*, 19 September 2000, p. 17). The fourteen leaders were pronounced guilty on 21 September and sentenced to twenty years in prison.

On 19 September 2000 a counter-terrorist operation, led by British and Swedish troops, undertook a raid in Kosovo which resulted in the capture of Serbs (some of whom are believed to be connected with the Yugoslav army's special forces), weapons and explosives.

On 20 September 2000 Milosevic addressed an election rally at a military airfield in Berane in north-eastern Montenegro. '[This was] the first time he has left Serbia since the Kosovo conflict and his first visit to Montenegro since May 1996' (*The Times*, 21 September 2000, p. 20).

President Milo Djukanovic:

If Milosevic decides to provoke a military conflict with Montenegro, then we would have no choice but to defend the state and our freedom ... It is more and more clear to Milosevic that his chances of winning at these elections in a legal way are minimal – they practically do not exist. Therefore, he is trying to scare the Yugoslav public with speculation about introducing a state of emergency ... Is it possible that things will go as far as a conflict and Milosevic will use some kind of pretext to declare a state of emergency?

(*IHT*, 21 September 2000, p. 6)

Mr Milosevic returned later on Wednesday [20 September] to Belgrade, where he and Mr Kostunica held rallies in different parts of the capital.

About 100,000 people gathered in the city centre and more were still arriving ahead of Mr Kostunica's rally ... In contrast Mr Milosevic addressed 15,000 people in a sports stadium.

(*IHT*, 21 September 2000, p. 6)

The opposition rally finally totalled around 150,000 (*Independent*, 22 September 2000, p. 14; *Telegraph*, 22 September 2000, p. 18).

In Kosovo ... the first batch of 2,000 extra troops started arriving to reinforce security ahead of the elections amid renewed threats of violence ... Some of the estimated 100,000 Serb minority will participate in Sunday's poll. Tuesday's [19 September] discovery of what Nato says was a Serbian terrorist cell in a major Serbian enclave and reports of clashes between Albanian Guerrillas and Serbian forces on Kosovo's doorstep, underlined the potential for trouble.

(*IHT*, 21 September 2000, p. 6)

In the first war crimes trial in Kosovo a Serb student was yesterday [20 September] sentenced to twenty years in prison for murder and rape committed ... last year [1999] ... A French judge ... joined Kosovo Albanian judges for the hearing under a United Nations programme designed to guarantee impartiality ... The verdict and sentence come six weeks after a court in the same Kosovo town ... cleared three Serbian men of murdering an ethnic Albanian last year. It was the first time the UN-run Kosovo courts had acquitted a Serb charged with killing a member of the majority Albanian population ... War crimes trials of fifteen other Serbs were stymied earlier this month [September] when they escaped from a UN-run detention centre in Mitrovica.

(*Guardian*, 21 September 2000, p. 17)

Federal prime minister Momir Bulatovic (in a televised interview in Montenegro given on 21 September): 'Under the constitutional law, the mandate of the president cannot be shortened. It will last until its expiry, which will be until mid-2001' (*Guardian*, 23 September 2000, p. 16)

Opposition lawyers have challenged this interpretation, claiming that constitutional changes made this summer require that the president should resign after calling elections ... In Montenegro ... A Yugoslav military policeman shot dead an off-duty Montenegrin policeman after an argument in a bar.

(*FT*, 23 September 2000, p. 5)

The UN mission in Kosovo announced on 22 September that 'witnesses' would stand outside polling stations in Kosovo to count the number who turn out to vote. The 'witnesses' were meant to provide a check on the predicted fraudulent official Serbian figures.

The end of the Milosevic era

The first round of the presidential election was held on 24 September. Also held were elections for the Yugoslav parliament (in which the ruling coalition retained its majority). In local elections in Serbia opposition parties predominated.

'The election in Yugoslavia "met all the requirements of international law," said observers from the Parliamentary Assembly of the Union of Belarus and Russia' (*CDSP*, 2000, vol. 52, no. 39, p. 4).

The distribution of seats in the Yugoslav Chamber of Citizens was as follows: Democratic Opposition of Serbia, fifty-nine; Socialist Party of Serbia and Yugoslav United left, forty-four; Socialist People's Party (Montenegro), twenty-eight; other parties (including the Radical Party and the Serbian Renewal Party), forty-seven (*The Times*, 9 October 2000, p. 14).

'Vuk Draskovic … [is] in Montenegro, where he has been in self-imposed exile after assassination attempts' (*Guardian*, 26 September 2000, p. 12).

'Mr Kostunica has overwhelming support among the young, urban population and Mr Milosevic among the rural and elderly who hark back to the old Yugoslav Federation' (Irena Guzelova, *FT*, 26 September 2000, p. 10).

Chancellor Gerhard Schröder of Germany (on 25 September, referring to the presidential election during a press conference in Moscow with Russian president Vladimir Putin): 'We agreed … that it looks as though Serbia and Yugoslavia have decided in favour of democratic change.'

On 25 September the Radical Party said that Kostunica had won in the first round (53.5 per cent to 37.9 per cent). The Serbian Socialist Party conceded that a second round was needed since Kostunica had won 45 per cent to 40 per cent. But the Yugoslav United Left claimed that Milosevic had won in the first round (by 56.3 per cent to 31.4 per cent).

The turnout in Montenegro was very low (less than 30 per cent). Those who did vote were largely pro-Milosevic.

The official Federal Election Commission (appointed by the Yugoslav parliament and containing few opposition representatives) reported preliminary figures on 26 September, based on a count of around 64 per cent of the vote: Kostunica, 48.22 per cent; Milosevic, 40.23 per cent. The final result was given on 28 September: Kostunica, 48.96 per cent; Milosevic, 38.62 per cent.

On 26 September the eighteen-party Democratic Opposition of Serbia, based on a count of 98.5 per cent of the vote, claimed that the respective figures for Kostunica and Milosevic were 54.66 per cent and 35.01 per cent. The following day a figure of 52.54 per cent was given for Kostunica, based on a count of 98.7 per cent of the vote.

'Each polling station produced multiple copies of agreed voting figures, signed and countersigned by Milosevic loyalists and the opposition' (*Independent*, 28 September 2000, p. 15). 'With the exception of a few places where they were denied access, there were representatives of all parties in each Serbian polling station … and in each they jointly counted the ballots, reporting the result to the Federal Electoral Commission' (*The Times*, 28 September 2000, p. 23).

According to opposition members of the Federal Election Commission, who were outvoted, the commission reduced the number of eligible voters in the country by 600,000 people, and made no effort to reconcile its results with those of the opposition, as it is supposed to do under the law.

(*IHT*, 29 September 2000, p. 4)

'In Kosovo Mr Milosevic claimed he had won 140,000 votes. Kfor ... says only 45,000 people voted and polling stations where votes were said to have come from never opened' (*Guardian*, 30 September 2000, p. 2). 'The opposition ... on Friday [29 September] said the commission had attributed to Mr Milosevic 140,000 non-existent votes from Kosovo ... The United Nations ... said only 45,000 minority Serbs had voted there' (*IHT*, 30 September 2000, p. 5). 'UN "witness" teams counted about 45,000 voters, almost all Serbs, going into polling stations [in Kosovo], Bernard Kouchner said last night [24 September] ... "The maximum number of voters was 44,167," Dr Kouchner said' (*Telegraph*, 25 September 2000, p. 11). (The commission claimed that 150,000 had voted in Kosovo in total.)

Vojislav Kostunica (26 September): 'We are talking about political fraud and blatant stealing of votes. This is an offer [a second round of voting on 8 October] which must be rejected.'

On 27 September an opposition rally in Belgrade attracted more than 200,000 people. Other rallies were as follows: Novi Sad, 35,000; Nis, 25,000; Kragujevac, 15,000; Kraljevo, 10,000 (*IHT*, 29 September 2000, p. 4)

On 28 September the Serbian Orthodox Church (headed by Patriarch Pavle) issued a statement addressed to 'Vojislav Kostunica, elected president of Yugoslavia': 'Vojislav Kostunica and all the people elected together with him, when they take over the control of the state, its parliament and its municipalities, [should] do so in a peaceful and dignified way.'

On 29 September an afternoon opposition rally attracted protesters estimated at around 20,000. There were also rallies later on in Belgrade and elsewhere in Serbia. There were reports of some factories, schools and colleges closing, of some taxi drivers and truck drivers blocking roads and of protests by some working in the state media. The opposition called for a campaign of civil disobedience, including a general strike, on 2 October.

A BBC correspondent was expelled from Serbia on 29 September for alleged bias in reporting.

On 29 September Kostunica suggested an internationally monitored recount.

On 29 September miners in Serbia's largest mine, at Kolubara south of Belgrade, began a strike. They were joined on 1 October by coal miners at the Kostolac mine in eastern Serbia. Coal is important in the production of electricity. ('The great opencast coalfields of Kolubara, some thirty miles south of Belgrade, provide the fuel to generate more than half of Serbia's electricity ... Some 17,500 people are employed in the Kolubara complex ... The miners in the Kolubara coal mines, whose strike was to give a decisive push to the revolution, told me their wages had shrunk after the war from an average of about DM

150 a month to as low as DM 70. The reduction was explained as a tax for postwar reconstruction': Timothy Garton Ash, *New York Review of Books*, 2000, vol. XLVII, no. 18, pp. 10–11.)

A German spokesperson reported on a telephone conversation that Chancellor Gerhard Schröder of Germany had with President Vladimir Putin on 30 September: 'They agreed that, in the election of Vojislav Kostunica, the will of the Serbian people for a democratic change in Yugoslavia had been clearly expressed.'

Relatively small rallies were reported on 30 September.

The USA said that an offer of mediation by Russia had been rejected by Milosevic.

Vladimir Putin (2 October): 'As president of Russia I am prepared to receive in the next few days in Moscow both candidates who have gone through to the second round … to discuss means of finding a way out of the current situation.'

> Mr Kostunica [2 October] strongly criticized both the USA and Russia for their handling of the crisis. He accused Washington of indirectly bolstering Mr Milosevic by insisting that he remained an indicted war criminal … Mr Kostunica described Russian policy as 'indecisive and reluctant'. He said: 'It could be described as taking one step forward and one step back. The Russians do not have a specific and concrete position on the situation in Yugoslavia.'
>
> (*FT*, 3 October 2000, p. 9)

On 2 October there began the campaign of civil disobedience, with strikes, rallies and road blocks. Support was patchy on the first day, with most in provincial cities and towns where the opposition parties are strongest.

The opposition claimed that on 2 October a computer disk was thrown from a window in the Yugoslav Statistics Office. The disk is said to have included election results from individual polling stations.

> Late Monday [2 October] Mr Milosevic sent the army's chief of staff, General Nebojsa Pavkovic, to the Kolubara mine to demand that the strikers return to work … But the miners said early Tuesday that they would remain on strike until Mr Milosevic accepted defeat … Before dawn on Tuesday morning … General Nebojsa Pavkovic came to warn the workers to stop their strike for the good of the nation. Intermittently yelling and cajoling, threatening punishment and promising a 10 per cent rise, General Pavkovic failed to end the strike … Mr Kostunica came here on Monday [2 October] and was greeted as 'president' … After Mr Kostunica's visit a former general, Momcilo Perisic, fired by Mr Milosevic and now an opposition leader, came Tuesday morning [3 October] to encourage the workers.
>
> (*IHT*, 4 October 2000, pp. 1, 4)

'Late Tuesday [3 October] the Belgrade prosecutor's office ordered the arrest of thirteen alleged organizers of the strike at the Kolubara mine' (*IHT*, 4 October 2000, p. 1). 'The [eleven] miners are members of the strike committee at Serbia's largest coal mine, Kolubara ... The two opposition leaders ... visited the mine on Sunday night [1 October]' (*Guardian*, 4 October 2000, p. 2).

A government statement was issued on 3 October:

> Any violent behaviour of individuals or groups that threatens citizens' lives, disrupts traffic and prevents industry, schools, institutions and health facilities from carrying out their normal work will be prosecuted by law ... Special measures will be taken against the organizers of these criminal activities. These measures will also apply to media that are financed from abroad and are breeding lies, untruths and inciting bloodshed.

On 4 October 2000 police failed to take over the Kolubara mines, foiled by the miners themselves and others who came in support. Kostunica visited the mines later in the day. The opposition have issued an 'ultimatum' for Milosevic to resign by 3 p.m. on 5 October, the time set for a large rally in Belgrade. There were four other demands, including the publishing of proper results by the constitutional court. Strikes spread.

Also on 4 October the constitutional court, after a challenge by the opposition, announced that 'part' of the first round of the presidential election had been annulled.

> The Milosevic-controlled Yugoslav constitutional court issued a declaration Wednesday [4 October] that one justice said nullified the election. The justice, Milutin Srdic, told Radio Free Europe that Mr Milosevic could remain in office until his term expires in July [2001] and that new elections would be held.
>
> (*IHT*, 6 October 2000, p. 1)

What may be described as a popular revolution took place on 5 October 2000. Crucial was the participation of workers, who joined other groups such as students and other intellectuals. Casualties were low. One demonstrator was reported dead, the result of an accident. One man died of a heart attack.

In the morning of 5 October the constitutional court declared that the first round of the presidential election had been annulled and that a fresh election was necessary.

What were generally described as 'hundreds of thousands' of demonstrators from Belgrade (perhaps half a million) and outside the capital took over key buildings, such as the Yugoslav federal parliament, the state-controlled television (Radio Television Serbia) and other television stations. Fires were started in the parliament and Radio Television Serbia buildings. The state news media Tanjug referred to 'President Kostunica'. Kostunica declared himself president.

The police offered little resistance and the army did not intervene. Some police and soldiers fraternized and even collaborated with the demonstrators.

'The new authorities ... may arrest him [Milosevic] on charges of corruption, attempted electoral fraud or even for ordering the police and army to fire on the demonstrators on 5 October – an order they ignored' (Tim Judah, *The World Today*, 2000, vol. 56, no. 11, p. 6).

Milosevic (in a recorded address broadcast on 6 October):

> I congratulate Mr Kostunica on his electoral victory and I wish much success to all citizens of Yugoslavia. I intend to rest a bit and spend some time with my family and especially with my grandson Marko and after that to help my party gain force and contribute to future prosperity.

(It was later revealed that army personnel, including chief of staff Nebojsa Pavkovic, had visited Milosevic and ordered him to meet Kostunica.)

Russian foreign minister Igor Ivanov (6 October): 'I passed on a message from President Putin and congratulated Kostunica on his victory in the presidential elections.'

Russian foreign minister Igor Ivanov (after meeting Milosevic in Belgrade on 6 October):

> During the talks Milosevic emphasized his intention to seek a solution in a peaceful and legal manner, to avoid the use of force. Being the leader of the largest political party in Serbia he intends to continue to play a political role in the country.

On 6 October the constitutional court announced that Kostunica had won in the first round of the presidential election, Belarus offered political asylum to Milosevic and the two Britons and the younger Canadian who had been arrested in early August were released from prison. The army announced that it would not intervene unless its bases and personnel were threatened. (On 6 October the army formally recognized Kostunica as commander-in-chief of the armed forces and as Yugoslav president: *EEN*, 2000, vol. 13, no. 1, p. 7.)

> In Belgrade the central bank yesterday [6 October] halted the sale of hard currency, presumably to maintain reserves and block capital flight ... Vojislav Kostunica ... yesterday started putting together an interim ruling structure called the 'crisis committee for Yugoslavia' ... a quasi-government to which they are inviting representatives of Montenegro ... The new president has also approached Vojislav Seselj and Vuk Draskovic ... Mr Kostunica plans to hold fully democratic elections in about a year and ask the new parliament to write a new constitution.
>
> (*FT*, 7 October 2000, pp. 1, 6, 12)

Kostunica was sworn in as president on 7 October 2000.

Milo Djukanovic, the Montenegrin president, said on the eve of Mr Kostunica's swearing-in on Saturday [7 October]: 'The past elections were illegal. We can talk to Mr Kostunica, however, not as the Yugoslav president but as the representative of the new political thought in Serbia.'

(*FT*, 9 October 2000, p. 8)

Djukanovic: '[I am willing to negotiate with Kostunica] not as president of Yugoslavia but as the representative of the democratic majority in Serbia' (*Telegraph*, 9 October 2000, p. 4).

The extraordinary events that brought down the fall of Milosevic last week were planned with defectors from elite Serbian police units, the opposition mayor who led the storming of parliament said yesterday [Sunday 8 October]. The apparently spontaneous capture of the Yugoslav parliament and state television was the result of a carefully planned strategy, said Velimir Ilijc, mayor of Cacak, an opposition stronghold ... At 7.30 a.m. on Thursday [5 October] a huge column of protestors set off from Cacak to Belgrade, led by Mr Ilijc. Most were farmers and peasants but among them, said Mr Ilijc, were Yugoslav army paratroops and plainclothes police defectors ... As they marched they were joined by others. When the column reached Belgrade there were 10,000 of them. It was they who led the storming of parliament and state television ... The police defectors broke police lines, opening the protestors' path to parliament ... The mayor insists that although it was his protestors who broke into parliament they were not responsible for the fire started in the building ... He did not tell the opposition of his plan to storm parliament, but he said he did co-ordinate with the Otpor student resistance movement and fans of Belgrade's Red Star football team.

(*Independent*, 9 October 2000, p. 12)

Police and soldiers from Yugoslavia's elite units staged a mutiny during Belgrade's day of revolution last week, according to a former member of one of the units involved ... More than 100 active or former soldiers ... actually spearheaded the storming of the federal assembly and the offices of state television RTS, liaising with sympathetic police inside ... The man around whom these security forces rallied on Thursday [5 October] – the day of Belgrade's revolution – was the ... mayor of Cacak.

(*Guardian*, 9 October 2000, p. 12)

People from Cacak, one of the most determinedly anti-Milosevic places in Serbia, were at the core of the tide of people who ... overran parliament and the state television centre. [Mayor] Velimir Ilijc [leader of the New Serbia Party] ... said two officers who were members of an elite police unit in Belgrade and two more in Cacak had helped to co-ordinate a mass defection of the police as the crowd, spearheaded by off-duty army paratroopers, rushed parliament … Among the workers, students and truck drivers, he had organized a core team of tough young men and, crucially, off-duty members of the police and the army, he said … Mr Ilijc said: 'We established a team of young professionals, paratroopers from the Yugoslav army and young policemen, and we co-ordinated this with the most elite units of the interior ministry police in Belgrade … We even had plainclothes police co-ordinating with nearby towns' … He said his personal agreement with two special policemen from Belgrade and two from Cacak had caused major elements of the police in the capital to join the side of the demonstrators.

(IHT, 11 October 2000, p. 7)

The mayor of Cacak, Velimir Ilijc, described to me how he and his group prepared their trip to Belgrade as if it were a military operation … There is doubtless some retrospective self-glorification in these accounts, but other witnesses agree that the boys from Cacak were there in the front line … [But] Cacak was not alone; there were many angry men from other provincial towns … The hard men from the provinces … were here to finish the job.

(Timothy Garton Ash, *New York Review of Books*, 2000, vol. XLVII, no. 18, p. 12)

Customs controls on the Serb–Montenegrin border were lifted on 7 October (*EEN*, 2000, vol. 13, no. 1, p. 4).

The whereabouts of Marko Milosevic, the son of [Slobodan Milosevic] … were unclear last night [8 October] after the millionaire underworld figure was reported to have flown into Moscow with his wife and infant son … [Slobodan Milosevic acknowledged] the victory of the Serbian insurgency against his regime on Friday [6 October] … Hours later the infant was whisked on to a Yugoslav Airline flight to Moscow, according to a Belgrade news agency, with his mother Zorica and notoriously brutish father. Marko Milosevic fled a lynch mob in his hometown of Pozarevac, south-east of Belgrade … His uncle, Borislav Milosevic, is the Yugoslav ambassador [to Russia] … The Marko family left behind scenes of looting [of his business properties].

(Guardian, 9 October 2000, p. 12)

Significant events on 9 October 2000 included the following:

1   The resignation of federal prime minister Momir Bulatovic.
2   The resignation of Serbian interior minister Vlajko Stojiljkovic, a post whose remit includes the police.
3   The Serbian parliament agree to hold fresh elections on 17 December 2000.

The power of the federal authorities is much smaller than that of the two republics of Serbia and Montenegro. The republics control most of the budget, including income taxes, and the police. They also appoint constitutional court judges, who play a big role in the many disputes arising from these complex arrangements.

(*FT*, 10 October 2000, p. 8)

'Mr Kostunica's coalition has formed a "crisis committee" that is a kind of parallel government to the Serbian authorities who were beholden to Mr Milosevic' (*IHT*, 10 October 2000, p. 1).

4   The EU unconditionally lifts most sanctions. These include the oil embargo and the ban on commercial air travel (which had already been suspended). But the EU was to 'maintain a freeze on state assets as well as a selective ban on visas to prevent ... Slobodan Milosevic and his aides from escaping with looted national wealth' (*IHT*, 10 October 2000, p. 1).

The EU would also provide aid estimated at about $2 billion (*IHT*, 10 October 2000, p.1; *Guardian*, 10 October 2000, p. 21). 'British officials circulated figures suggesting that up to Euro 4 billion was available to 2006' (*FT*, 10 October 2000, p. 8).

5   Marko Milosevic and his family are refused permission to enter China at Beijing airport. His plane returns to Moscow. ('He tried to enter the country with a diplomatic passport but no valid visa ... China and Yugoslavia have an agreement allowing holders of diplomatic passports to enter each other's countries without visas': *FEER*, 19 October 2000, p. 14.) (China had already recognized Kostunica's victory, belatedly, as was the case with Russia.)

6   The four Dutchmen arrested at the end of July 2000 are released from prison.

7   There are reports of employees turning against pro-Milosevic management and demanding their resignation.

[There have been] reports of a forceful takeover of the state customs office, major banks and nearly all key companies and factories remaining in pro-Milosevic hands ... Eager to shore up his power base Mr Kostunica is trying to install his own supporters in charge of the country's most important institutions, including the police, judiciary, banks and state-run companies.

(*IHT*, 11 October 2000, pp. 1, 7)

Workers' committees were yesterday [10 October] taking control of Yugoslav public sector organizations and throwing out managers appointed by Slobodan Milosevic ... The Zastava car factory, the Dunav insurance company and the big Genex trading company were among state-controlled businesses where employees battled to establish their authority ... Strike committees, workers' committees, lock-ins and lock-outs, Yugoslavia was yesterday awash with reports of workers revolting against their Milosevic-era managers and taking over the directors' suites. It happened in Novi Sad, in the state lottery company, in Nis, in the tobacco works, and in Belgrade

University, where teaching staff and students expelled the rector and his administrators.

(FT, 11 October 2000, p. 8)

Workers and activists ... rush to seize businesses, assets and lucrative senior jobs in an uncontrolled raid on the power of the old regime ... Since Monday [9 October] workers have been storming the offices of factories, banks, universities and the civil service ... and using threats and force to expel their old bosses ... At the weekend [7–8 October] activists had wrested control of the National Bank, the Serbian police and the customs office from Milosevic supporters ... Zarko Korac, a leading member of DOS [Democratic Opposition of Serbia] ... admitted that DOS was involved in some of the dismissals.

(The Times, 11 October 2000, p. 18)

'In ministries, newspapers and all manner of companies self-proclaimed crisis committees were taking over' (Tim Judah, *The World Today*, 2000, vol. 56, no. 11, p. 5). 'As the political parties met for coalition talks about a new federal government, self-appointed "crisis committees" in factories and offices sacked their former bosses – in the name of the people' (Timothy Garton Ash, *New York Review of Books*, 2000, vol. XLVII, no. 18, p. 8).

The Yugoslav president said yesterday [11 October] that 'I am having almost as much trouble from my friends as from my enemies' ... In the interview Mr Kostunica said that some of the members of the eighteen-party coalition that supported his presidential candidacy were making policy statements that have not been cleared with him and using extra-legal procedures to take control over certain ministries and companies that have been run by those close to Mr Milosevic. 'I cannot justify all that is going on,' he said. 'On the surface there is a peaceful democratic transition, but below the surface there is a kind of volcano, not so controlled ... Some members of the DOS [Democratic Opposition of Serbia] are not so much eating away at my authority. That they cannot do. The problem is that they are compromising that authority.' In particular, he and his aides said, the Democratic Party leader, Zoran Djindjic ... who leads the strongest party by far in the coalition, is moving to try to consolidate the popular revolt against Mr Milosevic, but in a way that might cause confusion. The best known example was Mr Djindjic's effort to put an ally and well-known businessman in charge of the customs office after ousting the old minister. While no one objected to the ouster, the appointment of Mr Djindjic's ally caused an uproar among other political leaders and it was rescinded in a day. In state-owned companies and banks Milosevic managers are being ousted, but sometimes by workers who were tired of political bosses. 'Some of this is spontaneous, some of it is not,' said Mr Kostunica. 'Some of it comes from within, and some from the outside. And some of these actions are from people who are in connection with or appear on behalf of DOS or even myself, which is not true. But all together it is something that worries me' … Mr Djindjic has also made announcements that Mr Kostunica had not approved. Mr Djindjic, for example, said that the Yugoslav army chief of staff, General Nebojsa Pavkovic, would be dismissed. But Mr Kostunica said Wednesday [11 October] that he had no intention of ousting General Pavkovic, who became a popular hero for his efforts to defend Kosovo, at least for now. Mr Kostunica said he had no interest now in stirring up a quiescent army while he and his allies try to ensure they control the Serbian police. Mr Djindjic also announced that Miroljub Labus, an economist, would become provisional prime minister of Yugoslavia in a technical government. But Mr Kostunica said Wednesday that he would choose a prime minister from Montenegro, as the constitution required, who would be a member of the Socialist People's Party, which won nearly all the Montenegrin seats because of an election boycott by the republic's president, Milo Djukanovic.

(Steven Erlanger, *IHT*, 12 October 2000, pp. 1, 4)

On 10 October French foreign minister Hubert Vedrine visited Belgrade and talked with Kostunica.

On 10 October 2000 the journalist Miroslav Filipovic was released from military prison. (He had been arrested in May 2000 and sentenced to seven years in prison in July 2000.)

The Serbian Socialist Party issued a statement on 11 October 2000:

The Serbian government will go on ruling the republic since it was elected on a four-year mandate [until September 2001] and it is the only body which can make legal decisions. The government will also ignore all the decisions of the so-called 'crisis committees' … State bodies, especially the prosecutor's office and the police, are obliged to take urgent action in accordance with the law against the organisers and perpetrators of illegal actions.

Talks on the formation of an interim government failed. The Serbian government refused to agree on the formation of a transitional government and appointed Mirko Marjanovic, the Serbian prime minister, to take over control of the interior ministry and thus police and security forces. The government demanded the reinstatement of four ministers and the regaining of control over state television.

Kostunica met senior army representatives on 11 October. The army warned of 'possible negative consequences of increased attacks and attempts to discredit certain individuals of the Yugoslav army'. ('Mr Kostunica said Wednesday [11 October] that he had no intention of ousting General Pavkovic, who became a popular hero for his efforts to defend Kosovo, at least for now. Mr Kostunica said he had no interest now in stirring up a quiescent army while he and his allies try to ensure they control the Serbian police': *IHT*, 12 October 2000, p. 4.)

Resignations on 11 October included the head of the electoral commission and the police commander in charge of defending the parliament building.

The United States' ambassador-designate to Yugoslavia visited Belgrade on 11 October.

(*FT*, 12 October 2000, p. 1; *The Times*, 12 October 2000, pp. 1, 18; *Independent*, 12 October 2000, pp. 1, 12; *Guardian*, 12 October 2000, pp. 1, 17; *Telegraph*, 12 October 2000, p. 18; *IHT*, 12 October 2000, pp. 1, 4.)

On 12 October the USA lifted its oil embargo and flight ban. James O'Brien, the special adviser to President Clinton for the Balkans, met President Kostunica.

'Mr Kostunica said Thursday [12 October] that he respected the Dayton agreement ... He also committed himself to United Nations resolutions that provide for wide Albanian self-government in Kosovo' (*IHT*, 13 October 2000, p. 11).

Kostunica (12 October): 'If the will of the people of Montenegro is to not belong to the federation, this will be respected.'

On 12 October Gorica Gajevic resigns from her post as secretary-general of the Serbian Socialist Party and is replaced by Zoran Andjelkovic. The increasingly split party called for an exceptional congress on 25 November 2000, with some members openly calling for the removal of Milosevic as party leader.

On 13 October the Serbian Socialist Party agreed to early parliamentary elections (to be held on 24 December 2000).

> After a week of talks allies of President Vojislav Kostunica and the Socialist Party of Serbia have reached an agreement in principle to share power in the Serbian republic until new elections are held in late December, according to leaders in the new democratic coalition. At a meeting Saturday night [14 October] seven representatives of Mr Milosevic's party, including the Serbian president Milan Milutinovic, told the democratic coalition that they had agreed to a power-sharing arrangement for the next ten weeks but still needed to 'consult' before they could sign the accord on Monday [16 October], the deadline set by Mr Kostunica's allies ... The agreement reflects the abandonment by the Socialists of a demand for control of the police and justice ministers, a sticking point that had held up a deal for the last week.
>
> (*IHT*, 16 October 2000, p. 2)

Also on 14 October 2000 Kostunica attended an EU meeting in Biarritz (France). The EU promised emergency aid worth Euro 200 million ($170 million) for things like food, medicine and fuel. 'Mr Kostunica said he was in favour of changing the name of the country from Yugoslavia to Serbia–Montenegro ... [and] of allowing the citizens of Serbia and Montenegro to express their will in a referendum' (*IHT*, 16 October 2000, p. 4).

'The Crown Prince of Yugoslavia, Alexander [II] Karadjordjevic returned to Belgrade yesterday [15 October] for a meeting with President Kostunica' (*The Times*, 16 October 2000, p. 17).

On 16 October a transitional power-sharing arrangement for Serbia was agreed upon. Fresh elections for the Serbian parliament would be held on 23 December 2000. The Serbian Socialist Party would retain the post of prime minister but the premier would have to take decisions in consensus ('consensually') with two deputy prime ministers, one from DOS and one from the Serbian Renewal Party. State television would be similarly run. The ministries of justice, finance, information and the interior (which is in charge of some 85,000 police) would be controlled jointly by DOS, the Serbian Socialist Party and the Serbian Renewal Party.

The Radical Party refused to take part in the arrangement (having been very critical of what it saw as anarchic conditions). No mention was made of the Serbian president, Milan Milutinovic, whose mandate runs until 2002.

The minister of defence and the army high command were not affected by the deal.

Kostunica has yet to appoint a new Yugoslav (federal) government and prime minister. Under the federal constitution the prime minister must be from Montenegro if the president is, like Kostunica, from Serbia.

President Kostunica visited Montenegro on 17 October 2000 but he failed to persuade President Djukanovic to take part in a federal government.

> Milo Djukanovic applauded democratic changes in Serbia ... but said he would take part in national institutions only after Yugoslavia's two republics redefined their relationship. That must await the results of early elections for the Serb republic's parliament, set for 23 December. Nevertheless, Mr Djukanovic said he and Mr Kostunica had agreed to continue talks on the new relationship between the two republics. His statement also referred to Mr Kostunica as president. Mr Djukanovic's government had declared last month's federal elections in Yugoslavia as illegal and had refused to recognise Mr Kostunica as president ... But the Montenegrin president's office in Podgorica said Mr Kostunica and Mr Djukanovic had agreed that problems between Montenegro and Serbia would be resolved through talks. 'The parties reached mutual consent on having all disputes that burdened our relations resolved through dialogue,' a statement said. Mr Djukanovic, however, remains angry over a plan by Mr Kostunica's allies to offer the federal prime ministership to his Montenegrin rivals [the Montenegrin Socialist People's Party] who had supported Mr Milosevic.
>
> (*IHT*, 18 October 2000, p. 4)

> Miodrag Vukovic, a senior adviser to President Milo Djukanovic, said: 'The present federation cannot be saved. What we want is a new partnership involving co-operation between two states. The new system could be something between a union and a confederation.' If that could not be achieved, complete independence would be the only choice, he said.
>
> (*IHT*, 19 October 2000, p. 7)

Mr Djukanovic ...[has proposed] that Montenegro and Serbia occupy separate seats in the United Nations, according to a 27 October letter he wrote to secretary-general Kofi Annan. Montenegrin sovereignty, Mr Djukanovic wrote, is the foundation 'of our initial proposal to President Kostunica, namely the proposal that acclaims the relationship of Montenegro and Serbia as an alliance of two internationally recognised states'.

(*IHT*, 22 November 2000, p. 5)

Kostunica has made it clear that he would respect the outcome of a referendum in Montenegro – and, for that matter, in Serbia, for the Serbs do not want to stay together with the Montenegrins at any price, in an unequal or sham confederation.

(Timothy Garton Ash, *New York Review of Books*, 2000, vol. XLVII, no. 18, p. 14)

'Kostunica has won tentative support from the Montenegrin Socialist People's Party' (*Independent*, 19 October 2000, p. 16).

'[On 17 October] Mr Milosevic's ... personal banker [was] voted out of office ... At a shareholders' meeting in a leading Belgrade bank, Borka Vucic was voted out as the bank's director amid disarray and her resistance to demands that she step down' (*IHT*, 18 October 2000, p. 4).

Shareholders at Serbia's largest bank [Beogradska Banka] voted to remove Borka Vucic, regarded locally as the Milosevic family's banker, as head of the company ... Ms Vucic has been instrumental in sanctions busting and is accused of siphoning state money and assets belonging to the Milosevic family to foreign banks. In July [2000] the authorities in Cyprus closed down the local branch of Beogradska, citing problems with its solvency, following allegations that the branch had played a key role in the illegal transfer abroad of about DM 6 billion in foreign exchange belonging to the former Yugoslav republic. The bank's president ... said that on Sunday [15 October] Ms Vucic broke into her office with a group of her armed men who disarmed the security guards and took control of the bank.

(*FT*, 18 October 2000, p. 11)

Last week ... Borka Vucic, a seventy-two-year-old woman who is a diehard ally of ... [Milosevic] ... was marched from her office by armed men ... Her successor at the bank says he is going to make public the bank's financial records since 1992 ... On Sunday night Ms Vucic returned to her old office in the dead of night for an hour, and it is now rumoured that she was returning to destroy incriminating evidence. Mr Milosevic was head of the Belgrade Bank in the eighties.

(*Independent*, Monday 17 October 2000, p. 13)

Slobodan Milosevic remains the boss of bosses at the apex of a criminal organization and has salted away more than $100 million, according to an investigation by the German Federal Intelligence Service (BND) ... The file on Mr Milosevic released yesterday [16 October] to the German press names a dozen senior Serbian politicians as cohorts in a mafia that has bled Yugoslavia dry for a decade or more. 'Considerable evidence indicates that Milosevic and his entourage constitute an organized crime structure and are engaged in drug dealing, money laundering and other criminal acts,' the report said. The file also alleges that about sixty people allied to [Milosevic] ... have been ruling the country and have prospered in the shadow of war and chaos. 'The near total control of key economic posts by Milosevic followers opened opportunities for illegal capital transfer for personal enrichment and financing for political plans – weapons purchases – and served as a camouflage for criminal activity – drug trade,' the report alleged. Among the Milosevic cronies named in the report are Dragan Tomic, parliamentary president, Mirko Marjanovic, the Serbian prime minister, and Dragan Kostic, the former minister of energy ... With the imposition of international sanctions on Yugoslavia eight years ago massive smuggling operations began ... The smuggling is said to have been controlled by Mr Milosevic and his cronies, who made vast profits from it.

(*Independent*, 17 October 2000, p. 13)

Slobodan Milosevic and his associates are criminals who have stashed at least $100 million in purloined funds abroad, German intelligence agents claim ... The German Federal Intelligence Service (BND) alleged that the sums thought to have been diverted – estimated to be 'at least three-digit millions of dollars' – could not have been obtained legally. Mr Milosevic's private assets extended to Russia, China, Cyprus, Greece, Lebanon and South Africa, the BND assessment said. In Switzerland, it estimated his holdings at $100 million.

(*Guardian*, 17 October 2000, p. 15)

'OSCE announced that it had invited Yugoslavia to join the group in time for its next ministerial meeting in Vienna on 27 November [2000]. Yugoslavia was dropped from the group in 1992' (*IHT*, 20 October 2000, p. 4).

Kostunica visited Bosnia on 22 October 2000, the first visit by a leader of Serbia since 1992. He first went to Trebinje in the Republika Srpska to attend, in a private capacity, the reburial of a Serb nationalist poet (a chetnik supporter), who died in the USA in 1943. Kostunica then visited Sarajevo. He declared support for the Dayton agreement. 'Mr Kostunica said ... that he was convinced an establishment and normalization of relations between Sarajevo and Belgrade "would be achieved very fast"' (*IHT*, 23 October 2000, p. 4).

A new Serbian government was agreed on 23 October.

The Serbian parliament approved the transitional government on 24 October. The prime minister is Milomir Minic, deputy chairman of the Serbian Socialist Party.

Kostunica (in an interview on Kosovo held on 24 October):

I am ready, how to say, to accept the guilt for all those people who have been killed, so I am trying to, taking responsibility for what happened on my part. For what Milosevic had done and, as a Serb, I will take responsibility for many of these, these crimes. Those are the crimes and the people that have been killed are victims. There are a lot of crimes on the other side and Serbs have been killed ... [In answer to the question whether Milosevic will ever stand trial] Somewhere, yes.

On 25 October Kostunica attended a summit of Balkan leaders in Skopje (the capital of the FYR of Macedonia), along with the leaders of Albania, Bosnia, Bulgaria, Croatia, Greece, the FYR of Macedonia, Romania and Turkey.

'The summit was organized at short notice by the South-Eastern European Co-operation Process, a group which brings together eight Balkan states as well as Turkey. The meeting was also attended by EU foreign policy chief Javier Solana' (*Guardian*, 26 October 2000, p. 18).

Some or all of the more than 900 ethnic Albanians from Kosovo imprisoned in Serbia for more than a year may be released in coming weeks ... President Vojislav Kostunica planned to propose a general amnesty for ethnic Albanians accused of illegal involvement in the Kosovo war in 1999. He would then seek parliament's approval of the measure ... Mr Kostunica ... has already attempted to arrange a pardon for ... Flora Brovina ... But Mrs Brovina has refused to leave jail unless all other ethnic Albanians are released.

(*IHT*, 26 October 2000, p. 4)

[There are] approximately 800 ethnic Albanians still being held in Serbian jails ... Initially Mr Kostunica linked the release of Kosovo Albanian prisoners to progress in tracking down an estimated 1,000 Serbs who had disappeared in Kosovo since the end of the war. More recently, however, his aides have said the president is considering a general amnesty for Albanian political detainees, to be submitted to the Yugoslav parliament in a few weeks.

(*IHT*, 1 November 2000, p. 5)

(Serbia's supreme court overturned the conviction of Flora Brovina on 7 June 2000 and referred the case back to the Nis tribunal. She had been convicted of terrorism by a court in Nis in December 1999 and sentenced to seven years in prison for alleged links to the KLA: *IHT*, 8 June 2000, p. 5. Flora Brovina was released from prison on 1 November 2000 on the orders of President Kostunica. 'In December last year [1999] Mrs Brovina was ... sentenced to twelve years in prison ... The sentence was quashed by the Serbian supreme court earlier this summer [2000]. A new trial was ordered and was due to take place on 16 November ... Mrs Brovina had earlier told her family that she would not leave jail unless her fellow inmates were released too': *Guardian*, 2 November 2000, p.

19. 'Three Albanian men were released with Dr Brovina and eleven more are due to be freed tomorrow [4 November]': *Telegraph*, 3 November 2000, p. 20. 'Flora Brovina ... has visited four prisons in Serbia where inmates are rioting ... [including] the Nis prison where she had been held. She was accompanied by Mr Kostunica's chief of staff ... an interior minister ... and the Serbian chief of state security (Radomir Markovic) ... Nearly 1,000 ethnic Albanians arrested during the Kosovo war are still being held in Serbian prisons ... Dr Brovina said they have not been targets and have not taken part in the riots and protests ... The Serbian authorities freed fourteen Serbs and one ethnic Albanian on Friday [10 November]': *IHT*, 11 November 2000, p. 6.)

On 26 October Yugoslavia was admitted into the Stability Pact for South-Eastern Europe.

Kostunica visited Russia on 27 October. President Putin: 'You have managed to escape the difficult situation without bloodshed and lead your country out of international isolation ... Very soon Russia will reestablish energy deliveries interrupted this year to Yugoslavia, including gas supplies.'

> Russia's natural gas monopoly, Gazprom, has cut off supplies because Serbia ... owes $300 million. To survive the winter Yugoslav officials have said the country urgently needs $600 million in energy assistance ... 'Half the country's population is living without electricity and heating,' the Yugoslav president was quoted as saying Friday [27 October] ... Mr Kostunica has suggested swapping commodities for the gas debt.
>
> (*IHT*, 28 October 2000, p. 5)

> Mr Putin said that energy deliveries, including gas, would be reconnected 'very soon' after being cut off earlier this year as a result of non-paid bills by Yugoslavia totalling at least $400 million. They [Putin and Kostunica] agreed to set up a group of experts to work on the issue ... Before leaving Mr Kostunica pledged to discuss commodities transactions to pay for the gas.
>
> (*FT*, 28 October 2000, p. 10)

Elections for Kosovo's thirty municipalities were held in Kosovo on 28 October 2000. The campaign was largely peaceful. The turnout among registered voters was 79 per cent among 913,179 eligible voters.

'Bernard Kouchner said Kosovo's first free elections had been considered successful around the world' (*IHT*, 8 November 2000, p. 13).

The vast majority of Serbs decided to boycott the elections and no Serb party participated. 'Almost a million Kosovo Albanians have registered to vote and about 1,000 Serbs ... To try to circumvent the boycott the UN administrator in Kosovo, Bernard Kouchner, will appoint Serbs to some municipalities' (*Guardian*, 28 October 2000, p. 19). 'Few of the 100,000 Serbs in Kosovo voted' (*FT*, 30 October 2000, p. 1). 'The poll was boycotted by Kosovo's 75,000-strong Serb minority' (*FT*, 1 November 2000, p. 9). 'There were also candidates from the Bosniak, Gorani, Turkish and Ashkalia–Roma minorities, but the process was boycotted by the 90,000 Kosovo Serbs, and Serbophone Roma, both as voters and candidates' (James Pettifer, *The World Today*, 2000, vol. 56, no. 12, p. 14).

There were three main parties:

The Democratic League of Kosovo (LDK) is led by Ibrahim Rugova. The party won 58.0 per cent of the vote and control of twenty-one municipalities.

The Democratic Party of Kosovo (PDK) is led by Hashim Thaci. The party won 27.3 per cent of the vote and control of six municipalities.

The Alliance for the Future of Kosovo (AAK) is led by Ramush Haradinaj. The party won 8 per cent of the vote.

Of the 869 seats in twenty-seven municipalities, the LDK won 504, while the PDK got 267.

As of 31 October three municipalities remained to be counted.

> All three main parties favour independence sooner rather than later. Mr Rugova's party is seen as the most moderate and enjoys widespread support … He preaches a message of non-violence, tolerance and co-operation with other parties. Mr Thaci's Party of Democratic Kosovo is seen as the most hard-line. Most of his supporters are young, but his popularity among mainstream Albanians has declined as many associate his party with a violent underworld of crime and corruption. Ramush Haradinaj's Alliance for the Future of Kosovo seeks to steer a road between the two.
>
> (Irena Guzelova, *FT*, 28 October 2000, p. 10)

'Mr Thaci's supporters include former guerrilla fighters who have been in effect running municipalities across Kosovo' (Irena Guzelova, *FT*, 31 October 2000, p. 10).

> The popularity of Mr Thaci and his now disbanded KLA appeared to eclipse Mr Rugova in the aftermath of the Serbian pullout from Kosovo … But disenchantment grew quickly with the KLA and its members. They were accused of taking over people's homes at the point of a gun and other violent crime, as well as violence against their political opponents. Some of their top leaders were said to be associated with organized crime and fomenting the climate of lawlessness, particularly in Kosovo's larger communities, that led to near daily killings.
>
> (*IHT*, 30 October 2000, p. 9)

> [The PDK is a] party formed by the KLA guerrillas who had fought the Serbian overlords … Since the United Nations took control of Kosovo the KLA has controlled twenty-seven out of the province's thirty municipalities … When Mr Thaci's KLA arrived in Nato's wake it seized as much power as it could get, in any way it could get it, and often abused it. That eventually provoked its massive and unexpected repudiation in Saturday's election outcome.
>
> (William Pfaff, *IHT*, 2 November 2000, p. 11)

The ex-KLA ... seized *de facto* control of several regions, relying on a mixture of intimidation and the prestige it enjoyed as the force which could claim to have succeeded in expelling the Serbs, with Nato's help, where Mr Rugova's pacifism failed. As the election results show, the guerrillas have squandered any popularity they enjoyed. They have seized businesses and properties, and often reacted arrogantly, or worse, when anyone objected. Criminal connections may be a help when pursuing underground feuds, but they are not an electoral asset.

(*The Economist*, 4 November 2000, p. 68)

All the Kosovo Albanians want independence. The new Serbian government insists that the province is Serbia's – as it remains in international law. Mr Kostunica has conceded, however, that the Serbian minority's claim is historic, whereas the Albanian majority's is a homeland claim.

(William Pfaff, *IHT*, 2 November 2000, p. 11)

Mr Thaci wants Kosovo to become independent as soon as possible and join Albania. Mr Rugova also wants independence but at a more cautious pace and for Kosovo to be a state in its own right, free of both Serbia and Albania.

(*Guardian*, 30 October 2000, p. 14)

Ibrahim Rugova (30 October):

The LDK cultivates tolerance and co-operation with other political groups. We will continue protection of minorities, which should be integrated into Kosovo institutions. But it is important to remember that this election had both a local and national context – which is independence for Kosovo.

Hashim Thaci (30 October): 'We will recognise the final result. Objectively, we did not expect such a result.'

However, while acknowledging defeat, Mr Thaci's party also complained that OSCE staff had turned a blind eye while their opponents threatened voters and workers in several municipalities across Kosovo. The party said it would lodge appeals against some of the results.

(*FT*, 31 October 2000, p. 10)

'[Mr Thaci's allegations include] charges that League officials posed as OSCE officials ... [and] had told voters to vote for them' (*The Times*, 31 October 2000, p. 20).

In Belgrade a senior member of ... President Vojislav Kostunica's reformist cabinet welcomed Mr Rugova's revival ... [But] Mr Kostunica's cabinet ...

on Sunday [29 October] released a statement saying the elections were invalid because the Serb minority had not taken part.

(*Guardian*, 31 October 2000, p. 14)

On 1 November 2000 Yugoslavia was readmitted to the United Nations.

'Mr Kostunica … yesterday travelled to Podgorica for talks with President Djukanovic for a meeting of the supreme defence council' (*Guardian*, 2 November 2000, p. 19). The Yugoslav supreme defence council met in Podgorica on 2 November 'with President Djukanovic in attendance for the first time in several years' (*EEN*, 2000, vol. 13, no. 1, p. 7).

On 4 November 2000 the Yugoslav parliament approved the new Yugoslav government. 'The federal administration has relatively little power but it does have a leading role in fostering international relations' (*Independent*, 6 November 2000, p. 14).

Of the sixteen cabinet posts DOS had nine, including economics, foreign affairs and the interior. The other seven portfolios were held by the Montenegrin Socialist People's Party (SPP), including the posts of prime minister, defence minister and finance. 'Mr Djukanovic was offered some post in the new government but declined' (*IHT*, 6 November 2000, p. 5).

Some cabinet details were as follows:

1   Prime minister, Zoran Zizic (deputy chairman of the SPP).
2   Deputy prime minister, Miroljub Labus (DOS). 'Miroljub Labus … [is] an economist who has worked in the United States. He belongs to the think-tank responsible for drawing up the DOS economic programme' (*Independent*, 6 November 2000, p. 14). 'He is chairman of a group of opposition economists and policy experts known as G17 Plus, which was instrumental in drawing up the government's programme' (*IHT*, 6 November 2000, p. 5).
3   Foreign minister, Goran Svilanovic (DOS; leader of the Civic Alliance). 'Goran Svilanovic … is a long-time human rights activist, a lawyer by education' (*Independent*, 6 November 2000, p. 14). 'Goran Svilanovic … belongs to the Civil Alliance, the legal brain of DOS. The Alliance has been the most prominent anti-war party in Serbia since 1991' (*Independent*, 7 November 2000, p. 14).
4   Interior minister, Zoran Zivkovic (DOS). He is the mayor of Nis, Serbia's third largest city.

'The ruling Montenegrin parties resolved last week that legal preparation for a referendum should be completed by the end of the year, and that the referendum should be held by 30 June 2001' (*EEN*, 6 November 2000, vol. 13, no. 1, p. 4).

On 10 November Yugoslavia became a member of OSCE.

Prison riots spread across Serbia yesterday [7 November] … Inmates are demanding better conditions and say they should all benefit from an amnesty promised by Mr Kostunica to political prisoners, mostly Kosovo Albanians ... The third riot in two days started yesterday ... Serb prisoners launched their revolt on Sunday [5 November] ... The Albanians have refused to join in the riots ... Mr Kostunica's ... administration moved quickly to announce an amnesty law for the hundreds of ethnic Albanians imprisoned during last year's Nato bombing. The law would affect political prisoners, mostly Kosovo Albanians, sentenced by the Milosevic regime for alleged 'terrorism'. There are also thousands of Serb draft dodgers and deserters who would benefit from the amnesty. Apparently the riots started after the Serb prisoners learnt that some 400 ethnic Albanians, roughly half of those still in Serbian jails, were quietly released.

(*Independent*, 8 November 2000, p. 15)

On 15 November 2000 Kostunica addressed the European parliament in Strasbourg. On the same day it was revealed that the EU had proposed (EU foreign ministers still having to approve the move) that the number of people on its entry ban list should be reduced by over a hundred. The approval of the Kostunica regime had been sought and the move was seen as a reward for those not using violence to try to prevent the revolution from succeeding. But it was still controversial. Among those benefiting were Rade Markovic (head of the Serbian secret police), Nebojsa Pavkovic (the army chief of staff) and Momir Bulatovic (the former federal prime minister).

On 17 November 2000 diplomatic relations were restored with the USA, the UK, France and Germany.

On 20 November former Socialist Party of Serbia high officials founded the Democratic Socialist Party (*EEN*, 2001, vol. 13, no. 2, p. 6).

[On 20 November] Slobodan Milosevic ... [made] an unexpected television appearance ... [and] urged his Socialist cronies to rally around him 'to save Yugoslavia' ... He urged his comrades to 'stay united' because, he said, they were the only ones who can save Yugoslavia from total disintegration.

(*The Times*, 22 November 2000, p. 21)

In a rare appearance this week on Yu Info, a state television channel he created, Mr Milosevic was seen urging party associates to maintain unity. 'There are scenarios to destroy the state, to destroy the economy, to destroy the party because it is the only guarantee for the defence of the national interests,' he declared. If the congress sent a message of unity 'the consequences in the elections on 23 December will be positive'. It was unclear where the televised meeting with party colleagues was held but viewers noted that the Serbian president, Milan Milutinovic – once thought ready to break with Mr Milosevic – was sitting meekly in the audience ... Former colleagues now concede that they have failed to generate enough strength to remove Milosevic. Zoran Lilic, a past president of Yugoslavia, who left the Socialist Party [of Serbia] a few weeks ago, has set up his own party ... The

SPS's former vice-president, Milorad Vucelic, who split with Mr Milosevic at the end of 1998, had been considered the most likely replacement as party president. Now he too is planning to form his own party and says he may not attend the congress ... Mr Vucelic belongs to a group calling itself the 'SPS founders', which has been calling for Mr Milosevic to resign in favour of a temporary secretariat to run the party. The group includes another former Yugoslav president, Borislav Jovic, and the former head of the Belgrade branch of the party, Slobodan Jovanovic ... The latest defector from the SPS is Ratko Markovic, a former deputy prime minister, who led the negotiations for autonomy in Kosovo in 1998 and 1999. He denounced Mr Milosevic for taking control of drafting all documents for the congress without consultation.

(*Guardian*, 23 November 2000, p. 15)

'Mr Milosevic on Tuesday [21 November] was declared the only candidate to lead the Socialist Party ... He seeks reelection as its president when the party meets in a special congress on Saturday [25 November]' (*IHT*, 22 November 2000, p. 5).

On 22 November it was reported that ethnic Albanian guerrillas had killed four Serb policemen in the Presevo Valley in an attack that had begun the day before. This was the latest incident in the valley. On 22 November one person (the residence's driver) was killed in a bomb attack in Pristina at the home of Yugoslavia's chief representative in Kosovo. He is head of the Yugoslav government's liaison committee with the international administration in Kosovo.

On 24 November Serbia gave Kfor seventy-four hours (starting 7 p.m.) to halt the attacks. Otherwise it would send police reinforcements into the buffer zone (where only lightly armed Serb police are allowed without Kfor permission). Serbia claimed that Kfor had agreed to the deadline (*IHT*, 25 November 2000, p. 1).

Xhemajl Mustafa, one of Ibrahim Rugova's closest advisors, was shot dead in Pristina on 23 November.

An EU–Balkan summit meeting was held in Zagreb on 24 November 2000. Albania, Bosnia, Croatia, Macedonia and Yugoslavia were formally invited.

A statement was released: 'It is a matter of priority to develop regional co-operation ... [including] political dialogue, regional free trade and close co-operation in the fields of justice and home affairs.'

The EU, which has taken prime responsibility for reconstruction and stability in the Balkans, will hold its first summit meeting with regional leaders on Friday [24 November] ... The EU is offering the main countries of the western Balkans – Macedonia, Croatia, Bosnia, Yugoslavia and Albania – Euro 4.65 billion from 2000 to 2006 ... It does not include Euro 200 million in emergency aid for energy, food and medicine ... for Serbia to help it get through the winter ... The European Commission had asked for Euro 5.5 billion through 2006 but could not get that much through the European Parliament. And of the current figure – which must cover seven years – about a quarter was already spent last year [1999], the first year of the plan ... The EU has also, at the beginning of this month, lifted nearly all customs duties for products from the region ... EU countries currently import from these Balkan countries less than 2 per cent of what they export to them ... The Europeans ... are negotiating agreements with these countries, called Stabilization and Association Agreements, that lay out reforms that could put these countries on the path toward joining the EU. In Zagreb Macedonia will sign such an agreement with the EU, while the host, Croatia, will formally begin its negotiations toward one ... The EU would not invite Milo Djukanovic as the head of a delegation, but only as part of the Yugoslav one. Mr Djukanovic got a special invitation from the French and 'special status', with a chance to speak, normally reserved for national leaders.

(*IHT*, 24 November 2000, p. 5)

(The Euro 4.65 billion aid package is worth around $4 billion: *IHT*, 25 November 2000, p. 2.)

The EU's fifteen governments decided last week ... to dole out Euro 850 million less to the Balkans than the European Commission had been seeking; this left a total ... of Euro 4.65 billion, of which nearly Euro 1 billion has already been spent. That would imply an annual average of Euro 600 million for Yugoslavia (including Kosovo), Croatia, Bosnia, Albania and Macedonia ... The EU has also assured Serbia's neighbours that the Euro 200 million the Serbs have begun to get is coming out of a special EU reserve.

(*The Economist*, 25 November 2000, p. 63)

'Ibrahim Rugova ... is staying at home ... Bernard Kouchner will, however, be attending' (*Independent*, 24 November 2000, p. 18). 'There were no Kosovo Albanian representatives' (*The Times*, 25 November 2000, p. 24).

President Djukanovic: 'The serious dilemma we are faced with is: do we follow the illusion of a common state, which in the meantime has been left with only a few compromised and abused functions, or the reality of two functioning states?' 'Mr Djukanovic described the current relationship as "unsustainable" and promised a referendum for Montenegrins on the issue during the first part of next year [2001]' (*Independent*, 25 November 2000, p. 15).

'The summit also saw Macedonia's signing of the first so-called Stabilization and Association Agreement with the EU – a new kind of agreement intended for western Balkan countries. Croatia also formally started negotiations on such an agreement' (*FT*, 25 November 2000, p. 6).

On 25 November Milosevic was re-elected as leader of the Serbian Socialist Party. 'Mr Milosevic, the sole candidate for party leader, got 85 per cent of the votes of 2,300 delegates at the special congress in Belgrade' (*Independent*, 27 November 2000, p. 15).

On 27 November Yugoslavia was readmitted to OSCE.

'Ethnic Albanian gunmen of the Liberation Army of Presevo, Medvedja and Bujanovic agreed yesterday [27 November] to extend a ceasefire until Friday [1 December]' (*The Times*, 28 November 2000, p. 21). 'The Yugoslav authorities agreed to give the alliance more time ... backing off from a threat to take matters into their own hands if Nato failed to stop rebel infiltration before the Monday [27 November] deadline' (*IHT*, 28 November 2000, p. 4).

> The Serbian ceasefire had been extended until Friday ... The UCPMB ... wants to unite three Albanian municipalities with Kosovo. The three towns were part of the province until 1957, when they were made part of Serbia ... A referendum held in 1992 voted for independence from Serbia.
>
> (*Guardian*, 28 November 2000, p. 16)

(On 28 November an 'indefinite' ceasefire was announced.)

On 28 November Mirjana Markovic made her first appearance in parliament.

> US Treasury Department investigators have concluded that at least $1 billion was spirited out of Yugoslavia by associates of Slobodan Milosevic ... and flowed through banks in Cyprus to other destinations, the Yugoslav central bank governor said in Belgrade [on 1 December]. 'It is apparently the money the former regime had transferred to Cyprus in the course of the 1990s' ... the bank governor said.
>
> (*IHT*, 4 December 2000, p. 5)

'[On 8 December] Yugoslavia's central bank governor [Mladjan Dinkic] accused the regime of former president Slobodan Milosevic of stealing more than $4 billion' (*Guardian*, 9 December 2000, p. 25).

On 8 December 2000 Hans Haekkerup, the Danish foreign minister, was named as the new head of UNMIK. He would replace Bernard Kouchner in January 2001.

An EU delegation arrived in Belgrade on 8 December 2000, urging collaboration with the war crimes tribunal in The Hague. Javier Solana (the EU's chief foreign affairs representative) was targeted by a small number of pro-Milosevic demonstrators.

On 9 December diplomatic relations were restored between Serbia and Slovenia.

Milosevic was interviewed on a private television station on 12 December 2000.

Dismissals in the diplomatic service announced on 15 December 2000 included Slobodan Milosevic's brother. Boris Milosevic was ambassador to Russia (*Independent*, 16 December 2000, p. 16).

> A Serb man died from gunshot wounds and another was injured during a night of violent protests against police and Nato-led peacekeepers in Kosovo ... Belgian peacekeeping soldiers fired warning shots in the air when a

crowd of angry Serbs tried to break into their compound in the northern town of Leposavic around midnight on Saturday [16 December] ... The crowd was protesting against the arrest of a Serb man for speeding and trying to run over a Kosovo police officer.

(*FT*, 18 December 2000, p. 7)

'Gunmen fired on a joint US–Russian patrol Sunday [17 December] as it tried to seal the boundary between Kosovo and a part of southern Serbia where ethnic Albanian rebels have been challenging Yugoslav forces' (*IHT*, 18 December 2000, p. 1).

'In an interview on Monday [18 December] Mr Kostunica said Belgrade had proposed ... that the zone be narrowed "to 1 or 2 kilometres" from the current 5 kilometres' (*IHT*, 20 December 2000, p. 5). 'The UN Security Council called Tuesday [19 December] for ethnic Albanian "extremists" from Kosovo to withdraw immediately from the boundary zone' (*IHT*, 21 December 2000, p. 7).

The UN Security Council condemned violence by ethnic Albanian extremists in the area [southern Serbia] and called for an immediate cessation of violence. The Security Council, meeting at the request of ... Vojislav Kostunica, late on Tuesday [19 December] asked the guerrilla groups, which have infiltrated a 5 kilometre demilitarized buffer zone on the Serbian side of the Kosovo border to leave. Meanwhile [on 20 December] British soldiers ... detained thirteen ethnic Albanians trying to smuggle arms into the area, known as Ground Safety Zone, from Kosovo ... Mr Kostunica says Nato-led peacekeepers have failed to prevent the guerrillas from crossing the border and has suggested that the security zone be narrowed.

(*FT*, 21 December 2000, p. 6)

'This month [December] Yugoslavia was admitted to the EBRD' (*FT*, 20 December 2000, p. 8). 'Our board of governors has approved Yugoslavia's membership. This should enable Yugoslavia to join the EBRD in early 2001, when we will open a Belgrade office and become the first international financial institution there' (Jean Lemierre, president of the EBRD, *IHT*, 30 December 2000, p. 13). 'Membership of the IMF and other international bodies is imminent' (Jean Lemierre, *Guardian*, 29 December 2000. p. 21). 'During the last two weeks of December [20 December 2000] the [IMF] board ... welcomed the Federal Republic of Yugoslavia ... back into the IMF' (Horst Köhler, managing director of the IMF, *FT*, 8 January 2001, p. 23).

The Serbian general election of 23 December 2000 and events thereafter

The general election in Serbia was held on 23 December 2000. The turnout was 58.8 per cent. There was a 5 per cent threshold for any party to be represented in the 250-seat parliament.

The Serbian government is, constitutionally speaking, where the real power lies. The Yugoslav authorities led by Kostunica will deal mainly with foreign affairs and foreign economic relations. Kostunica's influence will owe little to his powers under the constitution, which are limited, and a lot to the fact that he has a [very high] popularity rating.

(Tim Judah, *New York Review of Books*, 2001, vol. XLVIII, no. 2, p. 45)

Serbia has wiped the names of 900,000 Kosovan Albanians from the voting register ... Spokesmen in Belgrade vehemently deny the move advances independence or partition, claiming they were forced to abandon organizing the election in the Albanian parts of Kosovo because ... Kfor would not guarantee security if polling occurred ... A spokesman for ... Zoran Djindjic said Belgrade had set up just fifty polling stations in the province, in the Serb-dominated areas of Leposavic, Mitrovica, Lipljan and Zvecan ... Kosovan Albanians do not fully use their votes, he said, and Belgrade was trying to avoid a repeat of the voting fraud that occurred under Mr Milosevic, when he allegedly abused the unused Kosovo-Albanian votes ... According to ... the vice-president of Belgrade's Civil Alliance Party, today [23 December] will be the first time elections have bypassed the all-Albanian parts of Kosovo.

(*Guardian*, 23 December 2000, p. 13)

Despite the relatively low turnout, the eighteen-party DOS (Democratic Opposition of Serbia) coalition achieved its expected victory. In fact it won more than the two-thirds of seats necessary to change the constitution. Zoran Djindjic was to be prime minister. The detailed results were as follows:

1   DOS: 64 per cent of the vote and 176 seats.
2   Serbian Socialist Party: 13.7 per cent per cent of the vote and thirty-seven seats.

   'Milosevic's Socialists won only in Presevo ... Albanians boycotted the polls while angry Serbs stuck with Milosevic' (*Telegraph*, 26 December 2000, p. 15).

3   Serbian Radical Party (led by Vojislav Seselj): 9 per cent of the vote and twenty-three seats.
4   Serbian Unity Party (set up by the late Zeljko Raznatovic, also known as Arkan): 5 per cent of the vote and fourteen seats. This surprise result was helped by the relatively low turnout.
5   Yugoslav United Left (led by Mira Markovic): 0.38 per cent of the vote.
6   Serbian Renewal Movement (led by Vuk Draskovic); the party did not win enough votes to gain representation in parliament.

The head of the state security service, Rade Markovic, is to be dismissed. 'The police [was] built up by Mr Milosevic into a 100,000-strong force' (*Independent*, 26

December 2000, p. 15). Milosevic's police force is 80,000-strong (*The Economist*, 9 October 1999, p. 16). 'Mr Milosevic's security apparatus in Serbia includes 80,000 police and special forces members in a country of only 8 million' (*IHT*, 29 December 2000, p. 6).

> President Milo Djukanovic of Montenegro made his first visit to Belgrade in two years Monday [25 December] ... to attend a meeting of Yugoslav's supreme defence council, chaired by ... Vojislav Kostunica ... Mr Djukanovic is eager to have Mr Kostunica replace the Yugoslav Army commanders in Montenegro ... and to disband a special militarized police battalion.
>
> (*IHT*, 26 December 2000, p. 5)

The following day military figures associated with Montenegro were dismissed: General Milorad Obradovic, the commander of the Second Army, Admiral Milan Zec and Colonel Luka Kastratovic (who commanded a key military airfield in Montenegro). ('President Kostunica has purged the army ... with the sudden retirement of fourteen generals, including Dragoljub Ojdanovic, the former defence minister wanted by the Hague tribunal for war crimes ... [He was] indicted in May 1999 ... The presidential decree reshuffling the military top brass was issued over the weekend [30–1 December 2000] ... The list of retired generals includes Geza Farkas, head of the army intelligence service (KOS) under Milosevic, and one of his closest aides, General Alexander Vasiljevic. But Mr Kostunica stopped short of retiring the chief of staff, General Nebojsa Pavkovic ... Among the retired officers is Admiral Milan Zec, commander of the Yugoslav Navy, based in Montenegro. General Milorad Obradovic, the commander of the Second Army responsible for Montenegro, was transferred to Belgrade and replaced': *Independent*, 1 January 2001, p. 9.)

'Serbia plunged into its worst-ever energy crisis on Tuesday [26 December], which forced power cuts across the country' (*FT*, 28 December 2000, p. 4).

> The country's worst energy crisis ... [has a number of causes] ... Nine months of drought ... has lowered hydro-electric output to record lows. Serbia relies heavily on hydro power, although there are several big thermal plants ... The Milosevic regime kept energy prices low ... Over the past decade overall investment in the power system equalled the investment of one year in the Eighties. To make matters worse power stations were targeted during last year's Nato bombing. Then Mr Milosevic temporarily solved the energy crisis by importing electricity from neighbouring countries.
>
> (*Independent*, 29 December 2000, p. 13)

The crisis is caused by several factors: the disrepair of the electric system, Serbia's debts to several countries which supply it with electricity, a regional shortage of electricity, and a debt to Russia for natural gas that has prompted Moscow to reduce the flow. Low water levels have further reduced

Serbia's ability to produce hydroelectric power and cool generators, while the export of electricity during the summer by the Milosevic regime to pay back debt ... Macedonia, Albania and Greece, which bailed out the country last winter, are not creating enough electricity to supply Serbia this winter. Bulgaria is supplying the whole of Kosovo, which as an international protectorate will pay its bills.

(*Guardian*, 29 December 2000, p. 15)

[Zoran] Djindjic ... said [on 29 December 2000 that] the international authorities running the province would need five more years to create trust between Kosovo and Serbia ... 'During this period we will show the ethnic Albanians that co-operation with Serbia is in their own interest ... But if they make an enemy of Serbia they might as well jump in the Adriatic to get to the West. Because the only route to the West passes through Serbia.

(*IHT*, 30 December 2000, p. 4)

On 29 December 2000 President Boris Trajkovski of Macedonia visited Belgrade (*IHT*, 30 December 2000, p. 1).

'[On 30 December 2000] Nato peacekeepers in Kosovo mediated an agreement between Yugoslavia and the rebels to open another road in the contested area' (*IHT*, 2 January 2000, p. 5). 'Kfor won an agreement between Serbia and the ethnic Albanian rebels for both sides to remove checkpoints and pull back from their positions in Veliki Trnovac' (*Guardian*, 2 January 2000, p. 11).

'The formation of Serbia's reformist government was delayed yesterday [2 January] when the supreme court, responding to complaints lodged by opponents of the new government, ruled that elections must be reheld in nineteen of the country's more than 8,000 districts' (*FT*, 3 January 2001, p. 7).

Reformist allies of President Vojislav Kostunica of Yugoslavia won a rerun of Serbian parliamentary elections, according to results made public Thursday [11 January], paving the way for a new government. The vote, held Wednesday [10 January] at nineteen out of a total of about 8,700 polling stations, confirmed the outcome of the 23 December election.

(*IHT*, 12 January 2001, p. 4)

On 3 January 2001 the Yugoslav foreign minister, Goran Svilanovic, arrived in the USA. This was the start of an official visit. Goran Svilanovic (5 January 2001): 'There are possibilities to fully co-operate with the [Hague] tribunal and to prosecute all indicted personalities in co-operation with the tribunal on the territory of the Federal Republic of Yugoslavia' (*The Times*, 6 January 2001, p. 20; *Independent*, 6 January 2001, p. 17).

'Nine men suspected of membership of a radical ethnic Albanian guerrilla group were detained [on 6 January 2001] by British peacekeepers when they tried to enter Kosovo ... from the Presevo Valley area' (*Independent*, 8 January 2001, p. 13).

'The former head of Yugoslav customs, Mihail Kertes, who is under investigation for abuse of office, has gone missing and is rumoured to have fled to the Bosnian Serb republic' (*Telegraph*, 11 January 2001, p. 16).

On 12 January 2001 Mira Markovic flew to Moscow, seemingly to visit her son, Marko Milosevic.

On 13 January President Kostunica met Slobodan Milosevic for the second time (the first being on 6 October 2000). On the same day Bernard Kouchner's term of office in Kosovo came to an end. (His replacement, Hans Haekkerup, the former Danish foreign minister, started working on 15 January 2001.)

On 17 January Albania and Yugoslavia (Serbia) agreed to re-establish diplomatic relations (*EEN*, 2001, vol. 1, no. 2, p. 4).

On 19 January President Kostunica visited Sarajevo. '[This was] the first official trip by a Yugoslav leader to the Bosnian capital since it was torn apart by war in 1992' (*FT*, 20 January 2001, p. 7).

The United States lifted economic sanctions against Yugoslavia on Friday [19 January] ... The [executive] order lifted a ban on trade by easing sanctions on financial transactions, but left in place measures against some members of the former regime of Slobodan Milosevic or those implicated in political repression.

(*IHT*, 20 January 2001, p. 4)

'The United States will continue to impose sanctions on about eighty Serbs, including former president Slobodan Milosevic, his family and members of his entourage' (*IHT*, 19 January 2001, p. 1).

On 22 January the Serbian parliament met for the first time since the election.

On 23 January Carla del Ponte, the chief prosecutor at the war crimes tribunal in The Hague, met President Kostunica in Belgrade at the start of a three-day visit.

'Yugoslavia formally submitted its application to join the WTO' (*IHT*, 24 January 2001, p. 11).

Carla del Ponte (25 January 2001):

We [the tribunal] are the first who must have Milosevic on trial. I cannot wait for years until the fugitives are transferred ... Dialogue [with President Kostunica] was not possible ... My feeling is that he was practically forced to meet me. I tried for half an hour to explain about the tribunal. I had to sit and listen to his long complaints ... For half an hour I had to listen to things which I already knew since he had already said them to the press ... I tried to get into the dialogue but it was practically impossible. He obviously wanted to make a political declaration ... He can and must change his mind. Full co-operation with my office cannot be avoided if Yugoslavia wants full membership in the international community. If there is no co-operation new sanctions can be imposed ... I remain cautiously optimistic that obstacles such as the lack of domestic legislation which hinders the surrender of indicted fugitives to The Hague will soon be removed. I did not expect the immediate arrest of indicted war criminals, but I cannot wait years until fugitives are transferred to The Hague ... The important thing is that Mr Djindjic and others recognize the obligation to co-operate. They say they must implement a new law and need two or three months before they can be fully active in co-operation.

(*Independent*, 26 January 2001, p. 13; *Guardian*, 26 January 2001, p. 14)

'Carla del Ponte ... rejected Serbian accusations that the use of depleted uranium (DU) munitions in the 1999 Nato air raids against Serbia constituted a war crime' (*Independent*, 26 January 2001, p. 13). 'Mrs del Ponte said there was no scientific evidence to justify a war crimes inquiry into Nato's use of cluster bombs and munitions with depleted uranium in the Balkans: "At this time their use is legal"' (*Guardian*, 26 January 2001, p. 14).

('Carla del Ponte ... said yesterday [26 January] ... [that] Slobodan Milosevic should be investigated for the deaths of sixteen Serbian state television employees killed by Nato bombs in Belgrade in 1999 ... She claimed that Mr Milosevic had been warned of the air strike on the television station': *The Times*, 27 January 2001, p. 16. Carla del Ponte: 'Belgrade will not co-operate. They told me that we have no role there. If Slobodan Milosevic is ever to be tried it will never be in The Hague, only in Belgrade ... I received new information from Serbia that Nato advised Mr Milosevic ahead of time that the television station would be bombed. He then only told some of the directors, but he did not inform the working technicians so they could leave. So Mr Milosevic himself obliged people to stay in the building knowing it would be bombed so he could manipulate the situation against Nato. Our preliminary review of the bombing incident [on 23 April 1999] has come to the conclusion that there is insufficient cause so far to open an inquiry. We have asked the Serbian authorities for more evidence and if there is cause to open an inquiry we will do it. I have to say that this issue of Nato bombing arises all the time. How can this be a priority when each time I visit Bosnia-Hercegovina or Kosovo and observe the exhumation of thousands of bodies from mass graves? Our priority is prosecuting genocide and crimes against humanity. That is our goal now. Of course, the sixteen dead [at the bombed television headquarters] are not unimportant, but they cannot be my priority': *IHT*, 1 February 2001, p. 8.)

'Mr Kostunica ... [notes] that the tribunal has already set up an office in Belgrade' (*IHT*, 3 February 2001, p. 6).

Rade Markovic, the head of state security, resigns. He is replaced by Goran Petrovic.

Serbia's parliament yesterday [25 January] approved the formation of a reformist government. Prime minister Zoran Djindjic ... has promised a government based on transparency, the rule of law and liberal market reform ... Bozidar Djelic [is] Serbia's new finance minister ... The government will prepare a detailed economic programme in time for a European Union and World Bank donors conference scheduled for this spring. Before that Mr Djindjic hopes to secure a stand-by facility from the IMF of between $150 million and $200 million to help the reform process ... One of the first moves the government will make is to review earlier privatizations that gave management the possibility of buying companies at knock-down prices and reverse a recent wave of management buy-outs ... Mr Djindjic hopes that a law on privatization is likely to be ready in March, but the government is likely to take a cautious approach to privatization and decide what to do with each company on a case by case basis.

(Irena Guzelova, *FT*, 26 January 2001, p. 7)

Fighting has risen sharply between the Yugoslav military and ethnic Albanian guerrillas in the tense buffer zone ... with four Serbian soldiers reportedly wounded Sunday [28 January] and one killed Friday [26 January]. The casualties [were] the first for the military since they were deployed along the edge of the buffer zone two months ago ... The Yugoslav army and the Serbian police forces have dug in along the edge of the mountainous buffer zone and occasionally come in contact with the rebels, exchanging sniper fire. A Yugoslav soldier died of gunshot wounds Friday night.

IHT, 30 January 2001, p. 7)

On 1 February 2001 the government placed Slobodan Milosevic under twenty-four-hour police surveillance.

'A convoy carrying high-ranking US officials, including the ambassador to Belgrade, came under fire Tuesday [6 February] ... [in Presevo] ... Deputy prime minister Nebojsa Covic of Serbia ... said ethnic Albanians were responsible for the attack' (*IHT*, 7 February 2001, p. 4).

The region's two most senior US envoys came under fire from Albanian fighters ... James Pardew [is] the US special envoy to the Balkans and William Montgomery [is] the new ambassador to Belgrade ... On Monday [5 February] the demilitarized buffer zone was the scene of the fiercest fighting for three months between Serb forces and the Albanian rebels ... Sources in Belgrade said yesterday [6 February] that American diplomats had agreed the basics of a new Serbian government plan approved by the cabinet yesterday to cool tensions in southern Serbia, one of the most depressed areas of Yugoslavia, by sending economic aid and providing jobs in the public sector for Albanians.

(*The Times*, 7 February 2001, p. 14)

'The Yugoslav government offered more rights to ethnic Albanians living in [Presevo] ... But the peace proposal stopped short of granting autonomy or unification with [Kosovo]' (*Independent*, 8 February 2001, p. 16).

The plan calls for joint police forces of local Albanians and Serbs, in proportion to the ethnic groups' populations in the area. There are some 70,000 ethnic Albanians and 30,000 Serbs in the region. At present the local police are all Serbs. The plan also provides for the reintegration of ethnic Albanians into the local governing bodies and judiciary system, but falls short of giving autonomy to the region. In co-operation with international aid agencies and foreign governments, the area will get a badly needed economic boost.

(Independent, 23 February 2001, p. 15)

Serbia's new government has put together a peace plan that rules out autonomy or annexation but would demilitarize the area and grant Albanians civil rights stripped away under Slobodan Milosevic ... Nebojsa Covic ... author of the plan ... said the conflict [in Presevo] threatened to spread further among the 100,000 ethnic Albanians in southern Serbia or even into neighbouring Macedonia, where Albanians dominate the western regions ... His peace plan ... was approved unanimously ... by the governments of both Serbia and Yugoslavia ... It rules out annexation by Kosovo or autonomy for the areas where Albanians are in the majority, but it offers ethnic Albanians full representation in government and police structures and the judiciary in their communes and representation in the Serbian government. Albanian parties boycotted December [2000] elections for the Serbian parliament and so have no representation in Belgrade. The plan outlines a phased demilitarization of the entire region, indicating a withdrawal of Yugoslav army and police forces from the area and introduction of joint police patrols consisting of one Albanian and one Serb. Mr Covic said he would even consider unilateral withdrawal of Serbian forces, if 'someone could guarantee that the Albanians will not take advantage of it'. His plan would also offer an amnesty for members of the rebel army, along with economic development of the region with international aid. Members of the rebel force, which is known as the Liberation Army of Presevo, Medvedja and Bujanovac [Bujanovic], have rejected the plan, but not the idea of talks.

(IHT, 13 February 2001, p. 6)

'The plan stops short of autonomy and calls for the guerrillas to disband before Yugoslav forces withdraw' (*Guardian*, 24 February 2001, p. 15).

Two key laws to be adopted today and tomorrow [12–13 February] will clear the way for the prosecution of ... Slobodan Milosevic. The first law curtails the privileges of former Serbian presidents, effectively stripping Mr Milosevic of the immunity he hoped to enjoy. The law provides for a single security officer and one secretary to be placed at the disposal of a former president. No member of his family will enjoy any privileges. Ex-presidents can be stripped of these privileges if sentenced to more than six months in prison by any court, the text says. The second law will change the public prosecutors and judges all over Serbia … The previous law on privileges was introduced … by … parliament three years ago … It gave the former Serbian president and all members of his family a life-long entourage of dozens of state-paid bodyguards and secretaries and benefits that would see to all their needs for a lifetime.

(*Independent*, 12 February 2001, p. 12)

'Parliament … voted to reduce the ousted president's security detail to just one man from the previous level of about fifteen' (*Telegraph*, 14 February 2001, p. 19).

'The former head of Serbian state television … Dragoljub Milanovic … was arrested yesterday [13 February] on suspicion of knowing in advance of the Nato air raid that killed sixteen of his staff in April 1999' (*Independent*, 14 February 2001, p. 16).

Lawmakers in Serbia fired judges and prosecutors loyal to … Slobodan Milosevic … on Wednesday [14 February] and replaced them with others … The Serbian parliament … voted to replace dozens of supreme and municipal court judges, public prosecutors and other judicial officials. Some asked to be relieved of their duties, while others – loyal to Mr Milosevic's regime and often working under orders – were fired.

(*IHT*, 15 February 2001, p. 5)

'Parliament has also repealed Serbia's repressive public information law, passed in 1998 to fight the independent media' (*Telegraph*, 15 February 2001, p. 18).

Yugoslavia will deal the final blow to its communist past today [16 February 2001] when the federal parliament passes a bill to restore Yugoslav citizenship to members of the royal family … On 8 March 1947 the country's communist rulers stripped ten members of the Karadjordjevic family of their citizenship. The family fled to London in April 1941, when Nazi Germany invaded Yugoslavia. Three Karadjordjevics are still alive. They are Crown Prince Alexander, his aunt, Princess Jelisaveta and an uncle, also Prince Alexander.

(*Independent*, 16 February 2001, p. 15)

On 16 February 2001 a bus carrying Serb civilians from Serbia to Kosovo was blown up by a bomb. (Initial estimates put the number dead at seven, but the final toll was in double figures.) The bus was part of a convoy of buses escorted by Kfor troops. 'The attack … comes just two days after a Serb man was killed … when a gunman attacked … [a] bus … in the south of Kosovo' (*Guardian*, 17 February 2001, p. 2).

The new interior minister, Dusan Mihajlovic, had a run-in with gunmen in central Belgrade early Friday [16 February] and he warned later that organized crime gangs connected to the ousted Milosevic regime were targeting members of the new government. A gunman fired on the minister's security escort … The incident comes days after a jeep belonging to Cedomir Jovanovic, a key aide to prime minister Zoran Djindjic, was blown up … and the driver of the newly appointed state security chief, Goran Petrovic, was shot in the arm while on duty waiting in his car … Mr Mihajlovic said that sections of the police were connected to organized crime groups and to members of the former regime who were directing the attacks on the new government.

(*IHT*, 17 February 2001, pp. 1, 7)

On 18 February three Serb policemen were killed when their vehicle was blown up by land mines on the edge of the buffer zone. The policemen were on their way to deliver supplies to colleagues in the Presevo Valley.

On 23 February a Balkan summit was held in Skopje, the capital of Macedonia, attended by EU representatives. 'Concern about the destabilizing impact of the Presevo conflict overshadowed the summit's main agenda – to tighten economic links and ensure a continued flow of funding for cross-border projects under the Balkan Stability Pact' (*FT*, 24 February 2001, p. 7). '[On 23 February at the Balkan summit in Skopje] President Boris Trajkovski [of Macedonia]… and [President] Vojislav Kostunica … initialled a long-awaited treaty that defines the border between Macedonia and Serbia' (*The Economist*, 3 March 2001, p. 48).

On 24 February Rade Markovic, the former head of the secret police, was arrested in connection with an investigation into a road accident involving Vuk Draskovic on 3 October 1999. (See the entry for that date. Draskovic claimed it was an assassination attempt.) Also arrested were two other policemen, including Branko Djuric (the former chief of police in Belgrade).

Dragoslav Avramovic died on 25 February 2001 (*IHT*, 21 April 2001, p. 3).

The Yugoslav parliament has passed a long-awaited amnesty law that will free several hundred Kosovo Albanians held in Serbian prisons since the war in Kosovo in 1999 and clear thousands of draft dodgers and deserters from prosecution by the army … UN officials in Kosovo and human rights organizations have long called for the release of the 650 Albanians still in Serbian prisons, most of whom they regard as political prisoners … Human rights organizations have said they consider … 570 … of the remaining 650 Kosovo Albanians … [to be] political prisoners … The [650] prisoners were among about 2,000 transferred to Serbia at the end of the war in 1999 … The legislation was approved easily in both upper and lower houses on Monday [26 February]. It will provide amnesty to all convicted of conspiring against the state, but will not include those convicted of terrorism. In addition to the prisoners, the main beneficiaries of the law will be an estimated 28,000 young Serbs and Montenegrins, many of whom fled abroad to avoid serving in the army during the wars in Croatia, Bosnia and

Kosovo, according to justice minister Momcilo Grubac. Approximately 200 of the imprisoned Kosovo Albanians have been charged with terrorism, and their cases will be reviewed separately, Mr Grubac said. But the justice minister added that after reviewing the status of the prisoners, he had asked President Kostunica to pardon some who had been convicted of terrorism on insufficient evidence ... [Grubac] said that, in particular, a group of 143 men from the town of Djakovica had been convicted as a group, apparently without evidence, after several policemen were killed.

(*IHT*, 28 February 2001, p. 7)

'[On 27 February] Nato agreed to a "phased" reduction in the buffer zone ... Lord Robertson, Nato's secretary-general, said military advisers would work out how to plan a "phased and conditioned reduction of the ground safety zone"' (*Guardian*, 28 February 2001, p. 15).

Quashing any speculation that the new US administration under George W. Bush [president since 20 January 2001] was no longer willing to remain involved in the region ..., Colin Powell, US secretary of state ... said: 'We went in together and we will leave together.'

(*FT*, 28 February 2001, p. 8)

'The Belgrade prosecutor's office yesterday [28 February] ordered the first official investigation into allegations that Mr Milosevic smuggled 173 kilograms of gold out of the country last autumn [2000]' (*Independent*, 1 March 2001, p. 17).
'[This was] the first legal move against Mr Milosevic' (*Guardian*, 1 March 2001, p. 17).

Yugoslavia's public prosecutor on Wednesday [28 February] ordered an investigation into allegations that ... Slobodan Milosevic ... transferred huge amounts of gold out of the country ... The public prosecutor's office ordered the police to investigate news reports that Mr Milosevic had transferred nearly 173 kilograms (380 pounds) of gold ... worth $1.1 million ... to Switzerland between 21 September and 2 November last year [2000] ... The police were ordered to investigate whether funds from the sale of the gold were transferred to bank accounts in Cyprus and Greece suspected of belonging to Mr Milosevic or his associates ... Inquiries into Mr Milosevic's purchase of a house in an expensive Belgrade suburb are far more advanced.

(*IHT*, 1 March 2001, p. 7)

On 28 February prosecutors said they would ask the interior ministry to check reports that quantities of gold had been shipped from Belgrade to Switzerland, notionally in the name of Greek and Cypriot firms, in the weeks before and after Mr Milosevic's downfall last October [2000].

(*The Economist*, 3 March 2001, p. 48)

Serbia must pull back troops before Nato starts ceding control of the Kosovo buffer zone [Nato] secretary-general George Robertson said Wednesday [28 February] ... 'We are looking for urgent military advice on the proposal and on the principle of a conditioned release of some parts of the Ground Safety Zone' ... Heavy shooting erupted ... in southern Serbia ... on Wednesday ... Serb troops and Albanian militants clashed.

(*IHT*, 1 March 2001, p. 7)

'Three Yugoslav army soldiers were killed Wednesday ... when their vehicle ran over a mine on a road on the edge of the exclusion zone' (*IHT*, 8 March 2001, p. 4). 'Two Yugoslav army soldiers were killed' (*FT*, 8 March 2001, p. 36).

'A full bilateral political and economic co-operation agreement [was] signed [on 5 March 2001] with Yugoslavia/Serbia during Yugoslav president Kostunica's visit to Banja Luka' (*EEN*, 2001, vol. 13, no. 4, p. 6).

Nato ... decided yesterday [8 March] to let Serb security forces reenter a buffer zone along a part of the Macedonian border ... Lord Robertson, Nato secretary-general said it was 'the first step in a phased and conditioned reduction of [the ground security zone].'

(*FT*, 9 March 2001, p. 20)

'Nato said yesterday [8 March] Yugoslav forces would within days be allowed to retake the edge of the ground safety zone at the junction of the borders between Kosovo, Serbia and Macedonia' (*Telegraph*, 9 March 2001, p. 19).

Serb forces are not yet allowed by Nato–Kfor to enter the GSZ [ground safety zone] – now exploited by ethnic Albanian extremists as a base for attacking Serb policemen and for crossing between Kosovo and Macedonia to attack Macedonian police. If a ceasefire is agreed and Nebojsa Covic, deputy prime minister of Serbia, moves to implement a package of social, economic and political reforms for the impoverished local ethnic Albanian population, lightly armed Serb troops might be permitted to return to the Presevo Valley.

(*FT*, 10 March 2001, p. 7)

A Serb officer was killed on 9 March.

Nato and Yugoslavia agreed Monday [12 March] to let Yugoslav troops return to a small section of a buffer area on Serbia's tense border with Kosovo and Macedonia ... Yugoslav soldiers and interior ministry forces operating under negotiated rules and without helicopters, tanks or armoured personnel carriers, will enter a five-square-kilometre (two-square-mile) section of the zone in the next few days ... The area is an important smuggling route for men, weapons supplies and drugs ... Nato succeeded Monday in getting Albanian representatives to agree to a one-week ceasefire in the zone, but the Albanians added a clause saying they could not guarantee the safety of Yugoslav forces who move inside the buffer area. A key rebel commander who signed the document said ... 'I declare that my commanders and I cannot accept responsibility for spontaneous actions of local Albanian elements in Sector C of the ground safety zone' ... Lieutenant General Carlo Cabigioso, [the Italian] commander of ... Kfor peacekeeping troops in Kosovo ... announced the agreement after a meeting with a Serbian deputy prime minister, Nebojsa Covic ... in the border village of Merdare in northern Kosovo ... General Cabigioso said the Yugoslav side would submit a detailed military plan for his approval ... Mr Covic has been instrumental in drawing up a plan for improved relations with the ethnic Albanians of the Presevo Valley, promising better education and housing, and offering them places in local government and the police ... The [numbers of] Albanian militants are variously estimated from about 800 to several thousand.

(*IHT*, 13 March 2001, p. 6)

('[There are] about 2,000 rebels ... in the buffer zone': *Guardian*, 13 March 2001, p. 15.)

'The ceasefire [effective midnight] ... [is to last] until 19 March ... [The agreement] paves the way for the limited return of Serbian security forces into a sliver of land in the five-kilometre-wide buffer zone' (*FT*, 13 March 2001, p. 9).

A limited number of Yugoslav army and ministry of interior troops [would be allowed] into the buffer zone bordering the Former Yugoslav Republic of Macedonia ... an area of the Presevo Valley measuring three miles square up to the border with Macedonia ... A ceasefire agreement was signed by the commanders of the Liberation Army of Presevo, Medvedja and Bujanovac ... [But a] special envoy to Lord Robertson ... said it was 'open-ended' and intended to embrace all the Albanian extremist forces including the National Liberation Army operating against the Macedonian specials.

(*Times*, 13 March 2001, p. 21)

On 12 March Blagoje Simic, a former Bosnian Serb mayor, flew from Belgrade to surrender to the Hague war crimes tribunal. Since he has adopted Yugoslav citizenship, he became the first Yugoslav citizen to do so. There was speculation that the move was linked to Serbia's need to show a sufficient degree of co-operation with the Hague tribunal in order to avoid US aid penalties set to be introduced at the end of March.

On 12 March citizenship was formally restored to Crown Prince Alexander of Yugoslavia (*The Times*, 13 March 2001, p. 20). (On 27 February the Yugoslav parliament passed legislation to restitute property expropriated from the Karadjordjevic family after the Second World War and to give back Yugoslav citizenship to the family: *EEN*, 2001, vol. 13, no. 3, p. 5.)

'Yesterday [14 March] several hundred Yugoslav army soldiers and special police units swept into the buffer zone on Kosovo's boundary with Serbia, close to the Macedonian border' (*Independent*, 15 March 2001, p. 15).

'Yugoslav soldiers ... [entered the zone] under the watchful eyes of a handful of Kfor troops' (*Telegraph*, 15 March 2001, p. 22).

> Hundreds of Yugoslav army troops, monitored by international observers, poured into the southern area of Kosovo on Wednesday [14 March] ... into a 5-kilometre (3-mile) buffer zone bordering Kosovo ... Yugoslav troops are allowed to patrol a 25-square-kilometre (10-square-mile) area of the buffer zone in the Presevo Valley region of Serbia ... that is bordered by Kosovo in the west and Macedonia in the south ... Serb actions would be monitored by Nato officials ... The area that Serb soldiers entered Wednesday splits two separate guerrilla groups, one with about 800 rebels in the Presevo Valley and another of perhaps 100 rebels south of there in northern Macedonia.
>
> (*IHT*, 15 March 2001, p. 5)

'The United States ... vetoed Nato protection for thirty EU monitors, meant to observe a limited Serbian army movement back into the buffer zone' (William Pfaff, *IHT*, 17 March 2001, p. 10).

> Serbia will take steps to transfer non-Yugoslav citizens indicted for war crimes by the United Nations to the Hague tribunal, Vladan Batic, Serbia's justice minister said yesterday [20 March]. Speaking after a meeting with Carla del Ponte, the UN's chief war crimes prosecutor, Mr Batic also said he expected several more indictees to turn themselves in voluntarily. The United States has threatened Serbia with economic sanctions unless it begins to co-operate with the tribunal by 31 March.
>
> (*FT*, 21 March 2001, p. 10)

> The UN war crimes prosecutor for former Yugoslavia, Carla del Ponte, disclosed [on 21 March] that she was investigating allegations against Albanian armed groups in Kosovo and the self-styled Liberation Army of Presevo, Medvedja and Bujanovac (UCPMB).
>
> (*Guardian*, 22 March 2001, p. 11)

On 23 March 2001 a Bosnian Serb was arrested in Serbia and handed over to the war crimes tribunal in The Hague. Milomir Stakic, the former mayor of Prijedor in Bosnia, was wanted under a sealed indictment. '[He was] the first suspect to be surrendered by Yugoslav authorities' (*Guardian*, 24 March 2001, p. 17). 'The arrest and extradition of Milomir Stakic ... was apparently done without telling ... [President] Kostunica ... [who] said Mr Stakic's extradition was illegal under Yugoslav law' (*Guardian*, 31 March 2001, p. 14). 'Yugoslavian law forbids the handing over of its citizens to the Hague tribunal' (*Independent*, 24 March 2001, p. 14).

Nato will hand two sectors of the buffer zone between Kosovo and Yugoslavia back to the Belgrade government this weekend, Lord Robertson ... said last night [Friday 23 March]. Lightly armed Yugoslav troops would be free to move into the two sectors of the three-mile-wide ground safety zone between Kosovo and Montenegro and between Kosovo and southern Serbia.

(*Telegraph*, 24 March 2001, p. 20)

'Lord Robertson said an agreement had been reached with ... Kfor peace-keepers which would allow lightly armed Serb forces to enter two buffer zones along the northern and western border with Kosovo' (*Guardian*, 24 March 2001, p. 17).

Belgrade's army and police units yesterday [25 March] moved to take control of the Nato-imposed buffer zone separating Kosovo from Serbia proper. The deployments, made with Nato's blessing ... put Serb forces in control of most of the three-mile-wide buffer zone ... The Yugoslav deployment of more than 2,000 police and army troops are proceeding carefully under Nato eyes.

(*Guardian*, 26 March 2001, p. 13)

Hundreds of Yugoslav troops and Serb police occupied much of the buffer zone yesterday [25 March] after Nato commanders allowed them back ... Up to 2,000 members of the joint task force, comprising Yugoslav army troops and Serb special police, occupied most of the territory along the border between Kosovo and Montenegro and the boundary with Serbia proper.

(*Telegraph*, 26 March 2001, p. 12)

'Yugoslav army and Serbian police troops moved into a large section of a buffer zone around ... [Kosovo] on Sunday [25 March] in a Nato-approved operation' (*IHT*, 26 March 2001, p. 8).

Eight former associates of ... Slobodan Milosevic, including two of his top aides, have been detained by police on suspicion of corruption ... Among those arrested were Uros Suvakovic, a former head of Serbia's state security and lieutenant of ... Mirjana Markovic, and the former deputy chief of the secret police, Nikola Curcic ... The arrests bring to about fifteen the number of former associates in custody ... Mr Curcic was arrested on Saturday [24 March], the rest on Monday [26 March]. The Belgrade court said Mr Curcic was put under thirty-day detention on suspicion of revealing state secrets. Mr Suvakovic, Danilo Pantovic, a former senior foreign and interior ministry official, and Milos Loncar, another federal government official, are being investigated in connection with the purchase of the villa where Mr Milosevic lives. Four more officials are suspected of embezzling ... [money] from Serbia's health insurance funds.

(*Guardian*, 28 March 2001, p. 11)

'An Albanian died on Monday night [26 March] in clashes with Serbs in the buffer zone' (*Independent*, 28 March 2001, p. 13).

'Serb forces were reported to have killed an ethnic Albanian guerrilla leader in the Presevo Valley' (*Guardian*, 29 March 2001, p. 17).

> The Bush administration is prepared to certify that Yugoslavia is co-operating with the war crimes tribunal at The Hague, thus meeting the requirements of US law and allowing economic assistance to resume, administration officials said. The certification, which Congress requires by Saturday [31 March] in order for the money to flow, is likely to be accompanied by a cautionary note by the state department that Yugoslavia has not made a completely good-faith effort ... The certification law demands that the government live up to the Dayton Accords ... Congress appropriated $100 million for Yugoslavia last year [2000], half of it without conditions. Without certification Yugoslavia would be denied the remaining $50 million that has not yet been disbursed ... The government in Belgrade says ... Yugoslavia's constitution ... bans the extradition of citizens.
>
> (*IHT*, 30 March 2001, p. 5)

Slobodan Milosevic was arrested at his Belgrade villa in the early hours of Sunday 1 April 2001 and taken to prison for questioning. The drama started on Friday 30 March when police vehicles parked near the entrance to the villa. There followed an exchange of fire between police and Milosevic's supporters in the early hours of Saturday 31 March. No one was killed. Milosevic said he would 'not go to jail alive' and threatened to kill himself, his wife and his daughter. But negotiations proved effective. Although small numbers of Milosevic supporters had stationed themselves outside the villa for some time, there were no large rallies after the arrest. A number of those who tried to prevent Milosevic's arrest were themselves arrested, including some of his bodyguards. Milosevic's wife and daughter remained in the villa. After the initial failure to arrest Milosevic, President Kostunica, accompanied by leading government and military and police leaders (with whom there had been consultations), said that no one was above the law: 'If the state is to survive, no one can be untouchable. Whoever shoots at police must be taken to justice. Whoever receives a court order must obey.'

The Serbian justice minister, Vladan Batic, said Milosevic would be charged with abuse of power and financial corruption. 'The Yugoslav indictment says there is

> 'grounded suspicion' that Slobodan Milosevic 'committed crimes with the intention of securing benefits for himself and a certain number of persons, to secure to his SPS party property and other benefits with the aim of preserving that political party in power'. The indictment centres on the diversion of funds from customs accounts from 1994 onwards, supposedly to

fund state companies, which resulted in illegal cash payments to [certain individuals].

(FT, 2 April 2001, p. 7)

Slobodan Milosevic faces fresh charges for organizing an armed group of people and inciting them to fire on the police during the thirty-hour siege at his residence ... The police are also preparing criminal charges against Mr Milosevic's daughter, Marija, who fired a pistol as the police drove her father away to prison ... Three men suspected of firing on the police during the raid have been arrested ... They include ... an official of the Yugoslav Left party ... [and] another party official ... The three will be charged with obstructing the police and wounding four policemen, one seriously, when the police unit stormed the gates of the compound early Saturday morning [31 March] ... Members of Mr Milosevic's private security guard are also under investigation and have been detained ... Mr Milosevic in the end was surrounded by some of the most dubious characters from his Socialist Party and his wife's Yugoslav Left party, who seemed to have amassed a small arsenal of weapons and ammunition, which the police said were not part of any official security allowance.

(IHT, 3 April 2001, p. 5)

'Prosecutors said the charges against Mr Milosevic had been widened ... Yesterday [2 April] a new charge of "organizing a group and inciting persons to prevent actions by officials" ... was added' (*The Times*, 3 April 2001, p. 15). 'Charges are also being prepared, officials suggested, accusing the former president of having political opponents assassinated' (*Telegraph*, 3 April 2001, p. 11).

The state department said Monday [2 April] that US assistance would continue ... but secretary of state Colin Powell said that unless Yugoslavia continued to co-operate with the United Nations war crimes tribunal at The Hague, the United States would withhold support for an international donors' conference to help repair the Yugoslav economy. The decision means that for the time being a $50 million US aid programme for Yugoslavia will continue.

(IHT, 3 April 2001, p. 5)

The immediate effect of the US decision is to release $50 million of American aid, the second tranche of a $100 million package approved last year [2000]. It will also help to secure US support for a $260 million loan under negotiation with the IMF and for World Bank membership. The USA is also likely to look more favourably on an international donors' conference, sponsored by the World Bank and the EU, which is to be held later this spring, when Belgrade hopes to raise between $700 million and $1 billion.

(FT, 3 April 2001, p. 8)

The government estimates that it needs some $600 million this year [2001] in addition to $250 million already received ... Mladjan Dinkic, central bank governor ... expects about half of the new funds to come from the IMF, which is negotiating an agreement with Belgrade, and the World Bank. Most of the rest is likely to come from the EU. Beyond that Belgrade has high hopes of a donors' conference in the early summer at which long-term schemes, including reconstruction, are to be discussed. It also wants to clear the financial air by renegotiating $12.8 billion owed bilaterally to the London and Paris creditors' clubs.

(p. 18)

'Slobodan Milosevic denied charges of embezzling from the Yugoslav state yesterday [2 April], but ... conceded for the first time that he had covertly funded the Bosnian and Croatian Serb armies' (*The Times*, 3 April 2001, p. 15). 'He claimed in his appeal yesterday that the money had been secretly channelled to the war efforts of the unrecognized Serb Republic of Krajina and the Bosnian Serbs' (*Independent*, 3 April 2001, p. 13).

'Carla del Ponte, the chief [Hague] prosecutor ... said Monday [2 April] that she was getting ready to sign a new indictment of Mr Milosevic for the war in Bosnia' (*IHT*, 3 April 2001, p. 5). 'A spokeswoman at the Hague tribunal said that new indictments were being prepared against Mr Milosevic for war crimes committed in Croatia and Bosnia. He is already indicted for genocide and other crimes in Kosovo' (*Independent*, 3 April 2001, p. 13).

A Belgrade court on Tuesday [3 April] turned down Slobodan Milosevic's appeal to be released from custody, pending investigations on charges of corruption and abuse of power. Mr Milosevic had filed his own appeal, in which he argued that missing money had never gone into his own pockets but had been used secretly to pay for important state needs, including financing and arming breakaway Serbian forces in Bosnia and Croatia. It was the first time he had admitted secret state funding for the wars in Croatia and Bosnia ... A presidential truth and reconciliation commission ... [was] officially created on Monday [2 April] to look into the causes of the wars in Yugoslavia.

(*IHT*, 4 April 2001, p. 5)

Slobodan Milosevic:

The investigation document states that I incited the highest officials of the federal government to commit illegal acts and acquire gain for others from 1994 until 5 October 2000. But the people who profited were solely our state and people, the defence of our country and economy ... [The money was] not stolen by anyone ... As for the funds spent on weapons and ammunition and the other needs of the Bosnian Serb Republic Army and the Croatian Serb Republic Army, as these were state secrets they could not be shown in the budget, which is a public document. The same is true of the expenses for equipping the security forces and counter-terrorist forces.

(*Guardian*, 4 April 2001, p. 14)

'Yugoslavia's chief banker, Mladjan Dinkic, has estimated that $1 billion was transferred abroad during Mr Milosevic's rule' (*IHT*, 7 April 2001, p. 2).

British foreign secretary Robin Cook flew into Belgrade on 4 April.

'Yugoslavia will officially ask Interpol to issue an international arrest warrant for ... Marko Milosevic' (*IHT*, 5 April 2001, p. 5).

The UN war crimes tribunal on Thursday [5 April] formally presented Yugoslav authorities with its warrant for the arrest of former president Slobodan Milosevic for alleged crimes against humanity ... [The] registrar of the tribunal in The Hague submitted the warrant and the original indictment ... [relating to] atrocities allegedly committed by his forces against ethnic Albanians in Kosovo in 1998 and 1999.

(*IHT*, 6 April 2001, p. 8)

[The] court registrar tried to present a warrant ... to the Serbian justice minister, Vladan Batic. But Mr Batic said he could not accept it and sent him for a meeting today [6 April] with the federal justice minister, Momcilo Grubac.

(*Independent*, 6 April 2001, p. 14)

'Criminal charges were filed against Mr Milosevic's daughter Marija ... yesterday [5 April] for ... "endangering public safety and illegal possession of arms"' (*Guardian*, 6 April 2001, p. 15). 'Belgrade prosecutors were preparing a formal request to Interpol to issue an arrest warrant for Marko Milosevic' (*The Times*, 6 April 2001, p. 16).

'On Friday [6 April] a UN war crimes tribunal envoy handed Yugoslav authorities an arrest warrant for Mr Milosevic and said the country's justice minister promised to serve it on the jailed former president' (*IHT*, 7 April 2001, p. 2).

'After Mr Milosevic was taken to Belgrade's central jail, the new democratic government ordered his wife, Mira Markovic, to leave the residence ... the Villa Mir in the smart suburb of Dedinje ... that was built for Tito in 1979. She left yesterday [6 April]' (*The Times*, 19 April 2001, p. 19).

The wife and daughter of ... Slobodan Milosevic ... have been run out of the family's home town [Pozarevac] by former opposition activists ... Otpor [said it] would hold protests ... [if they] did not leave ... The two women left Pozarevac on Friday [6 April].'

(*Guardian*, 10 April 2001, p. 14)

'The EBRD yesterday [9 April] opened its office in Belgrade, from where it has agreed to help fund the Microfinance Bank of Yugoslavia, an institution which aims to kickstart the economy by lending to small businesses' (*FT*, 10 April 2001, p. 8).

> Nato decided yesterday [10 April] to allow Yugoslav forces back into another area of the Kosovo–Serbia buffer zone … Belgrade could return to Sector D, south-west of the Serbian town of Medvedja, from tomorrow [12 April] … In the past month three other buffer-zone sectors have been opened to Yugoslav soldiers and Serbian police officers. Kfor will remain in control of a fifth sector, adjoining the Presevo Valley where there have been clashes between Yugoslav security forces and ethnic Albanian rebels.
>
> (*Telegraph*, 11 April 2001, p. 18)

> As Colin Powell, the American secretary of state, began talks with other 'contact group' foreign ministers … the six republics of the former Yugoslavia announced agreement on a long-standing quarrel: how to split up the former federation's holdings of gold … Rump Yugoslavia [Serbia and Montenegro] has agreed with the four breakaway republics on the division of 46 tonnes of gold held in the Bank for International Settlements in Basle, Switzerland … Its total value is estimated at nearly \$440 million … The gold will be divided according to a formula suggested by the IMF. This will give 36.52 per cent to the present Yugoslavia, 28.49 per cent to Croatia, 16.39 per cent to Slovenia, 13.2 per cent to Bosnia and 5.4 per cent to Macedonia … Former president Milosevic had insisted on retaining all the assets … Meanwhile in Paris Mr Powell and Igor Ivanov joined four West European foreign ministers at the first meeting of the 'contact group' since September [2000] to look at outbreaks of violence now threatening Kosovo, Macedonia and Bosnia.
>
> (*The Times*, 12 April 2001, p. 22)

On 11 April a Russian Kfor soldier was shot dead while patrolling the border with Macedonia. Russia blamed Albanian militants.

> Yugoslav army doctors tested … Slobodan Milosevic on Thursday [12 April] after he was rushed to a military hospital from Belgrade's central prison complaining of chest pains [the previous evening]. The doctors found no evidence of heart disease, a senior government official said.
>
> (*IHT*, 13 April 200, p. 5)

(Milosevic was returned to prison on 13 April.)

Colin Powell, the US secretary of state, was meant to travel from Skopje (the capital of Macedonia) to Kosovo on 13 April. But bad weather meant that Kosovo leaders travelled to see him.

On 14 April a British Kfor soldier was killed when his vehicle ran over a land mine while patrolling the border with Macedonia.

The Nato secretary-general, George Robertson, on Sunday [15 April] praised the release by ethnic Albanian guerrillas in Serbia's Presevo Valley ... Three Serb men who had been held since last month [March] ... were handed over Saturday [14 April] to Nato-led peacekeepers. On Sunday the guerrillas also freed two Yugoslav soldiers whose seizure three weeks ago had complicated talks mediated by Nato on restoring peace in the area.

(*IHT*, 16 April 2001, p. 7)

Serbs blocked UN and Nato traffic in Kosovo for a second day Tuesday [17 April] to protest a new policy of collecting excise taxes on goods entering ... Kosovo ... Protesters put up roadblocks in Mitrovica ... and nearby border-area towns ... denouncing what they called 'customs points' intended to cut them off from Yugoslavia ... UN authorities in Kosovo ... said the new revenue posts were not customs points but rather only an effort to collect duty on cigarettes, fuel, liquor and luxury items previously untaxed. Kosovo is awash with black-market merchandise.

(*IHT*, 18 April 2001, p. 6)

'A car bomb exploded outside Yugoslav government offices on Wednesday [18 April] in Pristina, killing one Serb [a civil servant] and wounding four' (*IHT*, 19 April 2001, p. 4).

A Truth and Reconciliation Commission started work in Belgrade on 19 April 2001.

The former head of Serbian state television and a key associate of ... Slobodan Milosevic was released from detention Monday [23 April] ... without charges being filed ... two years after sixteen employees of the station were killed in a Nato air strike. Dragoljub Milanovic is suspected of 'endangering public security' and abusing his position by failing to evacuate the television workers despite indications that the state television station might be bombed.

(*IHT*, 24 April 2001, p. 5)

About 200 Yugoslav army officers and soldiers are either undergoing trial for alleged war crimes in Kosovo, will do so, or already have been tried, military officers said Tuesday [24 April]. The military has previously said that twenty-four soldiers were facing – or had faced – legal action on similar charges. Tuesday's announcement said that 183 army members were at some stage in the legal process.

(*IHT*, 25 April 2001, p. 5)

[On 25 April] 143 ... ethnic Albanians ... released from Serb prisons ... [return to Kosovo] ... The courts [in Belgrade] ... ruled Monday [23 April] that the sentences of the 143 men should be reviewed. New trials are considered highly unlikely ... More than 1,000 ethnic Albanians were imprisoned in central Serbia ... in June 1999 ... [A spokesman for] the Red Cross said 281 Kosovo Albanians are known to remain in Serbian prisons.

(*IHT*, 26 April 2001, p. 7)

[Serbia's] supreme court ruled on Monday that the original mass trial ... had followed 'faulty procedures' ... Still in prison are 281 Albanian prisoners. A further 3,526 people are still unaccounted for, including 2,746 Albanians, 516 Serbs, 137 Roma Gypsies and 127 others.

(*Independent*, 26 April 2001, p. 17)

A Belgrade court said it had delivered the UN tribunal's indictment for war crimes to ... Slobodan Milosevic ... in his Belgrade cell on Thursday [3 May] ... But the office of Mr Milosevic's lawyer said he had refused to accept the document [which] was left on the bars of his cell.

(*IHT*, 4 May 2001, p. 12)

'President George W. Bush told the [visiting] Yugoslav president [Kostunica] that US aid to the new democracy depended on Belgrade's co-operation with the war crimes tribunal investigating Slobodan Milosevic and other suspects' (*IHT*, 10 May 2001, p. 7).

The United Nations administration in Kosovo yesterday [14 May] unveiled a constitutional framework for provisional self-government in the province and announced elections to a legislative assembly for 17 November ... It gives the assembly powers in health, education and environment, but leaves ultimate executive authority with the UN's chief administrator, who will be able to dissolve parliament. International administrators will also retain power over taxes, the province's budget, judiciary and the Kosovo Protection Corps ... The move came as fighting continued for a third day between ethnic Albanian guerrillas and Yugoslav federal forces in the Presevo valley ... Disagreement emerged between Nato and the EU over handing back to full Serb control the so-called 'ground safety zone' in the Presevo valley, which separates Yugoslav and Nato-led troops in Kosovo. Some of the zone was handed back over two months ago to Belgrade. EU ministers had yesterday morning issued a statement saying the remaining parts of the valley would be handed over by 24 May, only to rescind it a few hours later because Nato had not formally agreed to the move.

(*FT*, 15 May 2001, p. 11)

Hans Haekkerup, the UN governor for Kosovo, promulgated a constitutional framework for the province. He laid out plans for an assembly, a government and elections to be held in November ... It [the plan] will let Kosovo's Albanians and Serbs – if the latter participate – run the territory until both are ready for the final status talks ... The future arrangements have no time limit and resolution of Kosovo's final status has been put off for the foreseeable future ... Kosovo's assembly will have 120 seats, including ten reserved for Serbs and ten for Kosovo's other minorities. The assembly will elect a president, who in turn will nominate a prime minister, who will form a government. The United Nations will still be responsible for the Kosovo Protection Corps ... Kosovars will be running their own day-to-day affairs ... The Serbian leadership in Kosovo rejected the constitutional framework out of hand, declaring that it will boycott the elections. The leaders wanted a veto in the parliament.

(*IHT*, 24 May 2001, p. 7)

On 14 May Hans Haekkerup, the former Danish defence minister who runs UNMIK ... the UN's interim administration mission in Kosovo ... promulgated what is called the Constitutional Framework. It means that the citizens of Kosovo will vote in a general election on 17 November. They will elect a 120-seat assembly in which ten seats will be reserved for Kosovo's Serbs and ten for the province's other minorities. The assembly will elect a president who, in turn, will nominate a prime minister who will form a government. The government will then take charge of the day-to-day running of Kosovo. But justice, law and order and security will remain with UNMIK ... The assembly and parliament ... will not be able to declare independence ... Kosovo's Serbs rejected the framework out of hand ... They have said they will not take part in the elections. But the Yugoslav president, Vojislav Kostunica, has urged the 100,000 or so remaining Serbs to keep their options open by, at least, registering to vote.

(*The Times*, Survey, 26 June 2001, p. 17)

(Hans Haekkerup announced his resignation on 28 December 2001. On 21 January 2002 it was announced that Germany's Michael Steiner would replace him.)

A seven-member presidency of the assembly will have control over procedure; it will include two members from each of the top two parties, one from the third party, as well as one from the Kosovo Serb community and one from a non-Serb minority group – the Roma, Ashkali, Egyptian, Bosnia, Turkish and Gorani. The government must include at least one Serb and one non-Serb minority representative in ministerial positions. The framework also provides for the appointment of a president of the assembly, a prime minister and ... a president of Kosovo ... Every major active political party is ethnically 'pure' ... The three main Albanian parties – Ibrahim Rugova's Democratic League of Kosovo, Ramush Haradinaj's Alliance for the Future of Kosovo and ... Hashim Thaci's Democratic Party of Kosovo – have agreed to take part in the [17 November] elections ... Few Serbs will vote ... The framework provides for the guaranteed community representation in the assembly. As the assembly treats all of Kosovo as a single electoral district and elects representatives on the basis of proportional representation, guaranteed representation should not be necessary. The provisions were apparently included because the Serbs are not expected to vote, but they will receive a minimum number of seats to encourage some sort of participation … The framework specifies that these seats will be distributed in proportion to the number of valid votes received by Serb parties in the assembly election … The framework provides for a president of Kosovo appointed by the assembly, in addition to the president of the assembly and a prime minister … Kosovo's future status will be determined 'through a process at an appropriate future stage which shall, in accordance with [UN Security Council] resolution 1244 (1999), take full account of relevant factors including the will of the people'.

(Simon Chesterman, *The World Today*, 2001, vol. 57, no. 11, pp. 20–2)

'Belgrade … urged the boycotting of local elections in Kosovo last year [2000] and is not encouraging Serbs to vote in the assembly elections scheduled for November [2001]' (Gareth Evans, *IHT*, 27 June 2001, p. 8).

At least two ethnic Albanians have been killed in fighting in the Presevo valley, southern Serbia, officials said. Clashes between ethnic Albanian guerrillas and Yugoslav security forces started on Saturday [12 May] in the village of Oraovica, just outside the buffer zone around Kosovo.

(*Independent*, 15 May 2001, p. 14)

Yugoslav troops and Serbian police clashed yesterday [15 May] with ethnic Albanian rebels … as they tried to retake … Oraovica, near a volatile buffer zone between Kosovo and the rest of southern Serbia … Oraovica [is] on the edge of the zone … The clashes began on Saturday [12 May] … Nato said that on 24 May Serb forces would move into the final 20 per cent of the three-mile-wide buffer zone between Kosovo and the rest of Serbia.

(*Independent*, 16 May 2001, p. 15)

'On 15 May the signing [took place] of constitutional arrangements for the transitional period leading to Kosovo autonomy. The Democratic Party of Kosovo chairman Hashim Thaci did not sign' (*EEN*, 2001, vol. 13, no. 5, p. 6).

The commander of Yugoslav forces that pushed ethnic Albanian rebels out of … Oraovica … said Wednesday [16 May] that fourteen insurgents were killed … Government troops entered the village of Oraovica late Tuesday [15 May], forcing ethnic Albanian militants to abandon it after four days of clashes … [The commander] also said that eighty members of the … Liberation Army of Presevo, Medvedja and Bujanovic had surrendered to Yugoslav troops. Meanwhile, the top commander of Nato-led peacekeepers in Kosovo … offered a safe haven Wednesday to ethnic Albanian rebels fighting in southern Serbia, provided they lay down their arms … As of 24

May the Yugoslav army would be allowed to move into the final 20 per cent of the five-kilometre-wide buffer zone, Nato said Tuesday.

(*IHT*, 17 May 2001, p. 7)

Nearly 100 suspected Albanian guerrillas ... rebels fighting Serb forces in the disputed Presevo valley ... gave themselves up to Nato-led peacekeepers yesterday [16 May] in response to an amnesty offer ... Under the terms of the amnesty those who cross back into Kosovo unarmed will be screened and freed if they have not been guilty of any serious crime ... Eighty rebels from the self-styled Liberation Army of Presevo, Medvedja and Bujanovic, or UCPMB, arrived at a border checkpoint ... to give themselves up.

(*Telegraph*, 17 May 2001, p. 20)

In Kosovo forty-five Albanian guerrillas surrendered to Kfor troops early yesterday. Their actions prompted the Kfor commander ... to offer an amnesty to other Albanian guerrillas willing to surrender before the 24 May deadline for Yugoslav troops to reoccupy the last piece of the buffer zone.

(*Guardian*, 17 May 2001, p. 11)

Ethnic Albanian rebels agreed with representatives of Serbia ... to demilitarize a divided village on the edge of a buffer zone with Kosovo ... The agreement [is] to pull out from Lucane – a key village contested since November [2000] ... The joint Serbian–Yugoslav force is scheduled to move into the last part of the zone on 24 May. Ahead of that hundreds of rebels have been slipping into Kosovo. Nato forces said more than 100 entered on Thursday [17 May] ... A Yugoslav army captain was killed and several of his men were injured in an attack in the buffer zone.

(*IHT*, 18 May 2001, p. 5)

The United Nations administration in Kosovo yesterday [18 May] cracked down on illegal border crossings, in a move aimed at restricting the activities of guerrillas fighting in neighbouring Macedonia and southern Serbia. The authorities are also preparing tough anti-terrorist laws that will let them outlaw proscribed groups ... Under the law due to be promulgated yesterday [18 May] people crossing the border illegally will be liable to heavy fines and up to one year in prison if they are involved in military activities. The law will fill a gap in Kosovo legislation under which the province's Nato-led forces found it difficult to detain guerrillas even when their involvement in fighting seemed clear ... The proposed anti-terrorist laws would allow the UN authorities to list banned groups and penalise any individual or companies dealing with them, including, for example, newspapers that accepted advertising or banks handling money ... The UN authorities have reported 21,000 refugees, mainly from Macedonia, fleeing to Kosovo in recent months ... The new constitutional framework announced this week ... [involves] some administrative powers ... [being]

transferred from the UN to a new Kosovo assembly on 17 November ...
The assembly's powers ... are restricted ... to control over education, health
and welfare.

(*FT*, 19 May 2001, p. 6)

Albanian guerrillas ... signed a pact to disarm and disband ... In southern
Serbia ... The commander of ethnic Albanian guerrillas signed a commitment to demilitarize, demobilize and disband his group by the end of the
month. The agreement was signed by Shefket Musliu, commander of the
general headquarters of the UCPMB guerrilla group in the Presevo valley
area next to the Kosovo border, and by the head of Nato's office in
Yugoslavia as a witness.

(*IHT*, 22 May 2001, p. 5)

Rebels based in the Presevo valley made an agreement to lay down their
arms and withdraw by the end of the month. The agreement was signed by
Shefket Musliu ... after a string of desertions over the past week. Yugoslav
army forces and Serbian police are due to begin deploying into a three-and-
a-half-mile wide strip of the Kosovo–Serbia border on Thursday [24 May].
The area, known as Sector B, is the last to be handed over to Yugoslav
control ... About fifty people have been killed in intermittent fighting
between the guerrillas and Serb security forces.

(*Telegraph*, 22 May 2001, p. 116)

Muhamed Xhemajli ... is known as the hardest of all the rebel commanders
... [He] was arrested late Monday [21 May] as he tried to enter Kosovo,
according to the Serbian deputy prime minister overseeing the zone,
Nebojsa Covic. Mr Xhemajli was the only ethnic Albanian rebel leader
operating in the territory between Kosovo and Serbia who refused to
disband and disarm his force before the entry of Serbian forces into the final
part of the zone ...[Xhemajli] is one of two commanders excluded from a
general amnesty and he is also wanted by international peacekeepers in
Kosovo who accuse him, or his men, of firing on peacekeepers.

(*IHT*, 23 May 2001, p. 5)

The last rebel commander in southern Serbia's Presevo valley was
captured ... Muhamed Xhemajli, better known by his *nom de guerre* of
Commander Rebeli, was arrested by soldiers of the Kfor international
peacekeeping force in Kosovo, although Kfor did not confirm the arrest.
Mr Xhemajli was the only commander of the UCPMB who refused to
honour an agreement to disarm and demobilize by the end of this month,
signed by Shefket Musliu, the rebels' leader. Mr Xhemajli's arrest was
reported as forty-three of his men turned themselves in to Russian and
American peacekeepers ... It brought the total of UCPMB fighters to have

given themselves up under an amnesty offered by Kfor to 280 since last Wednesday [16 May].

(*Independent*, 23 May 2001, p. 15)

Within twenty-four hours of signing an agreement to disband, ethnic Albanian guerrillas in Presevo ... appeared to have withdrawn from all but a few of their positions. Guerrilla commanders said only 150 men out of an estimated 2,000 gunmen remained in the region, eight days ahead of the 30 May deadline for their demobilization.

(*Guardian*, 23 May 2001, p. 13)

'Thousands of Serb troops will today [24 May] take control of a buffer zone bordering Kosovo with Nato's backing, after the withdrawal of 300 ethnic Albanian guerrilla fighters' (*FT*, 24 May 2001, p. 9).

'Yugoslavia sent 4,000 troops and police into the last section of a buffer zone around Kosovo on Thursday [24 May], squeezing a demoralized and dwindling ethnic Albanian rebel force into some final strongholds' (*IHT*, 25 May 2001, p. 5).

Between 4,000 and 5,000 Serb troops and paramilitary police moved into the last section of the ... buffer zone around Kosovo yesterday [24 May] ... after Albanian rebels agreed to disband and more than 400 gave themselves up under an amnesty offered by Nato-led Kfor ... An ethnic Albanian rebel commander ... was said to have been killed by a sniper. Belgrade claimed that he was a victim of Albanian in-fighting.

(*The Times*, 25 May 2001, p. 14)

'About 440 ethnic Albanian guerrillas from southern Serbia surrendered to Nato peacekeepers in Kosovo yesterday just before an amnesty deadline' (*Telegraph*, 25 May 2001, p. 14).

Serbian police yesterday [25 May] accused Slobodan Milosevic ... of ordering the destruction of evidence related to possible war crimes committed during the Yugoslav army's military campaign against ethnic Albanians in Kosovo in 1999. It was the first time that Mr Milosevic had been linked by Yugoslavia's new reformist authorities to war crimes in Kosovo, for which he has been indicted by a United Nations tribunal in The Hague ... Captain Dragan Karleusa, the deputy head of the police's organized crime section, told a Belgrade news conference that Mr Milosevic ordered his senior officials to 'clean up', and to remove all traces that could be linked to war crimes ... to clear up 'civilian victims, who could become the topic of possible investigations by the Hague tribunal'. Those present included his interior minister Vlajko Stojiljkovic, who is also wanted by The Hague. Police say they believe this meeting was only part of a large-scale operation to remove traces of thousands of civilian deaths ... Dusan

Mihajlovic, Serbia's interior minister, told the same news conference the meeting had 'most probably' been after 24 March 1999, when Nato began a bombing campaign ... [Karleusa] said police had reached their conclusion while investigating the discovery of a truck containing fifty corpses dumped in the River Danube during the air war. A driver who helped salvage the truck said the bodies – believed to be those of Kosovo Albanian civilians – included women, children and elderly men ... [Karleusa] said investigators had established that the freezer truck was pulled from the river on 6 April 1999 and that the police declared the case a state secret. The story broke in the local media only this month.

(*FT*, 26 May 2001, p. 8)

Dragan Karleusa ... said yesterday [25 May]: 'Slobodan Milosevic ordered Vlajko Stojiljkovic to take measures to remove all the traces that could lead to the evidence on crimes that have been committed' ... As many as 10,000 Albanians are thought to have been murdered by Mr Milosevic's security forces in Kosovo during the 1999 Nato air campaign ... Only 4,000 corpses have been discovered.

(*Independent*, 16 May 2001, p. 13)

'The bodies of 4,000 ethnic Albanians were exhumed in Kosovo after Yugoslav troops were forced to leave ... Over 3,000 ethnic Albanians are still missing' (*IHT*, 26 May 2001, p. 2).

'An initial "succession" agreement is signed in Vienna between five constituent members of the former Yugoslavia, providing for the sharing out of former Yugoslav assets' (*EEN*, 2001, vol. 13, no. 5, p. 7).

Tens of thousands of Serbs, including Yugoslavia's present rulers, will from today [2 June] have access to secret police dossiers ... Acting under a special decree, the Serbian government is making available to the public the files of 'internal enemies, extremists and terrorists' as defined by the regime of former president Slobodan Milosevic. The classification covers former opposition leaders who rule now, opposition sympathisers, prominent intellectuals, aid workers and journalists. Records were also kept on people who contacted foreigners or frequently travelled abroad. About 40,000 to 50,000 files are expected to be made available to the public ... But analysts say that Rade Markovic, the former head of the security service, had time to destroy many documents. He remained in office until January [2001], although Mr Milosevic fell from power on 5 October [2000].

(*Independent*, 2 June 2001, p. 15)

President Vojislav Kostunica appealed Tuesday [5 June] to his Montenegrin government partners to reconsider their opposition to ... a draft law that allows the extradition of war crimes suspects ... to the [Hague] tribunal ... The Montenegrins oppose the extradition of any Yugoslav citizen to the tribunal ... Late Monday [4 June] Mr Kostunica's office issued a statement asking the Montenegrins to reconsider, 'bearing in mind the highest national and state interests, primarily in regard to preserving the joint state' ... The leader of the Montenegrin faction [is] Predrag Bulatovic ... The Montenegrins in the Yugoslav government have tentatively agreed that the country needs a law on co-operation with the tribunal, but have resisted a clause permitting Yugoslavs to be handed over. They maintain that the tribunal is biased ... The national police chief said Tuesday [5 June] that investigators had started the exhumation of a mass grave site ... Two other suspected sites are also being investigated, said the police chief, Dusan Mihajlovic ... The disposal [had occurred] in 1999 of a truck containing eighty-six bodies in the Danube river ... The remains were removed from the river two weeks after the Nato air war against Yugoslavia and buried at the site that is now being searched. Mihajlovic said that Mr Milosevic would be 'the key witness' in the mass grave case.

(*IHT*, 6 June 2001, p. 7)

On 12 June 2001 prime minister Zoran Djindjic arrived in Sarajevo for a visit to Bosnia (*IHT*, 13 June 2001, p. 5).

On Wednesday [13 June] the police released details of a mass grave ... It is thought to contain the remains of eighty-six Kosovan Albanians killed in April 1999 and stored in a refrigerated lorry which was dumped in the River Danube ... About 4,000 Kosovan Albanians are still missing.

(*Guardian*, 15 June 2001, p. 15)

This week Serbian television carried footage of the excavation of a mass grave ... Serbia's interior minister said ... five or six mass graves have been located around Belgrade. International agencies estimate that bodies of about 3,000 people missing from Kosovo were either destroyed or taken to Serbia for disposal.

(*FT*, 15 June 2001, p. 7)

'A deeply divided Yugoslav government adopted a bill Thursday [14 June] on co-operation with the United Nations war crimes tribunal' (*IHT*, 15 June 2001, p. 5). 'The Socialist People's Party of Montenegro ... reluctantly dropped its objections' (*Guardian*, 15 June 2001, p. 15). 'The law must still go before the federal parliament ... Opinion polls show public resistance to Mr Milosevic's extradition has melted away' (*FT*, 15 June 2001, p. 7).

President George W. Bush (speaking in Poland on 15 June 2001): 'America's role is important, and we will meet our obligations. We went into the Balkans together, and we will come out together. Our goal must be to hasten the arrival of that day' (*IHT*, 16 June 2001, p. 4).

President Vladimir Putin of Russia visited Belgrade on 16 June 2001 and inspected Russian troops in Kosovo the following day. 'President Vojislav

Kostunica … told reporters that Mr Putin wanted a regional conference to re-affirm the inviolability of borders and the territorial integrity of countries in the area, as well as minority rights' (*Guardian*, 18 June 2001, p. 11).

> Yugoslavia's reformist leaders said Thursday [21 June] that they would with-draw a bill on co-operation with the United Nations war crimes court after they failed to resolve differences over the measure with their junior partner in government. The junior partner, the Montenegrin Socialist People's Party, said it was sticking to its stance of opposing any law allowing war crimes suspects like Slobodan Milosevic to be transferred to The Hague … Yugoslavia's reformist interior minister, Zoran Zivkovic, said … that the reform alliance would withdraw the bill and find other ways to co-operate with the tribunal.
>
> (*IHT*, 22 June 2001, p. 50)

'The federal government could issue a special decree … The eighteen-member DOS alliance was due to meet last night [21 June] to decide on ways of co-operating with the Hague tribunal' (*Independent*, 22 June 2001, p. 13).

> The latest opinion poll, published yesterday [21 June in Belgrade] showed that 46 per cent of those asked believed Slobodan Milosevic should be extradited to The Hague – the first time a majority has supported such a move … Human rights groups in Belgrade say they believe that the remains of up to 2,000 Kosovan Albanians may have been moved to Serbia. The interior minister mentioned a possible figure of 1,000 buried at three sites so far … The Albanians claim 4,000 people are still missing.
>
> (*Guardian*, 22 June 2001, p. 2)

> [On 22 June] the Yugoslav government … agreed on a decree … after it was forced Thursday [21 June] to withdraw a bill from parliament on co-opera-tion with the [Hague] tribunal because of opposition from its Montenegrin junior partners in the government. The decree will have the same legal effect as a law.
>
> (*IHT*, 23 June 2001, p. 2)

> A government decree … [was] drafted … yesterday [22 June] … Zoran Zivkovic, interior minister, said the decree, once adopted by the federal cabinet, would 'automatically become a legal measure that would enable all forms of co-operation with the UN war crimes court' … A cabinet session … was to take place today [23 June].
>
> (*FT*, 23 June 2001, p. 7)

Making a cosmetic concession to Belgrade's constitutional niceties … the word 'extradition' … [was dropped] from the decree. Instead, the process is described as a 'handing over'. The Yugoslav constitution forbids extradition of its citizens to foreign countries ... Legal experts based the decree on the fact that Yugoslavia is a member of the UN and is obliged to implement the laws of affiliated institutions.

(*Independent*, 23 June 2001, p. 1)

(Those in favour of extradition also point out that the war crimes tribunal is not a foreign country.)

'The Yugoslav government is due to pass a decree this morning [23 June] ... The Democratic Opposition of Serbia alliance ... enjoy a nine to seven majority ... within the cabinet' (*Guardian*, 23 June 2001, p. 1).

The decree entailing co-operation with the international war crimes tribunal in The Hague was adopted by the Yugoslav government on 23 June and went into force the following day.

> The decree handed authority for all extraditions to Yugoslavia's republics of Serbia and Montenegro and made clear that suspects need not first be tried in local courts ... On Saturday [23 June] only a few dozen Milosevic partisans stood outside the cabinet meeting to protest the decree ... Diplomats said that Mr Kostunica was unhappy with the decree but was willing to accept it.
>
> (*IHT*, 25 June 2001, p. 7)

'The decision on extradition will be taken by three judges from a district or high court, and any appeal must be made within eight days. Five supreme court judges must rule on the appeal within fifteen days' (*Guardian*, 25 June 2001, p. 2). 'The Serb government relied on an obscure and little-used article of Serbia's constitution that allows Serbia to reject federal law if it "threatens the interests of Serbia"' (*Telegraph*, 29 June 2001, p. 1).

> Yugoslavia's justice minister filed court papers Monday [25 June] seeking the extradition of Slobodan Milosevic to the International Criminal Tribunal for the former Yugoslavia ... The appeal ... [by] Mr Milosevic's lawyers ... is to be heard by the constitutional court ... [Socialist] Party members met Monday with President Kostunica ... [who] pronounced ... [the] extradition 'a lesser evil' than the country's impoverishment if foreign aid is withheld ... The United States said Monday it wanted more details from Belgrade on its plans for Mr Milosevic before deciding whether to take part in the aid donors' conference Friday [29 June] ... Foreign ministers of the EU said Monday the donors' conference would go ahead after Belgrade passed the decree ... The European Commission ... and the World Bank will jointly chair the conference in Brussels ... A poll released Monday ... said that half of the nation's citizens now favour Mr Milosevic's extradition, while one-third oppose. The remainder are undecided.
>
> (*IHT*, 26 June 2001, p. 7)

'EU officials said that even if pledges are made at the conference, "conditions will be set" for the release of any funds. These include delivering Mr Milosevic to The Hague' (*FT*, 26 June 2001, p. 6).

> Thousands of supporters of Slobodan Milosevic ... gathered in ... Belgrade last night [26 June] to resist his extradition ... Mr Kostunica ... [said] it would be better for war criminals to be tried in Belgrade, but pressure from Washington and the majority opinion of Serbia's democratic reformers had made this impossible.
>
> (*Telegraph*, 27 June 2001, p. 13)

> Seven governments ... yesterday [27 June] signed an agreement aimed at liberalizing trade in at least 90 per cent of goods trade between them. The move by Albania, Bosnia-Hercegovina, Bulgaria, Croatia, Romania, Macedonia and Yugoslavia marks the latest stage in efforts, under the EU's Stability Pact for South-Eastern Europe, to enhance stability in the region through economic growth. Moldova is expected to join the arrangement shortly. Croatia, Bosnia and Yugoslavia also reached agreement on measures to resettle the remaining 1.2 million refugees and displaced persons in their countries. Initiatives include reconstruction programmes and housing loan schemes.
>
> (*FT*, 28 June 2001, p. 8)

'The United States announced Wednesday [27 June] that it would attend the donors' conference' (*IHT*, 29 June 2001, p. 4).

On 28 June 2001 Slobodan Milosevic was handed over to the war crimes tribunal in The Hague.

'President Vojislav Kostunica ... was informed of the handover only after it happened ... The Serbian government ... had indicated earlier that it would opt to reject a constitutional court ruling to freeze the extradition process' (*IHT*, 29 June 2001, pp. 1, 4.).

> The decision [to extradite Milosevic] was taken a day before an international donors' conference in Brussels, called to raise over $1.25 billion for Yugoslavia ... The constitutional court had tried to freeze a government decree allowing his extradition. The court decision was based on a four–zero vote after presiding judge Milan Srdic resigned before the session began. The court had ordered all Yugoslav and Serbian state bodies to take no action on extradition until it had decided whether the decree was constitutional.
>
> (*FT*, 29 June 2001, p. 1)

'The court's four judges were all Milosevic appointees ... Mr Djindjic called its decision invalid. He said "The court's decision endangers the survival of the country" ' (*The Times*, 29 June 2001, p. 1).

Prime minister Zoran Djindjic said:

> The possibility of delaying the decree by the federal government presented us with the risk of unseen disgrace and humiliation for our country, as well as the danger that a number of countries could cancel their participation in the [aid] conference.
>
> > (*Telegraph*, 29 June 2001, p. 1)

'The extradition is unprecedented in international law. It marks the first time a head of state has been handed over to an international court ... About 2,000 supporters of Mr Milosevic protested in Belgrade's Republic Square, many of them elderly' (*Independent*, 29 June 2001, p. 1).

'About 3,000 pro-Milosevic supporters gathered' (*Guardian*, 29 June 2001, p. 1).

'An international donors' conference yesterday [29 June] pledged $1.28 billion to Yugoslavia ... pledges of aid which exceeded the original request for $1.25 billion' (*FT*, 30 June 2001, p. 1). (See 'Economy' for details.)

> Yesterday [29 June] Yugoslavia's prime minister resigned ... Premier Zoran Zizic, a leader of Montenegrin Socialists who have ruled in coalition with reformers since last November, said Mr Milosevic's transfer to The Hague had humiliated the nation and was a price 'beyond the level of dignity' ... Vojislav Kostunica ... is known to be furious about Mr Milosevic's extradition, lambasting it as 'undemocratic'. His Democratic Party of Serbia said it would separate from the eighteen-party alliance ... A couple of thousand of Mr Milosevic's supporters protested in front of the federal parliament ... Carla del Ponte, chief prosecutor at the United Nations tribunal ... [said about Milosevic that] ... 'Indictments for crimes committed during the conflict in Bosnia and Hercegovina and in Croatia are also in preparation' ... A charge of genocide is also being considered.
>
> > (*FT*, 30 June 2001, p. 6)

> Yugoslav prime minister Zoran Zizic [is] leader of the Montenegrin faction in the Yugoslav government, former allies of Mr Milosevic ... Mr Kostunica's party announced Friday [29 June] that it was breaking away from the alliance's parliamentary block in both the Serbian and Yugoslav parliaments ... Zoran Djindjic ... said his move had been backed by all the ministers in his government except one from Mr Kostunica's party ... He added that he had discussed the extradition with Mr Kostunica and had warned him that his government could not respect an order from the constitutional court – packed with Milosevic-era appointees – not to carry out the extradition ... About 6,000 supporters of Mr Milosevic ... massed in front of Belgrade's federal parliament ... Mr Milosevic formally received the charges against him Friday [29 June] ... Carla del Ponte said Mr Milosevic was formally served an amended list of charges ... [relating to] Kosovo in 1998

and 1999. The charges were expanded from the original indictment, she said, 'to cover more facts and additional victims' and may be amended again later to include the results of exhumations of mass gravesites recently discovered around Belgrade. Mrs del Ponte also said Mr Milosevic would likely face additional charges stemming from the wars in Bosnia and Croatia.

(*IHT*, 30 June 2001, pp. 1, 4)

'The Dayton peace accords committed Yugoslavia to co-operate with the international war crimes tribunal in The Hague' (*IHT*, 30 June 2001, p. 6). 'The former Yugoslav states were supposed to surrender war criminals under the 1995 Dayton accord' (*The Times*, 2 July 2001, p. 13).

'About 6,000 Milosevic supporters ... massed in front of Belgrade's federal parliament' (*Guardian*, 30 June 2001, p. 1).

'Some 3,000 supporters of Mr Milosevic ... massed in central Belgrade' (*Independent*, 30 June 2001, p. 1).

'Some 10,000 die-hard Milosevic supporters gathered in Belgrade last night [29 June]' (*Telegraph*, 30 June 2001, p. 1).

'On Saturday [30 June] Mr Kostunica formally announced that he did not know about plans for the extradition' (*The Times*, 2 July 2001, p. 13).

> The rift between the two was underlined yesterday [1 July] when Mr Kostunica's office issued a carefully worded statement denying he had any knowledge of Mr Djindjic's plans to extradite Mr Milosevic ... Mr Djindjic denied this, saying the president had been kept informed.
>
> (*FT*, 2 July 2001, p. 6)

Slobodan Milosevic (appearing for the first time, for about twelve minutes in all, before the international war crimes tribunal on 3 July 2001, having chosen to appear without defence lawyers):

> I consider this tribunal [a] false tribunal and indictments false indictments. It is illegal, being not appointed by the United Nations General Assembly. So I have no need to appoint counsel to [an] illegal organ ... That's your problem [in response to the question whether he wanted to exercise his right to have the thirty-two-page indictment read out to him] ... This trial's aim is to produce false justification for the war crimes Nato committed in Yugoslavia [in response to whether he pleaded guilty or not guilty: a plea of 'not guilty' was entered on his behalf] ... The aim of this tribunal is to justify the crimes committed in Yugoslavia. That is why this is a false tribunal, and illegitimate.

'The fifteen-nation [UN] Security Council ... set up the court in 1993' (*FT*, 4 July 2001, p. 1).

'Milosevic acknowledged the authority of the Hague tribunal when, as President of Serbia, he signed the 1995 Dayton accords' (*Independent*, 4 July 2001, p. 1). 'Five years ago he [Milosevic] had been happy to hand over Drazen Erdemovic, a war crimes minnow, for prosecution at the selfsame court' (Review, p. 3).

'He himself [Milosevic] implicitly recognized its [the tribunal's] authority when he signed the 1995 Dayton peace accords. They committed Serbia and other Balkan states to co-operate with the tribunal' (*The Times*, 4 June 2001, p. 4).

According to the updated appointment ... that was completed on Friday [29 June], prosecutors hold him and his four co-defendants responsible for the deportation of 740,000 people from the province [Kosovo]. They are also accused of ordering the murder of 600 named victims.

(p. 4)

Yugoslavia's former secret police chief and another senior security official ... were sentenced yesterday [6 July] to a year in jail on charges of revealing state secrets. A third senior security official got sixteen months ... The three were charged with allowing unauthorized people to see confidential papers while the information was being destroyed after Mr Milosevic's fall last October. Radomir Markovic, once ... head of state security, and his colleagues, Branko Crni and Milan Radonjic, will serve twelve months. Another security official, Nikola Curcic, got sixteen months ... The Serbian interior ministry said that about 800 Kosovo Albanians lay buried in mass graves in Serbia.

(*Guardian*, 7 July 2001, p. 16)

'Rade Markovic ... will also be tried on other charges' (*Telegraph*, 7 July 2001, p. 20).

Crown Prince Alexander of Yugoslavia has been told that he will be able to move back into his family's official residence in Belgrade ... Zoran Djindjic ... told the Yugoslav heir to the throne at a meeting in Belgrade that the way was clear for his 'family to return and live in their home'. The properties in question are the Stari Dvor (Old Palace) and Beli Dvor (White Palace) in Belgrade's fashionable Dedinje suburb.

(*The Times*, 10 July 2001, p. 11)

'Crown Prince Alexander of Yugoslavia ... said that Zoran Zizic, the care-taker federal prime minister, had telephoned him yesterday [12 July] to confirm officially that he will be able to use the Stari Dvor and Beli Dvor' (*The Times*, 13 July 2001, p. 17).

He [Alexander] and his wife, Princess Katherine, will move into the palace next week ... Alexander was born in 1945 at Claridges [the London hotel]. The British government proclaimed room 212 Yugoslav territory so that he would be born a Yugoslav. King Peter died in 1970.

(*Telegraph*, Friday 13 July 2001, p. 22)

> Crown Prince Alexander of Yugoslavia received the keys to his family's offi-
> cial residence in Belgrade yesterday [17 July] ... [in] a ceremony at the
> federal place granting him the use of the Stari Dvor and Beli Dvor ... The
> Crown Prince ... did not visit Belgrade until 1991.
>
> (*The Times*, 18 July 2001, p. 13)

On 13 July 2001 the Dutch government granted a visa (valid 19–21 July) to
Mirjana Markovic so that she could visit her husband in The Hague.

'Yugoslavia on Tuesday [17 July] named a Montenegrin official as the new
federal prime minister ... Dragisa Pesic was finance minister in the previous
Yugoslav cabinet' (*IHT*, 18 July 2001, p. 5).

> Since ... the first freezer truck of dead people [was] found in the Danube
> river in May [2001] ... nine more truckloads [have been discovered] ... The
> bodies – totalling as many as 1,000 now – are thought to be ethnic Albanian
> victims of Serbs during the 1999 war over the province ... The authorities
> in Belgrade have ... opened their first war crimes case at home against two
> men alleged to have killed nineteen people in Kosovo.
>
> (*IHT*, 1 August 2001, p. 5)

> The former head of Yugoslavia's state television station was charged yesterday
> [2 August] with responsibility for the deaths of sixteen staff when Nato
> bombed the building ... in April 1999 ... Dragoljub Milanovic is alleged to
> have known that Nato planned to attack the station and is accused of
> 'provoking the general danger' by deliberately failing to evacuate the premises.
>
> (*Telegraph*, 3 August 2001, p. 18)

'Prosecutors have charged Slobodan Milosevic's daughter Marija with endangering the public and the illegal possession of a handgun. She fired the pistol into
the air during the former president's arrest' (*The Times*, 11 August 2001, p. 11).

> Nato-led peacekeepers escorted fifty-four Serbs to their deserted village in
> north-western Kosovo on Monday [13 August] ... It was the first such orga-
> nized return of Serbs to Kosovo ... About 200,000 Serbs left Kosovo in the
> summer of 1999 ... Many of the 100,000 Serbs remaining in Kosovo live in
> enclaves protected by ... [Kfor troops].
>
> (*IHT*, 14 August 2001, p. 4)

Slobodan Milosevic was sixty on 20 August 2001.

> The former chief of Serbia's secret police, Radomir Markovic, has been
> charged with helping to plot the attempted murder of ... Vuk Draskovic
> and the murder of four opposition party staff members in a car crash in
> 1999, Radio B-92 reported Monday [20 August 2001].
>
> (*IHT*, 21 August 2001, p. 5)

A fresh political crisis has erupted in Serbia after the party of Yugoslav President Vojislav Kostunica threatened to pull out of the government ... The controversy blew up when Mr Kostunica last week accused Zoran Djindjic, prime minister, and his supporters of involvement in organized crime. In dozens of interviews since, Mr Kostunica and members of his Democratic Party of Serbia (DOS) have accused the Serbian government of colluding in and covering up evidence of corruption. The two DOS ministers in Mr Djindjic's cabinet have filed their resignations, but the party has stopped short of calling for a vote of no confidence, which would lead to new elections ... The dispute blew up after a former secret police official, Momir Gavrilovic, was killed in a gangland-style murder on 3 August, hours after he was allegedly spotted in Mr Kostunica's office. Mr Kostunica's party says he was shot because he possessed evidence about Mr Djindjic and his party's links to organize crime. The party followed these accusations with references to an article published in the Croatian newspaper *Nacional*, which claimed that Mr Djindjic had links to a businessman linked to lucrative tobacco smuggling rackets ... Mladjan Dinkic, governor of the central bank, noted that Mr Kostunica's party had failed to present any evidence for its claims against Mr Djindjic ... Other officials in the central bank and finance ministries have threatened to resign if Mr Kostunica's supporters gain the upper hand.

(*FT*, 23 August 2001, p. 6)

President Vojislav Kostunica's party yesterday [23 August] refused to rejoin Serbia's government from which it resigned last week in protest over alleged corruption ... 'The chain of criminality has remained unbroken, the narco-mafia untouched and the killings continue,' said Dusan Budisin, an official in Mr Kostunica's party.

(*Telegraph*, 24 August 2001, p. 19)

Last week ... Mr Kostunica's party announced its withdrawal from Mr Djindjic's government, ostensibly over its failure to tackle organized crime ... The two men met Tuesday [21 August] ... It was the killing of a former secret police officer, Momir Gavrilovic, on 3 August, hours after he visited Mr Kostunica's office, that set off the crisis ... [President Kostunica]: 'The fact is that crime has not been suppressed. It is rising and there are links, according to the assessment of the public, between the actions of certain segments of the state apparatus and the mafia, crime and certain clans' ... [Zoran Djindjic]: 'Some people and some parties, believing that they now have a chance for them to portray the government – and their rivals in the elections – as dishonest, corrupt people' ... On Tuesday [21 August] Dragan Karleusa, the deputy head of the organized crime unit of the Serbian police, revealed what he said were details of Mr Gavrilovic's dark past as a paramilitary fighter in Croatia and Bosnia, a debt collector and an assassin. For now these details appear to have deflected scandal away from the government ... Mr Karleusa said ... Mr Gavrilovic ... [who] had left the secret police in 1999, was gunned down on a Belgrade street. An unnamed member of the president's staff ... [said] that the former secret policeman had met with two of the president's advisers and had brought documents revealing government connections with organized crime. That information, which appears to have been untrue, was seen as a hit at Mr Djindjic. Later reports confirmed that Mr Gavrilovic did indeed meet with Mr Kostunica's aides, but apparently to discuss changes in the secret police, meaning that his slaying shortly afterwards might have been an attack on Mr Kostunica.

(*IHT*, 25 August 2001, p. 2)

[On 30 August 2001] Slobodan Milosevic made a second appearance before the war crimes tribunal in The Hague ... exuding contempt and defiance ... Carla del Ponte, the tribunal's chief prosecutor, confirmed for the first time that she would indict Mr Milosevic on 1 October for genocide in Bosnia and possibly Croatia.

(*The Times*, 31 August 2001, p. 10)

'Mr Milosevic ... again refused to recognize the legitimacy of the court and criticised the conditions in which he is held' (*Guardian*, 31 August 2001, p. 2).

'Slobodan Milosevic's daughter ... Marija Milosevic ... has joined the ... Serbian Radical Party ... [headed by] Vojislav Seselj' (*Guardian*, 31 August 2001, p. 2).

'The UN Security Council has voted unanimously to lift a three-year-old arms embargo on Yugoslavia, ending [on 10 September 2001] the last in a series of military and economic sanctions imposed on Belgrade during the past decade' (*IHT*, 12 September 2001, p. 5).

Serbian investigators said Tuesday [18 September] they had found [at least] 269 bodies in the largest of the five graves discovered since the downfall of President Slobodan Milosevic and said they believed the graves contained victims of the Kosovo conflict. Excavation of the grave at a police compound in the Belgrade suburb of Batajnica was completed Tuesday ... Another mass grave had been found earlier at the same site ... The Serbia authorities have so far found two mass graves in the east of the country and one in the west ... They started exhumations in June and have reported 427 bodies recovered to date [from the five graves] ... In Kosovo ... investigators have recovered more than 4,000 bodies at 400 sites.

(*IHT*, 19 September 2001, p. 8)

'Yugoslavia was voted back into Interpol yesterday [24 September] ... It was thrown out of the international police body in 1993' (*Telegraph*, 25 September 2001, p. 15).

'[On 27 September] Carla del Ponte, the United Nations chief prosecutor, signed a new indictment against Slobodan Milosevic for war crimes in Croatia' (*Independent*, 29 September 2001, p. 16).

On 26 October 2001 a court in Belgrade convicted three men of murdering Zeljko Raznatovic (alias Arkan) in January 2000. The man convicted of doing the actual shooting, Dobrosav Gavric (a former policeman), was jailed for twenty years. His accomplices (one still at large) were given fifteen years each.

> At his third pre-trial appearance [on 29 October] since his June transfer to The Hague … Slobodan Milosevic … remained defiant as the Kosovo indictment against him was expanded to include charges of responsibility for sexual assault and to add tens of thousands to the number of Albanians allegedly deported in 1999 … [He] has refused to read the Kosovo and Croatia indictments. Both were read aloud to ensure he had heard them … The revised Kosovo indictment alleges Mr Milosevic carried responsibility for the forced deportation of about 800,000 Kosovo Albanians – up from 740,000 in the original indictment. It adds charges, including responsibility for sexual assault, linked to the recent discovery of bodies in a mass grave near Belgrade … [Milosevic] has refused to appoint his defence counsel out of contempt for the court, prompting judges to appoint three lawyers … *amici curiae* ('friends of the court').
>
> (*Independent*, 30 October 2001, p. 15)

> Mr Milosevic … refused to enter pleas on the Croatia and Kosovo charges. On his behalf the court entered pleas of not guilty to a total of thirty-seven counts of crimes against humanity, breaches of the Geneva Conventions and violations of the laws or customs of war.
>
> (*Independent*, 31 October 2001, p. 6)

> A tribunal clerk took 110 minutes to read out an expanded, forty-two-page indictment against Mr Milosevic that added charges of sexual assault by his forces during the 1999 Kosovo conflict to those of persecution, mass murder and the forcible deportations of … ethnic Albanians … For a further eighty-five minutes the clerk read out a new indictment, accusing Mr Milosevic of thirty-two counts of extermination, murder, torture, unlawful imprisonment, deportation and persecution during the Croatian war [between August 1991 and June 1992].
>
> (*The Times*, 30 October 2001, p. 13)

> Slobodan Milosevic … bitterly denounced the UN court [set up by the Security Council] and repeated his refusal to co-operate with it in any way … The Croatia indictment has thirty-two counts of persecution, murder, plunder, unlawful imprisonment and other 'inhuman Acts'.
>
> (*Guardian*, 30 October 2001, p. 15)

'Prosecutors said they would file a third indictment against Mr Milosevic next week, including the most serious offence of genocide for the mass murder of Moslems in Bosnia' (*IHT*, 30 October 2001, p. 7).

> The constitutional court on Tuesday [6 November] scrapped a government decree providing for the handover of suspects to the UN war crimes tribunal, leaving Yugoslavia with no legislation on co-operation with the court. The Yugoslav authorities have insisted that such legislation is necessary for citizens to be handed over to the war crimes tribunal in The Hague. Their stance is disputed by Carla del Ponte, who says no special provision is needed to hand over suspects. The decree was passed in June to clear the way for the transfer of … Slobodan Milosevic and other suspects, after legislation regulating co-operation with the court failed to get through parliament.
>
> (*IHT*, 7 November 2001, p. 7)

> A pair of Bosnian Serb twins were flown to The Hague from Belgrade … The United nations war crimes tribunal praised the Serbian authorities, who handed over the suspects yesterday [9 November] … Predrag and Nenad Banovic are accused of beating and murdering detainees while they worked as guards at the Keraterm prison camp in … north-western Bosnia.
>
> (*IHT*, 10 November 2001, p. 7)

> More than 100 Serbian elite police officers blocked a main road into Belgrade with armoured cars Monday [12 November] in a dispute over co-operation with the UN war crimes tribunal … The officers protested that they had been tricked into arresting [Predrag and Nenad Banovic].
>
> (*IHT*, 13 November 2001, p. 3)

> A former senior Yugoslav navy officer flew to the Netherlands yesterday [12 November] to surrender to the UN war crimes tribunal, which had indicted him over the shelling of the Croatian city of Dubrovnik in 1991 … Miodrag Jokic [is] a former vice-admiral … Special police blocked a road in Serbia's northern Vojvodina province on Saturday [10 November] after fellow officers complained they had been duped into arresting [Predrag and Nenad Banovic].
>
> (*Guardian*, 13 November 2001, p. 15)

'Yugoslavia's elite security forces … the Red Berets … have gone on strike at their training camp in protest at the extradition of … Predrag and Nenad Banovic' (*Telegraph*, 13 November 2001, p. 13). 'About 100 … Red Berets yesterday [12 November] blocked the main highway that runs through Belgrade in a third day of protests against the extradition' (*Telegraph*, 13 November 2001, p. 18).

Serbia's top two intelligence chiefs resigned [on 14 November] in a row over co-operating with the UN war crimes court, and the government placed a mutinous special police unit under civilian police control. The government launched an investigation into protests and roadblocks by the so-called 'Red Berets' special police, previously part of the secret services. The Red Berets had demanded the resignation of the interior minister and refused to arrest any war crimes suspects until Yugoslavia passes special laws on extradition to The Hague. They say they were manipulated into arresting two Bosnia Serb war crimes suspects who were handed over to the tribunal last week, an act they see as illegal without such a law. Mr Djindjic accepted the resignations of intelligence head Goran Petrovic and his deputy Zoran Mijatovic, who denied any fault. However, he stood by Dusan Mihajlovic, the interior minister, who had offered to resign on Tuesday [13 November] to help defuse the row after more than 100 Red Berets blockaded part of the main road into Belgrade with armoured vehicles for most of Monday [12 November].

(*FT*, 15 November 2001, p. 12)

A mutinous division of the Serbian secret police refused to submit to civilian control Thursday [15 November] and vowed to deepen a protest over co-operation with the UN war crimes court ... Serbia began an investigation Wednesday [14 November] into the unit's behaviour and put it under the command of the civilian police force ... The Red Berets have demanded the resignation of the interior minister and have refused to arrest any more suspects until Yugoslavia passes special laws on extradition to The Hague ... Prime minister Zoran Djindjic said that the secret service had mishandled the situation in which the Red Berets were told the suspects were common criminals rather than war crimes suspects .. Mr Djindjic said the unit would be disbanded if it refused to submit to civilian control.

(*IHT*, 16 November 2001, p. 4)

'Yugoslavia's creditor governments, members of the Paris Club of creditors, agreed [on 16 November] to reduce the country's $4.6 billion debt by 66 per cent' (*IHT*, 17 November 2001, p. 13).

'Last week ... President Kostunica ... insisted that Belgrade would have to co-operate with the criminal tribunal in The Hague, and called for new laws to regularize the extradition of suspects' (*The Times*, Monday 19 November 2001, p. 17).

Elections were held in Kosovo on 17 November 2001 for the new 120-seat national assembly. There was a 5 per cent threshold for ethnic Albanian parties. The mandate was for three years.

'A provisional self-government will have broad powers over health, education and the economy. However, the UN's civilian administrator will retain a final say over taxes, the province's budget and the Kosovo Protection Corps' (*FT*, 17 November 2001, p. 9).

There are 1.25 million eligible voters and roughly 170,000 non-ethnic Albanians, mainly Serbs, have registered to vote. That includes 100,000 living outside Kosovo ... [Some] 100,000 Serbs remain in Kosovo ... Vojislav Kostunica agreed to call on Kosovo's Serbs to vote ... Since the UN took over Kosovo's administration in 1999 ... scores of Serbs have been murdered and 1,300 are still missing ... Serbs live in isolated enclaves guarded by Nato/Kfor troops.

(*FT*, 17 November 2001, p. 9)

'The remaining 100,000 [Serbs] live ... in isolated, UN-patrolled enclaves' (*Independent*, 19 November 2001, p. 12). 'Hardliners loyal to the Serbian Socialist Party ... are urging Serbs not to vote' (*The Times*, 17 November 2001, p. 20).

'International observers hailed the elections as a success ... The vote was overwhelmingly peaceful. Nato arrested two people suspected of intimidating voters and a grenade exploded on Friday night ... in Mitrovica' (*FT*, 19 November 2001, p. 12). 'OSCE hailed [the election] as a "great success"' (*Telegraph*, 19 November 2001, p. 14). 'The election was not completely problem free, and a handful of Serbs in ... Mitrovica tried to keep other Serbs there from voting' (*IHT*, 19 November 2001, p. 5).

'[Some] 46 per cent of mainly Serbian minorities cast their votes ... Overall turnout was 63 per cent' (*FT*, 19 November 2001, p. 12). 'The turnout was high at 65 per cent among Albanians and 46 per cent among Serbs living in Kosovo ... About 800,000 people went to the polls' (*Independent*, 19 November 2001, p. 12). '[There was an estimated] turnout of 65 per cent among ethnic Albanians ... The Serb turnout was an estimated 46 per cent among a community of about 180,000' (*The Times*, 19 November 2001, p 15). 'After the flight of almost 200,000 Serbs and other minorities, those remaining account for only 5 per cent of the population. But ... around 46 per cent voted' (p. 17).

The results were as follows: Democratic League for Kosovo (led by Ibrahim Rugova), 46.2 per cent of the vote and forty-seven seats; Democratic Party of Kosovo (led by Hashim Thaci) 25.54 per cent of the vote and twenty-six seats; Alliance for the Future of Kosovo (led by Ramush Haradinaj) 7.8 per cent.

Povarak (Return) was the main Serb party contesting the election. 'A coalition of parties representing Kosovo's minority Serbs' (*IHT*, 20 November 2001, p. 2). It won somewhat less than 11 per cent of the vote. It has twenty-two seats in the national assembly.

Ibrahim Rugova was thus victorious, although nowhere near the extent he initially estimated. (Soon after voting ended he seemed to expect an absolute majority in the assembly.) On 18 November Rugova declared: 'We take this opportunity once again to call for the formal recognition of the independence of Kosovo as soon as possible.'

'An agreement between the UN and Serbia that the province's final status will be tackled in the lifetime of the Kosovan parliament has enraged Albanian politicians' (*Guardian*, 19 November 2001, p. 14).

International attention has moved away from the Balkans and the West's preoccupation with the war on terrorism may have made quiet compromise easier. But the war has also sent useful signals to Kosovo. The first is that the West has not lost its will to defend its interests and use force to defeat extremism. The calculations by Albanian extremists, in Kosovo as well as Macedonia, that the West would be unwilling to take up arms again to oppose them have been dented. The second signal is that the new closeness between Russia and the West now also extends to the Balkans, and undercuts hopes by Serb nationalists of exploiting differences.

(*The Times*, editorial, 19 November 2001, p. 17)

The United Nations war crimes tribunal said Friday [23 November] that it had formally charged Slobodan Milosevic with committing genocide against the Bosnian people, the third and most serious indictment brought against [him] ... The latest charge will make the Serb nationalist the first head of state to stand trial for genocide, which is considered to be the most grievous of all war crimes ... The Hague tribunal defines genocide as 'acts committed with intent to destroy, in whole or in part, a national, ethnic, racial or religious group' ... The indictment ... charges Milosevic on twenty-nine counts for multiple crimes against humanity and breaches of the Geneva conventions during the 1992–5 war in Bosnia ... that left 200,000 dead and spawned one million refugees. The tribunal's indictment says that 'Slobodan Milosevic participated in a joint criminal enterprise, the purpose of which was the forcible removal of the majority of non-Serbs, principally Bosnian Moslems and Bosnian Croats, from large areas of the Republic of Bosnia and Hercegovina'.

(*IHT*, 24 November 2001, p. 5)

'The indictment reads ... "The total number of people expelled or imprisoned is estimated at over a quarter of a million"' (*Guardian*, 24 November 2001, p. 17).

The Danube will be officially reopened to shipping tomorrow [29 November] for the first time since 1999, when bombs dropped by Nato aircraft destroyed the bridges over the river ... Some parts of the Danube remain in need of clearance work and tenders will be published this week. Most of the cost of clearing the river has been met by the EU.

(*The Times*, 28 November 2001, p. 17)

Carla del Ponte (28 November 2001):

Ratko Mladic is residing in the Federal Republic of Yugoslavia under the official protection of the Yugoslav Army. As an officer of the Yugoslav Army, General Mladic is said to enjoy military immunity and he is being shielded from both national and international justice ... Working with prime minister

Djindjic and the Serbian authorities at the republic level we have experienced good results ... [But] co-operation at the federal level appears to be blocked for reasons of domestic politics.

(*Independent*, 29 November 2001, p. 17)

The Danube will be cleared of war debris by the middle of next year [2002], three years after Nato bombs destroyed many of the river's bridges in Serbia ... The European Commission last year [2000] agreed to fund 85 per cent of the Euro 26 million it will cost to clear the river.

(*FT*, 30 November 2001, p. 13)

Kosovo's new multi-ethnic assembly held its inaugural session yesterday [11 December], only to see a [temporary] walkout by the second largest party and the delay [until 13 December] of a presidential election ... reflecting a failure of the main Albanian parties to reach a deal on power-sharing ... The Democratic Party of Kosovo ... led by Hashim Thaci ... argued that the presidency of the assembly should not be elected until an overall governing coalition deal has been worked out.

(*Independent*, 11 December 2001, p. 14)

('Members of Kosovo's new parliament failed to elect a president yesterday [13 December] after rival parties refused to participate in the voting ... The DPK [Democratic Party of Kosovo] and ... the Alliance for the Future of Kosovo ... refused to vote ... A DPK spokesman said his group was prepared to vote for Mr Rugova but only after a power-sharing arrangement had been reached': *Independent*, 14 December 2001, p. 17. 'Kosovo's lawmakers failed to elect a president Thursday [10 January 2002] ... Two rival parties have been boycotting the vote unless a power-sharing agreement is reached': *IHT*, 11 January 2002, p. 4.)

[On 11 December] Slobodan Milosevic ... [made] his fourth appearance at the United Nations war crimes court ... Mr Milosevic refused to enter a plea to twenty-nine counts of genocide, complicity to commit genocide, crimes against humanity and other war crimes in Bosnia ... [The presiding judge entered] pleas of not guilty [on his behalf] ... Mr Milosevic ... is set to go on trial in February [2002], charged with war crimes in Kosovo. Another trial will be held of Serb atrocities in Croatia and Bosnia but the second trial date has not been set.

(*IHT*, 12 December 2001, p. 6)

The indictment alleges that Mr Milosevic 'exercised effective control or substantial influence' over the political officials and military officers who committed 'the widespread killing of thousands of Bosnian Moslems and Bosnian Croats' ... The prosecution ... had hoped to amalgamate charges for crimes in Kosovo, Bosnia and Croatia into one trial. Instead the court ruled that the Kosovo trial, scheduled to begin on 12 February, should proceed while the other two cases will be heard later.

(Independent, 12 December 2001, p. 14)

Slobodan Milosevic, at his [fifth and] last hearing before going on trial ... dismissed his judges as biassed ... Mr Milosevic's first trial ... is to start on 12 February [2002] ... He is charged in [connection with] the deaths of nearly 900 Kosovar Albanians, the deportations of 800,000 people and sexual assaults committed by Yugoslav army troops under his command.

(IHT, 10 January 2002, p. 5)

'Prosecutors yesterday [30 January] asked the United Nations war crimes tribunal to reconsider a decision to hold two separate trials for Slobodan Milosevic' *(FT,* 31 January 2002, p. 1). 'Prosecutors want a single trial, alleging that all the charges add up to a "criminal enterprise" to create a Greater Serbia' *(Guardian,* 31 January 2002, p. 12).

Slobodan Milosevic, finally allowed to speak in court, defended his actions during the Balkan wars and accused the UN war crimes tribunal Wednesday [30 January] of an 'evil and hostile attack' against him ... [He] asked the tribunal to free him immediately, but said he would return to face trial. 'This is a battle I will not miss,' he said ... During five earlier appearances ... Mr Milosevic was silenced every time he sought to give a statement.

(IHT, 31 January 2002, p. 4)

[He said] that he would defend himself at his war crimes tribunal ... Carla del Ponte ... argued that Mr Milosevic's plan to create a Greater Serbia underpinned all his crimes during the Balkan wars. They were 'one strategy, one scheme' to create a Greater Serbia by 'forced and violent expulsion of the non-Serb population', she said.

(Independent, 31 January 2002, p. 16)

'Prosecutors [also argued] that witnesses would only have to testify once' *(Independent,* 2 February 2002, p. 13). '[The war crimes tribunal] agreed yesterday [1 February] to combine indictments [against Milosevic] relating to three wars in the Balkans – Croatia, Bosnia and Kosovo – in a single trial' *(Independent,* 2 February 2002, p. 13).

The introduction of Euro notes and coins [on 1 January 2002] appears to be boosting previously weak banking sectors in parts of the former Yugoslavia as residents seek to convert cash DM savings ... Bank collapses and government seizures of hard currency savings drove many in former Yugoslavia away from the formal economy in the 1990s. Hopes are particularly high in ... Montenegro and ... Kosovo. Both used the DM, the preferred reserve currency across former Yugoslavia, as an official currency and are now introducing the Euro … Conversion rules were designed to push customers towards opening bank accounts. Both Kosovo and Montenegro require sums over DM 10,000 (Euro 5,112) to be changed through bank accounts.

(*FT*, 10 January 2002, p. 7)

Montenegro adopted the DM … in January 2000. And Kosovo's postwar rulers accepted the German currency as the main unit of exchange … In both places the authorities limited the amount of DMs people could exchange for Euro notes to DM 10,000 (Euro 5,100 or $4,550) per transaction. For anything larger you had to open a bank account. In Kosovo the results were spectacular: over 100,000 new accounts were opened last month [December 2001], compared with 1,000 in the previous eleven months, and more than DM 1 billion has been deposited since 2 January [2002] … Seven local banks [are] licensed to deal in Euros. Montenegrins, by contrast, were unimpressed by assurances that their 'under-the-mattress' savings – estimated by the central bank at DM 200 million, and five times as much by some economists – could now be taken to the bank without fear of hard questions. Only a few million DMs have been lodged in banks, but the price of property has risen as people have converted their German cash into bricks and mortar. It is a mystery where the full DM savings of Montenegro's 650,000 citizens have ended up: much of them, perhaps, in the relative anonymity of Italy. Street-wise Montenegrins believe their local fat cats offloaded their DMs some time ago – and they expect some of this money to return as foreign investment.

(*The Economist*, 12 January 2002, p. 38)

The Euro … has quickly become the *de facto* currency here [in Montenegro] and in other parts of the former Yugoslavia … A billboard near the Central Bank of Montenegro proclaims: 'The Euro. Our currency' … By the end of March stores will accept payment only in Euros … The Euro rush has been bigger than expected, perhaps because banks here have made it easy for people who want to hide their wealth … All anybody needs to do here is show their national identity card – no questions asked, no money tracing, no fees … In Serbia as well as Montenegro people can simply send their money in packs of DM 10,000, about $4,500, with couriers … Money laundering is also big business. Montenegro registered more than 500 offshore 'banks', a remarkable number for a country with only 700,000 inhabitants, and these are allowed to transfer money into and out of the country without disclosing the money's origins … This is a country where a very high share of the economy is 'unofficial', based on activities like cigarette smuggling and corruption as well as legitimate income that people hide from tax collectors … Central bankers here [in Montenegro] estimate that nearly 70 per cent of the money in circulation is in cash, but nobody really knows how much money is out there. Most of the people who lined up at the banks had no bank account at all, which in part reflects a deep distrust toward banks engendered by runaway inflation under the Milosevic regime. In 1993 a 500 billion dinar note was barely enough to buy a cup of coffee ... In Serbia bankers estimate that people converted as many as DM 800 million into Euros in the first two days after the notes became available this month [January 2002].

(IHT, 18 January 2002, p. 5)

THE ECONOMY

Milosevic was forced to change his attitude towards economic reform in certain respects through force of circumstances.

'In so far as he [Milosevic] has any economic ideas, he is wary of reform and suspicious of free-market capitalism' (*The Economist*, 23 July 1994, p. 42). 'Radical economic reform would strike at the heart of Mr Milosevic's power base, which rests on a vast web of political and economic patronage' (Michael Dobbs, *IHT*, 5 August 1996, p. 6). 'Economically, Serbia is run as a giant government cartel, with ministers and political leaders wielding enormous influence in both the public and so-called private sector.' It is claimed that 'political clientelism reaches even farmers, who are pushed into political activity as a condition for receiving the seeds they need' (Andrew Gumbel, *Independent*, 7 August 1996, p. 9). Dragoslav Avramovic, the governor of the Yugoslav National Bank, was dismissed in May 1996 because he called for an end to state monopolies and for privatization (Jane Perlez, *IHT*, 21 August 1996, p. 2). He later said that:

> They want things to stay as they are because they have the best of all worlds. You have companies run by general managers appointed by one political leader. These are feudal fiefs held by one man. If you privatize, you lose control – you convert your country from a tightly controlled society to an amorphous society where you do not know what to expect.

Avramovic reckoned that the economic system was dominated by 120 companies, whose heads were all government and political appointees and who represented Serbia's main producers, exporters, importers and the banks. Jane Perlez comments as follows:

> Milosevic ... has reverted to a more tightly controlled state-run economy ... because Mr Milosevic believes that economic power, even in the debilitated Serbian economy, is the most certain method of keeping political control, his critics assert ... Key elements of the Serbian economy (fuel, agriculture, exports–imports) were controlled by Mr Milosevic's cronies during the war, and remain so. The general manager of Progres, Serbia's biggest export enterprise and the leading importer of Russian gas, is prime minister Mirko Marjanovic. The speaker of parliament, Dragan Tomic, is the head of

Jugopetrol, Serbia's biggest fuel distributor. Because these companies represent an enormous source of wealth for these politicians, they oppose any notion of a market economy, Serbian economists say.

(*IHT*, 21 August 1996, p. 2)

New privatization legislation was passed in August 1991. It envisaged a state-dominated system favouring workers and managers and extensive state involvement (Bicanic 1996: 135–6). In the past few years private industry has been gaining ground, but there are no plans to pursue the vigorous privatization of big state enterprises (*The Economist*, 23 July 1994, p. 43).

The Serbian parliament has passed a law calling for the reappraisal of all privatized enterprises. In short, what little privatization has been achieved, less than 10 per cent of state enterprises, will be largely reversed (Laura Silber, *FT*, 29 December 1994, p. 2).

In the summer of 1994 an opposition party introduced in parliament a proposal for the revaluation of assets in enterprises in order to correct the 'injustices' of the privatization process during the previous period of hyperinflation, when managers bought shares at 'negligible' prices and thus assumed majority ownership of former social capital 'for a trifle'. 'The employees were unable to participate in the process because of their total pauperization.' The law was passed with some minor corrections.

As a result of the procedure of property revaluation, the great majority of enterprises in which ownership was previously transferred into private hands have been 're-socialized'. Briefly, by 1994 privatization was completed in 1,785 enterprises; under the property transformation revaluation act the privatization was annulled in 1,556 or 87 per cent of transformed enterprises, employing 80 per cent of the labour force in Serbia.

(Lazic and Sekelj 1997: 1064)

The forms of statization include the following (p. 1065):

1   The direct transfer of some big enterprises into 'public firms' (such as electricity, railway and airline, forestry, water supply, communications, and radio and television).
2   The creation of firms with 'mixed property' in which the state is practically the sole owner (such as steel, other metals and electronics).
3   The organization of 'mixed property' firms in which banks (under state control) hold the majority of shares. (Big banks themselves belong to this category. The state controls them via the founding capital of big enterprises which are in state ownership.)
4   Retaining the previous social ownership, without defined property rights. These firms are under managerial control, while managers are appointed by the state, usually indirectly through bank-controlled boards. During 1995 a majority of firms were 're-transformed' into this status.

The ruling Socialist Party of Serbia opposes privatization, while Montenegro favours it. Differences over this issue resulted in the federal law of 'transformation' (privatization) being withdrawn (*EEN*, 24 August 1995, vol. 9, no. 17, p. 2). A law already on the books empowers the government unilaterally to renegotiate the terms of sale of privatized firms and to take them back if the new owner objects (Business Central Europe 1995: 43).

But by September 1996 *The Economist* was able to comment:

> Milosevic ... seems set to dump his former socialist policies for 'swift and brutal' privatization. Plans are afoot to sell 30 per cent of Serbia's telecoms system, and the state oil and electricity companies will probably be next ... Milosevic believes the proceeds from these sales will keep him and Serbia's ruling political and economic elite afloat for some time.
>
> (*The Economist*, 31 August 1996, p. 37)

> The telephone service is the jewel in the crown of Serbia's modest move towards privatization. This liberalization is hardly voluntary. Privatization is still frowned upon by Serbia's ruling Socialist Party ... It is palatable now only because President Slobodan Milosevic has run out of other sources of cash.
>
> (*The Economist*, 7 September 1996, p. 80)

'Self-managed firms are now controlled directly – and incompetently – by the state' (*The Economist*, 14 December 1996, p. 44).

On 9 June 1997 an agreement was signed whereby 49 per cent of Serbia Telecom was sold to foreign companies, 29 per cent to Stet of Italy and 20 per cent to OTE of Greece. The Serbian government retained a 'golden share', giving it a veto over important decisions (*FT*, 10 June 1997, p. 30). ('Milosevic ... used most of the proceeds from Serbia Telecom to pay backlogs owed to workers and pensioners ahead of last month's elections for the Serbian parliament and presidency': *FT*, 20 October 1997, p. 2. 'The proceeds of the disposal went to pay overdue salaries and pensions, finance export-oriented companies and carry out emergency repairs to Serbia's crumbling infrastructure': *FT*, Survey, 27 January 1998, p. 14.)

The Serbian parliament passed a new privatization law in June 1997 aimed at selling off 5,000 small and medium-sized enterprises. The law aimed to attract foreign investment and 'pacify impoverished citizens by doling out free stakes'. The decision to take part in the programme would be left to enterprise managers (*Business Central Europe*, September 1997, p. 17). Phase one was to start on 1 November 1997 and last for thirty to fifty days. During this period enterprises would distribute up to 60 per cent of their capital to workers, pensioners and farmers, who could each receive up to DM 16,000 in free shares. Phase two would begin three months later and would last for six months, during which time enterprises could sell the rest of their shares on the open market (including foreign purchasers). (The privatization minister predicted that as much as 70 per cent of some 5,000 state enterprises would be privatized or be involved in the process of restructuring by 1999.) During phase three all shares left over would be transferred to a share fund managed by a government-appointed board. As for the proceeds of privatization, half would go to the development fund, while the remaining half would be split between the national pension fund and the unemployment office. The law left the question of whether to privatize or not to the enterprises themselves. Transactions involving more than 25 per cent of an enterprise's capital would be contingent on government approval, while 'strategic enterprises' would be the subject of special treatment (p. 26). Some 90 per cent of assets are state-owned. But there is a new privatization law, which earmarks seventy-five strategic enterprises for privatization (Business Central Europe 1997: 40).

A new privatization law went into effect on 1 November 1997. It called for 60 per cent of shares in state-controlled and socially owned enterprises to be distributed free to workers and managers, as well as public sector employees, pensioners and farmers. The state pension fund was to be allocated 10 per cent of the share capital in enterprises due to be privatized, while the remaining 30 per cent was first to be offered at a discount to employees before being made available to outside investors. But privatization was not to be made mandatory for state-controlled and socially owned enterprises and no deadline was set for completing the process. The law required privatization to be approved at enterprise level by an employees' assembly before it could go ahead (Kerin Hope, *FT*, Survey, 27 January 1998, p. 14).

'Serbia has been unable to sell off state companies to earn foreign money because of an international ban on investments' (William Drozdiak, *IHT*, 21 October 1999, p. 5).

> About 40 per cent of GDP is produced by the private sector but much of it is in the informal economy. There has been negligible progress on structural reforms. Nearly all large industrial enterprises continue to be in state hands, despite the 1997 privatization law in Serbia.
> (Willem Buiter, chief economist at the EBRD, *Guardian*, 12 October 2000, p. 29)

> While it is impossible to give a precise estimate of the size of the private sector, a rough estimate puts the private sector share of GDP at about 40 per cent, with most small-scale enterprises in private hands. The true size of the private sector may be significantly higher once the informal or illegal economy is taken into account ... In 1991 Serbia enacted a more restrictive law [than Montenegro], but many companies nevertheless continued with privatization, mostly through management–employee buy-outs and shares for pensioners. Amendments to the law in 1994 annulled many of the sales, and from 1995 onwards privatization ground to a virtual standstill. Serbia adopted a new privatization law in late 1997 with the aim of attracting foreign investors, but the large level of indebtedness of large state-owned enterprises has prevented much activity taking place so far ... About 80 per cent of the banking sector in Yugoslavia is owned by enterprises under social

ownership ... The country's large enterprises are largely unreformed and are characterised by substantial losses, soft budget constraints, widespread inter-enterprise arrears and barter arrangements. There are no effective bankruptcy procedures. While there is a competition law in place, it has not been applied.

(EBRD 2000b: 9)

'Most medium-sized and large firms belong to the state ... The black sector is estimated to account for as much as 70 per cent of the country's economic activity' (*The Economist*, 14 October 2000, pp. 31–2).

The government seized the Yugoslav subsidiary [of the US company ICN Pharmaceuticals] Friday [5 February 1999] and the police armed with assault rifles entered the plant Saturday [6 February] to impose new management. [Milan] Panic [the owner] is a former prime minister and political rival of ... Slobodan Milosevic ... The general manager ... [says that] the state-run health fund of Serbia owes the Yugoslav subsidiary more than $176 million that the government said in July [1998] it would not pay ... In seizing the factory the Yugoslav federal ministry of health alleged that the company had failed to make investments as required by a 1991 agreement to purchase the plant ... The factory is Yugoslavia's largest drug manufacturer and, until Friday, was its biggest privately owned company. Mr Panic bought 75 per cent control from the Yugoslav government in 1990. Following the seizure Friday the government claimed it now owns 65 per cent of the company.

(*IHT*, 10 February 1999, p. 5)

'Mr Panic, a naturalized US citizen from Serbia, was Yugoslav prime minister from 1992–3 but fell out with Mr Milosevic and founded an alliance of opposition parties in Serbia last year [1998]' (*FT*, 10 February 1999, p. 2).

Hyperinflation

Serbia has had to grapple with massive economic problems. Shortages have been severe and some basic products have been rationed. The cost of supporting the wars in Bosnia and Croatia has been variously estimated:

1   Around 20 per cent of Serbian GNP goes to the Bosnian and Croatian Serbs (Milos Vasic, *IHT*, 25 August 1993, p. 4).
2   The figure of 20 per cent is an official one. Some independent estimates put the proportion at closer to 40 per cent of GNP (Laura Silber, *FT*, 22 July 1993, p. 3).
3   Local economists and Western diplomats estimate that from 5 per cent to 20 per cent of Yugoslav GDP is spent on military and financial support for the Bosnian Serb forces (*IHT*, 5 August 1994, p. 1).

4   Around 75 per cent of the federal Yugoslav budget goes on defence (*The Times*, 22 October 1993, p. 21).

Table 5.2 shows the conquering of hyperinflation, although inflation began to rise again in 1998.

Although there have been varying estimates of the staggering figures for inflation, there is general agreement that at its peak Serbia's hyperinflation broke all known records worldwide:

1   Inflation reached almost 9,000 per cent in 1992 (United Nations, *World Economic and Social Survey*, 1996, p. 31). By the end of 1992 the annualized inflation rate was 20,000 per cent (United Nations, *World Economic Survey*, 1993, p. 44). Prices were rising at some 20,000 per cent a month at the end of 1993 (United Nations Economic Commission for Europe 1996: 170). The monthly inflation rate in the Federal Republic of Yugoslavia reached 180,000 per cent in December 1993 (United Nations Economic Commission for Europe 1994: 76).

2   'By January 1994 the rump Yugoslavia was suffering from a monthly inflation rate of 313 million per cent, breaking the world records set by Weimar Germany and post-World War II Hungary' (Steve Hanke, *Transition*, 1997, vol. 8, no. 1, p. 9). Inflation was 300 million per cent in December 1993 alone (Laura Silber, *FT*, 14 January 1997, p. 2). 'Under Milosevic in 1993 Yugoslav inflation was at the inconceivable annualized level of 286 billion per cent' (Ian Traynor, *Guardian*, 29 March 2001, p. 4). (By way of comparison the peak inflation rate in Germany during the Weimar Republic was 45,213 per cent in October 1923. Hyperinflation is generally considered to begin when the monthly rate is 50 per cent.)

3   The annual inflation rate reached 32,701,709 per cent by August 1993 (Bicanic 1996: 143), 64,422,464 per cent by September 1993 (United Nations Economic Commission for Europe 1994: 75) and 320 million per cent by December 1993 (*The Economist*, 23 July 1994, p. 43). Inflation 'once reached 6 per cent an hour' (*The Economist*, 14 December 1996, p. 43).

4   'The Yugoslav hyperinflation of 1992–94 was historically unique and significant due to its extreme peak and duration. At its peak, in January 1994, the monthly inflation rate reached 313 million per cent, thus becoming the second highest recorded inflation after the Hungarian inflation of 1945–46. In addition, the Yugoslav hyperinflation lasted twenty-four months so that, after the Russian hyperinflation in the 1920s, which lasted twenty-six months, it is the second longest ever recorded. During these twenty-four months, between February 1992 and January 1994, the price level rose by a factor of 3.6×10 to the power of 22, which is second only to the most severe Hungarian inflation (3.8×10 to the power of 27), but well ahead of any other ... [For example] 10 to the power of 10 in Germany of the 1920s ... The hyperinflation in the Federal Republic of Yugoslavia ... was associated closely with the disintegration of the former Yugoslavia, the ensuing

loss of monetary and fiscal control, wars in the region and the comprehensive international economic embargo imposed on the country. As inflation gained pace output in the FRY halved and the fiscal deficit reached 28 per cent of GDP' (Petrovic *et al*: 1999: 336). 'The fiscal deficit increased from 3 per cent of GDP in 1990' (p. 340). 'The money supply fuelled Yugoslavia's hyperinflation by monetizing various deficits' (p. 341). 'The Yugoslav hyperinflation ... was driven by excessive money supply that monetized various deficits that emerged upon the disintegration of the country' (p. 335).

Excessive money growth fuelled the hyperinflation. However, there are two important caveats to the monetary view. First, there is persuasive evidence of exchange-rate-based pricing, i.e. that money fuelled hyperinflation via exchange rate depreciation. Accordingly, this result suggests that prices might not be set in the money market ... but rather that they were indexed to the exchange rate. Second ... the money supply was not endogenous.

(p. 350)

A massive increase in the money supply (caused by the printing of money to cover enormous budget deficits) in an economy with falling output was the root cause of hyperinflation. A new 'super-dinar' was introduced on 24 January 1994 as part of an anti-inflation package. The new dinar was to be backed by gold and hard currency reserves and convertible into Deutschmarks at par. (The Deutschmark had come to dominate transactions during the hyperinflation.) New dinars could be exchanged at banks for Deutschmarks, but transfers of more than DM 100 required written notice and a waiting period. The government hoped that hard currency savings would be traded in for new dinars at banks. The old currency was to be used for an interim period (initially exchangeable at a rate of 13 million old dinars to one new one). There was to be a new guaranteed minimum wage of twenty new dinars a month, income in excess of this being taxed at a rate of 35 per cent. A steep rise in taxes, especially in the private sector, was another element of the stabilization package. There was also a steep rise in water, electricity and telephone charges.

The government used gold coins to pay farmers for the 1993 harvest. The farmers were the first to get gold coins if they wanted them instead of paper money or goods, but any citizen could buy the coins (*Business Central Europe*, October 1994, p. 22).

The United Nations Economic Commission for Europe (1994: 76) commented that 'it is uncertain whether the programme also includes the necessary cuts in budgetary expenditure which would be required to eliminate the underlying sources of inflationary pressure'.

But the early consequences of the introduction of the 'super-dinar' were encouraging. Tim Judah (*The Times*, 30 April 1994, p. 13) described the results after three months as 'impressive': the monthly rate of inflation had been brought down to zero; the uncontrolled printing of dinars had been brought to a halt; the new dinar had held its value; the authorities had been zealous in collecting taxes; production in March 1994 had increased by 22 per cent compared with the same period of 1993 (although the economy was operating at about a third of its pre-war level); empty shops had been replenished; real incomes had doubled; 'Dragoslav Avramovic, architect of the plan, is being hailed as a Serbian folk hero.' (Avramovic was governor of the Yugoslav National Bank and at some time in the past had worked for the World Bank.)

The Economist (7 May 1994, pp. 49–50) noted that by the end of 1993 industry was running at barely one-third capacity. But in February 1994 (according to the Serbian government) industrial production was up 12 per cent on the same period of 1993 and in March it was up 22 per cent. The use of the currency was fostered by a ban on foreign currency accounts but not on dinar accounts. (Avramovic also said that subsidies to the Bosnian and Croatian Serbs had been reduced.)

Laura Silber (*FT*, 3 June 1994, p. 3) saw signs of tentative improvement. Industrial output had grown over the previous four months; it rose, according to official figures, by 3 per cent in April 1994 compared with March, though this followed a 24 per cent increase over February.

There were harsh penalties for black-market hard-currency dealing, from three months to three years in prison. But while the printing presses had stopped, the enormous demands on the budget had not been eliminated (Laura Silber, *FT*, 9 May 1994, p. 4).

The results, said James Whittington, eight months after the 'super-dinar' was introduced, confounded critics and exceeded all expectations: (1) inflation was brought down to −0.8 per cent in March 1994 (in September the rate stood at 0.2 per cent); (2) the industrial production index in August 1994 was up 70 per cent over January; (3) average monthly wages rose from DM 30 in January 1994 to DM 200 in September; and (4) shops were surprisingly full.

But *The Economist* began to believe that the problems could soon reappear. 'It is hard to see how a second collapse can be avoided, perhaps in the autumn, as foreign reserves run out and inflationary pressures return' (*The Economist*, 23 July 1994, p. 43). Others saw signs of trouble: (1) the reappearance of the currency black market signalled a weakening dinar; (2) shop prices were showing inflationary pressures; and (3) by mid-1994 the money supply had begun to increase more quickly than the growth of foreign exchange reserves (James Whittington, *FT*, 6 October 1994, p. 3). After nine months' respite from hyperinflationary economic collapse, Serbia appeared to be on the brink of a second slump. The dinar was slipping, meat and cooking oil were again beginning to disappear from supermarkets, and prices were rising (*EEN*, 5 October 1994, vol. 8, no. 20, p. 8). The black-market rate for the dinar slipped to about 1.7 to the Deutschmark and prices were still rising (*Independent*, 20 December 1994, p. 9). The dinar went from 2.1 to 2.7 to the Deutschmark on the black market, while price controls were due to end on 1 April 1995 (*Independent*, 27 March 1995, p. 10). The dinar slumped to 4.5 to the Deutschmark on the black market, although it then strengthened to 2.6 to the Deutschmark (*FT*, 29 March 1995, p. 2). On 27 March 1995 dealers were selling the Deutschmark at varying rates around the country, from 2.7 to 5 dinars (*Transition*, 1995, vol. 6, no. 3, p. 18). 'An exchange rate based stabilization programme put a sudden end to extreme hyperinflation in early 1994, but growing fiscal and quasi-fiscal imbalances spurred renewed high open inflation in late 1994' (IMF, *World Economic Outlook*, June 1995, p. 55). Monetary policy was relaxed after July 1994 to counter the continued fall in production (United Nations Economic Commission for Europe 1995: 96). Inflation was running at 100 per cent by the end of 1995 and the exchange rate had slumped to 2.6 dinars to the Deutschmark. Some price controls were reintroduced (*Business Central Europe*, November 1995, p. 15; Business Central Europe 1995: 43). On 26 November 1995 the dinar was officially devalued to 3.3 dinars to the Deutschmark. 'Inflation, now steady at an underlying annual rate of about 120 per cent, is programmed to increase again' (*EEN*, 15 March 1996, vol. 10, no. 4, p. 4). The monthly inflation rate was 9.5 per cent in January 1996 and 16 per cent in February 1996. The annual inflation rate was 120.2 per cent in 1995. The official rate for the dinar of 3.3 to the Deutschmark came under pressure in mid-February 1996 as the parallel market reached a rate of 3.7 to the Deutschmark (*Business Europa*, April–May 1996, p. 52). The official exchange rate is 3.4 dinars to the Deutschmark, but over the past month it has slipped to 3.9 to the Deutschmark on the black market (*IHT*, 16 December 1996, p. 7). The exchange rate for the dinar has fluctuated on the black market, going from 3.8 to 5.0 and then 4.2 to the Deutschmark (*Independent*, 11 January 1997, p. 10).

The radical stabilization programme implemented in January 1994 was based essentially on a fixed exchange rate for the new dinar, but was not supported by wage controls. Consequently, there were large increases in real wages and, in the absence of compensating gains in productivity, in unit labour costs. Furthermore, in order to counter the continuing fall in output monetary policy was relaxed in mid-1994. The monthly rate of inflation started to climb rapidly, reaching an average of more than 8 per cent during the second half of 1995 (United Nations Economic Commission for Europe 1996: 96). Inflation accelerated during 1995, reaching some 105 per cent in the eleven months to November (p. 170). The acceleration of inflation in 1995 reflected the difficulties of controlling public expenditures while sanctions were still in place (p. 158). On 26 November 1996 the dinar was devalued by 69.7 per cent (p. 170).

On 15 May 1996 the lower chamber of parliament dismissed the governor of the Yugoslav National Bank, Dragoslav Avramovic, for criticizing the government over monetary policy and its attitude towards privatization and the terms of IMF membership. The dinar fell from 3.3 to 3.5 to the Deutschmark (*FT*, 16 May 1996, p. 2; *IHT*, 17 May 1996, p. 16).

'The dinar's black-market rate has plunged' (*The Economist*, Survey, 24 January 1998, p. 15).

On 26 January the dinar fell to 5.6 to the Deutschmark on the black market.

The slide in the dinar has been caused by a 50 per cent surge in money supply over the past six months as the Socialist government has attempted to ease a liquidity crisis and pay workers and pensioners ahead of parliamentary and presidential elections.

(Guy Dinmore, *FT*, 27 January 1998, p. 3)

After many protests the Serbian government has announced that it has decided to revoke a financial decree intended to raise taxes and prop up the ailing dinar. Under the decree all property and vehicle sales had to be transacted through the banking system rather than in cash. Companies could only pay employees up to 1,000 dinars in cash a month. Any excess had to be paid into bank accounts (*FT*, 23 February 1998, p. 3).

On 1 April 1998 the dinar was devalued by 45 per cent, from 3.3 to the DM to 6.0 to the DM.

Prior to the devaluation the dinar had been changing hands on the black market at 5.0 to 5.2 to the DM. Afterwards black market rates were 6.0 to 6.3 to the DM. Yugoslav economists had first called on the central bank to devalue the dinar in November 1997, when the spread between the official and the black market rate started to widen (*IHT*, 2 April 1998, p. 13).

Although the dinar was devalued by 45 per cent to 6 to the DM, an officially sanctioned dual rate of 6.3 already exists. State-run banks offer a 5 per cent discount on petrol and electricity bills for customers with foreign exchange. The central bank has tried to build up its foreign exchange reserves by demanding that commercial banks raise mandatory deposits with it (*FT*, 17 April 1998, p. 2).

'The dinar ... was trading at twenty to twenty-two [to one DM] on the black market yesterday [9 December 1999], down from seventeen to eighteen a week ago' (*Guardian*, 10 December 1999, p. 16).

The war in Kosovo, of course, had an adverse effect on the dinar, especially after Nato's bombing of Serbia's infrastructure in 1999. (See below.)

Other aspects of economic performance

There were heavy falls in GDP in the Federal Republic of Yugoslavia between 1990 and 1993. (See Table 5.2.) But the economy grew in 1994 and Serbia's ability to feed itself has always been a positive factor. The GDP growth rate fell sharply in 1998 and turned heavily negative in 1999. Positive growth resumed in 2000. In 2000 the level of GDP in the Federal Republic of Yugoslavia was still only 47 per cent of the 1989 level (EBRD 2001b: 59).

Further indications of the generally dreadful state of the economy are given below:

1   The Belgrade Institute of Statistics reckoned that 75 per cent of the population lived at a minimum subsistence level (*EEN*, 30 March 1993, vol. 7, no. 7, p. 7). Workers who earned the equivalent of DM 540 a month in 1990 were earning only DM 50 in June 1993. The UN High Commissioner for Refugees estimates that around 3 million of the 10 million people in the Federal Republic of Yugoslavia are at or below the poverty line (*Independent*, 3

September 1993, p. 10; 22 October 1993, p. 13). The Red Cross reckons that almost 3 million people (28.9 per cent of the population of the Federal Republic of Yugoslavia) live in poverty (*Independent*, 2 November 1996, p. 12).

Real wages in the Federal Republic of Yugoslavia fell by 5 per cent in 1991 and 50 per cent in 1992 (United Nations Economic Commission for Europe 1993: 226). In real terms the average monthly salary in Serbia is only a tenth of that of five years ago (*FT*, 18 December 1993). GNP per head has fallen to $350 from $3,060 in 1989. Some 60 to 70 per cent of the Serbian population live below the poverty line. More than half Serbia's factories have temporarily closed (*FT*, 22 July 1993, p. 3). Almost half the 2.4 million non-agricultural labour force are without a job, while the average monthly wage in 1993 fell to DM 10 from DM 550 in 1990 (*FT*, 26 January 1994, p. 3). Industrial production has fallen to a third of its level in 1990 and factories are operating at below half capacity. *Per capita* GNP has fallen from $2,148 to less than $1,000. Unemployment is running as high as 50 per cent, including those on 'forced holiday' (*FT*, 2 June 1994, p. 3). Currently *per capita* income is barely $900, compared with $2,700 in 1990 (*Independent*, 18 February 2000, p. 18). 'The average wage here [in Serbia] has fallen from $300 a month ten years ago to $80 today. Industrialization has been reversed; the share of agriculture in the economy has doubled' (*IHT*, 25 March 2000, p. 7). GDP per head fell to $1,400 in 1999, down from $2,700 in 1990 (*Business Central Europe*, April 2000, p. 48).

According to some estimates, the black economy makes up about a third of GNP. Taxes on corporate profits have already been abandoned in an attempt to encourage the black market into the registered private sector (*FT*, 6 October 1994, p. 3).

2   Real incomes in Serbia are a tenth of what they were three years ago and about 60 per cent of the labour force is out of work (*The Economist*, 14 August 1993, p. 69). Today 60 per cent of workers in industry, services and administration are unemployed. Industry is working at 20 to 30 per cent of its pre-war capacity. GNP has fallen by half since 1989, while 40 per cent of all economic activity is believed to take place on the black market. Only agricultural output and oil output have remained constant. Before the war Serbia produced up to a quarter of the oil it needed (*The Economist*, 12 February 1994, p. 36). Unofficially, the Federal Republic of Yugoslavia conducted foreign trade worth $1 billion in 1993, i.e. 20 per cent of the pre-war level. This was achieved despite sanctions and an economy functioning at only one-third of its previous capacity (*The Economist*, 2 July 1994, p. 34).

3   More than 1 million workers (about 40 per cent of the Serbian work force) have been laid off by closures but still receive 80 per cent of their former salary (*FT*, 1 June 1993, p. 3). Some 750,000 workers (25 per cent of the work force) are registered as unemployed and 1.2 million are on paid leave. GDP is now only a third of the 1990 level, while dramatic falls in industrial output mean that agriculture now accounts, officially, for more than 50 per cent of GDP. But the black economy may be the equivalent of 33 per cent

of GDP (*FT*, 14 February 1994, p. 2). Unemployment in the Federal Republic of Yugoslavia is officially put at 26 per cent. But in reality it is over 40 per cent and growing (*FT*, Survey, 27 January 1998, p. 13). Unemployment in Serbia is over 30 per cent and many workers are on forced leave with little or no pay (*FT*, 29 May 1998, p. 3).

'Unemployment remains around 50 per cent and workers in state companies, where production is often at a standstill, go unpaid for months on end' (Jane Perlez, *IHT*, 21 August 1996, p. 2).

4   There has been a heavy 'brain drain' from Serbia. One source cites an unofficial estimate of over 100,000 people, mostly educated and/or young (*FT*, 2 March 1994, p. 2). (About $1 billion of the current annual trade deficit of about $2 billion is covered by remittances from Serbs working abroad: *EEN*, 15 March 1996, vol. 10, no. 4, p. 4.) The economy shrank by about half during the war. Some 200,000 have emigrated, mainly skilled and well-educated people (Business Central Europe 1995: 43). *Per capita* income is about $1,000, down from more than $2,000 when Milosevic came to power in 1987 (Michael Dobbs, *IHT*, 5 August 1996, p. 6).

There are up to 650,000 refugees from Bosnia and Croatia in Serbia (*FT*, 6 August 1996, p. 7).

There are 500,000 Serbian refugees from Croatia and Bosnia in Serbia, including 150,000 from the Krajina region of Croatia. It is estimated that 100,000 predominantly young and well-educated people have left in search of decent jobs in the West during the past five years (*IHT*, 5 August 1996, p. 6). Since March 1991, an estimated 300,000 people, most of them young and educated, have left Belgrade and gone abroad (*IHT*, 27 November 1996, p. 6). 'More than 400,000 Serbs, many of them young and talented, have left the country in the last five years' (*IHT*, 11 December 1996, p. 6.) 'Many of Serbia's best, youngest and brightest – up to 350,000 people – have emigrated in the last decade' (*IHT*, 13 October 1999, p. 5). 'Damage from the war and international sanctions has nearly ruined the economy, accelerating an exodus of Serbia's best and brightest that has seen 300,000 educated professionals flee the country in the past ten years' (*IHT*, 25 October 1999, p. 6).

'Serbia has the highest number of refugees in the Balkans with almost 900,000 people displaced by wars in Croatia, Bosnia and now Kosovo' (Fiona Fox, *The World Today*, 2000, vol. 56, no. 4. p. 21). 'About 900,000 refugees and internally displaced persons live in Yugoslavia' (*Transition*, 2000, vol. 11, no. 6, p. 39).

'Even today an estimated half of the ethnic Serbs who once lived in Croatia remain refugees beyond its borders' (*IHT*, 28 December 1999, p. 8).

Though Yugoslavia and Croatia resumed diplomatic relations in 1996, only 20,000 of the estimated 300,000 refugees from Croatia have returned to their homes. Denied Yugoslav citizenship, the right to work, vote or own property, they survive on handouts and the charity of local relatives.

(*FT*, 30 December 1999, p. 4)

The [January 2000] election [in Croatia] was seen as a quiet but significant milestone for members of Croatia's slowly returning Serbian community. Before independence they represented 12 per cent of the population, but 100,000 still live in exile in Yugoslavia or in Bosnia.

(*Guardian*, 4 January 2000, p. 10)

Nato's bombing of Serbia's infrastructure in 1999, of course, had a profoundly adverse effect on Serbia's economy. (See below.)

The economic impact of the war in Kosovo and the Nato bombing campaign

Kosovo

The EU has estimated total reconstruction costs in the province at Euro 3 billion to Euro 4 billion over three years, while the European Investment Bank, the EU's investment arm, has estimated the costs of rebuilding all of Yugoslavia and neighbouring Macedonia and Albania at about $25 billion. But participants [at an international conference in Brussels] yesterday [13 July 1999] said the damage in Kosovo, particularly to infrastructure such as roads, bridges and utilities, was less severe than had been thought.

(*FT*, 14 July 1999, p. 2)

The EU has put a rough estimate on the cost of reconstructing Kosovo at around Euro 500 million ($506 million) (*IHT*, 14 July 1999, pp. 1, 8).

The World Bank estimates that the cost of repairing physical damage in Kosovo could be $1.5 billion or less, about half of some previous estimates (*IHT*, 28 July 1999, p. 4).

Nato forces that entered Kosovo, swiftly followed by 625,000 refugees, have found the physical damage to the province much less widespread than Western officials had claimed. International investigators have discovered evidence of atrocities committed against Kosovo's ethnic Albanian majority on a scale even greater than anticipated. But as beat up as Serb-led Yugoslav forces left some sections of the province – especially the western part – there are relatively few signs of damage from either the Serbs or the seventy-eight-day Nato bombing campaign throughout most of Kosovo. That observation is quantified in a UN disaster assessment provided this week ... 'The extent of the damage to housing has been overstated,' the UN report says. Sections of the province are every bit as devastated as feared. Whole neighbourhoods in the western cities of Pec and Djakovica are blackened shells, for example, and villages stretching to the mountains of Albania are charred rubble ... Several international agencies have released a report that called damage to housing and to health-care and water resources 'severe' in 141 of Kosovo's approximately 2,000 villages. But the damage is not wholesale. In a territory in which two-thirds of the population is described as urban, no cities other than Pec and Djakovica suffered widespread damage. And most of the countryside is not as battered as it appears from main roads. Across Kosovo up to 35 per cent of all homes have been damaged, according to the UN study, which found that 'only a small percentage have been totally destroyed'. And a third of the province – in the north, east and the area around the southern city of Prizren – suffered little damage, the report said. Utilities and infrastructure remain essentially intact ... There is almost no telephone service beyond Pristina ... Only one town, Srbica, lacks adequate water supplies, and the entire province has electricity ... A survey by the UN Food and Agriculture Organization found a 'severe deficit' in wheat, 80 per cent of Kosovo cornfields unplanted and that a third of large livestock had been killed or carried off into Serbia proper.

(*IHT*, 10 July 1999, p. 4)

The UNHCR, which during the war put the percentage of damaged homes as high as 50 per cent, now estimates it at 10 to 20 per cent ... Infrastructure like roads, railways, water and power supplies are mostly intact. The main loss is not in destroyed buildings, but in equipment looted by departing Serbs.

(*FT*, 13 July 1999, p. 23)

A World Bank study points out that Kosovo's problems have been compounded by a 50 per cent contraction in its economy from 1990 to 1995, which left it with a *per capita* income of $400 – lower than Albania, Europe's poorest country. The study says that growth in the six countries surrounding Yugoslavia – Bulgaria, Romania, Macedonia, Bosnia, Croatia and Albania – will be cut by 3 to 4 percentage points this year [1999] because of the conflict.

(p. 3)

Before the war about 50 per cent of Kosovo's population worked in agriculture. Albanian farmers mainly grew cereals and feed crops. State-owned vineyards in southern Kosovo produced wine for export by Serbian bottlers. Fruit and vegetable production flourished. But wheat yields declined as farmers lost access to bank credits after the province came under direct rule from Belgrade in 1989. State farms and dairy breeding units were neglected and irrigation systems fell into disrepair. Production of cash crops such as tobacco and sugar beet fell as local processing plants shut down. Remittances from the 400,000 ethnic Albanians working in northern Europe helped to maintain farmers' incomes. Although farms are small in Kosovo, ranging from 2 to 5 ha, almost every family owned a tractor. The biggest impact of the war has been on cereal production. This year's wheat crop amounted to about 110,000 tonnes, 35 per cent of the normal level ...

Maize production this year [1999] is estimated at about 55,000 tonnes, some 20 per cent of a normal crop ... An FAO report says that cattle numbers were halved because of the war, while numbers of small livestock and chickens had fallen by 80 per cent. It says modern animal units not destroyed by Serb forces appear to have suffered disproportionately from Nato bombing, either because they were used as shelters for Serb forces or because the units were mistaken for barracks ... UN officials estimate it will take two to three years to clear minefields and destroy bombs. Contamination of wells with petrol and dead livestock was widespread ... With farmers occupied over the summer [of 1999] with rebuilding their homes, vegetable production was ignored ... Production has shrunk at the Progress factory in Prizren, the province's biggest vegetable and fruit processor.

(Kerin Hope, *FT*, 21 October 1999, p. 40)

'UNMIK has chosen to treat ex-Yugoslav assets as the continuing property of the "Yugoslav" state' (James Pettifer, *The World Today*, 2000, vol. 56, no. 12, p. 15).

The mines of Kosovo, traditionally one of the major employers there, are owned by Serbs who now live in Belgrade. It was not clear how ownership of such properties would be decided until the final status of Kosovo was decided, he [UN secretary-general Kofi Annan] said.

(*IHT*, 21 October 1999, p. 7)

The problem for ... hundreds of Albanians who have seized control of factories across Kosovo is that they do not own their workplaces. It may in fact be some time before anyone is clear who owns businesses ... The [Pec] brewery remains, as far as anyone knows, the property of Mr Milosevic's nationalist state ... The Ramiz Sadu car component factory [in Pec] – which makes parts for the Zastava, formerly the Yugo – is technically the private property of Karic Brothers, close associates of Mr Milosevic, who were born in Pec. Still more complex are enterprises of a definitely federal Yugoslav nature or with foreign investment. Among these is Mobtel, the joint venture mobile telephone company between Karic Brothers and PTT, the state telephone company, which is 49 per cent owned by Greek and Italian interests ... Ahmet Shala, trade minister in the interim government, says the answer is simply to turn the clock back to 1985, before the abolition of the autonomy Kosovo enjoyed under the rule of Marshall Tito. Most of the companies in disputed ownership were then owned by Kosovo's autonomous government and so could be handed over to the new Kosovo authorities. Mr Shala aspires not only to recapture control of the important Trepca mining complex, Europe's largest lead and zinc producer, but even other mines owned by the Trepca company, which had a complex five-year deal with the Greek mining conglomerate Mytilineos. Mr Shala also points out that foreign investment in collaboration with Serbs was declared illegal by the Kosovars' underground government in 1992. The new authorities will consequently be within their rights to confiscate foreign-owned investments made since then, he says ... UNMIK [however] ... has not even started to examine the question [of state and private business ownership].

(Robert Wright, *FT*, 16 July 1999, p. 2)

There is no banking system and there are only murky ideas of ownership rights arising from Yugoslavia's unique system of social ownership and self-management ... Kosovo operates exclusively as a cash economy ... Transactions are carried out in the currency of choice, normally the DM, sometimes the US dollar. Change for small transactions can range from Swiss francs to Albanian lek ... For the moment there is no taxation of any kind – except the unofficial taxation of paying protection money – and utility charges are non-existent for the likes of electricity and water, when supplies are available ... [There is a] complete absence of any customs controls.

(Kevin Done, *FT*, 2 August 1999, p. 3)

On 27 September 1999 donor countries held a conference in Washington to discuss the UN's programme for the medium-term reconstruction of Kosovo. The work of reconstruction would be as much institutional as physical. UNMIK has been able to raise some revenues by charging customs duties, but it is intended to impose further taxes. The privatization of a number of small and medium-sized public companies should be considered by transferring ownership to workers, encouraging foreign strategic investors or by selling through auction. Current thinking was that large public enterprises should not be privatized until after elections in Kosovo. However, a pilot programme should take place in 2000 in which some enterprises could be sold by tender to strategic investors. There are an estimated 200 public companies, of which sixty-six could be classified as major enterprises. Financial advisers involved in the pilot programme would be provided with financial incentives and allowed to pick a certain number (perhaps ten) of the large enterprises for sale. Agricultural production had almost come to a standstill. A majority of livestock (including half the cattle) and most mechanical implements have been destroyed (*FT*, 28 September 1999, p. 6).

'In Kosovo ... food aid should compensate for a two-thirds drop in farm production' (Business Central Europe 1999: 37).

In 2000 the Kosovo consolidated budget was financed significantly with external grants (almost 50 per cent) ... Some 70 per cent ... [of] the budget for 2001 is expected to be financed by domestic revenues (primarily import duties, excises and sales tax), with donor contributions making up the balance ... The main outstanding legal and political issue relates to ownership of the so-called socially-owned enterprises (SOEs), which constitute the bulk of Kosovo's industrial sector. In late 2000 and early 2001 a handful of SOEs were tendered for management contracts. Local managers and employees generally resisted this move and it did not raise much interest among investors. More recently UNMIK circulated a proposal for the privatization of SOEs.

(EBRD 2001b: 21)

Serbia

'According to independent Serbian estimates, the direct damage to infrastructure, including industrial facilities, from the bombing was approximately $3–4 billion' (EBRD 2000b: 9).

'Little industrial damage was caused by 1999's bombing, which flattened less than 5 per cent of capacity. But infrastructure took a pounding' (Business Central Europe 2000: 40).

The G17 economic research organization estimated that it would have taken twenty-nine years for Yugoslavia to reach the level of economic prosperity it had in 1989. Today, the think tank asserts, it will take forty-five years – without a significant infusion of economic aid. The price tag for repairing the country after more than ten weeks of Nato's attacks is estimated to be somewhere between $50 billion and $150 billion.

(Daniel Williams, *IHT*, 7 June 1999, p. 9)

'The dinar has been losing value against hard currencies, currently trading on the black market at about 17.5 dinars per dollar and ten per DM' (*IHT*, 12 April 1999, p. 8).

On 25 August 1999 the government decreed the issuing of coupons for old age pensioners to pay for utility bills (*EEN*, 1999, vol. 12, no. 20, p. 4).

The first cold weather of autumn has produced shortages across Serbia ... Electricity blackouts that lasted at least two hours were imposed Tuesday [19 October] in Belgrade, Novi Sad and other cities across Serbia ... The seasonal cold snap has coincided with fresh signs of hyperinflation and food shortages ... Even in the capital there are evident supply problems with meat, sugar and cooking oil. Hyperinflation is creeping back, with prices rising at the rate of more than 150 per cent a year. The free-market value of the Yugoslav dinar has plummeted to less than one-third the official rate, prompting rumours that the government may soon devalue the currency ... [There is a] lack of foreign currency reserves held by the central bank, which cannot intervene to prop up its value. Serbia has been unable to sell off state companies to earn foreign money because of an international ban on investments, and efforts to collect some $3 billion in debts owed by Iraq and Libya have been fruitless ... In the past Mr Milosevic has shored up his political support by ensuring cheap fuel and food through lavish subsidies. But with its financial reserves almost depleted, the government is coping with the twin curses of shortages and soaring prices by blaming any hardships on Nato's bombing campaign and the panoply of international sanctions against Serbia ... Goran Pitic, a Serbian economist ... believes that Mr Milosevic has bought himself more time by appealing to Serbia's time-honoured sense of victimhood in faulting the outside world for his government's economic failures ... Hungary, which is concerned about the fate of ethnic Hungarians living in the northern province of Vojvodina, says for humanitarian reasons it is now willing to allow Russian gas to pass through its territory. But Budapest has sought assurances that Yugoslavia will repay about $20 million in overdue debts ... The first deliveries of Russian gas destined for Serbia's heating plants started arriving via Hungary on Tuesday [19 October].

(William Drozdiak, *IHT*, 21 October 1999, p. 5)

'In the past month the dinar has lost a third of its value against the DM, while the annual inflation rate is near 100 per cent' (*FT*, 30 October 1999, p. 5).

Dragoslav Avramovic (former governor of the central bank): 'Prices are increasing 10 per cent a week, which is 50 per cent a month' (*IHT*, 3 November 1999, p. 1).

A UN environmental team has found no evidence of an ecological catastrophe in Yugoslavia because of Nato's bombing, according to its leader. But he urged the West to help clean up significant hot spots of war-related pollution ... He said environmental damage in heavily bombed industrial towns like Pancevo, Krugevac and Bor needed immediate attention to protect the health of ordinary citizens.

(*IHT*, 29 July 1999, p. 2)

The report on the environmental impact of Nato's bombing campaign was published on 14 October 1999. It concluded that there had been no 'catastrophe' but recommended immediate action on four pollution 'hot-spots'. The report said that Nato had refused to co-operate in its investigation of the use of depleted uranium weapons (*FT*, 15 October 1999, p. 10).

Last year [1999] GDP fell by another 23 per cent, as Nato bombing banged the final nail into the coffin of Serbia's economy ... Inflation is deceptively tame on paper – the government says prices went up by 1.8 per cent in February [2000] ... The trouble is that, one way or another, the government financed last year's deficit by printing money. By the second half of the year inflation was rising ominously and the government tried to cover it up by introducing strict price controls. They stopped inflation, at least statistically ... But ... the products that never go up in price ... disappeared from the shelves long ago, because the price controls forced producers to make the same products under different names – but with higher prices. Some independent economists reckon that inflation has reached 20 per cent or even 30 per cent a month. And the collapse in the unofficial dinar exchange rate has piled on the pressure. Last year the exchange rate plunged three times faster than official prices went up. True, the dinar was relatively stable in the last few months of last year, thanks to a $300 million loan from China ... Whether that was really Chinese money or Serbian money sent abroad for safe-keeping remains a mystery. And the amount was only enough to support the dinar for a few months: last year only 45 per cent of imports were covered by exports.

(*Business Central Europe*, April 2000, p. 48)

(In December 1999 China provided Serbia with aid worth $300 million in the form of grants and soft loans: *The Economist*, 5 February 2000, p. 45.)

Rough estimates suggest that [Yugoslav] GDP in 1999 at official exchange rates was ... not much more than half the 1989 level. Recorded unemployment is over 30 per cent of the labour force and the true rate may be as high as 50 per cent. Real GDP fell by about 20 to 25 per cent in 1999 ... The agricultural sector, which accounts for nearly one-quarter of GDP, has been badly hit by drought in 2000, and the wheat crop, normally a significant export earner, will be well below average ... The level of external debt is still rising, mainly through the build-up of arrears, and currently stands at around $12–14 billion.

(EBRD 2000b: 8)

Very little progress has been achieved in economic liberalization. Price controls are widespread, with government control (either direct or indirect) over an estimated 60 per cent of all goods. Prices of utilities are well below cost-recovery levels. The economy is relatively protected, with a complicated system of extensive tariffs on imports. In Serbia as of mid-October [2000] a multiple exchange rate regime is in place: the official rate (currently six dinars equals one DM) is used for customs tariffs on the import of raw materials and for selling foreign currency to government enterprises. Higher exchange rates apply for others (for example, importers selling dinars to the central bank), although banks sometimes give preferential rates to selected enterprises. The current black market rate (mid-October) is around thirty dinars to one DM.

(EBRD 2000b: 8)

'Around 50 per cent of all prices are controlled at the moment' (*Business Central Europe*, November 2000, p. 21).

The economy after the fall of Milosevic

Since Mr Milosevic was overthrown in early October the people of Serbia have suffered prolonged electricity shortages and blackouts, as well as price rises for basic foods that brought inflation in October alone to 27 per cent, after the artificially restricted increases of 2 to 3 per cent a month under Mr Milosevic.

(*IHT*, 14 November 2000, p. 7)

'Milosevic allies enacted sweeping price liberalization' (*Telegraph*, 16 November 2000, p. 20).

'Property rights are unclear in many cases; the initial days after the election of President Kostunica saw the spontaneous ousting of some owners and the return of social ownership' (EBRD 2000b: 9).

'Only a few directors were sacked after a popular uprising ... A complex system of worker and state ownership of property has confused shareholder structures' (Irena Guzelova, *FT*, 13 December 2000, p. 10).

'The heads of some big banks and companies were booted out by employees ... but many more remain in place ' (Business Central Europe 2000: 40).

> Serbia ... can learn from all the other post-communist transitions. Mladjan Dinkic, a representative of the so-called G17 Plus group of economists who are already preparing for a democratic transition, told me they would combine Polish-style shock therapy with a more cautious privatization ... A crucial test – this we have learned from other transitions – is whether they can establish the rule of law in a highly criminalized society. This will determine whether Serbia becomes a little Russia or a civilized European country.
> (Timothy Garton Ash, *New York Review of Books*, 2000, vol. XLVII, no. 18, p. 14)

'The economic reformers behind ... Vojislav Kostunica says speedy privatization is a high priority' (*IHT*, 18 November 2000, p. 19).

'Yugoslavia will declare its dinar internally convertible as of 15 December and introduce a new series of bank notes' (*IHT*, 2 December 2000, p. 13). '15 December: the dinar becomes fully convertible' (*EEN*, 2001, vol. 13, no. 2, p. 6).

'The federal government, which the reformers have controlled since October, has stabilized the currency, initiated foreign trade liberalization and abolished the system of preferential customs duties' (*FT*, 27 December 2000, p. 6).

> Serbia's parliament yesterday [25 January 2001] approved the formation of a reformist government. Prime minister Zoran Djindjic ... has promised a government based on transparency, the rule of law and liberal market reform ... Bozidar Djelic [is] Serbia's new finance minister ... The government will prepare a detailed economic programme in time for a European Union and World Bank donors conference scheduled for this spring. Before that Mr Djindjic hopes to secure a stand-by facility from the IMF of between $150 million and $200 million to help the reform process ... One of the first moves the government will make is to review earlier privatizations that gave management the possibility of buying companies at

knock-down prices and reverse a recent wave of management buy-outs ...
Mr Djindjic hopes that a law on privatization is likely to be ready in March,
but the government is likely to take a cautious approach to privatization and
decide what to do with each company on a case by case basis.

(Irena Guzelova, *FT*, 26 January 2001, p. 7)

'Yugoslavia's banking sector has more than DM 10 billion ($4.81 billion) in
accumulated uncovered losses, equal to more than 40 per cent of the country's
GDP, the central bank said' (*IHT*, 3 February 2001, p. 12).
'Yugoslavia ... needs to reschedule an external debt of perhaps $12 billion ...
The Yugoslav state owes another $4.5 billion to its own citizens, whose hard
currency bank accounts are frozen, and as much again in debts denominated in
local dinars' (*The Economist*, 17 February 2001, p. 50).

This year's Serbian budget [was] passed in March [2001]. It targets a deficit
of ... 2 per cent of GDP, compared with 13 per cent of GDP last year
[2000]. For that to happen Yugoslavia must grow 5 per cent this year
[2001], and inflation fall to 30 per cent, compared to over 110 per cent in
2000. And spending must tumble. To set an example, the government has
frozen ministers' salaries and introduced salary caps for public companies ...
The number of taxes has been reduced from 250 to six, while penalties have
been laid down for tax evasion ... A new law passing through parliament
will pave the way for some 4,500 companies to be sold by tender and
auction to strategic investors ... Half of the workforce is now jobless and a
third of the population live below the official subsistence level.

(*Business Central Europe*, May 2001, pp. 45–6)

'In 2000 ... in the Federal Republic of Yugoslavia ... the ratio of external
debt to GDP was about 140 per cent' (IMF, *World Economic Outlook*, May 2001, p.
45).
'Yugoslavia's $12 billion international debt [is] one-and-a-half times the
country's GDP' (*Telegraph*, 5 April 2001, p. 19). 'Foreign debt now stands at 140
per cent of GDP' (*Independent*, 5 April 2001, p. 14). 'Servicing ... Yugoslavia's
total debt ... costs eight times current export earnings' (*Guardian*, 5 April 2001, p.
13). ' Foreign debt [is] about eight times the nation's present exports' (*The Times*,
5 April 2001, p. 20).

[On 12 June 2001] Yugoslavia was awarded a ten-month $249 million loan by
the IMF, the country's first lending programme since being ousted from the
Fund ... The government pledged to aim for 5 per cent economic growth this
year [2001] and to drive down inflation to as low as 30 per cent in Serbia and
6.5 per cent in Montenegro ... Yugoslavia was ejected from the IMF in 1992
... because former President Slobodan Milosevic refused to redistribute state
assets among the republics that had comprised the federation.

(p. 14)

[On 25 June 2001] the IMF ... [said Yugoslavia] was $9.7 billion in arrears to foreign creditors, $1.7 billion of which is owed to the World Bank ... It is estimated that the economy has shrunk by half since 1989, contracting by 15.9 per cent in 1999 alone. Unemployment was at 30 per cent and there were 600,000 refugees and other displaced people.

(*FT*, 26 June 2001, p. 6)

In a recent report the IMF ... noted that the government had embarked with 'impressive speed and commitment' on a series of important structural reform. It has liberalized extremely restrictive foreign exchange and trade regimes, freed most prices and begun to reform the tax system ... In the Serbian parliament the ultra-nationalist Radical Party's filibustering has delayed a new law on privatization by nearly two months.

(*FT*, 28 June 2001, p. 8)

Yugoslav officials say ... [aid] is needed to rebuild infrastructure (particularly the power grid), reshape the banking system, and support the transition to a market economy ... The Federal Republic of Yugoslavia will need to find $20.5 billion in external financing over the next five years if its economy is to recover from a decade of underinvestment, international isolation and war, the World Bank recently estimated ... The Federal Republic of Yugoslavia's membership in the World Bank was reestablished on 8 May [2001] ... In support of the Federal Republic of Yugoslavia's economic programme, on 12 June the IMF approved a stand-by credit of $249 million. The first instalment ($62 million) can be drawn on immediately; the remaining three instalments ($62 million each) could become available once quarterly reviews of the programme are concluded ... The country owes some $5 billion to Western governments in the Paris Club and another $7 billion to commercial lenders in the London Club. The most optimistic forecasts predict a GDP of $11 billion for the Federal Republic of Yugoslavia this year [2001].

(*Transition*, 2001, vol. 12, no. 2, pp. 35–6)

An international donors' conference yesterday [29 June 2001] pledged $1.28 billion to Yugoslavia ... pledges of aid which exceeded the original request for $1.25 billion ... The World Bank and EU hosted the conference ... According to the World Bank, an estimated 1.3 million, or 12 per cent of the population, live in absolute poverty ... Miroljub Labus, deputy Yugoslav prime minister ... insisted that substantial relief was needed for a foreign debt of $12.2 billion, or 80 per cent of GDP. He also added that Yugoslavia still required a further $3 billion over the next four years.

(*FT*, 30 June 2001, p. 1)

'His [Djindjic's] advisers explained that the funds pledged included $400 million awarded last winter. The remaining $900 million [is] for Serbia and Montenegro' (*FT*, 2 July 2001, p. 6). '[The] $1.28 billion ... is slightly more than the $1.25 billion the European Commission and the World Bank said was needed this year' (*IHT*, 30 June 2001, p. 1).

The reformist Belgrade government has already drawn up an economic 'recovery and transition programme' that requires funding of almost $4 billion over three to four years ... Inflation is 150 per cent and unemployment is 50 per cent. The World Bank's vice-president Johannes Linn said priorities would be balancing the budget, rebuilding the energy networks, clearing the Danube of bombing debris as well as reconstruction and social programmes.

(*Guardian*, 30 June 2001, p. 4)

RZB, umbrella bank of Austria's local Raiffeisen banks, has won the race to be the first foreign bank to open an office in Yugoslavia following last year's change of government. The Austrian bank has opened a subsidiary in Belgrade, Raiffeisenbank Jugoslavia, with an initial staff of fifty. The bank will focus on corporate banking initially, but expects to start servicing retail customers in September.

(*FT*, 31 July 2001, p. 9)

Economic reform has remained largely untouched. Ministers responsible for economic reform have sought to distance themselves from the bickering [between Kostunica and Djindjic] and have won widespread praise from international financial organizations for the speed and effectiveness with which they have overhauled public finances, greatly strengthened transparency and reformed the tax system ... A firm clampdown on cigarette and petrol smuggling has boosted the budget and enabled lower taxes, resulting in a 10 per cent increase in real wages. For the first time in more than ten years pensions and wages are being paid on time ... Serbia, a haven for smuggling into western Europe, has seen black market sales drop from 50 per cent of total market share in 2000 to about 17 per cent. Ministers are preparing laws designed to foster and protect investments, deal with bankruptcy and out-of-court settlements and guard against monopoly control and corruption. They are preparing a labour law which will make it possible to sack employees and are introducing tax breaks for overseas investors ... Ministers will meet creditors from the Paris Club on 12 November to begin talks to reschedule a $4.4 billion debt. Yugoslavia has debts of $12 billion, amounting to 140 per cent of GDP. Ministers are seeking a two-thirds write-off. Voters complain about price rises but strikes that were expected have failed to gain momentum ... The government ... [is to try] to sell its three largest cement plants towards the end of this year [2001].

(*FT*, 4 October 2001, p. 10)

'The same miners ... at the Kolubara pit [who opposed Milosevic] ... are on strike for higher wages. Otpor (Resistance) ... now speaks out on corruption in government' (*Telegraph*, 6 October 2001, p. 22).

'[On 5 October 2001] the first anniversary of the ousting of President Slobodan Milosevic ... Velimir Ilijc, the mayor of Cacak who played a leading role in the anti-Milosevic campaign, issued a "warning" to the new leaders over living standards' (*IHT*, 6 October 2001, p. 5).

'Yugoslavia's creditor governments, members of the Paris Club of creditors, agreed to reduce the country's $4.6 billion debt by 66 per cent' (*IHT*, 17 November 2001, p. 13).

> Ten years of isolation have been devastating for the Yugoslav economy, but entrepreneurship remains strong ... Privatization in Serbia has almost come to a standstill in the last couple of years. The current law, which allows insiders to retain about 60 per cent of the shares after privatization, needs to be changed. A new law on privatization is being prepared and is likely to emphasize a combination of tender sales and voucher privatization. A few large-scale privatizations should be initiated by early summer [2000]. The country's large enterprises are largely unreformed and accrue heavy losses. Soft budget constraints, widespread inter-enterprise arrears and barter arrangements are common ... Confidence in the existing banking system is minimal ... [The new reformist authorities in FR Yugoslavia have ... liberalized most prices: p. 28] ... The price of electricity, fuel, gas and some essential goods more than doubled in November [2000], but much higher increases are required to bring price levels close to world averages ... The [new reformist] authorities unified the exchange rate regime and have introduced a managed float from January 2001. Export surrender requirements have been abolished and the federal authorities are revising and simplifying the complicated tariff structure. The FR Yugoslavia has been formally invited to begin WTO accession negotiations.
>
> (EBRD 2001a: 62)

> The most dramatic progress in structural reform in the past year has been in FR Yugoslavia ... Price liberalization was the first step towards reform. This was initiated in the waning days of the previous government. By the middle of 2001 almost all prices other than those for bread, flour and utility services were liberalized. These measures were accompanied by strict stabilization policies by the central bank.
>
> (EBRD 2001b: 20)

> While the prices of 60 per cent of weighted goods in the consumer price index basket were formally administratively controlled, the Serbian government abandoned price controls and subsidies in late 2000, except for those applied to public utilities and bread.
>
> (p. 142)

> The price of electricity ... [was] well below cost-recovery levels ... The average price of electricity was raised by 60 per cent in April 2001 and by a

further 40 per cent in June. A further 15 per cent increase is planned for October 2001.

(p. 142)

'Other utility prices are being moved closer to cost-recovery levels' (p. 20). 'The federal authorities abolished the multiple exchange rate regime, replacing it with a managed float, and introduced current account convertibility' (p. 20).

Until last year [2000] a multiple exchange rate system was in operation, with access to foreign currency at the 'official rate' (1 dinar equal to 6 DM) restricted to favoured associates of the old regime. At the end of 2000 the National Bank of Yugoslavia unified the rates at a level around 30 dinars to 1 DM, close to the black market rate.

(p. 142)

During the first half of 2001 the federal authorities abolished almost all non-tariff import restrictions and introduced a new tariff schedule for imports ... Quantitative export restrictions have been maintained for some agricultural goods. FR Yugoslavia began negotiations in February 2001 for accession to the WTO and started preliminary discussions with the EU on a Stabilization and Association Agreement.

(p. 142)

'The Serbian government introduced wide-ranging reforms to the tax system in April 2001' (p. 142). In mid-2000 the private sector's share of (Yugoslav) GDP was roughly 40 per cent (p. 144).

Social ownership remains the dominant form of ownership in the enterprise sector ... At the end of June 2001 the Serbian parliament adopted a new law on privatization. The law specifies that at least 70 per cent of shares in state and socially-owned assets will be sold to private investors. Employees and other eligible citizens can retain up to 30 per cent of the shares, depending on how quickly the enterprise is sold. Any enterprise not sold within four years will be taken over by the privatization agency and sold or liquidated.

(p. 142)

'Under the new Serbian law, strategic investors can acquire majority shares' (p. 20). 'The banking sector is in crisis and fails to meet the needs of the real economy' (p. 142).

Poverty and inequality are widespread. According to World Bank estimates, absolute poverty is currently twice as high as it was in 1990 ... The rate of unemployment is estimated at around 30 per cent of the labour force, although many of those classified as unemployed work in the informal sector.

(p. 143)

Postscript

'Serbia and Montenegro agreed Thursday [14 March 2002] to remain part of a single federation and in the process the two sides dropped the name Yugoslavia ... The new union will be called Serbia and Montenegro ... The new agreement puts aside the referendum proposal. After three years each side can reconsider the agreement. Under the accord Serbia and Montenegro will have separate currencies and customs services. A common presidency, defence establishment, foreign ministry, human rights ministry and supreme court will join the two republics. New elections are scheduled for autumn to choose a parliament, which will in turn elect a president of the federation ... The EU foreign policy chief, Javier Solana, brokered the deal' (*IHT*, 15 March 2002, p. 1). 'The new union would have some weakish joint institutions, including a presidency, a parliament and five ministries, but each side would keep its own economic system' (*The Economist*, 23 March 2002, p. 42). '[There is need for] approval by the two republics' parliaments and the federal assembly ... Mr Djukanovic said that a system of rotating senior official positions "will ensure the protection of Montenegro's interests in international institutions", including alternative Montenegrin and Serbian representatives occupying a single seat at the UN ... Mr Djukanovic was quoted as saying he did not rule out a referendum being called in Montenegro to ratify the agreement' (*The Times*, 15 March 2002, p. 20). 'A constitution should come into force by the end of 2002 at the latest ... Serbia and Montenegro, the new name, will be organized under one parliament, president, council of ministers and court. The council will be responsible for foreign affairs, defence, international economic relations, internal economic relations and protection of human and minority rights. The economic systems of both republics will be eventually harmonized with EU rules' (*FT*, 15 March 2002, p. 6). 'Mr Solana said the deal marked an important step forward for the stability of the region and Europe", and promised this was "not an end of anything, but the beginning of a new chapter that we will write together and bring you membership of the EU" ... Both ... President Vojislav Kostunica and ... Milo Djukanovic will join EU leaders at their two-day summit in Barcelona which starts [on 15 March]' (*The Independent*, 15 March 2002, p. 20).

Bibliography

Periodicals

CDSP *Current Digest of the Soviet Press* (since 5 February 1992 *Post-Soviet*)
EBRD European Bank for Reconstruction and Development
EEN *Eastern Europe* (formerly *Eastern Europe Newsletter*)
EIU Economist Intelligence Unit
FEER *Far Eastern Economic Review*
FT *Financial Times*
IHT *International Herald Tribune*

Books and journals

Åslund, A. (1994) 'Lessons of the first four years of systemic change in Eastern Europe', *Journal of Comparative Economics*, vol. 19, no. 1.
——(1996) 'Introduction: the Balkan transformation in perspective', in I. Jeffries (ed.) *Problems of Economic and Political Transformation in the Balkans*, London: Pinter.
Åslund, A., Boone, P. and Johnson, S. (1996) 'How to stabilize: lessons from post-communist countries', *Brookings Papers on Economic Activity*, no. 1.
Bartlett, W. (1996) 'From reform to crisis: economic impacts of secession, war and sanctions in the former Yugoslavia', in I. Jeffries (ed.) *Problems of Economic and Political Transformation in the Balkans*, London: Pinter.
Ben-Ner, A. and Neuberger, E. (1990) 'The feasibility of planned market systems: the Yugoslav visible hand and negotiated planning', *Journal of Comparative Economics*, vol. 14, no. 4.
Bicanic, I. (1996) 'The economic divergence of Yugoslavia's successor states', in I. Jeffries (ed.) *Problems of Economic and Political Transformation in the Balkans*, London: Pinter.
Bideleux, R. and Jeffries, I. (1998) *A History of Eastern Europe: Crisis and Change*, London: Routledge.
Blanchard, O. (1994) 'Transition in Poland', *Economic Journal*, vol. 104, no. 426.
Bojnec, S. (1999) 'Privatization, restructuring and management in Slovene enterprises', *Comparative Economic Studies*, vol. XLI, no. 4.
Business Central Europe (1995) *The Annual*, London: The Economist Group.
——(1997) *The Annual: 1997–98*, London: The Economist Group.
——(1998) *The Annual: 1998–99*, London: The Economist Group.
——(1999) *The Annual: 2000*, London: The Economist Group.
——(2000) *The Annual: 2001*, London: The Economist Group.

Clague, C. (1992) 'Introduction: the journey to a market economy', in C. Clague and G. Rausser (eds) *The Emergence of Market Economies in Eastern Europe*, Oxford: Blackwell.

Clague, C. and Rausser, G. (eds) (1992) *The Emergence of Market Economies in Eastern Europe*, Oxford: Blackwell.

Crampton, R. (1994) *Eastern Europe in the Twentieth Century*, London: Routledge.

Daalder, I. and Froman, B. (1999) 'Dayton's incomplete peace', *Foreign Affairs*, vol. 78, no. 6.

Dyker, D. (1990) *Yugoslavia: Socialism, Development and Debt*, London: Routledge.

——(1992) *Yugoslavia*, Brighton: University of Sussex: Discussion Paper no. 04/92.

EBRD (1994) *Transition Report*, London: European Bank for Reconstruction and Development.

——(1995a) *Transition Report Update* (April), London: European Bank for Reconstruction and Development.

——(1995b) *Transition Report*, London: European Bank for Reconstruction and Development.

——(1996a) *Transition Report Update* (April), London: European Bank for Reconstruction and Development.

——(1996b) *Transition Report*, London: European Bank for Reconstruction and Development.

——(1997a) *Transition Report Update* (April), London: European Bank for Reconstruction and Development.

——(1997b) *Transition Report*, London: European Bank for Reconstruction and Development.

——(1998a) *Transition Report Update* (April), London: European Bank for Reconstruction and Development.

——(1998b) *Transition Report*, London: European Bank for Reconstruction and Development.

——(1999a) *Transition Report Update* (April), London: European Bank for Reconstruction and Development.

——(1999b) *Transition Report*, London: European Bank for Reconstruction and Development.

——(2000a) *Transition Report Update* (May), London: European Bank for Reconstruction and Development.

——(2000b) *Transition Report*, London: European Bank for Reconstruction and Development.

——(2001a) *Transition Report Update* (April), London: European Bank for Reconstruction and Development.

——(2001b) *Transition Report*, London: European Bank for Reconstruction and Development.

Economic Commission for Europe (1989) *Economic Reform in the European Centrally Planned Economies*, Economic Studies no. 1, New York: UN.

Economist (1998) Survey: 'The Balkans', 24 January.

Estrin, S. and Takla, L. (1992) 'Reform in Yugoslavia: the retreat from self-management', in I. Jeffries (ed.) *Industrial Reform in Socialist Countries: From Restructuring to Revolution*, Aldershot: Edward Elgar.

Financial Times (various surveys) Bosnia-Hercegovina: 21 October 1998; 14 December 1999.

——Central and Eastern Europe: 8 May 1998; 10 November 1999; 24 October 2000.

——Croatia: 30 May 1996; 28 May 1997; 7 July 1998; 10 July 1999.

——Macedonia: 7 July 1995; 15 November 1996; 17 December 1997; 19 February 2001.

——Montenegro: 10 July 2001.

——Slovenia: 30 March 1992; 30 March 1993; 12 April 1994; 6 April 1995; 26 March 1996; 28 April 1997; 18 May 1998; 7 June 1999; 11 July 2000; 9 July 2001.

——Yugoslavia: 18 June 1984; 21 December 1984; 21 June 1985; 17 December 1985; 17 June 1986; 16 December 1986; 22 December 1987; 22 June 1988; 6 December 1988; 29 June 1989; 5 December 1989; 6 July 1990; 17 December 1990; 27 June 1991; 27 January 1998 (Federal Republic of Yugoslavia).

Friedman, F. (2000) 'Dayton, democratization and governance: electoral dilemmas in Bosnia's peace and security', *International Relations*, vol. XV, no. 1.

Frydman, R., Rapaczynski, A., Earle, J. *et al.* (1993) *The Privatization Process in Central Europe*, London: Central European University Press.

Frydman, R., Gray, C., Hessel, M. and Rapaczynski, A. (1999) 'When does privatization work? The impact of private ownership on corporate performance in the transition countries', *Quarterly Journal of Economics*, vol. CXIV, no. 4.

Ghosh, A., Gulde, A.-M. and Wolf, H. (2000) 'Currency boards: more than a quick fix?' *Economic Policy*, October.

Gulde, A.-M. (1999) 'The role of the currency board in Bulgaria's stabilization', *Finance and Development*, September.

Havrylyshyn, O. and McGettigan, D. (1999) *Privatization in Transition Countries: Lessons of the First Decade*, Washington DC: IMF, Economic Issues no. 18.

Havrylyshyn, O. and Odling-Smee, J. (2000) 'Political economy of stalled reforms', *Finance and Development*, vol. 37, no. 3.

International Herald Tribune (various surveys) Central and Eastern Europe: 30 June 1999.

——Slovenia: 6 April 1995.

Jarvis, C. (2000a) 'The rise and fall of Albania's pyramid schemes', *Finance and Development*, vol. 37, no. 1.

——(2000b) 'The rise and fall of the pyramid schemes in Albania', *IMF Staff Papers*, vol. 47, no. 1.

Jeffries, I. (ed.) (1981) *The Industrial Enterprise in Eastern Europe*, New York: Praeger.

——(1990) *A Guide to the Socialist Economies*, London: Routledge.

——(ed.) (1992) *Industrial Reform in Socialist Countries: from Restructuring to Revolution*, Aldershot: Edward Elgar.

——(1993) *Socialist Economies and the Transition to the Market: A Guide*, London: Routledge.

——(1996a) *A Guide to the Economies in Transition*, London: Routledge.

——(ed.) (1996b) *Problems of Economic and Political Transformation in the Balkans*, London: Pinter.

——(2001) *Economies in Transition: A Guide to China, Cuba, Mongolia, North Korea and Vietnam at the Turn of the Twenty-First Century*, London: Routledge.

——(2002) *Eastern Europe at the Turn of the Twenty-First Century: a Guide to the Economies in Transition*, London: Routledge.

Johnson, S., La Porta, R., Lopez-de-Silanes, F. and Scheifer, A. (2000) 'Tunnelling', *American Economic Review*, Papers and Proceedings, May.

Koevski, G. and Canning, A. (1995) *Privatization in the Former Yugoslav Republic of Macedonia*, Edinburgh: Heriot-Watt University, Discussion Paper no. 95/10.

Kraft, E. (1995) 'Stabilizing inflation in Slovenia, Croatia and Macedonia: how independence has affected macroeconomic policy outcomes', *Europe–Asia Studies*, vol. 47, no. 3.

Lavigne, M. (2000) 'The years of transition: a review article', *Communist and Post-Communist Studies*, vol. 33, no. 4.

Lazic, M. and Sekelj, L. (1997) 'Privatization in Yugoslavia (Serbia and Montenegro)', *Europe–Asia Studies*, vol. 49, no. 6.

Lerman, Z. (1999) 'Land reform and farm restructuring: what has been accomplished to date?', *American Economic Review*, Papers and Proceedings, May.

McFarlane, B. (1988) *Yugoslavia: Politics, Economics and Society*, London: Pinter.

Malcolm, N. (1994) *Bosnia: A Short History*, London: Macmillan.

Mencinger, J. (1993) 'How to create a currency? The experience of Slovenia', *Weltwirtschaftliches Archiv*, vol. 129, no. 2.

Nellis, J. (1999) 'Time to rethink privatization in transition economies?', *Finance and Development*, vol. 36, no. 2.

Palairet, M. (2001) 'The economic consequences of Slobodan Milosevic', *Europe–Asia Studies*, vol. 53, no. 6.

Petrovic, P., Bogetic, Z. and Vujosevic, Z. (1999) 'The Yugoslav hyperinflation of 1992–94: causes, dynamics and money supply process', *Journal of Comparative Economics*, vol. 27, no. 2.

Pettifer, J. (1995) 'Macedonia: still the apple of discord', *The World Today*, vol. 51, no. 3.

Prasnikar, J. and Pregl, Z. (1991) 'Economic development in Yugoslavia in 1990 and prospects for the future', *American Economic Review*, Papers and Proceedings, May.

Radosevic, S. (1994) 'The generic problems of competitiveness at company level in the former socialist economies: the case of Croatia', *Europe–Asia Studies*, vol. 46, no. 3.

Rausser, G. (1992) 'Lessons for emerging market economies in Eastern Europe', in C. Clague and G. Rausser (eds) *The Emergence of Market Economies in Eastern Europe*, Oxford: Blackwell.

Roberts, E. (1999) 'Trouble ahead', *The World Today*, vol. 55, no. 12.

Sachs, J. (1994) *Poland's Jump to the Market Economy*, Cambridge, Mass.: MIT Press.

——(1997) 'An overview of stabilization issues facing economies in transition', in W. Woo, S. Parker and J. Sachs (eds) *Economies in Transition: Comparing Asia and Eastern Europe*, London: MIT Press.

Sachs, J. and Woo, W. (1994) 'Structural factors in the economic reforms of China, Eastern Europe and the former Soviet Union', *Economic Policy*, no. 18.

Sjöberg, Ö. and Wyzan, M. (eds) (1991) *Economic Change in the Balkan States: Albania, Bulgaria, Romania and Yugoslavia*, London: Pinter.

Swinnen, J. (1999) 'The political economy of land reform choices in Central and Eastern Europe', *Economics of Transition*, vol. 7, no. 3.

Thomas, R. (1998) 'Choosing the warpath', *The World Today*, vol. 54, no. 5.

United Nations (1993) *World Economic Survey 1993*, New York: United Nations.

——(1996) *World Economic and Social Survey*, New York: United Nations.

United Nations Economic Commission for Europe (1992) *Economic Survey of Europe in 1991–92*, New York: United Nations.

——(1993) *Economic Survey of Europe in 1992–93*, New York: United Nations.

——(1994) *Economic Survey of Europe in 1993–94*, New York: United Nations.

——(1995) *Economic Survey of Europe in 1994–95*, New York: United Nations.

——(1996) *Economic Survey of Europe in 1995–96*, New York: United Nations.

——(1997) *Economic Survey of Europe in 1996–97*, New York: United Nations.

——(1998a) *Economic Survey of Europe 1998*, No. 1, New York: United Nations.

——(1998b) *Economic Survey of Europe 1998*, No. 2, New York: United Nations.

——(1998c) *Economic Survey of Europe 1998*, No. 3, New York: United Nations. (Subsequent issues are not specifically quoted from, but data are used.)

Woo, W., Parker, S. and Sachs, J. (eds) (1997) *Economies in Transition: Comparing Asia and Eastern Europe*, London: MIT Press.

World Bank (1996) *World Development Report: From Plan to Market*, New York: Oxford University Press.

Zimmerman, W. (1995) 'The last ambassador: a memoir of the collapse of Yugoslavia', *Foreign Affairs*, vol. 74, no. 2.

Zizmond, E. (1993) 'Slovenia – one year of independence', *Europe–Asia Studies*, vol. 45, no. 5.

Index